PUBLIC
POLICY

PUBLIC POLICY

Politics, Analysis, and Alternatives

Third Edition

MICHAEL E. KRAFT AND
SCOTT R. FURLONG
UNIVERSITY OF WISCONSIN–GREEN BAY

CQ PRESS

A Division of SAGE
Washington, D.C.

CQ Press
2300 N Street, NW, Suite 800
Washington, DC 20037

Phone: 202-729-1900; toll-free, 1-866-4CQ-PRESS (1-866-427-7737)

Web: www.cqpress.com

Cover design: Anne C. Kerns, Anne Likes Red, Inc.
Photo credits:
AP Images: 2, 11, 18, 30, 41, 47, 64, 71, 86, 88, 96, 102, 129, 191, 202, 209, 241, 284, 302, 316, 325, 371, 428
California Department of Public Health: 249
Getty Images: 56, 114 (both), 124, 144 (both), 150, 157, 160, 172, 184, 213, 228, 268, 291, 323, 338, 345, 365, 382, 390, 395
Landov: 418
© 2007, The Washington Post/Michel du Cille: 244
Cover images: "Bank Crisis": AP Images/Mary Altaffer; remaining images: iStock

∞ The paper used in this publication exceeds the requirements of the American National Standard for Information Sciences—Permanence of Paper for Printed Library Materials, ANSI Z39.48-1992.

Printed and bound in the United States of America

13   12   11   10   09   2   3   4   5

Library of Congress Cataloging-in-Publication Data

Kraft, Michael E.
   Public policy : politics, analysis, and alternatives / Michael E. Kraft
and Scott R. Furlong.—3rd ed.
      p. cm.
   Includes bibliographical references and index.
   ISBN 978-0-87289-971-1 (alk. paper)
   1. Policy sciences—Evaluation. 2. Political planning—Citizen parti-
cipation. 3. Political planning—United States—Evaluation. 4. Public
administration—United States—Evaluation. 5. Evaluation research
(Social action programs)—United States.   I. Furlong, Scott R.
II. Title.
H97.K73 2009
320.60973—dc22
                                                      2009010938

FOR

SANDY

AND

DEBBIE, KYLE, AND DARCY

MICHAEL E. KRAFT

SCOTT R. FURLONG

Michael E. Kraft is professor of political science and public affairs and Herbert Fisk Johnson Professor of Environmental Studies at the University of Wisconsin–Green Bay. He is the author of, among other works, *Environmental Policy and Politics,* 4th ed. (2007). In addition, he is the coeditor of *Environmental Policy: New Directions in the 21st Century,* 7th ed. (2010), and *Technology and Politics* (1988), with Norman J. Vig; *Public Reactions to Nuclear Waste* (1993), with Riley E. Dunlap and Eugene A. Rosa; and *Toward Sustainable Communities: Transition and Transformations in Environmental Policy,* 2nd ed. (2009), with Daniel A. Mazmanian. He has taught courses in environmental policy and politics, Congress, and public policy analysis for more than thirty years.

Scott R. Furlong is dean of the College of Liberal Arts and Sciences and professor of political science and public affairs at the University of Wisconsin–Green Bay. His areas of expertise are regulatory policy and interest group participation in the executive branch, and he has taught public policy for more than fourteen years. His articles have appeared in such journals as *Public Administration Review, Journal of Public Administration, Research and Theory, Administrative Studies Quarterly,* and *Policy Studies Journal.*

BRIEF CONTENTS

CONTENTS

3 UNDERSTANDING PUBLIC POLICYMAKING   64

PART II ANALYZING PUBLIC POLICY

BOXES, FIGURES, AND TABLES

PREFACE

Health care costs are certain to soar in the coming decades as the baby boom generation ages and begins to demand an array of increasingly expensive medical services. In 2007 spending on health care rose at the lowest rate in nine years, providing some modest relief from what had been an unrelenting upward spiral in costs. Nonetheless, the total rose to $2.2 trillion, or 16.2 percent of the nation's gross domestic product. That was a record high. The United States spent $7,421 per person for health care in 2007, a rise of 6.1 percent over spending in 2006. The 2007 figures were released just before Barack Obama took office, after promising sweeping changes in health care policy during the 2008 presidential campaign . By February 2009, however, the Centers for Medicare and Medicaid Services reported that health care spending in 2008 rose to $2.4 trillion, a 9 percent increase from 2007. Projections show no end to the continuing rise in costs. What is the best way to deal with these ballooning health care costs, particularly in light of other trends—for example, increasing levels of obesity—that could drive up the costs even further? How should we protect the solvency of the Medicare trust fund as demands from baby boomers threaten to bankrupt it and jeopardize benefits for future generations? Indeed, what forms of health care and Social Security will be available to the generation of citizens now in their teens and twenties? What will the alternatives be?

Such public policy decisions touch nearly every aspect of daily life in the United States, although many people fail to recognize or fully understand their impact. Social Security reform, for example, may not seem terribly urgent to most young people today, but it undoubtedly will shape the quality of their lives decades down the road. This is why citizens need to understand not only how governments make policy choices but also how to evaluate those choices. We believe the reason to be politically aware is simple: policymakers are more responsive to the public's preferences and needs and, in some cases, are more effective when citizens take a greater interest in public affairs and play a more active role in the policy-making process. We hope this text stimulates interest and concern while equipping readers with the skills they need to think critically and creatively about policy problems.

The subtitle of this book—politics, analysis, and alternatives—explicitly expresses what we are trying to accomplish, which differs from conventional books on public policy. This text integrates three aspects of public policy study: government institutions and the policy-making process, the concepts and methods of policy analysis, and the choices that we make collectively about substantive public policies at all levels of government. Throughout, we focus on the interrelationship of government institutions, the interests and motivations of policy actors both inside and outside of government, and the role of policy analysis in clarifying public problems and helping citizens and policymakers choose among policy alternatives. These central themes are reinforced by providing students with the tools they need—how to find key information, how to use specific evaluative criteria, how to apply policy analysis methods, and how to assess the role of politics in policymaking—to investigate issues and carry out policy analysis on their own. We believe that this hands-on approach is the best way to teach the skills of analysis and give students not only an understanding of the conduct of public policy but also a way *into* the process.

A FOCUS ON POLICY ANALYSIS

By emphasizing the pervasiveness of public policy, we try to make its study a vital activity for students. They can better appreciate the power they wield to effect change in the system once they are armed with the tools of policy analysis. However, the logic of public policy and its study must be addressed before students encounter these powerful tools of the trade. In Part 1 we demonstrate that public policy choices are not made in a vacuum. Social, economic, political, and cultural contexts matter, as do the distinguishing characteristics of the U.S. government and the rationales behind government intervention. An understanding of the structure of institutions, the motivation of policy actors (both formal and informal), and the unique nature of the U.S. political system will allow students to comprehend the complexity of government while discovering opportunities for engagement with the process. We present multiple perspectives on the policy-making process, from elite theory to rational choice theory, but concentrate on the policy process model—a portrayal of policymaking as a sequence of key activities from agenda setting to policy implementation—that is used in the rest of the book. We hope these chapters encourage students to ask how decisions are made as well as why they are made in one way and not another.

Part 2 gets to the heart of the book and explains the approaches and methods of policy analysis, laying a foundation for dissecting and understanding public problems and policy choices. With careful application of the tools of policy analysis, students can interpret complex and conflicting data and arguments, evaluate alternative courses of action, and anticipate the consequences of policy choices. Specific cases—from tax cuts and cell phone use by drivers to immigration and urban traffic congestion—illustrate both the difficulty of policy analysis and its value in policymaking. Students learn how to find and interpret policy-relevant information and to acquire an understanding of the limitations to what government can do about public problems. The evaluative criteria at the book's core—a focus on effectiveness, efficiency, and equity—train students to think clearly about policy alternatives. Ethical considerations necessarily receive considerable attention as well as the more common concerns over effectiveness and efficiency. Case studies involving organ donation, profiling in relation to homeland security goals, national energy policy, and the morality of embryonic stem cell research give students the opportunity to grapple with controversial issues for which no policymaker has *the* answer.

Part 3 consists of six substantive policy chapters designed to illustrate and apply the concepts and methods introduced in the first two sections of the book. The six core policy areas—economics and budgeting, health care, welfare and Social Security, education, energy and the environment, and foreign policy and homeland security—represent a substantial part of contemporary U.S. policymaking and also present a diversity of economic, political, and ethical issues for analysis. This part of the text offers a clear picture of the issues that beginning analysts would encounter in policymaking or in the evaluation of all areas of public policy. For readers who want to probe more deeply into those policy areas that we discuss peripherally—for instance, criminal justice and civil rights and liberties—we recommend *Issues for Debate in American Public Policy,* which offers selections from the *CQ Researcher* and abundant references to current policy debates.

Consistent with the text's emphasis on analysis, we begin each policy area chapter with a brief illustration of a policy scenario (rising budget deficits and a deteriorating economy, the costs of health care and the gap between spending and results, the persistence of poverty in the United States, controversies surrounding implementation of the No Child Left Behind Act, conflicts over national energy policy and climate change, and the use of private contractors in the Iraq war) to spark student interest. A background section describes the public problems faced and the solutions chosen to date. We briefly summarize major policies and programs, discuss when and how they came into effect, review available policy evaluations, and suggest how students can investigate policy alternatives. At the end of each chapter, we offer a focused discussion of policy reform in terms of the key evaluative criteria used throughout the text: effectiveness, efficiency, and equity. These discussions link closely to the kinds of questions that can be asked about any proposal for policy change and how it might be addressed. In Part 4, a concluding chapter brings together the arguments of the text and looks to future challenges in public policy.

We made a great many changes throughout the text while preparing this third edition. We updated material in every chapter, particularly those that focus on substantive policy topics. In all chapters we incorporated new studies and interpretations and made use of new illustrations and case studies of policy controversies and actions. In addition, we sought throughout the text to improve the clarity of presentation and to update all references to Web sites and recommended readings.

SPECIAL FEATURES

To underscore the importance we place on active learning and critical engagement, we include two unique text boxes to guide students as they research policy problems: "Working with Sources" and "Steps to Analysis." The first type of feature identifies important sources of information and how to utilize them, providing step-by-step suggestions on how to make good (and critical) use of the information found on Internet sites—among other resources—that offer important data sources and policy perspectives. The "Steps to Analysis" feature invites critical thinking about specific policy problems. It demonstrates how to ask the urgent questions that drive policy analysis, then presents ways to narrow and refine these questions into feasible projects. To further direct students to the information they need, discussion questions at the end of each chapter get at, for instance, the "best" way to deal with health care concerns, environmental problems, education issues, or homeland security. These questions are followed by annotated suggested readings, suggested Web sites, a list of major legislation where appropriate, a list of keywords, and chapter notes. Students will find a reference list and a glossary at the end of the book as well.

A variety of ancillaries, updated and revised by Kevin Vonck, accompany this text. A companion Web site at www.cqpress.com/cs/publicpolicy offers students concise chapter summaries, practice quiz questions (modeled on the test bank questions), exercises that further the book's goals, annotated links that allow easy access to the Web sites found in the text, and much more. All of these features are keyed to each of the thirteen chapters in the text, and they will be updated regularly. Instructors should note that the quizzes and exercises on the Web site, as well as those in the text itself, provide the basis for potential assignments for students—quiz results can be e-mailed to instructors for credit, as can answers to exercises in the form of online response boxes. These can be used as models that instructors can adjust as necessary to concentrate on other areas of public policy. The instructor's resources—available at no cost to adopters—include a full test bank of approximately 300 questions that have been fully class tested and are available in Respondus format so instructors can generate multiple forms of customized tests that are fully compatible with course management systems. To assist in classroom preparation, PowerPoint lecture outlines for all thirteen chapters, as well as all the book's tables and figures in electronic format, also are available.

We have tried to make this text a distinctive and appealing introduction to the study of public policy while also maintaining a commitment to scholarly rigor. Our experience with students in many years of teaching tells us that they can handle demanding reading and exercises if these are linked firmly to concrete issues that affect society and students' personal lives.

Above all, the text emphasizes the urgency of making government more responsive to citizen concerns and equips students with the skills they need to understand policy controversies. Thus we hope the text inspires students to take a serious interest in government, politics, and public policy, and to participate enthusiastically in policy debates and decision making throughout their lives.

ACKNOWLEDGMENTS

Preparation of this text reflects contributions from many individuals and institutions. We are particularly grateful for support from the University of Wisconsin–Green Bay and our colleagues in the Department of Public and Environmental Affairs. Our students in Introduction to Public Policy, Public Policy Analysis, and other courses have taught us much over the years, especially about what they need to know to become informed citizens and effective policy professionals. We are also grateful to them for allowing the liberty of asking them to read drafts of the chapters.

We also appreciate the efforts of hundreds of creative public policy scholars whose work makes a book like this possible. Our citation of their publications is a modest way of acknowledging our dependence on their research and insights into policy analysis and policymaking. We thank Marc Eisner, Wesleyan University; Joseph Karlesky, Franklin and Marshall College; Paul Lewis, Arizona State University; and Margaret Stout, West Virginia University, for their critical appraisals and perceptive, helpful suggestions. Special thanks are also due to the skilled and conscientious staff at CQ Press: Brenda Carter, Charisse Kiino, Talia Greenberg, Allison McKay, and Lorna Notsch. As always, any remaining errors and omissions rest on our shoulders. We hope readers will alert us to any such defects and suggest changes they would like to see in future editions. Contact us at kraftm@uwgb.edu or furlongs@uwgb.edu.

MICHAEL E. KRAFT
SCOTT R. FURLONG

PUBLIC
POLICY

CHAPTER **1**

PUBLIC POLICY AND POLITICS

EVERY YEAR MILLIONS OF PEOPLE IN THE UNITED STATES GO TO theme parks, state and county fairs, and other events that feature thrill rides. According to the International Association of Amusement Parks and Attractions, in 2006 about 355 million people attended the country's approximately four hundred parks, with revenues conservatively estimated at $11.5 billion.[1] This is clearly a large industry that not only includes amusement park giants such as Walt Disney World and Six Flags, but also a variety of smaller, permanently placed operations. In addition, many travelling operations set up temporary ride attractions at events such as state and county fairs.

While these parks and attractions provide safe entertainment and recreation for most visitors, periodic accidents—some fatal—are reported every year. In the summer of 2007, for example, the feet of a thirteen-year-old girl were severed during the Superman Tower of Power ride in Six Flags Kentucky Kingdom amusement park in Louisville when a broken cable cord wrapped around them.[2] In some cases, accidents or deaths occur for no apparent reason other than the specific health of the visitor. This might be the case in a December 2007 death that occurred at Walt Disney World's Animal Kingdom Expedition Everest roller coaster, where a forty-four-year-old man, unresponsive when the cars pulled into the unloading area, was later pronounced dead.[3] When people go to these parks they intend to have fun, and accidents in such venues can generate all sorts of media coverage. No one thinks they can get injured in Disney World, home of Mickey Mouse, Goofy, the Seven Dwarfs, and other beloved characters. So one might ask, what kinds of controls or regulations are in place to ensure individual safety in these amusement centers?

The answer in this case is a bit complicated. It spans different government levels and agencies and is a good illustration of the complexity of policymaking. The U.S. Consumer Product Safety Commission (CPSC) is a regulatory agency responsible for ensuring public safety for a wide range of consumer products. The commission currently regulates over fifteen thousand products, ranging from lawn mowers to baby cribs. It also, not surprisingly, has some authority over

Amusement parks are a big business in the United States, and millions of Americans visit them each year, particularly large facilities such as Walt Disney World and the Six Flags parks. Yet the occasional accident is a reminder of the risk and possibly the need for government intervention to provide adequate assurance of public safety. The photo shows a carnival ride, called the Yo-Yo, which is similar to one that collapsed in May 2008, injuring all twenty-four people on the ride at the Calaveras County Fair and Jumping Frog Jubilee, about eighty miles from Sacramento, California.

amusement park rides. Specifically, the CPSC monitors the safety of the "portable amusement rides" that travel from one location to another and are set up for particular events, such as county fairs. What about rides associated with permanent amusement parks such as Six Flags? Government regulation of these rides occurs at the state level, and in some cases states have no authority. Some states require government inspection of park rides and others do not. Regulation may even vary within the state itself. Florida is a prime example. While some permanent parks are significantly regulated, those that hire more than one thousand employees are generally exempt from state regulations. (This includes places such as Universal Studios, Disney World, and Busch Gardens.) Why do you think these differences between and within states exist?[4]

Rep. Edward Markey, D-Mass., believes that there should be more systematic federal regulation of amusement park rides. Since 1999 he has introduced legislation that would give greater authority to the CPSC to regulate the industry, including "big theme" players such as Disney and Universal.[5] To date, he has not been successful getting this legislation passed, with opposition coming—not surprisingly—from the major theme parks, which claim that federal intervention is unnecessary, that these accidents occur rarely, and the risks are minimal.

How risky are these rides? According to Markey, people die on roller coasters at a higher rate per mile traveled than those travelling by plane, bus, or train. Rep. Cliff Stearns, R-Fla., states, on the other hand, that amusement park rides cause fewer injuries than fishing.[6] So who is right? The answer may be that both are, and it illustrates how information and data can be handled to communicate preferred positions. Policy analysts often use risk analysis to examine the extent of a problem and how it can affect a population. In the case of amusement park rides, according to a study by the National Safety Council, over 300 million visitors rode 1.8 billion rides and reported 1,783 injuries—or about one injury for every million rides.[7] Once again, one might ask if this is a significant number. For comparison purposes, about one person dies for every ten thousand ATVs currently in use, there are about seventy-five thousand lawn mower accidents each year, and a similar number of sledding accidents occur each year.[8] Based on some of these comparisons, should we be concerned about the safety of amusement park rides?

Another question might be whether government needs to be involved at all in the regulation of amusement park rides. It is clear that such accidents are not profitable, and the amusement park industry has a strong incentive to provide safe environments in order to continue attracting visitors. Might the self-regulation that currently occurs, particularly in the permanent parks, be sufficient to ensure safety? These are the kinds of questions to which elected and government officials must respond when making public policy.

While we are relatively certain that most people do not consider the role of government on their family vacation to Disney World, the examples above show that there are a variety of questions one might raise regarding the role of government. The regulation of amusement park rides is an example of the constitutional issue of federalism, how risk may affect decision making, and ultimately the role of government in a capitalist society. This example is quite common in public policy, as it relates to the diversity of issues that are examined. The ultimate outcomes can affect individuals directly.

The account of amusement park ride safety and its regulation tells us that public policymaking is complex and must consider many issues. They are resolved after long hours of research and debate, and they reflect many assumptions and calculations. In addition, a policy typically deals with a particular slice of American life, such as the family vacation, although it also may have important effects on the public's general well-being. Across the range of government activities today, it is no exaggeration to say that public policy deals with just about everything, affecting life in ways that are both obvious and sometimes difficult to recognize.

WHAT IS PUBLIC POLICY?

Public policy is what public officials within government, and by extension the citizens they represent, choose to do or not to do about public problems. Public problems refer to conditions the public widely perceives to be unacceptable and therefore requiring intervention. Problems such as environmental degradation, threats to workplace safety, or insufficient access to health care services can be addressed through government action; private action, where individuals or corporations take the responsibility; or a combination of the two. In any given case, the choice depends on how the public defines the problem and on prevailing societal attitudes about private action in relation to government's role.

For the amusement park ride example, governments at both the federal and state level share responsibility in some cases, and in others responsibility for safety is left to private businesses or individuals. There are ongoing debates over whether or not having the industry regulate itself in these situations is sufficient and when accidents do happen, those debates become much more public. When it comes to safety issues, government may decide to intervene, such as in regulation of medications, or allow for private industry to address the issue. For example, in 2001 Congress decided to reject proposed workplace safety regulations developed by the Clinton administration. The Occupational Safety and Health Administration (OSHA) had sought to impose ergonomics rules in an effort to reduce repetitive motion injuries, but Congress concluded that the mandatory rules were too burdensome and costly for U.S. businesses. It preferred to allow each business to determine the safest work environment for its employees on its own.

The term *policy* refers in general to a purposive course of action that an individual or group consistently follows in dealing with a problem (Anderson 2006). In a more formal definition, a policy is a "standing decision characterized by behavioral consistency and repetitiveness on the part of both those who make it and those who abide by it" (Eulau and Prewitt 1973, 465). Whether in the public or private sector, policies also can be thought of as the instruments through which societies regulate themselves and attempt to channel human behavior in acceptable directions (Schneider and Ingram 1997).

The language used to discuss public policy can be confusing. Analysts, policymakers, and commentators sometimes speak without much clarity about intentions (the purposes of government action); goals (the stated ends to be achieved); plans or proposals (the means for achieving goals); programs (the authorized means for pursuing goals); and decisions or choices, that is, specific actions that are taken to set goals, develop plans, and implement programs (Jones 1984). These elements of public policy can be found in many different legal expressions such as laws, executive orders, regulations, and judicial rulings. They also can be seen in the way that policymakers, such as presidents, governors, or legislators, describe how they view public policy in any given area. Both the legal statements and the actions of policymakers can define what public policy is at any given time. We find it useful as well to distinguish between **policy outputs** (the formal actions that governments take to pursue their goals) and **policy outcomes** (the effects such actions actually have on society).

To pull some of these perspectives together, we offer this definition: *Public policy* is a course of government action or inaction in response to public problems. It is associated with formally approved policy goals and means, as well as the regulations and practices of agencies that implement programs. Looking at public policy this way emphasizes the actual behavior of implementing agencies and officials, not merely the formal statements of policy goals and means found in laws and other expressions of government policy. As we will stress throughout the book, this view means that students of public policy need to seek out the information that can tell them what policy actually is at any given time.

Any level of government, whether federal, state, or local, may be involved in a particular policy effort because social problems, and the public demand for action on them, manifest themselves from the local to the national level. At the local level, failing public schools, high crime rates, crowded highways, or air pollution might attract enough attention to spur the school board, mayor, or city council to find remedies. At the national level, concern about inequitable access to health care or the country's heavy reliance on imported oil may galvanize policymakers and lead to policy development.

Whatever the level of government, proponents of policy actions seek a multitude of goals that also affect all members of society. For laws that govern personal conduct, such as speed limits, policies aim to restrict individual behavior as a way to protect lives or prevent injuries and property damage; that is, the goal is to promote the public's welfare or common good. After government enacts the laws, public policies also affect how the mandated services aimed at the public good, such as police protection, public education, or national defense, are provided. Direct government payments are another form of public policy, and they affect people's lives on the individual and societal level. Social Security checks for senior citizens, agricultural subsidies for farmers, and research grants to universities sustain long-term individual and collective well-being.

Public policies reflect not only society's most important values but also conflict between values. Policies represent which of many different values are given the highest priority in any given decision. David Easton (1965) captured this view in his often-quoted observation that politics is "the authoritative allocation of values for a society." What Easton meant was that the actions of policymakers can determine definitively and with the force of law which of society's different and sometimes conflicting values will prevail. Examples can be found in nearly every walk of life: Should the federal government further raise auto fuel efficiency standards to reduce emissions of greenhouse gases and cut U.S. dependence on imported oil, even if doing so raises the cost of buying a car? Or should such decisions be left to the marketplace and individual choice? Should government continue to recognize a woman's right to choose to have an abortion or restrict the choice and instead promote the rights of the fetus?

Because public policy often deals with tough questions like these, reflecting conflicts over fundamental human values, the resulting policies are going to affect people's lives. For these reasons, we designed this book with several goals in mind. The first is to help readers develop a fuller understanding of public policy and the ways governments make policy decisions. The second goal is to encourage readers to look ahead to the implications of policy choices. The third is to foster critical thinking about public policy and possible alternative courses of action. Because this goal is so important, we introduce basic concepts related to policy analysis throughout the text. The aim is to equip readers with essential skills in analytical thinking that will enhance their understanding of policy issues and make possible more effective participation in the policy process.

Developing a critical, analytical approach to policy issues has many advantages over simply learning the details of policy history, understanding the present legal requirements in various programs, or gaining an overview of current policy debates. Such knowledge is important, but it is inherently limited, in part because public policies and debates over them continually change, making earlier accounts less useful. In contrast, those who learn the basic principles of policymaking and policy analysis will have a better grasp of *why* governments make their decisions and be better able to identify the strengths and weaknesses in present policies as well as in proposals to change them. Individuals can apply these skills to the wide range of problems everyone faces as citizens and in their personal lives and careers.

DEFINING BASIC CONCEPTS

It is useful at this point to clarify several additional concepts in the study of public policy. These include government, politics, and policy analysis. Although these terms are in common usage, no universal definition exists for any of them.

Government

Government refers to the institutions and political processes through which public policy choices are made. These institutions and processes represent the legal authority to govern or rule a group of people. In the United States, the federal Constitution describes the government's institutions, which include Congress, the president, the various agencies of the executive branch, and the federal court system. Each is granted specific but overlapping legal authority to act under a system of separation of powers, which we discuss in chapter 2. At state and local levels, parallel government institutions develop policy for citizens within their jurisdictions, guided by the authority granted in state constitutions and in state and local statutes and ordinances. The American system of governance adheres to the principle of federalism, also discussed in chapter 2; in a federal system the national government shares authority with the states and local governments. Quite often national policies, such as those dealing with environmental protection, are implemented chiefly by the states through an elaborate system of intergovernmental relations in which the federal government grants legal authority to the states to carry out national policies. In other policy areas, such as education, crime control, and land-use regulation, state and local governments play the dominant role.

Politics

Politics concerns the exercise of power in society or in specific decisions over public policy. It has several different but complementary meanings. It is used to refer to the processes through which public policies are formulated and adopted, especially to the roles played by elected officials, organized interest groups, and political parties. This is the politics of policymaking. Politics can also be thought of as how conflicts in society (such as those over rights to abortion services or immigration restrictions) are expressed and resolved in favor of one set of interests or social values or another. Politics in this case refers to the issue positions that different groups of people (gun owners, environmentalists, health insurance companies, automobile companies) adopt and the actions they take to promote their values. These collections of individuals with similar interests often become active in the policy-making process. So politics is about power and influence in society as well as in the processes of policymaking within government. It concerns who participates in and who influences the decisions that governments make and who gains and who loses as a result. Harold Lasswell (1958) put it this way: Politics is about "who gets what, when, and how."

In the United States and most other democracies, politics is also related to the electoral processes by which citizens select the policymakers who represent them. In this sense, politics concerns political parties and their issue agendas and the political ideologies, philosophies, and beliefs held by candidates for office, their supporters, and their campaign contributors. The precise relationship of politics to public policy may not always be clear; defenders and critics of specific policy actions may offer arguments based in economics, history, ethics, philosophy, or any number of other ways we use to think about what is in the public interest. Still, no one doubts that electoral politics is a major component of the policy-making process.

Politics exerts this strong influence on policymaking in part because elected officials necessarily must try to anticipate how their policy statements and actions might affect their chances for reelection. Policymakers are therefore sensitive to the views of the groups and individuals who helped them win office in the first place and whose support may be essential to keeping them in office. These political incentives motivate public officials to pay particular attention to the policy preferences of their core constituencies, especially the activists, while also trying to appeal to the general electorate. For Republicans, the core constituencies include business interests, political conservatives, farmers, and suburban and rural residents, among others. For Democrats, the core constituencies are labor interests, environmentalists, African Americans, political liberals, residents of urban areas, and others.

Politics is also one of the principal reasons public policy is so riddled with conflict and why it can be so difficult to analyze. Consider the debate over smoking and its health effects. In recent years the federal government has sought to discourage smoking out of concern for its adverse effects on public health (Derthick 2005; Fritschler and Hoefler 1995). Yet while the Office of the Surgeon General and the Food and Drug Administration (FDA) take this position, the Department of Agriculture has continued its longtime policy of subsidizing tobacco farmers. Similarly in conflict with the antismoking message is a long-standing policy to sell cigarettes at discount prices in military commissaries. When the Pentagon tried in 1996 to end this subsidy of tobacco products to discourage troops from using them, the tobacco industry lobbied Congress to block the plan.[9]

Clearly, tobacco policy today—whether higher cigarette taxes meant to curtail smoking, public advertising campaigns to warn children and teenagers about the dangers of smoking, or actions to regulate tobacco as a drug—is both complex and controversial. Decisions are influenced by a public that is divided on the issue, by the actions of interest groups that represent the tobacco industry, and by public health studies that are used by other groups to press for further government action to reduce smoking. These various points of view and studies are parts of the contentious process of setting new policy directions.

It would be wrong to assume, however, that such conflicts merely reflect inconsistencies in government policies, or worse, that they demonstrate bad faith. In fact, the process of resolving conflicts helps to determine where the public interest lies. These conflicts illustrate the different public interests that U.S. policymakers attempt to meet. Promoting a health agenda through decreasing smoking will lead to a healthier society and a reduction in health care costs for both the individual and the nation. But the family farm is revered in the United States, and Congress has enacted many policies to protect it. The tobacco industry has been able to play upon this public interest of protecting farmers in its lobbying efforts. Such conflicts exist in nearly all policy areas.

Whether the debate is over tobacco support and public health, state support for colleges and universities, or the imposition of automobile fuel economy standards, government officials, interest groups, and active citizens promote their views about what to do, and they bring all kinds of information to bear on the decisions. Naturally, the different participants in the policy process can and do disagree vigorously about the kinds of public policies that are needed and the proper role of government in addressing the problems.

The policy-making process within government provides abundant, although not necessarily equal, opportunities for all of these participants, or policy actors, to discuss problems; to formulate and promote possible policy solutions to them; and to press for formal adoption by legislatures at the national, state, and local levels. Politics, as we defined it above, is evident throughout this process.

Ultimately, executive agencies and departments, such as the Environmental Protection Agency (EPA), the Department of Defense, the Department of State, or a local police or public health department are responsible for implementing what the legislators enact. Here too politics is often evident as an agency may reflect the political values and priorities of a president or governor, or try to respond to the views of other elected officials. For example, the EPA, OSHA, and the State Department under President Bill Clinton in the 1990s reflected different priorities and positions than they did during President George W. Bush's administration, and these will be different from President Barack Obama's administration.[10]

Policy Analysis

Analysis means deconstructing an object of study, that is, breaking it down into its basic elements to understand it better. Policy analysis is the examination of components of public policy, the policy process, or both. Put another way, it is the study of the causes and consequences of policy decisions. Duncan MacRae and James A. Wilde (1979, 4) have called policy analysis "the use of reason and evidence to choose the best policy among a number of alternatives." Policy analysis uses many different methods of inquiry and draws from various disciplines to obtain the information needed to assess a problem and think clearly about alternative ways to resolve it. The same information also shapes public debate and deliberation over what actions to take. At heart, policy analysis encourages deliberate critical thinking about the causes of public problems, the various ways governments and/or the private sector might act on them, and which policy choices make the most sense. Doing so requires not only knowledge of government and politics but also the ability to evaluate the policy actions. Chapter 6 discusses the major evaluative criteria used to make such judgments.

THE CONTEXTS OF PUBLIC POLICY

Public policy is not made in a vacuum. It is affected by social and economic conditions, prevailing political values and the public mood at any given time, the structure of government, and national and local cultural norms, among other variables. Taken together, this environment determines which problems rise to prominence, which policy alternatives receive serious consideration, and which actions are viewed as economically and politically feasible. Some aspects of the policy environment, such as the U.S. system of separation of powers and the nation's free-market economy, are relatively stable. Others, such as which party controls the White House and Congress, the public mood or political climate, and media coverage of policy-related developments, can vary considerably over time. To underscore how these variables shape the policy-making process, we offer a brief description of the social, economic, political, governing, and cultural contexts of public policy.

Social Context

Social conditions affect policy decisions in myriad ways, as is evident in controversies over phenomena as diverse as urban sprawl, inner-city crime rates, and immigration. Moreover, social conditions are dynamic, not static. The population changes because of immigration, growth in nontraditional households, and lower or higher birth rates. These social changes in turn alter how the public and policymakers view and act on problems ranging from crime to the rising cost of health care. Today, for example, elderly Americans make up the fastest growing segment of the country's population. Their needs differ from those in other cohorts—or age groups—of the population, and they are more likely than younger citizens to demand that government pay attention to them. One critical concern is Social Security. As the elderly population continues to increase, policymakers face difficult challenges, particularly how they can ensure the system's solvency as greater numbers of people begin to draw benefits. Fifty years ago, Social Security was a government program that posed no special risk to budgetary resources. Now, however, public officials recognize that they must find politically and economically realistic ways to deal with an aging population and the imminent retirement of the baby boom generation, those Americans born between 1946 and 1964.

How citizens relate to one another in their communities also influences public policymaking. People tend to place a high value on having homes and private spaces where they and their families can feel secure. In some areas, the desire for security has led to the rise of "gated communities." Do the gates create a mental barrier as well as a physical one? Conflicts also arise between communities. Even without gates, suburban growth—often at the expense of older, urban cores—continues almost unabated, creating economic and social tensions between cities and their suburbs.

Some of these trends have prompted public officials at all levels of government to think more about the "livability" of their communities over the next few decades. One solution is sustainable development—communities in which social, economic, and environmental concerns are approached in an integrated and comprehensive manner. President Clinton established the Office of Sustainable Development to develop "bold, new approaches to achieve our economic, environmental, and equity goals" (President's Council on Sustainable Development 1996). Even without the help of the White House, however, public officials and local leaders in communities across the nation are searching for innovative approaches to bring about sustainability. In the process, they are looking at public policies designed to affect urban growth, transportation, air and water quality, recreational opportunities, and the location of new industry and businesses, housing, and schools (Mazmanian and Kraft 2009; Paehlke 2010; Portney 2003).

Economic Context

The state of the economy has a major impact on the policies governments adopt and implement, as the sharp economic downturn of 2008 and 2009 clearly demonstrated. Economic policy deals with inflation and unemployment, but the economy itself affects the development of many other programs. For example, a strong economy often

Among the social contexts that influence public policy development is the diversity of the American population, which has been enriched by immigration over the years. Because they may be unfamiliar with the political process and reluctant to get involved, immigrants sometimes have to be encouraged to participate. The photo shows Ana Maria Archila giving instructions to volunteers from a group called Make the Road New York, in the Queens borough of New York City, in February 2008. The grassroots immigrant activist organization was sending out teams to canvas the area, knock on doors, and urge people to vote.

leads to lower unemployment, which in turn reduces the need for welfare and comparable assistance programs. The federal and state governments all claimed credit for reform policies that reduced the welfare rolls in the late 1990s, but could this change have occurred without a strong economy and near-record low rates of unemployment? The welfare reform example illustrates how a change in economic conditions can affect the dynamics of public policymaking. As the United States shifts from a traditional industrial economy to one based on providing information and services, many similar impacts on public policy will become apparent.

Another way to appreciate the influence of the economic context is to consider budgetary politics. For years the United States has operated in the red, with the government spending more money than it was collecting in taxes and other revenues. Congress has tried many ways to reduce the deficit, including the Balanced Budget and Emergency Deficit Control Act of 1985 and a proposed constitutional amendment mandating a balanced budget. Policymakers were particularly concerned because the continuing deficits meant they could not enact any new policy initiatives since no money was available to pay for them. Nor could they continue to fund programs without increasing taxes, always a politically unattractive option.

This situation changed in 1998, when President Clinton announced a federal budget surplus for the fiscal year and projected surpluses for years to follow. In 1992 the federal government had registered a record deficit of $290 billion, but by fiscal 2000 it had a record surplus of $237 billion, a result of the expanding economy and tax revenues. The dynamics of the policy-making process changed dramatically. Rather than thinking about how to save money to reduce the deficit, by 2000 members of Congress and candidates for federal office were preoccupied with various proposals for how to spend the surplus or to reduce taxes.

The economic context shifted once more early in the Bush administration. In 2001 the president proposed and Congress approved a massive tax cut that greatly reduced government revenues. The tax cut, combined with a broad economic slowdown in 2001 and 2002, the economic toll of the September 11, 2001, attacks and the subsequent war on terrorism, and a large increase in defense spending plunged the U.S. government back into deficit. These conditions, combined with the dramatically weaker economy in late 2008 and early 2009 and massive federal spending on economic recovery actions, led to astonishing projections by the Congressional Budget Office that in 2009, and possibly for years to come, the deficit would be over one trillion dollars. Many state governments also found themselves dealing with unexpected deficits as a result of the economic slowdown. At the federal and state level, policymakers struggled once more with tough decisions on program priorities and budget cuts.[11]

Political Context

It is impossible to understand public policy without considering politics, which affects public policy choices at every step, from the selection of policymakers in elections to shaping how conflicts among different groups are resolved. To appreciate the political context, one must be aware of the relative strength of the two major parties; the influence of minor parties; ideological differences among the public, especially the more attentive publics such as committed liberals and conservatives; and the ability of organized interest groups to exert pressure. It is equally important to consider how much interest the public takes in the political process, its expectations for what government ought to do, and the level of trust and confidence it has in government. For example, both in the United States and in other industrialized nations there has been a notable erosion of public trust in government in recent decades (Dalton 2004), typically because of historical events such as the Vietnam War and the Watergate scandal that called government activities into question. This trend affects not only the way people are likely to judge government programs and what public officials do, but also the way the press covers public policy debates and actions.

In addition, it is evident that increasingly Democrats and Republicans, liberals and conservatives, hold sharply different views about the legitimacy of government action and which policies are acceptable to them. During the 1990s partisan differences widened, and on many policy issues ideological polarization between the parties made government action difficult. This polarization and the seemingly endless bickering among politicians as they try to resolve their differences and find acceptable solutions to society's problems make the public even more critical of government and the political process (Hibbing and Larimer 2005).

The student of public policy also needs to recognize, however, that political labels such as liberal and conservative are not always reliable guides to predicting specific policy positions. That is, it is simplistic to assume that conservatives always want smaller government and that liberals prefer the opposite. Most conservatives argue for less government intrusion into the economy and decision making within business and industry, but they often favor a strong government role to achieve certain social goals, such as reducing crime or banning abortions and gay marriages. Liberals, on the other hand, rally against government threats to civil liberties and individual rights but are among the first to call for government regulation of business activity to protect consumers and workers, or to control air and water pollution.

Party labels themselves may be poor indicators of positions taken on policy issues. Within the major political parties one can find ideological differences among members: some Democrats, particularly southerners, are conservative, and some Republicans, particularly those from the Northeast, are moderate to liberal, although many fewer today than several decades ago. The same is true within the minor or "third" party organizations such as the Green Party or the Reform Party, which has served as a vehicle to promote the divergent views of Texas billionaire and presidential candidate H. Ross Perot, former Minnesota governor Jesse Ventura, and conservative commentator Patrick Buchanan.

Because the United States has a weak party system, individual politicians not only run their own campaigns for office but also promote their own ideas. Many feel little obligation to support the official party position on policy issues, especially when electoral forces in their constituencies differ from those influencing the national party. In the same vein, the political context can vary greatly from one state to another, or even from one community in a state to another. Some states and cities tend to favor conservative policies, while others support liberal policies. Much depends on the alignment of party and ideological forces in the particular jurisdiction, in addition to the social and economic contexts.

Among the policy implications of the prevailing political context in the United States is the continual challenge of reconciling partisan and ideological differences. Policy actors who cannot agree on what action to take may decide to do nothing, allowing social problems to continue unchanged; or they might reach a temporary compromise that falls short of an ideal solution. It is not at all unusual in the U.S. political system to see enactment of such policy compromises, which may contain broad or vaguely worded components. The details, where the greatest conflicts often occur, are worked out later, typically by the rulemakers and managers in the executive branch agencies.

Governing Context

The U.S. government is highly complex, and its structure has a major impact on public policymaking. The authority to act is widely dispersed among institutions and policy actors. As a result, the time needed to resolve differences can be lengthy. In addition, the inevitable compromises lead to policies that may be less focused or coherent than many would wish.

The separation of powers mandated by the Constitution requires that any policy developed at the national level be acceptable to a majority of Congress and to the president. Policymakers in both institutions must therefore find common ground. In recent decades, the search for consensus has been difficult because of divided government, with one political party in control of the White House and the other in control of one or both houses of Congress. Strong philosophical differences among policymakers over the role of government and the need to satisfy differing political constituencies often make them unwilling to compromise. Even with unified government, as the United States has in 2009 and at least until 2010, it can be difficult to reach a compromise. Pundits often talk about the need for a filibuster-proof Senate, which would require a sixty-seat majority of the president's party. If policymakers dig in their heels and do nothing, outdated and ineffective policies will continue in force, and consideration of new and possibly more effective policies will not progress.

Under the U.S. political system, the federal government and the states share governing responsibilities. Prior to the New Deal, these institutions had defined areas of governance. The situation is less clear today; more often than not, state and federal government responsibilities overlap. For example, state governments traditionally were responsible for education policy, but since 1960 the federal government has become more involved in education. It provides billions of dollars in education grants to state and local governments and subsidizes student loan programs in higher education, but the funds can come with many strings attached. Newer legislation, such as No Child Left Behind, increases federal involvement in education policy by pushing for evaluation of success in the nation's schools, including setting standards for what students should know.

In addition to overlapping responsibilities, the states and the federal government face other problems of divided authority that arise when federal and state agencies try to determine what they need to do to put a policy into effect. Sometimes, the federal government is willing to share governing responsibility, but not money. For example, the federal government has granted authority to the states to implement many environmental programs, such as those falling under the Clean Water Act, but the states say that the funds from Washington are insufficient to cover the costs of their new duties. Throughout the 1990s, states frequently grumbled about these so-called unfunded mandates. Congress made some efforts to limit the practice in regard to future mandates but did little about the previously approved mandates. It is clear that the states have a larger role today in the development and implementation of public policy. State and local governments have been forced to step in to fill the gap left by a shrinking or inattentive federal government. This devolution of authority to the states provides opportunities for innovation; however, it may also produce a "race to the bottom" as states compete with one another to save money. The evidence on the effects of such devolution is mixed to date (Donahue 1997; Rabe 2010).

Americans sometimes complain that "government can't get anything done." In light of the complexity of the U.S. governance structure, with its overlapping responsibilities and political disagreements, a more accurate statement might be that it is a minor miracle that policies get enacted and implemented at all.

Cultural Context

Political culture refers to widely held values, beliefs, and attitudes, such as trust and confidence in government and the political process, or the lack thereof. Political culture also includes commitment to individualism, property rights, freedom, pragmatism or practicality, equality, and similar values, some of which are distinctly American. These values are acquired through a process of political socialization that takes place in families, schools, and society in general, and that at times seems to reflect popular culture and television (Putnam 1995, 2000). Scholars have found that such political cultures not only vary from nation to nation but from state to state within the United States, and even from one community to another, as one might expect in a diverse society. These cultural differences help to explain the variation in state (and local) public policies across the nation (Elazar 1984; Lieske 1993) and also account for some of the differences in voting between "red" states (Republican) and "blue" states (Democrat). Some states, such as California and Massachusetts, often enact progressive policies, while others, such as Texas and Mississippi, are reliably conservative in their policy enactments. Similarly, some cities, such as San Francisco, New York, and Boston, have notably liberal cultural values and policies, while others, such as Dallas, Phoenix, and Salt Lake City, are much more conservative in both their values and policy actions.

At times, the policies under consideration are linked directly to cultural perspectives. For example, former secretary of education William Bennett and writer James Q. Wilson have connected what they see as a decline in public morality to crime, abortion, and education. Those who believe that the ideals of right and wrong have not been given sufficient weight in U.S. society tend to promote stricter punishments for convicted criminals. Those who believe in deterrence feel that education and opportunity can reduce crime. Recurring battles over family planning programs, abortion rights, and international population policy reflect cultural conflicts, especially over the role of women in society, that have yet to be resolved.

Cultural conflicts also affect public judgments about government officials and their conduct and may influence the policy-making process. President Clinton's impeachment by the House of Representatives in 1998 and his subsequent trial in the Senate clearly demonstrated the differences of opinion over his fate. Many conservatives wanted to punish Clinton for what they saw as his immoral behavior as well as violations of law, such as lying to a grand jury. In contrast, many liberals were willing to overlook Clinton's sexual misconduct and attempts to hide it because they placed a higher value on his contributions to government and public policy, which they believed substantially enhanced the nation's well-being. The conflicts between the two sides significantly affected the policy process during the investigation, impeachment, and trial—and for months afterwards—by deflecting attention from policy proposals and weakening support for White House initiatives. These conflicts also show that, for many political and policy issues, citizens and policymakers must decide how much weight to give to competing social values such as the relative importance of personal and professional behavior.

These conflicts have translated into constraints on policymaking. While not a new issue, partisanship is more apparent than before at both the state and national level. Members of Congress have observed that partisan rancor, ideological disputes, and decreased willingness to compromise on policy issues have made policymaking far more difficult than it was only a decade ago (Dodd and Oppenheimer 2009). As a result, government often finds itself deadlocked, completely unable to deal effectively with issues. The inability to solve public problems further erodes the public's trust in government and diminishes its willingness to get involved in the political process.[12]

THE REASONS FOR GOVERNMENT INVOLVEMENT

When the public and policymakers believe that government needs to intervene to correct a social problem, they create or alter policies. But this does not mean the matter is settled permanently. The rationales offered for government involvement in public policy were highly contested in the past, and they continue to be today. The arguments for and against government intervention in the economy and in people's lives draw from political philosophies and ideologies, specific beliefs about policy needs, and the positions that are advocated by political parties and interest groups. These arguments often are advanced during the processes of agenda setting (to discourage or encourage action), policy formulation (where the specific form of intervention is designed), or policy legitimation (where the rationale for intervention may be debated). The three leading, and somewhat overlapping, rationales for government intervention are: political reasons, moral or ethical reasons, and economics or market failure. The last of these rationales warrants a longer discussion than the others because it is often thought to be more complex.

Political Reasons

The public and policymakers may decide that government should intervene to solve a problem for political reasons. The reasons vary, but often they reflect a notable shift in public opinion or the rise of a social movement pressing for action. After the 1954 Supreme Court decision on public school segregation in *Brown v. Topeka Board of Education* and the rise of the civil rights movement, for example, the federal government began to act on civil rights. President Lyndon Johnson persuaded Congress to adopt new policies to prevent discrimination against minorities, including the Civil Rights Act of 1964. In the 1960s the federal government began the Medicare program after more than twenty years of public debate in which critics argued that such actions were not legitimate for government and that they constituted a step toward "socialized medicine." During the 1960s and 1970s the federal government also substantially increased its involvement in consumer protection, automobile safety, and environmental protection because of rising public concern about these issues.

Moral or Ethical Reasons

In addition to the power of public opinion or a social movement, certain problems and circumstances may dictate that government should be involved for moral or ethical reasons. In other words, government action is seen as the right thing to do even without public pressure. Some portion of the population or members of an organized interest group may be unwilling to witness suffering from poverty, hunger, or human rights abuses, either at home or abroad, and want the government to do something about it. They may join groups to lobby policymakers or contact them directly to persuade them to take action.

There are many examples of government acting primarily for moral or ethical reasons. As we discuss in chapter 9, Social Security was adopted to ensure that the elderly, disabled, and the minor children of deceased or disabled workers had sufficient income and would not suffer from the ravages of poverty. Debate over the future of the Social Security system continues this moral argument. Similar moral values lie behind the United States' long-standing support of family planning programs and economic assistance in developing nations. These operations have been defended as essential to promoting much-needed economic development that could rescue people from desperate poverty. The Bush administration offered many different reasons for its decision in 2003 to invade Iraq, but here too parallel moral arguments were advanced, including the need to remove dictator Saddam Hussein from power and to promote the growth of democracy and freedom in that nation.

Economics and Market Failures

In a pure capitalist or market system, most economists would not consider the plight of family farmers who cannot compete with large agribusiness or the challenges that face many other small businesses a legitimate reason for government intervention. They would argue that government intrusion into the marketplace distorts the efficiency with which a competitive market economy can allocate society's resources. In such a market, voluntary and informed exchanges between buyers and sellers allow them to meet their needs efficiently, especially when large numbers of people are involved, so that the market operates fairly. In this world, competition sets the fair market value on houses, cars, and other goods.

Economists acknowledge, however, that a situation known as **market failure** warrants government intervention. A market failure occurs when the private market is not efficient. Market failures fall into four types: the existence of monopolies and oligopolies, externalities, information failure, and inability to provide for the public or collective good.

A monopoly or oligopoly exists when one or several persons or companies dominate the market and can control the price of a product or service. Examples abound. It is a rare community that has more than one cable television operator or electric power company. Monopolies of this kind are called "natural" or "technical" because they are essentially unavoidable. There would be little sense in having multiple cable TV operators or power companies in an average-size city if greater efficiency can be achieved by having a single company invest in the necessary infrastructure. Governments usually accept this kind of monopoly but institute regulations to ensure that the public is treated fairly. Yet the balance between government regulation and economic freedom for the monopoly is the subject of ongoing debate.

Externalities are the decisions and actions of those involved in the market exchange that affect other parties, either negatively or positively. A **negative externality** occurs when two parties interact in a market and, as a result of that interaction, a third party is harmed and does not get compensation. Pollution is a negative externality. For example, consumers enter into an agreement with the utility to provide electricity. In the absence of government regulation, the utility may decide to use the least expensive fuel, most likely coal. When coal is burned, it sends pollutants into the atmosphere, which settle downwind and may cause health problems to a third party. The third party, not the two parties interacting in the electricity market, pays the costs of those health problems. Ideally, the health care costs associated with electricity production would be considered part of the cost of production, and government intervention may ensure that this happens. Through environmental regulation, the government requires utilities to install pollution-control technology on their plants to limit the amount of pollutants emitted.

A **positive externality** occurs the same way as a negative externality, but the third party gains something from the two-party interaction and does not have to pay for it. Higher education is a positive externality. Some policymakers argue that because society benefits from a well-educated population, it should be willing to provide financial support to encourage people to continue their education. Many state governments subsidize higher education tuition for their local institutions. For example, Georgia has a HOPE (Helping Outstanding Pupils Educationally) Scholarship Program, which provides tuition for students who graduate from high school with a 3.0 average within a certain core curriculum and maintain that average in college (Georgia Student Finance Commission 2005). In essence, this benefit increases students' incomes and enables them to afford more schooling.

Information failure is the third kind of market failure. According to the theories of market operation, to have perfect competition willing buyers and sellers must have all of the information needed to enter into a transaction or exchange. When the information is not fully or easily available,

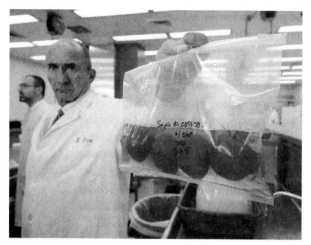

Once a rarity, the United States has experienced an unusually high number of food contamination scares in the last few years. Despite the role of the Food and Drug Administration (FDA) and the Department of Agriculture in trying to ensure a safe food supply, public anxiety has risen after publicity about possibly dangerous tomatoes and, more recently, peanut butter products. As a result, policymakers are considering whether the nation needs a new food safety agency or a stronger FDA to protect public health. The photo shows Mark Roh, the FDA's acting regional director, holding a bag of tomatoes being tested for salmonella bacteria at the agency's southwest regional research lab in Irvine, California, in June 2008. Microbiologists at the site were working to trace the origin of a multistate salmonella food poisoning outbreak. Ultimately, the source turned out not to be tomatoes but rather jalapeño peppers from Mexico.

a market failure may occur. At times, the consumers' lack of complete information about a product or service does not present a major problem: consumers can adjust their buying behavior if they believe there is something wrong with the goods or services they purchased. When the lack of information leads the consumer to suffer significant financial or personal loss, the government may step in. A clear example of such government intervention is its regulation of prescription and over-the-counter pharmaceuticals. Without government, consumers would find it impossible to figure out whether medical drugs are safe and effective. The Federal Food and Drugs Act of 1906 established the modern FDA and authorized it to test proposed drugs to ensure their safety and efficacy. Another FDA example is the public warnings or recalls of particular food items that may be causing sickness, such as alerts provided in the summer of 2008 regarding possibly contaminated tomatoes and jalapeño peppers and the peanut butter scare in early 2009. Chapter 8 discusses how well the FDA does its job.

A fourth kind of market failure occurs when markets cannot provide for the **public good,** also called the **collective good.** A public or collective good is defined by two criteria: the ability to exclude someone from getting the good and the ability to jointly consume the good. Exclusion within the U.S. economy typically occurs through pricing. If an individual can charge for a good or service, then he or she can exclude someone from getting it. Goods that can be jointly consumed are those in which one person's consumption does not prevent another from also consuming it. The two criteria can be displayed as a typology (see Table 1-1) of private goods and public goods that clarifies the range of what analysts call collective goods.

A pure private good, as defined in the table, refers to a good that is private and for which there is no market failure. It represents the normal, day-to-day interactions between the private sector and consumers. The other three kinds of goods refer to nonprivate or public goods, and they signal conditions that may require government intervention to alleviate the market failure.

Toll goods can be jointly consumed, and exclusion is feasible. An obvious example is a utility such as electricity or cable services. One person's use of cable services does not preclude another person's use, but a cable company's charges may exclude low-income individuals. Earlier, we identified such goods as natural monopolies. To keep essential services affordable, government intervenes by regulating prices. For years public utility commissions regulated prices that electric companies could charge their consumers. Experiments in electricity market

TABLE 1-1 Private Goods and Public Goods	No Joint Consumption	Joint Consumption
Exclusion Is Feasible	1 Pure private goods Examples: DVD players, automobiles, houses	2 Toll goods Examples: cable TV services, electrical utilities
Exclusion Is Not Feasible	3 Common pool resources Examples: air, water, grazing land, oceans, fisheries, wildlife	4 Pure public goods Examples: national defense, public parks

deregulation have tried to create more competition and choices for consumers, but they have not always succeeded. California's energy crisis in 2000 and 2001, when electricity was in short supply, was widely attributed to the state's failed experiment with such deregulation and to fraudulent action by some power companies.

Common pool resources are goods that cannot be jointly consumed and for which exclusion is not feasible. For example, environmental scientists write about a "tragedy of the commons," which comes about from use of natural resources such as air, water, grazing land, fisheries, and the like. The tragedy is that each individual seeks to maximize his or her use of the common pool resources without regard to their degradation or depletion because no one owns them. Such individual behavior may lead to the loss of the resources for all, even when each person would benefit from their continued use. To ensure the preservation of these shared goods, government intervenes. It requires individuals to have a license to fish, which may preclude some from partaking in the good, but the funds raised through the licensing fee can be used to restock the fishery. Government may also set catch limits on different species to prevent overfishing, and it requires ranchers to pay a fee to allow their cattle to feed on public grazing land. For common pool resources, government's role is to develop policies to ensure their continuance or sustainability. Without government, the public would likely deplete these goods.

Finally, **pure public goods** can be jointly consumed, and exclusion is not feasible. They would not be provided at all without government intervention because the private sector has no incentive to provide them. National defense and public parks are examples. For these kinds of goods government intervention is necessary to ensure the general public has them.

These three reasons for government intervention—political, moral and ethical, and economic or market failure—are not exhaustive. Other reasons may present themselves, and these three may not be mutually exclusive; that is, policymakers may favor government action for one or more reasons at the same time. The reasons also may change over time: policies are adopted and changed in a continuous cycle, which is part of society's response to public problems and efforts to find solutions. Government intervention is simply one of these options. When such intervention no longer works or no longer makes sense, policies may be changed in favor of private action or free markets once again. Much of the movement toward deregulation of financial markets in the 1980s and of energy markets in the late 1990s reflected such views. The adverse consequences of deregulation prompted a new round of public debate over what kind of government intervention best serves the public interest.

WHY STUDY PUBLIC POLICY?

As the discussion throughout this chapter has indicated, the study of public policy occurs in many different organizations and for diverse reasons. Policy analysts both in and outside of government have a professional concern for public policy. That is, they work on developing public policy solutions by studying public problems and various policy alternatives or choices that might be made. Scholars at universities and research institutions share some of the same interests as policy analysts, but they may also be concerned with building general knowledge and advancing theory, for example, of the policy process or the performance of government institutions. We will revisit these approaches to the study of public policy, especially policy analysis, in chapter 4.

For citizens who lack such professional reasons but who have strong personal interests in government and public policy, the U.S. political system affords numerous opportunities to become involved. Such interests alone are a good reason to study public policy, but it is not the only one. Studying public policy may help citizens sharpen their analytic skills, decide what political positions and policies to support, and how best to evaluate democratic governance. It may encourage students to consider careers in public policy, law, or government. Two additional reasons are presented here: citizens' ability to participate in policy processes and their ability to influence policy decisions.

Citizens' Ability to Participate and Make Choices

The United States is a representative democracy. Its citizens elect delegates to act for them, but that is not necessarily the end of citizen participation. Within democracies, citizens may speak out on policy development and government actions. Lack of knowledge about public problems, policies, government decisions, or politics does not normally keep people from acting in this way, but they can participate more effectively by improving their understanding of the issues. During political campaigns, candidates for public office state their positions on the issues through speeches and advertisements in hopes of persuading voters to support them. Voters who study public policy are better equipped to understand the candidates' policy ideas and to evaluate them—that is, to determine what impacts they are likely to have and whether they are desirable. If elections are to turn on informed assessments of the issues rather than how good the candidate looks on camera, policy knowledge of this kind is essential.

Citizens can also join with others in an interest group to learn more about public policy. Scholars often observe that the **logic of collective action** suggests that a single individual would be irrational to join an interest group when almost no personal gain follows (Olson 1971). The enormous growth of citizen lobbies over the last several decades, however, clearly indicates that agreement with a group's goals persuades many people to sign up and participate (Berry 1997, 1999). Interest groups operate at all levels of government, and one of their roles is to educate policymakers and citizens about public policy issues. For example, many of them—from the National Rifle Association to the Sierra Club—commission policy studies and use them in the political process to advance their views (Wolpe and Levine 1996; Cigler and Loomis 2007). Nearly all of the major groups maintain Web sites that offer issue briefings and facilitate communication with public officials. The box "Working with Sources: Interest Groups on the Web" addresses the role of such groups in shaping public policy.

At state and local levels citizens may have the opportunity to get more directly involved in policymaking through referendums, initiatives, or participation in public hearings and meetings (Cronin 1989). A referendum is a law proposed by a state or locality for voters to approve or reject. An initiative is much the same, but a group of citizens organizes the effort to place it on the ballot. About half the states allow citizen-generated initiatives. Naturally, the voters can better determine whether to support or oppose a ballot measure if they understand the proposal and its possible effects. Obtaining that information and developing a sound position on the issues is often a challenge for the average voter; it is also one reason critics argue that many initiatives lead to bad public policy, especially when insufficient thought goes into the drafting of the proposals or the public acts emotionally or in response to misleading media advertisements (Ellis 2002).

Public meetings afford perhaps the greatest opportunity to participate directly with other citizens and public officials to learn more about local problems and decide what to do about them. Notices of such meetings and hearings are posted in the local newspaper or on pertinent Web sites. The box "Working with Sources: The Public's Political Knowledge" is an introduction to a primary government source.

Citizens' Ability to Influence Policy Decisions

The ability of citizens to participate in decision-making activities can often lead to influence over the decisions that result. Policymakers and others involved in the policy process need information to understand the dynamics of a particular problem and develop options for action. As we show throughout this text, when examining policy alternatives policymakers and other actors often make use of policy analysis. The more that citizens are aware of such studies and their implications, the better equipped they are to play an effective role in policymaking and help to shape the decisions that are made. One of the major objectives of this text is to help readers improve their capacity for reading and interpreting such policy studies.

We also want to build understanding of the policy-making process itself and alert readers to the many opportunities they have to make their views known. Most readers may recognize that Congress has chief responsibility for making public policy. However, they may not be as alert to the critical role that administrative agencies play in implementing the laws that Congress enacts. Whether the Centers for Medicare and Medicaid Services in the Department of Health and Human Services or the Office for Civil Rights in the U.S. Department of Education, such agencies have enormous influence over how programs are run and the services they deliver to citizens. Citizens may be particularly able to influence government decisions at the state and local levels where policymakers and administrators are easier to reach.

Whether at the national, state, or local level, citizens who wish to be effective need to be alert to the politics of any given situation. They need to know who the major policy actors are and the motives behind the positions they take. We provide many examples in the chapters that follow. A simple one concerns reform of the Social Security system. Someone who wants to change it must recognize the interests of AARP (formerly known as the Association for the Advancement of Retired Persons), an interest group with more than thirty-nine million members over the age of fifty. AARP members have strong views on Social Security, can easily be mobilized to contact policymakers, and vote at a higher rate than other segments of the population. Not surprisingly, members of Congress and other policymakers tend to pay attention to AARP and take the group's positions on Social Security seriously.

WORKING WITH SOURCES

INTEREST GROUPS ON THE WEB

Interest group Web sites are treasure troves of policy information, but a word of warning is in order. Visitors to these sites need to be cautious about how they approach the materials and policy recommendations they find. Information on these sites is always selective; it may be limited in scope and biased in ways that a näive reader may not discern. Policy briefings and reports made available by such groups therefore merit careful and critical reading, and our goal here is to teach you how to be alert to the general political orientation of the group sponsoring the site. We start by asking about the credibility of the studies and reports you find there.

Visit the American Petroleum Institute (API) Web site (www.api.org)*, the major trade association for the oil industry, and access reports and data regarding its positions on energy issues by selecting the link for Policy Issues. Then click on the Global Climate Change link. From there, select the link for Regulation/Legislation, where you will find API's testimony before Congress on energy issues, letters sent to members of the House and Senate, and reports API commissioned on the effects of a climate change bill. Note especially the language API uses to support its position that

the nation should be cautious about the impact of climate change bills on energy supplies, costs, and jobs. It emphasizes the need to find policies that are "environmentally effective, economically sustainable and fair" and to "support the deployment of readily available energy technologies and sources such as clean burning natural gas."

For a contrasting view, visit the Natural Resources Defense Council (NRDC) Web site (www.nrdc.org) and follow the link to Curbing Global Warming and then to Repowering America, where you will see a summary of the NRDC position on limiting global warming and a link to the full report on repowering America and curbing global warming.

How credible is the information you found on the two Web sites? Does either supply references to authoritative sources for the information presented, such as government reports or studies published in scientific or scholarly journals? How else can you judge the facts and issue positions on these pages? By comparing the different positions and the language used to defend them, can you determine which group offers the most defensible stance on energy use and climate change?

*Note: Web sites are changed and upgraded frequently. The sites provided throughout this text are meant to be current; however, design changes may require you to investigate a site more thoroughly than originally assigned.

THE PRACTICE OF POLICY ANALYSIS

There is one last topic we would like to introduce in this chapter. This is the value of policy analysis as a way of thinking about public policy. As we noted earlier, policy analysis is usually described as a systematic and organized way to evaluate public policy alternatives or existing government programs. Often it involves applying economic tools and other quantitative methods or measures. Policy analysis may therefore seem to some students of public policy to hold little relevance to anyone except policy specialists, but in reality everyone uses such analysis in many day-to-day activities. Buying a car, selecting a particular college course, or deciding on a restaurant for dinner all require thinking about the pros and cons associated with the available choices, including how to spend money.

THE PUBLIC'S POLITICAL KNOWLEDGE

As indicated throughout the text, the enormous amount of information available through Web sites makes citizen activism more feasible than ever before. After all, the potential for activism is facilitated by information as well as by individual motivation to get involved. Reliance on Web sources, however, also presents a challenge: how to manage the huge amount of information.

In 2000 the federal government launched FirstGov, which has since evolved to USA.gov (www.usa.gov), an official portal to U.S. government Web sites. Its mission was to make government more accessible and seamless and to make it easier for citizens to find the services they seek and to complete transactions online. A new search engine developed specifically for accessing such material is capable of sifting through about fifty-one million pages of information from national, state, and local governments in a fraction of a second.

A simple exercise indicates how useful USA.gov can be. Go to the site, look under the Citizens list of links, and select Family, Home and Community. Next, select Community Resources and click Public Service and Volunteer Opportunities. Select Volunteer.gov and use one of the search options to find a list of organizations in your community that are seeking volunteers.

A more challenging illustration of how to navigate through USA.gov involves a different kind of citizen participation: voting. Once again, look under the Citizens link and select the link for Voting and Elections. Select U.S. Senators. Select one of the senators to visit their Web site. Senators maintain different types of Web sites, but all will have information about the senator, and many will have links to issues they care about or perhaps even their voting records. The sites will also provide information on how the senator may be able to help you. This is called "constituency service" and is a critical part of an officeholder's job while serving in office.

The Many Uses of Policy Analysis

Policy analysis can be used throughout the policy process, but it becomes especially important in the formulation of policies and evaluation of programs after they are implemented. In assessing a public problem, policy analysis may assist in describing its scope, such as the percentage of public schools that are failing. When developing alternatives and choosing a direction, a decision maker can use analysis to assess the feasibility of the choices based on economic, administrative, political, and ethical criteria. The same methods can be used to evaluate a program to determine its effectiveness or whether it has achieved its expected results.

In short, policy analysis represents an attempt to dissect problems and solutions in what is usually described as a rational manner. By this, practitioners mean that they bring information and systematic analysis to bear on policy issues and try to show how a given set of goals and objectives might be achieved most efficiently. Public policy goals and objectives are usually determined in a political process—for example, how much the government is willing to pay for health care services for the elderly—but analysis can help policymakers weigh competing ideas about how best to deliver such services.

Policy analysts argue that their systematic analyses should be given serious consideration as a counterweight to the tendency of public officials to make policy choices based on their partisan positions, ideology, or support from important constituencies and interest groups. They point to inconsistencies in public policy or to what some would describe as unwarranted or inefficient policy actions. For example, why does the federal government give subsidies to farmers growing tobacco while it also tries to reduce smoking? Why does Congress continue to subsidize mining and timber harvesting on public lands that causes environmental damage and costs taxpayers more than the revenues these activities earn? Why do members of Congress vote to spend public money on particular projects they favor (such as a highway or bridge in their district) and at the same time complain about the government's wasteful spending? The answers lie mostly in interest group and constituency pressures that elected officials find difficult to resist, particularly when the general public fails to take an interest in such decisions.

Citizens' Use of Policy Analysis

Ordinary citizens and organizations also can benefit from policy analysis. Citizens with an interest in public policy or the political system may make decisions based on their general political views; for example, liberals usually favor government regulation to improve the environment. But most people would understand the benefit of a focused study of a particular program or proposal that put aside personal political views. Perhaps the liberal environmentalist will come to question whether regulation is the best way to achieve environmental goals. A conservative might be moved to reassess whether stringent laws that put first-time drug offenders in prison for years make sense.

It is not unusual for individuals or interest groups to use information developed through policy analysis to reinforce the arguments they make to government policymakers. An organization will often dangle its latest research or analysis to convince policymakers that the group is correct in its beliefs. For example, the following information was gathered from the Sierra Club's Web site, www.sierraclub.org, advocating policies for cleaner air. The quotations come from a *Washington Post* article summarizing studies that the group included to reinforce its position on maintaining stringent clean air standards.

- "A study published in today's issue of the *Journal of the American Medical Association* concludes that people living in the most heavily polluted metropolitan areas have a 12 percent increased risk of dying of lung cancer than people in the least polluted areas."
- "Air pollution levels have declined significantly during the past 20 years because of stepped-up enforcement of clean air laws, yet levels of fine particle emissions in New York, Los Angeles, Chicago and Washington are at or exceed limits set by the Environmental Protection Agency."
- "Previous research by Harvard University and the American Cancer Society strongly linked these fine particles to high mortality rates from cardiopulmonary diseases such as heart attacks, strokes and asthma. Until now, however, scientists lacked sufficient statistical evidence to directly link those emissions to elevated lung cancer death rates."

By citing these analytical—presumably objective—studies, the Sierra Club hopes to move the direction of clean air policy toward stronger air quality standards.

The Sierra Club's opponents in the business community will circulate information, sometimes from the same studies, that bolsters their arguments about the uncertainty inherent in such health assessments and the high costs imposed on society if environmental policies and regulations are overly restrictive. For example, in 2002 the U.S. Chamber of Commerce made this statement on its Web page, www.uschamber.com, dealing with environmental and energy issues: "The U.S. Chamber's objective is to ensure that air quality standards are based on: a market-based approach rather than the out-dated command-and-control structure; sound, publicly available science; and a balancing of environmental protection and the needs of communities and business." Note in particular the emphasis given to "sound" science and to the need to balance environmental protection against the needs of communities and business. In this usage, "sound" is a buzzword signaling a distrust of the kind of science often used to support clean air and other environmental standards. Business groups contend that such scientific studies use methods that are frequently flawed and lead to unjustified regulations.

Presented with conflicting assumptions and interpretations, students of public policy need to be aware of the sources of information and judge for themselves which argument is strongest. This book provides the tools and techniques to help students make informed judgments. In particular, chapters 4 through 6 cover the major approaches to policy analysis and some of the methods, such as cost-benefit analysis and risk assessment, that make clear what the studies say and how the findings relate to policy choice.

For policymakers, policy analysis is an essential tool for the development of public policy and its evaluation. For citizens interested in public affairs, it provides a way to organize thoughts and information to be able to better understand the alternatives presented and the possible implications of these choices. Individuals do not have to know how to conduct complex economic analysis to recognize the importance of using a wide range of information when making decisions; they just need to be able to think about problems and solutions from different perspectives. The box "Steps to Analysis: How to Interpret Policy Studies" offers some suggestions for how to interpret the policy studies you encounter.

How to Decide Which Policy Is Best? Using Multiple Criteria

As the examples cited in this section suggest, much of the controversy over public policy, from international affairs to protection of public health, reflects conflicts over which values are most important. Does protection of national security warrant some infringement on individual rights? If so, to what extent? Should we continue or expand public programs (such as support of health services under Medicaid) even when they become very costly? Should we be more alert to the cost of military weapons systems, or should cost play no role in decisions to buy the weapons? When programs in any area (such as national defense, agricultural subsidies, environmental protection, or the war on terrorism) are not as effective as they should be, should we end them, or at least change them so they are likely to be more effective?

All of these questions suggest that citizens, analysts, and policymakers need to be aware of the multiple criteria that can be used to judge the merit or value of government policies and programs, and of proposed policy alternatives. We suggest that four criteria in particular deserve serious consideration: effectiveness, efficiency, equity, and political feasibility.

STEPS TO ANALYSIS

HOW TO INTERPRET POLICY STUDIES

Policy analysis is pervasive and critically important for the policymaking process at all levels of government. To determine which studies are credible and which are not, and which might be used as a basis for making policy decisions, students of public policy need to hone their analytical skills. How to do this? One way is to ask questions such as the following:

- What is the purpose of the study, and who conducted it?
- Does it seek and present objective information on the nature of the problem and possible solutions?

- Does the information seem to be valid, and what standard should you use to determine that?
- Is the report's argument logical and convincing?
- Does the report omit important subject matter?
- Does the study lay out the policy implications clearly and persuasively?

We will address these kinds of questions throughout the book when summarizing particular studies.

Effectiveness refers to whether a current policy or program or one that is being considered is likely to work. That is, how likely is it that the policy's goals or objectives will be achieved? In many policy areas, such as the environment, national defense, or energy, effectiveness may be affected by a proposal's technical or administrative feasibility. That is, it makes a difference whether a proposal is technically possible (for example, cheap, abundant, and clean energy sources) or whether an agency can adequately implement it.

Efficiency refers to what a policy or policy proposal costs in relation to its expected benefits to society. It also is sometimes described as a desire to realize the greatest possible benefit out of the dollars that government spends. Thus, considering a policy proposal's economic feasibility means asking whether it is "affordable" or will be considered a good use of public funds in an era when all programs compete for such funds.

Equity refers to the consideration of what constitutes a fair or equitable policy choice. It may be a way to consider how a program's costs and benefits are distributed among citizens (that is, fairly or not). Think of who benefits or gains from decisions to raise or lower taxes, whether it would be fair to have taxpayers pick up the full bill for college tuition at public colleges and universities, or who would be most affected by a decision to reinstate a military draft. The criterion of equity is also a way to think about who is allowed to participate in policy-making processes, such as who gets to vote or who gets to speak at a public hearing. That is, it is about whether the process is open and fair to all concerned.

Political feasibility concerns how government officials and other policy actors appraise the acceptability of a proposal. Most often, references to political feasibility reflect a judgment about whether elected officials (for example, members of Congress or state legislators) are willing to support a policy proposal. In a democracy, policymakers must consider the preferences and potential reactions of the public, interest groups, and other government officials when developing policies.

These criteria are not meant to be exhaustive. Others, such as ethical acceptability or consistency with political values such as individual freedom or civil liberties, may also be relevant, depending on the issue at hand. In addition, these criteria may not have equal weight in the decision-making process. Public officials acting on national defense and foreign policy issues, for example, rarely consider economic costs as paramount in reaching decisions. Personal freedom might be the primary consideration for some when considering policies in areas such as abortion rights, gun control, crime, and the privacy of e-mail and cellular telephone communications. Chapters 4 through 6 examine these criteria and the tools used to evaluate them more fully.

CONCLUSIONS

This chapter introduces the basic concepts of the study of public policy and policy analysis. It lays out the reasons for citizens, policymakers, and scholars to study both the policy-making process and the substance of public policy. It describes the contexts in which public policy debates and decisions take place: social, economic, political, governing, and cultural. And it reviews the major justifications or rationales for intervention by government in the form of public policy. The chapter explains the role of policy analysis in government policy-making processes and the need for citizens to think critically about the sources of information that are used to justify or to challenge policy action. Understanding the most frequently used criteria for evaluating public policy proposals—such as effectiveness, efficiency, and equity—is a good place to begin. Students of public policy also need to learn how to distinguish objective analysis from biased analysis. The suggestions on this point made here are augmented by many in the chapters to come.

The remainder of Section I continues an analysis of the big picture: the institutions involved and ways to approach public policy. Chapter 2 introduces the government institutions and actors involved in policymaking and how they interact. Chapter 3 explains the prevailing models and theories used to study public policy, focusing on the policy process.

Section II is a departure from other policy texts in its thorough coverage of policy analysis. In addition to an overview of policy analysis, chapter 4 presents the many different ways practitioners carry it out. Chapter 5 stresses problem analysis, or understanding the nature of public problems, their causes, and solutions. It also considers the various policy tools available to governments and how to think creatively about policy alternatives. Chapter 6 describes the leading methods of policy analysis and summarizes the most frequently used criteria to judge the acceptability of policy proposals.

The six chapters of Section III combine the material from the first two sections to delve into substantive policy topics. Each chapter follows the same format to illustrate how to think critically and constructively about public policy. These chapters highlight the nature of the problem, provide background on policy development, discuss different perspectives on policy change, and indicate how students might think about and assess the issues. Chapter 13 is a brief conclusion that emphasizes the role of citizen participation in policy choices.

The end of each chapter includes discussion questions to assist students in examining the implications of the material, short lists of suggested readings and useful Web sites, and key words. Because of the transitory nature of the Internet, readers should expect that some Web addresses will need to be updated. At the end of the book is a reference list for all of the works cited in the individual chapters.

DISCUSSION QUESTIONS

1. Do you agree with the "logic of collective action"? Do you think that people have nothing to gain by joining interest groups? What do you think people gain by participating in interest groups like the Sierra Club or the National Rifle Association?

2. How much government intrusion into daily life is acceptable? Is the reduction in personal freedom worth the benefits that the policy provides to society? What kinds of policies are acceptable and unacceptable in America? Is this the same in other nations?

3. Of the various evaluative criteria discussed in the chapter, effectiveness and efficiency are most often discussed. Why is equity not considered as often? For what types of policy issues should equity be a primary concern? Using these examples, how would you evaluate equity concerns?

4. The federal government inserted itself directly and massively into the economy during the economic crisis of 2008 and 2009, largely by trying to bail out or rescue corporations at risk of failure, including many banks and other financial institutions and the U.S. auto industry. Discuss the economic, political, and moral reasons behind the government's decision to do this.

SUGGESTED READINGS

James E. Anderson, *Public Policymaking: An Introduction,* 6th ed. (Boston: Houghton Mifflin, 2006). A leading text on the policy process that describes multiple perspectives on politics and policymaking.

Charles O. Jones, *An Introduction to the Study of Public Policy,* 3rd ed. (Monterey, Calif.: Brooks/Cole Publishing Company, 1984). An older but still useful text on politics and policymaking.

Michael Moran, Martin Rein, and Robert E. Goodin, eds., *The Oxford Handbook of Public Policy,* paper ed. (New York: Oxford University Press, 2008). Part of the ten-volume series *Handbook of Political Science,* this volume comprehensively surveys the major approaches to public policy from the perspective of political science.

Deborah Stone, *Policy Paradox: The Art of Political Decision Making,* rev. ed. (New York: W. W. Norton, 2002). An original and provocative assessment of the role of policy analysis in the political process.

Carl E. Van Horn, Donald C. Baumer, and William T. Gormley Jr., *Politics and Public Policy,* 3rd ed. (Washington, D.C.: CQ Press, 2001). A unique, perceptive analysis of politics and policymaking in the U.S. system.

SUGGESTED WEB SITES

www.appam.org/home.asp. Home page for the Association for Public Policy Analysis and Management, with useful links to the study of public policy and management, graduate education in the field, and public service careers.

www.apsanet.org. Home page for the American Political Science Association, with information on academic study of public policy and related fields in the discipline.

www.ipsonet.org. Policy Studies Organization home page.

www.policylibrary.com/index.html. Policy Library home page, with links to worldwide policy studies.

www.publicagenda.org. A guide to diverse policy issues and public opinion surveys.

www.usa.gov. The federal government's portal to government sites.

KEYWORDS

NOTES

1. International Association of Amusement Parks and Attractions, "U.S. Amusement Park Attendance and Revenue History," available at www.iaapa.org/pressroom/Amusement_Park_Attendance_Revenue_History.asp.

2. For more information, see "Report: Parks Shut Down Drop-Tower Rides after Teen Loses Feet," available at www.cnn.com/2007/US/06/22/six.flags.accident/index.html.

3. See the Theme Park Insider at www.themeparkinsider.com/accidents/list.cfm.

4. To explore these state differences some more, check out the Saferparks Web site at www.saferparks.org.

5. For more information, see "Bill Seeks Federal Oversight of Theme Park Attractions," *Orlando Business Journal,* November 30, 2007, available at www.bizjournals.com/orlando/stories/2007/12/03/story2.html.

6. "Theme Park Regulation Crippled," *Washington Post,* December 6, 2007.

7. National Safety Council, "Fixed Site Amusement Ride Injury Survey, 2005 Update," September 2006, available at www.nsc.org/research/publications.aspx.

8. United States Consumer Product Safety Commission, "2006 Annual Report of ATV Related Deaths and Injuries," February 2008; University of Michigan Health System, "Lawn Mower Safety Could Save Life and Limb this Summer," June 2, 2003, available at www.med.umich.edu/opm/newspage/2003/lawnmower.htm; "University of Michigan Health System" and "Winter Sports Safety," available at www.med.umich.edu/1libr/yourchild/wintsafe.htm (December 2006).

9. See Eric Schmitt, "Tobacco Lobby Tries to Keep Pentagon Cigarette Subsidy," *New York Times,* October 20, 1996, 1, 12. The Pentagon's analysts estimated that the tobacco subsidy cost the Defense Department $384 million a year in health expenses and $346 million a year in lost productivity.

10. See, for example, a critical review of the way the Bush administration ran OSHA: R. Jeffrey Smith, "Asleep on the Job: OSHA Career Officials Say Bush Appointees Ignored Danger and Favored Employers," *Washington Post National Weekly Edition,* January 5–11, 2009.

11. See Mary Dalrymple, "Many Divisions Yield Gloomy Forecast for Upcoming Appropriations Season," *CQ Weekly,* May 18, 2002, 1294–1297. The volatile economy in 2002 and again in 2009 made budget projections of this kind more difficult than usual.

12. Morris Fiorina argues that most Americans are moderate in their political views and not as polarized as the political activists and party leaders. See Fiorina (with Samuel J. Abrams and Jeremy C. Pope), *Culture War: The Myth of a Polarized America* (New York: Pearson Longman, 2004).

CHAPTER 2

GOVERNMENT
INSTITUTIONS AND
POLICY ACTORS

IN AN ACCOUNT THAT WOULD FUNDAMENTALLY ALTER NATIONAL policy on cleaning up toxic waste sites around the nation, the *New York Times* on August 2, 1978, carried a front-page story on the now infamous Love Canal, near Niagara Falls, New York. The paper reported that twenty-five years after the Hooker Chemical Company stopped using a local canal as an industrial dump, "82 different compounds, 11 of them suspected carcinogens, have been percolating upward through the soil, their drum containers rotting and leaching their contents into the backyards and basements of 100 homes and a public school built on the banks of the canal."[1] Once Americans became aware of the health dangers posed by toxic and hazardous wastes such as those found at Love Canal and many other locations, their concern was instrumental in the enactment of federal policies to reduce the risks.

At times since then, however, the leading federal program for controlling the most serious of the nation's abandoned or uncontrolled hazardous waste sites, the Comprehensive Environmental Response, Compensation, and Liability Act (CERCLA), popularly known as Superfund because of a large fund used to pay for cleanup costs, has been at a standstill. Critics have condemned the law for the slow and costly cleanup of those sites and claim some of its provisions stimulate more litigation than cleanup. For the skeptics, including many in the business community, Superfund is a poster child for what is wrong with complex, inflexible environmental regulatory programs. Environmentalists, however, view Superfund as a vitally important program that correctly imposes demanding standards for the cleanup of chemical waste sites to protect the public's health. They also applaud the law's stringent liability standards that force polluters to pay for the cost of cleanup. Largely because the critics and defenders of the law see the issues so differently and are so determined to have their respective ways, Congress has been unable to agree on how to modify Superfund so that it can achieve its goals more effectively and efficiently (Kraft 2010; Portney and Stavins 2000).

A fence around the contaminated Love Canal dump site in New York State illustrates the danger that toxic chemicals in the area posed for nearby residents. Many found that the chemicals were seeping into their basements and creating unsafe living conditions. Love Canal became emblematic of the risk posed by thousands of such sites around the nation. In 1980 Congress approved the Comprehensive Environmental Response, Compensation, and Liability Act, better known as Superfund, to identify, assess, and clean up the worst of these sites. Yet in recent years Congress has been deadlocked over the policy, with little agreement on how it should be changed to meet contemporary needs. This chapter explores the institutional and political reasons why government often finds it difficult to act quickly in response to such public problems.

The policy impasse evident in the case of Superfund can be found in many other policy areas. For example, Congress was also divided over dealing with health care policy during the Clinton administration in the early 1990s and about prescription drug coverage and other health policy issues in the early 2000s. To cite another example, members of Congress were unable to reach agreement from 2001 to 2005 on a national energy policy, despite recognition that the nation had become dangerously dependent on imported oil and as a result faced significant economic and national security risks. In August of 2005 they finally approved a portion of what the Bush administration had recommended, chiefly subsidies to expand domestic production of fossil fuels and increase use of nuclear power. In December of 2007 they added new requirements to improve automobile fuel efficiency. Yet by 2008 Congress was again trying to formulate national energy policies, and the debate continued into 2009, when both Congress and the Obama administration agreed that major changes were still needed, in part to deal with rising concern over climate change. Other examples of such policy stalemate or piecemeal action abound. For instance, politicians and policy analysts have recognized for years that changes are necessary in both the Social Security and Medicare programs in order to maintain their solvency, yet nothing significant has occurred. In all of these policy areas, conflict was simply too great to permit members of Congress to act (or act fully) on the problems the nation faced.

When political decision makers are unable or unwilling to compromise in a way that permits public policy action, the result is **policy gridlock.** It occurs for many reasons: high levels of partisanship and ideological conflict, disagreements among policymakers and influential interest groups over policy goals and means, a lack of consensus among the public, and the complexity of the problems. Whether the public is worse off or better off because of gridlock depends on the particular policy conflict, but few doubt that the public views a government stalemate negatively or that it is a source of political cynicism about a political process in which leaders often appear unwilling to act (Hibbing and Theiss-Morse 1995, 2002; Hibbing and Larimer 2005).

Most people see policy gridlock of this kind as a failure of government, and in many ways it is. But it is also true that U.S. political institutions were designed with the clear intention of making actions on public policy—and therefore the expansion of government authority—difficult. The chosen institutional structure reflected the prevailing political values and culture of late-eighteenth-century America. At that time only about four million people lived in the United States, most of them in rural areas and small towns. In 2008 the population was close to 305 million, with the overwhelming majority of people living in large metropolitan areas and their suburbs. At its founding, the nation faced relatively few public problems, and most people believed that it was more important to maintain their freedoms than to create a powerful government that could act swiftly in response to national problems. Many critics of the U.S. system wonder whether its political institutions are even capable of responding effectively to the highly complex and interdependent problems the United States faces at home and abroad, from maintaining a strong economy to dealing with climate change or global terrorism (Chubb and Peterson 1989; Ophuls and Boyan 1992).

Understanding this system of government and how policy actors maneuver within it is essential for students of public policy. It enables us to assess the constraints on policy development and the many opportunities that nevertheless exist within the U.S. political system for solving public problems through creative policy action. The complexity of many contemporary problems, such as urban sprawl or failing public school systems, also hints at the crucial role that policy analysis plays, or can play, in designing effective, economically feasible, and fair solutions.

This chapter surveys the major institutions and actors involved in making public policy in the United States. It begins with a brief account of the growth of government over time, then looks at the interrelationship of policy actors and their institutions and how political incentives as well as constitutional and legal constraints affect their behavior. The next chapter deals with the policy-making process and how policy analysis can clarify issues and choices.

GROWTH OF GOVERNMENT

Most people recognize that government today is much larger than it was at the nation's founding, and that it is also much more likely to affect their lives, from regulation of broadcast media to provision of loans for college education. They may disagree, however, as liberals and conservatives often do, on whether such government involvement is a good thing or not. Most people value the services that government provides, but many also complain about government and the programs it creates, particularly their costs and effectiveness. As the nation continued in an economic recession in 2009, we saw additional calls for federal government action to help revitalize the economy. The Obama administration and Congress also are very likely to take on the challenge of dealing with the nation's health care needs, particularly insurance for those not covered or covered insufficiently. These actions may increase the size of government even more, and as we noted in chapter 1, we already have greatly increased federal spending and the deficit in recent years. So how did government come to be so big and, at least in some views, such an intrusive force in the lives of citizens?

The original U.S. government was quite small, as was the nation itself. The first Congress, representing thirteen states, had sixty-five representatives and twenty-six senators. The bureaucracy consisted of three cabinet-level departments (War, Treasury, and Foreign Affairs, to which one more, Justice, was added). In contrast, today there are fifteen departments, numerous bureaus and agencies, and about 2.7 million civilian federal employees, counting civil servants and postal workers (Office of Personnel Management 2005). Despite widespread belief to the contrary, the federal government's size, measured by employees and not budgets, has been relatively stable since the 1970s. Indeed, it decreased during the 1990s, and has seen only a small increase since 2000. However, at the same time, the number of federal contractors and grant recipients has increased substantially since 1990, and particularly since the early 2000s. As Brookings Institution scholar Paul Light has argued, this group constitutes a kind of "hidden" federal workforce and disguises the true size of government today.[2] Much of the rest of the recent growth in government employees has been in the states. Still, viewed in the broad sweep of history, it is important to understand why government has grown to its present size.

Obviously, part of the growth of government results from the expansion of the United States in physical area and population. The population has increased more than seventyfold from the initial four million residents at the time of the first census in 1790. The population today is also heavily urban and well educated compared to that of 1790, and it occupies land from coast to coast as well as in Alaska and Hawaii. Demographics and geography, however, cannot fully explain the growth of government, which has more to do with the changing nature of public problems and citizen expectations for government services than it does with the nation's size.

One major reason for government's increasing size is that American society has become more complicated. This added complexity, which comes in part from advances in science and technology, has led to many kinds of government intervention, from regulation of television, radio, and satellite communications to airline safety; none was a reason for concern a hundred years ago. Few people today would argue that government should not be in the business of regulating air safety, or food and drug safety, or automobile safety, or environmental protection, all for similar reasons. Indeed, as scientific knowledge about the technological risks posed by nuclear power or toxic chemicals increases, the more likely the public is to demand government policies that offer protection from unacceptable dangers (Andrews 2006a; Lowrance 1976).

Another reason for the growth of government is the public's acceptance of business regulation. Even though politicians still like to talk about the free-market economy, the United States has moved away from it to a regulated, or mixed, economy. Nowhere does the Constitution mention the power to prevent monopolies, provide for safe food and drugs, or require limits on child labor, but all of these policies are in effect, to varying degrees, today. They resulted not only from legislation but also from the Supreme Court's expansive interpretations of the commerce and the necessary and proper clauses of the Constitution.

Viewed from a historical perspective, policy change on government regulation has been astonishing. Congress has enacted regulatory statutes that, prior to the Progressive Era of the late nineteenth and early twentieth centuries, would have been considered improper exercises of government authority. By then, however, social pressure for reform was strong enough that government had the backing to correct some of the excesses flowing from rapid industrialization in the 1800s. These included the prevalence of unsafe food and drugs and dangerous working conditions, and the domination of entire industries by monopolies. These social pressures also spurred major advances in business regulation during President Franklin Roosevelt's New Deal (Harris and Milkis 1996). At first resistant to New Deal legislation, the Supreme Court eventually ruled many of these acts constitutional. In doing so, the Court reflected society's endorsement of these new powers of government.

Attitudes have also changed about government's role in social welfare. Again, under the New Deal the federal government signaled its responsibility to provide a minimal level of support for certain individuals, including the poor, farmers, and the elderly. By that time many states had already developed such social programs for certain categories of individuals (Skocpol 1995). President Lyndon Johnson's Great Society agenda expanded those commitments in the 1960s. As government moved into the area of social welfare support, it also grew to administer these programs. For example, Social Security today is the single largest government program and requires a large organization to administer it.

America's role in the world has also contributed to government growth. After World War II (1941–1945) the United States emerged as a superpower and took a larger role in world affairs. The government had to grow to keep up with the new responsibilities in foreign affairs and national defense, which has meant not only an increase in the budget and personnel of the Departments of Defense and State, but also in agencies with peripheral connections to international affairs, such as the Environmental Protection Agency and the Departments of Commerce and Agriculture.

In addition, the size, scope, and cost of certain projects mean that only the government can undertake them. They may come about because of a market failure, as discussed in chapter 1, or changes in public expectations of government. Some individuals and organized groups therefore argue that for social or economic progress to occur, government needs to become involved. No other entity, they say, can perform the functions of government, especially space exploration and other scientific research and development, including work in the areas of defense, energy, and health.

Finally, Americans must accept some responsibility for the growth of government. Citizen demands for government action continue to rise. Americans tend to be ideologically conservative but liberal in practice with respect to provision of government services, from police protection to health care for the elderly. One can see the evidence throughout the federal rule-making process, which is a good indicator of government growth.

> [T]he American people have developed a habit that is the ultimate cause of rulemaking. To reduce significantly the number of rules written by agencies, someone or something must persuade the American people to stop turning to government as a means of achieving their aspirations or solving their problems. (Kerwin 1999, 276)

The Tenth Amendment of the Constitution declares: "The powers not delegated to the United States by the Constitution, nor prohibited by it to the States, are reserved to the States respectively, or to the people." These powers are often called the reserve powers of the states and are the basis for their right to legislate in many areas. Despite the federal government's involvement in public policy issues that were formerly the states' exclusive domain, state and local governments also have grown substantially over the past fifty years. Moreover, the trend toward devolution to the states (discussed later) has meant that many of these governments now are often at the leading edge of policy development.

The effects of government growth are many. First, government policies affect most of what people do every day. Second, government growth has led to an entire occupational sector. Not only are governments at all levels major employers, but also their buying power has a substantial impact on numerous economic sectors that rely on government programs and spending. Third, the scope of government increases the likelihood of conflicting public policies and greater difficulty in addressing society's problems. Fourth, policymaking in a large, complex government organization takes more time and effort—to analyze problems, discuss alternatives, decide on solutions, and implement programs—than in a smaller entity. When such efforts do not succeed, the result is policy stalemate or gridlock, the phenomenon to which we referred at the chapter's opening. This is a major reason why we emphasize in this chapter how the government's **policy capacity**—its ability to identify, assess, and respond to public problems—might be improved.

GOVERNMENT INSTITUTIONS AND POLICY CAPACITY

Many students are already familiar with the major U.S. government institutions. Even so, a brief review of their most notable features and the implications for public policymaking may be useful.

The reason is that the way institutions are designed and structured is critical to how they function, as are the rules they adopt for decision making. Both affect their policy capacity.

The nation's Founders created a system of checks and balances among the institutions of government, primarily to ensure that government could not tyrannize the population. That is, power would not be concentrated enough to pose such a threat. The formal structure of government they established more than two hundred years ago remains much the same today. The U.S. system is based on a tripartite division of authority among legislative, executive, and judicial institutions and a federal system in which the national government and the states have both separate and overlapping authority. Each branch of the federal government has distinct responsibilities under the Constitution but also shares authority with the other two. This system of separated institutions sharing power had the noble intention of limiting government authority over citizens and protecting their liberty, but the fragmentation of government power also has a significant impact on policy-making processes and the policies that result.

Fragmented power does not prevent policy action, as the routine administration of current national policies and programs as well as the development of new policies clearly indicate. Moreover, when conditions are right, U.S. policy-making institutions can act, sometimes quickly, to approve major policy advances. Often they do so with broad bipartisan support (Jones 1999; Mayhew 1991). Recent examples include the enactments of the USA PATRIOT and No Child Left Behind Acts in 2001 and the Energy Policy Act of 2005. What conditions lead to such substantial policy changes in a system that generally poses significant barriers to such action? It is an intriguing question to ponder, and one that this chapter explores.

Despite policy successes, the fragmented U.S. political system generally makes it difficult for policymakers to respond to most public problems in a timely and coherent manner. The same can be said about the constitutional mandate for a federal system in which the states share power with the national government. The fifty states and about eighty thousand local governments chart their own policy courses within the limits set by the Constitution and national law. In one, perhaps extreme, example of what can happen in a local government, Jeffrey Pressman and Aaron Wildavsky (1979) found a minimum of seventy clearance points necessary before the Economic Development Administration in Oakland, California, could successfully implement a policy. The probability of reaching agreement at each point was low, and of success across all of the potential veto points practically nil. Stalemate occurs in organizations such as this because of constitutional design and government structure. Fortunately, the situation is not so dire in most local governments; they find ways to move programs along.

Stalemate at the national level usually increases during periods of divided government, when one political party controls the presidency and the other at least one house of Congress (Thurber 1991; Ripley and Franklin 1991). The reasons are clear: members of the same political party tend to have similar beliefs concerning the scope of government and the direction of policies, but the two major parties often hold strongly conflicting views on these matters. Although divided government makes agreement and cooperation difficult, policymaking can proceed even under these circumstances. In fact, David Mayhew (1991) argues that divided government has a limited impact on the enactment of major public policies at the national level. A good illustration is one of the most expansive laws ever written, the Clean Air Act Amendments of 1990, approved in a period of split-party control of the

White House and Congress. During the Carter administration (1977–1981), on the other hand, Democrats controlled both the White House and Congress, but President Jimmy Carter was ineffective at getting his priority legislation through Congress. The Democrats took control of the presidency and both houses of Congress in 2009 with a popular president who appeared to want to bring the parties together to address problems. Time will tell how this unified government will work to develop policies to solve the nation's problems, particularly those related to the economy.

Fragmented power can lead to other concerns. For example, state policies, such as California's stringent air quality laws and Massachusetts' universal health care plan, sometimes result in significant advantages for their citizens that people living in other states do not enjoy. In addition, serious conflicts can develop between the federal government and the states. In the 1950s and 1960s the federal government enacted legislation banning segregation in response to state Jim Crow laws that denied African Americans equal rights. But even passage of the federal Civil Rights Act of 1964, which ended legally sanctioned discrimination, did not resolve all of the conflicts (Williams 1987). A number of southern states refused to implement the federal statutes, resulting in continued civil rights abuses in those states.

It should be said, however, that the ways government institutions are structured and how they make decisions are not immutable. They can be changed, and occasionally they are, as citizens and policymakers seek to improve government performance or try new approaches to decision making. In fact, most of the time policymaking involves action that falls between gridlock and innovation. The norm in U.S. politics is **incremental policymaking,** especially for relatively noncontroversial policies. Incremental policy changes are small steps, often taken slowly. They are adjustments made at the margins of existing policies through minor amendments or the gradual extension of a program's mandate or the groups it serves. The Head Start preschool program is a good example of incremental change, made possible because it is seen as a success.

Presidents can play a role in pushing for change, and they sometimes favor dramatic shifts in policies or the structures of government. President Johnson pushed strongly in the early to mid-1960s for enactment of new civil rights policies discussed above as well as a War on Poverty. He also was instrumental in the passage of the federal Medicare program in 1965. In response to the September 11, 2001, attacks on the United States, President George W. Bush proposed creation of a new cabinet department to prevent future terrorist attacks. The Department of Homeland Security represented the largest reorganization of the executive branch since World War II. It brought together twenty-two agencies and their approximately 170,000 employees. By 2008, the department grew to more than 200,000 employees and had an annual budget of about $50 billion.[3]

Figure 2-1 provides an overview of the U.S. political system, with a focus on its proactive elements—Congress, the president, and the rest of the executive branch. State governments are organized in a similar manner. The figure illustrates the different institutions and policy actors who play a role in public policy development and implementation. It can be read in two somewhat different ways. First, it serves as a reminder that the U.S. system imposes substantial barriers to a top-down, unilateral approach to making public policy. Second, it shows the many different points of access the system affords to policy advocates. State and local governments dominate in many policy areas, such as education and crime control. They also

Federal, State, and Local Agents of Policymaking and Avenues of Policy Formation

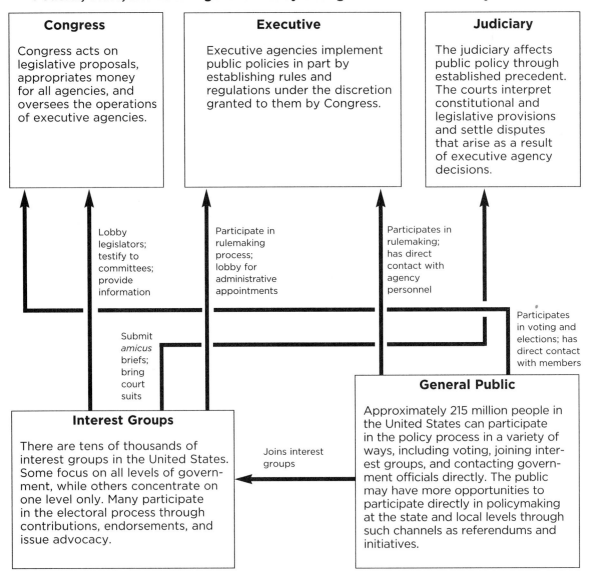

Congress

Congress acts on legislative proposals, appropriates money for all agencies, and oversees the operations of executive agencies.

Executive

Executive agencies implement public policies in part by establishing rules and regulations under the discretion granted to them by Congress.

Judiciary

The judiciary affects public policy through established precedent. The courts interpret constitutional and legislative provisions and settle disputes that arise as a result of executive agency decisions.

Lobby legislators; testify to committees; provide information

Participate in rulemaking process; lobby for administrative appointments

Participates in rulemaking; has direct contact with agency personnel

Participates in voting and elections; has direct contact with members

Submit *amicus* briefs; bring court suits

General Public

Approximately 215 million people in the United States can participate in the policy process in a variety of ways, including voting, joining interest groups, and contacting government officials directly. The public may have more opportunities to participate directly in policymaking at the state and local levels through such channels as referendums and initiatives.

Interest Groups

There are tens of thousands of interest groups in the United States. Some focus on all levels of government, while others concentrate on one level only. Many participate in the electoral process through contributions, endorsements, and issue advocacy.

Joins interest groups

FIGURE 2-1

The U.S. government is a highly complex system with multiple actors at all levels and multiple interactions among these different levels. But the system is also fragmented; public policy decisions can often be made within any of the units described. Because of this dispersal of power, the general public and interest groups alike have numerous points of access to decision-making organizations and thus may be able to influence policy decisions. This diagram illustrates these connections for the national level of government. It is also important to recognize that similar points of access occur at the state and local government levels. All state governments have a similar tripartite separation of powers with legislative committees and state level agencies. Local governments also disperse power in a variety of ways that provide opportunities for groups and citizens to access policymakers.

sometimes intervene when the federal government chooses not to act. For example, faced with federal inaction, many states have adopted climate change policies that try to reduce use of fossil fuels (Rabe 2004 and 2010).

The next section discusses the major features of the U.S. government system, beginning with federalism and followed by the institutions of the federal government. The chapter continues with "informal" policy actors, those outside of government who shape public policy, including the general public and organized interest groups. The purpose of this review is twofold: first, to reacquaint readers with the basic components of government, and second, to encourage them to think about the choices that are represented in these arrangements. Why is government structured one way and not another? What difference does the structure of government make for public policymaking and the substance of public policy? What changes in government might be desirable in terms of improving performance, especially the effectiveness, efficiency, and equity of policies? Or in improving the responsiveness of government to the U.S. public?

FEDERALISM

As noted earlier, the Framers of the U.S. Constitution designed a system of government in which power is divided between the national government and the states (and, for some purposes, Indian tribes).[4] Both the national and state governments have the authority to enact laws or public policies. We focus here on the history of federalism, the federal-state relationship, the continuing controversies over the proper allocation of responsibility between the federal government and the states, and the variation among the states in their capacity for public policy innovation.

The Evolution of Federal-State Relations

During the early history of the United States, disputes arose over how much power the national government should have and what should be left to the states. As the national government attempted to assert itself on issues such as the establishment of a national bank and the rules of interstate commerce, its authority was challenged. The Supreme Court, led by Chief Justice John Marshall, supported an expanded role of the national government. Yet, as disagreement over the spread of slavery to new states and the subsequent Civil War showed, major conflicts persisted over interpretation of the national government's powers.

The relationship between national and state governments in policymaking has evolved since the nation's founding. In the late eighteenth century the functions or responsibilities of each level of government were quite distinct. State governments, for example, were responsible for education and transportation policies. The national government limited itself to larger issues such as national defense and international trade. Little integration of the two levels of government existed. This state of affairs is often referred to as **dual federalism,** and it persisted throughout the nineteenth century, in part because the federal government's activities remained fairly limited.

In the twentieth century federal-state relations changed significantly, especially in response to the Great Depression of the 1930s. President Roosevelt's legislative program, known as the New Deal, was an expansive economic recovery program that began to break down the imaginary barriers between national and state policy. It was not unusual to see the national government become involved in what were traditionally considered state responsibilities. Thus, dual federalism over time evolved into **cooperative federalism,** as collaboration on policymaking between the national and state governments increased. Many large-scale federal programs begun in the 1960s and 1970s, another period of government growth, relied on such a model. The federal clean air and clean water programs, for example, involved a mix of national and state responsibilities, with the national government setting environmental protection standards and the states carrying out most implementation actions.

Much of the cooperation that occurred between the national and state governments was a result of additional monies being provided to the states through **block grants** and **categorical grants.** Block grants are transfers of federal dollars to the states where the states have substantial discretion in how to spend the money to meet the needs of their citizens. Categorical grants also involved the transfer of federal dollars to the states, but in this case the funding must be used for specific purposes. During the 1970s and 1980s critics of increasing federal power urged the states to retake some of their policy-making responsibilities. President Richard Nixon's "new federalism" initiatives in the early 1970s were designed to move away from categorical grants and toward block grants to give the states more discretion in how they used the funds. States were grateful for the federal funds but also concerned about the expectations that such funding carried. How would such stipulations affect the states' autonomy in designing and managing their own policies?

The devolution of policy to the states continued under President Ronald Reagan. His conservative philosophy and political rhetoric gave a significant boost to the trend already under way to restore greater authority to the states. Although many states welcomed this change, they also worried about the subsequent decrease in federal dollars coming into their treasuries. In addition, the national government had discovered a new way to enact popular policies without paying for them: it gave implementation responsibilities to the states. Federal policymakers received political credit for the new programs without spending federal tax dollars. These **unfunded mandates**—federal requirements placed upon the state governments without funds for implementation—added stress to the relationship between the national and state governments. That relationship continues to evolve.

In 1995 Congress enacted the Unfunded Mandates Reform Act to limit future financial impacts on the states, but conflict over policymaking in a federal system did not vanish as a result. For one thing, the legislation Congress passed was not implemented very effectively. Congress continued to approve new mandates for which insufficient money was made available. Additionally, the act did not remove the extensive mandates for state action that were already in place. Continued conflict between the federal government and the states could be seen in 2001 over federal education policy, specifically, the No Child Left Behind program. Debate focused on the impact on the states of mandatory national standards for promoting primary and secondary school students to the next grade. Supporters of the standards wanted to ensure that students had the skills and knowledge to compete nationally and internationally. Few questioned the goal of improving the quality of the nation's schools, but many had doubts about imposing federal standards in a policy area that has traditionally been a state responsibility. According to the Department of Education, $387 million was authorized for the states to develop and implement the tests, but many state officials complained that the federal funds were insufficient to meet their responsibilities under the act.[5]

State Variation in Policy Capacity

Both of the major political parties seem interested in continuing the **decentralization** of power to the states, that is, the transfer of policy authority from the federal government to the states. The focus, however, has shifted to asking whether the states have the capacity to handle additional responsibilities. The issues that arise in this debate parallel the book's main evaluative criteria. For example, critics of decentralization are concerned about the implications for program effectiveness, efficiency, and equity because they recognize that the fifty states are quite different from one another both in their capacity to act on policy issues and in the kinds of policies they enact.

The states also differ in fundamental ways such as physical size, population, extent of industrialization, and affluence. Moreover, each state and

The text discusses the principle of federalism and the importance of state and local governments in setting public policy. Sometimes state and local governments are the first to take action, particularly when there is no agreement at the national level about what policies are needed. This has been the case with smoking in public places, use of cell phones by drivers, climate change policy, and healthy eating. The photo shows an employee putting up new menus featuring calorie counts at a Subway restaurant in June 2007 in New York. New York was the first city in the country to require certain fast food restaurants to list calorie counts next to menu items and to do so in type that is at least as large as that used for the item's price. In July 2007 a New York ban on the use of trans fat–laden cooking oils in restaurants also took effect.

region has a distinctive history and culture that shape policy actions (Elazar 1984; Lieske 1993). What may work well and be acceptable to residents of Wisconsin or Minnesota might not be appropriate or feasible in Texas or Mississippi. Some states have extensive state parks and other recreational facilities, while others have strict vehicle inspection programs to promote highway safety. A number of states, such as California, Colorado, New York, and Vermont, do not permit smoking in restaurants, and California in 2008 became the first state to ban the use of trans fats in restaurants; New York City had adopted a similar restriction in 2006, and other cities followed suit.[6] There is nothing inherently negative about such policy variation among the states; indeed, throughout the nation's history Americans have celebrated the rich diversity of state cultures and policy preferences. However, when a state's policies are so different from others that its residents may be deprived of essential human needs or federally protected rights, the federal government is likely to intervene. One might argue that this was the justification for No Child Left Behind: to ensure certain minimal expectations for students regardless of where they get their education.

Those who favor increasing state authority tend to believe that the states are capable of handling additional responsibilities and are better equipped than the federal government at defining their citizens' needs. Indeed, for some, the states are the "new heroes" of American federalism, with greater capacity for policy innovation and closer ties to citizens than a national government in which many have lost their faith. Studies show that over the past several decades state legislatures and bureaucracies have become more skilled than they were before at dealing

WORKING WITH SOURCES

STATE PUBLIC POLICIES

One way to become familiar with public policy variation among the fifty states is to explore what several of them have done in a particular policy area, such as education, health care, environmental protection, economic development, or criminal justice. The Web site for the Council of State Governments (www.csg.org) provides links to all fifty state government home pages, which in turn have links to major policy areas. The council also has extensive news reports on policy activities that affect the states, including policy innovation. Reading about different policy actions within the states is one of the best ways to become informed about state capacity for policy development and to see how the states differ from one another in this regard.

Visit the council's Web page, click on Western Region at the top of the page, and select California, then About CA, Environment and Resources, Air Resources Board, and Climate Change. Here you can examine the different policies that the state of California is considering or implementing to deal with climate change. Included here is an executive order signed by Gov. Arnold Schwarzenegger to reduce greenhouse gas emissions over a period of years.

The federal government, on the other hand, has yet to set such limits and may have a different perspective on how to address climate change. To learn about federal policies related to climate change, go to the Environmental Protection Agency's Web site at www.epa.gov and click on Climate Change. Read about some of these policies to address the issue.

Now that you have explored policies in both California and the federal government, think about these questions:

- Based on what you have read, how does the issue of climate change rank in terms of priority in California compared to the federal government?
- What are some of the major similarities and differences in the approaches to addressing these environmental problems?
- What aspects of climate change policy are left entirely up to California? For which ones do they share authority with the federal government? Why are certain actions left to the state and others shared or left to the federal government?

with policy issues (Hedge 1998). Their new capacity comes from growth in their professional staffs and expertise, including the ability to appraise policy needs and evaluate programs with greater accuracy. Depending on its economic conditions, a state could also act on public problems because it may have sufficient funds to do so, from transfer of federal dollars and state taxation (Bowman and Kearney 2005). The best evidence supporting these arguments can be found in the many innovative and effective measures states have taken over the past several decades in various areas (Borins 1998; Rabe 2010; Teske 2004). For example, state and local governments are mainly responsible for highway safety, and states have been at the forefront in requiring seat belt and speed limit laws. The box "Working with Sources: State Public Policies" indicates where readers can locate information about variation among the states in public policy.

Nevertheless, analysts have several reasons to remain skeptical of how much more decentralization of federal power to the states is desirable:

- Policy performance varies from state to state, and citizens may suffer the consequences.[7] For example, some states fail to fully test drinking water or to enforce clean air and clean water laws, even though they are violating federal environmental laws (Rabe 2010).
- States with more money and greater expertise than others can design better programs and offer more services to their citizens.
- Business and industry interest groups may exert more influence at the state than at the national level because of the states' eagerness to attract businesses and jobs. One example is automobile manufacturers in Michigan.
- Decisions may be less open and less visible at the state level, despite the closer proximity of government to citizens.
- Many public problems, such as air and water pollution, cross state boundaries, suggesting that a higher level of government is needed to address them adequately.
- Only the federal government has sufficient resources to support policy activities such as scientific research for environmental protection and health care.

It seems likely that public debate over the proper distribution of authority between the states and the federal government will continue. The question at the heart of the controversy is which level of government is best suited to address different kinds of public policies. That question has no automatic answer, however, and each person's position is likely to be influenced by his or her beliefs about the role of government in society, particularly the national government. As public policy students become acquainted with evaluative criteria and how they apply to public policy questions, the appropriate level of government to address them may become apparent.

SEPARATION OF POWERS

One of the distinguishing characteristics of the U.S. Constitution is the separation of powers. Governing power is shared among the three branches of government: legislative, executive, and judicial. This arrangement reflected the Founders' experience of living under what they saw as the tyranny of the British monarch. As we stated earlier, they feared that unrestrained government authority could abuse citizens' rights, and they believed that the checks and balances built into a system of separated powers would ensure that no one branch of government would have enough power to threaten liberty. In fact, under this system, the legislative and executive branches must cooperate to accomplish almost anything, and this is not always easy to achieve (Jones 1999). Most people would agree that the goal of preventing tyranny is a worthy one, but the separation of powers has added to the complexity and difficulty of policymaking, and to gridlock.

The number of policy actors within the U.S. government and their overlapping responsibilities contribute to the complexity, making it difficult to figure out who is responsible for any particular government action. Think about oversight of the financial and housing markets and issues of subprime mortgages that helped lead the nation into a recession in 2008, which in turn was a major factor in a worldwide economic slowdown. It seems clear that agencies such as the Securities and Exchange Commission (SEC), which is formally charged with overseeing corporate accounting, and housing agencies such as Fannie Mae and Freddie Mac, which provide some oversight to the mortgage and housing market, were remiss—but why? Did Congress fail to provide adequate financial support for the agency to exercise oversight or fail to urge it to use its oversight authority? Or consider the investigations of terrorist threats to the nation prior to September 11 and the seeming inability (or unwillingness) of the Federal Bureau of Investigation (FBI) and other intelligence agencies to share information and cooperate (Sanger 2002; Van Natta and Johnston 2002). Or, finally, think of climate change, by its very nature a national and global problem. Yet it has been the states, not the national government, that have taken the lead on this issue, with over half of the states adopting some form of action on climate change by 2008, particularly measures requiring use of renewable energy sources. Indeed, the Bush administration tried repeatedly to block such state action when it considered some of those efforts to infringe on federal power (Rabe 2010; Rabe and Mundo 2007).

Difficulty in policymaking is a reflection of the government's capacity to respond to public problems in light of divided institutions and authority and the political conflicts that inevitably arise over how best to deal with those challenges. In other words, it is not easy to identify and define problems, develop suitable solutions, and approve the solutions in such a fragmented governing system. The following sections explore the branches of the national government, each branch's major characteristics, and the implications of these characteristics for policymaking. In general, all state governments have similar systems and must deal with comparable complexity and difficulty within their own policy processes.

Legislative Branch

The legislative branch of the United States is a **bicameral** (two-house) Congress, consisting of the House of Representatives and the Senate. The two chambers differ from each other in both their composition and operating style. The House, with members elected every two years from separate districts within each state, is the more representative or democratic chamber of the two. It has 435 voting members, each representing about 680,000 constituents.[8] Senators serve six-year terms, giving them more independence than House members. Moreover, with only one third of its members up for reelection every two years, the Senate is also more insulated than the House from short-term political forces. Each state, regardless of its size, elects two senators, so that the one hundred members serve quite different constituencies. California's senators, for example, represent more than thirty-six million people, while the senators from Delaware represent about 850,000. The Senate also allows its members more freedom to debate issues than does the House. Senators have the right to **filibuster,** or to talk for an extended period of time in hope of delaying, modifying, or defeating a proposal. One of the more famous examples occurred when Sen. Strom Thurmond of South Carolina conducted the longest filibuster in history in his attempt to prevent passage of the Civil Rights Act of 1964. Threats of a filibuster can force policy compromises as members try to prevent having all other business grind to a halt. The box "Working with Sources: Congress" gives you the opportunity to see how the bicameral legislature often leads to different bills on the same general area and explore why this may be the case.

Article I of the Constitution spells out Congress's powers, but the most important today are its lawmaking and budgetary responsibilities. In addition to passing legislation, Congress each year must appropriate the funds necessary to run government programs. To accomplish these tasks, both chambers operate under a system that allows for division of labor and policy specialization.

WORKING WITH SOURCES

CONGRESS

As stated in the text, policy gridlock sometimes occurs because of differences within our bicameral Congress. The two houses, the Senate and House of Representatives, may have significant differences in the development of a law even when controlled by the same party. To illustrate this, go to the THOMAS Web site (http://thomas.loc.gov), where you can access a wide range of information on Congress. Click on Search Bills and Resolutions. In the search field, type in HR 6 and make sure to select 109th Congress on the right side. The bill you will examine is the Energy Policy Act, signed into law by President George W. Bush in August of 2005. Specifically, you will compare the versions that passed the House and Senate prior to going to conference committee. The House bill is labeled HR 6 EH and the Senate bill is HR 6 EAS. Once you access these bills, go to Title II, the Renewable Energy provisions, and examine these provisions in each bill.

- Which house's version seems to take renewable energy more seriously? What are some of the major similarities and differences between the two versions?
- Why do you think there are such large discrepancies in these two versions? What is it about the two legislative bodies that may lead to such divergence?
- You can click on HR 6 PP to see the final version after the conference committee action. Is this bill more like the Senate or the House version?

Policy development is concentrated within this elaborate system of committees and subcommittees, each of which is chaired by the party holding a majority of seats in Congress.

Each of the two hundred committees and subcommittees has specific jurisdiction over certain public policies and the executive agencies that administer them. Each has a substantial staff that can bring experience and expertise to bear on lawmaking and on oversight and investigations of the executive agencies. Bills introduced into either chamber are referred to a committee for consideration. If the committee chooses to move ahead on the legislation, it typically conducts public hearings to acquire information on the advantages and disadvantages of the proposed law. Executive branch officials and experts from academia, think tanks, and interest groups may be invited to Capitol Hill to testify. (It is easy to find verbatim accounts of testimony through services available at most college libraries, such as the LexisNexis congressional database.) Eventually, the committees accept, modify, or reject the legislation. For bills that are to move forward, the committees submit reports on their findings and recommendations to the full chamber for consideration. To become law, a bill must pass both chambers in identical form and be signed by the president. Presidents may **veto** or reject a bill approved by Congress, and Congress in turn may override the president's veto with a two-thirds vote in both houses. Normally, Congress has a difficult time overriding a presidential veto.

The fragmentation of authority among the committees in Congress can pose an obstacle to policymaking, but there is an upside as well. The large number of committees and subcommittees creates multiple venues for highlighting public problems and considering policy proposals. In this way, almost any issue, from energy conservation to child care, can gain attention on Capitol Hill, and possibly by the media as well. During 2007, for example, Rep. James McGovern, D-Mass., and Sen. Daniel Akaka, D-Hawaii, got the House of Representatives to consider a bill that would impose civil and criminal penalties for fossil thefts from government lands. The law, in essence, gives fossils protections similar to those of cultural and archeological resources.[9] One has to wonder what effect the popular Indiana Jones films have on people's thinking about this kind of legislation.

Often the committees, or the full House and Senate, fail to agree on policy proposals, and policy gridlock results. It is tempting to fault members of Congress for inaction, but the causes of policy disagreement and stalemate are easy to understand. The parties are deeply divided ideologically, and on major issues—from health care policy to Social Security reform—members are lobbied intensely by organized interest groups as well as political activists within their parties. Moreover, when Congress is divided on public policy, the nation often is as well. As a representative political institution, Congress reflects the larger society, for better or worse. In a sense, Congress struggles continuously with its dual roles of representation and lawmaking (Davidson, Oleszek, and Lee 2009).

This tension is evident in the policy behavior of members of Congress. Incumbent members usually seek reelection and are overwhelmingly successful in retaining their seats. As David Mayhew (1974) has argued, because of their electoral incentive, members are strongly motivated to stay in the spotlight; take positions on the issues, even if they do nothing about them; and claim credit for public policy actions, particularly those that materially benefit the district or state. These pressures mean that members often introduce bills, make speeches, and distribute press releases on many issues, even when the legislation has no chance of moving forward. In many ways, Congress is a loosely connected assembly of 535 elected officials who, because of the electoral incentive, often go their own way. If they do not act as teammates, policy action that requires agreement may be stymied.

To rein in this natural tendency toward political individualism, Congress relies on the elected leadership within each house, which is organized by political parties. The majority party dominates the House and Senate agendas and decision-making processes to a substantial degree. Historically, the party leadership has been instrumental in overcoming ideological and regional divisions within Congress and forging consensus; it also negotiates with the president on potentially divisive policy issues (Jones 1999; Sinclair 2008). As parties have weakened, however, the leadership role is less evident, and individual members of Congress rely on their substantial personal staffs to develop policy. Policy formulation of this kind is particularly likely in the Senate, where members have larger staffs and attract greater media coverage than do House members.

In recent years both the House and the Senate have been closely divided in party membership, which forces the two major parties to work together to fashion legislative compromises. Party control of each chamber remains highly important, however, as demonstrated vividly in 2001, when Sen. James Jeffords of Vermont left the Republican Party to become an independent and voted with the Democrats. His action gave the Democrats majority control of the Senate for a time, which in turn meant that President George W. Bush faced more difficulty securing the approval of Congress for his legislative initiatives and budget proposals. More recently, in 2006 Democrats took control of the House as well and increased

During an election campaign voters may be led to think that their selection of the president largely ends the process of establishing a new administration. Yet a president appoints thousands of individuals to key positions in a new administration, among the most important of them the heads of the fifteen cabinet departments. The photo shows President-elect Barack Obama, center, flanked by his education secretary–designate Arne Duncan, right, and Vice President-elect Joe Biden, during a visit with students at the Dodge Renaissance Academy in Chicago in December 2008. Prior to becoming the secretary of education, Duncan served for eight years as the superintendent of schools in Chicago.

their majority in the Senate, providing President Bush with an even greater hurdle to leap in order to pursue his policy preferences. As a result of the 2008 elections, Democrats increased their majorities further in both houses, gaining twenty-one seats in the House and eight seats in the Senate.

Executive Branch

The federal executive branch is responsible for carrying out the laws enacted by Congress. It is made up of the president, the vice president, the White House staff, and the federal bureaucracy. Although presidents do not make laws, they are actively involved in agenda setting, policy formulation and adoption, and implementation (Anderson 2006; Jones 1999). Other than the vice president, the president is the only federal official who is elected nationally. In effect, the president embodies the U.S. government, symbolizes U.S. culture and values, and speaks for the nation abroad. As such, he commands enormous public and media attention that gives him unequaled influence in agenda setting and policy leadership. For example, President George H. W. Bush got discussions started on revising the Clean Air Act. His interest in amending the law and being an active player in its formulation broke a decade-long logjam and in 1990 eventually led to one of the most sweeping environmental laws ever enacted (Vig and Kraft 2010). Presidents Ronald Reagan in 1981 and George W. Bush in 2001 were equally successful in focusing national attention on the need to substantially cut federal taxes.

As we discuss in chapter 7, their success in gaining congressional approval for the tax cuts dramatically affected economic policy, including growth in federal budget deficits and the national debt.

In addition to the president, the entire White House staff and the **Executive Office of the President** (EOP) are intimately involved in policy development. The EOP consists of the White House offices and agencies that assist the president in the development and implementation of public policy. Among other offices, these include the Office of Management and Budget (OMB), the Council of Economic Advisers, the National Security Council, the Council on Environmental Quality, and the Office of Science and Technology Policy. Together, these offices constitute a "mini-bureaucracy" that provides the president and his staff with vital information and policy ideas in their respective areas. The EOP keeps the president informed about the plethora of policies being considered in Congress or implemented in the federal bureaucracy, giving him opportunities to influence policy direction. In most policy areas, the president's agenda and his positions, particularly on domestic issues, reflect his party affiliation and political ideology, as well as the constellation of constituencies most important to his party and—if he is in his first term—his reelection. Democratic and Republican presidents tend to adopt distinctive policy positions on most issues because of their differing philosophies of governance and the particular array of interests the parties represent. George W. Bush's support for reform of the Social Security system in 2004 emphasized the development of personal or private retirement accounts—an idea that deeply split Congress, largely along party lines.

The federal bureaucracy constitutes the bulk of the executive branch. It includes all of the agencies and offices that fall under each of the cabinet departments and other offices and agencies whose mission is to develop and implement policy in specialized areas. The best known of these are the fifteen **cabinet-level departments,** each of which is managed by a secretary appointed by the president and confirmed by the Senate.

Each cabinet department includes subsidiary agencies, some of which may be better known than their home departments. For example, the Federal Aviation Administration (FAA), which has primary responsibility for aviation safety, is part of the Transportation Department; the Food and Drug Administration (FDA), responsible for ensuring the safety of food and medicine, is part of Health and Human Services; and the FBI, charged with protecting and defending the United States from foreign and domestic threats, is the investigative arm of the Justice Department. The bureaucratic agencies issue reports and studies that enable the public to follow the agencies' activities in their special policy areas, much of which can be found on agency Web sites (see the box "Working with Sources: Executive Departments and Agencies").

Each agency makes policy within its specialized area through the interpretation of legislative language and development of regulations that are essential to policy implementation. Career federal officials in the agencies have considerable authority to shape public policy, even though ultimate responsibility for policymaking rests with the president's appointees at the top of each agency and department. The career officials work closely with the White House to ensure that agency and department policy decisions are consistent with the president's programs and priorities, at least where the decisions are not strictly limited by statutory specifications. As a result, the U.S. bureaucracy is more politicized than bureaucracies in many other developed nations, and its policies can change significantly from one administration to the next.

WORKING WITH SOURCES

EXECUTIVE DEPARTMENTS AND AGENCIES

Often, a number of different agencies may develop and implement policy related to a particular problem. A good example is tobacco policy, where a wide range of agencies are responsible for various policies. To examine tobacco policy from an agricultural perspective, go to the Department of Agriculture Web site at www.fsa.usda.gov/FSA/webapp?area=home&subject=toba&topic=landing. For a different view, go to the U.S. surgeon general's Web site at www.surgeongeneral.gov/tobacco. The Alcohol and Tobacco Tax and Trade Bureau has a different attitude regarding tobacco policy, available at www.ttb.gov/tobacco/index.shtml. Finally, the Federal Trade Commission's Bureau of Consumer Protection has a role in tobacco policy. To access this information, go to www.ftc.gov/bcp/bcpap.shtm.

For each agency, consider the following questions:

- What is its main purpose regarding tobacco policy?
- How does it pursue these policies? In other words, what government tools, such as regulations and subsidies, does the agency use to meet its goals?
- What contradictions do you see among these policies?

The shift from President Bill Clinton to President George W. Bush is a good illustration. Bush's appointees to executive agencies and his administration's policies were decidedly more conservative than those of his predecessor. Such differences were notable even in the selection of individuals to serve in a voluntary capacity on scientific advisory committees to executive agencies such as the FDA and the Centers for Disease Control and Prevention (CDC). Such advisory committees are intended to help inform government decisions in public health and other policy areas. The Department of Health and Human Services alone has more than 250 advisory committees of this kind. Because their interpretation of scientific evidence can push policy decisions one way or another, presidents and cabinet officials take a keen interest in who serves on these committees.[10] The beginning of the appointment process of the Obama administration shows movement back toward more liberal appointees.

Such a shift in political ideology also makes it difficult for the administration to fill important agency positions. A case in point is appointing the commissioner of the FDA. For the first two years of the George W. Bush administration, the FDA had no commissioner because Democrats and Republicans in Congress could not agree on the appropriate qualifications for the head of the agency. Democrats said they would oppose candidates with close ties to industries the FDA regulates, including those associated with drugs, medical devices, food, and cosmetics. Republicans reportedly insisted that the nominee support conservative positions, for example, on halting sale of RU-486, the so-called abortion pill. In October 2002 Bush nominated Mark McClellan, an internist and associate professor at Stanford University, who had bipartisan credentials and a pragmatic rather than ideological approach to FDA issues. McClellan left the agency, however, in early 2004 to head the Centers for Medicare and Medicaid Services. Dr. Lester M. Crawford replaced him, first as acting commissioner until the Senate confirmed him in July 2005. Crawford in turn resigned as FDA commissioner in September 2005, following a series of controversial decisions at the agency, particularly over nonprescription sales of emergency contraceptives for women ("morning after" pills).

Outside of the cabinet departments are the numerous independent executive and regulatory agencies. One of the best known is the Environmental Protection Agency (EPA), an **independent executive agency** with an appointed administrator who has major policy-making and implementation responsibilities for environmental policy. Independent agencies differ from cabinet-level departments chiefly because they are responsible for a more focused policy area. Other examples include the National Aeronautics and Space Administration (NASA); the Central Intelligence Agency (CIA); and the Nuclear Regulatory Commission (NRC), which oversees the civilian use of nuclear energy, including power plants and the high-level waste they produce.

The **independent regulatory commission** (IRC) is yet another breed of executive agency. Like cabinet secretaries, the commissioners are appointed by the president and confirmed by the Senate, but for fixed and staggered terms. These fixed terms are intended to insulate IRC decision making from political pressure from the president or Congress. In addition, most IRCs are responsible for the economic regulation of certain industries. For example, the Federal Communications Commission (FCC) regulates the broadcasting industry, and the SEC regulates the financial markets. An IRC focuses on one industry, and therefore its scope of authority tends to be narrow.

Although each agency operates within its own area of expertise, what it does can be in conflict with another agency. For example, the EPA, intent on its mission to reduce pollution, for years wanted automobiles to have onboard pollution controls to cut emissions coming from engines. The National Highway Traffic Safety Administration (part of the Transportation Department), concerned with its mission of safe automobile travel, believed that such a mechanism would make cars more susceptible to explosion. Table 2-1 lists the fifteen federal cabinet departments and a selection of executive agencies.

Judicial Branch

The federal judiciary is made up of the nine-member Supreme Court, thirteen **circuit courts of appeals,** and ninety-four **federal district courts,** as well as special courts such as bankruptcy courts, a court of appeals for the armed services, and a court of federal claims. Although many would not think of them as policymakers, the courts play a vital role in the process by inter-preting the policy decisions made by others; indeed, the courts often have the last word on policy. The major distinction between the judiciary and the other two branches is that the courts' policymaking is *reactive* rather than *proactive*. Unlike Congress and the executive branch, which can initiate policy, the federal courts offer rulings and opinions only on cases brought before them. Yet these rulings may dictate policy far beyond the actual cases. Consider the Supreme Court's ruling in *Brown v. Board of Education of Topeka* (1954), which overruled the precedent of "separate but equal" public schools, thereby ending legally sanctioned segre-gation; or the Court's decision in *Roe v. Wade* (1973), which struck down state laws that made abortion a crime. Although each was an important case in its own right, the Court's ruling in each had greater policy implications than perhaps initially anticipated.

TABLE 2-1	Federal Cabinet Departments and Major Agencies

Executive Departments	Selected Major Federal Agencies
Department of Agriculture	Central Intelligence Agency
Department of Commerce	Consumer Product Safety Commission
Department of Defense	Environmental Protection Agency
Department of Education	Equal Employment Opportunity Commission
Department of Energy	Export-Import Bank of the United States
Department of Health and Human Services	Federal Communications Commission
Department of Homeland Security	Federal Deposit Insurance Corporation
Department of Housing and Urban Development	Federal Reserve System
Department of the Interior	Federal Trade Commission
Department of Justice	National Aeronautics and Space Administration
Department of Labor	National Science Foundation
Department of State	Nuclear Regulatory Commission
Department of Transportation	Peace Corps
Department of the Treasury	Securities and Exchange Commission
Department of Veterans Affairs	United States Postal Service

The federal courts' functions shape public policy in many ways. The courts serve as gate-keepers by deciding who has *standing to sue* (the legal term for the right to bring suit), the right to appeal to the federal courts, or whether a dispute is "ripe," or ready for review. The courts also set standards for review, including whether they will defer to the expert judgment of administrative agencies or review an agency's decisions more critically. Courts interpret the Constitution, statutory language, administrative rules, regulations, executive orders, treaties, and prior court decisions regarded as **precedent**—using prior court decisions to help make a current decision. The policy language in these various documents may be ambiguous or vague, or new situations may arise that the architects of the language failed to anticipate. The courts have the final say on what the law means, unless Congress revises the law to make its purpose clearer. Finally, courts also have some discretion in choosing a judicial remedy, such as imposition of fines, probation, or incarceration (O'Leary 2010).

The federal courts, therefore, are more constrained in their policy-making roles than Congress and the executive branch. In addition to having to wait for a suitable case, judges must anchor their rulings in law or precedent, not personal beliefs or interest group politics as elected officials are free to do. The legitimacy of the courts depends upon the public's willingness to abide by judicial rulings. If judges deviate too far from acceptable legal rationales for their decisions, they risk losing citizens' confidence. Still, judges clearly differ in their judicial philosophies, or the bases they use for decision making. Some are more conservative or liberal than others, and analysts tend to describe the federal courts, especially the Supreme Court, in terms of the justices' ideological or philosophical leanings.

Federal judges are nominated by the president and confirmed by the Senate, but their jobs are for life, if they choose to stay in them. For that reason, the senators, along with interest groups and the public, scrutinize their views on public policy issues when they are nominated. Presidents usually get the judges they want appointed to office, but the Senate sometimes blocks nominees it finds unacceptable, often for ideological reasons. Given the typical lengthy service of a federal judge, a president's influence on public policy continues for decades after he leaves office.

WORKING WITH SOURCES

THE FEDERAL JUDICIARY

As mentioned in the text, federal justices serve life terms and can leave lasting legacies for the presidents who appointed them. This is especially true at the U.S. Supreme Court, whose decisions and opinions guide the entire federal judiciary. To learn more, go to www.oyez.org/oyez/frontpage and click on the Justices link. You can click on any of the justices to get biographical information, such as how long they served, which president appointed them, and other information. Note the length of time that these justices served on the Court. From each justice's site, you can click on Opinions to read the arguments written by individual justices. Another way to examine the

Court's influence on public policy is to look at a series of cases dealing with a particular public policy issue—for example, abortion. From the front page of the site, under Browse Cases, click on By Issue and then Privacy. You will see a few choices, one of which is Abortion. Some of the cases you may want to examine are *Roe v. Wade, Webster v. Reproductive Health Services,* and *Planned Parenthood v. Casey.* How has the Court's position on this issue changed since 1973? Note that Justice William H. Rehnquist was involved in all three of these cases over this twenty-year period. Was he ever in the majority? Did his views change?

President George W. Bush's nomination in 2005 of John Roberts for the position of Chief Justice of the Supreme Court and, to a lesser extent, Samuel Alito, appointed in 2006, are cases in point. Roberts was easily confirmed by the Senate and assumed the position at age fifty, so he can be expected to serve on the Court for many years to come. President Bush's appointments to the federal appeals courts have had a similar effect on the courts' shift to the right, an effect that is likely to last for years because they were among the youngest justices ever nominated.[11] The box "Working with Sources: The Federal Judiciary" provides an opportunity to examine what types of Supreme Court decisions, and the justices who made them, have affected public policy.

Under the U.S. system of separated powers, it is essential that the three branches of government cooperate to ensure policy enactment and effective implementation. Indeed, policy results from the interaction of the branches rather than their separate actions. Constitutionally, the legislature may be the branch responsible for policymaking, but many other policy actors must also be involved. It is clear that each branch has a strong capacity to analyze public problems and devise solutions to them, but equally clear that building consensus among diverse policy actors with different political incentives and constituencies, although necessary, is rarely easy.

INFORMAL POLICY ACTORS AND POLICY CAPACITY

So far, this chapter has dealt with the formal government institutions involved in making public policy. It is easy for citizens to understand these institutions and the people who work in them. This next section discusses other players in the policy-making process, including the public itself (indirectly and directly) and organized interest groups. In addition, we discuss a theory of how the formal and informal actors work together in the development of policy.

Public Opinion and Policymaking

As one would expect in a democracy, public opinion is a major force in policymaking, even if it constitutes an indirect or passive form of action on the public's part. Public opinion influences what elected officials try to do, especially on issues that are highly salient, or of great importance to voters, or on those that elicit strong opinions, such as abortion rights or gun control. Although public opinion is rarely the determinative influence on policymaking, it sets boundaries for public policy actions. Policymakers cross those boundaries at their own risk. The broad direction of public policies therefore tends to reflect the concerns, fears, and preferences of the U.S. public (Page 1992; Manza, Cook, and Page 2002).

The common definition of **public opinion** is what the public thinks about a particular issue or set of issues at any point in time (O'Connor and Sabato 2006), but what is meant by "the public" is not always clear. The attentive public can be distinguished from the general public. The attentive public, typically less than 10 percent of the public, includes those who are apt to take an interest in a particular problem or policy. They are more likely than other people to become informed about the issues and to get involved in some way. Actions and communication from either of these groups may influence policy development, but the general public's opinions tend to shape only the overall direction of policy, while the views of the attentive public, especially of organized interests, tend to have a greater impact. This influence can be especially pronounced for policies with low salience for the general public.

Public opinion is usually expressed as the aggregate or sum of the individual attitudes and opinions of the adult population. Poll takers measure it through interviews, typically conducted over the telephone, with a random sample of the adult population. (In a random sample, each person in the population has an equal chance of being selected.) If standard opinion research methods are followed, a typical survey or poll of about a thousand to twelve hundred adults will be accurate to within about three percentage points, meaning that the result is only three percentage points higher or lower than it would be if the entire U.S. population had been interviewed. Before accepting a poll's results as accurate, however, the public policy student needs to ascertain whether the survey followed proper methods. For example, were the questions objective or did they lead those responding to a particular position? Was a random sample used (Asher 2007)? Internet polls and other self-selected surveys almost always fail to meet these standards, as do many polls commissioned by interest groups, where leading questions are common. The box "Steps to Analysis: Public Opinion" highlights some sources of public opinion data and shows how one might critically examine the questions and other methods used in surveys.

Americans have numerous ways and opportunities to voice their opinions, so policymakers at all levels of government need to be aware of the shifting beliefs of the population. Beyond answering polls or surveys, people can express their opinions through their political participation, which may include not just voting, but attending meetings, writing or speaking to government officials, joining interest groups, and backing referendums and initiatives placed on state or local ballots. These are forms of direct citizen involvement in policymaking, and many states permit their use. In 2004, for example, voters in Colorado approved by a margin of 54 to 46 percent a statewide ballot referendum on renewable energy use that the state legislature had defeated three times. The measure mandates that 10 percent of the state's

| STEPS |
| TO |
| ANALYSIS |

PUBLIC OPINION

An enormous amount of contemporary poll data can be found on the Internet. Several specific examples illustrate the kind of material you can find and how you might evaluate it. If the particular poll data we discuss here are not available when you access the site, try to find comparable information in the newer polls that appear regularly.

Go to the Public Agenda Web site (www .publicagenda.org) and select the Abortion link. Under the public opinion category, select People's Chief Concerns. Then click the link to one of the findings reported on the site: "Americans are divided on whether they are pro-choice or pro-life, but slightly more than half say abortion is morally wrong." The site refers to a 2002 poll sponsored by the Gallup Organization that asked the following question: "With respect to the abortion issue, would you consider yourself to be pro-choice or pro-life?" The results were as follows: 47 percent of the sample selected "pro-choice," 46 percent chose "pro-life," and 7 percent said they were not sure or mixed. What conclusions would you draw from these data about public opinion on abortion? Do you think the question was fairly worded?

Next, go back to the People's Chief Concerns page and click on the link "Views on abortion have not changed significantly since the 1970s." Poll results here are from a Gallup/CNN/*USA Today* poll from January of 2003. That survey reported that of the U.S. population, 57 percent state that abortion should only be legal under certain circumstances, 24 percent that it should be legal, and 18 percent that it should be illegal. The question was: "Do you think abortion should be legal under any circumstances, legal only under certain circumstances, or illegal in all circumstances?" Both surveys suggest that the public is divided on the subject of abortion. What do you think of the results? Which of the two sets of results do you think is more valid?

energy must come from wind and solar power by 2015. Some twenty-eight states had enacted such renewable energy portfolio requirements by late 2008 (Rabe 2010; Rabe and Mundo 2007). Votes on initiatives and referendums may also reflect public anger or frustration about an issue and not necessarily constitute good public policy. In another example from 2004, voters in Arizona approved Proposition 200, a ballot measure that was intended to slow the rate of illegal immigration into the state. Among other actions, it requires public employees to report illegal immigrants to federal authorities or face criminal charges. Not surprisingly, critics question the legitimacy and likely effectiveness of such laws. In 2008, California voters passed a referendum that bans same-sex marriage even after a California court ruled that a previous gay marriage ban passed by the legislature was unconstitutional.

It makes sense intuitively that public opinion should be important in a democracy, even if in a less direct way than a ballot initiative. The truth is, however, that most citizens pay relatively little attention to government, politics, and public policy. They are preoccupied with their families, jobs, homes, and other matters that are important to them on a day-to-day basis. As a result, they may not be well informed on policy issues, and they may have few strong opinions about them. Such opinions are often characterized as being low in both saliency and intensity. Saliency refers to how centrally important an issue is for an individual;

intensity refers to the strength of the opinion, or how firmly it is held. Both qualities are important for predicting whether and how likely people are to act on their opinions. For example, most people express views sympathetic to environmental protection, but they do not act like environmentalists in their energy use, consumer purchases, and so forth. Because environmental policy is a low-salience issue, it is also not as likely as other issues to shape people's votes during election years (Guber and Bosso 2010).

Stability is another dimension of the opinions that people hold. It refers to the continuation of an opinion over time. Public opinion can be fleeting and change quickly, and it can be influenced by current events and the way issues are presented in the media and by public officials. A good example is what public opinion analysts call the "rally 'round the flag" effect, which occurs among citizens when an international crisis stirs patriotic feelings and more than usual support for the president and other national leaders. President Bush clearly benefited from the effect following the September 11 attacks; the evidence could be seen in his soaring approval ratings. As this discussion indicates, it is often difficult to figure out just what citizens want from government and what policy proposals they are prepared to endorse. Yet, the more stable public opinion is on an issue, the more likely policymakers are to pay attention and consider the public's views when making decisions.

Partly because so few Americans approach government and public policy with a clear, strong political ideology, they find it easy to hold inconsistent views on the role of government. Ideologically, a majority of Americans tend to be somewhat conservative; that is, they prefer limited government and, when offered the choice, less bureaucracy and regulation, at least in the abstract. This same majority, however, is likely to demand that government provide a great many services, from regulation of foods and drugs and environmental quality to provision of public education and police protection. The way people react to any given policy proposal depends greatly on *how* it is presented to them. When pollsters ask people about concrete policy programs, they generally find considerable public support for them. At the same time, politicians can elicit public sympathy if they attack government, bureaucracy, regulation, and taxation in a very general or abstract manner.

Despite the public's often weak grasp of policy issues, there are reasons to believe that, given the opportunity, citizens can take a keen interest in public affairs, inform themselves on the issues, voice their opinions, and influence public policies. Especially at the local level, citizens can and do get involved, and they can have a major voice in public policy (Berry, Portney, and Thomson 1993). Even in highly technical areas such as nuclear power and nuclear waste policy, studies suggest a substantial potential for citizen involvement and influence (Hill 1992; Dunlap, Kraft, and Rosa 1993). Moreover, governments have ways to encourage citizens to become more involved if they wish (Ingram and Smith 1993). Local communities that are trying to become more sustainable, for example, have created numerous opportunities for citizens to play a central role in the process (Mazmanian and Kraft 2009; Portney 2003).

Interest Groups and Public Policy

Organized interest groups are a major influence on public policy, and by most measures their numbers and activities have soared since the 1960s (Berry 1997; Cigler and Loomis 2002). The number of citizen groups, or so-called public interest groups, such as the Sierra Club, the

Organized interest groups play a major role in the policymaking process through lobbying of public officials. Most people's views about lobbyists are rather negative and reflect what they see as the undeserved power of special interests such as Wall Street bankers and automobile manufacturers. Yet many newer businesses involved in health care services, major league sports, and Internet communications are increasingly part of the lobbying scene in Washington, D.C., and in state capitals. Here, major league baseball commissioner Bud Selig and Lucy Calautti, an MLB lobbyist, prepare before Selig's testimony during a 2008 House Oversight and Government Reform Committee hearing on players' abuse of steroids, human growth hormone, and other performance-enhancing substances.

National Rifle Association, the Christian Coalition, or Mothers Against Drunk Driving, has risen significantly during this period, but so has the number of what are usually termed *special interest groups,* those with a direct economic stake in public policy, such as organized labor, business groups, and professional associations. A good example is Google, a dominant Internet presence. In 2002 it spent almost nothing on lobbying, but by 2008 it spent some $1.5 million, and its activities in Washington, D.C., go well beyond traditional lobbying. It works with Washington think tanks, nonprofit organizations, and many others on some issues of obvious importance to its business, such as copyright laws and temporary visas for foreign technical workers, but also on broad concerns related to the future of the Internet and new technologies.[12] Most groups are involved in direct lobbying of policymakers, indirect or grassroots lobbying aimed at mobilizing the public or the group's supporters, and public education campaigns. Some also engage in electioneering, such as endorsement and support for candidates for office, and in litigation, or challenging government action in the courts.

Lobbying is probably the most visible group activity, but it is not what people often suspect— illegal pressure of some kind. Groups lobby legislators mainly by supplying information on their policy views or summaries of policy-related studies they have conducted. They may testify in legislative committee hearings, meet with individual members or their staffs, and urge their members and supporters to write or call legislators (Levine 2009). All of this activity generally is intended to support policy proposals the group favors, oppose those it does not, or keep certain issues or policy alternatives off the legislative agenda. Groups also lobby executive branch agencies by submitting studies and recommendations during formal public comment periods on proposed regulations, as well as through frequent and informal communication with agency officials. In both the legislative and executive arenas a great deal of interest group activity consists of trying to block proposals (Kingdon 1995). A good example is the intense efforts by accounting companies during 2002 to water down proposed new regulatory oversight of the industry. The proposed regulations came about because the public was outraged over the behavior of the Arthur Andersen accounting firm during the Enron debacle, among other accounting scandals of 2001 and 2002 (Spinner 2002). While the regulations passed, they were likely less restrictive on the accounting firms than they would have been without their lobbying efforts.[13] More recently, as part of the historic federal economic revitalization measures of 2008 and 2009, lobbyists from a wide range of sectors sought financial help from the federal bailout, including

WORKING WITH SOURCES

INTEREST GROUP POLICY STRATEGIES

Organized interest groups are pervasive in the policy process. Public interest groups tend to lobby for activities they believe will benefit the entire population. In contrast, special interest groups, particularly economic but also sometimes ideological, support actions that tend to benefit only members of their organization. To examine some of these differences more fully, go to the Web sites of the U.S. Public Interest Research Group (www.uspirg.org) and the Nuclear Energy Institute (www.nei.org). Once there, consider the following:

- Is it clear from the two organizations' mission statements who the organizations represent?
- What are some of the groups' most recent accomplishments, and how do they affect their membership?
- What types of political tactics do these groups use to promote their ideals? Are there any differences?

the Big Three automakers. The box "Working with Sources: Interest Group Policy Strategies" explores the mission, activities, and achievements of two prominent organizations, one usually described as a public interest group and the other as a special interest group.

Many groups issue studies, reports, and news releases. They sometimes produce commercials that air on television and radio or appear in newspapers and on Web pages and are intended to educate the public. That is, groups provide information and perspectives on public policy issues and try to win the public to their side. Many interest groups participate actively in the electoral process. They openly endorse candidates for office, contribute money and other resources to their campaigns, and sponsor issue advocacy advertisements that are intended to affect voter opinion on the issues and, the groups hope, their votes. These efforts are aimed at getting people who are sympathetic to the particular group's positions elected or reelected and defeating those who oppose its positions. Groups also use litigation as a policy tool. They may file a suit against an agency because of a ruling or regulation and try to get the courts to change the policy. In the late 1990s, for example, the American Trucking Association sued the EPA over its proposed higher standards for ozone and particulate matter, which the association charged would adversely affect the trucking industry. The case went all the way to the Supreme Court, and the justices affirmed the EPA's regulations.

The lobbying directed at executive agencies is often intense; after all, the businesses and other groups have a great deal at stake. When administrative agencies implement policy, they write rules and regulations, including specific standards that affect business operations. These rules can have a major impact on business and industry, as well as on ordinary citizens. The federal Administrative Procedure Act of 1946 (APA) requires that the rule-making process follow due process of law and be open and fair. Because of the importance of these administrative decisions, interest groups often discuss the issues informally with agency officials. For example, television executives talk to officials at the FCC about requirements for digital television broadcasting standards and the schedule for their implementation. In the late 1990s labor union representatives were keenly interested in the ergonomics regulations to promote worker safety being developed by the Occupational Safety and Health Administration.

Business, labor, and other interests act more formally through the rule-making process as well, particularly when a proposed rule or regulation is open to public comment. The APA requires that agencies considering the issuance of regulations first propose them and allow for public comments before adopting and implementing them. The content of these comments varies widely, ranging from opinions on the rule's importance to extensive analysis of the rule's likely consequences, technical merits, costs, and benefits. Although anyone may provide comments to administrative agencies under these circumstances, the vast majority of comments come from interest groups that are directly affected by the agency's policy. Therefore, if the FAA proposes a rule to require that all children under the age of two be seated in a child safety seat on airplanes, one would expect the airlines, and perhaps groups representing consumers, to provide most of the public comments.

The role of interest groups in the U.S. system of government is important for understanding the policy-making process. It also raises questions that are fundamental to a democracy. For example, are ordinary citizens well represented in the activities of interest groups, or do certain groups and segments of the population, such as corporate interests and the wealthy, have privileged access at the expense of others? To what extent should the activities of interest groups be restricted in some way to promote policy developments that serve the public interest? There is little question that interest groups are omnipresent and highly influential in the policy process at all levels of government and within all branches. Yet analysts disagree on whether such restrictions would promote the public's interest or are consistent with constitutional guarantees of assembly and free speech (Berry 1997; Cigler and Loomis 2007).

Policy Subgovernments and Issue Networks

Much policymaking occurs in less formal settings or venues and involves policy actors within particular issue areas, such as national defense, communications, agriculture, forestry, or energy. Political scientists refer to these informal arrangements as **subgovernments** or **issue networks** (Heclo 1978; Lowi 1979; McConnell 1966; McCool 1990). *Iron triangles* was another term often used to describe these arrangements because of the supposed power and autonomy of their three components: congressional subcommittees, an executive agency, and an outside economic interest group, such as cotton farmers or oil companies. These subgovernments usually operate under the radar of most citizens and are less likely than the more formal institutions to be influenced by citizen values or policy preferences.

The reality is that decision making about many programs and policies tends to be highly specialized. Because of the complexity of public problems and policies, and the often detailed knowledge required to understand them, specialization will no doubt continue to be the norm. One group of policy actors specializes in health care policy; another quite different group acts in defense policy, financial regulation, or environmental protection. Each develops its own, distinctive channels of communication, even terminology, to discuss policy issues. The areas of specialization, and the people and institutions active in them, are known as issue networks, subgovernments, or subsystems to reflect the fact that decision making takes place below the level of the full system of government (Anderson 2006; Freeman 1965; Thurber 1996a). For example, defense procurement decision making (how much to spend on weapons systems and which to buy) involves the congressional armed services committees, the Department of Defense, and the private defense contractors who build the weapons. All tend to favor increased spending for defense, and they work together toward provision of defense systems, usually without much involvement, oversight, or criticism by those who are not part of the subgovernment or network.

Historically, the subgovernments have been exceptionally powerful in setting U.S. policy, particularly in areas of limited interest to the general public, such as agricultural subsidies, mining and forestry, weapons procurement, and highway and dam construction. Today, however, the subgovernments are less autonomous and generally operate with more visibility and "outside" participation. More policy actors are involved, sometimes hundreds of different institutions and individuals. Use of the term *issue network* rather than *subgovernment* reflects this evolution in U.S. policymaking (Heclo 1978). Nevertheless, these networks or subsystems are still important. To varying degrees, their participants remain preoccupied with narrow economic interests; they may afford limited participation beyond the core members; and they may be able to resist external influences (Anderson 2006). If nothing else, it is clear that much U.S. policymaking involves informal networks of communication in which prevailing policy ideas and the evaluation of new studies and information shape what is likely to be acceptable to the major policy actors (Kingdon 1995). Fortunately for students of public policy, it is much easier today to gain access to those networks and to see what the specialized policy communities are considering and where change may be possible.

IMPROVING POLICY CAPACITY

This chapter demonstrates that the design of U.S. government institutions and the conflicting demands of the nation's citizens make governing a difficult, though by no means impossible, task. The history of U.S. public policy development in many areas, as we will show in chapters 7 through 12, indicates a robust capacity for policy formulation, adoption, and implementation. The proof is in the extensive collection of public policies in operation today. Much the same can be said about the policy capacity of state and local governments. Although some are clearly more capable than others, considerable policy innovation and successful implementation is apparent at this level as well (Borins 1998; Hedge 1998).

Does policy capacity need to be improved? Almost certainly. By any measure, the challenges that governments at all levels will face in the future will require an even greater ability than they now possess to analyze complex problems and develop solutions. Whether the problems are worldwide terrorism; economic recessions; natural hazards such as hurricanes; global climate change; or public needs for education, health care, and other social services, governments will have to do a better job of responding to these needs.

Consider one recent example. When a devastating hurricane struck New Orleans and other Gulf Coast areas in September 2005, critics described the responses by federal, state, and local governments as woefully inadequate. Hurricane Katrina killed over one thousand people and left a far larger number injured or homeless, many of them residents of poor and minority communities. The storm also destroyed countless businesses. Government agencies had to drain severely flooded neighborhoods, restore public services over a wide area, assist hundreds of thousands of residents displaced by the storm, and rebuild damaged levees and other structures across a wide stretch of the Gulf Coast. It was perhaps the worst natural disaster in U.S. history in terms of economic impact, costing between $100 and $150 billion, according to the Congressional Budget Office.[14] While governments cannot prevent hurricanes, they can do much to improve their capacities for emergency preparedness and disaster relief. One lesson from Katrina is that governments might have avoided the enormous human and economic toll had they made smarter decisions over the previous decade.

What about the capacity of citizens to participate in public life? Here too there is much that can be done, and we will return to the subject in chapter 13. In brief, it is easy to argue that in a democracy citizens should be given extensive opportunities to participate in policymaking. Yet some analysts worry that citizens have too little time and too little interest to inform themselves on the issues so that they can participate effectively. Others focus on what measures might be taken to assist citizens in learning more about the issues and encouraging their participation. From either perspective, questions arise. For example, is it a good idea to create more state and local referendums to allow direct citizen participation in lawmaking? Many cities and states do that, and as we stated earlier, some highly innovative policies have been enacted through such direct citizen participation. But there is also a risk that such direct democracy can fuel public prejudice and allow special interest groups to have undue influence on the results (Cronin 1989; Ellis 2002).

So what is the best way to encourage citizen participation in government processes? It seems clear that additional citizen participation may enhance policy capacity at the state and local levels, but some programs designed to involve citizens are more effective than others. Most scholars today recognize the desirability of going beyond the conventional hearings and public meetings to offer more direct and meaningful citizen access to policymaking. Citizen advisory committees, citizen panels, and similar mechanisms foster a more intense citizen engagement with the issues (Beierle and Cayford 2002). Governments at all levels continue to endorse collaborative decision making with local and regional stakeholders, especially on issues of urban planning and management, natural resource use, and the like.

Whatever the form of public involvement, its effectiveness needs to be considered. Increasing citizens' voices in policymaking can come at some cost in terms of the expediency of policy development and implementation. In other words, it can slow down the policy process and make it more difficult to resolve conflicts. Even with these qualifications, however, the successful involvement of the public in local and regional problem-solving processes, and in electoral processes, is encouraging for the future. Enhancing civic engagement in these ways might even help to reverse a long pattern of citizen withdrawal, not only from politics but also from communities (Bok 2001; Putnam 2000; Skocpol and Fiorina 1999). The enormous outpouring of support for Barack Obama in the 2008 presidential election, particularly by young voters, testifies to the potential of greater citizen involvement in the future, and also to the diversity of mechanisms for such involvement, from traditional organizational politics to Web-based recruitment, fund-raising, and communication (Dalton 2009).

CONCLUSIONS

This chapter covers a lot of ground, from the constitutional design for U.S. government to the way policy actors within the major institutions interrelate when dealing with public problems and policymaking. It stresses not only the difficulty of governing and the potential for policy gridlock but also the many strengths of the U.S. political system. These strengths are found at all levels of government, but especially in the states' growing policy capacity and their efforts at policy innovation in recent years.

Knowing how government is organized and makes decisions is the foundation for the study of public policy, but equally important is understanding the political incentives that motivate and influence how policy actors relate to one another. Armed with these tools, students of public policy can see why government sometimes works and sometimes does not, and what needs to be done to improve government's capacity for analyzing public problems and developing solutions to them. In the same vein, the chapter suggests that few changes would do more to enhance democracy than finding ways for U.S. citizens to become better informed about public policy and more engaged with government and the policy process.

DISCUSSION QUESTIONS

1. Do you think the U.S. government's system of checks and balances is a detriment to policymaking? Why or why not? How could we amend current checks—such as use of the filibuster in the Senate or lifetime terms for federal judges—to make better public policy?

2. Do states have sufficient capabilities in policymaking to assume a greater role in the federal system of government? Or is the present balance of power between the national government and the states about right?

3. What advantages did the Obama administration have in developing public policy as it entered office in 2009? Discuss major successes and the reasons for the policy development success. In what areas was policymaking more difficult? What contributed to these obstacles?

4. Is the American public capable of playing a more active role in the policy-making process than it currently does? Or would greater public involvement in policymaking pose risks to the quality of decision making? Why do you think so?

5. What role does interest group information play in policymaking? What do you see as the potential positives and negatives of having groups provide this information to policymakers? What might policymakers want to take into account when receiving information and data from interest groups?

SUGGESTED READINGS

Sandford Borins, *Innovating with Integrity: How Local Heroes Are Transforming American Government* (Washington, D.C.: Georgetown University Press, 1998). An analysis of the potential for state and local government policy innovation, with examples of successful action.

Allan J. Cigler and Burdett A. Loomis, eds., *Interest Group Politics,* 7th ed. (Washington, D.C.: CQ Press, 2007). A leading volume on interest group activity in U.S. politics. Includes some of the best current work in the field.

Roger H. Davidson, Walter J. Oleszek, and Frances E. Lee, *Congress and Its Members,* 12th ed. (Washington, D.C.: CQ Press, 2009). The leading text on Congress and a treasure trove of information on the role of Congress in policymaking.

David M. Hedge, *Governance and the Changing American States* (Boulder, Colo. Westview, 1998). A leading text on state government and recent changes in state policy capacity.

Charles O. Jones, *Separate but Equal Branches: Congress and the Presidency,* 2nd ed. (New York: Chatham House Publishers, 1999). A valuable assessment of the relationship between Congress and the presidency.

SUGGESTED WEB SITES

www.ciser.cornell.edu/info/polls.shtml. Cornell University Web site that lists all major public opinion companies, with links to the Gallup Organization, Roper Center, *New York Times*/CBS, *Washington Post,* National Opinion Research Center at the University of Chicago, and National Election Studies at the University of Michigan. Includes the major state and regional polling organizations.

www.csg.org. Council of State Governments, with links to all fifty states as well as public policy issues and think tanks; includes suggestions for state legislation .

www.publicagenda.org. A nonpartisan opinion research organization Web site that includes reports from national firms on public policy issues such as race, health care, privacy, drug abuse, crime, the economy, poverty, welfare, the environment, immigration, and others. Includes a good collection of colorful graphs, tables, and advice on how to read public opinion polls.

http://thomas.loc.gov. The Library of Congress's Thomas search engine for locating congressional documents.

www.usa.gov. Federal government Web portal, with links to online services for citizens, businesses, and governments, and links to federal, state, local, and tribal government agencies. Includes links to all fifty state government home pages and national associations dealing with state and local issues.

www.uscourts.gov. Portal to the U.S. judiciary system.

www.whitehouse.gov. White House home page, with links to the president's stand on various policy issues, news, appointments, speeches, and more.

KEYWORDS

bicameral 44	independent executive agency 50
block grants 40	independent regulatory commission 50
cabinet-level departments 48	issue networks 58
categorical grants 40	lobbying 56
circuit courts of appeals 50	policy capacity 35
cooperative federalism 40	policy gridlock 32
decentralization 41	precedent 51
dual federalism 39	public opinion 53
Executive Office of the President 48	subgovernments 58
federal district courts 50	unfunded mandates 40
filibuster 44	veto 45
incremental policymaking 37	

NOTES

1. Donald G. McNeil Jr., "Upstate Waste Site May Endanger Lives," *New York Times*, August 2, 1978, A1.

2. Measuring the size of government is not easy. Should it include only government employees or also count those in the private sector who produce goods and services for the government under contract? For an assessment of government size, see Paul C. Light, *The True Size of Government* (Washington, D.C.: Brookings Institution, 1999); and Christopher Lee, "Big Government Gets Bigger: Study Counts More Employees, Cites Increase in Contractors," *Washington Post*, October 6, 2006, A21. See also Scott Shane, "In Washington, Contractors Take on Biggest Role Ever," *New York Times*, February 4, 2007, 1, 24. The *Times* article provides detailed estimates of the rise in contractor activities in the 2000s; the amounts spent on their contracts; and other actions by contractors, such as money they spent on lobbying and on campaign contributions.

3. The Bush reorganization left the CIA and FBI largely unaffected. This decision was somewhat surprising because criticism of the two agencies' failure to share their knowledge of terrorist activities prior to the September 11 attacks was the impetus for the president's plan. For a description of the reorganization proposal, see Adriel Bettelheim and Jill Barshay, "Bush's Swift, Sweeping Plan Is Work Order for Congress," *CQ Weekly*, June 8, 2002, 1498–1504. The estimate for employees and budget in 2008 comes from Dana Hedgpeth, "Congress Says DHS Oversaw $15 Billion in Failed Contracts," *Washington Post* online edition, September 17, 2008. DHS is often characterized as one of the least effective federal departments and agencies.

4. For many policy activities, Indian tribes constitute sovereign entities that deal directly with the federal government rather than with the states where tribal land is located.

5. For assessments of how well the legislation on unfunded mandates has worked in several different policy areas, including education, see Bill Swindell, "Political Pendulum Swings Back to 'Unfunded Mandates,'" *CQ Weekly*, April 10, 2004, 844, 853.

6. In addition to state policies preventing smoking in restaurants and other public places, many localities have passed ordinances to do the same. On the trans fat bans, see Jennifer Steinhauer, "California Bans Restaurant Use of Trans Fats," *New York Times*, July 26, 2008, 1, A10.

7. Antismoking campaigns illustrate the wide variation in policy action from state to state. One study found that only six states spent even the minimum amount on programs designed to prevent or stop smoking, as recommended by the Centers for Disease Control and Prevention. Most states spent less than half the recommended level, and two supported no antismoking programs at all with their portion of the $206 billion national settlement against U.S. tobacco companies. See Greg Winter, "State Officials Are Faulted on Anti-Tobacco Programs," *New York Times*, January 11, 2001, A20.

8. In addition to the 435 members, the House of Representatives has four delegates and a resident commissioner, bringing the total to 440. These five positions were created by statute. Puerto Rico elects a commissioner, and Congress has approved nonvoting delegates for the District of Columbia, Guam, the Virgin Islands, and American Samoa. See Roger H. Davidson, Frances E. Lee, and Walter J. Oleszek, *Congress and Its Members*, 12th ed. (Washington, D.C.: CQ Press, 2009).

9. See Avery Palmer, "Protecting Dinosaur Fossils Takes Ages Too," *CQ Weekly* online edition, May 19, 2008, 1307–1317, http://library.cqpress.com/cqweekly/weeklyreport110-.

10. See Rick Weiss, "Political Science: HHS Panels Are Made Over in Bush's Image," *Washington Post National Weekly Edition*, September 23–29, 2002, 29. See also Sheryl Gay Stolberg, "Bush's Science Advisers Drawing Criticism," *New York Times*, October 10, 2002, A28.

11. See Charlie Savage, "Appeals Courts Pushed to Right By Bush Choices," *New York Times*, October 29, 2008, 1, A14.

12. See Julie Kosterlitz, "Google on the Potomac," *National Journal*, June 21, 2008, 54–55.

13. A sign of their success may be found in a proposal by the Bush administration to sharply limit an expected rise in the budget for the Securities and Exchange Commission. The budget increase was to help the SEC implement the new corporate antifraud legislation, the Sarbanes-Oxley Act, which the president signed in mid-2002. See Stephen Labaton, "Bush Seeks to Cut Back on Raise for S.E.C.'s Corporate Cleanup," *New York Times*, October 19, 2002, 1, B14. In early 2003 the SEC staff recommended a softening of the proposed rules for regulating lawyers and accountants. The staff's recommendations came on the heels of intense lobbying by prominent law firms, bar associations, and leading accounting firms and trade groups. See Stephen Labaton and Jonathan D. Glater, "Staff of S.E.C. Is Said to Dilute Rule Changes," *New York Times*, January 22, 2003, C1, 11.

14. The CBO estimate combines costs for Hurricane Katrina and Hurricane Rita, a less-damaging storm that struck several weeks later. See "Statement of Douglas Holtz-Eakin, Director, Macroeconomic and Budgetary Effects of Hurricanes Katrina and Rita," testimony before the Committee on the Budget, U.S. House of Representatives, Congressional Budget Office, October 6, 2005.

ON AUGUST 1, 2007, THE I-35 WEST BRIDGE BETWEEN MINNEAPOLIS and St. Paul, Minnesota, collapsed into the Mississippi River, causing thirteen deaths, numerous injuries, and major transportation headaches for the Twin Cities. The story, widely broadcast because of its high drama, raised a number of questions regarding the aging of the United States' infrastructure and the potential risks associated with neglecting such issues. Unfortunately, maintaining existing infrastructure is not a subject that normally draws much public and political attention. Building new highways, bridges, and stadiums generates more interest because such projects represent growth in a community. Infrastructure repair, on the other hand, is kind of "boring" and more likely to be associated with merely keeping the status quo.

Providing a strong infrastructure, though, is extremely important to the nation. If it is not done, there can be significant economic impacts, property damage, and—as in Minneapolis— injury and loss of life. How large is this problem? According to the Department of Transportation, 12 percent of all bridges in the United States (nearly seventy-five thousand) are classified as "structurally deficient." Concerns about the nation's power-grid infrastructure have been raised consistently over the past few years. The air traffic control system is hopelessly out of date, causing not only flight delays but potentially making air travel more dangerous. Many of the nation's dams are also at risk, and their failure can cause extensive property damage and loss of human life. The American Society of Civil Engineers (ASCE) gave the nation a grade of D in its Report Card for America's Infrastructure, and that is not including the effect of infrastructure on homeland security, where there is limited information available.[1]

Initially, it is not hard to understand why many of these infrastructure problems are being ignored. The replacement of a bridge or dam or the rebuilding of major highway systems or water pipes in a water supply system can cost millions and perhaps billions of dollars. The

The nation's aging infrastructure, such as highways, bridges, water lines, and electrical transmission lines, rarely gets much political attention, and as a result, problems have been long neglected. However, when major accidents occur, press coverage increases dramatically, and sometimes public policy changes as well. The collapse of the I-35 West bridge between Minneapolis and St. Paul, Minnesota, in August 2007 killed thirteen people and injured about eighty others. The photo shows vehicles stopped on the bridge on the east bank of the Mississippi River after the collapse. The economic stimulus package that Congress approved in February 2009 included funding to deal with aging highways and bridges, which members hoped also would create thousands of jobs across the country.

ASCE estimated that it would cost $1.6 trillion over a five-year period to bring the nation's infrastructure up to "good" condition. This would obviously represent a significant investment and a large amount of money even in government budgetary terms. Perhaps a different way to examine the issue, though, is to ask why certain policy problems get addressed and funded while others continue to remain under the radar. Over the past few years the federal government has spent significant amounts of money on prescription drug coverage for Medicare recipients, the war in Iraq, and various farm subsidies. Why has there not been much attention paid to infrastructure issues, at least to the extent needed?

This is the kind of question often studied by policy analysts. The Mississippi River bridge collapse generated a lot of news coverage and drew attention to the issue of infrastructure repair and maintenance for a period of time. But will this notice lead to new policies or budgets? Do interest groups or other actors pressure the government to do something about aging infrastructure? As we enter an Obama administration, there appears to be interest in infrastructure spending, but most of the rhetoric has been based on how such spending will help create jobs and speed economic recovery rather than on the infrastructure needs themselves. How do we make sense of these decisions and learn how governments might be moved to adopt more sensible and far-sighted policies in the future? The answer lies in studying the policy-making process. Knowing something about agenda setting, policy formulation, policy legitimization, and policy implementation can help in understanding why certain problems get addressed and others do not, and of how politics in the broadest sense influences the decisions that are made.

This chapter offers some insight into this policy-making process. Chapter 2 showed how the structure and rules of U.S. government institutions create certain political incentives that push policymakers toward the kinds of decisions reflected in choosing one policy problem over another. This chapter introduces several theories that further explain why policymakers reach decisions like these. After a brief consideration of five competing approaches, this chapter focuses on the policy process model, which is widely used in the study of public policy. It is particularly helpful for clarifying the role of policy analysis in the design and formulation of the most appropriate policy actions government can take and in evaluating how well those policies work once they are implemented.

As we argued in chapter 2, policymaking in the U.S. political system is inherently difficult because of the institutional dispersal of power, the multiplicity of policy actors, and the sharp conflicts that often arise over what policy actions to take. Policy analysis can help to resolve the conflicts by clarifying the issues and bringing reliable information to bear on the decision-making process. It is especially useful when dealing with complex public problems—such as economic forecasts—that are not easy to understand and when policymakers need to make the best estimates they can about a proposal's likely effectiveness, costs, and fairness.

THEORIES OF POLITICS AND PUBLIC POLICY

Social scientists use theories and models—abstract representations of the real world—to understand the way things work. They can create meaning out of what otherwise might seem to be a complicated and chaotic world in which nothing makes sense and all acts are random. Theories generally attempt to explain why certain things happen the way they do—in the case of policy theories, why certain policies are adopted. Models tend to be more descriptive in nature and are less concerned with explanation. The theories discussed here pertain to the world of government, politics, and public policy, and they provide the concepts and language that facilitate communication with others about these subjects. They also help to focus people's attention on the most important factors that affect government decision making. Political scientists use several different theories and models to explain and describe the nature of policy-making and the policies that result. Among the most common are elite theory, group theory, institutional theory, rational choice theory, political systems theory, and the policy process model (Anderson 2006; McCool 1995).

Each offers a different perspective on the principal determinants of decision making within government and, therefore, on what people might regard as the major forces that shape the direction and content of public policies. Social scientists use these theories to explain politics and policymaking, and students can use them to better understand how policies are made and why we get one policy rather than another. In other words, when asked why the United States has one kind of economic, agricultural, health care, or education policy and not another, the answer depends in part on which theory is used to offer insights into these choices.

Elite Theory

Elite theory emphasizes how the values and preferences of governing elites, which differ from those of the public at large, affect public policy development. The primary assumption of elite theory is that the values and preferences of the general public are less influential in shaping public policy than those of a smaller, unrepresentative group of people, or elites (Dye 2001; Dye and Zeigler 2003). These policy actors may be economic elites—foundations, wealthy people, corporate executives, Wall Street investment bankers, and professionals such as physicians or attorneys. They may be cultural elites, such as celebrated actors, filmmakers, recording artists, or other media stars. Elected officials constitute an elite as well, as do other influential policy actors, such as scientists and policy analysts. Elite theory, then, focuses on the role of leaders and leadership in the development of public policy.

We can see the application of elite theory by looking at those who dominate in public policy decisions. A single power elite or establishment is seldom at the center of all policy decisions, because different elites tend to dominate in different policy areas. For example, one elite may be influential in foreign policy, another in defense policy, and others in areas as diverse as health care, agriculture, financial regulation, and education. One elite may compete with another to win attention for its concerns or to secure a superior level of funding for the programs it favors. Still, by emphasizing the power of these groups, elite theory demonstrates that the U.S. policy-making process may not be as democratic as many believe it to be. Critics of President George W. Bush's energy and environmental policies were convinced that they were shaped with the interests of a corporate elite in mind, particularly those representing large manufacturing interests; oil and natural gas producers; electric power companies; and mining, timber, and similar interests (Kraft and Kamieniecki 2007). At the same time, conservatives often blame the liberal cultural elites of Hollywood and New York for what they see as lax moral standards in today's society.

The role of different elites is particularly evident in the subgovernments or issue networks described in chapter 2 (Baumgartner and Jones 1993; Kingdon 1995). This kind of elite dominance is in part a function of the low salience of policymaking within these subgovernments or issue networks. Most people outside of the narrow circles that are concerned about a matter, such as the Federal Communications Commission's regulation of the television and telecommunication industries, would have little reason to pay attention to the issues or to participate in policy decisions. In fact, most members of Congress also tend to defer to their colleagues who work regularly on these issues. Much the same can be said for the input and influence that legislators seek from agribusiness on U.S. farm policy, the defense industry on weapons procurement policy, and pharmaceutical companies on health care policy. Parallels to these kinds of subgovernments, or narrow policy communities, also exist at state and local levels.

Group Theory

Group theory sees public policy as the product of a continuous struggle among organized interest groups (Baumgartner and Leech 1998; Cigler and Loomis 2007). In contrast to elite theory, supporters of group theory, particularly those who call themselves pluralists, tend to believe that power in the U.S. political system is widely shared among interest groups, each of which seeks access to the policy-making process. That is, they say power is pluralistic rather than concentrated in only a few elites. In this view, some groups provide countervailing power to others—for example, labor unions versus manufacturing interests—as they lobby legislators and executive officials and appeal to the broader public through issue advocacy campaigns. This balance helps to ensure that no one group dominates the policy process. It is reasonable to assume, however, that the groups with greater financial resources, recognition, access to policymakers, and prestige are likely to have more influence than others. At the opposite end of the spectrum are those people—such as the poor and homeless—who are not well organized, lack significant political resources, and are inadequately represented in the policy process. When people speak of "special interests" influencing government decisions, they are using the concepts of group theory. Examples include efforts by the music recording industry to protect copyrights by restricting Internet access to MP3 music files, and by the food industry to prevent government from requiring manufacturers to list ingredients by percentage of food products, an action favored by consumer groups.[2]

A modern variant of interest group theory, the **advocacy coalition framework** (ACF) focuses on the "interactions of competing advocacy coalitions," particularly within a policy subsystem such as agriculture, telecommunications, or environmental protection (Sabatier and Jenkins-Smith 1993). Each coalition consists of policy actors from different public and private institutions and different levels of government who share a particular set of beliefs about the policies that government should promote. In the clash between advocates for health care reform and health insurance companies, for example, each coalition tries to manipulate government processes to achieve its goals over time. Whether and to what degree the coalitions reach their objectives depends on forces in the rest of the political system and the larger society and economy that either provide opportunities or throw up obstacles. The ACF framework posits that policy change can occur over time, as each coalition uses its resources to change the views or policy beliefs of leading policy actors. Proving this concept, environmentalists to some extent have persuaded the business community to think about long-term goals of sustainable development. In turn, the business community has been able to persuade many actors in this policy arena that new policy approaches such as market incentives, collaboration, and information provision are more attractive than conventional regulation, which they view as burdensome and ineffective (Mazmanian and Kraft 2009).

Many students of public policy argue that group theory tends to exaggerate the role and influence of organized interest groups in policymaking and to underestimate the leadership of public officials and the considerable discretion they have in making policy choices. It is easy to believe that lurking behind every policy decision is a special interest group eager to have its way, but assigning too much power to organized groups oversimplifies a more complex dynamic in policymaking. Public officials also frequently use organized interest groups to promote their own political agendas and to build support for policy initiatives. The relationship between groups and policymakers is often a subtle, two-way exercise of influence (Kraft and Kamieniecki 2007).

When specific industries decide to lobby for or against a particular policy, they often become critical actors in the policy-making process. A recent example is support for the production of ethanol. As fuel prices increased, ethanol industries and many farmers' groups lobbied hard and successfully for legislation to encourage ethanol production through federal subsidies. But as food prices increased sharply in 2008, organizations such as the Grocery Manufacturers Association were critical of these policies, which they argued were responsible for rising food prices.[3] Both of these perspectives have been important in the discussion of ethanol as an alternative fuel and the potential consequences associated with its production, particularly from food crops. In addition to these arguments, environmentalists believe that the use of ethanol made from corn and other food grains offers no real advantage over that the of fossil fuels such as gasoline in terms of net energy consumption and release of greenhouse gases that contribute to global warming.

Institutional Theory

Institutional theory emphasizes the formal and legal aspects of government structure, which we discussed in chapter 2. Institutional models look at the way governments are arranged, their legal powers, and their rules for decision making. These rules include basic characteristics such as the degree of access to decision making provided to the public, the availability of information from government agencies, and the sharing of authority between the national and state governments under federalism. A major tenet of institutionalism is that the structures and rules make a big difference in the kinds of policy process that occur and which policy actors are likely to be influential in them. Enactment of the farm bill of 2002 and again in 2008, for example—with its very generous agricultural subsidies—illustrates the power in the Senate of less populous agricultural states such as Iowa and South Dakota. Because the Constitution provides that each state has two senators, these less populous states have as much voting power in the Senate as the far more populous New York and California.

The term *institution* can have many meanings. It refers to "both the organizations and the rules used to structure patterns of interaction within and across organizations" (Ostrom 2007, 22). Therefore, in addition to a focus on organizations such as legislatures, courts, or bureaucracies, the term encompasses how people within organizations relate to one another and to those in other organizations—that is, the rules that govern their behavior. Many kinds of institutions can influence public policy: markets; individual firms or corporations; national, state, and local governments; voluntary associations such as political parties and interest groups; and foreign political regimes. Analysts use institutional theory to study how these different entities perform in the policy-making process as well as the rules, norms, and strategies used by individuals who operate within particular organizations, such as the U.S. Congress or the federal court system.

Although formal institutional analysis can become quite complex, institutional theory is a simple reminder that procedural rules and certain aspects of government structure can empower or obstruct political interests. A common axiom is that there is no such thing as a neutral rule. Rules have real consequences for the ways decisions are made, helping some and hurting others. They can make some groups more influential than others and some policy outcomes more likely than others. For example, the Nuclear Waste Policy Act of 1982 set out a formal, detailed process for selecting the nation's first repository for the radioactive wastes produced at nuclear power plants. The act included the stipulation that public hearings should be held near any site under serious consideration. That legislative provision resulted in extensive opportunities for public comment on the plan, which was widely condemned across the country. Congress was forced to revise the act in 1987 to focus on a single site at Yucca Mountain, Nevada (Dunlap, Kraft, and Rosa 1993).

Rational Choice Theory

Rational choice theory, also called public choice and formal theory, draws heavily from economics, especially microeconomic theory, and often uses elaborate mathematical modeling. A highly developed and rigorous theory, rational choice has been widely applied to questions of public policy (Ostrom 1998, 2007; Schneider and Ingram 1997). Analysts have used it to explain actions as diverse as individual voter decisions and the calculations of public officials as they face national security threats. It assumes that in making decisions, individuals are rational actors; that is, they seek to maximize attainment of their preferences or further their self-interest. The theory suggests that analysts consider what individuals value, how they perceive a given situation, the information they have about it, various uncertainties that might affect the outcome, and how a particular context or the expectations of others—for example, rules and norms—might affect their actions. The goal is to deduce or predict how individuals will behave under a variety of conditions.

Rational choice theory tries to explain public policy in terms of the actions of self-interested individual policy actors, whether they are voters, corporate lobbyists, agency officials, or legislators. David Mayhew (1974) provided a simple illustration in his classic text, *Congress: The Electoral Connection.* Mayhew asked what kind of behavior one might expect from members of Congress if their only incentive were reelection. He found that this simple assumption about individual motivation could reveal a great deal about the way members behaved and even about what kinds of public policy actions such a Congress would be likely to produce. Mayhew found that the "electoral incentive" caused members to advertise themselves, claim credit, and take positions on the issues. This is not to imply that members of Congress and other politicians do not have many concerns other than getting reelected, including a genuine desire to promote the public welfare. Mayhew's example simply highlights the explanatory power of rational choice theory. It forces people to think about the core motivation of individual political actors and its consequences for the larger political system and for public policy.

The critics of rational choice theory argue that individuals are not always single-minded pursuers of their own self-interest. The critics also question the narrow and rigid assumptions that underlie the theory, such as the ability of individuals to behave rationally when they may lack pertinent information, or when decision makers have different and unequal information—a condition called information asymmetry (Green and Shapiro 1994; Shepsle and Bonchek 1997). Some say that the theory gives too little emphasis to the willingness of individuals to engage in collective action pursuits, such as joining public interest groups or participating in community organizations (Stone 2002).

Even so, rational choice theory provides insights into political behavior

Rising gasoline prices in recent years have imposed hardships on many Americans, especially in mid-2008 when record prices convinced many to rethink the kind of vehicles they use, consider taking mass transit rather than driving, share rides with others, or walk or use a bicycle instead of a car whenever possible. Even though prices dropped sharply by the end of 2008 because of the global economic recession, many continue to favor such alternatives as bicycling. The photo shows a resident of Southern California pumping air into his bike's tires before riding home on April 20, 2006, another period in which high gasoline prices were common.

that can affect the design of public policies. It is especially useful to formulate predictions of how agency officials and the objects or targets of policy actions are likely to respond to policy initiatives (Schneider and Ingram 1997). For example, economists say that to persuade individuals to significantly reduce their fuel consumption would take a hike in the gasoline tax of 50 cents or more per gallon. Anything less would likely not alter the consumers' behavior because they would see the incentive as too small to make a difference in their personal welfare. Recent increases in gasoline prices, although not tax related, seem to support this idea. As gas prices increased in 2008 and passed $4.00 per gallon in many places, people turned more to mass transit, bicycles, car pools, and more efficient automobiles to get around.

Political Systems Theory

Political systems theory is more comprehensive, but also more general, than the other theories. It stresses the way the political system (the institutions and activities of government) responds to demands that arise from its environment, such as the public opinion and interest group pressures that we discussed in chapter 2 (Easton 1965). Systems theory emphasizes the larger social, economic, and cultural context in which political decisions and policy choices are made, such as a general preference for limited government or low taxes.

Systems theory is a formal way to think about the interrelationships of institutions and policy actors and the role of the larger environment. It also supplies some useful terms, such as *input, demands, support, policy outputs, policy outcomes,* and *feedback.* In systems theory, these terms operate in formal models. Input into the political system comes from demands and support. Demands are the claims individuals and groups seeking to further their interests and values make on the political system. For example, a union calls for safety regulations in the workplace. Support signifies the acceptance by individuals and groups of the actions of government as well as the actions' legitimacy. Support is evident when people obey the law and respect the system's rules and procedures and when they vote in elections and express trust and confidence in institutions and leaders. For example, there was support for the establishment of workplace safety regulations when the AFL-CIO made it a legislative priority and President Richard Nixon agreed to back legislation on the subject (Kelman 1980).

In this theory, the political system responds to demands and support in the process of policymaking and produces outputs (decisions, law, and policies) that over time may create real changes (called policy outcomes) in the situations that prompted the demands and support in the first place. Systems models incorporate yet another element—feedback from these kinds of outputs and outcomes—that can alter the environment and create new demands or support. An example is strong public support for additional policies to protect nonsmokers, such as bans on smoking in restaurants, which followed other antismoking policies over the past four decades. In this example, an important policy outcome is that exposure of nonsmokers to dangerous secondhand smoke was reduced.

Systems theory is a simple way to portray how governments respond to society's demands on them. It proposes an almost biological model of politics suggesting that governments and public officials react to the political climate much as organisms respond to environmental stimuli. As the environment changes—for example, the economy deteriorates or the public becomes distressed with crime rates or corporate malfeasance—individuals and groups are moved to make demands on government to deal with the situation. Once government acts, the system readjusts in light of the particular decisions and their effects.

Each of these theories is helpful. Each offers a distinct conceptual lens through which to view politics and public policy, highlighting particular features of the political and institutional landscape. Yet none by itself is completely satisfactory. We believe another approach—the policy process model—is more useful than the others, in part because it can incorporate the most valuable elements of each of the others. It also has the advantage of portraying the activities of government and policymaking more clearly and using language that most people can understand intuitively. This chapter and the rest of the book make extensive use of the policy process model, also called the policy cycle model (Anderson 2006; Jones 1984).[4]

THE POLICY PROCESS MODEL

The policy process model posits a logical sequence of activities affecting the development of public policies. It depicts the policy-making process and the broad relationships among policy actors within each stage of it. The model can also be helpful to understand the flow of events and decisions in different cultures and institutional settings; in other words, the concepts and language are general enough to fit any political system and its policy processes.

Table 3-1 presents the model as a set of six distinct, if not entirely separate, stages in policymaking, in keeping with the way the model is discussed in most textbooks. Sometimes the term **policy cycle** is used to make clear that the process is cyclical or continuous, rather than a one-time set of actions. Instead of a top-down listing of each stage, it could be presented as a series

TABLE 3-1	The Policy Process Model	
Stage of the Process	What It Means	Illustrations
Agenda setting	How problems are perceived and defined, command attention, and get onto the political agenda.	Energy problems rose sharply on the agenda in 2001. The Bush administration defined them in terms of an insufficient supply requiring more oil and gas drilling rather than conservation to reduce demand.
Policy formulation	The design and drafting of policy goals and strategies for achieving them. Often involves the use of policy analysis.	The 2001 tax cut reflected conflicting economic assumptions and forecasts and differing estimates of future impacts on domestic programs.
Policy legitimation	The mobilization of political support and formal enactment of policies. Includes justification or rationales for the policy action.	The 2002 and 2008 farm bills reflected intense lobbying by farming interests and environmentalists to build a compromise bill all could support.
Policy implementation	Provision of institutional resources for putting the programs into effect within a bureaucracy.	Implementation of the federal Endangered Species Act has lagged for years because of insufficient funding, which reduced its effectiveness.
Policy and program evaluation	Measurement and assessment of policy and program effects, including success or failure.	Efforts to measure the effectiveness of the 1996 welfare reform policy and of the experimental use of vouchers to improve public education have produced mixed results.
Policy change	Modification of policy goals and means in light of new information or shifting political environment.	Adoption of new national security, airport security, and immigration reforms following the terrorist attacks of 2001.

Sources: Drawn primarily from Charles O. Jones, *An Introduction to the Study of Public Policy,* 3rd ed. (Monterey, Calif.: Brooks/Cole, 1984); and Garry D. Brewer and Peter deLeon, *The Foundations of Policy Analysis* (Homewood, Ill.: Dorsey Press, 1983). The original policy process model can be traced to Harold Lasswell's early work on the policy sciences, "The Policy Orientation," in Daniel Lerner and Harold D. Lasswell, eds., *The Policy Sciences* (Stanford: Stanford University Press, 1950).

of stages linked in a circle, because no policy decision or solution is ever final. Changing conditions, new information, formal evaluations, and shifting opinions often stimulate reconsideration and revision of established policies. In addition, in the real world these stages can and do overlap or are sometimes skipped. In other words, policies might be formulated before they are high on the political agenda, or it may be impossible to differentiate policy formulation from legitimation.

Despite these complications, the policy process model captures important aspects of policymaking that correspond to political reality, as review of the six components—or stages—of the model makes clear. Moreover, policy analysis can potentially affect each of the stages; that is, methods of policy analysis can provide knowledge and insights that might influence every stage of policymaking, from how the agenda is set and policies are formulated to how existing programs are evaluated and changed. For example, economic and budgetary analysis had a powerful influence on the decision to add a prescription drug program to Medicare in 2003. Further analysis showed a much higher cost for the program than what was initially presented to Congress, and some questioned whether legislators would have been as enthusiastic about supporting it had they been fully informed from the beginning. Yet another possibility is that the members were so eager to provide this benefit to a politically powerful constituent (the elderly) that no policy analyses would have dissuaded them from doing so; politics sometimes trumps even the best policy analysis.

Problem Definition and Agenda Setting

Governments at all levels in the United States deal with many different public problems and policies each year. But how do the problems generate interest to begin with? That is, why do people pay attention to them, or why are they considered important enough to solve? And why do some problems, such as crime, command so much attention while others, such as population growth, tend to be ignored? If a problem does rise to a level of visibility, as gas prices did in 2008, who determines that it is the government's responsibility to address it rather than leave it to individuals and the private sector? These questions are at the center of the problem-definition and agenda-setting stage of the policy process. In many ways, this step is the most critical of all. If a problem is not well defined, and if the public, the media, and policymakers cannot be persuaded to pay attention to it, it may go unresolved, even if society continues to suffer the ill effects.

Defining a Problem. It might seem relatively easy to identify a problem, to define it objectively, and to ensure that politics does not enter into the equation. If the issue is juvenile violence and school killings, for example, who would not agree that these are serious problems and that society should do everything possible to prevent them? But are the causes of the problem equally clear? Perhaps they include easy access to firearms and the media's tendency to emphasize violence. Analysts may need to look for other causes as well. What about the rise of bullying in school? Or the effect of two-income and single-parent homes? Or, perhaps, what some Americans see as the moral decay in society, which some blame on the ban of prayer in schools?

As these examples illustrate, defining a problem and determining its causes are not always simple tasks, and the search for answers usually reflects a number of different perspectives. How one defines a problem also goes a long way toward shaping the solution offered. As John W. Kingdon (1995, 110) stated, "Problem definition and struggles over definition turn out to have important consequences." **Problem definition** may also come with some distinct biases. As Deborah Stone (2002, 133) put it:

> Problem definition is a matter of representation because every description of a situation is a portrayal from only one of many points of view. Problem definition is strategic because groups, individuals, and government agencies deliberately and consciously fashion portrayals so as to promote their favored course of action.

In other words, "Where you stand depends on where you sit." A person's perspective and background determine how he or she defines a problem and relates to it. Personal ideology and values are likely to influence how the problem is defined or even if the individual considers a situation to be a problem at all. Internet pornography, for example, is thought of as an issue about protecting children or about protecting basic civil liberties, with very different implications. The financial rescue plan that Congress adopted in late 2008 was initially described as a Wall Street *bailout,* a distinctly less appealing definition from the perspective of those who favored it.

This is what political commentators mean when they refer to how issues may be "framed" or "spinned." Those who favor one view of a problem or one kind of solution use language that describes the problem or the policy action in a framework that reflects their perspective. Their opponents act similarly to convey a different perspective. Those who favor government support for family planning services, for example, frame the issue as a matter of individual rights or a health care service that government should provide. Opponents of family planning might frame the issue in moral terms and argue that government should not fund such services, especially for minors.[5] In a prominent example in 2005, President Bush initially spoke of creating innovative "private" Social Security accounts. But when Democrats successfully criticized the move as "privatization" of the system (which voters feared), the Bush administration switched to calling the accounts "personal" rather than private.

Making comparisons is part of problem definition (Kingdon 1995). Americans might think gasoline prices and taxes are too high and argue for relief (as many did when gas prices rose sharply in 2008); but if they compared the price of gasoline in the United States to that in Europe and Japan, where prices are significantly higher because of government taxes, they might conclude that U.S. prices are in fact quite low (Parry 2002). In recent comparisons of test scores with students in other countries, American students lagged behind in mathematics.[6] This finding raised concerns about the quality of education in the United States. As these examples suggest, the way problems are defined and measured is not neutral; nor is it without important implications for whether and how public policies are formulated and implemented.

The different actors and institutions (formal and informal) reviewed in chapter 2 are almost always deeply involved in problem definition (Rochefort and Cobb 1994). Reports by executive agencies are crucial in supplying information on a problem and how it is changing over time. Congressional committees frequently hold hearings on public problems and invite testimony from various experts. Congressional advisory bodies, such as the Government Accountability Office (GAO), issue authoritative reports on nearly all public problems, from oil imports to health care. Even interest groups get involved. Most interest groups work hard not only to interpret the policy studies but also to supply other information that portrays a problem as they prefer to see it. For example, Common Cause, a public interest group concerned with honest and accountable government, has for years highlighted the implications of election campaign financing as a problem and called for its reform; the group celebrated its success when President Bush signed the Bipartisan Campaign Reform Act of 2002. The private sector also defines public problems. In the early years of radio, broadcasters became concerned about the anarchy of the airwaves, a problem they believed needed a solution. It eventually led to the government's licensing of airwave frequencies to the broadcasters.

By supplying new, and often objective, information on the nature of a problem and its implications, policy analysts can help to steer political debate toward a rational assessment of the scope of the problem, its causes, and possible solutions. A study of urban sprawl, for example, might highlight the adverse impacts on highway congestion, land use, and water supplies, and suggest how better growth management could minimize those effects. The findings and recommendations of such a study would no doubt differ significantly from the arguments of real-estate developers and pro-growth public officials, as Atlanta, Georgia, and other high-growth metropolitan areas have learned in recent years (Jehl 2002; Murray 2002).

Setting the Agenda. Defining a problem is not enough; the public and policymakers must recognize it as a problem, and it must rise high enough on the agenda that action becomes likely. At that point, the search for solutions, or policy formulation, begins. Yet it is by no means easy for societal problems to reach agenda status, because at any given moment many issues are competing for social and political attention. Some make it onto the agenda and some do not (Birkland 1997; Cobb and Elder 1983).

Because of the competition for agenda space, many problems that government could potentially address never capture its attention and are neglected. Population growth is a prime example. The United States is growing as fast as or faster than any other industrialized nation in the world. Its growth rate (about 1 percent a year) is ten times that of most European nations, partly because of its generous immigration policies. The Census Bureau projects that the U.S. population (305 million in early 2009) is likely to rise to 438 million by 2050, depending on the rate of immigration; this is a gain of 133 million people over its size in 2009, or the equivalent of adding about four states the size of California to the nation.[7] Except for a few cities and regions, however, population growth has never been an issue that commanded much attention from either the U.S. public or its elected officials.

The implications are plain. The mere existence of a problem is no guarantee that it will attract government attention or be addressed. Indeed, the term *nonissues* best distinguishes those problems that fail to gain attention from those that do. Some issues are intentionally kept off the agenda by those who oppose acting on them, as was true of civil rights in much of the South during the 1950s and 1960s. Others, such as population growth and energy use, often have been ignored by an indifferent public and policymakers. For the former, what some scholars call *agenda denial*, E. E. Schattschneider (1960, 71) explained the phenomenon:

> All forms of political organization have a bias in favor of the exploitation of some kinds of conflicts and the suppression of others because *organization* is the *mobilization of bias*. Some issues are organized into politics while others are organized out.[8]

When policymakers begin active discussions about a problem and potential solutions, the issue is said to be "on the agenda." Scholars distinguish between a **systemic agenda,** of which the public is aware and may be discussing, and an **institutional agenda,** or government agenda, to which policymakers give active and serious consideration (Cobb and Elder 1983). John W. Kingdon's (1995, 3) definition of the agenda captures the meaning of the institutional agenda. It is, he said, "the list of subjects or problems to which governmental officials, and people outside of government closely associated with those officials, are paying some serious attention at any given time." The term *agenda,* therefore, means the subjects that gain such attention and become possible objects of policy action. There is no official or formal listing of such an agenda; rather, it becomes evident in the subjects that elected officials choose to discuss, the media cover prominently, and interest groups and other policy actors work on at any given time.

Agenda setting is central to the policy process: if an issue does not attract the appropriate attention, chances are it will languish without government response. Therefore, the public policy student needs to understand what facilitates the movement of certain issues onto the agenda. Obviously, policy-making elites in government can define a problem and raise its visibility. Members of Congress or the president may highlight a particular concern or issue they want

---

WHAT'S ON THE AGENDA?

Budget issues are one of those items that are always on the government agenda because all levels of government must develop and pass a budget before they can provide services to their constituents. You can examine how different levels of government address budgetary issues using an array of Web resources. First, go to the White House Web site at www.whitehouse.gov. From here you can browse a number of links or try searching on Budget to see the president's priorities. You can do the same for any state. Access a state site from the Council of State Governments at www.csg.org. For example, you can go to the Pennsylvania governor's site and search on Budget. You could then compare one state's budgetary issues with another. In some cases, you can go down yet another level and examine local government budget issues as well. As you analyze these sites, keep these questions in mind:

- What is the budgetary situation for the entity being examined? Is there a surplus or deficit?
- What kinds of tax proposals are being discussed? Are tax increases or decreases being proposed? What are the reasons and justifications for these proposals?
- Are there any new programs being proposed? Are there budgetary figures provided, and if so, do these figures make sense for what is being proposed?

For another exercise in agenda setting, visit some government and media Web sites and look for the issues the sites emphasize and assign the most space. Starting at the national level, go to the White House site and see if you can determine what is on President Obama's agenda. Visit your governor's site to do the same for your state or the mayor's or local government's site for your community. To reach your state government page, go to the Council of State Governments at www.csg.org. From that site, select a region at the top of the page and then select a state within the region. Either select the governor's office or look for a link to local government to find your city and then the mayor's office.

Next, sample one or more of the leading media sites to determine which issues their journalists believe merit the most coverage. Choose from ABC, CBS, CNN, NBC, and other television networks, and the *New York Times, Washington Post,* or your city's newspaper. Here are the major links:

abcnews.go.com
www.cbsnews.com
www.cnn.com
www.msnbc.msn.com
www.newyorktimes.com
www.washingtonpost.com

Do the government and media sites overlap, or do they cover different issues? Can you think of major problems—national, state, or local—that the media and elected officials are ignoring? What do you think are the reasons for this neglect?

---

addressed, as President Lyndon Johnson did in the 1960s for civil rights and President Bush did in 2001 for education reform. Governors or mayors do the same at the state or local level. Government agencies that deal with a particular problem can also raise awareness and move related issues onto the agenda. The media, by deciding which issues to report on or not, also highlight public problems and may sway public opinion about them. Interest groups likewise emphasize those problems of greatest concern to them and try to define them according to their own political values and goals. The box "Steps to Analysis: What's on the Agenda?" is an exercise in determining what issues are currently attracting the government's attention.

Determinants of Agenda Setting. Some issues make it to the agenda automatically. They are mandated, or required, actions with which government must deal. Examples include passing the annual budget, legislating to reauthorize existing programs, and acting on a president's or governor's nominees for executive appointments. These issues alone probably take up most of the time that policymakers have available, leaving little to the discretionary issues. So what determines which of the optional issues receive attention and possibly policy action? In one of the best attempts to answer that question, Kingdon (1995) points to the intersection of three largely independent sets of activities in what he calls the problem, policy, and political "streams" that flow through society. When the streams converge, they create opportunities to consider certain issues. Whether they successfully move to the political agenda and are acted on is sometimes in the hands of influential policy entrepreneurs, or leaders who invest much of their time and resources in the issue.

The problem stream refers to the various bits of information available on the problem, whom it affects, and in what ways. Government reports and other studies are a valuable resource. They are released frequently and can assess the magnitude of the problem, both in terms of how serious it is and how widespread. Some issues, such as airline security or the safety of nuclear power plants, warrant attention because of their potential harm to large numbers of people. Information about a problem or a possible solution works both ways: it may either help an issue make it to the agenda or prevent it. Acid rain and global warming did not become agenda items until a sufficient amount of information had been collected to document the problems. Policymakers may not, however, spend time on a problem if the technology is not available for a solution. Sometimes the failure or inability of the private sector to address an issue will get it on the agenda. For example, the private sector cannot deal with poverty in the United States or provide Social Security for the elderly. The scope of the problems makes them candidates for the national policy agenda. Finally, government programs may have spillover effects that spur concern about another area.

A focusing event, such as a crisis, usually improves an issue's chance of getting on the agenda, in part because of the exceptional media coverage it receives. The terrorist attacks of September 11, 2001, clearly altered the agenda status of airport and airline security in extraordinary ways. Likewise, natural disasters such as Hurricane Katrina in 2005 or the Midwest floods in 2008 can focus attention on the risk to the public well-being caused by hurricanes, floods, and earthquakes; Katrina clearly did so for hurricanes, and it stimulated a government response. These focusing events are sometimes linked to powerful national priorities, such as defense, public safety, and public health, that may spur government action.

The policy stream refers to what might be done about the problem—that is, the possible alternative policies. Legislators and their staffs, executive agency officials, interest groups, academics, and policy analysts all may develop policy proposals. Often, the ideas are floated as trial balloons—potential solutions—to see how they are received. Some become the subjects of speeches, press releases, legislative proposals, hearings, and study reports. The policy ideas tend to circulate within the specialist communities, or issue networks, of those most concerned about the problem, and with the public through books, magazines, the broadcast media, and the Internet. Kingdon (1995) compares this process to evolution because only the fittest ideas survive. Policy alternatives that are inconsistent with the current political climate, the "unfit," may be dropped from consideration temporarily and incubated until the climate improves. Those that fit better with the political climate may receive serious attention from policymakers and other policy actors. What Kingdon calls the "criteria for survival" are what this text refers to as evaluative criteria, such as economic feasibility and political acceptability. Chapter 6 addresses these criteria.

The political stream refers to this political climate or public mood. It is evident in public opinion surveys, the results of elections, and the activity and strength of interest groups. For example, Ronald Reagan's election in 1980 abruptly changed the political climate by greatly increasing the acceptability of conservative policy ideas. George W. Bush's election in 2000 did much the same thing, and there has already been a dramatic shift with Barack Obama's election in 2008 that will likely continue in upcoming years. Although it is never easy to decipher the political mood of the nation—and it can change quickly—elected officials have a well-developed ability to detect a shift in public attitudes, especially in their own constituencies.

When these three streams converge, policy entrepreneurs have their best chances to move problems and policy ideas onto the agenda and step closer to approval. Moreover, policy entrepreneurs may help to bring about such a convergence. They may be inside government or outside; they may be official policymakers or one of the legions of unofficial policy actors, such as interest group leaders. The president holds a unique position as a powerful agenda setter, in part because of the enormous media attention the office receives. At the state or local level, the parallel would be a governor or mayor.

As chapter 2 noted, however, one of the intriguing characteristics of the U.S. political system is the dispersal of power, meaning that policy leadership can come from many sources. At the national level, congressional committees and subcommittees are often hotbeds of innovative policy ideas precisely because members and their staffs are not only continually seeking ways to improve public policy but also to enhance their own visibility and compete with the other major party. Policy think tanks and interest groups are rich sources of policy proposals. Indeed, as the next three chapters explain, one of the major purposes of policy analysis is to conduct studies that evaluate the potential of new policy ideas. When the politically astute activist think tanks and interest groups put their weight behind these studies, influential policymakers and their staffs are likely to read them and take note of the results. Colleges and universities, professional associations, state and regional think tanks, citizens' groups, and the business community are also sources of policy ideas.

Another way to think about why one issue may gain agenda status while another does not is to look to the particular issue's characteristics, especially its salience and potential for conflict (Walker 1977). Salience refers to the issue's relative importance to the general public and conflict to the level of disagreement over it. The logic here is that policymakers would rather deal with a problem the public believes is important than with one that people are ignoring. In addition, policymakers prefer to avoid conflict and so will tend to shy away from contentious issues. Therefore, one would expect that the issue with the best chance of getting on the agenda would be one that is highly salient but low in conflict, and the one with the worst chance would have low salience and high conflict. Table 3-2 illustrates these differences. Why do the items fall into the text blocks as shown? Can you think of other illustrations of the salience-conflict view of agenda setting? What other examples of policy issues might fit into the text blocks shown in the table?

TABLE 3-2	Influences on Agenda Setting	
	Level of Conflict	Level of Issue Saliency
HIGH	HIGH Crime, gun control, abortion rights	LOW **Worst chance** Population growth, energy, health care reform
LOW	**Best chance** Airline safety	Pork-barrel projects, such as research grants, water projects, agricultural subsidies

Policy Formulation

Policy formulation is the development of proposed courses of action to help resolve a public problem. As noted, policy alternatives are continually being studied and advocated as part of the policy stream and constantly being evaluated against the prevailing standards for policy acceptance. Among the standards for policy acceptance are economic cost, social and political acceptability, and likely effectiveness in addressing the problem. Policy analysis is abundant at this stage of the policy process, as the leading policy actors (formal and informal) look for information and ideas that will allow them to pursue their goals. The next three chapters deal with policy analysis in depth, but here it is sufficient to note that formulation is a technical as well as a political process. Policies that are carelessly formulated—for example, by using inadequate data, questionable projections, or unreasonable assumptions—may fail. A recent case of failure is California's deregulation of its energy market. The state made a series of disastrous decisions in designing a policy that eventually cost its residents some $30 billion in excess electricity charges and forced one of the state's major utilities into bankruptcy (Brennan 2001). Another widely cited example is the decision to launch the war in Iraq in 2003. Toward the end of his term of office, even President Bush conceded that it was based on faulty intelligence that suggested Saddam Hussein's government posed a serious risk to the security of the United States because it apparently had weapons of mass destruction. No such weapons were ever found (see chapter 12).

Who is involved in policy formulation? Chapter 2 discussed the formal policy actors in government, such as legislators, chief executives, and agency officials, who are especially influential at this stage. In most policy areas the appointed and career officials in a bureaucracy are among the most experienced and knowledgeable policy actors. They have the technical information needed to develop policy and the political knowledge that comes from working in the policy arena. Their expertise can cut both ways, however. On the one hand, it can be enormously valuable in formulating new policy approaches. On the other hand, current officials who are strongly wedded to traditional policy approaches may be concerned about the implications of new policies for their offices, resources, and careers. In short, agency officials may be conservative about policy proposals and favor only incremental changes, while those outside the agency are willing to experiment with innovative policy designs.

In addition to agency expertise, legislators and executive branch officials have access to many other sources of information and advice as they formulate public policy proposals. The president, for example, draws not only from his White House staff but also from the Executive

Office of the President, which includes specialized agencies such as the National Security Council, the Council of Economic Advisers, the Council on Environmental Quality, and the Office of Management and Budget. The last serves as a well-staffed, centralized policy clearinghouse for the White House. Legislators, particularly at the national level, also have sources of expertise and advice. Working for Congress are the GAO (a diversified program evaluation office), the Congressional Research Service (for policy research), and the Congressional Budget Office (for budgetary and economic analysis). These offices are supplemented by extensive staffs that serve the several hundred committees and subcommittees where policy formulation is concentrated. Executives and legislators at state and local levels have fewer resources for policy formulation, but the larger states and cities may nevertheless be well equipped to address the kinds of questions that arise during formulation.

Interest groups are active contributors to policy formulation. Like the bureaucracy, interest groups have a great deal of information at their disposal to provide background or specific solutions to problems. This information ranges from technical details about the problem to judgments about whether a proposal is likely to have political support. But interest groups also attempt to shape policy to serve their own economic or political needs. One example of self-serving economic lobbying came to light during consideration of President Bush's proposed national energy policy. A secret task force, headed by Vice President Dick Cheney, formulated the energy plan, which strongly favored drilling for oil in the Arctic National Wildlife Refuge, among other locations. Environmentalists complained bitterly that the recommendations reflected what they saw as the undue influence of energy industry lobbyists, some of whom were among the top donors to the Bush election campaign. The evidence seemed to support the accusations: the Cheney task force was in close contact with energy industry officials, including executives from the Enron Corporation, and its final report strongly favored their positions (Van Natta and Banerjee 2002). The box "Steps to Analysis: Appraising Policy Formulation" suggests some questions that might be asked about the reliability and fairness of the process of formulation as it applies to any area of public policy.

Policy Legitimation

Policy legitimation is defined as giving legal force to decisions, or authorizing or justifying policy action. It may come from a majority vote in a legislature or a formal executive, bureaucratic, or judicial decision (Jones 1984). From some perspectives, the process of legitimation includes the legitimacy of the action taken, that is, whether it is thought to be a proper exercise of government authority and its broad acceptability to the public and/or other policy actors.

Legitimation as a step in the policy process is at once both simple and complex. It is simple when it merely means that a recognized authority considered and approved a policy proposal. A bill becomes a law at the national level if both houses of Congress approve it and the president signs it, but does that process necessarily imply that the measure was legitimated? This question may be especially pertinent for the large number of policy measures that are part of omnibus legislative packages, or the government's growing tendency to adopt budget riders, which are policy actions attached to mandatory appropriations bills. These riders often are buried deep within budget bills precisely to avoid legislative scrutiny and public criticism (Davidson, Oleszek, and Lee 2009).

STEPS
TO
ANALYSIS

APPRAISING POLICY FORMULATION

What steps would you take to determine whether a policy proposal was properly formulated in any area of concern, such as health care, education, national security, or the economy? One issue that was in the news in 2008 was a high-profile discussion raised by a number of college and university presidents regarding whether to reopen the debate over the appropriate drinking age. The discussion quickly turned into claims that these presidents were advocating such a policy. There are a number of sites available for examining this question. The Amethyst Initiative provides its perspective at www.amethystinitiative.org. For a contrary perspective, try Mothers Against Drunk Driving at www.madd.org. You may also want to do a Google search on "drinking age" to get additional information. Use the following to help guide your thinking on policy formulation:

1. Start by examining the assessments of the problem to determine whether they were based on appropriate data and analysis.
2. Next, try to find out who was involved in the formulation process, who dominated it, and whether any serious conflicts of interest existed. You could also review the main assumptions made and any analysis that was used to determine whether they were valid.
3. In your judgment, were the policy alternatives examined sufficiently and evaluated fairly?

The complex view is that legitimation requires more than a majority vote or legal sanction by a recognized authority. Policy legitimacy or acceptability in this sense flows from several conditions: the action is consistent with the Constitution or existing law, it is compatible with U.S. political culture and values, and it has demonstrable popular support. Legitimation also may follow from a process of political interaction and debate that involves all major interests and a full and open airing of the issues and controversies (Lindblom and Woodhouse 1993). A careful assessment of any policy analyses or other technical studies might be part of this process of discussion and debate. So too might public participation through public meetings, hearings, and citizen advisory bodies, or endorsement by respected community or national leaders. Sometimes lawmakers call on cultural elites, athletes, and other celebrities to convince the public of the worthiness of the issue under consideration. During the past few years, for example, congressional committees heard testimony on various issues from actors Michael J. Fox, Dennis Quaid, and Julia Roberts; model Christie Brinkley; singer Kevin Richardson of the Backstreet Boys; and former heavyweight boxing champion Muhammad Ali. In one illustration of the power of celebrity status, in September 2005 the late novelist Michael Crichton was invited to testify before the Senate Environment and Public Works Committee, largely because in his novel *State of Fear* he suggested that the science behind climate-change concerns was too weak to justify government action—a position long argued by Sen. James M. Inhofe, R-Okla., who at that time was the chair of the committee.

Policies that are adopted without such legitimation face serious hurdles. They may well fail to command public support, affected interest groups may oppose them or even challenge them in court, and their implementation could be adversely affected. As discussed earlier, the Nuclear Waste Policy Act of 1982 is an example of a failed policy. Congressional proponents of the act seriously misjudged the public's willingness to accept high-level nuclear waste repositories, the spent fuel from nuclear power plants. They also misjudged the public's trust and confidence in the Department of Energy, the bureaucracy in charge of the program. The policy's backers were so determined to speed up the process of repository location and construction that they rejected the advice from Congress's own Office of Technology Assessment, which had warned that public concern and opposition would scuttle the program's success. Similar issues arose during revision of the act in 1987, when Congress voted to study only one possible site in the nation, at Yucca Mountain in Nevada, over the strenuous objections of the state (Kraft 1992). Nevada was still fighting the federal government's actions in 2008, and controversy heightened when presidential candidate Barack Obama said that he opposed the storage of nuclear waste at Yucca Mountain.

Policy formulation has both technical and political elements, but the process of policy legitimation is mostly political. Nevertheless, policy analysis is still applicable at this stage; assessment of a policy's political feasibility and social acceptability remains relevant. Analysis of public opinion on the policy is also useful, as is measuring interest group support and opposition. Ethical analysis is both appropriate and helpful to determine what is fair and equitable in a policy decision or how it affects individual freedom or liberty. These kinds of questions arise frequently in public debates over welfare reform, access to higher education, patients' rights, family planning and abortion, fetal stem-cell research, and many other issues. The box "Steps to Analysis: Judging Policy Legitimation" poses some questions that might be asked about the process of legitimation in any political venue.

Policy Implementation

For many, the passing of a law by the U.S. Congress, a state legislature, or a city council signals the end of the policy process. In reality, it is just the beginning of government activity that ultimately will affect citizens and businesses more than they may realize. When Congress enacted the Clean Air Act Amendments of 1990, did industry automatically comply and stop polluting the air? When Congress lifted the federal highway speed limit of fifty-five miles per hour, were drivers immediately allowed to legally drive seventy miles per hour? The obvious answers to both of these questions is "no." Once a policy is formulated and adopted, it must be implemented.

According to Charles Jones (1984), implementation is the "set of activities directed toward putting a program into effect." Three activities—organization, interpretation, and application—are particularly important to successful implementation. Organization is the establishment of resources, offices, and methods for administering a program. Interpretation means translating the program's language—the plans, directives, and regulatory requirements—typically found in a law or regulation into language that those affected can understand. Application is the "routine provision of services, payments, or other agreed upon program objectives or instruments" (Jones 1984, 166). In other words, **policy implementation** depends on the development of the program's details to ensure that policy goals and objectives will be attained. One of the primary mechanisms agencies use to implement the laws is regulation. A

STEPS TO ANALYSIS

JUDGING POLICY LEGITIMATION

It is never easy to judge whether a policy proposal had been fully legitimated as it was considered for approval. Among other evidence, analysts would look for information that indicated public support for the action, that the views of major interest groups were considered, that policymakers took enough time to think carefully about their decisions and the consequences, and that appropriate information was used in making decisions.

A May 2008 article in the *Washington Post* discusses the issue of protecting the North Atlantic right whale and a National Oceanic and Atmospheric Administration (NOAA) final rule that was blocked by the White House.[1] The major question being asked was whether politics trumped scientific expertise, an issue that was raised a number of times during the George W. Bush administration. Organizations such as the Union of Concerned Scientists have raised this as a concern, and you can see its perspective at www.ucsusa.org. You can find some information on the right whale at the NOAA Web site at www.nmfs.noaa.gov/pr/species/mammals/cetacea ns/rightwhale_northatlantic.htm and alternative views from the World Shipping Council at www .worldshipping.org and the International Fund for Animal Welfare at www.ifaw.org/images_custom/ publications/AnimalFactSheets/4-ProtecWhales .pdf. Consider this case and try to determine whether the government's decision met expectations noted in the text for policy legitimation.

- What is the appropriate balance between science and politics in making decisions? How do you determine which is more important? Should a president or other policymaker defer to the experts?
- Was sufficient consideration given to the views of major interests, such as the shipping industry and conservation groups?
- Is delaying an appropriate step to take if disagreement exists? What might be the purpose of delaying?
- From a legitimacy perspective, how do you balance economic and conservation interests?
- Did policymakers give sufficient consideration to other alternatives?

[1]Juliet Eilperin, "White House Blocked Rules Issued to Shield Whales," *Washington Post,* May 1, 2008, A3.

---

regulation, which has the force of law, is simply the rule that governs the operation of a particular government program.

Policy implementation is a crucial stage of the policy process because it is where one sees actual government intervention and real consequences for society (Mazmanian and Sabatier 1983; Goggin et al. 1990). For example, the Occupational Safety and Health Act (OSH) is a relatively short law that governs workplace health and safety in the United States. The law itself provides few details on how the Occupational Safety and Health Administration (OSHA) is to go about the business of protecting workers. It has been the implementation of the OSH Act, rather than its adoption, that has most directly affected workplace health and safety conditions. Critics of OSHA often have blamed it for weak implementation decisions. For example, a review of the agency's actions from 1982 to 2002 concluded that it frequently declined to seek prosecution of industries responsible for workplace deaths even when employers were found to have willfully violated safety standards. Later assessments drew much the same conclusion about OSHA's implementation of the law throughout the George W. Bush administration.[9] Much the same could be said about the Consumer Product Safety Commission, which has been chronically underfunded and understaffed. Its weaknesses came to the forefront when its failure to protect the nation's consumers from toxic Chinese toys and similar threats in recent years became headline news.[10]

Executive branch agencies implement most public policies within the United States. The traditional view was that they and their personnel were nonpolitical administrators who simply carried out the will of the legislature by following the established guidelines, with no say in the policy beyond its execution. This viewpoint, however, is unrealistic and fails to take into consideration the influence agencies and their administrators have in formulating policy and the discretion they have in its implementation.

Because of this degree of discretion, agency decisions often reflect the political philosophy and preferences of the chief executive who appointed the agency's administrators. Chief executives try to place in the top agency jobs people who agree with them on matters such as interpreting the law, deciding on agency priorities and budget allocations, and choosing which policy tools to use. In addition, debates that occur during policy formulation often continue during implementation. A good example was the conflict between the Bush White House and the intelligence agencies over conduct of the war in Iraq.[11] These conflicts continued long after the president decided to invade Iraq in March 2003. At times, the executive's enthusiasm for the law, or lack thereof, becomes apparent when it comes time to write the rules. When the Federal Election Commission began to set standards for implementing the controversial campaign finance reform law of 2002, the law's sponsors in Congress complained that the rules "would severely undermine the new law" (Mitchell 2002).

All government agencies and programs depend on a continuing supply of money to operate and carry out the various activities of policy implementation. The federal government uses an annual budget process that begins with the president's budget recommendations to Congress and ends with Congress passing appropriations bills, without which, according to the Constitution, no money can be spent. In between these two steps, Congress decides whether to accept or modify the president's budget and in what ways. Some of those decisions depend on performance assessments, judgments about how well the agencies are implementing their programs. The programs that have proven successful probably have an easier time securing the same or larger budgets; those seen as less so may have to get along with less money. State governments often use a biennial budget process rather than an annual one and usually make adjustments in the second year. The overall process is similar to what occurs at the national level. Ultimately, agency budgets reflect a compromise between what the chief executive wants and what the legislature is willing to give.

Policy Evaluation

The last two stages of the policy process are evaluation and change. **Policy evaluation,** or program evaluation, is an assessment of whether policies and programs are working well. In particular, analysts look for evidence that a program is achieving its stated goals and objectives. For example, did a welfare reform policy reduce the number of people on welfare? Do the programs

In its rush to house victims of Hurricane Katrina in 2005, the Federal Emergency Management Agency (FEMA) ordered thousands of trailers and mobile homes. However, their construction was hurried, with few detailed specifications and with insufficient oversight by FEMA. As a result, many of the temporary housing units turned out to have excessive levels of formaldehyde, a dangerous chemical. The photo shows some of more than 7,500 mobile homes owned by FEMA being stored at the Hope Municipal Airport near Hope, Arkansas. In March 2008 they were being tested for formaldehyde, and about half of them had levels higher than those found in the average home. In some cases, the levels were high enough to put possible residents at an increased risk of cancer and respiratory illnesses.

have unanticipated consequences, particularly any that are viewed as harmful? For example, in the rush to house victims of Hurricane Katrina in 2005, the Federal Emergency Management Agency (FEMA) ordered nearly $3 billion worth of trailers and mobile homes, only to discover later that many of those temporary housing units had excessive levels of formaldehyde, a dangerous chemical. That outcome was attributed to FEMA's weak contracting with the manufacturers, inconsistent regulation, and use of low-quality plywood imports from China. FEMA's specifications for the units amounted to only twenty-five lines of print and did not address the safety of those who would occupy the housing.[12] Evaluation involves judging a program's success in terms not only of the program's policy outcomes but also its legitimacy or need, regardless of how well it is working, especially for controversial programs such as family planning or affirmative action.

Of the many reasons governments engage in policy and program evaluation, costs may be among the most important. Government programs are usually expensive, and policymakers, who must be accountable to the voters, want to know if the results are worth the money—a question that lies at the heart of policy analysis. In addition to costs versus benefits, analysts have many other methods for evaluating policies and programs, but as with policy formulation, legitimation, and implementation, evaluation is not merely about technical studies of program results. It also involves political judgments about a program's worth, decisions that are likely to be of great interest to all policy actors involved. In this sense, programs are continually, if often informally, evaluated by members of Congress, interest groups, think tanks, and others.

Policy Change

Should government expand a program or reduce its scope? Should the administrators try a different policy approach? Questions like these may follow the evaluations and lead to **policy change,** which refers to the modification of policy goals, the means used to achieve them, or both; the change could be minor, moderate, or extensive. Termination of a policy or program is one of many kinds of changes that might be considered, although it is rare. Most often a policy or program undergoes incremental change in an attempt to make it more effective or to meet the objectives of its main constituencies and other policy actors. A clear illustration is Congress's decision in 2002 to expand agricultural crop subsidies. Just six years earlier, Congress had decided to phase out the same subsidies. This 1996 policy change failed to satisfy agribusiness interests, and they pressured Congress to reinstate, and substantially increase, the subsidies. When the farm bill came up for congressional action again in 2008, Congress still kept the subsidies, even in the face of extensive studies that have highlighted their adverse consequences for the economy, food production in developing nations, and the environment.

The farm bill demonstrates that the policy process never really ends. What is thought to be a resolution of a problem through policy adoption at one point is later evaluated and judged to be unacceptable. Interested parties then advocate changes. Another round of the policy cycle begins as the newly recognized needs reach the political agenda and a different policy is formulated and adopted. There is nothing wrong with this process. Indeed, all public policies can be considered to be experiments in which government and the public learn what works well and what does not. Even major policy reforms in welfare, education, immigration, and taxation, among other areas, have not always produced the changes the reformers had in mind, and further assessment and policy change often is needed (Patashnik 2008; Sabatier and Jenkins-Smith 1993).

INSTRUMENTS OF PUBLIC POLICY

We have reviewed the various stages of the policy process model in the sections above. A related topic concerns the options that government policymakers have available at any point in this process, whether it is formulation, legitimation, or implementation. This is the role that government might play in addressing public problems, and especially the policy alternatives among which policymakers can choose. We put this discussion at the end of the chapter because it serves as a transition to what we go on to consider in chapters 4 through 6 on the perspectives and insights of policy analysis.

As we indicated earlier, one of the first decisions to be made is whether government should intervene at all to deal with a problem or simply leave its resolution to individual action or the marketplace. For example, governments chose for years not to regulate smoking in public places, and then chose to do so in an escalating series of actions as scientists learned more about the health consequences of exposure to secondhand smoke. Similarly, most cities and states chose to do nothing about rising levels of childhood obesity because they determined this was largely a matter of private or family choice. By 2009, however, cities

Among the many options that policymakers can consider as they respond to various public problems is government management, in which government directly delivers services to the public or manages the resources at issue. Examples include the operation of public schools, national defense, most local government services such as police and fire protection, and national parks. The photo shows a lone bison crossing a road ahead of a group of snowmobilers in Yellowstone National Park, Wyoming, in 2003. As part of its management of the park, the federal government struggled with the challenge of reconciling the use of snowmobiles in the park with protection of wildlife and provision of quiet and scenic vistas for winter visitors.

and states across the nation were intervening in varying ways, from prohibiting certain kinds of foods in school vending machines and cafeterias to mandating physical exercise for students.[13] Chapter 1 described the most common rationales for such intervention, which include political reasons, moral reasons, and market failures. Complicating the decision about government action is that liberals and conservatives often disagree—sometimes heatedly—about what course to take, and especially about whether government or private action is most appropriate.

Should citizens and policymakers decide that government intervention is indeed necessary, they can choose from a diverse menu of possibilities. We have provided a number of examples in the chapter. Policymakers consider many questions when deciding which **policy instrument** to use to address a particular issue or problem. The most obvious is whether the instrument will be effective in addressing the problem, but others include its political acceptability, technical feasibility, economic impact, and long-term effects. Chapter 5 examines policy alternatives in some detail. The following sections explain the most common policy tools that governments use.

Regulation

One of the best-known policy instruments, regulation, encompasses several different kinds of government actions, including the laws that legislatures enact and the rules bureaucracies adopt. Regulations are government decrees that either require or prevent citizens from doing something. Particular requirements ensure compliance by individuals, corporations, and other units of government. Typically, the regulations impose sanctions, such as fines or imprisonment, for failure to comply. For the most part, citizens and corporations adhere to these legal requirements voluntarily, but the means are available to enforce the regulations when necessary.

Government Management

Governments use the direct services or direct management of resources as instruments of public policy. Education, defense, public parks, and most municipal services, such as police and fire protection, are examples of policies that governments implement by providing the service directly to citizens. Governments offer most of these services because they need to be provided in a specific way, such as making national park lands available to all for a modest fee. Today, it is not unusual for governments, especially at the local level, to contract out a wide variety of services and pay private companies to provide them.

The questions of which government services might be handled by private businesses and whether doing so is a good idea are the subjects of ongoing public policy debate. According to James E. Anderson (2006, 17), "privatization supports transferring many government assets or programs to the private sector and contracting with private companies to handle many public services, whether the collection of garbage or the operation of prisons." Policymakers evaluate the options by using criteria such as effectiveness, cost, and accountability to the public, and the public sector remains responsible for ensuring the quality of the work, even though the private sector is providing the services. To date, many services and programs that were once part of the public sector have been privatized or contracted out, including solid waste collection, jail and prison management, firefighting, highway construction and maintenance, and much more (Savas 2000). But even before the privatization movement, the government relied on the market to provide services. A clear example is that the government has always contracted with private companies in the defense industry to build aircraft, tanks, ships, and missiles.

Taxing and Spending

Governments also use their ability to tax and spend to achieve policy goals and objectives. One form of spending policy is the direct payment of money to citizens. Social Security is an obvious example: the federal government transfers money from people who are working to retirees or others who are covered by the system's rules. Governments also provide monetary payments as a way of promoting certain activities. For example, under welfare reform, the federal government provides money to the states to distribute as they see fit to those needing assistance, but the states must show that they have reduced the welfare rolls or risk losing some of this federal funding.

Governments also use tax policy to promote or discourage certain activities. For example, the federal government promotes home buying by allowing homeowners to deduct their mortgage interest from their taxable income. Many state governments have increased the tax on cigarettes not only to discourage smoking but also to raise revenue for other programs. For example, in the 1990s California launched a two-pronged attack on teenage smoking by raising the cigarette tax and using the additional revenue for antismoking campaigns targeted to teenagers. The action seemed to be effective, as cigarette sales fell substantially.

Market Mechanisms

Governments can take advantage of market mechanisms as a form of public policy. Using the market may be an explicit decision by government not to intervene in any way but instead to allow the laws of supply and demand to work. For the most part, the government has chosen not to regulate electronic commerce on the Internet, or even to impose taxes on Internet purchases, much to the dismay of local merchants who have found themselves losing market share to Amazon.com and other companies.

Governments also actively use market incentives rather than other approaches to achieve policy goals. For example, when Congress passed the 1990 Clean Air Act Amendments, it required a certain amount of reductions in sulfur dioxide and nitrogen oxides, which are precursors to acid rain. In the past, Congress may have used regulation as the tool to achieve these reductions, but under the 1990 act the government is using marketable permits to get the reductions. The permits, which are emission allowances, are provided to companies based on their previous emissions levels, but with the target of lower emissions over time. Companies then decide how to use these permits; they can buy, sell, trade, or bank the permits, using whatever strategy allows them to meet the emissions targets at the least cost. If companies can emit less pollution than they have allowances for, they can sell their additional permits to companies for which emissions reductions are more difficult and more costly (Freeman 2006). This market mechanism, also called "cap and trade," has been suggested as one way to address the release of greenhouse gases that lead to global climate change, and a number of cap and trade bills have been introduced in Congress in recent years.

Education, Information, and Persuasion

Another policy instrument available to the government is educating citizens while attempting to persuade them to behave in a certain way. Following a natural disaster in the United States, the president usually makes a personal appeal to Americans to support relief efforts. This kind of message is called exhortation, or a hortatory appeal (Schneider and Ingram 1997), and the bully pulpit can be an effective instrument of public policy under certain circumstances. Public opinion polls, however, have shown that trust in government and its leaders has decreased over the past thirty years (Nye, Zelikow, and King 1997), although the pattern was reversed temporarily following the September 11 terrorist attacks (Mackenzie and Labiner 2002). As trust decreases, so too does the effectiveness of persuasion as a public policy instrument. People may not comply with a request of a public official if they question the official's justification in making it or the government's overall legitimacy.

Providing information to the public can be a powerful policy instrument. Anne L. Schneider and Helen Ingram (1997) call it a "capacity building" tool with the potential to inform, enlighten, and empower people through training, education, technical assistance, and other ways of making information available. Use of this instrument has increased in recent years and is common in the areas of health, safety, and environmental protection (Graham 2002). For example, the Food and Drug Administration requires nutritional labeling as a way of informing consumers about the substances in their food and allowing them to make decisions on healthy eating. The Environmental Protection Agency each year collects and makes available on its Web site information about emissions of toxic chemicals from industries around the nation. In creating this policy in 1986, Congress hoped, with some success, that publicizing toxic emissions would give businesses an incentive to correct their pollution problems (Graham and Miller 2001).

POLICY TYPOLOGIES

Policymakers are likely to think about policy options in terms of the tools at their disposal. For example, what will be more effective in reducing toxic chemical emissions, regulation or information provision approaches? Which instrument will work better to cut fuel consumption, regulation (raising vehicle fuel efficiency standards) or a market incentive (imposing a larger gasoline tax)? Public policy scholars think about the different kinds of policies that governments adopt and why they do so for a slightly different reason (McCool 1995). The goal is to understand the basic differences among policies and the political conditions that lead to one kind of policy rather than another. To that end, this chapter concludes with a review of the best-known and most frequently cited typology, developed by Theodore Lowi (1964).

According to Lowi, all government functions can be classified into three types: distributive, redistributive, and regulatory. Individual programs or grants that a government provides without regard to limited resources or zero-sum situations (where one group's gain is another's loss) are characterized as **distributive policies.** Examples include college research grants, weapons procurement, agricultural subsidies, highways and bridges, and other public construction projects. Many people label these kinds of programs *pork barrel,* the term used to describe the attempts of elected officials, such as members of Congress, to provide government programs and services that directly benefit their constituencies. Such politicians are said to excel at "bringing home the bacon." These kinds of policies are often noncontroversial because they tend to be visible only to those directly involved, and members usually do not seriously question each other's pet projects because to do so may jeopardize their own. One might expect these kinds of policies to be particularly attractive when spending limits and budget deficits are viewed as unimportant, because the potential exists for most members of Congress to get something out of this kind of spending. But even in fiscally difficult times elected officials may continue to support costly distributive policies. One particular project sarcastically labeled as the "bridge to nowhere" received a lot of media attention with the selection of Alaska governor. Sarah Palin as the Republican vice-presidential nominee in 2008. The bridge was proposed to link a small island in Alaska to the mainland at a cost of $223 million.[14] The direct electoral rewards of providing such benefits to their states and districts appear to override politicians' concerns about the budget.

Conflict is what makes **redistributive policies** different from distributive policies. For every redistributive policy, winners and losers are associated with its approval, which makes such policies controversial and difficult to adopt. Because redistributive policies provide benefits to one category of individuals at the expense of another, they often reflect ideological or class conflict. Some examples include welfare, Social Security, affirmative action, and tax policy. A proposed tax cut may benefit chiefly upper-income taxpayers while eroding services that assist lower-income citizens because of reduced government revenue. If a company adopts an affirmative action policy in hiring women or racial minorities, these groups may benefit at the expense of others.

Lowi's final policy type is **regulatory policy.** According to Kenneth Meier, a leading scholar of regulation, "Regulatory policy is government restriction of individual choice to keep conduct from transcending acceptable bounds" (Meier 1993, 82). This definition covers a wide range of government activities, from protecting consumers to ensuring environmental quality. The range is so broad that some scholars divide regulatory policies into two subcategories. The first, **competitive regulation,** is mostly associated with regulating specific industries and their practices, such as computer software and communications companies. The second, social or **protective regulation,** protects the general public from activities that occur in the private sector (Ripley and Franklin 1991; Eisner, Worsham, and Ringquist 2000).

Competitive regulatory policy includes the licensing of radio and television broadcasting and antitrust actions, such as the Justice Department's suit against Microsoft Corporation in the late 1990s for monopolistic practices. Protective regulatory policy includes consumer protection and workplace health and safety rules, such as those administered by the Consumer Product Safety Commission and the Occupational Safety and Health Administration. These kinds of policies are controversial because they require the government to intervene in the activities of private businesses, often leading to increased operating costs or restrictions on corporate behavior.

Lowi's policy typology provides a simple but helpful way to classify different kinds of government programs and policies. The characteristics associated with each type allow the student of public policy to understand the debate surrounding the issue, why policies may or may not gain approval, how they might be implemented, and the public's acceptance of them.

CONCLUSIONS

This chapter describes the leading theories used to explain the politics of policymaking. It focuses primarily on the policy process model and explores each of its stages, noting the roles of different policy actors and the potential for policy analysis in each. We believe this model enables the public policy student to formulate effective questions about the policy process. It also aids in evaluating the information and arguments used to advance certain policy proposals or to criticize existing programs. The models and theories introduced here are the tools for figuring out what policy actors are doing at any given time and why they are doing it.

The next three chapters explore in more detail some of the themes touched on so far. They cover the nature of policy analysis and its growth over time, particularly through the rise of independent think tanks and the expansion in interest group analysis and policy promotion.

They introduce concepts and methods for measuring and analyzing public problems and thinking creatively about possible policy alternatives for dealing with them. They elaborate on the leading criteria for evaluating policy proposals and the range of policy analysis methods that can provide information about the likely effects of those proposals.

DISCUSSION QUESTIONS

1. With a current public policy example, use the theories of politics (such as elite, group, or rational choice) to help explain why a particular policy choice was selected. How do the assumptions associated with these theories help to explain the outcome?

2. Under what circumstances might U.S. public policy be made mostly in accordance with the wishes of the American people? What kinds of policy decisions reflect the public's preferences? What kinds do not?

3. What steps within the policy process model present the greatest challenges? Are the most formidable challenges presented by the institutional processes, the policy actors, or the nature of the policy itself?

4. What specific factors get most issues onto government agendas? Do you think that most issues on local, state, and national agendas are propelled there because of the political interests of legislators (pork-barrel projects), or in response to the needs of the public? Why or why not?

5. Considering the various policy instruments discussed in this chapter, how would you determine whether one (for example, regulation, market incentives, or public education) is more appropriate in a given situation than another?

SUGGESTED READINGS

Thomas A. Birkland, *An Introduction to the Policy Process: Theories, Concepts, and Models of Public Policy Making,* 2nd ed. (Armonk, N.Y.: M. E. Sharpe, 2006). An accessible and insightful text that describes the U.S. policy-making process.

John W. Kingdon, *Agendas, Alternatives, and Public Policies,* 2nd ed. (New York: HarperCollins College, 1995). A classic analysis of agenda setting in U.S. politics, with exceptional insight into the policy process, particularly agenda setting.

Charles E. Lindblom, *Inquiry and Change: The Troubled Attempt to Understand and Shape Society* (New Haven: Yale University Press and New York: Russell Sage Foundation, 1990). An original and perceptive treatment of the role of policy analysis in the process of problem solving and policymaking.

Charles E. Lindblom and Edward J. Woodhouse, *The Policy-Making Process,* 3rd ed. (Upper Saddle River, N.J.: Prentice Hall, 1993). A unique text on the policy-making process that links it to policy analysis.

SUGGESTED WEB SITES

The Web sites listed at the end of chapter 1, especially those of major government institutions and public opinion surveys, are also useful here. Sites for the leading policy think tanks are listed at the end of chapter 4. In addition, see the following for the study of public policy and policymaking:

www.ipsonet.org. The Policy Studies Organization's home page.

www.napawash.org. The National Academy of Public Administration's home page, with links to events and academy publications on government and public policy.

www.policyagendas.org. The Web site for the Policy Agendas Project, with an extensive database; permits users to graph the agenda status of policy issues over time to highlight some of the dynamics of policy change described in this chapter. Sponsored by the Center for American Politics and Public Policy and supported by the University of Washington, Pennsylvania State University, University of Texas at Austin, and the National Science Foundation.

www.usa.gov. The citizen portal for USA.gov is the default, with links to news, government studies and reports, consumer action, and government e-services.

KEYWORDS

advocacy coalition framework 68	policy formulation 80
agenda setting 76	policy implementation 83
competitive regulation 92	policy instrument 88
distributive policies 91	policy legitimation 81
elite theory 67	political systems theory 71
group theory 68	problem definition 74
institutional agenda 76	protective regulation 92
institutional theory 69	rational choice theory 70
policy change 87	redistributive policies 92
policy cycle 72	regulatory policy 92
policy evaluation 85	systemic agenda 76

NOTES

1. For more information on the Report Card for America's Infrastructure, including information on individual state issues, go to www.asce.org/reportcard/2005/index.cfm. For a useful appraisal of the problem, with measures of its extent and the likely cost to address it, see also Burt Solomon, "The Real Infrastructure Crisis," *National Journal,* July 5, 2008, 14–20.
2. See Cindy Skrzycki. "U.S. Sees No Percentage in Food Content Labeling," *Washington Post,* June 14, 2005, D01.
3. For more information, see Shawn Zeller, "Grassley and Food Manufacturers Go Toe-to-Toe on Ethanol," *CQ Weekly* online edition, June 2, 2008, 1456–1456, at http://library.cqpress.com/cqweekly/weeklyreport110-000002886111.
4. The policy process model is not without its critics. Some argue that it should be replaced by a more accurate and genuinely causal model of policy activities that lends itself to empirical testing and the incorporation of a broader variety of policy actors and behavior. See Paul A. Sabatier and Hank C. Jenkins-Smith, eds., *Policy Change and Learning: An Advocacy Coalition Approach* (Boulder, Colo. Westview, 1993); and Paul A. Sabatier, ed., *Theories of the Policy Process,* 2nd ed. (Boulder, Colo. Westview, 2007). We disagree with the critique. The policy cycle model can be useful for describing the diversified players in the policy game and for alerting observers to pertinent actions that contribute to understanding public policy and politics. One should not, however, treat the stages in the model as anything more than helpful constructs.
5. For a review of how the two major parties used such strategies in recent election contests, see Matt Bai, "The Framing Wars," *New York Times Magazine,* July 17, 2005, 38–45, 66–71.
6. See the data provided at the Public Agenda Web site: www.publicagenda.com/issues/factfiles.cfm?issue_type=education.

7. See the Population Reference Bureau's "2008 World Population Data Sheet" (Washington, D.C.: Population Reference Bureau, 2008), at www.prb.org; see also the Census Bureau's frequently updated projections at www.census.gov.

8. On the subject of nonissues and decisions to keep issues off the agenda, see Peter Bachrach and Morton S. Baratz, *Power and Poverty: Theory and Practice* (New York: Oxford University Press, 1970). We think the agenda-setting theories of John Kingdon, Frank Baumgartner, and Bryan Jones offer equally, if not more, useful insights on the process. See John W. Kingdon, *Agendas, Alternatives, and Public Policies,* 2nd ed. (New York: HarperCollins College, 1995); and Frank R. Baumgartner and Bryan D. Jones, *Agendas and Instability in American Politics* (Chicago: University of Chicago Press, 1993).

9. See David Barstow, "U.S. Rarely Seeks Charges for Deaths in Workplace," *New York Times,* December 22, 2003, A1, A21; Stephen Labaton, "OSHA Leaves Worker Safety Largely in Hands of Industry," *New York Times,* April 25, 2007, 1, A20; and R. Jeffrey Smith, "Asleep on the Job: OSHA Career Officials Say Bush Appointees Ignored Danger and Favored Employers," *Washington Post National Weekly Edition,* January 5–11, 2009.

10. For example, see Eric Lipton, "Safety Agency Faces Scrutiny Amid Changes," *New York Times,* September 2, 2007, 1, 20.

11. For example, see Douglas Jehl, "Report Says White House Ignored C.I.A. on Iraq Chaos," *New York Times,* October 13, 2005, A10.

12. Spencer S. Hsu, "Hazardous Haste: The Rush to House Katrina Victims Resulted in Trailers That Endanger Health," *Washington Post National Weekly Edition,* June 2–8, 2008, 6–7.

13. See Patricia Leigh Brown, "Bake Sales Fall Victim to Push for Healthier Foods," *New York Times,* November 10, 2008, A15.

14. For additional examples of what many might consider "pork," see Scott Bittle and Jean Johnson, *Where Does the Money Go?* (New York: HarperCollins, 2008); and the Heritage Foundation's "Top 10 Examples of Government Waste," at www.heritage.org/research/budget/bg1840.cfm.

CHAPTER 4

POLICY ANALYSIS:

AN INTRODUCTION

ON SEPTEMBER 12, 2008, A RUSH-HOUR METROLINK COMMUTER TRAIN in the San Fernando Valley northwest of downtown Los Angeles ran a red light and collided head-on with a Union Pacific freight train, killing 25 people and injuring more than 130 others, many severely. It was the deadliest train accident in Metrolink's history and the worst in the nation since 1993. Investigators discovered that the commuter train's engineer failed to brake before the accident and that he had been sending text messages on his cell phone moments before the collision. Since February 2007, engineers and drivers had been prohibited from using cell phones while operating trains and buses in Los Angeles County, but the ban was not well enforced. Within a week of the accident, the California Public Utility Commission temporarily banned the use of all cellular devices by anyone at the controls of a moving train, noting there were no federal or state rules specifically regulating the use of cell phones by on-duty train personnel.

California state legislators quickly proposed a ban on text messaging (reading, writing, or sending) by all drivers, an action already taken by a number of states and cities and under consideration by others. By January 2009, seven states, including California, prohibited texting by all drivers, and nine others banned texting by novice or teenage drivers. A widely cited 2006 study reported that over 19 percent of drivers text message while at the wheel, and the number is far higher—over 37 percent—for drivers eighteen to twenty-seven years of age. Is there a good case for banning the use of cell phones for texting while driving? Would the bans be effective? Should the action be extended to any use of hand-held cell phones, talking or texting, while driving? What about use of hands-free cell phones in cars, since studies suggest the real distraction is not holding the phone but talking on it, which carries a risk equivalent to driving with a blood alcohol level at the legal maximum?[1]

In early 2009, the National Safety Council called for a total ban on cell phone use while driving, saying the use of cell phones increases the risk of an accident four-fold. At the time, no state in the nation banned all cell phone use while driving, although six states banned hand-held cell phone use while driving, eleven localities in seven states banned any cell phone use while driving, and seventeen states and the District of Columbia restricted cell phone use by novice drivers. Of the 270 million cell phone users in the United States, some 80 percent say they talk on the phone

New Jersey's ban on cell phone use by drivers went into effect on July 1, 2004, but police cannot stop a driver like this state resident simply for talking on the phone while driving. Use of a cell phone while driving is subject to a $250 fine, but only if a driver is stopped for another traffic offense. As the text indicates, there has been much concern in recent years about the risk of traffic accidents when drivers use a cell phone, but states and cities have taken different policy actions to discourage cell phone use in moving vehicles.

while driving.[2] Would you favor the safety council's recommendation to ban all cell phone use while driving? What about texting while driving? What should be done about other distractions in the car? Washington, D.C., approved a cell phone restriction in 2005 that also bans driving while "reading, writing, performing personal grooming, interacting with pets or unsecured cargo or while playing video games."[3] Is that going too far? As drivers and citizens, everyone should ask how policymakers can ultimately reach decisions like these that are effective, fair, and reasonable. This chapter demonstrates that policy analysis may be able to help answer such questions.

Chapter 3 elaborated on the policy process model, which is particularly useful for understanding how policy analysis contributes to government decision making. Whether in testimony before legislative committees, studies and reports on the Internet, or articles and reports, policy analysis is usually performed at the policy formulation stage. Here, policymakers search for the proposals they believe hold promise for addressing public problems. But policy analysis is also used throughout the policy-making process, starting with defining the nature of the problem right through implementing and evaluating policies within administrative agencies.

This chapter examines the nature and purposes of policy analysis, including basic steps in the policy analysis process. It also surveys the diverse ways in which analysts and research organizations engage in their work. The next two chapters go into greater detail on how analysts study public problems and seek solutions to them, using different methods and criteria to evaluate what might be done. No one expects these chapters to make students instant analysts; rather, their purpose is to convey the challenge of understanding and solving public problems and the need for clear, critical thinking about public policy, whether the issue is public support for higher education or government action to combat terrorism. Readers should learn what policy analysis is all about, how to question the assumptions that analysts make about their work, and how analysis is used in support of political arguments. We also try to direct readers to a variety of information sources about public policy and provide some guidelines for using them.

THE NATURE OF POLICY ANALYSIS

As discussed in chapter 1, the term *policy analysis* covers many different activities. It may mean examining the components of the policy-making process, such as policy formulation and implementation, or studying substantive public policy issues, such as regulation of cell phone use, or both. Policy analysis usually involves collecting and interpreting information that clarifies the causes and effects of public problems and the likely consequences of using one policy option or another to address them. Because public problems can be understood only through the insights of many disciplines, policy analysis draws from the ideas and methods of economics, political science, sociology, psychology, philosophy, and various technical fields (Anderson 2006; Weimer and Vining 2005).

Most often, policy analysis refers to the assessment of policy alternatives. According to one scholar, it is "the systematic investigation of alternative policy options and the assembly and integration of the evidence for and against each option" (Jacob Ukeles, quoted in Patton and Sawicki 1993, 22). Policy analysis is not intended to make policy decisions but rather to inform the process of public deliberation and debate. As in the case of cell phone use in cars, analysis can provide useful information and comparisons. Ultimately, however, the public and its elected officials must decide what course of action to take.

Policy analysis, then, is part science and part political judgment. Doing analysis often means bringing scientific knowledge to the political process, or "speaking truth to power" (Wildavsky 1979). To put it in a slightly different way, policy analysis involves both descriptive or empirical study, which tries to determine the facts of a given situation, and a normative or value-based assessment of the options. Policy analysis can never be reduced to a formula for solving public problems, but as we will show, it can bring valuable information to both policymakers and the public. In those cases where public involvement in decisions is important, analysis also may enhance the democratic process (Ingram and Smith 1993). A good example is the effort in hundreds of communities in the United States to take sustainable development seriously and to implement "smart growth" policies after extensive opportunities for public participation in the design of those policies (Mazmanian and Kraft 2009; Portney 2003). Of course, in some policy areas, particularly those where national security is involved, where quick decisions must be made during a crisis, or where the public is likely to be poorly informed or highly emotional, public involvement is more problematic.

By now it should be clear that the study of public policy and the conduct of policy analysis are rarely simple matters. Public problems are usually complex and multifaceted, and people are bound to disagree intensely over how serious they are, what might be done about them, and the role of government in relation to the private sector. Some problems, such as global climate change or the challenge of terrorism, are monumental. Others, such as how best to provide for a high-quality public school system or limit urban sprawl, may be a bit easier to grasp. But they still are not simple. If they were, the course of action would be clear and not very controversial—removing snow and collecting trash, for example. Unfortunately, dealing with most public problems is not so straightforward.

So what exactly does policy analysis do? One of its primary functions is to satisfy the need for pertinent information and thoughtful, impartial assessments in the policy-making process. The information may not be widely available, or citizens and policymakers may not be able to understand it sufficiently. This is particularly true when decisions must be made quickly because of impending deadlines or when the issues are politically controversial. Essentially, policy analysis involves looking ahead to anticipate the consequences of decisions and thinking seriously and critically about them. It is an alternative to "shooting from the hip" or making snap decisions based on ideology, personal experience, or limited or biased assessment of what should be done.[4] Even though such policy analysis is an intellectual activity, it takes place within a political setting (Dunn 2004). The way the analysis is done and its effects on decision making reflect that basic political reality.

The role of politics is readily apparent in policy areas such as guaranteeing abortion rights, controlling illegal immigration, and including evolution in public school science curricula—a subject of great controversy in Kansas, Pennsylvania, and other states in the 2000s. These issues touch on fundamental questions of values, and people may hold intense views on them. It is no surprise therefore that politics sometimes trumps policy analysis when decisions are made on such issues. Yet the political nature of policymaking is also evident in nearly every policy area, from setting foreign policy objectives to reforming the welfare system. Policy choices usually reflect some combination of political preferences and various assessments of the problem and possible solutions to it. Policy analysis can help to clarify the problem, the policy choices available, and how each choice stands up against the different standards of judgment that might be used, such as those we emphasized in chapter 1: effectiveness, efficiency, and equity. Ultimately, however, policymakers and the public choose what kinds of policies they prefer to have.

STEPS IN THE POLICY ANALYSIS PROCESS

The most common approach to policy analysis is to picture it as a series of analytical steps or stages, which are the elements in rational problem solving (Bardach, 2009; MacRae and Whittington 1997). According to models of **rational decision making,** one defines a problem, indicates the goals and objectives to be sought, considers a range of alternative solutions, evaluates each of the alternatives to clarify their consequences, and then recommends or chooses the alternative with the greatest potential for solving the problem. This process is similar to the way most of us make everyday decisions, although we do it much more casually.

Often, the so-called **rational-comprehensive approach** to analysis and decision making is not possible, and the less demanding **incremental decision making** is substituted. Still, essentially the same steps are involved. The only difference is that incremental decision making is more limited than the rational-comprehensive approach in the extent of analysis required; often it means making modest changes in policy or making them gradually. In political settings incremental decision making is a more realistic approach, given ideological and partisan constraints and the ever-present pressure from interest groups and other constituencies. All can restrict the range of policy options to be taken seriously (Anderson 2006; Lindblom and Woodhouse 1993).

Table 4-1 summarizes the major steps in policy analysis and the kinds of questions analysts typically pose. It also illustrates how each stage of analysis might apply to a particular policy problem. Each step is considered briefly here as a summary description of what policy analysis aspires to do. Chapters 5 and 6 examine each of these steps in greater detail. Note as well how these steps in the analysis process relate to the stages of the policy-making process discussed in chapter 3. Defining and analyzing problems is usually part of the agenda-setting stage of policymaking, and sometimes so is the construction of policy alternatives, especially if some potential alternatives are not considered seriously at all. Usually, however, the formal construction of alternatives is part of policy design and hence fits into the policy formulation stage of policymaking. Development of evaluative criteria also can be part of policy formulation, but it mainly falls into the stage of policy legitimation or approval. Assessing alternatives similarly can take place during both the formulation and legitimation stages of policymaking as policy actors consider which solutions they prefer and which will succeed politically. The same is true of the last stage of analysis, drawing conclusions. Analysts and policymakers may draw conclusions about preferred policy alternatives as policy is formulated, debated, and adopted. Since the policy-making process is continuous, these analytic steps also can be found in the implementation, evaluation, and policy-change stages of policymaking as current policies are assessed critically and alternatives considered.

Define and Analyze the Problem

The first step in any policy analysis is to define and analyze the problem. Everyone knows what the word **problem** means, but for policy analysts the term specifically refers to the existence of an unsatisfactory set of conditions for which relief is sought, either through private means or from the government. Analysts therefore need to describe that set of conditions, usually through the collection of pertinent facts or data on its magnitude or extent. For example, who is affected by it and how seriously? How long has the situation existed and how might it

TABLE 4-1	Steps in the Policy Analysis Process	
Steps	**Type of Questions**	**Illustrations**
Define and analyze the problem	What is the problem faced? Where does it exist? Who or what is affected? How did it develop? What are the major causes? How might the causes be affected by policy action?	How is cell phone use related to auto accidents? What is the potential to reduce accident rates through policy action? How does cell phone use compare to other distractions while driving, such as use of navigation systems or talking to passengers?
Construct policy alternatives[a]	What policy options might be considered for dealing with the problem?	To reduce drivers' cell phone use, should state governments institute fines? Should states try to educate drivers on cell phone use? Is it technologically feasible to disable cell phones in a moving car?
Develop evaluative criteria	What criteria are most suitable for the problem and the alternatives? What are the costs of action? What will the costs be if no action is taken? What is the likely effectiveness, social and political feasibility, or equity?	What criteria are most important for regulation of cell phones? What options might be most effective in discouraging drivers from using phones? Will people find these options acceptable? Is it ethical to restrict individual behavior to achieve a social goal?
Assess the alternatives	Which alternatives are better than others? What kind of analysis might help to distinguish better and worse policy alternatives? Is the evidence available? If not, how can it be produced?	Are fines or education more likely to reduce drivers' cell phone use? How successful are the efforts of states and localities to regulate cell phone use? What evidence is needed to answer these questions?
Draw conclusions	Which policy option is the most desirable given the circumstances and the evaluative criteria? What other factors should be considered?	Should state governments impose stiff fines? Would fines be accepted as a legitimate action? How might the action be made more acceptable?

[a]Most models of the policy analysis process place the task of developing policy alternatives after the stage of identifying evaluative criteria. See Carl V. Patton and David S. Sawicki, *Basic Methods of Policy Analysis and Planning*, 2nd ed. (Englewood Cliffs, N.J.: Prentice Hall, 1993). The precise order may not matter because the two stages tend to occur together anyway, but we think most analysts would consider policy alternatives first and then the criteria to use in judging their merits. Studies of the policy-making process, such as John Kingdon's book *Agendas, Alternatives, and Public Policies*, 2nd ed. (New York: HarperCollins College, 1995), suggest that alternative policies are discussed in various policy communities and then judged according to various criteria to determine their acceptability and which are likely to make it to a short list of ideas to be taken seriously.

change over the next several years or decades? How amenable is it to intervention through one means or another? The goals and objectives of such intervention, whether private or governmental, may not be clear to all concerned.

It may also be necessary to clarify what is meant by the set of conditions, to define it clearly, and to develop accurate measures of it. If the problem is homelessness in the United States, for example, an analyst would need to be clear about what is meant by homelessness, how to determine the extent of it, and who is affected by it. A great deal of information has been

The United States and other developed nations have long provided economic assistance to help developing countries deal with the poverty; this has included funding public health services, although funding has fallen well short of the levels the developed nations have pledged in support. The public and policymakers often are skeptical about foreign aid and its effectiveness, and as a result, many private organizations, such as the Bill and Melinda Gates Foundation, have stepped in and offered their own aid. The photo, from 2006, shows Tatomkhulu-Xhosa, left, explaining to Bill and Melinda Gates, right, how he has lived with and been treated for tuberculosis (TB) in recent years at the Khayelitsha Site B Clinic in Cape Town, South Africa. The Gateses were in South Africa to learn more about efforts to fight TB and HIV/AIDS in the country.

gathered on this problem. The federal government says a homeless person is one who "lacks a fixed, regular, and adequate nighttime residence" and who has a "primary nighttime residence" in a supervised public or private shelter or similar institution that provides temporary residence.[5] In 2007, the National Alliance to End Homelessness estimated that nearly 672,000 U.S. residents were homeless, representing a decrease of about 10 percent from 2005. The number (and percentage) of homeless varied greatly from state to state, as did the percent change from 2005. In light of the very large number of home foreclosures in 2008 and 2009, it is widely expected that homelessness is once more on the rise. In earlier studies, the federal government estimated that about 40 percent of the homeless were African American, nearly four times their percentage in the population. Some 23 percent were veterans, 57 percent had suffered from mental illness at some point in their lives, and 62 percent had problems with alcohol and 58 percent with drugs.[6] For most public problems, analysts will want to develop quantitative measures of this kind. Many are readily available in government reports and other sources.

Beyond gathering basic information about the problem, analysts want to identify its causes, which is not always an easy task. Without a good idea of how and why the problem came about, however, it is difficult to think usefully about possible solutions to it. This kind of diagnosis of the problem is akin to what a physician does when a patient is ill or what a mechanic does when a car is not running properly. The importance of the diagnosis is clear if one looks at how policymakers are trying to cope with an issue as large as global terrorism. Without an understanding of the causes of terrorism—and they may be too numerous to deal with—policy actions are unlikely to be effective. To use a more concrete example, one has to first diagnose the reasons for failing public schools before a solution can be sought. Otherwise, there is little reason to believe that specific actions will improve the quality of education in those schools.

A long-standing dispute over international development assistance speaks to the importance of careful measures and analysis of any public problem. Economic assistance to developing countries from twenty-two donor nations, including the United States, ran about $104 billion in 2007, or about 0.28 percent of the donor nations' combined gross national income. Although well below the level to which these nations had committed themselves in the 1990s, the total is nonetheless substantial; the United States alone contributed about $22 billion.[7] Donors contribute such funds because they believe such assistance will help stimulate economic growth in the receiving nations and save millions of lives through investment in health care services, education, and sanitation. Yet some recent studies indicate that, despite over $1 trillion in loans since the 1960s, many developing nations have shown little gain in per capita economic growth, and some have seen the health and welfare of their populations worsen. One explanation is that some portion of the aid was lost to corrupt and ineffective governments, a problem that has proven to be difficult to address.[8]

So now the question is: Should donor nations cease economic assistance because some of it has been misused? Some critics say yes, but looking at the overall statistical portrait misses seeing the real success stories in economic assistance, which are abundant. One lesson would seem to be that economic aid is more likely to work when it comes in relatively small, well-targeted, and tightly controlled investments rather than in large sums delivered to a government that may waste it. One leading economist argues, for example, that a $25 billion investment in fighting malaria, tuberculosis, and other preventable diseases could save eight million lives a year in developing nations. The money would be spent on concrete measures such as vaccines, antibiotics, and AIDS prevention.[9]

Construct Policy Alternatives

Once analysts believe they understand the problem, they begin to think about alternative ways of dealing with it. The policy typologies introduced in chapter 3 suggest several different approaches, such as regulation, subsidies, taxing and spending, market incentives, and public education or information provision. The point is that government has a finite number of actions from which to choose. Based on the available inventory of possibilities, analysts could construct a set of policy options for further study and consideration, such as the relative advantages of regulation and market incentives for reducing the use of toxic chemicals. Chapter 5 introduces some useful ways to lay out a range of policy alternatives.

Constructing policy alternatives is perhaps the most important stage in the policy analysis process. If analysts and policymakers cannot think of creative ways of solving problems, conventional approaches that may no longer be appropriate will continue to be used. Early in the process, therefore, analysts are called upon to think imaginatively and critically about how the problem might be addressed, both within government and outside it. One approach that has gained increasing acceptance is privatization, the transfer of public services from government to the private sector. Such private sector solutions, recommended by many policy analysts and organizations, and sometimes endorsed by the government, are said to be more appealing, and perhaps more effective, than reliance on a government agency. Some communities have even turned over management of their public schools to private companies. A few years ago, many people supported a partial privatization of the Social Security system. Under this plan, workers would be allowed to manage a portion of their payroll taxes instead of having all of the money go into the general Social Security system, where they have no control over the investment or rate of return. Neither idea was given much consideration a decade ago, and after the sharp downturn in the stock market in 2008, even partial privatization may be considered to be too risky today. Yet these examples illustrate that the search for possible policy alternatives can produce new ideas that gain a measure of public acceptance. Chapter 5 also suggests some fruitful ways for students of public policy to think creatively about generating policy options.

Choose the Evaluative Criteria

When the policy alternatives have been identified, the analysis shifts to assessing their potential. This task calls for deciding on suitable evaluation criteria. As chapter 1 discussed, this text focuses on effectiveness or the likely success of proposals in solving the problem at hand, the economic costs and efficiency of proposals, and the implications for social equity. There are, however, many other appropriate criteria, such as political, administrative, and technical feasibility; environmental impacts; ethical considerations; and any number of political values, such as personal freedom, against which to assess policy proposals. These are further explored in chapter 6 and summarized in Table 6-1, on page 154.

No matter how long a list of potential evaluative criteria analysts might develop, some criteria will be more appropriate for a given problem than others. For example, for years the United States has been considering a missile defense system for protection against a ballistic missile attack. On what basis should analysts evaluate the proposal, particularly in relation to other national security needs? One criterion would have to be technical feasibility. Can the missile defense system, which is based on highly complex computer software and state-of-the-art technology, do what it is supposed to do? Another would be the costs. The Pentagon spent more than $55 billion on the system between 1983 and 1999, and some $100 billion over four decades, with relatively few positive results.[10] Moreover, the cost of a fully deployed system depends on how extensive a shield the government decides to construct. Estimates by the Congressional Budget Office in 2000 put the cost at between $30 and $60 billion through 2010, but the ultimate cost could easily be much higher.[11] Indeed, some estimates put the total cost by the year 2025 at well over $200 billion. Is this outlay of money reasonable in light of the gains to the nation's defense and the risk that the technology might not work as planned? How would an analyst go about determining the answer?[12]

Plenty of information is available about the missile defense system, but a good deal of it is contradictory, and analysts disagree heatedly about the core issues, such as technical feasibility. In his campaign for the presidency, Barack Obama said that he supported deploying a missile defense system when the technology is proven to be workable, suggesting that he doubted that the current system would measure up. Any assessment of the desirability of creating and funding a system as technically complex as missile defense would be a demanding undertaking. Nevertheless, policymakers and analysts need to ask the questions and try to find answers. Because multiple criteria for evaluating such proposals exist (and for good reason), students of public policy need to be aware of them and be prepared to consider which criteria are best suited to making the correct choices for society.

For some policy actions—for example, whether and how to control gun ownership—the evaluative criteria would likely include political values. Personal rights will be weighed against other needs, such as protecting the public's safety and well-being. As this example indicates, conflicts may arise among criteria. The war against terrorism that began after the September 11 attacks raises similar questions. On what basis should policy analysts, citizens, and policymakers judge the suitability of policy options, such as military action against terrorist bases or economic development assistance to poor countries? Or the short-term national security implications of destroying terrorist operations versus the longer-term need to deal with the root causes of terrorism?

In some policy disputes, much of the battle between proponents and opponents of government action is over which criteria to use as well as which conclusions to draw. In 2001 and 2002 energy companies and environmentalists invoked numerous competing criteria to evaluate the proposal to drill for oil and natural gas in the Arctic National Wildlife Refuge. These included economic costs, national security, environmental protection, and technical feasibility. The two sides in this conflict also reached different conclusions as each of these criteria was considered. As this example shows, policymakers, analysts, and lobbyists of one stripe or another bring their ideological biases to these debates. Those beliefs tend to frame their selection of evaluative criteria and therefore their assessment of the problem and the solutions they are willing to consider.

Assess the Alternatives

With evaluative criteria at hand and a collection of possible courses of action to take, analysis turns to **assessing alternatives.** That is, the analysts ask which of the several alternatives that might be considered seriously is most likely to produce the outcome sought—whether it is to reduce the crime rate, improve the plight of the homeless, raise educational quality, or protect the environment. This exercise involves making judgments about how well each policy option fits in relation to the most relevant criteria. The analysts might rank the options in terms of overall desirability or consider them in terms of each criterion, such as effectiveness, economic cost, and equity.

Some authors refer to this stage of the process as projecting the outcomes or assessing impacts (Patton and Sawicki 1993; Starling 1988). A number of different methods or tools are used to do this, and they are discussed at length in chapter 6. They range from cost-benefit analysis to ethical analysis. Given their frequent use in policy studies and debates today, it is important even for the beginning student of public policy to understand these methods and their strengths and limitations.

Analysts have many ways to present the alternatives so that policymakers and other interested parties can understand the analysis and the choices they face. For example, if three policy options are offered for consideration, the analyst might present each in terms of its likely effectiveness, economic efficiency, and equity. Trade-offs are inevitable in this kind of decision making. Only rarely does a given policy option rank highest on all of the evaluative criteria. It is far more likely that one option is judged to be most effective but another to be cheaper or more equitable in its effects. Analysts therefore attach weight to each criterion. For example, is equity more important than efficiency in promoting cleanup of hazardous waste sites? Should governments focus on the most dangerous sites first or try to ameliorate the conditions at several sites at once? Or should the resources be directed to sites that have a disproportionate impact on poor and minority communities? Would doing so promote greater equity (Ringquist 2006)? As analysts consider more than a few conflicting bases for assessing policy options, the necessity for weighting criteria increases.

Draw Conclusions

Most studies draw conclusions about what kind of policy action is desirable, and some strongly advocate a particular position on the issues. Many studies do not recommend a single policy action. Rather, the analysts summarize their findings and draw conclusions about the relative merits of competing policy proposals but leave the choice of policy action to policymakers and the public.

Whichever approach is taken, all analysis is of necessity partial and limited. That is, analysis cannot ever be complete in the sense of covering every conceivable question that might be raised. It also cannot be free of limitations, because every method or tool that might be used is subject to some constraints. Policy analysts need to develop a robust ability to deal with uncertainty, which comes with the territory.

The later chapters consider these challenges and how to deal with them. Students will become familiar with the range of methods employed in the practice of public policy and how to use the different approaches, and therefore will be better prepared to cope with the challenges. For example, the amount of information available might be so overwhelming that finding the desirable course of action seems impossible; or there may be so little that no one can draw firm conclusions. Analysts may be faced with conflicting studies and interpretations that start with varying definitions of the problem and evaluative criteria that render their conclusions and recommendations difficult to compare and judge.

At this stage, we urge students to learn to ask critical questions about the information they collect, especially regarding its validity. Where did the information come from, and how reliable is the source? Is there any way to double-check the facts and their interpretation? Do the information and analysis seem on their face to be believable? Are there any signs of bias that might affect the conclusions that the study offers? If two or more studies contradict one another, what are the reasons? Is it because of conflicting political ideologies, differences in the preferred policy actions, or disagreement in the way the problem is defined? Are the authors too selective in deciding what information should be presented and what can be left out? By gathering information from multiple sources and comparing different interpretations, students might find it easier to determine which of the studies is the most credible. Chapter 1 touched briefly on the need to develop these critical skills in appraising public policy information and studies, and the point is stressed throughout the book.

The best policy studies are those that are also sensitive to political reality. Their authors have made a special effort to understand the information needs of decision makers and the public, whether at the local, state, or national level. A common complaint within policy studies is that much analysis goes unread and unused either because it does not address the questions that decision makers think are important or because it is not communicated effectively to them so they can consider it. Analysis that is designed from the start to address these kinds of questions is far more likely to have an impact on the policy process (Bardach 2009; Lindblom and Cohen 1979; Weiss 1978).

TYPES OF POLICY ANALYSIS

No matter what kind of public problem needs a solution, from airline safety to urban air pollution, there is usually no shortage of policy studies that might apply. Some come from government offices themselves, such as the Government Accountability Office and the Congressional Research Service, or from executive agencies and departments such as the Food and Drug Administration or the Department of Labor. Policy analysis is also becoming common in state government agencies (Hird 2005). A great number of studies, however, come from interest groups and independent policy research institutes or think tanks, many of which advocate specific political agendas (Rich 2004). The abundance of policy studies reflects not only the dramatic rise in the number of think tanks since the 1970s but also the even more striking increase in the number of interest groups that seek to shape public opinion on the issues and affect the policy process. This shift in the political environment is most evident at the national level, where policy researchers and interest groups pay rapt attention to the debates in Congress and the activities of administrative agencies. Policymakers at this level of government are the targets of thousands of studies released each year. Even at state and local levels of government, particularly in the larger states and cities, policy studies and advocacy are common.

Prominent think tanks, interest groups, and policy-oriented law firms and consulting companies tend to establish their offices in Washington, D.C., or in state capitals, but organized interest groups are found all over the United States. Whether they are environmental activists, corporate trade associations, professional organizations, or unions, they all have a stake in policy decisions made by government, and most set up a public or governmental affairs office to monitor pending legislation or agency actions.

Scholars have noted the rise and influence of think tanks in particular, given their visibility in contemporary policymaking (Rich 2004). Carol Weiss's study of these organizations attributes their dramatic growth and popularity to several trends and needs. First, government policymakers and the public need to understand and cope with complex problems. Second, policymakers find it useful in a time of political cynicism to demonstrate the reasonableness and rationality of their positions and actions, and policy analysis symbolizes an acceptable, or proper, procedure. Third, policy officials value independent research and analysis as supplements to the knowledge and skills within government and see the analyses as helping to persuade skeptical politicians and citizens. Fourth, certain interests who believe they are underrepresented in government circles seek to make their views known and promote their causes (Weiss 1992).

Whatever the reason for their rise, policy analysis organizations continue to thrive in the United States because of the character of government institutions and the political process. Fragmentation of government authority creates many opportunities for both interest group lobbying and policy analysis conducted outside of government. As political parties have weakened, interest group and think tank activity has strengthened. Forced to deal with intricate and interlinked problems, policymakers continually search for pertinent expertise, and the studies by think tanks and interest groups are often as influential as the analysis conducted within government agencies.

The leading think tanks, such as the Brookings Institution, the American Enterprise Institute for Public Policy Research, the Urban Institute, the Center for Strategic and

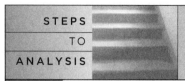

THINK TANK POSITIONS ON POLICY ISSUES

All think tanks conduct analysis and advocate positions on public policy issues, but some of these groups are committed to political or ideological standpoints that affect their analyses and recommendations. Welfare reform is one issue that think tanks of varying political persuasions have studied. The federal welfare reform law, the Personal Responsibility and Work Opportunity Reconciliation Act of 1996, eliminated the Aid to Families with Dependent Children (AFDC) program and created one called Temporary Aid for Needy Families (TANF). The new law had three primary goals: to reduce dependence on welfare and increase employment, to reduce poverty among children, and to strengthen marriages and reduce the number of illegitimate births.

The various studies of welfare reform reached different conclusions about its success. But why? One reason is that the studies reflect the political slant of the think tanks. Another is that they sometimes addressed different questions. Are the welfare caseloads being reduced? Are the caseload reductions permanent? Are fewer people living in poverty? Are children better off as a result of welfare reform? The following summaries come from two think tanks that represent distinctive positions on the ideological spectrum: the conservative Heritage Foundation and the liberal Center on Budget and Policy Priorities. What conclusions can you draw about how these two policy research organizations evaluate welfare reform? What are the similarities and differences in their positions?

WHAT DOES THE HERITAGE FOUNDATION SAY ABOUT WELFARE REFORM?

- According to the Census Bureau, 3.5 million fewer people live in poverty today than in 1995.
- Some 2.9 million fewer children live in poverty today than in 1995. The poverty

rate for African American children has fallen to the lowest point in U.S. history.
- Hunger among children has been cut roughly in half according to the U.S. Department of Agriculture.
- Welfare caseloads have been cut in half and employment for the most disadvantaged single mothers has increased from 50 percent to 100 percent.
- The explosive growth of out-of-wedlock childbearing has come to a virtual halt.

Source: Robert Rector and Patrick F. Fagan, "The Continuing Good News about Welfare Reform," Heritage Foundation, February 6, 2003. Available at www.heritage .org/Research/Welfare/bg1620.cfm.

WHAT DOES THE CENTER ON BUDGET AND POLICY PRIORITIES SAY ABOUT WELFARE REFORM?

- Overall, the number of single parents who now work has risen markedly.
- Those who work generally earn low wages and remain poor. The Center for Law and Social Policy found that former welfare recipients tended to earn between $6 and $8.50 per hour.
- Many families that left welfare do not receive Medicaid or food stamps even though they are eligible for these programs.
- Many people who left welfare did so not because they found a job but because they were terminated from the program for failing to meet its requirements.
- Teen pregnancy and nonmarital birth rates did fall in the 1990s, and the proportion of low-income children living in two-parent families rose. It is unclear how much, if at all, TANF policies affected these trends.

Source: Martha Coven, "An Introduction to TANF," Center on Budget and Policy Priorities, January 13, 2003. Available at www.cbpp.org/1-22-02tanf2.htm.

International Studies, and the Heritage Foundation, are well endowed financially and can afford large professional staffs. Many receive significant and continuing support from foundations and industry or from government agencies for whom they conduct research under contract.[13] These research institutes are therefore generally well equipped to distribute their analyses throughout government, the Washington policy community, academia, and major media outlets nationwide (Ricci 1993; Weiss 1992). At the end of the chapter is a list of Web sites for think tanks and for other sources of policy studies. See the box "Steps to Analysis: Think Tank Positions on Policy Issues" for a comparison of the findings of two prominent think tanks, the conservative Heritage Foundation and the liberal Center on Budget and Policy Priorities, on welfare reform.

The large number of think tanks and active interest groups almost guarantees that the public and policymakers will suffer from information overload as they try to digest the surfeit of reports and studies available on any public policy topic. Hundreds of books and thousands of articles, papers, pamphlets, and seminar and workshop reports flood Washington and state capitals every year. Yet, as noted biologist Edward O. Wilson (1998, 269) observed, we "are drowning in information, while starving for wisdom." The future, he said, will belong to those capable of synthesizing information to make it usable. They will be the people "able to put together the right information at the right time, think critically about it, and make important choices wisely." Another name for Wilson's synthesizers is *policy analysts*. Analysis, however, comes in a great many flavors, and policymakers and the public need to be able to differentiate the more worthy from the less worthy.

One way to do that is to understand the different kinds of policy studies or policy analyses available today, a matter addressed briefly in chapter 1. Policy analyses fall into three broad categories: scientific, professional, and political. All serve valid purposes, but they have varying goals and objectives and use different methods. Table 4-2 summarizes the distinctions among the three perspectives.

Scientific Approaches

Some individuals, particularly academics, study public policy for scientific purposes, that is, to build general understanding of public problems and the policy-making process. They seek "truth" through scientific methods, regardless of whether the knowledge is relevant or useful in some immediate way. For example, social science studies in the scientific category typically are not intended to influence public policy directly. Their purpose is, as one author put it, "to deepen, broaden, and extend the policy-maker's capacity for judgment—not to provide him with answers" (Millikan 1959, 167). On a substantive issue such as climate change, natural and social scientists may be interested mainly in clarifying what we know about climate change and its probable effects on society, not in recommending policy action.

Professional Approaches

As we have seen in this chapter, others study public policy for professional reasons, such as conducting policy analyses for government agencies, think tanks, or interest groups. Many policy analysts, both in and out of government, are committed to producing the best analysis

| TABLE 4-2 | Orientations to Policy Analysis | | | |

Type of Analysis	Objectives	Approaches	Limitations	Examples
Scientific	Search for "truth" and build theory about policy actions and effects	Use the scientific method to test hypotheses and theories; aim for objective and rigorous analysis; policy relevance less important than advancing knowledge	May be too theoretical and not adequately address information needs of decision makers	Academic social scientists and natural scientists, National Academy of Sciences, Intergovernmental Panel on Climate Change
Professional	Analyze policy alternatives for solving public problems	Synthesize research and theory to understand consequences of policy alternatives; evaluate current programs and their effects; aim for objectivity, but with goal of practical value in policy debate	Research and analysis may be too narrow due to time and resource constraints; may neglect fundamental causes of public problems	Brookings Institution, Urban Institute, American Enterprise Institute, Government Accountability Office
Political	Advocate and support preferred policies	Use legal, economic, and political arguments consistent with value positions; aim to influence policy debate to realize organizational goals and values	Often ideological or partisan and may not be credible; may lack analytic depth; level of objectivity and rigor varies	Sierra Club, AFL-CIO, Chamber of Commerce, National Rifle Association, Heritage Foundation, Cato Institute

Sources: Drawn in part from Peter House, *The Art of Public Policy Analysis* (Beverly Hills, Calif.: Sage Publications, 1982); and David L. Weimer and Aidan R. Vining, *Policy Analysis: Concepts and Practice,* 4th ed. (Upper Saddle River, N.J.: Prentice Hall, 2005).

possible, and they adhere to strong professional norms for economic analysis, modeling of complex situations, and program evaluation. The comparison of the Brookings Institution and the American Enterprise Institute (AEI) in the box "Working with Sources: Comparing Think Tanks" nicely illustrates the kinds of topics addressed by such analysts and how they express their purpose. Even though Brookings and AEI are usually described as left and right of center, respectively, both can be categorized as engaging in professional analysis.

Political Approaches

Some analysts may be as rigorous in the methods they use as the professionals, but they are also committed to specific policy values and goals and sometimes to ideological and partisan agendas. As one would expect, they try to emphasize the studies and findings that help to advance those values and goals. This kind of policy study can be described as political, rather than professional or scientific. Analysts who work for interest groups or activist organizations, such as Common Cause, the National Organization for Women, the American Legislative Exchange Council (a conservative organization that advises state legislators), the Christian

Coalition, or the National Rifle Association, are especially likely to have this orientation. So too are those who work for political parties and ideological groups, such as the Americans for Democratic Action, the American Civil Liberties Union, or the American Conservative Union. The two think tanks compared in the Steps to Analysis box on page 108, the Heritage Foundation and the Center on Budget and Policy Priorities, fit into this category of political policy analysis because of their strong commitments to conservative and liberal policies, respectively.

It may be difficult to distinguish this kind of politically oriented policy study from policy advocacy, but as Deborah Stone (2002) argues, it is also impossible to completely separate even rigorous policy studies from the political processes in which they are imbedded. Analysis, she asserts, is itself "a creature of politics," and often it is "strategically crafted argument" designed to advance particular policy values.

Even if such arguments are persuasive, readers need to keep in mind their distinct perspectives and appreciate the differences among the studies and arguments. As is often true in human affairs, critical judgment is needed to assess what organizations and analysts say about public policy. Some studies will present stronger scientific evidence than others, and some positions will demonstrate more passion than others, but everyone needs to determine how credible the information is and its implications for public policy.

As Table 4-2 indicates, some think tanks, such as the Heritage Foundation, should be placed in the political category because they have explicit ideological missions. For example, the Heritage Foundation Web site indicates that its purpose is to "formulate and promote conservative public policies based on the principles of free enterprise, limited government, individual freedom, traditional American values, and a strong national defense." It also calls itself a "research and educational institute—a think tank," but its mission statement makes clear that it is hardly neutral on political values.

Much the same can be said for the Cato Institute, the Competitive Enterprise Institute (CEI), and parallel think tanks on the left side of the political spectrum. The CEI Web page is more explicit than Heritage about its mission: the organization "is not a traditional 'think tank,'" it says. It is "not enough to simply identify and articulate solutions to public policy problems," and it is "also necessary to defend and promote those solutions. For that reason, we are actively engaged in many phases of the public policy debate."

WHAT KIND OF ANALYSIS IS NEEDED?

No matter what policy area is involved, there is never a single correct way to conduct a policy study or one set of methods or tools to use. The next two chapters have more to say about appropriate methods and tools, but here it is worth emphasizing that, regardless of whether the policy research falls into the scientific, professional, or political category, analysts face important choices about the kind of assessment needed for a given study and what approaches to use.

Deal with Root Causes or Make Pragmatic Adjustments?

One of the basic questions that all analysts must answer is whether they should focus on the **root causes** of public problems or examine policy actions that might ameliorate a pressing problem

WORKING WITH SOURCES

COMPARING THINK TANKS

Policy research institutes, or think tanks, differ in many ways. Some are large and cover many policy issues, while others are small and highly specialized. Some aim for professional analysis of the issues, and others promote a policy or ideological agenda. Here, we highlight two prominent Washington think tanks that are well regarded for their analyses of policy issues. They also reflect different political philosophies: the Brookings Institution is usually characterized as slightly left of center, and the American Enterprise Institute as right of center.

As you read the think tanks' descriptions below, pay attention to specific language in their mission statements that point to their political philosophy and to possible bias in their analyses. Reviewing the topics that each covers, and the way those topics are summarized, can you detect differences between the two organizations in what they think is important, and the kinds of policies they will likely favor?

THE BROOKINGS INSTITUTION

Web site: www.brookings.edu (contains about twenty-five thousand separate items)

Founded: 1922

Orientation and mission: Aims to "conduct high-quality, independent research" and based on that research to "provide innovative and practical recommendations." Its experts "focus on strengthening American democracy; advancing the economic and social welfare, security and opportunity of all Americans; and securing a more open, safe, prosperous and cooperative international system." It maintains that its research agenda and recommendations "are rooted in open-minded inquiry and our scholars represent diverse points of view." Its more than two hundred resident and nonresident scholars

"research issues; write books, papers, articles and opinion pieces; testify before congressional committees and participate in dozens of public events each year."

Sources of funding: Financed largely by an endowment and through support of philanthropic foundations, corporations, and private individuals. Also undertakes unclassified government contract studies.

Broad research programs:

Economic studies: Monitors the global economy and seeks answers to economic policy issues both in the United States and worldwide. Research is designed to increase the public's understanding of economic operations and how to improve programs and policies.

Foreign policy: Work focuses on global challenges in the twenty-first century, including economic globalization and threats to U.S. security. Scholars seek to help policymakers and the public address these issues effectively.

Global economy and development: Experts examine issues surrounding globalization within three key areas: the drivers affecting the global economy, ways to eliminate world poverty, and the rise of new economic powers such as China and India.

Governance studies: Explores the formal and informal political institutions within the United States and other democracies to determine how well they work and what might be done to improve their operations.

Metropolitan policy program: Aims to redefine the challenges facing metropolitan areas in the United States and promotes solutions that can help communities become more inclusive, competitive, and sustainable.

THE AMERICAN ENTERPRISE INSTITUTE FOR PUBLIC POLICY RESEARCH

Web site: www.aei.org (large collection of studies and reports)

Founded: 1943

Orientation and mission: Describes itself as "a private, nonpartisan, not-for-profit institution dedicated to research and education on issues of government, politics, economics, and social welfare." Says that its purposes are "to defend the principles and improve the institutions of American freedom and democratic capitalism—limited government, private enterprise, individual liberty and responsibility, vigilant and effective defense and foreign policies, political accountability, and open debate." Notes that its work is addressed to "government officials and legislators, teachers and students, business executives, professionals, journalists, and all citizens interested in a serious understanding of government policy, the economy, and important social and political developments."

Sources of funding: Supported primarily by grants and contributions from foundations, corporations, and individuals.

Topics covered:

Energy and environmental studies: Emphasizes the need to design environmental policies that protect democratic institutions and human liberty as well as nature. Program covers climate change, energy policy, the Clean Air Act, biotechnology, and agriculture.

Financial markets: Covers banking, insurance and securities regulation, reform of accounting operations, corporate governance, the mortgage and housing credit markets, consumer finance, and regulatory reform.

Health care: Includes Medicare reform, health care coverage for the uninsured, FDA regulation, the use of private sector solutions to health care problems, and global health issues.

International trade and finance: Focuses on international economic institutions such as the World Bank, the impact of globalization on developing countries, free trade agreements, and reform of international financial institutions.

Tax and entitlement reform: Puts emphasis on international taxation of corporate income, income distribution, and marginal tax rates, as well as the effect of taxation on investment, savings, and entrepreneurial activity. Includes work on the long-range solvency of Social Security.

Telecommunications and information technology: Focuses on telecommunications and information technology (IT) regulation, including U.S. and foreign regulatory and antitrust policy on IT, and how government policies can affect innovation, consumers, and economic welfare in general. Includes studies on regulation of broadband access and wireless services, competition among long-distance providers, and reform of the Federal Communications Commission.

The U.S. and world economies: Includes studies of the national budget, monetary policy, and international markets, including the 2009 financial crisis.

Sources: Taken from the Web sites for Brookings and AEI. The statements are summaries of what each presents as its mission and current (2009) areas of research.

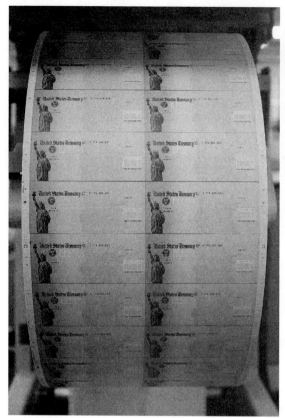

Among the public policy alternatives that received a great deal of attention in 2008 and 2009 were a variety of economic stimulus measures intended to help stabilize the U.S. economy and provide jobs to millions of Americans. Not all of the measures proved to be popular; many people grew tired of the government's efforts to bail out failing financial institutions and other businesses. People were more receptive to federal efforts to provide direct payments to households and to create jobs repairing highways, bridges, and utility lines. The photo on the left shows economic stimulus checks being prepared for printing in May 2008 in Philadelphia, Pennsylvania. The second shows workers with Shaw Pipeline repairing a water pipe in San Francisco, California, in February 2009 following a local report that found the city's infrastructure and buildings to be vulnerable to a major earthquake.

but do nothing about its underlying causes. Political scientist James Q. Wilson argued for the latter view in his influential book *Thinking about Crime* (1977, 55–59). The "ultimate causes cannot be the object of policy efforts," he said, because they cannot be changed. As he explained, criminologists, for example, know that men commit more crimes than women, and younger men more than older ones. It is a scientifically correct observation, Wilson said, but not very useful for policymakers concerned about reducing the crime rate. Why not? The answer is that society can do nothing to change the facts. So rather than address the root causes of crime, he suggested that policymakers concentrate on what governments can do to reduce the crime rate, or deal with what some call the **proximate causes,** or immediate causes, of the problem:

> What is the condition one wants to bring into being, what measure do we have that will tell us when that condition exists, and what policy tools does a government (in our case, a democratic and libertarian government) possess that might, when applied, produce at reasonable cost a desired alteration in the present condition or progress toward the desired condition? (59)

In contrast, the distinguished scholar Charles E. Lindblom (1972, 1) wrote that the kind of policy analysis illustrated by Wilson's statement can become a "conservative and superficial kind of social science" that fails to ask fundamental questions about the social and economic structures of society. It considers, according to Lindblom, "only those ways of dealing with policy that are close cousins of existing practices," and therefore reinforces a prevailing tendency to maintain current policies and practices even when they may be unsuccessful in addressing the problem.

Analysts who favor Lindblom's perspective would examine the fundamental or root causes as well as the proximate causes of public problems. These analysts would not dismiss as fruitless idealism the possibility of taking action on the root causes of problems in some circumstances. For example, the George W. Bush White House announced in July 2005 that the president's energy bill, then nearing approval in Congress, would help to address "the root causes of high energy prices," chiefly by expanding domestic production of energy.[14] Critics of the controversial energy bill were just as quick to suggest that the root cause most in need of attention was the nation's increasing appetite for energy, and that intensive programs fostering energy conservation and efficient energy use were needed more than an increase in supply. Both sides were correct in emphasizing the need to address not just the high price of energy in 2005 but the underlying causes of the problem.

Even an incremental adjustment in policy that does not look seriously at root causes can make a big difference. Consider the imposition of a national minimum drinking age of twenty-one that was intended to combat the high percentage of automobile accidents attributable to alcohol, especially among younger drivers. In 1984 the federal government decided to deny a percentage of federal highway funds to states that refused to comply with the minimum drinking age requirement. An assessment of the policy's results in Wisconsin showed that it had "immediate and conclusive effects on the number of teenagers involved in alcohol-related crashes." Accident rates declined by 26 percent for eighteen-year-olds and 19 percent for nineteen- and twenty-year-olds (Figlio 1995, 563). Similarly, an Insurance Institute for Highway Safety study released in 2003 showed that states that raised their speed limits to seventy miles per hour or higher during the 1990s experienced remarkable increases in people killed in traffic accidents. The study reported that between 1996 and 1999 alone the higher speeds led to almost 1,900 deaths. To the insurers, this is persuasive evidence that the trend toward higher highway speeds should be reversed. Even a small reduction in speed would save lives.[15] Other analysts have examined comparable questions, such as whether legislation mandating the use of bicycle helmets helps to reduce bicycling fatalities (Grant and Rutner 2004).

Comprehensive Analysis or Short-Term Policy Relevance?

Should analysts use the most comprehensive and rigorous approaches available to ensure the credibility of their results, even though doing so may take longer and cost more? Or should they aim for a less comprehensive and less rigorous study that might provide pertinent results faster and cheaper, even at some risk of the credibility of the results? The answer depends on the nature of the problem under consideration. The most complex, controversial, and costly policy choices might require the most comprehensive analysis, while more limited studies might suffice in other situations.

Academic scientists (social and natural) tend to favor rigorous, comprehensive studies. They place a high value on methodological precision because they believe that only demanding scientific investigations produce knowledge that inspires confidence. Sometimes, however, a study can take so long to complete that it has less impact on policy decisions than it might have had if the results were known earlier. For example, the federal government sponsored a decade-long study of the causes and consequences of acid rain, at a cost of $500 million. Although widely viewed as first-rate scientific research, the study also was faulted for failing to address some critical topics in time to influence the major decision makers. By most accounts, it had less influence than it should have had on the adoption of the Clean Air Act Amendments of 1990, the first national effort to deal seriously with acid rain (Russell 1993). Chapter 10 discusses another example—the exhaustive studies carried out in selected cities of the impact of school voucher programs. Because of the different assumptions and methodologies, the studies offer conflicting conclusions. That complication aside, communities with problem school systems can use the studies to take action, even though the studies are still under way and some questions are unanswered.

Professional policy analysts are often distinguished from social science researchers in part because of the analysts' interest in applied policy research. The professionals are far more likely to aim their research at policymakers and other policy actors. Indeed, their studies often come with an "executive summary" that is designed to permit busy decision makers to quickly see the gist of the study's findings. The executive summary is typical of think tank studies and the more comprehensive studies and reports from special commissions or government agencies, such as the Environmental Protection Agency and the Government Accountability Office.

Analysts associated with advocacy organizations in the "political" category shown in Table 4-2 are the most likely to emphasize short-term policy relevance. They also typically bring a strong commitment to the values embodied in the organization. It is not surprising that the studies by the Natural Resources Defense Council or the Sierra Club are unabashedly pro-environment, while those by the National Rifle Association or the Nuclear Energy Institute support gun ownership and nuclear power, respectively. Such policy advocacy does not necessarily mean that the studies are invalid; many are just as well done and valuable as those released by ostensibly more objective research institutes. One recent assessment of the liberal Center on Budget and Policy Priorities, for example, described its analyses as "academically rigorous" yet clearly "intended to influence lawmakers, aides, lobbyists and journalists." The center has become, the author noted, "a powerful source of knowledge that helps out-of-power Democrats counter White House experts at the Office of Management and Budget."[16] Because of these kinds of political commitments, however, reports from advocacy organizations warrant a critical reading to detect any possible bias (Rich 2004).

Consensual or Contentious Analysis?

Should analysts adhere closely to consensual norms and mainstream public values, or should they challenge them and propose new values or new ways of thinking about the problem under consideration? Political theorist Martin Rein (1976) argued for what he called a value-critical approach to policy research, urging analysts to be skeptical and distrust orthodoxy. He advocated approaches to policy study that made the analyst a "moral critic" who questions the value and belief assumptions behind policy research. He suggested three ways to engage in such research, with increasing degrees of critical inquiry: using consensual or mainstream approaches, using contentious or value critical approaches, and—the most radical—using paradigm-challenging approaches. Most contemporary policy analyses fall into the first category, a much smaller number into the second, and a negligible number into the third. Yet one could argue that many public policies today are very much in need of bold new thinking and radical challenges, much as Rein suggested in the mid-1970s. Consider the case of health care policy, the subject of chapter 8. With sharply rising costs and widespread dissatisfaction with access to and delivery of health care services today, some analysts and policymakers are beginning to suggest the need for radical change. This includes consideration of government-provided health insurance for all Americans.

Most analyses are consistent with mainstream values because they are likely to be more socially and politically acceptable than radical studies. Indeed, because many government agencies, and outside groups under contract to an agency, conduct the analyses, the "client," who has specific and concrete expectations, may limit the scope of any inquiry. Academic studies, with analysts hired by a university or an independent research institute, are less likely to be constrained by short-term bureaucratic or corporate needs. The same can be said for studies by policy institutes or interest groups that fall toward the left and right ends of the political spectrum. These groups often favor actions that embody more radical changes in policy and public values. For example, the conservative Heritage Foundation was instrumental in shaping the policy agenda of Ronald Reagan's presidency, which broke with mainstream approaches in many areas such as environmental protection. Throughout the 1990s and 2000s the libertarian Cato Institute released dozens of studies that supported its belief in individual rights and limited government.

Reliance on Rational Analysis or Democratic Politics?

Policy analysts are trained to engage in the rational assessment of public problems and their solutions, and they often use economic analysis and other quantitative methods to find the most logical, efficient, and (they hope) effective ways to deal with public problems. But should analysts also try to foster **democratic political processes,** such as citizen involvement (deLeon 1997; Gormley 1987; Jenkins-Smith 1990)? As noted, some advocates of policy analysis believe that public problems and policy choices are so complex that technical scientific analysis is essential to reach a defensible decision. These views sometimes conflict with the expectation that the public and elected officials are ultimately responsible for choosing the policy direction for the nation. In short, as citizens, we value rigorous analysis, but we also expect democracy to prevail unless there is some good reason (for example, national security) to limit public involvement.

Consider the case of nuclear waste disposal in terms of this dilemma. Federal government analysts and most of those working for the nuclear industry and technical consulting companies have relied on complex risk assessment, a form of policy analysis dealing with threats to health and the environment. Nearly all of the studies concluded that risks from the radioactive waste to be housed in a disposal facility are minor and manageable, even over the thousands of years that the proposed repository at Yucca Mountain, Nevada, is to contain the waste without significant leakage. Critics of the government's position, however, including the state of Nevada and many environmental groups, countered that the scientific questions are far from settled and that the public's concerns about nuclear waste have not been satisfactorily addressed. They called for a decision-making process that allowed for greater citizen involvement and consultation, no matter how long it would take to build public trust (Dunlap, Kraft, and Rosa 1993; Wald 2002). Proponents of the waste site in turn assert that the critics merely reflect the common NIMBY (Not-In-My-Backyard) syndrome; they argue that local opposition to such waste repositories and other unwanted facilities is inevitable and cannot be the sole basis for a policy decision.

How can this kind of tension between reliance on technical analysis and democracy be resolved? The management of nuclear waste is by definition a serious issue: the United States produces it and must find a safe way to store it for thousands of years. That objective points strongly to the need for the best kinds of policy analysis before making a final decision. By most standards, Yucca Mountain probably meets those expectations. At the same time, these decisions affect millions of people, not only in Nevada but all those who live along the transportation corridors across the nation. In light of the events of September 11, 2001, the possibility of terrorist attacks on the waste shipments raises a new concern. Does the best solution lie in more analysis of these various risks and better management by the federal government and the states? Or should more weight be given to the public's fears and concerns, and should policymakers turn to a more open and democratic political process for making the necessary choices?

Other Aspects of Policy Analysis

The differences among the fundamental types of policy research are evident in the great variety of academic journals and other professional outlets, many of which are available on the Internet. Some publications, for example the *Journal of Policy Analysis and Management*, emphasize the economic aspects of public policy, while others, such as the *Policy Studies Journal* and the *Review of Policy Research,* stress institutional and political factors. A few journals, such as *Philosophy and Public Affairs,* examine the ethical aspects of public policy, and nearly every law journal discusses the legal considerations of public policy. We urge students to browse the Web sites as well as the journals in their campus libraries to see what information is available on different topics. Most think tanks and advocacy organizations (and most government agencies) publish their studies, either in full or summarized, on their Web pages as well as in journals, books, and reports.

The primary focus of this text is substantive policy analysis, which aims at answering questions such as what effects school voucher programs have on the quality of education, or whether regulation of cell phones in cars reduces accident rates. But a great deal of work in the public policy field, especially by political scientists, focuses instead on describing how government and policymakers actually behave. Such work tries to address questions such as how Congress makes decisions on defense policy or agricultural subsidies, and how the White House influences agency regulatory decision making (Anderson 2006).

The perspectives and approaches of policy analysis apply to institutional issues as well as to substantive policy questions (Gormley 1987). This kind of analysis is especially helpful for examining proposals for institutional change. For example, institutional policy analysis might address a question such as what consequences could result if environmental protection policy were to be decentralized to the states (Rabe 2006)? Or, in light of controversies over the 2000 presidential election, what kinds of ballots are most likely to minimize voter error and be counted accurately?

Ethical issues in the conduct and use of policy studies deal with honesty and scruples. For example, what ethical obligations do analysts have to design and conduct their studies in a certain manner? To what extent are they influenced by the source of funding, particularly when the funds come from interest groups with a stake in the outcome, such as the tobacco companies that want to learn about the impact of antismoking initiatives? Does the analyst work primarily for the client who pays for the study, or does the analyst have a duty to represent the larger public interest (Weimer and Vining 2005)? At a minimum, most analysts would agree that they are obliged to be open and transparent about their values and policy preferences, their funding sources, the methods they use, the data they collect, and any critical assumptions they make in the analysis of the data and the conclusions they reach (Bowman and Elliston 1988; Tong 1986). Chapter 6 goes further into the criteria, including ethical standards, that can be used to evaluate policy alternatives.

CONCLUSIONS

The example at the beginning of the chapter on cell phone use and driving shows the challenge of making policy decisions when so many questions can be raised about the problem and the implications of taking action. Yet most students and practitioners of public policy are convinced that analysis can advance solutions by clarifying the problem, collecting information, and suggesting ways to make decisions. For that reason, this chapter surveys the practice of policy analysis and shows how it relates to the policy-making process and to politics in general.

Today, analysis is ubiquitous, and it enters policy debate everywhere it occurs. Analysis is conducted in formal think tanks, interest groups, executive agencies, and legislative committees at all levels of government. Its thoroughness, objectivity, and purpose vary markedly, as one might expect. Students of public policy therefore need to be alert to the strengths and weaknesses of particular policy studies and prepared to question everything: the assumptions, the methods, and the conclusions. At the same time, however, students need to explore the many available sources of policy information and to think creatively about how to become engaged with contemporary policy problems.

DISCUSSION QUESTIONS

1. Consider the case of using cell phones while driving a car, whether for talking or texting. Given the information provided in the chapter, would you favor restricting drivers' use of hand-held cell phones? What about hands-free cell phones? How would you defend this policy choice?

2. Much of the policy analysis that is used in public debates today comes from interest groups committed to one side of the issue or another, or from think tanks that espouse a particular ideology. Do you think these commitments make the quality of the analysis suspect? Why or why not?

3. Review the two contrasting think tank positions on welfare reform presented in the Steps to Analysis box on page 108. Which do you think is more persuasive? Why is that?

4. Should policy analysts try to deal with the fundamental causes of social problems such as crime, poverty, or homelessness, or aim for a more pragmatic and limited approach that may be more realistic and more politically acceptable? Why do you think so?

SUGGESTED READINGS

James E. Anderson, *Public Policymaking*, 6th ed. (Boston: Houghton Mifflin, 2006). One of the best general treatments of the U.S. policy-making process.

Eugene Bardach, *A Practical Guide for Policy Analysis: The Eightfold Path to More Effective Problem Solving*, 3rd ed. (Washington, D.C.: CQ Press, 2009). A short but readable guide to the essentials of policy analysis, particularly for practitioners.

Carl V. Patton and David S. Sawicki, *Basic Methods of Policy Analysis and Planning*, 2nd ed. (Englewood Cliffs, N.J.: Prentice Hall, 1993). One of the leading texts in policy analysis, with a focus on methods for basic or quick analysis.

Deborah Stone, *Policy Paradox: The Art of Political Decision Making*, rev. ed. (New York: W. W. Norton, 2002). An imaginative critique of conventional policymaking and policy analysis, with an emphasis on the role of politics and values in policymaking.

David L. Weimer and Aidan R. Vining, *Policy Analysis: Concepts and Practice*, 4th ed. (Upper Saddle River, N.J.: Prentice Hall, 2005). A widely used text in policy analysis that draws heavily from economics.

SUGGESTED WEB SITES

www.aei.org. American Enterprise Institute for Public Policy Research, a major policy research institute that tends to favor conservative positions.

www.alec.org. American Legislative Exchange Council, a national conservative research institute that assists state legislators in advancing the principles of limited government and free markets.

www.brookings.edu. Brookings Institution, a major policy research organization that is usually described as somewhat left of center or liberal.

www.cato.org. Cato Institute, a libertarian think tank.

www.cbpp.org. Center on Budget and Policy Priorities, a liberal policy research organization that focuses on fiscal policy and its effects on low- and moderate-income families and individuals.

www.cei.org. Competitive Enterprise Institute, a conservative think tank and advocacy organization.

www.csis.org. Center for Strategic and International Studies, a think tank that focuses on global challenges and foreign and defense policy issues.

www.heritage.org. Heritage Foundation, a conservative think tank.

www.hudson.org. Hudson Institute, a conservative think tank.

www.lib.umich.edu/govdocs/frames/psthinfr.html. A comprehensive guide to think tanks and other political research centers.

www.movingideas.org. A guide to liberal think tanks and policy research.

www.publicagenda.org. Nonpartisan briefings on policy and polling; news, legislation, and studies; and research sources.

www.public-policy.org. Center for Public Policy, with links to conservative policy organizations.

www.rand.org. RAND Corporation, the first organization to be called a think tank.

www.rff.org. Resources for the Future, a think tank specializing in economic analysis of environmental and natural resource issues.

www.urban.org. Urban Institute, a leading policy research center that deals with diverse urban issues such as housing, poverty, employment, health, crime, and the economy.

LEADING GENERAL JOURNALS OF PUBLIC POLICY

Journal of Policy Analysis and Management
Journal of Policy History
Journal of Public Policy
Policy Sciences
Policy Studies Journal
Review of Policy Research (formerly *Policy Studies Review*)

MAJOR PROFESSIONAL NEWS WEEKLIES WITH POLICY COVERAGE

CQ Weekly
National Journal

KEYWORDS

assessing alternatives   105
democratic political processes   117
incremental decision making   100
problem   100

proximate causes   114
rational-comprehensive approach   100
rational decision making   100
root causes   111

NOTES

1. See Gina Kolata, "Accidents Much More Likely When Drivers Hold a Phone," *New York Times,* February 13, 1997, 1, A14. The estimated equivalence to driving under the influence of alcohol came from a study published in the *New England Journal of Medicine* that analyzed some twenty-seven thousand cell phone calls. The estimate of the percentage of drivers text messaging while driving comes from a Nationwide Insurance study cited in Eric Konigsberg, "City Council Bill Would Ban Text Messaging While Driving," *New York Times,* August 14, 2008, A16. More recent simulation studies at the University of Utah confirm that the distraction from cell phone use is unique and is no different whether the phone is hand-held or hands-free. See Tara Parker-Pope, "A Problem of the Brain, Not the Hands: Group Urges Phone Ban for Drivers," *New York Times,* January 13, 2009, D5. Australian studies confirm that uses of hand-held and hands-free phones while driving pose similar risks. See Jeremy W. Peters, "Hands-Free Cellphone Devices Don't Aid Road Safety, Study Concludes," *New York Times,* July 12, 2005, C3.

2. See Joan Lowy, "Safety Council: Ban Cell Phones While Driving," Associated Press release, January 12, 2009. Other data on the issue can be found at the Web site for the safety council: www.nsc.org.

3. See Damien Cave, "Note to Drivers: Lose the Phone (and Lipstick)," *New York Times,* October 1, 2005, A14; and Katie Hafner and Jason George, "For Drivers, a Traffic Jam of Distractions," *New York Times,* March 3, 2005, E1.

4. Practical policy analysis is also sometimes referred to as "quick analysis" or "quickly applied basic methods," but the intention is to offer an analytical and objective assessment of the issues, even when policymakers must make decisions quickly. See Robert D. Behn and James W. Vaupel, *Quick Analysis for Busy Decision Makers* (New York: Basic Books, 1982); and Carl V. Patton and David S. Sawicki, *Basic Methods of Policy Analysis and Planning,* 2nd ed. (Englewood Cliffs, N.J.: Prentice Hall, 1993).

5. See the Department of Housing and Urban Development Web page for the "Federal Definition of Homelessness": www.hud.gov/homeless/definition.cfm.

6. National Alliance to End Homelessness, "Homelessness Counts: Changes in Homelessness from 2005 to 2007," available at www.endhomelessness.org/content/article/detail/2158. The earlier estimates come from "Homeless in America: A Statistical Profile," *New York Times,* December 12, 1999, Week in Review Section, 3. The *Times* report relied on statistics supplied by the Department of Housing and Urban Development, which came from surveys and interviews conducted in 1995 and 1996 with adults who used services for the homeless, such as shelters. This database indicated that 32 percent of the homeless were female and 68 percent male. Some 12 percent of the homeless were between seventeen and twenty-four years of age, and 80 percent were between twenty-five and fifty-four years of age, but no data were available in this survey on homeless children.

7. The data are taken from the Organization for Economic Cooperation and Development (OECD) report "Debt Relief Is Down: Other ODA Rises Slightly," released on April 4, 2008, and available at www.oecd.org.

8. See, for example, Sharon LaFraniere, "Africa Tackles Graft, with Billions in Aid in Play," *New York Times,* July 6, 2005, A1, A6.

9. Michael M. Weinstein, "The Aid Debate: Helping Hand, or Hardly Helping?" *New York Times,* May 26, 2002, Week in Review Section, 3. The many successful projects were highlighted in a 2002 tour of sub-Saharan Africa by Secretary of the Treasury Paul H. O'Neill and rock star Bono of U2, an active proponent of economic assistance to poor nations. Some of the economic studies on the consequences of aid programs can be found in Joseph Kahn and Tim Weiner, "World Leaders Rethinking Strategy on Aid to Poor," *New York Times,* March 18, 2002, A3. The United Nations Millennium Development Goals include cutting the rate of extreme poverty in half by 2015 and calling on nations like the United States to dramatically increase foreign assistance to poor nations.

10. Richard W. Stevenson, "Missile System Passes a Test as a Target Is Destroyed," *New York Times,* October 4, 1999, A18. A review of the missile tests through early 2005 indicated that the government's ten tests resulted in five hits, but some of them were under "scripted conditions" that may not truly indicate the system's reliability. Despite much criticism, planning for the missile system continues. See David Stout, "Rocket Fails to Launch in Test Run," *New York Times,* February 15, 2005, A11.

11. James Dao, "Amid Applause, Caution Urged on Missile Defense," *New York Times,* July 16, 2001, A8; and James Kitfield, "The Ultimate Bomb Shelter," *National Journal,* July 8, 2000, 2212–2223.

12. For a recent attempt by a critic of the system to lay out the issues and provide some answers, see Richard L. Garwin, "Holes in the Missile Shield," *Scientific American,* November 2004, 70–79. See also Christopher Drew, "Soaring Costs Jeopardize Missile Defense Systems," *New York Times,* March 18, 2009, B5.

13. For example, many organizations and think tanks on the right end of the political spectrum have received substantial funding from foundations supporting conservative causes and publications. Among the most notable are

the John M. Olin Foundation, Scaife Family Foundation, Koch Family foundations, Lynde and Harry Bradley Foundation, and Adolph Coors Foundation. For an assessment of how such conservative foundations have affected public policy debate, see the report by People for the American Way, "Buying a Movement," available at the organization's Web site: www.pfaw.org. For an assessment of how industry-funded think tank studies, including those supported by Koch Industries, influence environmental policy debates, see Curtis Moore, "Rethinking the Think Tanks," *Sierra,* July–August 2002, 56–59, 73. For an objective overview of the role of conservative foundations, see Shawn Zeller, "Conservative Crusaders," *National Journal,* April 26, 2003, 1286–1291.

14. The statement was made by White House spokesperson Scott McClellan and is reported in Carl Hulse, "As Energy and Highway Bills Near Completion, Congress Gives Itself a Hand," *New York Times,* July 29, 2005, A16.

15. Danny Hakim, "Study Links Higher Speed Limits to Deaths," *New York Times,* November 24, 2003, A12.

16. See Andrew Taylor, "Democrats' Go-To Guy Gets the Facts Straight," *CQ Weekly,* March 7, 2005, 552–553.

CHAPTER 5

PUBLIC PROBLEMS AND POLICY ALTERNATIVES

IN LATE NOVEMBER 2005, PRESIDENT GEORGE W. BUSH TRAVELED TO El Paso, Texas, to tour the Rio Grande River on the U.S.-Mexican border. His purpose was to symbolize a policy shift that his administration introduced that month. Instead of his earlier emphasis on finding a way for U.S. business to continue employing illegal immigrants on a temporary basis— a "guest worker" program—he now spoke of keeping such undocumented workers out of the country. "We've got a comprehensive strategy that says we're going to enforce this border," the president said. "We're going to prevent people from coming here in the first place."[1]

The president's new strategy emerged as Congress prepared to consider legislation that addressed border security and immigration, historically one of the most politically contentious policy problems facing the United States. With the president's standing in public opinion polls at new lows and conservatives in his own party demanding a different approach to deter illegal immigration, he had few choices but to change policy directions. For their part, Democrats accused the president of delaying action on immigration reform for too long. "It is time for President Bush to resist those on the right who rely on fear tactics to prevent our broken system from being fixed," said Sen. Edward M. Kennedy, D-Mass. "True immigration reform" would have to be more comprehensive and more realistic than the president's proposals, he added, "strengthening our security while bringing an underground economy above ground."[2]

The growing national debate over immigration has been emerging over the past decade, and reflects widespread belief that previous immigration control laws had failed to deal effectively with the problem. For example, despite a 1986 federal law that created penalties for businesses that knowingly hired illegal or undocumented workers, employers continued to do so, and the former Immigration and Naturalization Service largely stopped enforcing the law.[3] More fundamentally, there was little agreement on what the problem of illegal immigration really was about. To some it was captured by reports in 2005 that the number of illegal immigrants in the United

Immigration continues to be one of the more intractable public policy issues the United States faces, and it is sure to be debated once again in Congress in coming years. Although the weakening economy diminished the urgency of the issue in 2008 and 2009, one result of a decision that Congress made during the Bush administration will be around for a long time: a 700-mile-long fence on the U.S.-Mexican border. Supporters favored the fence as one more tool to limit immigration and protect U.S. national security interests. Opponents have argued that the costly fence will be ineffective. The photo shows a U.S. Border Patrol agent standing near a segment of the recently completed 18-foot-tall border security fence in July 2008 at the Santa Teresa Port of Entry in New Mexico near El Paso, Texas.

States had soared to well over ten million people and was growing rapidly, at an estimated half a million each year; much of the growth has been in the West and South. Among other concerns, they focused on the high cost to the states of providing education and medical care for undocumented workers and their families. Others worried that a high rate of illegal immigration suggested that U.S. borders lacked the security that is essential to prevent entry by potential terrorists. Still others, particularly business owners, were inclined to minimize the problem, saying that the health of the U.S. economy depended on immigrant workers and would suffer without their contribution; some also cited the economic benefits to the immigrants' home countries of their employment here. The Pew Hispanic Center, a nonpartisan research organization, estimated that 10 percent of restaurant workers in the United States, 25 percent of domestic help in private households, and nearly 60 percent of crop workers were in the country illegally.[4]

What should the United States do today about illegal immigration? To some extent the problem diminished significantly with the souring U.S. economy in 2008 and 2009, particularly within the construction industry, as immigrants found it difficult to secure work and returned to their home countries.[5] But the long-term concerns remain nonetheless. So should the nation provide for a selective guest worker program to fill jobs for which there are no U.S. workers available, an idea favored by business and labor groups? Should it strengthen the borders, especially the 1,933-mile boundary with Mexico, and add physical barriers beyond the 700 miles of fence already authorized by Congress in 2006 and under construction? Should the government increase the number of Border Patrol agents to control illegal entry?[6] Should it provide a form of amnesty to at least some of the illegal immigrants already in the nation if they meet requirements such as five years of residency and work, and payment of taxes? Should the laws that prohibit hiring illegal immigrants be toughened, for example, by requiring employers to verify the legal status of new employees? There are few clear answers, in part because policy actors hold sharply divergent views on immigration, emotions on the subject often run high, and both Democrats and Republicans are acutely aware of the political risks of staking out a position on the issue. Immigration was not a subject of intense interest during the 2008 presidential campaign, but it is likely that President Barack Obama will chart a different course on the problem than did President Bush.[7]

As we argued in earlier chapters, policy analysis is no panacea for a political system vulnerable to emotional and shortsighted decision making, all too evident in the history of immigration policy; but it can, under the right conditions, help to counteract such tendencies and push the policy process toward more thoughtful and effective actions. This chapter focuses on two elements in policy analysis: how to define and analyze public problems and how to think about possible solutions. It also suggests some strategies for studying public problems and for finding useful information.

PROBLEM ANALYSIS

The beginning of any policy study involves a description of a problem. Sometimes the problem—and perhaps even its causes—is obvious. For example, if the problem is teenage smoking and how to curtail it, one can find abundant information about the number of teenage smokers, why they choose to smoke, and the implications for lifelong smoking habits and the associated health problems that accompany them. Some states, most notably California, have used that information to adopt educational programs aimed at prevention and other policies that have successfully reduced the rate of teenage smoking.

To consider another example, highway safety experts have known for some time that using seat belts greatly reduces deaths and injuries from traffic accidents. They also know that the extent of compliance depends on how stringently the states enforce the seat belt laws. In 2007 the national average for seat belt use in the United States was estimated at 82 percent for front-seat passengers. But more than one thousand people would survive automobile accidents if that rate were increased to 90 percent or more. The rate of seat belt use varies considerably from state to state. Twelve states achieve a rate of 90 percent or more, among them California, Hawaii, Illinois, Michigan, Oregon, Texas, and Washington. But a number of states have rates well below 75 percent, among them Arkansas, Kentucky, Massachusetts, Mississippi, and New Hampshire. Compliance with seat belt laws also varies by age. It is highest for children, presumably because every state requires that children use seat belts. It is lowest for younger drivers ages sixteen to twenty-four.

Based on this information, law enforcement agencies and highway safety councils have concluded that one of the best ways to further reduce accident death rates is to make the seat belt laws tougher. Indeed, studies confirm that mandatory seat belt use laws are effective in reducing traffic fatalities, and that primary enforcement is more effective than secondary (where police officers can issue a citation only if a motorist is pulled over for another traffic infraction).[8] Although the safety councils consider advertising campaigns, or persuasion, to be relatively ineffective policy strategies, they nonetheless favor their use as one way to help increase the rate of seat belt use among younger drivers.[9]

These examples show how simple some kinds of **problem analysis** can be. The problems are relatively straightforward, and the information needed to make a policy choice is at hand, thanks to national surveys that collect it. Evaluations of previous policy actions, such as the ineffectiveness of persuasion to achieve compliance, may also inform decision making. Although few public problems are entirely without controversy, there are also many, such as the two examples discussed, about which reasonable people from all political ideologies can agree on what actions to take. Such agreement is made easier when the facts about the problem are readily available and easily understood.

The Nature of the Problem

Most public problems are not so simple; nor is the path to policy action as clear as trying to reduce smoking or increase seat belt use. Nevertheless, the first step in policymaking is the same whether the problem is straightforward or complicated: define and analyze the problem. Problem analysis involves trying to answer the basic questions about the nature of the problem, its extent or magnitude, how it came about, its major causes, and why it is important to consider as a matter of public policy. At heart, addressing these kinds of questions requires students of public policy to think critically and creatively about the problem. What does it entail? What is already known about it? What are the possible solutions? It also requires them to begin gathering the necessary information. The logic of information searches and useful strategies are discussed in this chapter.

Public problems are often difficult to understand. The challenge is even more daunting given that we are bombarded daily with limited, biased, and conflicting messages in numerous electronic and print formats. Whether the sources are talk radio, Internet blogs, published reports, policy analyses, or position statements issued by interest groups or policymakers, one of the most vexing issues is how to interpret information that comes to us without a meaningful

DILBERT: © Scott Adams/Dist. by United Feature Syndicate, Inc.

Many public problems today are highly complex, and both analysts and the public may find them difficult to understand. The challenge is compounded when proponents of varying perspectives offer selective and conflicting data and interpret the data differently. The cartoon refers to the need to have a meaningful context for data interpretation. What it calls "contextual data" can help people put a public problem into a perspective with which they are familiar and encourage them to ask pertinent questions. Among these questions are how a particular problem compares to other kinds of societal problems, the problem's causes and effects, the people or groups most affected by it, the actions on it that are possible, and whether one action is preferable to another because it is more likely to be effective, efficient, or fair. Individuals are better able to raise and address such questions once they acquire the analytical skills that the text tries to build in readers.

context. The "contextual data," or background information, to which the cartoon refers is essential to make sense of a problem, to see how it compares to other concerns in our personal lives or in society, and to estimate what effects a proposal or action might have. One of the purposes of this text is to assist readers in building analytical skills so they are better able to understand policy information and learn how to ask pertinent questions.

Definitions and Measures. An essential step in the policy process is to define the problem. The definitions enable those seeking a solution to communicate with one another with a degree of precision that otherwise might not be possible. For example, if analysts are studying the plight of the poor in the United States, they need to define what poverty means. Is being poor only a matter of having insufficient money or income, or does it include other characteristics, such as the lack of certain skills or abilities? Should poverty be defined in relative terms (poorer than others) or in absolute terms (unable to meet essential human needs)? In 2007 the U.S. government said that about thirty-seven million Americans were poor, or about 12.6 percent of the population. That same year the U.S. Census Bureau released a dozen alternative measures of poverty, nearly all of which would give a higher count than the official federal poverty rate.[10] In 2008 the federal government placed the poverty line for a family of four in the forty-eight contiguous states at $21,200 (it is higher in Hawaii and Alaska), and the number is important. It determines who is eligible for federal aid programs such as the Head Start preschool program, food stamps, and children's health insurance, among others.[11] Real consequences for real people result from this particular definition. Sometimes a quick literature search, discussed later in the chapter, will reveal both the usual definition of the concept and any debate that surrounds it.

Public policy arguments also turn on **operational measures** of problems. Rather than refer to poverty in the abstract, analysts want to know how many people live in poverty and their demographics. If discussing educational quality in the public schools, analysts want to see test scores and other student evaluations to determine if a problem exists in the schools and how the schools in one community compare to those in another. If the subject is violent

Energy use and climate change emerged as significant issues in the 2008 presidential election, and Congress adopted several measures as part of its 2009 economic stimulus plan to encourage the use of alternative energy sources, including solar, wind, and biofuels. Some of the most creative efforts to use energy more efficiently and to develop new, less polluting sources of energy have taken place on college and university campuses. This 2006 photo shows a Carleton College student holding a sample of biodiesel in front of a grease container. The college cafeteria's used cooking oil is converted into biodiesel fuel for campus vehicles. In 2004 the Northfield, Minnesota, campus was the first in the nation to install a utility-grade wind turbine to supply about 40 percent of the campus's electrical needs and to reduce its greenhouse gas emissions.

crime, the analysts need statistics about the number of crimes committed nationally and in local communities, and whether the crime rate is increasing or decreasing. In recent years, Congress considered establishing an independent, Web-based, and comprehensive national indicator system that would bring together high-quality data on the economy, society and culture, and the environment. Led by the National Academies, a consortium of two hundred institutions and individuals worked on a "State of the USA" document of this kind (U.S. Government Accountability Office 2004). The plan became a reality in 2008, with the establishment of a nonprofit and privately funded institution, the State of the USA, Inc., whose Web site was launched in 2009 (http://stateoftheusa.org). The organization promises a comprehensive collection of "credible, relevant data" on a wide range of public problems at an "easy-to-use and continually updated" site.[12] Of course, such data already exist in many different locations, particularly government agencies.

Quantitative measures are abundant for most contemporary public problems (Miringoff and Miringoff 1999). How much statistical information needs to be provided is a matter of judgment, but at a minimum most issue papers or problem analyses would include some basic descriptive statistics. One descriptive type is the frequency count, such as the percentage of the population at different income levels or the number of people in a survey who respond one way or another. Another type is the mean, or average, measure of a group or category, such as the average score on an examination. An alternative is the median of a variable, which is the point where one half of the group lies above and one half below. One such example is the median price of homes sold in different regions of the nation. Some idea of the range of variation (the standard deviation) or the correlation or relationship between two variables, such as race and income, may be useful as well.

Statistical information can be displayed in many ways in a report. These include tables that show frequency counts or percentages of what is being studied, such as the percentage of different age groups in the population who smoke. Information can be superimposed on maps to show geographic variations such as rates of urban growth or the income levels for adjacent urban and suburban areas. Graphic figures—pie charts or bar charts—are common, as are line figures that show how the magnitude of a problem changes over time, such as the number of people without health care insurance from 1970 to 2008 (Ammons 2009; Berman 2007).

There is an art to choosing how best to display quantitative information. At a minimum, reports should aim for clarity. But some visual displays are also more likely to capture the reader's attention than others. The use of computer-generated color graphics allows a range of different formats, both in written form and in PowerPoint or similar presentations. The best advice generally is to keep the audience and purpose clearly in mind when choosing the format of a report or presentation.

The use of quantitative data also carries some risks. Analysts need to be alert to the possibility of inaccurate data in a report or an invalid measurement that does not truly capture the problem (Eberstadt 1995). For example, are the SAT or ACT scores of graduating seniors an appropriate gauge of school quality? Are they an accurate indicator of students' ability to do well academically in college? Critics have long charged that these so-called aptitude tests have built-in biases that significantly affect the results. They say that students who grow up in affluent homes with well-educated parents are likely to score higher than others because of personal experience rather than innate intelligence or academic abilities (see chapter 10). Perhaps more important than SAT scores is the fact that many other elements, such as personal ambition and hard work, affect performance and success in college (which college admissions officers know well). In response to such criticism, the SAT test was modified in 2002.

Another conventional indicator that has come under criticism is the gross domestic product (GDP), which measures the sum total of goods and services produced in the economy. Politicians use the GDP as an indicator of public well-being, or the lack of it. They invariably applaud a rising GDP and express concern over a sagging GDP, but many critics argue that it is seriously flawed as a measurement. Environmentalists, for example, say it does not account for the use of natural resources. Cutting down old growth forests adds positively to the GDP because it is an economic activity, but economists do not subtract the loss of irreplaceable old trees or the damage to forest ecosystems that depend on them. Some economists have proposed developing a new method called the genuine progress indicator (GPI) to substitute the GDP and more accurately reflect human well-being (Cobb, Halstead, and Rowe 1995; www .rprogress.org). At least a few governments are beginning to think seriously about using this new and perhaps more accurate way to evaluate the economy.

Naturally, not all human concerns, such as happiness or sense of well-being, can be reduced to quantitative measures. Analysts can, however, make use of surveys that ask people whether they are happy, enjoy living in their communities, believe their children's schools are doing a good job, and so forth. Where public problems cannot be measured directly, this kind of survey data may be a useful substitute. Economists also say that people can be asked to estimate the dollar value of many activities for which no market value exists. Their responses can help to calculate whether certain actions, such as preserving open space or planting trees, are justifiable uses of tax dollars.

An illustration of how to develop quantitative indicators is found in the effort of communities to become sustainable. Critics have derided *sustainable development* as a fuzzy if not meaningless term. Even so, communities around the country, and many colleges and universities, have adopted it as a goal, and many have selected quantitative indicators of sustainability to see whether they are making progress toward that goal over time (www.sustainablemeasures.com). The residents and policymakers are clear enough about what sustainability means—the integration of economic, social, and environmental goals—that they are able to engage the public and work cooperatively in thinking about the future of their communities (Mazmanian and Kraft 2009; Portney 2003). The box "Working with Sources: Sustainable Development Indicators" provides further information about sustainable communities and sources of information for various indicators of sustainability.

The Politics of Problem Definition. Defining and measuring problems is not merely an exercise in analysis. People often disagree about a problem and what should be done about it. As Deborah Stone (2002, 133) says, there are "no fixed goals" in the policy process; instead, policy actors fight over "competing conceptions of abstract goals." Moreover, she says, "problem definition is never simply a matter of defining goals and measuring our distance from them. It is rather the strategic representation of situations." By this, she means a description of any given situation will vary, depending on a policy actor's perspective. The process becomes strategic, or political, because "groups, individuals, and government agencies deliberately and consciously fashion portrayals so as to promote their favored course of action."

One simple example of what Stone means concerns the irradiation of meat intended for human consumption, a process the federal government approved in 2000. The largest U.S. irradiator of ground beef lobbied members of Congress to define irradiated meat as "pasteurized." A farm-state senator inserted the provision into a major agricultural bill at the last minute. Obviously, the meat processor believed that the word *pasteurized* would be more acceptable to the public than *irradiated.* At the time the legislative language was proposed, the U.S. Department of Agriculture and the Food and Drug Administration had yet to agree that meat that is irradiated would qualify as pasteurized.[13]

Similar political, or strategic, actions occur in nearly every major policy area, from Social Security reform to energy policy. As noted earlier, supporters of partial privatization of Social Security switched from using the term *private* to describe individual accounts to *personal* when they learned that the latter was more acceptable to the American public than the former. Similarly, there was disagreement over whether the term *crisis* should be used to describe the Social Security problem. The White House thought so and used the word repeatedly; Democrats countered that Social Security was indeed a problem for the future (one that could be solved through modest policy changes), but they insisted that it was not an immediate crisis.

Some analysts might challenge Stone's view of the inherently political nature of problem analysis, but students of politics would probably agree with her. The evidence supports the observation that policymakers and interest groups will do whatever they can to set the policy agenda in their favor by defining problems their way. Political scientists have thoroughly studied such activities (Baumgartner and Jones 1993; Kingdon 1995; Rochefort and Cobb 1994).

WORKING WITH **SOURCES**

SUSTAINABLE DEVELOPMENT INDICATORS

Analysts and activists have developed a collection of indicators that allow a community, region, or nation (or a college or university) to measure its progress toward sustainability. These indicators typically involve some commonsense measurements, such as the number of people and automobiles in the geographic area of concern, energy and water consumption, greenhouse gas emissions, and the like. Some less obvious but equally useful social and economic indicators include the percentage of households that can afford to buy an average-priced house, high school graduation rates, and extent of citizens' community involvement (Mazmanian and Kraft 2009). The availability of these kinds of statistics has allowed communities across the nation to convert the abstract concept of sustainable development into something that citizens and policymakers can easily understand. By developing quantitative measures, communities are able to compile a kind of sustainability status report and to track progress over time toward shared community goals. The following Web sites compile sustainability statistics:

www.aashe.org. Association for the Advancement of Sustainability in Higher Education (AASHE), an association of colleges and universities in the United States and Canada working to promote sustainability in all sectors of higher education.

www.moea.state.mn.us/sc/index.cfm. State of Minnesota Sustainable Communities Program, which includes definitions and measures of sustainability and state policies through the Office of Environmental Assistance to encourage sustainable communities.

www.rprogress.org. Redefining Progress, an organization devoted to the use of new measurements of progress and environmental, social, and economic sustainability.

www.smartcommunities.ncat.org. Smart Communities Network, which emphasizes ways to create more energy-efficient communities that work toward sustainable development. This organization focuses on alternatives to urban sprawl, congestion, and intensive resource consumption, and includes "success stories" of communities that are working toward those goals.

www.sustainablemeasures.com. Sustainable Measures, a unique and comprehensive collection of sustainability indicators, with clear explanations of why some are more useful than others. Includes a database of indicators and extensive links to work on sustainability.

The best way to understand the kind of information collected at these sites is to visit one and look for particular indicators. For example, go to the Sustainable Measures site and select the link to Indicators of Sustainability to see a description of the qualities of indicators the site's analysts think are important. Read their description of a "sustainable community indicator check list" for a point-by-point review of what is important in selecting indicators to use for this purpose. Or visit the AASHE site to see what colleges and universities are doing to become more sustainable, such as becoming more energy efficient and trying to reduce greenhouse gas emissions. As you visit these sites, you might ask why some focus on some issues more than others. For example, why does Redefining Progress emphasize the necessity to rethink conventional views of economic growth? Why does the state of Minnesota emphasize financial and technical assistance to communities and public education?

Still, most analysts would likely argue that resolution of a public problem—homelessness, crime, poor-quality schools, urban sprawl, energy needs, nuclear waste disposal—depends at least in part on the ability to clarify the nature of the problem, collect the most pertinent data, and foster a public debate over what might be done about it.

Anticipating the Future. One other aspect of defining and measuring problems deserves mention. Any consideration of the present state of affairs must be grounded in an assessment of how it is likely to change over time. What will the problem look like in several years or decades? Forecasts, or projections, usually involve an extrapolation of current trends, but that is only one method for looking ahead.

Examples of forecasting include economic projections (will the nation have a surplus or deficit in five years or ten years?), population estimates (how large will the U.S. population be by 2025 or 2050?), and future energy needs (how much will we need, and on what sources are we likely to rely?). Such projections are especially helpful if they reveal how that change will likely unfold with or without policy intervention. For example, if the nation adopted tough energy conservation measures, to what extent would that action reduce the otherwise increasing reliance on imported oil?

Such forecasting has become an integral part of the public debate over energy and environmental problems; the anticipated rise in Medicare and Social Security benefits as the baby boom generation ages; and economic policy, such as the assumptions made about government spending and taxation over time. As with other forms of policy analysis, it is always necessary to look at the assumptions that lie behind the forecasts to judge their validity. Circumstances also change, and a forecast made in one year may not be as useful in subsequent years.

Thinking about Causes and Solutions

Any assessment of a public problem requires thinking about its **causes,** how it came about, and why it continues. The answers make a big difference in whether and how public policy might resolve the problem. For example, consider the dramatic rise in prison populations in the United States from 1970 to 2005, when they more than quadrupled to over two million inmates and now cost the nation more than $64 billion a year. The United States imprisons a larger proportion of its citizens than any other country in the world. But why was there an increase of this magnitude in the prison population, especially at a time when crime rates generally were on the decline?

Part of the answer is that states passed tougher sentencing laws and the public was willing to continue building prisons—often at the expense of funding for higher education. In many states, the growth in the prison population can be traced specifically to new laws that put even nonviolent drug offenders in jail and to the adoption of "three-strikes-and-you're-out" laws. These laws mandated long sentences, even life sentences, on conviction for a third-felony offense, even for a relatively innocuous crime.[14] In one case, a California shoplifter charged with stealing $153 worth of videotapes was sentenced to fifty years in prison because of his prior convictions. Many are questioning the wisdom of sentencing drug offenders to prison terms, both in terms of the justification for the harsh penalties and the costs of keeping them in prison. For example, former Republican governor Mike Huckabee of Arkansas noted that the long mandatory sentences were "good politics but bad public policy," adding that the system is locking up "people we are mad at but not afraid of." [15] Nearly half a million drug offenders were in prison in the early 2000s, many on a first conviction for possession; this represents a tenfold increase since 1980. [16]

How might this trend be reversed? One way is to change the laws that led to the growth of the prison population in the first place. In 2000, in California, where one in three prisoners in the state was incarcerated for a drug-related crime, the voters did just that. They approved a state referendum requiring that first- and second-time nonviolent drug offenders be put into treatment centers instead of prison, a move that is expected to reduce the prison population by about thirty-five thousand inmates a year. [17]

In a related move, many states and private organizations have endorsed "reentry programs" that are designed to help released prisoners readjust to society and avoid committing new crimes. Support for such programs has grown remarkably over the last decade, and they have been endorsed by both liberal activist groups and conservative Christian organizations. In a fitting culmination of this movement, in 2008 President Bush signed the Second Chance Act, which made such rehabilitation a fundamental goal of the federal justice system. The act—which, among other things, authorizes funding for matching grants to state and local governments and nonprofit organizations to provide drug treatment, education, housing, and employment services—passed Congress with unanimous bipartisan support. [18]

As discussed in chapter 4, most policy studies focus on what can be called proximate, or immediate, causes of public problems, such as the reasons for rising prison populations. The greater challenge is to deal with the root causes of problems. Taking policy action might be more difficult than it was in California because of long-standing public attitudes and habits that are resistant to change. For example, consider urban traffic congestion. Why does it exist? The obvious answer is that too many people are driving their cars on a limited number of roads at any given time. In addition, Americans are driving more miles per year—to go to work or school, to shop, and for other purposes. Is the solution to build more highways? Or is it to think about ways to reduce the use of automobiles in urban areas, where congestion is greatest? Some urban designers and environmentalists offer a more radical solution, at least for new communities: build cities with adequate mass transit and where people can live closer to where they work. Many states and communities are adopting "smart growth" policies with similar ambitions for managing anticipated growth over the next several decades. Use of such systems seems to depend on people's calculations of relative cost. When gasoline prices spiked to well over $4 per gallon in 2008, mass transit systems saw a substantial increase in ridership. [19]

Most public problems have multiple causes; therefore, people disagree over which is the most important and which ought to be the object of public policy. Liberals and conservatives may disagree about the causes of poor school performance, crime, environmental degradation, or anemic economic growth, and what might be done about them. Smart students of public policy learn how to deal with the politics and often overheated rhetoric that can sometimes cloud an objective review of the evidence.

Problem analysis can begin with making an explicit list of the goals and objectives of various policy actors and a determination of what might be done to reach them (Patton and Sawicki 1993). The objectives may include a specific measure of what is to be achieved, such as improving access to health care services, reducing the rate of teenage smoking, or curbing drunk driving. When analysts think of potential solutions to public problems, they try to identify the opportunities for

MAJOR COMPONENTS OF PROBLEM ANALYSIS

Define the problem. If the problem is educational quality, what does that mean? In other words, what is the exact nature of the education problem under study? Has quality declined? Is it lower than many people believe it ought to be? Is it lower in the United States than in other developed nations?

Measure the problem. Find a way to measure the problem that is consistent with the way it is defined. This step is sometimes called "developing an operational definition." What kinds of quantitative indicators are available from reliable sources? What is the best measurement to use for educational quality: Student scores on standard examinations? Other measures of student learning? Indicators of the quality of a school's faculty?

Determine the extent or magnitude of the problem. Using available indicators, try to determine who is affected by the problem and by how much. Try to answer these kinds of questions: What groups in the population suffer from the problem being studied, how long have they been affected by it, and to what extent are they affected? For example, how does educational quality vary from one school district or state to another? From urban districts to suburban districts? From schools in less affluent neighborhoods to those in more affluent areas?

Think about the problem's causes. How did the problem come about, and why does it continue? What are the leading causes of the problem, and what other causes should be considered? Knowing the causes of a problem is critical to developing solutions to it. How has educational quality changed over the past several decades, and why?

Set goals or objectives. What should be done about the problem, and why? Are certain goals and objectives of paramount importance, widely agreed upon, and economically or socially feasible? Over what period of time should the goals and objectives be sought? For educational quality, what goals or objectives are most appropriate? If quality is to be improved, how much progress should be expected for a given period of time?

Determine what can be done. What actions might work to solve the problem or to reach the specified goals and objectives? What policy efforts might be directed at the causes of the problem? What variables can be affected by such efforts? If the goal is improving educational quality to a certain extent, what needs to be done? Improving teacher quality? Reducing class sizes? Changing the curriculum?

Sources: Carl V. Patton and David S. Sawicki, *Basic Methods of Policy Analysis and Planning,* 2nd ed. (Englewood Cliffs, N.J.: Prentice Hall, 1993); and authors. Patton and Sawicki devote a full chapter to steps in defining a problem. For other treatments of problem diagnosis, see Grover Starling, *Strategies for Policy Making* (Chicago: Dorsey Press, 1988).

policy intervention. They attempt to imagine how a change in public policy might affect the problem; for example, would raising the price of cigarettes reduce the rate of teenage smoking?

Finally, sometimes analysts want to describe the benefits and costs of trying to solve the problem. They look at how the consequences of policy action, positive or negative, are distributed across population subgroups, such as those in certain regions, occupations, or social groups—in other words, who gains and who loses if the problem is resolved. Politicians and other major policy actors are sometimes very clever about addressing these kinds of distributive concerns. They are almost always interested in knowing about them. They may speak about solving public problems as though the entire nation will benefit equally, but the reality is that some segments of the population are more likely than others to enjoy the benefits of acting on a problem, and some are more likely than others to pay the costs. So students of public policy would be wise to think about how to present such information in any studies they complete. The box "Steps to Analysis: Major Components of Problem Analysis" summarizes basic elements in problem analysis. The list can also be a guide to what questions might be addressed in preparing a problem analysis or issue paper.

HOW TO FIND INFORMATION

To perform problem analysis and the other activities related to it, analysts need to collect reliable information. Indeed, good information is critical to successful analysis, but where does one find it? This chapter provides some guidelines. The Web sites listed at the end of each chapter and mentioned within the chapters are sources of extensive data on specific problems, as are articles in academic journals, books on the subject, and the better newspapers and professional newsweeklies. Because the substantive policy chapters in the book provide many particular examples about using the data in policy studies and arguments, the information here is intended to be fairly general.

Most university libraries have a variety of Internet search tools available that can greatly simplify an information search. One of the best search tools, however, is available to anyone. This is Google (www.google.com), which can return many useful links for specific public policy inquiries. Google Uncle Sam is a specialized tool for searching government Web sites, and Google News can search some 4,500 news sites. However, the online databases available through college and university libraries are different. They often contain full-text articles and can be searched by subject matter, title, or author. Card catalogs, generally online today, can be searched in the same way. Consider health care policy and the role of managed care organizations, which are addressed in chapter 8. To identify articles or reports on public satisfaction or dissatisfaction with health maintenance organizations (HMOs), use Google or a similar search engine by typing in the keywords *HMOs, public, satisfaction,* and *complaints* to find a suitable list of studies and public opinion surveys. To vary the search—for example, to find material on whether patients find it difficult to obtain referrals to medical specialists—add or substitute keywords such as *cost, patients, referrals,* and *specialists.*

A good way to begin preparing issue papers and problem analyses is with an overview of a subject from sources such as the *New York Times,* the *Washington Post,* the *Wall Street Journal, CQ Weekly,* or *National Journal.* These and similar newspapers and newsweeklies provide valuable information about current policy debates, particularly on a national level, and some background on the nature of the problem. For a broader historical perspective on public policy actions to address the problem, CQ Press's annual *Almanac* and its quadrennial volume *Congress and the Nation* are invaluable. Similar sources can be consulted for information at the state and local levels, and most can be found in college and university libraries.

The main concern at this point of a search is to find enough information to understand the basics about a given policy problem. How much information is enough? If the initial search yields three or four high-quality articles that provide an idea of the history of the problem, describe the policy efforts and recent controversies, and cover the different points of view about desirable policy actions, that may be sufficient to proceed. At this point, the researcher should be able to determine what else he or she needs to know to complete the assessment and then seek more detailed sources of information. An intense literature search could be profitable at this stage because the researcher knows what to look for and can focus on the best sources.

Most college and university libraries have access to online sources, such as LexisNexis Academic, that include indexing and abstracting services. One of the most useful for public policy research is the congressional database LexisNexis Congressional. It includes an index to, and abstracts of, nearly all congressional documents, from testimony at committee hearings to committee reports on proposed policies. Those documents are excellent sources for the most current analyses of public problems and policy actions. For example, the records of testimony by policy experts at committee hearings may also offer excerpts from their latest research findings before they are available elsewhere. LexisNexis Academic also covers documents that include statistical data, but this database is by no means restricted to statistical analysis. Rather, it covers any description of a problem that includes numbers, such as population trends, crime rates, or the success of welfare reform. LexisNexis also includes extensive databases for legal research. Major university and college libraries are also government depository libraries and have many documents on paper if they are not available online.

Another way to locate pertinent information is to visit the Web site for the government agency most directly related to the issue. For example, the Department of Energy is the first place to look for nuclear waste controversies, for the nation's energy demands and its reliance on imported oil, or for projections of future energy needs. For environmental issues, see the Environmental Protection Agency or the Department of the Interior; for health and welfare issues, see the Department of Health and Human Services. At the state and local levels, the same logic applies: visit the Web sites of the local or state government agencies that deal with the subject matter. In addition, the Web sites for the major interest groups active in the policy area often have extensive reports and commentaries, as do the sites for policy think tanks. Many of those Web sites also incorporate search engines that allow you to quickly locate important documents. Comprehensive Web sites such as www.publicagenda.org and others listed at the end of chapter 4 offer a portal to many of the most useful public policy sites.

In addition to LexisNexis, other indexing and abstracting services are available to help locate articles, government reports, and other major documents. Which are most useful depends on the subject being studied. For most of these sites, users need to gain access through a library with a subscription to the service. Among the most helpful for public policy in general are Academic Search Premier (EBSCO), Worldwide Political Science Abstracts, JSTOR (a database of major scholarly journals), the Social Sciences Full Text, and ProQuest Newsstand (which covers local newspapers). Some similar services are available without a subscription, such as the Government Documents Catalog or the GPO Access for online services (www.access.gpo.gov), and the Library of Congress's Thomas Web site for legislative research (http://thomas.loc.gov). Most libraries have research guides that outline these services and discuss how best to use them.

If possible, students should arrange visits to government and other offices to obtain information and interview policy actors. At the local level especially, policymakers and other actors often welcome a visit by someone who is interested in what they are doing. Advance preparation is essential for this strategy. Students should know what information they are seeking and who is most likely to be able to provide it. Reading local newspaper coverage of the issue would be a good place to begin.[20]

Beyond conducting a search and locating the documents, one of the most challenging aspects of a literature review is the interpretation of the information gathered. As the text has emphasized throughout, policy analyses vary greatly in quality and they are often prepared as ammunition in policy debates, with selective and sometimes misleading summaries and commentaries. Just because a statement appears in print or on the Web is no guarantee that it is true. It is always essential to find out the source of the information, the reliability of the author or organization, any critical assumptions that are made in a study or report (such as what is included or omitted), and any interpretations that might not be justified. At a minimum, the student researcher will want to determine whether the facts are current and accurate.

This description of how to find pertinent policy information is intended to be a general introduction to policy research. The real excitement in policy studies comes from having a strong interest in a particular policy area and learning where to find the information about it. For example, the student who is passionate about equal pay for women in the workforce will find the search for appropriate data and studies exhilarating. For the researcher worried about declining opportunities to download music and videos from the Internet, the hunt for information about copyright laws and restrictions on using downloaded files will be easy and a real learning experience.

CONSTRUCTING ALTERNATIVES

After problem analysis has yielded a good sense of what the problem is, how extensive it is, why it occurs, and what the goals are for resolving it, the next step is to think about courses of action. Chapter 6 introduces a range of relevant criteria for evaluating policy options and some of the tools of analysis that can provide the requisite information to evaluate the policy alternatives. This section focuses on how to develop the list of alternatives that merit such further consideration. It emphasizes learning how to think creatively about public policy, particularly when ineffective policies and programs need to be replaced.

What Governments Can Do

So how do analysts know which alternatives to consider? As we discussed in chapter 3, the starting point is to see what governments are doing or can do. Among their options, governments can regulate, subsidize, ration, tax and spend, contract out, use market incentives, privatize, charge fees for service, educate, create public trusts, and commission research (Patton and Sawicki 1993; Anderson 2006). Table 5-1 summarizes these activities and illustrates them with examples.

If current policies are not working well enough and a change is needed, analysts might suggest modifying the present policies or trying a different policy approach or strategy. Present policies could be strengthened; for example, the federal government could raise standards and penalties for clean air or water policies. Or policymakers could fund programs at a higher level, which might permit improved research, better enforcement, and better public information campaigns. Analysts and policymakers also consider alternatives to conventional regulatory policies, as was done for many environmental policies during the 1980s and 1990s (Mazmanian and Kraft 2009; Vig and Kraft 2010). These might include a combination of market-based incentives, public information campaigns, and various forms of what the Bill Clinton administration called "regulatory reinvention," which are more flexible and efficient policy reforms.

TABLE 5-1	What Government Can Do

Action	Illustrations
Regulate	Licensing, inspection, enforcement of standards, application of sanctions.
	Specific examples: environmental, health, and workplace safety regulations; corporate financial regulations.
Subsidize	Loans, direct payments or benefits, tax credits, price supports.
	Specific examples: student loans; subsidies to farmers; dairy price supports; low interest loans for disaster recovery.
Ration	Limit access to scarce resources.
	Specific examples: permits for backpacking in national parks; the Oregon Health Plan's limitations on coverage of health care services.
Tax and spend	Tax an activity at a level that encourages or discourages it.
	Specific examples: allowing home mortgage deductions to encourage home ownership; imposing cigarette taxes to discourage smoking.
	Spend money on preferred programs.
	Specific examples: defense weapons, prisons, AmeriCorps, public higher education.
Contract out	Contract for government services from the private sector or buy products for government agencies.
	Specific examples: contracts for defense weapons procurement and for the Iraq economic rebuilding initiative; purchase of computers and fleet vehicles for federal or state governments or public schools.
Use market incentives	A special category of taxation or imposition of fees that creates incentives to change behavior and achieve goals and objectives.
	Specific examples: raising gasoline taxes to encourage conservation of fuel and reduce carbon dioxide emissions; tax rebates for purchasing hybrid vehicles or installing solar or wind power sources.
Privatize	Transferring public services from government to the private sector.
	Specific examples: turning over management of public schools to private companies; partially privatizing the Social Security system by allowing individuals to manage a portion of their retirement savings.
Charge fees	Fees for select services.
	Specific examples: hunting and fishing licenses; requiring students to pay to ride the school bus; college tuition.
Educate	Provide information to the public through formal programs or other actions.
	Specific examples: formal public meetings; public education services; food safety labels; information on toxic chemical releases; automobile fuel efficiency labels.
Create public trusts	Holding public property in trust for citizens indefinitely.
	Specific examples: local land conservation trusts; state and national parks and recreation areas.
Conduct research	Conduct or support research and development.
	Specific examples: National Science Foundation support for academic studies; defense and environmental research; medical science research through the National Institutes of Health.

For some policies and agencies, policymakers might try different institutional approaches, such as a new way to organize the bureaucracy in charge. Reorganization was proposed in 2002 for the much-maligned Immigration and Naturalization Service (INS), widely considered to be one of the least effective federal agencies. The George W. Bush administration endorsed a plan to replace the INS with two new agencies, one for immigration services and the other for enforcement. Both new agencies were incorporated into the new Department of Homeland Security. The first is now called U.S. Citizenship and Immigration Services, and the second is named the Border and Transportation Security Directorate. Along with agency reorganization, the present federal-state relationship, some form of which pervades most policy areas, can also be changed. For example, many policies during the 1980s and 1990s were further decentralized, giving the states greater authority to make decisions and allocate funds.

Many state and local governments are trying another interesting institutional reform option. They make routine government services available online, from providing tourist information to supplying government forms that can be filled out by computer. Governments report improved efficiency, and the users say they are more satisfied with the results and think more highly of the agencies than before.[21] The federal government is also moving in this direction and has instituted an Internet portal for all federal information at USA.gov (www.usa.gov).

For many policy areas, actions are rooted in one of two views of the problem being confronted, what might be called **supply and demand perspectives.** If analysts believe a problem such as energy scarcity results from an insufficient supply of energy, they would likely recommend the policy alternative of increasing supply. They would consider actions to boost supplies of energy, whether from fossil fuels (oil, natural gas, and coal), nuclear energy, or alternative energy such as wind or solar power. The actions might include changes in rules that control exploration on public lands, various tax credits and incentives, and support for research that could speed up the introduction of new energy sources. The Bush administration took this position in its national energy policy proposal of 2001, much of which was approved by Congress in 2005. But what if the problem is too much demand for energy rather than too little supply? Policymakers might consider energy conservation and efficiency measures, such as increasing fuel economy standards for cars or providing tax credits for high-mileage hybrid vehicles, which use a combination of electric batteries and a gasoline-powered engine. The most likely scenario would be a combination of the supply and demand perspectives.

In addition to considering which policy options will work best or be more efficient or fair, policymakers also have to think about the philosophical and ideological aspects. Conservatives and liberals, and Republicans and Democrats, differ significantly in the kinds of policy solutions they favor. On the Bush energy bill, for example, Republicans in Congress strongly favored a supply-side approach, while most Democrats supported conservation measures to reduce demand. On health care policy, Democrats want federal government programs to help pay the cost of prescription drugs, and Republicans reject that approach in favor of drug insurance policies offered by private companies and subsidized in part by the federal government.

The same kinds of philosophical differences pervade other areas of domestic policy. Early in the Bush administration in 2001, a debate took place over so-called ergonomics regulations for the workplace. The Clinton administration had proposed broad, mandatory rules—favored by organized labor—to reduce workplace injuries such as neck strain and carpal tunnel syndrome, which result from repetitive motions such as lifting, bending, and typing.[22] A National Academy of Sciences report requested by Congress estimated that about one million of these injuries occur each year in the workplace, resulting in seventy million doctor visits annually and costing the nation's economy about $50 billion.[23] The Bush administration and Republicans in Congress opposed the Clinton rules as excessively burdensome and costly, as did business interests. The business groups said the rules would cost $120 billion to put into effect, although the Clinton administration argued the cost would be only $4.5 billion. In 2001 Congress nullified the Clinton rules, and a year later the Bush administration proposed a replacement policy based almost entirely on voluntary action by companies to reduce repetitive-motion injuries on the job.[24]

Policy Typologies as Analytic Tools

Chapter 3 introduced a typology that analysts can use to consider whether another kind of policy might be appropriate if the previously adopted policy or the one being given the most attention proves to be unsuitable. For example, if a regulatory policy is not working or is no longer politically feasible, the policymaker could consider either self-regulation or distributive policy actions, such as subsidies or incentives.

In a related effort, Anne Schneider and Helen Ingram (1997) developed an intriguing typology as part of their work on **policy design.** The term refers to the careful consideration, during the policy formulation stage, of the role of government "agents" and the "target population"— those who receive benefits or who are the objects of government regulation. Schneider and Ingram argue that, for public policies to stand a chance of working, they must be thoroughly grounded in an understanding of the attitudes and motivations of the policy actors who will decide how the policies are implemented and whether they have the desired effects. Underlying this view of policymaking is a variation of rational choice theory: if policy actors are rational beings who respond to the incentives and disincentives incorporated into a given policy, then the policymakers should be able to design policies that encourage people to behave in the way that is needed.

Viewed from this perspective, policy tools, according to Schneider and Ingram, are "the elements in policy design that cause agents or targets to do something they would not otherwise do with the intention of modifying behavior to solve public problems or attain policy goals" (1997, 93). The choice of such tools, they say, reflects different views of how people behave and what might lead them to change their behavior. They distinguish five such policy tools, which are summarized in the box "Steps to Analysis: Policy Design Tools." Governments can invoke their authority and ask for compliance, provide incentives or inducements to elicit compliance, apply sanctions or penalties for noncompliance, try to inform and enlighten the public and promote learning, and exhort people to change their behavior. The choice of which tools to use and how depends on the analysis of a given case and the process of political deliberation and debate that usually occurs at the stage of policy formulation and adoption.

Although it may seem an abstract exercise in rational choice theory, this policy design approach is quite effective and offers many insights into human behavior that can help analysts and policymakers figure out what kinds of policy action will likely succeed. Consider a situation that was unfortunate for California in 2001. Electricity prices in the state rose dramatically in 2000 and 2001 as a consequence of a poorly conceived state energy deregulation policy and a short-term shortage of electricity, which was brought about in part by the power companies' manipulation of the energy supply. As one solution, state policymakers adopted the nation's largest energy conservation program, with a strong focus on incentives for individuals to conserve energy. For example, those who cut their previous electricity use by 20 percent or more would earn a special rebate of 20 percent on their 2001 energy bills in addition to the direct savings they enjoyed from using less electricity. The state called this a "pay-to-conserve" program.

POLICY DESIGN TOOLS

Policy design is the consideration of a variety of possible approaches, instruments, or tools that may be appropriate for a given policy problem. The tools described here derive from anticipating how different policy actors are likely to respond to what governments attempt to do. They are similar to the list we provide in Table 5-1 for what government might do to address any public problem. This typology, however, seeks to categorize different policy tools in a way that highlights key differences among them.

Authority tools. Governments use their authority to urge or require people to behave in a certain way. The use of such tools, not always effective or democratic, depends on the perceived legitimacy of government. These tools may be particularly suitable during times of crisis, when favorable responses by the public are more likely.

Inducements and sanctions. Governments provide incentives or penalties to appeal to individuals' rational pursuit of their self-interest. Inducements encourage people to act in a certain way because they will gain from doing so. Sanctions are negative incentives or penalties that are thought to discourage behavior that is inconsistent with policy goals.

Capacity-building tools. Governments make available training, education, information, and technical assistance, and they can aim to inform or enlighten and thus empower people, either those in the target population or policy agents.

Hortatory tools. Governments invoke images and values through speeches, proclamations, and other communication to exhort people to behave in a certain way.

Learning tools. Governments can encourage policy agents and target populations to participate and learn, for example, through citizen advisory panels and collaborative processes.

How might government use these different tools? Which seem to be the most useful? Consider a specific problem, such as the use of cell phones by drivers, discussed in chapter 4. Which of these tools might be the most effective in reducing cell phone use by drivers? How about the use of seat belts in cars? Which of these tools is most likely to encourage drivers and passengers to "buckle up" and thus reduce their risk of injury or death in the event of an accident? Why do you think so? Or consider the case of immigration reform discussed at the beginning of this chapter: Which of these tools can help reduce the rate of illegal immigration or to address another component of the problem?

Source: Adapted from Anne Larason Schneider and Helen Ingram, *Policy Design for Democracy* (Lawrence: University Press of Kansas, 1997).

State policymakers were counting on individual incentives to alter consumer behavior that has proved difficult to change. California's policy is a good example of what Schneider and Ingram mean by offering inducements that persuade individuals to adjust their behavior because they realize they will be better off by doing so. In this particular case, hortatory tools—the governor and news media urging people to conserve energy—probably also made a difference, as Californians were determined to break out of their energy crisis. The policymakers had calculated that 10 percent of the public would take advantage of the pay-to-conserve program, but by November 2001 more than one third had done so. The financial inducement worked in part because rising energy prices provided a powerful financial incentive for individuals to save energy.[25]

Many other public policies are equally dependent on assumptions about how those affected by policy rules will behave. Traffic laws, for example, depend on drivers' willingness to stop at red lights and to abide by the posted speed limit. When people do not respond as expected, additional sanctions may be necessary. Jurisdictions impose substantial fines and other penalties for driving under the influence of alcohol as a way of discouraging this behavior. Some states maintain the death penalty for severe crimes in hope that it will deter criminals. Here too the assumption is that a person contemplating a criminal act would adjust his or her behavior with the understanding of the possible punishment.

These examples show that policy typologies, such as that proposed by Schneider and Ingram, can be useful when thinking about a government's possible courses of action. In conjunction with other analytic techniques, typologies like these can help analysts focus on the condition they are trying to bring about and what changes in human behavior may be necessary. Then they can consider various policy actions that may provide the necessary incentives.

CREATIVE THINKING ABOUT POLICY ACTION

Beyond considering policy typologies or variations on existing policies, students of public policy can try other techniques to expand the list of alternatives. Carl V. Patton and David S. Sawicki's book *Basic Methods in Policy Analysis and Planning* (1993) offers a pertinent discussion of how to apply **creative thinking** to policy action. Among other strategies, Patton and Sawicki suggest the following: no-action analysis, quick surveys, literature reviews, comparison to real-world situations, passive collection and classification, use of analogies and metaphors, brainstorming, and comparison with an ideal.

No-action analysis begins with the status quo, or present policy, as a kind of baseline. It does not suggest that governments do nothing about a given problem, but that keeping present policies or programs, or defending them, may be a viable option. Many will favor this strategy during times of budget constraints, when programs are vulnerable to cutbacks or elimination. A clear example is the idea of keeping Amtrak alive by continuing its government subsidies because the national passenger train system is an alternative to travel by car or airplane. Nearly every other developed nation subsidizes its railroads, but in the United States public and political support for passenger trains is limited. The level of support is so low that expanding Amtrak may not be a viable option, but keeping it going may prove to be an important decision because its demise would no doubt make it difficult to develop passenger rail systems in the future. The no-action option may also be a useful point of departure for considering other alternatives. One advantage of such choices is they are *not* the status quo, which may be unacceptable to critics of the current program. The greater the dissatisfaction with the status quo option, the more likely policymakers and the public are to favor a search for alternatives and give them serious consideration.

Quick surveys involve talking with people in a particular policy network or searching through hearings transcripts, minutes of meetings, newspaper accounts, and the like for pertinent information about a problem and policy alternatives. The idea here is that people familiar with the issues have probably raised many alternatives, and interviewing them, distributing questionnaires to them, or reviewing what they have written or said on the issues should produce a short list of possible policy alternatives. This technique could be particularly useful at the local level, where gaining access to principal policy actors is a real possibility.

In recent years hundreds of public schools across the nation have tried to discourage students from eating junk food and encourage the eating of healthy food as one way to deal with rising levels of childhood obesity. The obesity epidemic among both adults and children in the United States has led to many calls for better nutrition and more exercise as preventive health measures. The photos show a Nettelhorst Elementary School student digging into a salad bar during lunch in March 2006 in Chicago, Illinois. The revamped lunch program at the school, "Cool Foods," is part of the Healthy Schools Campaign. The second photo shows a high school senior doing schoolwork while eating healthy snacks at Mission High School in April 2004 in San Francisco, California. The San Francisco school district was one of the first in the nation to introduce vending machines with healthy alternatives in their schools.

A **literature review** is an examination of books, journal articles, Internet sites, and other sources. The purpose here is to look for policy alternatives that have been proposed or considered previously. This kind of search could extend to a survey of the options that policymakers have considered or adopted in other policy areas as well. For example, the National Environmental Policy Act required that government agencies conduct an environmental impact analysis, and make it public, before making major decisions such as building highways. Can an impact analysis be applied elsewhere? In other words, why not require that specific studies or reports be conducted and made public prior to reaching a final decision in many other areas of public policy?

Consider an intriguing law that Congress enacted in the 1980s, the False Claims Act Amendments, which encourages whistle-blowers to air their concerns about improper actions such as fraudulent contracts with the government. The law provides that those who blow the whistle, or come forward with such accusations, may receive up to a quarter of the money that the government recovers. This can be a substantial amount. After nearly three decades, the act—which imposes triple damages on companies that commit fraud—produced over $12 billion for the federal treasury. It also provided $1 billion for hundreds of whistle-blowers who reported the abuses. One individual who reported a former employer's fraud received tens of millions of dollars. A Justice Department spokesperson said the law was "highly effective in ferreting out individuals and companies that commit fraud." [26]

Rather than think only about abstract ideas, analysts might ask what has worked well in specific, or real-world, situations, and therefore what might be considered an effective alternative to the present policy. Analysts would also want to know which alternatives have been tried elsewhere and found wanting. This kind of information is likely to be available because one of the great virtues of the U.S. federal system is that the fifty states and their approximately eighty thousand local governments often demonstrate great creativity in addressing public problems. As Supreme Court Justice Louis D. Brandeis observed long ago, "A single courageous State may, if its citizens choose, serve as a laboratory; and try novel social and economic experiments without risk to the rest of the country." [27] Today, states frequently engage in innovative public policy actions. If several states have experimented with welfare reform, then other states or the federal government might look to them for ideas about what to consider. Indeed, the federal welfare reform measure of 1996 was based largely on what Wisconsin and a few other states were already doing. Many states and communities took action on global climate change in the face of the federal government's inaction. Many sources can be consulted for information on state or local policy innovation, including associations of state administrators and state legislative bodies, which often follow and evaluate state and local policy experiments. Analysts can also look to what other nations have tried to do about a particular problem and evaluate their success.

Similar to the quick survey approach, passive collection means finding out what others have suggested in a given policy area. Analysts might speak with a program's clients or administrators, advocates of various positions, and organizations that have taken a position on the issues. Do they offer creative ways of dealing with the problem that depart from present practices? Do those closely associated with a given policy area believe that some policy alternatives are politically infeasible because they have been raised and rejected earlier? Finding out these answers now can save analysts time and effort later.

Another approach is to look at parallel situations in other policy areas for ideas about what might be done. What seems to be a new problem may present many of the same issues as an earlier one. Analysts need to be alert to possible analogies. By listing and thinking about the attributes of the present problem, they may see its relationship to other problems. For example, measures to deal with the rights of disabled persons have borrowed concepts and language from analogous civil rights legislation from the 1960s. Another approach to using analogies is to imagine oneself in the position of a client served by a given program. As a client, how do you respond to present policies? What would you like changed?

Another example concerns a problem peculiar to college towns. What might a city do about old couches that wind up on open-air porches, where inebriated students deliberately set them on fire during celebrations? Boulder, Colorado, home to the University of Colorado, borrowed from the practice in analogous areas of regulatory policy. It decided to ban the placement of upholstered furniture outside of a dwelling, much to the dismay of students who liked the comfortable furniture on their porches. The measure applies only to the University Hill neighborhood of Boulder, a residential area near the campus that had been the scene of previous couch burnings. Other campus towns—including Fort Collins, Colorado; Normal, Illinois; and Blacksburg, Virginia—have adopted similar ordinances. The Boulder law carried penalties of ninety days in jail and fines of up to $1,000.

A popular technique to encourage creative thinking in public policy or in organizational change is **brainstorming,** which usually takes place in an informal meeting of people who share an interest in finding solutions to a given problem. In the brainstorming session the participants bounce ideas around with the goal of producing a list of possibilities. Ideas are offered and recorded as they are made, with no attempt to criticize or evaluate them. The freewheeling discussion of the issues should produce creative thinking and numerous suggestions. In the second phase of the meeting, the participants pare down the suggestions to come up with a shorter list of alternatives worthy of further consideration. Brainstorming can also take the form of written suggestions rather than verbal responses in open meetings. Some variations on the brainstorming theme suggest that creativity is enhanced when some structure is introduced into the discussions (Goldenberg, Mazursky, and Solomon 1999).

Sometimes analysts compare policy alternatives with an **ideal situation.** For example, as part of smart growth planning or sustainability efforts, many communities hold "visioning" meetings in which residents are encouraged to think about the community they want for the future: What kind of residential neighborhoods would it have? What kind of downtown? What kind of recreational opportunities? The goal is to envision an ideal future and use that vision to generate ideas for moving in the desired direction. Too often in public policy debates, the participants assume that an ideal situation is unattainable and therefore not worthy of serious consideration, but excluding the ideal guarantees that it will never come about. By encouraging the expression of an ideal, analysts can ensure that at least the more pragmatic ideas that do receive consideration are evaluated in terms of how close they come to the ideal.

Any one of these strategies for generating a list of policy alternatives should help an analyst to think clearly about how to solve a problem. At this point in the process, neither the cost nor the political feasibility of a particular option is the primary concern; rather, it is to think critically about the problem and try to imagine the various ways to address it. Chapter 6 suggests methods for evaluating the various policy options. In this chapter, however, the emphasis is on fostering the most creative thinking possible, especially if conventional policy action is thought not to be working well and alternatives are needed.

Consider this example. Studies have shown that the rate of obesity among children and teenagers is rising quickly, as are the rates of early-onset heart disease and Type 2 diabetes. Chapter 8 discusses the serious health consequences for the individuals and the significant costs to society if these conditions persist. So what might be done beyond encouraging people to eat healthier diets? Some states have thought about what public schools can do to reduce the availability of foods that contribute to the problem. They proposed restrictions on fast-food franchises in public schools and the imposition of a tax of several cents per can on soft drinks, which are loaded with sugar and calories. Predictably, soft drink makers opposed the initiatives and pointed instead to a sedentary lifestyle as the culprit. In 2001 California enacted legislation to eliminate junk food from schools by 2004, a move applauded by public health officials. By late 2008, some five hundred to six hundred school districts across the nation had policies that limited the amount of fat, trans fat, sodium, and sugar in food that was sold or served in school cafeterias, with some of the strictest prohibitions in elementary schools.[28] Are these kinds of responses the right way to act? Would you favor such a move? If not this kind of action, what else do you think might reduce the high levels of obesity among children and teenagers?

CONCLUSIONS

John Gardner, the founder of the nonprofit organization Common Cause and a longtime political reformer, once said, "What we have before us are some breathtaking opportunities disguised as insoluble problems."[29] That is a fitting thought for this chapter on problem analysis and the creation of policy alternatives. It conveys a sense of optimism about how to face any public problem, from inadequate performance of public schools to an inability of local governments to deal with urban sprawl. Rather than complain, analysts, policymakers, and citizens could try to figure out just what the problem is and why it exists, gather some basic information about it, and think about what might be done. As challenging as many public problems are, they are also opportunities to consider the role of government—and the private sector—in fresh ways and to imagine possibilities for changing unsatisfactory circumstances.

This chapter provides an overview of problem analysis. It discusses some of the perspectives and methods that can help analysts—whether professional or beginner—to identify, define, and measure problems. The chapter also notes some strategies for finding information about public problems. Finally, it offers some ways to generate alternative policy options that can later be evaluated against whatever standards or criteria apply. Problem analysis takes place within a political context that often leads to a proliferation of competing diagnoses and recommendations and sometimes to outright misleading and inaccurate portrayals of the problems faced. The skillful analysts learn to deal with the situation. They know how to conduct a critical review and appraisal of whatever studies and reports they find on a subject. Developing a healthy sense of skepticism, however, need not mean a loss of idealism or the willingness to think creatively about public policy change.

DISCUSSION QUESTIONS

1. Consider the case of illegal immigration presented at the beginning of the chapter. What is the nature of the immigration problem? What kinds of evidence would you want to see to decide how best to deal with it? Where would you go to get that evidence?

2. Early in the chapter, we discussed an example of policy studies involving seat belt use, and variation among the states and among groups in the population. What actions would you recommend to increase seat belt use, especially by young drivers? Why do you think those actions would be successful? Can you think of any creative solutions that have not been tried so far?

3. How would you determine whether a particular source of information on policy issues is reliable or not? What would you look for that could distinguish a solid, professional analysis of an issue from one that is weaker or biased?

4. What kinds of measures do you think would be the most accurate in determining whether public high schools are performing well or not? The SAT or ACT scores of graduating seniors? National achievement test scores in a variety of subject areas? State test scores? Something else?

SUGGESTED READINGS

Frank R. Baumgartner and Bryan D. Jones, *Agendas and Instability in American Politics* (Chicago: University of Chicago Press, 1993). A major work on agenda setting, with many insights into the policy-making process and policy change.

Evan Berman, *Essential Statistics for Public Managers and Policy Analysts,* 2nd ed. (Washington, D.C.: CQ Press, 2007). A useful overview of basic statistics that can be applied in policy analysis.

Anne L. Schneider and Helen Ingram, "Policy Design: Elements, Premises, and Strategies," in *Policy Theory and Policy Evaluation,* ed. Stuart Nagel (Westport, Conn.: Greenwood, 1990). A shorter version of Schneider and Ingram's argument in *Policy Design for Democracy.* Not easy reading, but well worth the effort.

———, *Policy Design for Democracy* (Lawrence: University Press of Kansas, 1997). One of the best treatments of policy design, with particular attention to incentives that policies provide to government officials and target populations to achieve policy success.

SUGGESTED WEB SITES

www.fedstats.gov. A site that provides easy access to a vast amount of federal data on policy problems, organized by agency as well as substantive policy area.

www.gao.gov. U.S. Government Accountability Office, a treasure trove of reports on government agencies and programs, especially evaluation studies.

www.gpoaccess.gov. Access to the federal government's printing office site for location of government documents.

www.lib.umich.edu/govdocs. University of Michigan site that provides a comprehensive set of links to statistical resources on the Web organized by subject area—health, environment, education, energy, science, transportation, military, housing, economics, agriculture, business, and more. Links within each area lead the user to extensive lists of agencies and programs. The site is updated frequently.

www.publicagenda.org. Nonpartisan briefings on policy and polling; a digest of news, legislation, and studies; and research sources.

http://thomas.loc.gov. The Library of Congress's Thomas search engines for locating congressional documents. Thomas is one of the most comprehensive public sites for legislative searches.

www.usa.gov. Portal for federal government Web sites.

KEYWORDS

brainstorming	146	no-action analysis	143
causes	133	operational measures	129
creative thinking	143	policy design	141
ideal situation	146	problem analysis	127
literature review	144	supply and demand perspectives	140

NOTES

1. See Richard W. Stevenson, "Bush, Touring the Border, Puts Emphasis on Enforcement," *New York Times,* November 30, 2005, A29.
2. Ibid. For further assessment of the issue and a discussion of pending immigration bills in Congress, see Michael Sandler, "Immigration Debate Focuses on Those in U.S.," *CQ Weekly,* November 7, 2005, 2963–2964.
3. Seth Stern, "An Uneasy Deal with Illegal Workforce," *CQ Weekly,* March 14, 2005, 620–626.
4. Ibid. For current figures, see the Pew Hispanic Center at http://pewhispanic.org.
5. Julia Preston, "Decline Seen in Numbers of People Here Illegally," *New York Times* online edition, July 31, 2008.
6. The construction of the border fence has drawn considerable criticism but continues nonetheless. See Randal C. Archibold and Julia Preston, "Despite Growing Opposition, Homeland Security Stands by Its Fence," *New York Times,* May 21, 2008, 1, A20.

7. Julia Preston, "Immigration Cools as Campaign Issue," *New York Times* online edition, October 28, 2008.

8. David J. Houston and Lilliard E. Richardson Jr., "Reducing Traffic Fatalities in the American States by Upgrading Seat Belt Use Laws to Primary Enforcement," *Journal of Policy Analysis and Management* 25, no. 3 (2006): 645–659.

9. The data on seat belt usage come from "Seat Belt Use in 2007—Use Rates in the States and Territories" (Washington, D.C.: National Highway Traffic Safety Commission, National Center for Statistics and Analysis, May 2008). See also Matthew L. Wald, "U.S. Presses States for Strict Seat Belt Laws, *New York Times,* March 5, 2004, A12; and Wald, "Urging Young to Buckle Up, Officials Try Switch in Tactics," *New York Times,* May 20, 2002, A18. Wald cites a study stating that 52 percent of teenagers killed in automobile accidents were not wearing seat belts. This rate is twice that of all people killed in automobile accidents.

10. "Counting the Poor," *New York Times* editorial, April 17, 2007.

11. See Louis Uchitelle, "How to Define Poverty? Let Us Count the Ways," *New York Times,* May 26, 2001, A15, A17; and Jonathan Weisman, "Measuring the Economy May Not Be as Simple as 1, 2, 3," *Washington Post,* August 29, 2005. The federal government's guidelines for who qualifies as poor can be found at http://aspe.hhs.gov/poverty/08Poverty.shtml.

12. The Web site is http://stateoftheusa.org.

13. Elizabeth Becker, "Bill Defines Irradiated Meat as 'Pasteurized,' " *New York Times,* March 5, 2002, A18.

14. "Nation's Inmate Population Increased 2.3 Percent Last Year," *New York Times,* April 25, 2005, A14, Associated Press release. As of mid-2004, the nation's jails and prisons held over two million people. Despite a falling crime rate, the prison population remains high, in part because of the tough policies enacted in the 1980s and 1990s. See also Carl M. Cannon, "America: All Locked Up," *National Journal,* August 15, 1998, 1906–1915.

15. *The Diane Rehm Show,* National Public Radio, February 18, 2003.

16. Ironically, the longer sentences and the increase in the prison population are not deterring people from committing crimes. The recidivism rate is rising in part because, to save money, state governments cut back on rehabilitation programs such as drug treatment, vocational education, and classes that help prepare convicted criminals to return to society. See Fox Butterfield, "Study Shows Building Prisons Did Not Prevent Repeat Crimes," *New York Times,* June 3, 2002, A11. See also Steven Raphael and Michael A. Stoll, eds., *Do Prisons Make Us Safer? The Benefits and Costs of the Prison Boom* (New York: Russell Sage Foundation, 2009).

17. Evelyn Nieves, "California Gets Set to Shift on Sentencing Drug Users," *New York Times,* November 10, 2000.

18. Erik Eckholm, "U.S. Shifting Prison Focus to Re-entry into Society," *New York Times,* April 8, 2008, A23.

19. Clifford Krauss, "Gas Prices Send Surge of Riders to Mass Transit," *New York Times* online edition, May 10, 2008.

20. For an overview of methods that can be used to obtain policy information, see Carl V. Patton and David S. Sawicki, *Basic Methods of Policy Analysis and Planning,* 2nd ed. (Englewood Cliffs, N.J.: Prentice Hall, 1993), chapter 3; and Janet Buttolph Johnson, H. T. Reynolds, and Jason D. Mycoff, *Political Science Research Methods,* 6th ed. (Washington, D.C.: CQ Press, 2008). Patton and Sawicki offer a helpful guide for arranging and conducting interviews with policymakers. Any recent social science methods text will discuss how to construct and use questionnaires as well as how to conduct interviews. See, for example, Earl Babbie, *The Practice of Social Research,* 10th ed. (Belmont, Calif.: Wadsworth, 2003).

21. Rebecca Fairley Raney, "From Parking to Taxes, a Push to Get Answers Online," *New York Times,* April 4, 2002.

22. See James C. Benton, "Washington's Repetitive Stress over Ergonomics Rules," *CQ Weekly,* February 26, 2000, 401–405. The article cites the following industries as most affected by musculoskeletal disorders: airline, airport, and terminal services; buses, commuter rail lines, and taxis; trucking and warehousing firms; hospitals, clinics, doctors' offices, and nursing homes; car, truck, aircraft, boat, and railroad car makers; and meatpackers, dairies, grain mills, bakeries, and packaged food makers.

23. Steven Greenhouse, "Ergonomics Report Cites Job Injuries," *New York Times,* January 18, 2001, C6.

24. Rebecca Adams, "Intense Lobbying Gets Under Way over Whether to Block Ergonomics Rules," *CQ Weekly,* February 10, 2001, 328–329; and Steven Greenhouse, "Bush Plan to Avert Work Injuries Seeks Voluntary Steps by Industry," *New York Times,* April 6, 2002, A1–A12.

25. See Timothy Egan, "Once Braced for a Power Shortage, California Now Finds Itself with a Surplus," *New York Times,* November 4, 2001, A17.

26. See Associated Press, "For Some Whistle-Blowers, Big Risk Pays Off," *New York Times,* November 29, 2004, A17. A nonprofit organization called Taxpayers Against Fraud Education Fund maintains an extensive Web site on the False Claims Act at www.taf.org.

27. *New State Ice Co. v. Liebmann,* 285 U.S. 262, 311 (1932).

28. See Patricia Leigh Brown, "Bake Sales Fall Victim to Push for Healthier Foods," *New York Times,* November 10, 2008, A15.

29. Quoted in a *Science* magazine editorial by Donald Kennedy, March 22, 2002, 2177.

CHAPTER **6**

ASSESSING POLICY ALTERNATIVES

ONE OF THE MOST MEMORABLE DEVELOPMENTS OF 2008 THAT AFFECTED nearly everyone in the United States was an unexpected, sharp increase in the cost of gasoline. The price of a barrel of oil on the international market soared to $147, and the price of a gallon of gasoline in the United States rose to well over $4 by the middle of the year, chiefly because rising worldwide demand exceeded supply. Even though prices plummeted by the end of the year as world economies slowed and demand for oil dropped, the short-term effect was widespread economic pain, not just in filling the gas tank but in the cost of everything we buy because of shipping costs. The nation's response to higher fuel prices was immediate and concrete. People began abandoning trucks and sport utility vehicles in favor of more fuel-efficient cars, and automakers struggled to bring such vehicles to market more quickly than planned. The price of real estate in distant suburbs fell even more than housing in general did as people decided that long and expensive commutes were no longer such a good idea. Demand for mass transit rose so much that many cities doubted that they could cope in the short term.[1]

Not surprisingly in an election year, the rapid rise in fuel costs sparked a national political debate over how best to respond to the problem, including competing proposals to lower the federal gasoline tax to ease the burden on consumers (a so-called gas tax holiday favored by presidential candidates John McCain and Hillary Clinton and opposed by Barack Obama); increase fuel efficiency requirements (which had just been raised in late 2007); and promote energy conservation, efficiency, and the use of alternative or renewable fuels through boosts in federal research and tax credits.[2] Among these proposals was an argument to increase drilling for oil on public lands, particularly those lands that had long been off limits to the oil companies: those located in the Arctic National Wildlife Refuge (ANWR) in Alaska and offshore on

The sharp rise in gasoline prices in 2008 assured that candidates would have to address the issue during that year's congressional and presidential elections. Aside from proposals to deal directly with gasoline prices, the subject of drilling off the nation's coastal areas was discussed often. Offshore drilling pits those who favor use of domestic supplies of oil against others worried about environmental impacts as well as continuing dependence on fossil fuels as energy sources. The rare and endangered blue whale shown here is one of at least four seen feeding near oil rigs eleven miles off shore near Long Beach, California, in July 2008. Once rarely seen along California's coastline, blue whale sightings have increased in recent years, possibly because climate change is affecting their food supply. Increased drilling in offshore areas could threaten the blue whales, the largest animals on the planet.

the outer continental shelf. Republicans discovered that the offshore drilling issue resonated well with voters in 2008, and they pushed it hard throughout the summer and into their national presidential nominating convention, where they made the chants "drill, baby, drill" and "drill here, drill now" readily recognizable signposts of their commitment to increasing the nation's domestic energy supply. Democrats remained opposed to offshore drilling for much of the year, but they eventually countered with their own proposal to allow such drilling, although with substantial restrictions.

This fascinating energy debate included nearly every criterion and method that policy analysts typically use to assess policy alternatives. There were questions raised about economic costs, national security, environmental risks, the role of federal and state governments, and the value of relying on market forces versus government regulation. There were also questions about whether to subsidize oil companies to encourage more exploration, the technical feasibility of offshore drilling (partly because of a shortage of drilling rigs), and the likely effectiveness of such drilling: if and when it would produce substantial quantities of oil and how much it would affect the price of gasoline and the nation's dependence on foreign oil. Each side pointed to arguments that bolstered its position, and each challenged the other's assumptions and portrayals of the situation.

It was a fairly typical, even if unenlightening, policy debate. It illustrated well the tendency of policymakers and their staffs to use policy studies more to reinforce and advocate existing positions and as ammunition against opponents than to think realistically about what is possible and the trade-offs involved (Sabatier and Jenkins-Smith 1993; Weiss 1978; Whiteman 1995). In this context, consider one particular study that did get some attention during the 2008 debate, even if it changed few minds. The Department of Energy (DOE) reported in 2007 that new drilling in the offshore areas would not have a significant effect on oil production before 2030, and that the ultimate effect on prices would be "insignificant" because oil is traded globally and the amounts would be too little to affect worldwide prices.[3]

Whether policymakers use them well or not, policy analyses like this one by the DOE are integral to the modern policy-making process precisely because the issues often are complicated and involve highly technical questions well beyond the expertise of elected officials. At the core of such analyses are a clear delineation of the criteria developed for judging policy alternatives and the application of available tools and methods to provide information essential to decision making. Yet as the case of energy policy shows well, even the best studies may be trumped by political necessity.

This chapter reviews the leading evaluative criteria used today as well as the methods of policy analysis most commonly employed. These methods range from cost-benefit analysis that addresses economic criteria to political and institutional assessments that estimate political or administrative feasibility. The combination of clear evaluative criteria and careful analysis should make it easier to determine whether one policy alternative is better than another. Policy analysts and those involved in making policy choices want to know whether one alternative is more likely than another to be more effective, or whether one will be cheaper. They want to ask as well about differences in equity or fairness, such as how these alternative policy options will distribute their costs or benefits across the population. That is, will some groups (such as wealthy or retired citizens) gain more than others, and will some (such as the middle class or those in the workforce) pay more than others for that policy? It is the purpose of policy analysis to provide that kind of information, and it is up to policymakers and the public to decide what to do with it.

EVALUATIVE CRITERIA FOR JUDGING POLICY PROPOSALS

Evaluative criteria are the specific dimensions of policy objectives (what policy proposals seek to achieve) that can be used to weigh policy options or judge the merits of existing policies or programs. Evaluative criteria can also be regarded as justifications or rationales for a policy or government action. The use of explicit evaluative criteria establishes relatively clear standards that can keep policy analysis objective and focused on the issues of greatest concern to the analyst, the intended audience, or the client. Such standards also allow users to rank alternatives in order of their preferences. It makes sense to choose the criteria that fit a given policy area and set of circumstances. Obviously, some criteria make more sense for judging access to health care services than they would for determining whether Congress should cut agricultural subsidies. In addition, as Brian W. Hogwood and Lewis A. Gunn (1984) argued, policy analysis for the real world is always contingent on the political and institutional context of policy debate and is influenced by available resources and time.

The dimensions of policy objectives that are most often the target of inquiry and political argument include effectiveness, costs, benefits, risks, uncertainty, political feasibility, administrative feasibility, equity or fairness, liberty or freedom, legality, and (sometimes) constitutionality. This is quite a long list, however, and analysts seldom address all of these elements in any single study. Chapter 1 suggested the usefulness of focusing on three of these criteria: effectiveness, efficiency, and equity. Concern about effectiveness, or how well a policy is working, is nearly universal. Because most public policies, from defense to education, spend public money, analysts consider efficiency—what clients get for their money—to be just as important. Many also argue that equity, which concerns the fairness of government programs in relation to the needs of different groups in the population, should always be a concern. Of all the criteria discussed in the text, these three capture the most politically important standards used to judge policy proposals today.

It should be said that policymakers, interest groups, and analysts often favor use of one criterion over another without being very clear about why they do so. In the case of the energy policy debate summarized above, for example, advocates of offshore drilling emphasized the need to expand domestic oil supplies, a component of effectiveness. They said little about the relative efficiency of that strategy in relation to other policy options. On the other side of this debate, environmentalists challenged the likely effectiveness of a drilling strategy but also underscored what they considered to be unacceptable environmental risks. Neither side made equity considerations a prominent part of their argument, although some opponents of drilling did note that U.S. consumption of oil was disproportionate to its population size (and hence unfair in a global context) and solutions lay more in decreasing our reliance on oil, whether produced domestically or imported. In the practical world of politics, policy actors use the arguments they think will best make their case without necessarily trying to address every consideration or every criterion.

Table 6-1 lists these three criteria along with five others often used in policy analysis and policy debate. The table gives the meaning of each criterion and the limitations in using it as a standard of judgment. It also indicates the type of public policies for which it is most apt. Critics such as Deborah Stone (2002) underscore the inherent ambiguities and problems of interpretation associated with such criteria. These qualities need not prevent their use in practical policy analysis, but they do suggest the need to be alert to such limitations in how they are applied.

TABLE 6-1	Selected Criteria for Evaluating Public Policy Proposals		
Criterion	**Definition**	**Limits to Use**	**Where Most Likely Used**
Effectiveness	Likelihood of achieving policy goals and objectives or demonstrated achievement of them.	Estimates involve uncertain projection of future events.	Virtually all policy proposals where concern exists over how well government programs work.
Efficiency	The achievement of program goals or benefits in relationship to the costs. Least cost for a given benefit or the largest benefit for a given cost.	Measuring all costs and benefits is not always possible. Policy decision making reflects political choices as much as efficiency.	Regulatory policies, such as workplace safety and environmental protection; consideration of market-based approaches.
Equity	Fairness or justice in the distribution of the policy's costs, benefits, and risks across population subgroups.	Difficulty in finding techniques to measure equity; disagreement over whether equity means a fair process or equal outcomes.	Civil rights, disability rights, tax equity, access to health services and higher education.
Liberty/ Freedom	Extent to which public policy extends or restricts privacy and individual rights and choices.	Assessment of impacts on freedom is often clouded by ideological beliefs about the role of government.	Proposed national identification cards, restrictions on Internet use, property rights, abortion rights, regulatory actions that constrain choices of corporations and individuals.
Political feasibility	The extent to which elected officials accept and support a policy proposal.	Difficult to determine. Depends on perceptions of the issues and changing economic and political conditions.	Any controversial policy, such as gun control, immigration, stem cell research, or subsidies for oil and gas drilling.
Social acceptability	The extent to which the public will accept and support a policy proposal.	Difficult to determine even when public support can be measured. Depends on saliency of the issues and level of public awareness.	Any controversial policy, such as crime control or abortion rights.
Administrative feasibility	The likelihood that a department or agency can implement the policy well.	Involves projection of available resources and agency behavior that can be difficult to estimate.	Expansion of agency duties, use of new policy approaches or new technologies, policies with complicated institutional structures.
Technical feasibility	The availability and reliability of technology needed for policy implementation.	Often difficult to anticipate technological change that would alter feasibility.	Science and technology policy, environmental and energy policies, telecommunications, defense policies.

Typically, when these criteria are used, they must be expressed in terms of operational measurements or indicators, such as those discussed in chapter 5. For example, analysts usually speak of efficiency in terms of dollar cost in relation to the value of benefits expected to be realized from a government action, such as improved workplace safety that might follow adoption of federal ergonomics standards. Effectiveness can be measured in terms of the likelihood of reaching a specific policy objective, such as reducing automobile accident rates by 20 percent over a five-year period. For most of these criteria, multiple indicators are available, and analysts normally use several to compensate for the limitations of any one of them. Some criteria, however, involve making qualitative judgments rather than using such indicators, for example, when questions of equity arise or when the debate turns on the loss of personal liberty for the benefit of the larger public welfare. The personal liberty issues range from controversies as diverse as gun control, freedom of religious practice, mandatory use of helmets for motorcycle riders, restrictions on private property rights, and actions to constrain possible terrorists. Indeed, they are a frequent subject of debate in nearly all areas in which government authority may impinge on individual rights.

Most policy debates resemble the battles over energy policy in 2008; they involve multiple and competing criteria. Policymakers and analysts want policy action to be effective, but they also want to minimize costs, or to promote the most equitable solution, or to maintain individual rights. It is a rare policy action that can maximize each of these criteria simultaneously. Those concerned with public policy must therefore figure out which criteria are most important and use those preferences to rank policy alternatives from best to worst. In a more formal exercise, policy analysts might assign weights to each of the various criteria to reflect their relative importance. Then multiple criteria can be used at the same time to assess the attractiveness of different policy options. A brief discussion of the most frequently used criteria should clarify their meanings and suggest how they might be used in policy analysis.

Effectiveness

The need for the effectiveness criterion is evident in the all-too-frequent complaints about the failure of government programs. Analysts and policymakers speak of what does and does not work, about policy success and the lack of it. In a narrow sense, effectiveness refers to reaching the stated goals and objectives. For a program already in existence, evaluation of its effectiveness usually turns on whether it has achieved the expected results or policy outcomes. For example, is the Clean Air Act improving air quality? Has a city's use of school vouchers raised the quality of education (see chapter 10)? Or do federally funded abstinence-only programs to prevent teenage pregnancy—which have been enthusiastically backed by conservatives—actually produce measurable benefits? Nonpartisan analyses suggest that they do not, and as a result states increasingly are turning down federal funds offered for these programs.[4]

Assessments like these require that analysts develop suitable indicators or measurements for the specified outcomes. For a proposed policy rather than an existing program, they try to estimate the likelihood that such goals and objectives would be attained if the proposal were adopted. For example, policymakers at both the federal and state level have proposed a number of seemingly strong measures to combat junk e-mail or spam. Most of us would cheer any new policy of this kind that would actually work. But one obvious question regarding these proposals is just that: Will they be effective in limiting spam, which by one recent count totals over one hundred billion messages each day, and in some areas constitutes more than 90 percent of Internet traffic?[5] There are many reasons to doubt their efficacy. Indeed, a year after a major federal antispam law was adopted, the frequency of junk e-mail actually increased.[6]

The view of effectiveness we summarize here is a little narrow, however, because programs usually have multiple goals and objectives and may succeed at some and fall short on others. Moreover, some objectives may be attainable only over a long period of time, making assessment of short-term outcomes problematic. Another limitation is that estimating the probability that a proposal will be effective, or more effective than the present policy, requires a forecast of future conditions and events, an uncertain activity at best. In addition, analysts must learn to deal with a political environment in which politicians often exaggerate the weaknesses of current programs and tout the strengths of alternatives based more on ideological beliefs than any assessment of empirical evidence of program effectiveness.

On the plus side, the federal Government Performance and Results Act of 1993 requires regular evaluations of all existing programs and demonstrations of their performance or achievements. The act encourages agencies to focus on results, service quality, and public satisfaction, and it mandates annual performance plans and reports. The political mood in Washington, D.C., and across the nation creates a strong expectation that new policy proposals be able to meet the same standards of effectiveness as policies already in place or improve upon them. The economic downturn of 2008 and the subsequent soaring federal deficit and national debt strongly reinforce these expectations at both the federal and state levels. With scarce budgetary dollars, policymakers are likely to be attentive to program effectiveness. Analysts who evaluate policy proposals in terms of likely effectiveness or who try to measure the achievements of existing programs therefore find a ready audience for their assessments.

Costs, Benefits, and Efficiency

If policy effectiveness is nearly universally expected in contemporary policymaking, so too is an interest in keeping the cost of government programs within reason. Whether efficiency is a specific measurement of costs in relation to benefits or gaining the most benefits for a fixed cost, the criterion amounts to the same thing. It strongly encourages analysts to think about the overall costs and benefits of existing programs and the various proposals to change them or substitute something different.

Essentially, efficiency is a way of justifying government action on the basis of economic concepts. Sometimes efficiency is expressed in terms of the relative virtues of government intervention and the operation of a free market in promoting societal welfare. As we discussed in chapter 1, government involvement may be called for when the market economy cannot adequately protect the public's well-being, for example, from crime, threats to national security, or urban air pollution. Efficiency is prized in the United States. As Deborah Stone (2002, 61) says, it is "an idea that dominates contemporary American discourse about public policy." Its role reflects the high value Americans place on a smoothly functioning market economy and the promotion of economic well-being.

The logic of efficiency in the allocation of scarce government resources is compelling. From an economist's perspective, fiscal resources must be used to best meet human needs—in other words, to increase the well-being of members of society. When the costs of programs are greater than the benefits, the possible alternative uses of the labor, capital, and materials are foregone, depriving society of their value (Patton and Sawicki 1993; Weimer and Vining 2005). Thus, if the government spends more on one activity—for example, prescription drug expenses under

Medicare—than is needed to gain the benefits of the action—better health for senior citizens—it will have fewer resources for other services, such as public education and national defense. A striking case that illustrates the argument came to light in late 2005 in a *New York Times* exposé of the New York State Medicaid program. The state's Medicaid spending on prescription drugs had doubled within five years, rising to $3.8 billion in 2005, in part because the state was unwilling to constrain the soaring costs of prescription drugs. As reporter Michael Luo put it, "New York lacks even the most basic controls that dozens of other states and private health insurers have used." [7] Among other examples of wasteful spending, the state was paying millions of dollars for prescription drugs for which far cheaper over-the-counter

With rising gasoline prices and the high cost of owning a car, particularly in urban areas, many people are using mass transit, ride sharing, walking, and biking as alternatives. Governments are supporting these developments by increasing spending on mass transit and encouraging the use of bicycles. These SmartBikes, shown at a station in Washington, D.C., in August 2008, are available to individuals who purchase an annual subscription and are then returned to the station for others to use. Those who subscribe to the service (for about $40 per year) have unlimited access to the bikes. The program is modeled after similar ones in Europe that have proved to be enormously popular.

equivalents were available. It was also paying for some expensive drugs that experts said were largely ineffective and rarely approved for use in other states.

As the Medicaid spending example illustrates, application of the principle of promoting efficiency can be difficult, yet it is by no means impossible. Consider another example. In 2008 the federal Centers for Disease Control and Prevention found that the job productivity lost because of premature deaths from smoking amounted to $97 billion, and that the nation's medical costs related to smoking were some $96 billion, for a total cost of $193 billion annually due to smoking. It also reported that 438,000 people in the United States die prematurely from smoking or exposure to secondhand smoke, and another 8.6 million have a serious illness caused by smoking.[8] Should government do more to restrict smoking to reduce these costs, particularly to lower the rate of smoking among young people? Or should smokers be left alone to make their own choices? During the 2000s, many states raised cigarette taxes, in part to discourage smoking and in part to raise revenue to offset budget deficits. The national average cost for a pack of cigarettes, counting all taxes, rose to about $5 in 2009 but in New York City new taxes drove the price higher than $9 a pack.[9]

Calculating these kinds of social benefits and costs is not always easy, particularly when they must be expressed in dollar terms, although economists have developed a number of methods for doing so, as we will see later in the chapter. One could ask, for example, how analysts might estimate the economic and social advantages of illegal immigration as well as the costs that such immigration imposes on the United States and on the nations from which immigrants come. Can it be done? Should it be done? We can appreciate that putting a dollar value on costs and benefits in this case can be a challenge intellectually and politically. But what about a qualitative consideration? Either way, making the costs and benefits of policy action more explicit and more understandable should contribute to making smarter choices simply because the public and policymakers can be better informed.

Critics of the use of efficiency as a criterion argue that one important constraint is the fact that benefits and costs are not equally distributed among the population. Often, the benefits of policies such as agricultural subsidies or subsidized tuition for college students go to particular groups in the population, but all taxpayers bear the costs. For regulatory policies, such as controls on polluting power plants, the larger society receives the benefits, but the corporate owners of the plant and the stockholders bear the costs. The implication of this critique is that analysts need to inquire into the distribution of benefits and costs as part of any attempt to examine economic efficiency and its acceptability. This is a subject addressed in the next section, about equity.

In fact, no matter what reservations are expressed about using the efficiency criterion in policy analysis and decision making, political reality dictates that it be addressed in some form. The smart analyst can find ways to do so that are reasonable and fair. Moreover, the great weight placed on policy costs today opens the door for creative ways to get policymakers and the public to think about the consequences of proposals under consideration. Actions that seem justifiable on some grounds might appear far less desirable once the costs of action are taken into account.

Equity

The term *equity* has at least two different meanings in contemporary policy debates: process equity and outcomes (end-result) equity. The first refers to the decision-making process that is used. Is it voluntary, open, and fair to all participants? If so, analysts and citizens might judge the results to be equitable even if some people ultimately fare better than others by gaining benefits such as higher education, better jobs, greater income, nicer houses, and so forth. This view is often associated with the political philosopher Robert Nozick and his book *Anarchy, State, and Utopia* (1974). Those who hold these views tend to believe strongly in the rights of individuals and the freedom to use and dispose of their resources as they see fit. They resist government efforts to promote equality beyond assuring equal opportunity to participate in society's decisions. As this description suggests, political conservatives identify strongly with the concept of process equity.

John Rawls promoted quite a different conception of equity, particularly in his book *A Theory of Justice* (1971). Rawls argued that equity or fairness refers to just outcomes or the fair distribution of societal goods such as wealth, income, or political power. His reasoning is that political institutions and social structures, such as racism and other forms of discrimination, affect the achievement of such goods. In other words, the acquisition of societal goods is not solely a function of the individual qualities of ambition, talent, and a strong work ethic. People who hold this view are more likely than others to favor government intervention to promote the equitable distribution of society's resources. Political liberals tend to identify with the concept of outcomes equity.

Equity criteria are likely to be central to any consideration of redistributive policies, such as tax reform, welfare reform, efforts to enhance access to education or health services, and assistance to the poor. They may also crop up in other policy areas where the debate and decisions turn on who gains and who loses as a consequence of policy action. The policy analyst might want to ask who receives the benefits of policy action, who does not, and who pays for the costs of the program. *Who* in this context means not individuals, but different groups or categories of people. They can be wealthy, middle class, or poor; city dwellers or suburbanites; ordinary people or huge corporations. Equity issues are pervasive in policy disputes, from tax reform proposals to actions that might restrict access to higher education—such as raising tuition levels.

In 2002, for example, the Republican-controlled U.S. House of Representatives voted to make permanent a 2001 decision to temporarily repeal the estate tax, a federal tax on property that is imposed when the owner dies and paid by the heirs to the estate. The estate tax, also sometimes called a "death tax," was repealed as part of the negotiated tax cuts made early in the George W. Bush administration in 2001, but the repeal was slated to expire in 2010. Making the tax repeal permanent will be costly to the federal government, and by some standards its effect can be considered inequitable.

Democratic analysts, for example, said the repeal would cost the U.S. Treasury about $740 billion from 2010 to 2020, with most of the benefits going to the very wealthy at a time when the government will need additional resources to provide for health care and retirement benefits to the baby boom generation, among other expenses. They criticized the estate tax repeal as fiscally irresponsible as well as unfair to the average taxpayers who will have to make up the difference in lost revenue. Some of the nation's wealthiest citizens, such as Microsoft founder Bill Gates and other members of a group called Responsible Wealth, supported that view. They argued that the estate tax should remain to avoid the buildup of "heredity wealth," which they believe will harm democracy. Republicans and many conservative analysts argued, in contrast, that there was little sense in having the estate tax reimposed in 2010 after a period of repeal. Why eliminate the tax for only a short period of time, which could confuse estate planning and lead to unfair impacts on different groups in the population?[10] Supporters of the repeal also defended it in terms of the benefits for the heirs to family farms and small businesses who find themselves capital-rich but cash-poor.

Those favoring action on the estate tax short of its full repeal, such as raising the amount of an estate that would be exempt from the tax, could find some comfort in certain Internal Revenue Service (IRS) studies. IRS data indicate that only about 2 percent of estates were subject to the tax in 1999, when the exemption was only $650,000. Moreover, half of the estate taxes collected in 1999 came from only 3,300 estates, or 0.16 percent of the total. One economist who examined the impact of the estate tax in recent years concluded that the widely circulated stories of "family farms and businesses broken up to pay the estate tax are basically rural legends; hardly any real examples have been found, despite diligent searching." [11] With the level of estates to be subject to the tax rising to $2 million in 2006, and set to rise to $3.5 million in 2009, even fewer estates would face any tax at all.[12] Many members of Congress argued that these limits could be raised to deal with the burdens the estate tax places on families with farms or small businesses. Those who favored outright repeal of the estate tax, however, showed little interest in such a compromise. What is fair or equitable in this case? Is it fairer to repeal the estate tax or to leave it in place? Would raising the limit on estates that are subject to the tax represent a reasonable compromise between the competing arguments?

Some public policy alternatives historically have been evaluated using ethical criteria rather than economic efficiency, political feasibility, or other standards. Government support of stem cell research and use of the death penalty are examples of this. This photo shows people in Paris, France, holding banners reading, "Halt to the death penalty" as they attend a July 2008 protest to denounce the death penalty in the United States. By 2009 a number of U.S. states—including Colorado, Kansas, Maryland, Montana, Nebraska, New Hampshire, and New Mexico—were considering ending use of the death penalty not so much on ethical grounds but rather because of the cost involved. The high cost is largely attributable to expensive prosecution requirements and mandatory and lengthy appeals.

Ethics and Political Values

In a classic essay on the role of principles in policy analysis, political theorist Charles W. Anderson (1979, 173) argued that there are "certain fundamental considerations that must be accounted for in any policy evaluation." This "repertoire of basic concepts" includes "authority, the public interest, rights, justice, equality and efficiency." They are, Anderson said, not simply an analyst's preferences but "*obligatory* criteria of political judgment."

In the practical world of policy analysis, some of Anderson's requisite criteria or standards of policy judgment are likely to be ignored. Indeed, some political scientists argue that it is unnecessary or even improper for policy analysts to include ethical or normative dimensions in their work. They say this in part because they think ethics and normative values, such as liberty or equality, are beyond the bounds of rational analysis. Or it may be that they believe analysts are incapable of objective analysis because they inevitably inject their personal biases into any such assessment. Some also argue that analysis of normative values is unnecessary because the political process exists to address and resolve ethical and value disputes (Amy

1984). An easy rejoinder to the last argument is that explicit analysis of ethics and values could greatly enhance the quality of argument and debate in policy-making bodies. No doubt, it is easier for analysts to stress criteria such as effectiveness and efficiency, where an assessment can be based on hard data such as measurable costs and benefits. Normative issues, however, deserve serious consideration. As Anderson (1979) argues, analysis that ignores basic issues such as the role of government authority, individual rights, or the public interest is incomplete and inadequate.

Policy debates over privacy, property rights, copyright laws, research on human stem cells derived from embryos, and many other contemporary issues clearly require an assessment in terms of normative and legal criteria, not just economics. Even for a seemingly technical subject such as nuclear waste disposal, it is both possible and necessary to analyze ethical issues such as the effects on future generations, whether it is fair for governments to offer monetary compensation to communities if they agree to host a waste repository, and how much public involvement in decision making should be required (Kraft 2000; Shrader-Frechette 1993; Weiss 1990).

As this review of evaluative criteria indicates, there are many different bases on which to analyze policy. Students of public policy should be aware of the range of standards that are applied and alert to their strengths and limits and the trade-offs between them. Sometimes, promoting the public's welfare, for example, through food safety or environmental protection policies, imposes a cost on individuals and corporations. Restrictions on their freedom or liberty may be justified by the public's gains. Conversely, at times the protection of individual rights and liberties is so important that society is willing to tolerate activity that many find abhorrent. Thus Internet pornography is protected because of the First Amendment's free speech guarantees, and the Constitution extends elaborate protections to those accused of criminal behavior, even for horrific crimes such as serial murder or terrorism.

The use of diverse evaluative criteria can help in another way. Too often policymakers, analysts, and commentators make statements that reflect their strong ideological beliefs when they discuss pending policy choices. Liberals know what they like and dislike and apply those philosophical standards to the full range of contemporary policies, and conservatives do the same, although both sides would have much to gain from dispassionate assessments of current government programs and proposed policies. An objective analysis of this kind could be grounded in one or more of the evaluative criteria described in this chapter. Doing so does not mean that citizens and policymakers need to abandon their convictions about what government should or should not be doing. Rather, it means that they ought to be sure they have the facts about a given issue, be it school vouchers, gun control, or health care alternatives, and that they think about a range of considerations in addition to their personal values and policy beliefs. They will have an easier time defending the position they take, and the policy positions they endorse will stand a better chance of success.

USING THE METHODS OF POLICY ANALYSIS

This last section of the chapter surveys the most frequently used methods of policy analysis and highlights their strengths and most significant weaknesses or limitations. The suggested reading list at the end of the chapter provides substantial coverage of analytic methods. Those wishing to read further will find this list a good place to start. The leading methods of policy analysis draw heavily from economics and focus on the evaluative criterion of efficiency, particularly for cost-benefit and cost-effectiveness analyses (Weimer and Vining 2005; Dunn 2004). The ideas found in these and related methods are useful even for nontechnical analysis. The methods are tools for critical thinking about public policy that anyone can use.

By now, however, it should be clear that public policy evaluation is about more than economics. It is also about effectiveness, equity, liberty, and, fundamentally, about politics. As stated earlier, analytic methods can be used to clarify problems and policy choices, but decisions about which policies to adopt or maintain are up to policymakers and, ultimately, up to the public that elects them.

The overview of analytic methods that follows groups them into four categories. One is economic approaches that include cost-benefit analysis, cost-effectiveness analysis, and risk assessment methods. Another is decision making and impacts, which includes forecasting and impact assessment. A third is political and institutional analysis, which includes assessment of political feasibility as well as policy implementation and program evaluation. The last category is ethical analysis, where the concern is consideration of the ethics of policy action.

ECONOMIC APPROACHES

As discussed earlier in the chapter, economic analysis pervades the study of public policy, and for good reason (Weimer and Vining 2005). Public policies can be expensive, and in ways that are sometimes not so obvious to the public and policymakers. Use of economic approaches can help us understand the real costs of government programs and the trade-offs involved in choosing one policy alternative over another. As we have seen, however, economic analysis also has its critics, who worry that too much emphasis can be placed on the dollar value of government action and too little on what they see as the necessity of addressing some public needs regardless of cost. A review of the most frequently used economic approaches is helpful for appreciating both the strengths and limitations of such methods.

Cost-Benefit Analysis

Most readers are already familiar with **cost-benefit analysis,** also called benefit-cost analysis, and they use the techniques even if they do not use the terms. When a high school senior decides which college to attend, he or she probably makes a list of the advantages and disadvantages of each important option. One college offers a stronger program in the student's area of interest, but it is expensive. Another is affordable but falls a little short on the number of courses in the anticipated major. In addition, the student considers the differences in the range of campus activities, housing, sports facilities, and other qualities of college life. How to make this decision? The student, probably with the help of a counselor and parents, weighs the advantages and disadvantages of each, perhaps writing them down in several columns to compare the choices. Cost-benefit analysis is simply a more systematic method for doing the same thing.

One economist described cost-benefit analysis as follows:

> It seeks to determine if the aggregate of the gains that accrue to those made better off is greater than the aggregate of losses to those made worse off by the policy choice. The gains and losses are both measured in dollars, and are defined as the sums of each individual's willingness to pay to receive the gains or to prevent the policy-imposed losses. If the gains exceed the losses, the policy should be accepted according to the logic of benefit-cost analysis (Freeman 2000, 192).

He added that in some respects cost-benefit analysis is "nothing more than organized common sense," even if the term usually refers to a more narrowly defined and technical calculation.

The usefulness of thinking in terms of what public policies and programs cost and what society gets from them should be clear enough. Consider the enormous costs inflicted by Hurricane Katrina in 2005. Over 1,300 people lost their lives, and many thousands lost their homes and businesses, suffered pain or trauma, or had their lives otherwise uprooted. The economic impact on both New Orleans and the nation was substantial, and it continued for some time. In addition, highways, utilities, schools, and other public structures in New Orleans and other cities had to be rebuilt at considerable expense. What would it have taken to provide greater protection for the New Orleans area by building stronger flood levees and improving the city's emergency preparedness capacity? Surely a great deal less than $100 billion. Most estimates were in the range of a few billion dollars. Indeed, following Katrina, one expert on cost-benefit analysis, Harvard economist W. Kip Viscusi, said the comparison of costs and benefits "was not a close call." Instead, it was "a no-brainer that you do this," meaning to invest in a much larger flood-prevention effort.[13]

Short of Category Five hurricanes, there are plenty of examples of routine policy decisions that are equally instructive on the value of thinking about costs and benefits. Consider this one. The U.S. Air Force's B-2 stealth bomber is a marvel of high technology capable of delivering precision bombs to distant targets, but it has been problem-prone from its beginning. In addition to costing $2.2 billion each in total development costs, B-2 bombers are among the most expensive planes to maintain. The air force has been spending $150 million per year in maintenance costs on *each* of the bombers. It employs a thousand workers to keep the fleet of twenty-one bombers ready for service. Despite this huge investment, the average B-2 bomber has been available for combat duty only about 30 percent of the time, well short of the air force target of 60 percent availability.[14] After years of operating without a major accident, in February 2008 a B-2 bomber crashed shortly after takeoff from Andersen Air Force Base in Guam, a loss valued at $1.2 billion—a figure the air force uses as its estimate of each plane's cost. Is the B-2 a good use of defense dollars? Could the money be better spent on other aircraft or different defense programs? Many supporters of the military argue strongly in favor of the B-2 because of its unique and essential capabilities, and they do not dwell on the aircraft's cost or reliability problems. Critics of the B-2 focus on the costs and its poor reliability and tend to ignore its distinctive military advantages. Which of the two groups makes the stronger argument?

Conducting a cost-benefit analysis is relatively straightforward in theory. The analyst (1) identifies all the important long-term and short-term costs and benefits; (2) measures the

CONDUCTING A COST-BENEFIT ANALYSIS

Conducting a cost-benefit analysis can be a fairly simple or quite complicated process, depending on the issue. In general, an analyst completes the following procedure:

1. Tries to identify all of the important costs and benefits;
2. Measures those costs and benefits that can be expressed in dollar terms and either estimates or acknowledges those that cannot be measured easily;
3. Adjusts the measurements for changes in value over time;
4. Sums up and compares all the costs and benefits and concludes whether the costs outweigh the benefits or vice versa.

Let us apply these steps to a policy example.

1. Identify all important costs and benefits. Consider the U.S. federal gasoline tax, which is the lowest among the world's industrialized nations. Those who support raising it contend that doing so would yield many tangible benefits, among them lowering the country's dependence on imported oil. It would reduce urban air pollution and improve public health; reduce carbon dioxide

emissions and the risk of climate change; cut back on traffic congestion and drive time; and lessen traffic accidents, thereby saving lives and preventing injuries. A higher gas tax could yield all of these benefits and substantially increase government tax revenues by internalizing the social costs of driving and providing an incentive to people to drive fewer miles or seek alternative forms of transportation. Raising the gas tax, however, imposes direct costs on drivers and on a variety of services that depend on transportation, and it can have a particularly adverse impact on low- and moderate-income citizens who have few alternatives to using automobiles, and on those who live in sparsely populated areas where they are obliged to drive.

2. Measure those costs and benefits that can be expressed in dollar terms. Because a complete cost-benefit analysis of raising the gasoline tax can become exceedingly complicated, we consider a recent study that took on only part of the challenge. In a paper prepared for Resources for the Future (RFF), Ian Parry and Kenneth Small examined many of these costs in an effort to determine the "optimal" level for a gasoline tax in the United States. Although economists cannot easily measure all of the benefits noted, they have estimated that

tangible costs and benefits in monetary terms; (3) uses a discount rate, which adjusts for changes in value over time, to ensure that all are expressed in commensurable terms; (4) estimates the intangible or qualitative considerations; and (5) aggregates, or totals, the costs and benefits. This total is expressed in one of two ways: as the net benefit (benefits minus costs) or as the ratio of benefits to costs (the benefits divided by the costs). The box "Steps to Analysis: Conducting a Cost-Benefit Analysis" indicates how it is done. Public policy students might try to apply these methods to a particular problem—perhaps a current campus issue such as whether to expand parking lots or to provide incentives to students, faculty, and staff to use other means of transportation to reach the campus. In this particular case, thorough analysis suggests the virtue of trying to discourage automobile use on economic as well as environmental grounds (Toor and Havlick 2004).

the pollution damages amount to about 40 cents a gallon, the carbon dioxide emissions 6 cents a gallon (estimates vary widely here), traffic congestion about 70 cents a gallon on average, and traffic accidents at 60 cents a gallon, for a total of $1.76 a gallon. To take into account that gasoline taxes actually tax the fuel purchased as opposed to the distance that is traveled and some of the negative economic effects of raising fuel taxes, the analysts lowered this amount to about $1.00 per gallon (Parry 2002).

3. Adjust the measurements for changes in value over time. In this example, no such adjustment is made. All costs and benefits are assumed to apply to the present. Conceivably, however, one could make such adjustments for those benefits expected to come only in the future, such as the value of reducing expected climate change from buildup of carbon dioxide emissions. The adjacent text discusses how such "discounting" of future benefits is done.

4. Sum up and compare all the benefits and costs and conclude whether the costs outweigh the benefits or vice versa. The study reached its

conclusion about an optimal level of taxation without considering the economic costs of dependence on foreign oil, which another study estimated to be around 12 cents a gallon; the military costs of defending access to Middle Eastern oil fields; or the damage caused by the production, transportation, and use of gasoline—such as oil spills and leaking storage tanks. Some environmental groups have tried to estimate all of those effects and, not surprisingly, came out with a much higher total. Still, according to the RFF analysis, the $1.00 per gallon optimal tax that would internalize the major social costs is more than twice the average combined federal and state taxes on gasoline in the United States, which in 2002 totaled about 40 cents per gallon.

Would you change any of the major social costs considered in this analysis? Are there other costs and benefits that should be considered if the gasoline tax is to be raised? Do you think that economists can fairly estimate the dollar value of things like improved public health because of reduced air pollution or the value of time lost by those stuck in traffic? Does the conclusion of the study present a cogent argument for raising gasoline taxes?

Source: Ian W. H. Parry, "Is Gasoline Undertaxed in the United States?" *Resources* 148 (summer): 28–33.

Some of the limitations of cost-benefit analysis are evident even in the brief summary provided here and in the fuel-tax example used in the box. Determination of what costs and benefits are important enough to be included is in part a judgment call. Measuring them in monetary terms is easier for some costs and benefits than others. The analyst may emphasize costs because they are more identifiable and measurable. What the benefits turn out to be is less certain and may be realized only after a period of time. Economists often try to estimate **opportunity costs,** which refer to the value of opportunities that are forgone when time or resources are spent on a given activity. For example, being stuck in traffic imposes an opportunity cost on drivers because they could be doing something more productive with their time. Federal regulations that require companies to spend more than necessary on safety or environmental regulations impose an opportunity cost because this money might have been invested in additional research, plant modernization, enhanced employee benefits, and so forth.

Using a **discount rate** allows analysts to determine the value of future benefits today, but the choice of the rate, essentially an estimate of inflation over time, clearly can have a profound impact on the results. For example, consider the present value of $100 earned a hundred years from now with varying assumptions of a discount rate. At a 1 percent discount rate, that $100 is worth $36.97; at 2 percent, $13.80; at 3 percent, $5.20; and at 5 percent, only $0.76. As these calculations illustrate, distant benefits may be of minimal value in current dollars, and a cost-benefit analysis can therefore yield wildly different results depending on the rate selected.

Because the choice of a discount rate can have a great effect on how one appraises policy options, that choice underlies innumerable conflicts over government policy decisions, from protection against hurricanes like Katrina or efforts to reduce the risk of future climate change. The benefits of preventing damage from hurricanes or of slowing or halting global climate change are real and often substantial, but they occur so far in the future that discounting the benefits to today's values tends to minimize them in a cost-benefit calculation. In contrast, the costs of hurricane damage mitigation or dealing with climate change can be quite large, and they will be paid for in today's dollars. These complications lead economic analysts to suggest other methods for discounting in a responsible way that consider long-term costs and benefits.[15] Yet, as noted above, at least one calculation in the aftermath of Katrina did employ such discounting and nonetheless concluded that the benefits of a massive investment in disaster prevention could easily have been justified on economic grounds.[16]

Another vulnerable part of the process of cost-benefit analysis is the estimate of intangible human costs and benefits, such as well-being, aesthetic preferences, or even the value of a life. Some analysts choose not to include them at all in a cost-benefit analysis and instead highlight that omission in reporting the results. Others prefer to use available economic methods to estimate intangible or nonmarket values and then include them in the cost-benefit analysis. For example, economists use techniques known as **contingent valuation methods,** which are essentially questionnaires or interviews with individuals, designed to allow an estimate of the dollar value of the time spent stuck in traffic or the preservation of lakes or forests. If done well, such methods can provide a useful estimate of the value people attach to certain intangibles. The use of **sensitivity analysis** can minimize to some extent the weaknesses inherent in cost-benefit analysis. When the calculations are "sensitive" to a basic assumption such as the chosen discount rate, the analyst can report on several different rates, and the reader can choose the assumptions that seem most reasonable.

Even with its obvious limitations, cost-benefit analysis is a powerful tool that is widely used in government decision making. It forces analysts and policymakers to define what they expect government action to do (produce benefits) and to consider the costs associated with that action. If done properly, cost-benefit analysis can help justify public policy that might otherwise be ignored or challenged. Consider this example. During the 1980s the Environmental Protection Agency asked for a reduction in the amount of lead allowed in gasoline from 1.1 grams per gallon to 0.1 grams. The benefits of controlling lead in the environment include a reduction in adverse health and cognitive problems in children, a lowered level of high blood pressure and cardiovascular disease in adults, and reduced automobile maintenance costs. Not all of those benefits could be measured, but counting those that could produced a benefit-cost ratio of 10 to 1 (Freeman 2000, 194). That calculation helped gain approval for eliminating lead in gasoline despite opposition from automobile companies and oil refineries and the Ronald Reagan administration's concerns about the action.

Critics of cost-benefit analysis claim that the method can be abused if only some costs and benefits are considered and inappropriate measures are used to estimate their value (Stone 2002; Tong 1986). Their concerns are genuine, even though in the real world of policy debate, it is likely that analysts on both sides of the policy question will carefully scrutinize any cost-benefit analysis. Moreover, the Office of Management and Budget (OMB) has set out elaborate guidelines that federal government agencies are expected to follow for the conduct of such studies.

OMB's Office of Information and Regulatory Affairs (OIRA) has been in charge of this process since President Reagan's 1981 executive order mandating that economic analysis be used to justify proposed regulations. Each successive president has established a similar review process, albeit with differing guidelines and expectations, and the agencies have improved their ability to conduct them. Under legislation approved in 2000, OIRA is also charged with establishing guidelines for how agencies ensure the accuracy of the data on which regulations are based.[17] Despite these expectations and procedures, the public policy student should always ask about the underlying assumptions in a cost-benefit analysis and how the costs and benefits were estimated. As noted in several other examples, such as the ergonomics rule, estimates of a new government regulation's future costs often reveal very wide ranges, indicating that the analysts used quite different assumptions and calculations.

Cost-benefit analysis is used less in areas of public policy where such measurements are not readily available. Even in these areas, however, one could carry out a kind of qualitative cost-benefit analysis in which the important benefits and costs are listed and considered, but without an attempt to place a dollar value on them. Such an exercise might allow citizens, analysts, and policymakers to think comprehensively about the pros and cons of government policies for which they have either no dollar estimates of costs or only partial information.

Cost-Effectiveness Analysis

Sometimes the concerns about the ability to measure the benefits of a policy action are so significant that cost-benefit analysis is not useful. For example, many policies, such as health regulations, highway safety, or medical research, may prevent disease or devastating injury, or may save lives. But how do analysts place a dollar value on human life and health? Government agency officials and analysts, along with insurance companies, have methods for estimating how much a life is worth, even though many critics object in principle to making such calculations (Tong 1986). The advantage of **cost-effectiveness analysis** is that it requires no measurements of the value of intangible benefits such as human lives; it simply compares different policy alternatives that can produce these benefits in terms of their relative costs. That is, analysts are asking which actions can save the most human lives given a fixed dollar cost, or which dollar investments produce the greatest benefits.

For example, in the early 1990s Oregon created a prioritized list as part of the Oregon Health Plan, which chiefly serves the state's Medicaid beneficiaries. The plan ranked 709 medical procedures "according to their benefit to the entire population being served." Coverage was to be provided for all conditions that fell above a threshold on the list, and the state legislature was to determine the cut-off points each year on the basis of estimates for health care services and budget constraints. The state used a cost-benefit methodology to establish the list, consulting fifty physician panels and surveying the Oregon public. The choices were based on factors such as the likelihood that treatment would reduce suffering or prevent death, the cost of care, and the duration of benefits. In effect, the state was trying to determine how to get the greatest benefit to society from the limited resources available for health care. As might be expected, the state's innovative approach was highly controversial, and the federal government initially rejected it, but it later approved a modified form.[18] Is such a cost-effective approach to state health care benefits a good idea? What are its strengths and weaknesses?

Similar comparisons are also common in safety and environmental regulation, where the cost of the regulations in terms of lives that would be saved is often ten, one hundred, or even one thousand times greater than other actions that could be taken. In these circumstances, critics of regulation cite the wide disparities in costs to argue against the adoption of measures aimed at, for example, improving workplace safety or eliminating toxic chemicals from the environment. Or they suggest that the same benefits might be achieved by taking other, sometimes far cheaper, action (Huber 1999). One recent example concerns directives from the Federal Emergency Management Agency (FEMA) in 2004 that pressed cities and states in earthquake-prone areas, including Memphis and other communities close to the New Madrid seismic zone (located near parts of Arkansas, Illinois, Indiana, Kentucky, Mississippi, Missouri, and Tennessee) to set building construction standards comparable to those required in California. Yet according to critics, FEMA proposed the plan "with almost no consideration of costs and benefits," even though the risk of a major earthquake in this area was only one-tenth to one-third that of California's. The critics suggest that the same money invested in such health and safety measures as highway upgrades, flu shots, and heart defibrillators could save many more lives.[19]

Should government always choose the cheapest way to gain benefits? Consider the cost of producing electricity. If the government's goal is to minimize the cost of electricity, policymakers could favor all actions that keep these costs down, including extensive use of nuclear power and coal. Citizens, however, might find the consequences less desirable than cheap electricity. For example, in 2002 the Bush administration favored a change in government regulations that would permit coal companies in West Virginia to fill valleys and streams with rock and dirt from mountaintop mining because that is the cheapest method of slag removal. An alternative method is to haul away the debris and bring it back later to restore the mountain when the mining is finished. The companies defended their proposal as a way to reduce the cost of producing electricity in the region. Many local residents objected strenuously, even though the proposal would help provide jobs in a state that has long been among the nation's poorest. The new jobs would result from lowering coal-mining costs, making West Virginia more competitive with other mining states.

Risk Assessment

Risk assessment is a close relative of cost-benefit analysis. Its purpose is to identify, estimate, and evaluate the magnitude of the risk to citizens from exposure to various situations such as terrorism, natural hazards such as hurricanes, or radiation from nuclear waste. Reducing risks conveys a benefit to the public, and this benefit can be part of the calculation in a cost-benefit analysis. But societal risks vary widely in their magnitude, and that is the reason to try to identify and measure them; the more significant risks presumably should receive a higher priority for government action. Risks are associated with many activities in daily life, such as driving a car, flying in an airplane, consuming certain foods, smoking cigarettes, drinking alcohol, and skiing down a mountain, among others. Most of life's risks are fairly minor and not especially alarming, although people may worry a great deal about some of them, such as hazardous waste, toxic chemicals, and radiation.

Consider this example of risk assessment. In late 2002 the Federal Aviation Administration (FAA) proposed a new regulation that would require airlines to build safer seats to reduce the risk of severe injury or death in the event of an accident. Under the proposal, the airlines would have fourteen years to develop and install the new seats, at an estimated cost of $519 million. The seats would have better belts, improved headrests, and stronger anchors to hold them to the aircraft floor under the stress of an accident. The FAA's risk assessment indicated that the new seats would prevent an estimated 114 deaths and 133 serious injuries in the twenty years after the regulation took effect.[20] Was the FAA's risk assessment reasonable? Is it possible to project accident rates, injuries, and deaths over twenty years when the technology of aircraft design and other elements in aviation safety, not just the seat design, are likely to change?

Some examples of risk analysis are simpler to understand and judge. In 2004 the National Highway Traffic Safety Administration (NHTSA) proposed a major change in side-impact crash standards for cars and trucks. The automobile industry was already moving toward a voluntary commitment to equip most new vehicles with side-impact protection, and many luxury cars already have the added protection. But NHTSA wanted to speed up the change and make the standards mandatory. It estimated that adding side airbags to cars would save seven hundred to one thousand lives a year but cost the automobile industry between $1.6 billion and $3.6 billion, presumably with most of the expense passed along to consumers.[21] Was this a reasonable action to protect the American public?

Risk assessments of this kind are widely used today in part because of public fears of certain technological risks and the adoption of public policies to control or reduce these risks. Workplace safety and food safety are two examples. Risk assessments are also prepared to estimate and respond to national security risks, such as terrorist attacks or other threats to the United States. Based on such assessments George Tenet, then CIA director, testified before Congress in late 2002 that, despite the expenditure of vast sums of money and a greatly expanded government effort to combat terrorism, the risk of another domestic attack was as serious as it had been before the September 11 aircraft hijackings.[22] Throughout the cold war period, from the late 1940s to about 1990, defense and security analysts regularly made assessments of the risk of nuclear war and other security threats. They continue to conduct similar studies today.

Risk is usually defined as the magnitude of adverse consequences of an event or exposure. As noted, the event may be an earthquake, flood, car accident, nuclear power plant accident, or terrorist attack, and an exposure could come through contaminated food, water, or air, or from being in or near a building or other structure under attack (Andrews 2006b; Lowrance 1976; Perrow 2007). The public's concern about risk has deepened in recent years as the media has increased its coverage of these situations. Books on this topic seem to sell well, another indicator of public concern.[23]

Professionals view risk as a product of the probability that the event or exposure will occur and the consequences that follow if it does. It can be expressed in the equation $R = P \times C$. The higher the probability of the event or exposure (P), or the higher the consequences (C), the higher the risk. Some risks, such as an airplane crash, have a low probability of occurring but high consequences if they do. Others, such as a broken leg from a skiing accident, have a higher probability but lower consequences. People tend to fear high-consequence events even if their probability is very low, because they focus on what *might* happen more than on its likelihood. Partly for this reason, there is often a substantial difference between experts and the lay public in their perception of risks. Public fear of nuclear power and nuclear waste (which experts tend to think are small risks) is a good example (Slovic 1987). But people also underestimate much more significant risks, including climate change, natural disasters, and medical calamities such as pandemics.[24] Even experts sometimes seriously misjudge risks, as the National Aeronautics and Space Administration (NASA) did in managing the space shuttle program. After two catastrophic accidents, in 2005 NASA recalculated the risk of a major failure during a space shuttle mission using probabilistic risk assessment that combined actual flight experience, computer simulations, and expert judgment. It put the risk at a very high 1 in 100.[25]

The tendency of people to misjudge the probability of various events is evident in the purchase of lottery tickets. When the Powerball jackpot rose to about $240 million at one point in 2005, people turned out in droves to buy tickets, even though Powerball hopefuls were forty times more likely to die from falling out of bed than to win even a portion of the lottery jackpot. The odds of winning the full amount were less than 80 million to 1, while the risk of dying by falling out of bed was 2 million to 1. The risk of dying in an automobile accident was enormous in comparison, at 5,000 to 1.[26] People also greatly underestimate risks associated with the U.S. food supply. The Centers for Disease Control and Prevention reported in 2005 that the nation experiences seventy-six million food-related illnesses each year and five thousand deaths.[27]

If risk assessment is the use of different methods to identify risks and estimate their probability and severity of harm, **risk evaluation** is a determination of the acceptability of the risks or a decision about what level of safety is desired. Typically, higher levels of safety, or lower risk, cost more to achieve. **Risk management** describes what governments or other organizations do to deal with risks, such as adopting public policies to regulate them (Presidential/Congressional Commission on Risk Assessment and Risk Management 1997).

Analysts use many different methods to conduct risk assessments, and they range from estimating the likelihood of industrial accidents to calculating how much radioactivity is likely to leak from a nuclear waste repository over thousands of years. For some assessments, such as the risk of automobile accidents or the likely injury to children from deployment of airbags during an accident, the task is relatively easy because plenty of data exist on the actual experience of drivers, vehicles, and airbag deployment. As a result, insurance companies can figure out how much to charge for car insurance once they know the age of the driver, what kind of car it is, and where and how far it is driven each day. For other estimates, the lack of experience means that analysts must depend on mathematical modeling and computer projections, for example, to project the risk of climate change and the consequences for society if average temperatures rise, rainfall patterns shift, or severe storms occur more frequently.

As with cost-benefit analysis, conservatives and business interests tend to strongly favor the use of risk assessment methods for domestic policy conflicts. They believe that many risks that government regulates are exaggerated and that further study will show they are not worth the often considerable cost to society (Wildavsky 1988; Huber 1999). It is equally likely, however, that risk assessments will identify genuine and serious risks to public health and welfare that merit public policy action.

Many risks also involve a difficult balancing act when it comes to government intervention or even personal choice. An issue that rose to prominence after the September 11 attacks was the risk of bioterrorism, particularly in light of the anthrax scare of late 2001. Experts knew that, even though smallpox had been eradicated from the world as a communicable disease, small stocks of the virus still existed and might fall into the hands of terrorists. Under this scenario, would it be a good idea to vaccinate the U.S. public against smallpox, without evidence that such an attack is likely to occur? Does the small risk of exposure warrant mass vaccinations, or should the nation wait until there is at least one verified case of smallpox before initiating a huge medical campaign? The cost of the vaccinations is not the only issue here; another is the concern about unnecessarily alarming the U.S. public and subjecting people to the risk of the vaccine's serious side-effects. When the smallpox vaccination was still mandatory in the United States (prior to 1972), it killed several children each year and left others with brain damage.[28] Recent estimates suggest that if the entire nation were vaccinated, between two hundred and five hundred people would die from the vaccine, and thousands more would become severely ill.[29]

What should policymakers and citizens do about the smallpox risk and the vaccination question? In 2002 public health scientists recommended that the health care and emergency workers most at risk of exposure to the virus—the so-called early responders in the case of a suspected smallpox case—be vaccinated. The general public would be vaccinated only if an outbreak occurred. The idea was to minimize the public's risk of an adverse reaction to the vaccine, but the public would remain unprotected, at least initially. Is this proposal a good idea? What are its limitations and its benefits?[30]

The great loss of life and severe property damage inflicted by Hurricane Katrina in New Orleans and other Gulf Coast areas in late August 2005 also illustrate the policy challenges of risk assessment and risk management. How much more should state and local governments do to try to anticipate the risks of natural hazards such as hurricanes, earthquakes, and floods? If emergency preparedness officials and others are able to forecast such events, and thus provide some basis for judging the severity of possible risks, what obligations do the various levels of government have to protect their citizens? In retrospect, many state and local officials in the Gulf states in 2005, and many in the federal government as well, either did not pay sufficient attention to the risk of major hurricanes in the area, or they failed to implement adequate disaster preparedness measures. Even when the levees in New Orleans collapsed after Katrina struck the city, responsible officials in Louisiana and in Washington, D.C., did not act quickly enough. Warnings about flood waters entering the city were misunderstood or ignored. The consequences in the case of Katrina and a later storm, Rita, were tragic because most of the loss of life and damage could have been prevented with better planning and a more timely response to the flooding. That need still exists because forecasts suggest that the intensity of the 2005 hurricanes may be repeated in future years.

DECISION MAKING AND IMPACTS

Throughout the text we have emphasized the centrality of decision making in the study of public policy. The methods discussed in this section focus on formal ways to model the choices that

The severe recession of 2008–2009 produced unusual and difficult demands on federal policymakers, including how to respond to requests by failing industries for government assistance. After numerous and costly federal bailouts of financial institutions, policymakers and the public became more skeptical about industry appeals for aid. Nowhere was this resistance more evident than with renewed requests by the U.S. auto industry for federal loans. Shown here, left to right, are then chair and CEO of General Motors Richard Wagoner, United Auto Workers president Ron Gettelfinger, president and CEO of the Ford Motor Company Alan Mulally, and chair and CEO of Chrysler LLC Robert Nardelli testifying before the Senate Banking, Housing, and Urban Affairs Committee on December 4, 2008, on behalf of a $34 billion bailout for the U.S. auto industry. The executives had returned to Capitol Hill after their initial efforts were rebuffed amid public outcry over their extravagant salaries and lavish corporate spending, including flying to Washington in private corporate jets.

policymakers face as well as techniques to consider how information about possible future events can be brought into the decision-making process. By introducing new perspectives and information in this way, the hope is that policymakers and the public can better determine which policy alternatives hold the most promise.

Forecasting

In chapter 5 we discussed the logic of forecasting in terms of understanding how present problems, such as public demand for Social Security and Medicare benefits, might change over time as the number of senior citizens increases. We also referred to it just above in our discussion of the risk of hurricanes striking the Gulf Coast states. Forecasting can be defined as "a procedure for producing factual information about future states of society on the basis of prior information about policy problems" (Dunn 2004, 130). That is, forecasting methods allow analysts to anticipate what the future is likely to hold based on their understanding of current conditions and how they expect them to change over time. This information can be exceptionally valuable because public problems are dynamic, not static. In other words, when policymakers aim at public problems, they face a moving target.

In the cases of Social Security and Medicare, each program produces annual reports that include updated estimates of future demand for these services as well as estimates of the economic gap between the cost of providing the services and the expected revenues to cover those costs. Agency officials and other experts say both programs face enormous shortfalls in the future. They also argue that making long-term forecasts that look ahead seventy-five years, even with some degree of uncertainty, is essential to provide critical information for policymakers.[31]

For example, the population of the United States was about 305 million in late 2008, but what will it be in twenty-five or fifty years? The U.S. Census Bureau (www.census.gov) has a population clock that reports continuously on the changing U.S. and global populations. It also offers several different projections of the nation's future population. All of those projections depend on a series of assumptions about the average number of children each woman is likely to have, the rate of immigration, and other factors. The bureau offers three different scenarios, with alternate assumptions. The medium projection is most widely cited, and it indicates that the United States has been growing by about 1 percent a year. At that rate, the bureau has estimated a U.S. population of 357 million in 2025 and 439 million in 2050.[32] Cities and states that are growing more rapidly than the nation as a whole (for example, Arizona, California, Florida, and Nevada) find their specific forecasts helpful in determining how to cope with the anticipated demand for public services.

Projections of what is usually called geometric or exponential growth, such as population growth, are fairly easy once one knows the rate of growth. It is the same equation used to determine compound interest: $A_n = P (1 + i)^n$, where A is the amount being projected, n is the number of years, P is the initial amount, and i is the rate of growth. The formula is quite handy for determining how much a given amount will grow in one, five, or ten years. A savings account deposit of $100 ($P$) that grows at 3 percent a year will be worth $103 after one year, $116 at the end of five years, and $134 after ten years. To consider a different example, to determine how much a house that is now valued at $200,000 will cost in ten years, one need only decide what the rate of annual increase is likely to be (3 percent? 5 percent? 8 percent?) and the formula will provide an answer: at a 5 percent annual rate of increase, the house will cost $326,000 in ten years. As these examples illustrate, even a small rate of annual increase can produce great changes over time.[33]

Most forecasting is more involved than the examples provided here, but the principles are the same. Forecasting can include a variety of quantitative methods, such as econometric models for estimating future economic growth and job creation. Qualitative, or intuitive, methods are also widely used. These include brainstorming, the so-called Delphi method of asking experts to estimate future conditions, scenario development, and even simple monitoring of trends that looks for signs of change (Patton and Sawicki 1993; Starling 1988).

As one might guess, whether quantitative or qualitative, forecasting methods are necessarily limited by available data, the validity of the basic assumptions made in projecting the future from present conditions, and how far out the projection goes. A look backward to earlier forecasts is sobering.[34] Quite often the futurists have been dead wrong in their projections, sometimes spectacularly so. Population biologist Paul Ehrlich in his 1968 book *The Population Bomb* forecast global famine and exhaustion of natural resources within decades if uncontrolled population growth continued. Other examples abound. During the 1970s, electric power companies believed that energy demand would grow indefinitely at 6 percent to 7 percent a year. They planned for and built power plants that turned out not to be needed, in some cases driving the power companies into bankruptcy. In a strikingly wrong, but telling, statement about the future, in 1899 the head of the U.S. Patent Office suggested that everything important had already been invented.

Lest we think that forecasts about technological change are inevitably better today, it is worth noting that even as late as 1990, few analysts anticipated the explosive demand for home personal computers. Development of the Internet throughout the 1990s was a major reason for that rapid growth, as were falling computer prices and the development of easy-to-use Web browsers. Even in the business community, where the ability to make such forecasts is essential for a company's success, hundreds of major firms and thousands of start-up companies greatly overestimated the demand for Internet business services, and many did not survive the dot-com implosion of the late 1990s. A more recent example is the failure of the major automobile companies to anticipate higher fuel costs and greatly reduced public demand for trucks and sport utility vehicles, a change so great that, combined with a recession and tight credit markets, threatened their very existence as corporations. To compensate for these kinds of egregious fore-casting errors, most analysts recommend using a number of forecasting methods, in the hope that a few of them will come up with comparable findings and increase confidence in the results. Even with the qualifications that should always accompany forecasting studies, being able to anticipate societal changes and prepare for them is a far better strategy than being surprised when problems develop.

Impact Assessment

During the highly contentious debate in 2002 over oil and gas drilling in the Arctic National Wildlife Refuge, proponents of drilling repeatedly cited a 1990 economic study suggesting that opening the refuge for commercial oil production would create some 735,000 jobs. Independent economists said that number was suspect because the assumptions on which it was based were probably no longer valid. Indeed, a separate study prepared for the Department of Energy in 1992 indicated that approximately 222,000 jobs would result, but only when ANWR reached peak production; the jobs would be chiefly in construction and manufactur-ing. Environmentalists argued that the correct number was lower still, perhaps 50,000 jobs. The wide variation in estimates of job creation may seem to indicate that analysts are unable to forecast economic impacts very well, but the real lesson is probably that studies of this kind may be seriously flawed because of the fanciful assumptions they make. The use of studies ten years after their completion may be equally faulted, because policy advocates may pay little attention to whether the initial assumptions are still valid. Instead, they are probably more interested in scoring political points in a highly contentious debate than in arriving at a sound estimate of these jobs. During yet another ANWR debate in Congress in 2005, the same, dated estimate of 735,000 jobs was still being used by drilling proponents.

The jobs impact study is one kind of **impact assessment.** Others include technology impact analysis, environmental impact analysis, and social impact analysis. They are similar in that ana-lysts share an interest in trying to project or predict the consequences of adopting a policy pro-posal or taking some other form of action. Robert Bartlett (1989, 1) describes the approach this way: "Impact assessment constitutes a general strategy of policymaking and administration—a strategy of influencing decisions and actions by a priori analysis of predictable impacts. A sim-ple, even simplistic, notion when stated briefly, making policy through impact assessment is in fact an approach of great power, complexity, and subtlety."

Much like forecasting, the purpose of an impact assessment is to see if analysts can system-atically examine the effects that may occur from taking a certain action. That action may be drilling for oil in ANWR, introducing or expanding the use of new Internet technologies, cre-ating gated residential communities for security-conscious home buyers, or deploying a national missile defense system. No matter what the subject, the analyst tries to identify possi-ble impacts and the likelihood they will occur.

Impact assessments are not new. Federal law has required environmental impact analyses since the National Environmental Policy Act (NEPA) was passed in 1969. The logic was sim-ple and powerful. Before governments undertake major projects that are likely to have signifi-cant effects on the environment, policymakers ought to identify and measure those impacts, and they also ought to consider alternatives that may avoid the undesirable effects. The law's strength is in its requirement that the impact assessments be made public, which creates an opportunity for environmental groups and others to influence agency decision making. The agency, in turn, is forced to deal with a concerned public and to respond to the information produced by the impact assessment. The hope was that the combination of information and political forces would "make bureaucracies think" and dissuade them from making poor decisions that could harm the environment. Evaluations of NEPA indicate that it has been quite successful on the whole (Caldwell 1998).

POLITICAL AND INSTITUTIONAL APPROACHES

At this point in the chapter the reader may be wondering whether policy analysis ever considers more than economic and technical estimates. The answer is clearly "yes." Political scientists in particular are likely to use political and institutional approaches to understanding proposed policy alternatives and to evaluating existing programs. Such studies are often more qualitative than the methods discussed so far, but they may also be just as rigorous and just as valuable for understanding public policy.

Political Feasibility Analysis

Political feasibility, a criterion for evaluating suggested policy changes, is the extent to which elected officials and other policy actors support the change. No formula is available for estimating political feasibility. Even experienced and thoughtful observers of politics acknowledge how difficult it is to determine the level of support that might be forthcoming for a proposal in local or state government, or at the national level. It may be easier to recognize the actions that are unlikely to fly politically. For example, a steep rise in the federal gasoline tax would seem to lack feasibility, particularly when gas prices were high in mid-2008. But by late 2008, when they had dropped considerably, the idea no longer seemed so inconceivable, particularly in light of rising needs to repair and improve roads, highways, and bridges. Imposing strong restrictions on gun ownership would bring a formidable challenge by the National Rifle Association, and therefore is viewed as politically difficult. Significantly curtailing Social Security benefits, or substantially raising the age at which people can qualify for benefits, would likely lack feasibility because senior citizens are superbly organized and would see any such proposal as against their interests and would resist such changes. At the margins of policy debate, however, it may be possible to anticipate how slight changes in proposed legislation or regulations, or an alteration in the political or economic environment, can create a majority in favor of action. Sometimes a shift on the part of a few legislators or a marginal change in policymaker perceptions of what the public will support makes the difference in the success or failure of a policy proposal.

Some simple determinations, however, can provide a good idea of political feasibility. Analysts could begin by identifying the policy actors who will likely play a significant role in the decision. These actors may be members of a city council or a state legislature, or they may be members of Congress. To the formal policymakers, analysts would add other players, such as representatives of major interest groups and administrative officials, for example, the mayor, the governor, and top officials in a pertinent bureaucracy. For each of the

Each major policy actors, analysts try to determine their positions on the issues, perhaps by investigating their previous stances. Sometimes, it is possible to estimate their positions based on their party affiliation, general political attitudes, and where they stand on comparable issues. Finally, an estimate can be made of their level of interest in the particular decision (how salient it is to them), and the intensity of their views or their motivation to get involved in the decision. These factors are likely to be shaped by the level of interest and preferences of the constituencies they represent, which in turn are influenced by how much the media cover the controversy and how the issues are presented. All of this information can be pulled together to estimate political feasibility.

Analysts need to bear in mind that not all policy actors are equal in influencing feasibility. Relatively small groups with intensely held views on a subject are often capable of defeating proposals that have the broad support of the U.S. public. Gun control is a policy area where this has long been the case. For a great many public policy disputes, especially those that do not rise to the highest levels of visibility, political feasibility is likely to depend on the views of a small number of people and organizations.

Implementation Analysis and Program Evaluation

The discussion of **implementation analysis** and the related program evaluation is brief because these methods are covered to some extent in the chapters that follow. As is the case with assessment of political feasibility, these methods draw far more from the disciplines of political science and public administration than is true for most of the others reviewed here. Implementation occurs after policy adoption, and it deals with how an administrative agency interprets a policy and puts it into effect. Policies are almost never self-implementing, and many circumstances affect success: the difficulty of the problem being addressed, the statute's objectives and legal mandates, and multiple political and institutional factors. These factors include an agency's resources, the commitment and skills of its leadership, the degree of public and political support, and influence from external constituencies (Goggin et al. 1990; Mazmanian and Sabatier 1983).

Implementation analysis is based on the assumption that it is possible to identify the particular circumstances either in advance of a policy's adoption or after it is implemented. In the first case, the analysis can help in the design of the policy to ensure that it can be implemented well. In the second, the analysis can document how well implementation has gone and the aspects of the policy or the parts of the implementing agency that are responsible for any success or failure. Policies can then be modified as needed.

Program evaluation focuses more on policy results or outcomes than on the process of implementation. Analysts use a number of methods to identify a program's goals and objectives, measure them, gather data on what the program is doing, and reach some conclusions about the extent of its success. As with other policy analyses, the intention is to complete those tasks in a systematic way that fosters confidence in the accuracy of the results (Rossi, Freeman, and Lipsey 2004). The studies sometimes make a real difference. For example, analysis revealed that, after years of increased funding, the nation's most popular program to discourage drug use among schoolchildren was ineffective. As a result, the U.S. Department of Education announced that its funds could no longer be used on the Drug Abuse

Resistance Education, or DARE, program, which had paid for police officers to visit schools to convey antidrug messages.[35]

ETHICAL ANALYSIS

As noted in this chapter, many policy analysts view **ethical analysis,** or the systematic examination of ethical or normative issues in public policy, as problematic. Because they are not quite sure how to do it and sometimes fear that entering the quagmire of ethics compromises the objectivity of their analysis, they often leave ethical issues to the policy advocacy community. Ethical issues most definitely are raised as part of policy debate, but they may not receive the kind of careful analysis that we have come to expect for economic issues or even for political and institutional issues (Tong 1986).

Two examples, however, illustrate the need for ethical analysis. The first involves family planning programs. The George W. Bush administration, much like other Republican administrations since the mid-1980s, was under pressure from antiabortion groups to curtail U.S. contributions to the UN Population Fund. The fund supports family planning programs around the world, but some people accuse it of condoning abortions. It has repeatedly denied those charges and has assured the U.S. government that none of the nation's funds would be used in support of abortion, which U.S. law forbids. Responding to political pressure from the antiabortion lobby, in 2002 Bush withheld $34 million from the UN program, which amounted to 13 percent of the agency's total budget. According to an agency spokesperson, the effect of a $34 million cut "could mean 2 million unwanted pregnancies, 800,000 induced abortions, 4,700 maternal deaths, and 77,000 infant and child deaths." [36] Note the qualification of "could mean" in this statement. It is difficult to project the consequences of the budget cut because other groups might make up some of the difference of the funds withheld. For example, the Population Fund and other organizations concerned about family planning services could ask their members for increased donations for this purpose. Even so, one could ask how likely the Bush administration's action was to achieve its goal of reducing abortions. If the consequences were even close to what the UN official indicated, was the administration's action largely symbolic and political, but one with detrimental consequences for public health? Can the decision be justified in terms of moral or ethical criteria?

The second example concerns the dramatically altered circumstances of airline travel in the aftermath of September 11. Federal law now requires random searches of individuals and carry-on luggage at the initial security checkpoint. Federal officials were concerned that if they adopted a system of passenger profiling based on demographic characteristics—that is, groups of people who might require special screening, such as young Arab men—they would violate principles of civil liberties. Civil libertarians argue that racial or ethnic profiling should be unacceptable in a free society that values diversity, and many find that view persuasive. The federal government opted for a system of random checks without profiling, but many experts say that while such a system has little chance of preventing hijacking, it imposes high costs and inconvenience on travelers. What is the most acceptable way to promote airline security? Does profiling travelers violate their civil liberties? Even if it did, is this practice a justifiable use of government authority to protect the country?

STEPS TO ANALYSIS

ETHICAL ANALYSIS: THE CASE OF ORGAN DONATION

A recent assessment of human organ donation to save lives contained some striking data and offered a creative solution, but one with ethical implications. Every day in the United States, more than seventy people receive an organ transplant, but about seventeen die because there are not enough donor organs to meet the demand. In 2008 there were more than ninety-seven thousand people in the nation waiting for a transplant. People's dire medical conditions do not allow them to wait indefinitely. Indeed, since 1995 more than forty-five thousand Americans have died while waiting for a suitable donor organ to become available.

The shortage is not because people are opposed to organ donation in principle. In fact, the overwhelming majority of Americans (85 percent) approve of organ donation. But few have made an explicit decision to donate by signing a donor card. Hence, in most cases their organs, such as hearts, kidneys, lungs, and livers, are not allowed to be used for transplantation.

So how might the number of available organs be increased? Current U.S. policy requires an affirmative step of signing an organ donation card (and generally notifying family members of one's intention). But what if the policy were flipped so that the default position is that organs are suitable for donation unless an individual opted out by signaling that he or she did *not* want to be an organ donor, for example, because of strong religious beliefs? What difference would that make?

Experience in Europe provides some answers. Two quite different approaches are used for what could be termed a "no-action default" policy, where an individual's failure to make a decision results in a given condition. But some nations (Austria, Belgium, France, Sweden, and others) rely on "presumed consent," where people are deemed organ donors unless they have registered not to be. Others follow the U.S. approach, where "explicit consent" is required; that is, no one is assumed to be an organ donor unless they have registered to be one. In Europe, the effective percentage of organ donors in the first case is nearly 100 percent, but in the second case it ranges from 4 to 27 percent. The implication is that a change in approach within the United States could result in thousands of additional organ donations a year, and thus in thousands of lives that would be saved.

Should the United States change its policy to one of presumed consent? Issues of individual freedom and social equity or justice are central to how one answers that question. What arguments, particularly those grounded in ethical concerns, would you make in support of that change? Should the United States continue to rely on the explicit consent model? What arguments would you make in support of this position?

What does this exercise tell you about the possibility or desirability of analyzing ethical issues in public policy? Should analysts try to address ethical issues like this? Can that be done as professionally as conducting cost-benefit analysis or assessing political feasibility?

Sources: Eric J. Johnson and Daniel Goldstein, "Do Defaults Save Lives?" *Science* 302, November 21, 2003, 1338–1339; www.organdonor.gov (official U.S. government Web site for organ and tissue donation and transplantation); and www.unos.org (United Network for Organ Sharing).

Other contemporary policy issues, such as human cloning and embryonic stem cell research, raise similar ethical and value concerns. By mid-2001, two dozen states had adopted laws to govern research on embryos and fetuses, and nine of them chose to ban any experiments involving human embryos. Was this position reasonable? Opponents of these laws argue that they could seriously impede important medical research.[37] Indeed, in 2002 California enacted legislation to explicitly allow research on stem cells that are obtained from fetal and embryonic tissue, a direct repudiation of federal limits on such research imposed by the Bush administration in 2001 (though lifted by President Obama in early 2009). When he signed the law, Gov. Gray Davis was joined by the late actor Christopher Reeve, who became a booster of embryonic stem cell research after a riding accident left him paralyzed in 1995. Antiabortion groups and the Roman Catholic Church opposed California's action.[38]

California went even further in 2004. Voters approved a state ballot proposal, Proposition 71, that authorized the state to spend $3 billion over the next decade for embryonic stem cell research, creating by far the largest such program run by any state in the nation. The decision makes California one of the most important centers for embryonic stem cell research in the world, but for some the action did not resolve the ethical dilemmas inherent in such research. If reputable policy analysts cannot provide guidance to the public and policymakers, debate over issues like embryonic stem cell research can deteriorate into emotional name calling. Equally important, as Reeve and other supporters of the California initiative argued at the time, the ban kept U.S. health researchers from making discoveries that could pay significant dividends in the improved treatment of disease. Partly because of these controversies, medical researchers turned to studying the potential of using adult stem cells rather than those derived from human embryos or fetal tissue. Under the Obama administration it is likely that both kinds of stem cell research will be funded.

The Steps to Analysis box "Ethical Analysis: The Case of Organ Donation" offers an intriguing policy question for which ethical analysis would seem to be appropriate.

CONCLUSIONS

This chapter introduces and describes the leading evaluative criteria in the study of public policy, with special emphasis on effectiveness, efficiency, and equity concerns. It also briefly reviews the major kinds of policy analysis and their strengths, weaknesses, and potential contributions to the policy-making process. Students of public policy should understand that analysts select from these criteria and methods, with significant implications for the breadth and utility of their findings. They should also be alert to the assumptions and choices made in such studies and ask how they affect the validity of the conclusions reached.

The chapter makes clear that policy analysis is both a craft and an art. The craft comes in knowing the methods of policy analysis and how to apply them in specific situations. The art lies in selecting suitable criteria for policy assessments, in recognizing the limitations of the available methods, and in drawing and reporting on appropriate conclusions. An artful policy analyst recognizes and is sensitive to the public mood and the political and institutional context in which the analysis is conducted and reported. He or she may also find ways to use policy analysis to empower citizens and motivate them to participate in the democratic process (deLeon 1997; Ingram and Smith 1993).

Some critics of policy analysis complain that analysts tend to view politics—that is, public opinion, interest group activity, and the actions of policymakers—as an obstacle to adopting the fruits of their labors, which they believe represent a rational, and therefore superior, assessment of the situation (Stone 2002). It is possible, however, to view the relationship of policy analysis and politics in a different light. Analysis and politics are not incompatible as long as it is understood that analysis by itself does not and should not determine public policy. Rather, its purpose is to inform the public and policymakers so that they can make better decisions. A democratic political process offers the best way to ensure that policy decisions further the public interest (Lindblom and Woodhouse 1993).

DISCUSSION QUESTIONS

1. Which of the many evaluative criteria are the most important? Economic costs or efficiency? Policy effectiveness? Equity? Why do you think so? Are some criteria more important for certain kinds of policy questions than for others?

2. How would you go about applying cost-benefit analysis to one of the following issues: (1) instituting a campus program for recycling paper, aluminum cans, and similar items; (2) getting a city to build bicycle lanes on selected streets to promote safety for cyclists; (3) increasing the number of crossing guards at roadway intersections close to elementary schools? What steps would you go through and what kinds of data would you need to conduct such an analysis?

3. Choose one of the following examples relating to the use of ethical analysis: budgets for family planning programs, restrictions on using embryonic stem cells for medical research, or profiling in airport security screening. How would you apply ethical analysis to clarify the policy choices involved in that case?

4. If you had to forecast changing student demand for programs of study at a college or university for the next ten to twenty years, how would you do that?

5. What are the most important factors to consider in conducting a political feasibility analysis? Take a specific example, such as raising gasoline taxes to reduce reliance on imported oil, cutting mandatory prison sentences to lower the cost of keeping nonviolent offenders in custody, or capping student tuition payments to permit greater access to higher education.

SUGGESTED READINGS

Eugene Bardach, *A Practical Guide for Policy Analysis: The Eightfold Path to More Effective Problem Solving,* 3rd ed. (Washington, D.C.: CQ Press, 2009). A concise and helpful handbook on the basics of conducting and presenting policy analysis in the real world.

Kenneth N. Bickers and John T. Williams, *Public Policy Analysis: A Political Economy Approach* (Boston: Houghton Mifflin, 2001). A brief text on policy analysis using the perspective of political economy, or how individual preferences and values are translated into collective policy choices.

Brian W. Hogwood and Lewis A. Gunn, *Policy Analysis for the Real World* (Oxford: Oxford University Press, 1984). An older text with good advice about how to conduct and use practical policy studies.

David L. Weimer and Aidan R. Vining, *Policy Analysis: Concepts and Practice,* 4th ed. (Upper Saddle River, N.J.: Prentice Hall, 2005). One of the leading policy analysis texts, drawing heavily from economics.

SUGGESTED WEB SITES

www.appam.org/home.asp. Association for Public Policy Analysis and Management, with guides to public policy education.

www.opm.gov/qualifications/standards/Specialty-stds/gs-policy.asp. The U.S. Office of Personnel Management Web page, offering a description of policy analysis positions in government.

www.rff.org/cost-benefitanalysis.cfm. Selected cost-benefit analyses done at Resources for the Future.

www.sra.org. Society for Risk Analysis, with links to risk-related sites.

www.wfs.org. World Future Society, with links to publications on future studies such as *Futurist* magazine.

www.whitehouse.gov/omb. Office of Management and Budget, with guidelines for conducting cost-benefit analyses and risk assessments.

KEYWORDS

contingent valuation methods   166
cost-benefit analysis   162
cost-effectiveness analysis   167
discount rate   166
ethical analysis   177
impact assessment   174
implementation analysis   176

opportunity costs   165
political feasibility   175
risk assessment   168
risk evaluation   170
risk management   170
sensitivity analysis   166

NOTES

1. Lena H. Sun, "On the Mass Transportation Bandwagon: Record Ridership Shows Continued Popularity of Leaving the Driving to Someone Else," *Washington Post National Weekly Edition,* December 15–21, 2008, 35; and Peter S. Goodman, "Fuel Prices Shift Math for Life in Far Suburbs, *New York Times,* June 25, 2008.
2. On the gas tax holiday debate, see John Maggs, "Tax-Holiday Blues," *National Journal,* May 10, 2008, 64–65. Few economists favored the proposal; in fact, both conservative and liberal economists joined in opposing the gas tax suspension. Polls at the time also showed that a majority of Americans opposed lowering the gas tax.
3. Energy Information Administration, "Impacts of Increased Access to Oil and Natural Gas Resources in the Lower 48 Federal Outer Continental Shelf" (Washington, D.C.: Department of Energy, 2007), available at www.eia.doe.gov/oiaf/aeo/otheranalysis/ongr.html.
4. See Jane E. Brody, "Abstinence-Only: Does It Work?" *New York Times,* June 1, 2004, D7; and Rob Stein, "Not That Kind of Sex Ed," *Washington Post National Weekly Edition,* December 24, 2007–January 6, 2008, 34. A congressionally mandated study by Mathematica Policy Research in 2007 found that elementary and middle school students in such programs were just as likely to have sex in subsequent years as those who did not participate in the programs.
5. The estimates come from Michael Specter, "Damn Spam," *New Yorker,* August 6, 2007, 36–41.
6. See Tom Zeller Jr., "Law To Bar Junk E-Mail Encourages Flood Instead," *New York Times,* February 1, 2005, 1, C8. See also Saul Hansell, "California Is Set to Ban Junk E-Mail," *New York Times,* September 24, 2003, C1, C9.
7. Michael Luo, "Under New York Medicaid, Drug Costs Run Free," *New York Times,* November 23, 2005, 1, A26.

8. "Targeting Tobacco Use: The Nation's Leading Cause of Preventable Death, at a Glance 2008" (Washington, D.C.: Centers for Disease Control and Prevention), at www.cdc.gov/nccdphp/publications/aag/osh.htm.

9. Associated Press release, "New York's Cigarette Tax Climbs to Highest in the Nation," June 2, 2008.

10. See Carl Hulse, "House Supports Permanent End to Estate Tax," *New York Times,* June 7, 2002, 1, A17.

11. Paul Krugman, "For Richer: How the Permissive Capitalism of the Boom Destroyed American Equality," *New York Times Magazine,* October 20, 2002, 62–67, 76–77, 141–142.

12. See David Cay Johnston, "Few Wealthy Farmers Owe Estate Taxes, Report Says," *New York Times,* July 10, 2005, 15.

13. See Jonathan Rauch, "The Loss of New Orleans Wasn't Just a Tragedy. It Was a Plan," *National Journal,* September 17, 2005, 2801–2802.

14. James Dao, "16 of 21 B-2's Have Cracks Near Exhaust, Officials Say," *New York Times,* March 20, 2002, A19. Other military aircraft are exceedingly expensive as well. The air force F-22 fighter cost $200 million per plane in 2000, and the tilt-rotor Osprey aircraft, a kind of combination helicopter and plane, cost $83 million each—and was plagued with operating problems. See Tim Weiner, "How to Build Weapons When Money Is No Object," *New York Times,* April 16, 2000, Week in Review, 3.

15. See Paul R. Portney, "Time and Money: Discounting's Problematic Allure," *Resources* 136 (summer 1999): 8–9. See also Paul R. Portney and John P. Weyant, eds., *Discounting and Intergenerational Equity* (Washington, D.C.: Resources for the Future, 1999).

16. Rauch, "The Loss of New Orleans."

17. The new guidelines for agency scientific data were pushed through Congress as a rider attached to a fiscal 2001 appropriations bill in late 2000, largely at the request of business and industry groups, and signed by President Bill Clinton. Business groups have long maintained that many government regulations are based on faulty data, and the law will make it easier for them to challenge regulations they view as burdensome. See Rebecca Adams, "OIRA Directs Guidelines on Data Quality," *CQ Weekly,* March 23, 2002, 827.

18. See Richard Conviser, "A Brief History of the Oregon Health Plan and Its Features," released in 1996, available at www.oregon.gov/OHPPR/docs/histofplan.pdf. The Oregon experience is examined in detail in Peter J. Neumann, *Using Cost-Effectiveness Analysis to Improve Health Care: Opportunities and Barriers* (New York: Oxford University Press, 2004).

19. See Seth Stein and Joseph Tomasello, "When Safety Costs Too Much," *New York Times,* January 10, 2004, A31.

20. The proposal can be found at the Federal Aviation Administration Web site: www.faa.gov.

21. Danny Hakim, "U.S. Proposes Tougher Crash-Safety Tests," *New York Times,* May 13, 2004, C1, 6.

22. See David Johnston, "C.I.A. Puts Risk of Terror Strike at 9/11 Levels," *New York Times,* October 18, 2002, 1, A12.

23. For example, a book published a year after the September 11 terrorist attacks discusses public anxiety over unfamiliar and highly publicized risks and attempts to assess the true risk: David Ropeik and George Gray, *Risk: A Practical Guide for Deciding What's Really Safe and What's Really Dangerous in the World Around You* (Boston: Houghton Mifflin, 2002). The book sold briskly at Amazon.com and Barnes and Noble's online site.

24. For a comparative review of the major risks facing the U.S. population, see Bruce Nussbaum, "The Next Big One," *Business Week,* September 19, 2005, 35–45.

25. See William J. Broad, "NASA Puts Shuttle Mission's Risk at 1 in 100," *New York Times,* July 26, 2005, A16.

26. The odds are taken from Larry Laudan, *The Book of Risks: Fascinating Facts about the Chances We Take Every Day* (New York: John Wiley and Sons, 1994), as cited in a May 20, 1998, CNN news story, when an earlier Powerball lottery jackpot reached $175 million.

27. The report, "Food-Related Illness and Death in the United States," can be found at the Centers for Disease Control and Prevention Web site: www.cdc.gov/ncidod/eid/vol5no5/mead.htm.

28. Gina Kolata, "With Vaccine Available, Smallpox Debate Shifts," *New York Times,* March 30, 2002, A8.

29. The estimates were reported by Susan Okie in "The Smallpox Tradeoff," *Washington Post National Weekly Edition,* May 13–19, 2002.

30. The options that were being considered in 2002 are discussed in a Center for Infectious Disease Research and Policy newsletter, available at www1.umn.edu/cidrap/content/bt/smallpox/news/acipupdate.html. In July 2002 the federal government decided to vaccinate about a half-million health care and emergency personnel rather than the fifteen thousand it originally believed necessary. See William J. Broad, "U.S. Expands Plan for Administering Smallpox Vaccine," *New York Times,* July 7, 2002, 1, 16.

31. Edmund L. Andrews and Robert Pear, "Entitlement Costs Are Expected to Soar," *New York Times,* March 19, 2004, A13.

32. The Census Bureau Web page has these kinds of forecasts, for example, in its National Population Projections release of 2008, based on the 2000 census. An easier way to see the estimates for the United States and to compare them to other nations is to view the annual World Population Data Sheet published by the Population Reference Bureau and available at its Web site: www.prb.org.

33. A compound interest calculator is available on the Web at http://javascript.internet.com/calculators/compound-interest.html. To use it, enter an amount of money, an interest rate, and the number of years the money will be invested, and immediately see how much the initial amount changes over this time period.

34. Burt Solomon, "False Prophets," *National Journal,* December 11, 1999.

35. Kate Zernike, "Antidrug Program Says It Will Adopt a New Strategy," *New York Times,* February 15, 2001, A1–A23. Several years later, a panel convened by the National Institutes of Health reviewed evidence on the causes of youth violence and also concluded that "scare tactics" such as those used in the DARE program do not work. However, the panel did find that a number of other intervention programs offer promise. See Associated Press, " 'Get Tough' Youth Programs Are Ineffective, Panel Says," *New York Times,* October 17, 2005, 25.

36. See Barbara Crossette, "U.N. Agency on Population Blames U.S. for Cutbacks," *New York Times,* April 7, 2002, A11. Similar calculations are made regularly by the Alan Guttmacher Institute, the policy analysis arm of Planned Parenthood. Its studies are available at www.agi-usa.org.

37. Sheryl Gay Stolberg, "Washington Not Alone in Cell Debate," *New York Times,* July 23, 2001, A12.

38. Associated Press, "California Law Permits Stem Cell Research," *New York Times,* September 23, 2002.

CHAPTER 7

ECONOMIC AND BUDGETARY POLICY

ON FEBRUARY 28, 2008, PRESIDENT GEORGE W. BUSH WAS HOLDING A PRESS conference; not surprisingly, given the state of the U.S. economy at the time, the president faced numerous questions regarding economic issues such as inflation, unemployment, and the housing crisis, among other topics. At one point a reporter brought up the possibility of gasoline prices rising to four dollars per gallon. Before the interviewer could finish, President Bush asked for clarification of the statement. The reporter's response that "a number of analysts are predicting four dollar per gallon gasoline this spring when they reformulate" seemed to catch the president off-guard. His response, "That's interesting, I hadn't heard that," seemed incredulous to many economic and political analysts and was fodder for late-night comedians in the days and weeks to follow. As most people now know, gasoline at four dollar per gallon became a reality a couple of months later. Many saw the president as out of touch with the economic realities of the nation and not fully understanding or admitting the extent of these concerns.

It being a presidential election year, the last thing Republicans wanted was a suffering economy going into November. Presidents are often held accountable for economic hardships of the nation, yet they rarely receive any credit during economic boom times. The reality is that the economy is extremely complex, and presidential policies can only have a limited effect. Nevertheless, politicians will try to claim credit or avoid blame. They may also use or not use certain words (political spin) in describing the economy. For example, the term *recession* is avoided like the plague and is sometimes referred to as the "R word" because of the potential implications that such an admission may carry. Avoiding terms is not limited to elected leaders. Federal Reserve Board Chair Ben Bernanke continually refused to use the term *recession* until he finally admitted its possibility in April 2008, but even this was tempered with a statement about economic growth picking up later in the year.

At the top of Barack Obama's policy agenda, even before he assumed office on January 20, 2009, was what government might do to help the ailing economy. This was a daunting task in light of the severity of the economic downturn, which at the time was getting worse from week to week. Here, President-elect Obama meets with members of his economic team, including treasury secretary nominee Timothy Geithner (fourth from the left), Council of Economic Advisers director nominee Christina Romer (second from the right), director of the Domestic Policy Council (DPC) nominee Melody Barnes (far right), and chief of staff nominee Rahm Emanuel (third from the left) on January 5, 2009, at the transition office in Washington, D.C. Economic policy remained Obama's primary concern for the first several months of his presidency.

It is clear that 2007 and 2008 were not stellar years for the U.S. economy by almost any of the traditional measures used, and 2009 is shaping up to be even worse. In addition, there were a number of major developments that illustrated poor economic times, such as the weakness of the dollar, the home mortgage and housing crisis, and the emergency acquisition of the Bear Stearns Bank and Trust by JP Morgan Chase and Co. Through all of this, most of the American public was suffering with increasing prices for gasoline, food, and just about everything else, and getting little relief through higher wages. It was clear that the economy was going to be a major issue of the presidential election as Sens. John McCain, R-Ariz., and Barack Obama, D-Ill., argued about the merits of lifting the federal gasoline tax, whether the United States should remove the ban on off-shore oil drilling as a way to reduce gasoline prices, and ways to create jobs and stimulate consumer spending.

In addition to the immediate implications of a weak economy, there continue to be longer-term issues associated with U.S. economic performance. Deficit spending rose rapidly in 2008, with the Congressional Budget Office (CBO) projecting over a trillion-dollar deficit in 2009 and the national debt over $10 trillion. Entitlement spending continues to eat up an increasing portion of the entire budget, and certain programs such as Medicare and Social Security in particular face dire financial straits in the future.[1] Infrastructure funding is insufficient for the needs of the nation, emergency spending continues to be necessary as the floods of 2008 showed convincingly, and billions continue to be spent, often off-budget, on the wars in Iraq and Afghanistan. Add to this the bailouts of the financial and housing industry and the economic stimulus package offered by President Obama and it becomes clear that the nation will be "in the red" for a long time to come.

The economic health of the nation and more specific issues such as the federal deficit change all of the time. For example, deficit projections can easily change because they are based on a series of assumptions that may not hold over time. Moreover, the projected deficits become less reliable as one begins to extend the forecasts out two, five, or even ten years. The CBO does provide such projections, however. According to these estimates, the United States can expect a nearly $1.2 trillion deficit in 2009, a $700 billion deficit in 2010, and a $234 billion deficit in 2015, with no surpluses projected for the next ten years.[2] Yet these budget projections are not necessarily reliable. As we discussed in chapter 6, long-term forecasting of this kind can be accurate only to the extent that the initial assumptions continue to be reasonable. What might change to make them unreasonable? For one thing, economic growth may be less than projected, which would lead to less revenue coming into the Treasury. For another, new laws could be enacted that would require more government spending, a decrease in taxes, or both. Tax cuts that were implemented under the Bush administration that were set to expire in 2010 may be extended. Or natural disasters such as Hurricane Katrina or the 2008 floods might require the federal government to spend a great deal more money to assist victims and reconstruct damaged areas. Or a prolonged recession and a change in political leadership may dictate particular economic policies. Any one of these scenarios could throw off future deficit (or surplus) projections.

Another issue to consider is how policymakers think about these economic projections. In particular, do they consider them to be serious enough to require strong action? In recent years the answer seemed to be "no." For example, the federal deficit does not appear to be a major concern to policymakers. The recent deficits have occurred during a time of a Republican administration and, for the most part, a Republican Congress. Traditionally, Republicans tout their fiscal conservatism and budget austerity when campaigning for office and administering government. Instead, the so-called tax-and-spend Democratic Party has been the more vocal of the two regarding budgetary policy. Democrats assert that the current budget deficit projections pose a major fiscal risk to the economic future of the United States, and they have been quick to blame the policies of the Bush administration for the country's budget woes. But as noted above, how much blame can fairly be attributed to the administration? Bush administration officials would surely have argued that the deficits can be traced to events over which they had little control. Among them have been a downturn in the economy, the September 11 attacks, and the subsequent government responses to those events, including the war on terrorism. They also have long argued that the broad-based tax cuts approved in 2001 were expected to spur economic growth and thus increase federal revenues. Most of these events could not have been predicted, and the tax cuts continue to be popular. Yet neither President Bush nor Congress showed much restraint in government spending. In fact, many economists and policymakers, including President Obama, are advocating greater government spending to help alleviate the downtrodden economy. Is it any wonder, then, that budget deficits have grown sharply in recent years?

This chapter explores how economic policy attempts to address such issues as the deficit and other goals of economic policy. It assesses economic policy in the United States through a broad review of the powers of government to influence the economy, including the role of the budget. The chapter concentrates on the major goals that policymakers attempt to promote while coping with the inevitable value conflicts and policy choices. The tools and approaches of policy analysis are as appropriate to assessing economic policy as they are to the other policy areas covered in the chapters that follow.

BACKGROUND

Managing national deficits and debt is only one of the economic and budgetary tasks to which the federal government must attend on a continuous basis. For much of the latter part of the twentieth century, the federal deficit dominated discussions regarding economic policy, and it clearly had major impacts on the nation's capacity to support other policy actions. Indeed, massive tax cuts at the beginning of President Ronald Reagan's administration in 1981 and the subsequent decline in government revenues greatly constrained spending by the U.S. Congress across a range of public programs. In addition, the U.S. national debt soared during the 1980s.

Economic policy is critical to all other government functions, but most people probably do not recognize it as readily as they do other substantive policy areas such as the environment, education, or welfare. One reason is that the general public does not connect actions such as tax cuts with attempts to influence economic growth or unemployment. In addition, so much attention is given to the Federal Reserve Board's monetary policy and its impact on the economy that the public tends to forget that the government's fiscal policies—its taxing and spending decisions—also have major impacts on the economy. A cut in tax rates or a decision to spend more money on highway construction—both forms of fiscal policy—can have significant effects on the nation's economy. It is generally only during extremely difficult economic times that the population pays much attention to government activities as they relate to economic policy. For example, in 2008, as the nation's economy continued in a recession, interest in tax rebates, the role of the government in the home mortgage crisis, and other economic policy issues became more salient. And in 2009, as Congress debated a huge economic stimulus package, these discussions and proposals became front-page news.

Economic policymaking is crucial to almost everything the government does. In a narrow sense, economic policy is the development of particular programs and policies that are intended to affect economic conditions in the nation, such as reducing unemployment or increasing economic growth. Public policy students should be aware, however, that the development and implementation of other public policies also have substantial effects on the economy and subsequently on the economic policies that the government pursues. For example, conservatives argue that too much government regulation to protect the environment retards economic growth. Because one of government's major economic goals is to encourage such growth, conflict between the two policy goals is likely. For this reason, as well as others, environmentalists emphasize the idea of sustainable development, which they believe can help to reconcile economic and environmental goals that may be at odds.

Since the 1980s, the United States has generally been burdened by large federal deficits. According to the CBO, the projected deficit by early 2009 is over a trillion dollars, meaning that the government plans to spend a trillion dollars more than it will bring into the Treasury during the 2009 fiscal year.[3] Economists often debate the potential impacts of deficits, and sometimes politicians will make choices knowing that little money is available. In the early 1990s, budget austerity constrained proposals of any grand ideas about what the government should be doing, such as reforming the health care system. Until 2009, such austerity had not occurred in the twenty-first century, with government continuing to expend funds on a range of activities—both foreign and domestic—without regard for their fiscal implications. Perhaps this is because things can change quickly in the world of economic policy. During the 1990s an unprecedented eight years of strong, sustained economic growth replaced budget deficits with projections of budget surpluses. In 2001 the nation struggled with an economic recession, and in 2002 growth slowly returned, but with less confidence that the United States would see the robust and sustained growth of the 1990s any time soon. More recent history would seem to bear this out.

From the Great Depression of the 1930s to the present, government has been intimately involved in trying to control, or at least influence, the economy. Policymakers have moved away from the free-market, "hands-off" approach to the economy endorsed by Adam Smith, an eighteenth-century political economist who believed that government should not intervene in the economy and unrestrained free markets best promote economic well-being. Since the Great Depression, however, the public and government officials have shown little tolerance for wide swings in the economy, which historically had cycled through periods of economic boom and recession as market forces dictated. In recent years, policymakers have adopted a "hands-on" approach to managing the economy that avoids wild fluctuations and produces steady economic growth.

To achieve these and other goals, the government uses fiscal policy—the sum of all taxation and spending policies—as well as the monetary policy tools of the Federal Reserve Board (the Fed, as it is called) to influence the U.S. economy. It does so with varying degrees of success. In addition, government regulation of business has become prevalent since the Depression. Business regulation also increased in the 1960s and 1970s, as citizens demanded more government assurances that health, safety, and the environment would be protected. These regulations have major effects on the budget and economic goals of the United States. The looming deficits in the late twentieth century worried public officials and introduced another major goal for them to consider as they developed economic policy.

When the traditional indicators of economic growth suggested a healthy economy during the 1990s, policymakers were eager to find ways to maintain that strength. With the economic downturn of 2000 through 2002, and again in 2007 into 2009, policymakers were just as concerned with making policy choices that could return the nation to economic good times, particularly with the consideration of tax cuts and government spending to stimulate economic growth. Both options could have significant impact on the size of the projected deficit over the next several years and the extent to which this deficit is reduced or increased.

GOALS OF ECONOMIC POLICY

Policymakers try to promote various goals and objectives in relation to economic policy. Government officials in Congress, the White House, and the Treasury Department, and those who sit on the independent Federal Reserve Board have a number of tools to use in pursuing these goals. What is taking place at the federal level is paralleled in states and localities, as their public officials attempt to promote certain economic goals, such as the growth of local and regional businesses. State and local governments also regulate business practices related to health, safety, the environment, and consumer protection, much as the federal government does. A public scare over contaminated peanut butter products in early 2009 pointed to one processing facility in Georgia that, despite repeated warnings and citations over the years, continued in operation and knowingly distributed peanut butter tainted with Salmonella bacteria. Such cases remind us of the role that government plays in ensuring a safe food supply. Yet such regulation may impose costs on businesses, influence economic competition, and affect a range of other economic values. In some circumstances, the different goals conflict with each other, which may explain the failure of the state of Georgia to take stronger action against the peanut processing facility. Ultimately, the federal government ordered an extensive recall of affected products that had sickened over five hundred people and led to eight deaths in forty-three states. A congressional committee also announced it would begin an investigation of what it called an "alarming" development.[4] Yet the major economic goals that government attempts to promote are nonetheless fairly constant. They are economic growth, low levels of unemployment, low levels of inflation, a positive balance of trade, and management of deficits and debt.

Economic Growth

Economic growth means an increase in the production of goods and services each year, and it is expressed in terms of a rising gross domestic product (GDP). Such growth usually means that, on average, people's incomes increase from year to year. Many benefits flow from economic growth. First, a strong economy is likely to add to the government's tax revenues. As mentioned, one of the major contributing causes of the budget surpluses of the late 1990s was strong economic growth and the tax revenues it generated. A low rate of economic growth can be a sign of an impending recession, which is generally defined as negative growth over two or more consecutive quarters. Like the federal government, many state governments benefited from economic growth for years and enjoyed budget surpluses. In other years, such as 2002 and again in 2007–2009, those states saw the opposite effect as their economies slowed and state tax revenues declined, prompting budget cuts in many programs, including higher education.

Second, economic growth may make redistributive programs palatable because people are more likely to accept policies that redirect some of their money to others if they have experienced an increase in their own wealth. Economic growth also allows more people to receive benefits or increases in existing benefits from government programs. For a simple explanation, imagine the government is dealing with four areas of expenditures in a given year. If in the following year the economy grows, the budget pie becomes larger. From a budgeting perspective, this means that each of the four areas also can become larger. But if there is little or no economic growth, in order for one program to gain it must take from one or more of the other three programs, which will likely cause political conflict.

From 1996 to 2000 the GDP increased from one year to the next by at least 3.6 percent, and consumer incomes also increased. Growth in GDP was more modest from 2001 to 2007, ranging generally between 1 and 3 percent annually.[5] Vigorous economic growth and the resulting tax revenues, while obviously welcome news, also send up warning flags. If the economy grows too fast, it could lead to damaging levels of inflation, which the government seeks to avoid. Theoretically, high levels of growth cause wages to go up; and, if people have more money, they can spend more on houses, cars, and other goods. Higher prices usually follow strong consumer demand, particularly for products or services in scarce supply. A high level of economic growth may lead to a budget surplus, at which point government needs to make decisions regarding how to deal with it. Should spending be increased? Should taxes be cut? Should the funds be used to reduce the federal debt? Or perhaps it is some combination of such policy decisions. On the other hand, low levels of growth can contribute to a budget deficit, which raises different questions on how to address the budget shortfall. This situation will be addressed in the focused discussion at the end of the chapter.

Low Levels of Unemployment

Low unemployment, or **full employment,** has obvious benefits to the economy as well as to individuals. In the United States, jobs and people's ability to help themselves are regarded as better alternatives to government social programs to assist the poor. Americans are more comfortable than citizens of many other nations in helping individuals find jobs and use their abilities to improve their standard of living than they are providing public assistance, and therefore, Americans have chosen low levels of unemployment as a policy goal.

Unemployment not only harms the people without jobs but also has two deleterious effects on the economy and the government's budget. First, the more people who are unemployed, the fewer people are paying income or Social Security taxes, so that means less revenue is coming into the Treasury to pay for government programs. Second, the unemployed may be eligible for a number of government programs geared toward people with low incomes, such as Medicaid, food stamps, or welfare payments. So the government needs to pay out more money when unemployment levels rise. Most of these programs are entitlements, meaning that the government is required to pay all those who are eligible. If this number is higher than expected, budget estimates will be thrown off.

The severe economic crisis in 2009 cost millions of people their jobs as factories, retail stores, and many other businesses laid off employees to cope with a rapidly shrinking demand for products and services, not only in the United States but globally. The hundreds of people waiting in line at this job fair in San Mateo, California, in February 2009 were representative of similar scenes nationwide. California's unemployment rate jumped to 10.1 percent in January, the state's first double-digit jobless reading in a quarter century. By March 2009, the nation's unemployment rate was more than 8 percent, with about 650,000 people being added to the ranks of the unemployed each month.

In recent years, the United States has succeeded in keeping unemployment levels at a reasonable rate. Unemployment in the United States stayed between 4 and 6 percent between 1997 and 2007, but it increased to more than 8 percent in 2009.[6] When unemployment rates are very low, businesses may find it difficult to hire qualified employees. For a recent college graduate, that is good news; jobs are plentiful and opportunities abound. But low unemployment levels can be problematic for local or state economies because businesses cannot expand without an available labor supply, and that constrains economic development. Businesses may be forced to offer generous incentives to attract and keep their most valued employees. In turn, the businesses may demand that local and state policymakers reduce their tax burdens or provide some other financial benefits.

Although the overall unemployment rate has been low in recent years, the rate is not distributed evenly across the population. For example, African Americans and young people continue to have much higher rates of unemployment than the national average. The rate for African Americans has been about twice as high as the national average (around 8.3 percent in 2007), and the rate for people sixteen to twenty-four years old has hovered close to 11 percent. The Bureau of Labor Statistics compiles this kind of data for the Labor Department. See the box "Steps to Analysis: Employment and Unemployment Statistics," where you can explore variations in unemployment statistics by demographics and geographic location, particularly differences among the states.

EMPLOYMENT AND UNEMPLOYMENT STATISTICS

The Labor Department's Bureau of Labor Statistics is the primary agency responsible for collecting data on employment and unemployment. You already know that the rates vary by geography and demographics. To see these distinctions, go to the following Web site: www.bls.gov/CPS. The opening page provides current statistics regarding employment and unemployment. What is the current unemployment rate in the United States?

Now look at some of the more detailed state statistics and see what differences you can find. You can access state-level unemployment data at the Local Area Unemployment Statistics site: www.bls.gov/LAU. Select two or three states from different regions of the country (such as Alabama, New York, and Washington) and see what differences exist by state. You can click on the dinosaur icon to see historical data by state. What is the trend for each state regarding unemployment? Are there regional differences? Why do you suppose these differences exist?

Another aspect of employment that influences public policy is the changing character of jobs in the U.S. economy and in other advanced, industrialized nations. During most of the twentieth century, many of the best jobs for those without a college education were in manufacturing, but a shift from this traditional sector to the service economy has occurred, and, in general, jobs in the service sector do not pay as much as factory jobs. Workers at fast food restaurants or sales personnel in retail stores may earn the minimum wage or just a little more. Many workers who had jobs that paid quite well, often supported by unions, now see fewer positions of this kind, as competition from abroad and greater efficiencies in production have reduced the need for skilled labor. Some of these workers have been forced to move to the service sector to find employment.

The past several decades have witnessed a significant increase in the two-income family even in the face of higher divorce rates and the increasing number of single-parent families. Several reasons can be cited for this change. First, many families need the income that two wage earners bring home to maintain their lifestyle, to pay for their children's education, or to provide other benefits to their families. Second, more women are entering the workforce than in the past. This is because they want careers and have greater job opportunities than before. Even with the large influx of women into the workforce over the past thirty to forty years (see Table 7-1), the number of jobs available continues to grow for people with the right qualifications. The expanding labor force and job opportunities result from a healthy economy.

Low Levels of Inflation

A simple definition of inflation is an increase in the costs of goods and services. Inflation is an inevitable part of the U.S. economy, but policymakers try to keep it under control—that is, no more than about 3 percent a year. If wages are increasing at the same rate, the rising prices of goods and services carry little significance to most people. They would be of greater concern, understandably, for those on fixed incomes. If inflation continues and grows worse, however, it

TABLE 7-1	Labor Force Participation for Females, Aged Twenty and Older, 1970–2007 (in percentages)

Year	Rate
1970	43.3
1975	46.0
1980	51.3
1985	54.7
1990	58.0
1995	59.4
2000	60.6
2005	60.4
2007	60.6

Source: Department of Labor Bureau of Labor Statistics, Current Population Survey, www.bls.gov/cps/cpsatabs.htm.

eventually affects all citizens, which is probably why government policymakers often seem more concerned with inflation than unemployment. To demonstrate this tendency, one has only to check the various government responses and political rhetoric that have occurred as gasoline prices rise. In some cases, state policymakers proposed suspending their state gasoline taxes, and even members of Congress suggested that the federal government partially suspend its excise taxes. These actions were in direct response to the public outcry about the rising price and the potential political fallout of not doing anything about it.

In the recent past, the United States had a good record on inflation. During the past ten years, inflation, as measured by the **Consumer Price Index** (CPI), was between 2 percent and 4 percent, although in 2008 it reached 5 percent before plummeting to a negative number at the end of the year. The 2 to 4 percent level is one that most government policymakers can accept as tolerable. What is interesting is that many believe that even this small number may overstate the actual level of inflation because of the way the CPI is calculated. A commission headed by Michael Boskin, who served as President George H. W. Bush's chief economic adviser, found that the CPI overstates inflation by about 1.1 percent.[7] Why should this seemingly small discrepancy matter? Many government programs such as Social Security are tied directly to the CPI as the official measure of inflation. Increases in Social Security benefits are based on the calculated CPI. If these inflation estimates are reduced by 1 percent, it would save the government a substantial amount of money in cost-of-living adjustments over a sustained period. The box "Working with Sources: The Consumer Price Index" explains how the CPI is calculated.

Positive Balance of Trade

A positive **balance of trade** is an economic goal related to the role of the United States in an international economy. Many argue that the goal should be for the nation to export more than it imports, which would be a positive balance of trade. Another way of stating this is the United States would prefer to sell more goods to other nations than it is purchasing from them (in terms of the total dollars). For a number of decades, the nation has failed to meet this goal; in fact, it has had a large negative balance of trade. Among the many reasons for this state of affairs

WORKING WITH SOURCES

THE CONSUMER PRICE INDEX

The Consumer Price Index (CPI), the statistic most frequently used to measure inflation in the United States, represents the average change in price over time of a market basket of consumer goods and services. The Bureau of Labor Statistics makes this calculation by collecting data on goods and services from across the country. They can be consolidated into eight major categories, shown below.

Category of Goods	Examples
Food and beverages	breakfast cereal, milk, coffee, chicken, wine, full-service meals and snacks
Housing	rent of primary residence, owners' equivalent rent, fuel oil, bedroom furniture
Apparel	men's shirts and sweaters, women's dresses, jewelry
Transportation	new vehicles, airline fares, gasoline, motor vehicle insurance
Medical care	prescription drugs and medical supplies, physicians' services, eyeglasses and eye care, hospital services
Recreation	televisions, cable television, pets and pet products, sports equipment, admission fees to national parks
Education and communication	college tuition, postage, telephone services, computer software and accessories
Other goods and services	tobacco and smoking products, haircuts and other personal services, funeral expenses

It should be noted that some economists have argued that the CPI overestimates the actual inflation rate. This may be true, for example, if the CPI does not take into consideration the fact that consumers may substitute similar goods when prices increase. There are other inflation measures used as well. One is the GDP Deflator, which measures the cost of goods purchased by consumers, government, and industry. This measure is not based on a fixed basket of goods but is allowed to vary based on changing consumption patterns. Which of these do you think is the most useful measure? To learn more about inflation and its indicators, visit the Bureau of Labor Statistics site at www.bls.gov/bls/inflation.htm.

Source: "Consumer Price Indexes: Frequently Asked Questions," Department of Labor, Bureau of Labor Statistics, at www.bls.gov/cpi/cpifaq.htm#Question%206.

are the large amounts of oil imported into the United States (more than half of what the nation uses in gasoline and other oil-based products), the desire of consumers to purchase foreign products such as Japanese or German electronics, and the relative weakness in other countries' economies that translates into their inability to purchase U.S. goods. In addition, labor is cheaper in many parts of the world than it is in the United States, which has led to what critics maintain is an export of jobs to nations that produce the clothing, toys, and many other consumer goods that Americans buy at home. (See the box "Steps to Analysis: Globalization, Job Loss, and Benefits" for an exploration of this topic.) This situation would seem to be problematic, but others question that conclusion, asking whether it matters that the United States

---

STEPS TO ANALYSIS

GLOBALIZATION, JOB LOSS, AND BENEFITS

According to the International Monetary Fund (IMF), globalization refers to "the increasing integration of economies around the world, particularly through trade and financial flows." It can also refer to the transfer of labor or people across international borders. While many see globalization as positive in promoting worldwide economic development, others are concerned about the negative effects, particularly on the trade deficit and job loss in the United States. Globalization allows businesses to find more efficient ways to produce goods and services, which ultimately can lead to lower prices and more opportunities for individuals. But these benefits may not be shared by all.

In the United States, one of the major issues involves job loss that may have occurred as a result of policies such as the North American Free Trade Agreement (NAFTA) and other treaties and agreements that foster economic globalization. Cheaper labor costs abroad may lead businesses to move their production efforts to other countries. For example, between 2000 and 2003 nearly three million factory jobs were lost in the United States, including jobs in such high-tech areas as computers and electronics (Cooper 2004). A story appearing on CNN.com actually lists a large number of companies, including Coca-Cola, Microsoft, Procter and Gamble, and Time Warner, that are either sending jobs overseas or employing overseas labor (see www.cnn.com/CNN/Programs/lou.dobbs .tonight).

This is an area where one might see a conflict between the criteria of efficiency (such as efficient economic investment) and equity (job losses for American workers and gains in other nations).

1. Why might businesses choose to move their jobs overseas? Might there be efficiency arguments for keeping these jobs in the United States? What are they?

2. What economic benefits are provided as a result of globalization, including the movement of jobs? What are the economic costs?

3. As we have discussed, equity often is a matter of perspective. What are the different equity issues that arise relating to globalization and job exports?

To further explore this issue, review the following Web sites, which offer different perspectives regarding globalization. Make sure you recognize who is sponsoring these sites and what they are promoting:

www.exportingourjobs.com

www.ntu.org/main/press_papers.php?PressID=645&org_name=NTU

www.workingamerica.org/jobtracker

In addition, the *CQ Researcher* and the Government Accountability Office have published articles on exporting jobs: Mary H. Cooper, "Exporting Jobs," *CQ Researcher*, February 20, 2004, 7; U.S. Government Accountability Office, "Offshoring of Services," GAO-06-5, November 2005.

---

has a negative balance of trade. These issues also relate to the increasing globalization of the world economy. One of the biggest reasons for the rise in gasoline prices, discussed earlier, has much to do with the greater demand for oil from nations such as China as they begin to further develop their economies.

Those concerned about negative trade balances, often referred to as "protectionists," answer with a number of reasons why the United States should attempt to rectify the situation. First, they see the negative balance as evidence that U.S. goods are not as competitive as foreign goods. If this assertion is correct, a number of U.S. industries and jobs may be at risk. Second, certain industries are crucial to the nation's security and economic well-being. For example, steel manufacturing may be seen as critical for national security because steel is essential to support the military. Third are the equity considerations with regard to trade. Some countries place prohibitive tariffs or quotas on U.S. goods that prevent American companies from competing on an equal footing. Protectionists say that in fairness to domestic industries, the United States should impose similar trade restrictions. On the political side, policymakers need to support industries (and unions) where jobs may be threatened by trade imbalances.

Some analysts argue, however, that negative balances are not necessarily a problem for the United States. They believe that if it makes economic sense for a country to import more than it exports, the government should not intervene; after all, if the countries involved in the trade relationships do not see mutual benefits, they will not make the trades. Economists often use the theory of comparative advantage versus comparative disadvantage when analyzing international trade issues. Countries that produce a good particularly well and have the comparative advantage should overproduce that good and export the excess to a country that does not produce the same good very well. By the same token, a country should import goods that it does not produce as well (comparative disadvantage). For example, the United States is a prime producer of wheat and should therefore take advantage of this capacity by overproducing and selling the excess to countries, such as Saudi Arabia, that do not produce wheat very well or at all. The United States does not produce oil very efficiently and therefore should be importing this product from another country because it is cheaper to do so. This argument is just one that free-traders cite to promote their point of view.

Managing Deficits and Debt

Even with the budget surpluses of the late 1990s, the United States still had a large **national debt** to pay off, and that debt has increased as the nation has returned to deficit spending. The national debt, which is the accumulation of all of the deficits the nation has run, recently was considerably more than $10 trillion. Like any other borrower, the United States must pay interest on its debt. In 2007 this interest amounted to over $430 billion and constituted one of government's largest single expenditures ever.[8] This expenditure was interest only; no principal was repaid. The problem for the nation is the same as a credit card holder paying only the minimum amount billed every month: when the interest due is added, the payment the following month will be very close to the original amount. During the years of budget surpluses, most policymakers believed the federal government should have used at least part of the surplus to begin paying down the national debt, even if they disagreed over how much of a commitment to make to this goal.

Limiting the occurrences of federal deficits and the amount of the national debt are serious goals for the United States because they show fiscal responsibility. In other words, they demonstrate the ability to live within one's means, an important political goal. The jury is still out about the economic impact of having deficits and debt. Deficits require the government to borrow from private investors, which makes less money available for private investment. Finally, the interest the government is paying on the national debt is money that cannot be spent on other government programs—it is money that in a sense is paying for nothing. Once the debt is reduced or eliminated, more money becomes available for other government programs or tax reductions. Years of deficit spending did not, however, seem to harm the nation's overall economic situation, so it is fair to ask whether ensuring balanced budgets is an important goal. Many Republican lawmakers supported the Bush administration's proposals to decrease taxes without major reductions in spending, which can increase the deficit and the national debt. Their stance on fiscal policy was unusual for conservatives, who more often than not argue against deficit spending.

For a few years, U.S. economic policy regarding deficits and debt appeared to be moving in the direction of decreasing debt, but as more recent events have shown, these policies can change quickly in different circumstances. Will strong economic growth return, or will the nation continue to have slower rates of growth—or even enter another recession? What about the ever-increasing demands on entitlement programs? It is clear that rosy forecasts about budget surpluses and debt reduction have changed dramatically and plunged the nation back into a situation where deficit policy—alternatives for how to decrease the deficit—may once again take on a dominant role in government policymaking.

Interrelationships of Economic Goals

It is difficult to discuss major economic policy goals without also considering how they interrelate. The relationship between inflation and full employment is a frequent subject of debate. For many years, economists assumed these two goals were in conflict because they believed a certain level of unemployment would keep inflation under control. This theory made economic sense: when a larger number of people are out of work, the demand for products should go down, and with a decrease in demand should come a decrease in prices. The opposite effect should occur when unemployment is low; more people with money to spend fuels the demand for products, and prices go up. The economic problems of the 1970s changed this view when the United States experienced high levels of both unemployment and inflation.

Another often-discussed relationship is that of economic growth and inflation. This connection is of particular interest to the Fed, which is responsible for monetary policy in the United States. The Fed traditionally is concerned with inflation in the economy, and it often implements monetary policy to control it. In general, most policymakers (and citizens) see economic expansion in the United States as positive, but the Fed looks at the potential of higher prices as a possible negative consequence. If the economy is growing too fast, the Fed argues, people have more disposable income to spend, and the demand for products increases and leads to an increase in prices—inflation. The Fed therefore uses its powers to attempt to slow down the economy—for example, by raising the interest rate—to keep inflation in check.

The third relationship is between federal deficits (and debt) and the other economic indicators. With high deficits or debt, less money is available for private investment, which limits economic growth and perhaps exacerbates unemployment. The discussion here does not exhaust the relationships among these economic goals, but it should make clear that the government cannot conduct its economic policies in a vacuum; rather, it must take many factors into consideration before choosing to pursue a particular economic goal.

TOOLS OF ECONOMIC POLICY

Governments have a variety of policy tools to help them achieve their goals and deal with economic issues. **Fiscal policy** is a term that describes taxing and spending tools, but governments have other mechanisms, such as regulations or subsidies, that can also be effective. In addition, monetary policy, which is the Fed's responsibility, is another major tool of economic policy. The Fed tends to receive more media attention than other economic policymakers in the federal government, but it is only part of the picture. This section examines the various tools used to influence the economy and some of the consequences invariably associated with these choices.

Fiscal Policy

The president and Congress conduct fiscal policy when they make decisions concerning taxing and spending. At the federal level, major changes in fiscal policy often start with a presidential initiative. The president cannot act alone in this area but must work with Congress to make any major changes. The primary tool of fiscal policy is the budget process that the government goes through every year. During this process, policymakers decide how much money should be spent on government programs ranging from highway building and maintenance to national defense and education. Policymakers frequently reconsider provisions of the tax code, reducing some taxes and raising others. Tax changes and government expenditures are the major tools of fiscal policy, and policymakers use them to achieve certain economic and other public policy goals.

In a recession, for example, government policymakers would attempt to stimulate economic growth. To do this, the president and Congress have two basic choices: cut taxes or increase spending. Reducing the federal income tax puts more money into citizens' pockets, and, with that extra cash, people will likely buy more goods. The demand for products, in turn, requires companies to increase their production, which means hiring additional employees, driving down unemployment, and giving people paychecks so they can make purchases. Theoretically, these activities should promote economic growth and pull the nation out of recession. Similar to a tax cut, a tax rebate has been used in recent years to provide citizens with additional money in response to an economic downturn. Eligible taxpayers in 2008, for example, received as much as $600 for individuals and $1,200 for those filing jointly. A boost in government spending would have a similar impact. The increase in spending—for example, to build new highways—creates jobs, and these new workers are able to buy goods and services. Thus the cycle begins again. The Obama economic stimulus package in 2009, as an example, included a number of items to rebuild infrastructure and invest in energy conservation activities that could produce jobs. When the economy is running "too hot," government can use the opposite tactics to address the situation. Raising taxes takes disposable income away from individuals and limits their purchasing power. The subsequent decrease in demand should reduce the level of inflation.

Although using fiscal policy makes sense from an economic perspective and appears to be a logical way to manage or control swings in the economy, elected officials may see the matter differently. A politician campaigning for office finds it easy to support lower taxes "to get the economy moving again," but what happens to a politician who campaigns on a platform of controlling inflation by *raising* taxes? The individual will probably face a hostile public and lose the election, even if the economic policy decision is sound in terms of its impact on the nation's economy.

The Reagan administration introduced a different form of fiscal policy in 1981. Officials argued that a shortage of investment in the United States was the cause of the sluggish economy and rising deficits, and that the answer was **supply-side economics.** According to this theory, the government could increase economic growth by cutting taxes, especially for the richest individuals. The largest tax cuts went to the wealthy because, the administration assumed, they would use the additional resources to invest in the economy—building or expanding businesses, hiring more employees, and so forth—which would stimulate the economy, decrease unemployment, and increase the tax revenue collected. While not specifically calling it "supply-side economics," President George W. Bush's tax policies upon entering office in 2001 were similar in their efforts to provide greater tax relief to the rich as a way of promoting economic growth.

Monetary Policy

Monetary policy is a pivotal component of economic policy in the United States. Indeed, the chair of the Federal Reserve Board is widely considered to be among the most powerful positions in the nation's capital because of its influence on economic policymaking. Monetary policy differs from fiscal policy in several ways. First, it tries to deal with economic fluctuations by controlling the amount of money in circulation, also referred to as the "money supply." Second, the Fed implements the policy itself rather than responding to initiatives from the president and Congress. In other words, the Fed is relatively independent of the government's political institutions. Its independence is deliberate and intended to remove politics from these kinds of economic decisions. Third, the Fed's mechanisms typically affect the economy more quickly than the tools of fiscal policy. Fourth, unlike the decision making that occurs in Congress or the executive branch, most of the Fed's deliberations take place behind closed doors. This practice is controversial, given the American political culture of open decision making and political accountability.[9] In light of that tradition, it was something of a surprise when Bernanke agreed in March 2009 to be interviewed on the widely viewed television news program *60 Minutes,* the first such interview of a Fed chair in more than two decades. Bernanke clearly believed that the economic crisis called for him to speak out to reassure the American public of the Fed's critical role in the economic recovery.

When trying to influence the economy, the Federal Reserve will either increase or decrease the amount of money in circulation. If the economy is in a recession, the Fed can make money available to stimulate growth. During times of inflation, the Fed may cut back the money supply. In general, the Fed tends to be an inflation hawk and will take action to curtail it even at the risk of hindering strong economic growth. The Federal Reserve has three primary tools at its disposal to try to influence the economy: open-market operations, changing the discount (interest) rate, and changing the reserve requirements. Table 7-2 shows how the Fed uses these tools under different economic circumstances.

Open-market operations occur when the Fed decides to buy or sell U.S. Treasury bonds. The discount rate is the rate the Fed charges member banks to borrow money from the Federal Reserve Bank. Changes to this rate subsequently have an impact on the interest that banks charge their borrowers. The reserve requirement is the amount of money (a percentage of its deposits) that member banks must keep on reserve; in other words, the banks cannot use this money for any other purpose. Changes to the reserve requirement affect how much money banks can lend out and therefore either stimulate or suppress economic growth.

TABLE 7-2	Tools of Monetary Policy	
Economic Condition	Federal Reserve Tools	Projected Results
If the economy is overheated, inflation is too high, or similar expectations exist.	The Fed can decrease the money supply by: Selling government securities to the general public. Increasing the discount rate to member banks. Increasing the reserve requirement that banks must deposit.	People will buy bonds and have less disposable income with which to buy products. Member banks will have to increase their interest rates, making it more expensive to borrow money. Banks will have less money to lend. The decrease in the supply of money available to loan will likely increase interest rates, making it more expensive to borrow.
	All of these activities will result in taking money from consumers, reducing the demand for products, slowing the economy, and reducing inflation.	
If the economy is sluggish, low levels of economic growth prevail, or high levels of unemployment exist.	The Fed can increase the money supply by: Buying government securities from the general public. Decreasing the discount rate to member banks. Decreasing the reserve requirement that banks must deposit.	The Fed will buy securities from the general public, using funds from its reserves. This will put money in the sellers' pockets, and they will be able to buy more products. Banks will drop their interest rates, making it cheaper to borrow money and stimulating new spending and growth. Member banks will be provided with an additional "supply" of money that they can lend to consumers; this will reduce the interest rate and stimulate spending and growth.
	All of these activities result in giving more money to consumers, increasing the demand for products, and increasing economic growth.	

Regulation

Government regulation is rarely used explicitly to achieve economic goals, but it is a tool that can affect these goals, as we noted earlier with regard to food safety regulation and the peanut butter recall of 2009. The government has used regulatory policies for many years. In 1887, Congress created the Interstate Commerce Commission as a way of regulating the growing monopolistic railroad industry and to protect the public from unfair practices. Additional policies were developed throughout the early twentieth century, but a major infusion of regulation occurred as a result of President Franklin D. Roosevelt's New Deal program. The New Deal created a number of programs and agencies whose goals were to manage the U.S. economy during the Great Depression of the 1930s. Most of these early actions were economic regulatory policies—those whose primary intention was to regulate the potential monopolistic practices of business. The policies were somewhat limited in that most of them tended to regulate a single industry.

Since the 1970s, government has produced more social or protective regulatory policies, which generally are not concerned with monopolies. The primary goals of social or protective regulation are not usually based on economics; rather, they are enacted to protect society from unsafe business practices and products (Harris and Milkis 1996). Social regulatory policies range from ensuring clean air and water to providing a safe workplace to promising safe consumer products. Social regulatory policies differ from economic ones in a number of ways. One major distinction is that these policies tend to affect multiple industries rather than just one. For example, a workplace safety standard developed by the Occupational Safety and Health Administration (OSHA) is a requirement placed upon all businesses. These policies tend to increase the scope of government and can affect business production. An unintended consequence may be an increase in the cost of doing business, which in turn may lead to price increases (inflation), unemployment, or a diminished ability to compete with other nations in the global economy. As an example, the OSHA ergonomics standard that was halted by congressional Republicans in 2001 had cost estimates ranging from $5 to $18 billion a year (Skrzycki 2003), mainly because of the broad impact such a regulation could have on just about every workplace. For these reasons, many analysts and policymakers, as noted in chapter 6, favor the use of cost-benefit analysis or cost-effectiveness analysis to help policymakers understand the consequences of regulatory policies or proposed regulations.

Many conservatives asserted in the 1970s that excessive environmental regulation and health and safety regulation were responsible for holding back economic growth. The logic here is that businesses have to spend money to comply with environmental requirements, making fewer dollars available to them for investment and expansion (Freeman 2006). Such thinking had a powerful effect on the Reagan administration in the 1980s, and fostered its antiregulatory policy actions.

Chapter 3 defined *regulation* as any government decree that forces or prevents a particular activity, but other kinds of government mandates can also directly or indirectly affect economic policy. For example, the United States has a minimum wage law that requires employers to pay at least a certain amount to their employees. The federal minimum wage in early 2009 was $6.55 per hour; it was set to increase to $7.25 on July 24, 2009, but many states have minimum wages greater than the federal level. For example, on January 1, 2009, the rate in California was $8.00 per hour, $7.50 in New Mexico, and $7.30 in Ohio. The policy exists for good reasons, but it clearly has economic policy ramifications. When the minimum wage goes up, employers may decide either to hire fewer people or to lay off a part of their workforce. If enough employers take these actions, the rate of unemployment goes up. On the other hand, higher wages will provide individuals with more income, spur economic growth, and perhaps lead to inflation. These results are not stated goals of minimum wage policy, but they could be the consequences. Another example is the implementation of security changes following the September 11 terrorist attacks. Additional security measures were required at airports, aboard airplanes, and elsewhere. A new tax on airline tickets helped to pay for the enhanced security requirements. The additional costs did not stop people from flying, but the tax shows how an unrelated policy can have economic impacts.

Incentives, Subsidies, and Support

In addition to fiscal policy, monetary policy, and regulation, governments have other tools to achieve economic goals. These tools may be applied to a particular industry or individual businesses to promote that industry, or they may favor a particular location. State and local governments trying to encourage regional economic development and growth might provide a tax break to a company willing to locate in their area. They do this because they believe the additional jobs created by a new industry will make up for any loss in their tax base. Sometimes this

Among other tools, economic policy relies on the provision of incentives or subsidies to achieve the nation's goals. Some of the major beneficiaries of these economic subsidies have been large farming and timber operations. The photo shows a Weyerhaeuser employee in February 2006 giving instructions about which tree stump to use to rig the next guideline to the yarder on a piece of company land east of Onalaska, Washington. Washington State's timber industry was expected to see about $10.7 million in tax breaks during the next fiscal year because of legislation that would cut the state business and occupation tax for companies that cut and manufacture timber products into wood products and sell timber products wholesale.

projection is correct, and sometimes it is not.

At the federal level, Congress provides what is often called "corporate welfare" to large corporations to promote an industry. This assistance comes in the form of subsidies and tax incentives, sometimes called **tax expenditures.** While some may argue with how such an expenditure is defined, according to a study conducted by the Cato Institute, the 2006 fiscal year budget contained more than $92 billion in corporate welfare expenditures. The Cato report cites a number of examples of such expenditures, including $21 billion in agricultural subsidies that mainly go to agribusiness.[10] These kinds of support programs influence economic policy in a number of specific ways. First, government expenditures have a direct effect on the size of the budget and potentially affect deficit and debt policy. Second, tax incentives or breaks reduce the revenue the government collects, thereby limiting what it can spend. Third, if the policies are adopted to improve an industry's performance, they should lead to growth in a particular business or industry and to subsequent economic growth and higher employment rates. In the area of international trade, such programs may allow domestic companies to be more competitive abroad and perhaps improve the nation's balance of trade. Although many of these programs benefit certain businesses and industries, they also constitute another tool government has for managing the economy.

Tax Policy

Nothing generates as much political debate as discussions about raising taxes, in part because tax policy has important consequences for the public. Given their preferences, politicians would like to avoid the topic altogether. The Internal Revenue Service (IRS), the agency responsible for collecting the federal income tax, rarely receives high marks in public opinion polls. Indeed, public resentment of the IRS runs so high that over the past decade Congress has forced it to adopt a friendlier posture in its dealings with taxpayers, both individuals and corporations.[11] Still, compared to people in other developed nations, Americans are taxed at a lower rate. The reason is that the other nations have to tax at a high rate to provide for a much greater level of government-provided services, such as national health insurance and retirement benefits. According to the Organisation for Economic Co-operation and Development (OECD), the

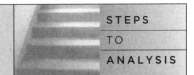

VARIABLES IN MAKING TAX POLICY

STEPS
TO
ANALYSIS

The government has a number of ways to raise $1 million through taxes, but which is best? Policymakers must think about this question when designing tax policy, and many variables may affect the ultimate decision. B. Guy Peters (2006) notes five major characteristics of taxation: collectability, fiscal neutrality, buoyancy, distributive effects, and visibility. To these we can add the ideals of horizontal and vertical equity. Each addresses different policy analysis concerns.

Collectability: the ease of collecting the tax and its ability to generate the needed revenue. This is concerned with administrative feasibility and effectiveness, in this case meaning the ability to meet the goal of collecting enough revenue to meet expenditures.

Fiscal neutrality: whether the system gives preference to one kind of revenue or expenditure without good reason. Think of a tax loophole as something that is not fiscally neutral. As implied by the name, fiscal neutrality is an equity issue. Why should one kind of expenditure or revenue be treated differently?

Buoyancy: the ability of the tax to keep up with inflation and economic growth. Buoyancy is mainly an efficiency issue in that revenues increase automatically with inflation without any policy changes being necessary. This has political feasibility concerns as well in that new tax proposals may not be necessary with a buoyant tax.

Distributive effects: the impact of the tax on different groups in the population. Who is most affected by the tax, for example, low-income or high-income households? This is mainly an equity criterion.

Visibility: the extent to which the tax is visible or acceptable to the general public. This is mainly a political feasibility criterion.

Horizontal and vertical equity: the degree to which the tax system is fair or equitable. Horizontal equity means that people who make the same amount of money pay the same amount in taxes. Vertical equity means that people with different income levels pay different amounts in taxes. As the name implies, this is an equity issue.

Think of some of the different kinds of taxes you currently pay or proposals about which you have heard. How do they stack up against these criteria? Some examples:

- Local property taxes
- Increases in federal and state gasoline taxes
- Movements to more consumptive taxes such as a national sales tax
- Increases in cigarette and alcohol taxes

Go to the President's Advisory Panel for Tax Reform at http://govinfo.library.unt.edu/taxreform panel. Here you can view the panel's November 2005 report on tax reform. Take a look at the executive summary of the report and see how the panel's proposal might be evaluated using the criteria above.

Source: B. Guy Peters, *American Public Policy: Promise and Performance,* 6th ed. (Washington, D.C.: CQ Press, 2006).

total tax rate in the United States in 2006, expressed as a percentage of GDP, was about 28 percent, while in France it was 45 percent, and in the United Kingdom and Canada it was 33 and 37 percent, respectively.[12]

On its face, the goals of tax policy are quite simple. The government (at whatever level) wants to collect enough revenue to meet its expenditure demands. The problems arise when governments try to decide *how* to tax citizens and corporations. Governments have several different ways to raise revenue, such as income taxes, property taxes, and sales taxes. They might be able to collect similar amounts of revenue using different tax methods but, because other factors need to be considered, governments turn to policy analysis for help. Tax policy is highly susceptible to policy analysis because the criteria discussed throughout the book—effectiveness, efficiency, equity, political and administrative feasibility, and others—can clarify the effects of adopting one kind of taxation relative to another. What kinds of taxes are the most politically acceptable? Which are the most equitable in spreading the burden of taxation among different groups of citizens? Will any given tax generate enough revenue, a measure of effectiveness? Will it be administratively simple to collect? The box "Steps to Analysis: Variables in Making Tax Policy" defines the different factors policymakers need to consider when selecting an appropriate tax policy.

Another question that analysts might ask is whether a proposed tax is regressive or progressive. A **regressive tax** applies the same rate of taxation to all individuals regardless of their income or socioeconomic standing. A **progressive tax** is based on the philosophy that higher earners should pay higher taxes both in terms of actual dollars and as a percentage of income. Most sales taxes are regressive in nature because they treat all income the same. A poor person buying $50 worth of items pays the same amount in sales tax as a millionaire buying the same dollars' worth of goods. Payroll deductions such as Social Security and Medicare taxes are also regressive in that the rates of taxation do not vary by tax bracket, and these taxes in particular have major effects on take-home pay. Income taxes, on the other hand, tend to be progressive. As income increases, the wage earner not only pays more actual dollars in taxes but may also graduate to a higher tax bracket and pay taxes on a larger percentage of income. Recent changes in the tax system lowered the tax brackets and reduced their number as well, making the system less progressive than it used to be.

THE BUDGET PROCESS AND ITS EFFECT ON ECONOMIC POLICY

The budget process is so complex that even a book-length treatment of how it works would not exhaust the topic. The short introduction to the process provided here is intended to make the public policy student aware of the multitude of decisions that are made each year during the budget process and their implications. The federal government's fiscal year begins on October 1 and ends on September 30 of the following year, but at any given time policymakers and government staff may be working on two or three different budgets for various years. Figure 7-1 provides a sketch of the major sequences of decisions in this process.[13]

Assumptions and Planning

The first major step in developing a budget occurs many months before the government implements the actual plan. During this stage, economic analysts in the executive branch and high-level policymakers begin the process of setting the budget's major taxing and spending goals. In addition, they develop assumptions about the economic conditions of the country, such as the growth rate and unemployment levels. These assumptions are necessary to sketch out a budget that will be implemented more than a year later. The problem with making assumptions is that conditions change and the assumptions may turn out to be wrong once the budget is implemented. For example, if policymakers assume that unemployment will be 4 percent and instead it is 6 percent,

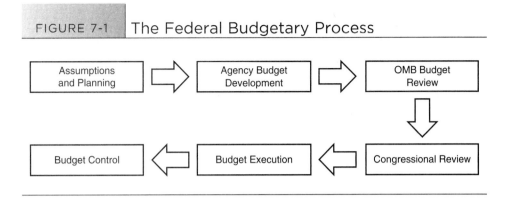

FIGURE 7-1 The Federal Budgetary Process

that difference has a major impact on the budget. Less revenue will be collected, and expenditures will likely rise to pay benefits to the unemployed. Another critical assumption is whether the economy will grow and by how much, which affects the anticipated revenues from income taxes. Eventually, however, the analysts develop their estimates of the total budget, and this information is communicated to the federal agencies so they can develop their individual budgets.

Agency Budget Development

Most of the specific work in budget development occurs at the agency level. Each agency is responsible for preparing the estimates for funding in the coming year based on its current programs as well as any new initiatives it would like to implement. Most agencies consist of bureaus or subagencies, and budget preparation begins with them and then is sent up the hierarchical chain until it reaches the highest level of the agency. Because agencies are enthusiastic about their programs, they will likely attempt to increase their budgets from year to year, a process often referred to as "incrementalism." They also recognize that they are part of a presidential team, and some will win and others will lose in the budget process. Once the agency has signed off on the budget proposal, it proceeds to the next step.

OMB Budget Review

The Office of Management and Budget (OMB) is a presidential agency that has the primary responsibility for reviewing all agency budgets and ensuring that they conform to the administration's policies and agenda. Inevitably, the agency's budget request will be higher than the amount OMB initially planned to provide it. At that point, OMB and the agency begin negotiations to settle on an amount. OMB holds hearings in which each agency defends its budget and provides a rationale for its programs and funding. The OMB director receives the final report of these hearings and negotiations and makes changes before delivering the entire package to the president for review. If agency heads are unhappy with the way OMB treated their submissions, they may attempt to make their case with the president.

The executive budget not only provides the financial information for and about the government and its programs but also sends a strong signal to Congress regarding the president's priorities for the coming year. For example, if the presidential budget includes an increase in environmental spending or a cut in defense spending, Congress can expect to see a number of substantive policy changes in these areas. Once the president and White House advisers complete their review, the presidential budget is delivered to Congress for the next stage of the process.

Congressional Review

The president initiates the budgetary process, but Congress's role in budget development is equally if not more important. Congress uses a two-step process for considering the president's budget recommendations. In the first step the House and Senate Budget Committees formulate what is called a "concurrent budget resolution" that sets out the total amount of spending, the total revenues, and the expected surplus or deficit for the coming fiscal year. Part of this resolution specifies the total spending in nineteen categories, such as national defense, agriculture, and energy, with spending levels for each. This budget blueprint for the year is to guide the House and Senate Appropriations Committees as they formulate more detailed bills that specify how much money the government can spend on specific programs (Davidson, Oleszek, and Lee 2007). Usually, these committees rely on the president's budget as a baseline for starting the budget discussion, but sometimes a president's budget is declared DOA—dead on arrival. The two Appropriations Committees work primarily through their subcommittees, which are set up to mirror the functional units of government such as defense, energy and water development, agriculture, and education. The members of Congress who serve on the Appropriations Committees typically gain substantial expertise in their areas of specialization, and with this information they can influence budget and spending decisions. The subcommittees hold hearings on the budget proposals and mark up their respective budget areas. Upon completion of the subcommittee work, the appropriations bills, like other legislation, move to the full Appropriations Committee and then to the full House or Senate.

What Congress and the president contribute to budget development, in terms of which institution has the primary responsibility, has shifted back and forth throughout U.S. history based on the ebb and flow of power between these branches of government. Major changes occurred in 1974 with the passage of the Congressional Budget and Impoundment Control Act. Congress enacted this legislation to recapture some of the budget authority it had lost to the White House in previous years. The act had a number of noteworthy provisions. First, it created congressional Budget Committees to facilitate the coordination of budget development within the legislative branch. These committees are responsible for setting overall taxing and spending levels (Thurber and Durst 1993). Second, it created the Congressional Budget Office (CBO), a legislative agency responsible for providing Congress with economic and budget information. In the past, Congress often had to rely on the president's OMB estimates and assumptions, and some members were concerned about the potential for political manipulation of the process. The CBO is a nonpartisan organization that most neutral observers believe provides the more accurate assessments of economic and budget issues. If nothing else, Congress now has its own independent assessment of economic assumptions and budget forecasts.

Once Congress passes the budget, the bill goes to the president for signature or veto in twelve separate appropriations bills that reflect the functional divisions in government. At this point, the president's options in regard to the budget are limited: accept and sign the appropriations bills or veto one or more of them. Many presidents have asked for **line-item veto** authority, a budgeting tool that would allow the president to delete specific items from an appropriations bill without rejecting the whole bill. Most state governors have this power. The Republican Congress in 1996 provided President Bill Clinton with a version of the line-item veto, sometimes referred to as "enhanced rescission authority," that he used a number of times in subsequent years. The Supreme Court, however, struck down the line-item veto law as unconstitutional, stating that it violated the constitutional provision requiring all legislation to be passed in the same form by both houses of Congress and sent to the president in its entirety for signature or veto. The Court said by vetoing part of a bill, the president was changing its form.[14]

In recent history, particularly under divided government, partisan politics has made enactment of the budget an excruciating task. The White House favors its version of federal spending priorities, and Congress may disagree strongly. If a president is prepared to exercise the veto option, the president can force Congress to negotiate or risk being held accountable for a breakdown in the budget process. If a budget is not passed by October 1, then technically the government must shut down.

A dramatic example of what can happen if both sides dig in their heels occurred in 1995 when Congress, completely in Republican hands for the first time in forty years, attempted to use the budget to push its conservative agenda, which included substantial cuts in many government programs that were strongly opposed by the Democratic minority. When Congress sent its budget to President Clinton for his signature, he took the opportunity to confront the Republicans on what he believed was the wrong direction for the country. He refused to sign the budget, and the result was that the government officially closed—on two separate occasions. When such quarrels occurred in the past, the government shut down for merely days, with only minor ramifications. In this situation, however, the stalemate between President Clinton and the Republican Congress lasted for almost a month (Thurber 1996b). The other trend in budget politics is for Congress to pass large omnibus bills, often pork-laden, that include many programs the president supports and some not. Presidents find it almost impossible to veto these bills. The federal highway bill that was enacted in 2005 and included hundreds of millions of dollars of new expenditures is an example of such an omnibus bill.

Typically, however, the president and Congress are able to reach agreement on a budget, even if neither is completely satisfied with the outcome. Sometimes Congress enacts continuing resolutions that allow government agencies to operate while the budget negotiations carry on. When the president signs the final appropriations bills, the budget they represent becomes law, and the next step of the process begins.

Budget Execution and Control

Once Congress and the president approve a budget, the various government agencies execute it by spending the money to implement the programs receiving budget support. This spending goes for personnel, day-to-day supplies, and providing services and payments to those who qualify under the agency's programs, such as farm price supports or Social Security. Each agency typically decides what mechanisms to use to spend its allotted budget.

The final step in the process, and one to which most people pay little attention, is budget control. After the fiscal year is over, the Government Accountability Office (GAO) is responsible for ensuring that the money was spent legally and properly. In many ways this amounts to an audit of the entire government. The GAO reports its findings to Congress, and the members may use the results to reward an agency or hold its metaphorical feet to the fire.

ECONOMIC POLICY: SUCCESSES AND FAILURES

In the past few decades a number of economic policies have been proposed and implemented. These policies have enjoyed varying degrees of success in achieving their stated goals. Some also have unintended consequences, that is, impacts that were neither planned nor foreseen when the policies were designed and implemented. This section considers several of the most significant of these economic policy actions.

Ronald Reagan's and George W. Bush's Tax Cuts

Tax cuts are always politically popular with citizens, but presidents will make economic arguments for proposing such policies. When President Reagan took office in 1981, he faced an economy that by many measures was in a recession. Economic growth was low, both inflation and unemployment were high, the deficit was rising, and the country's morale was low. Reagan championed supply-side economics, which its adherents claimed would encourage investment and economic growth. The political problem for the president was how to sell the idea to a dubious Democratic House of Representatives.

Reagan's electoral mandate—he won 489 electoral votes to President Jimmy Carter's 49—was a major reason for his ability to secure passage of the Economic Recovery Tax Act of 1981. The $162 billion tax cut included a 23 percent reduction in personal income taxes, cuts in the highest tax rate, and major cuts in business taxes (Peterson and Rom 1988). The result was more money in the pockets of individuals, especially the wealthy. The hope of the supply-siders was that this new money would be used to invest in and expand the economy. After a recession in the early 1980s, the U.S. economy indeed began to grow in 1983. Unemployment decreased and inflation was held in check, so the tax cut and other Reagan economic policies achieved in part many of the administration's economic goals.

One criticism, however, lingers to this day. The president's policies, usually called Reaganomics, created unprecedented increases in the nation's deficit and debt. The national debt went from about $1 trillion in 1981 to well over $5 trillion by the late 1990s. The Reagan administration had hoped that the additional tax revenue generated through economic growth would pay for its spending priorities, including the rise in defense spending. This did not happen. Higher interest rates imposed by the Fed's monetary policy during the 1980s took back part of the money Reagan's fiscal policy had provided. In addition, domestic spending did not slow down enough to offset the potential loss in revenue created by the massive tax cuts. Although the Reagan administration redefined tax policy in many ways, it also helped to create a different problem in terms of economic goals. In fact, it was during this period that policymakers learned to pay more attention than ever before to deficit and debt management in economic policy. Many proposals and policies were offered to address the deficit problem generated by the Reagan policies.

Taking office in 2001, President Bush, like President Reagan, faced a sputtering economy, and his vision for tax policy was an across-the-board tax cut. Much like the Reagan cuts, a significant portion of this cut would go to the nation's richest citizens, which Bush did not see as a problem because they pay a significant percentage of federal taxes. As president, Bush was able to work with the Republican-controlled Congress to enact tax legislation that not only lowered tax brackets but also provided a rebate check of $300 or $600 to many taxpayers during the summer of 2001. The

A customer shops for flat screen televisions at Best Buy in Guilderland, New York, in January 2008. At the time, policymakers in Washington were discussing a $150 billion economic stimulus package that might include $800 tax rebates for individuals and $1,600 for married couples. The checks were expected to arrive by late spring, and people could choose to spend the money as they wished. Some said they would use the rebate checks for a big-ticket item like a flat-panel TV, but most indicated they would use the money to pay down their credit card debt or to save for the future. Despite the 2008 stimulus policy, the economy was not jump-started. In fact, it got much worse by the fall of 2008, a reminder that setting economic policy involves uncertain estimates of what effects such spending bills are likely to have on the nation's economy.

weakening economy helped persuade Congress to approve the bill; as noted earlier, a similar one also passed in 2008. The move was politically popular and from an economic standpoint could be an effective way to spur economic growth. Programs to further reduce taxes were implemented during the Bush administration, including a movement to repeal the estate tax (discussed at length in chapter 6). In most cases, such taxes only affect the richest 2 percent of the population.[15] Responding to President Obama's budget plan submitted in early 2009, Congress voted to extend middle class tax cuts and allow tax cuts to those making more than $250,000 to expire at the end of the year. As you might imagine, policymakers in the two major parties are divided over whether letting these taxes expire constitutes a tax increase or not.

As already noted, however, the 2001 tax cut had implications beyond the attempt to stimulate the economy. President Bush entered his second term of office with an increasing deficit. Administration officials said that the growing deficit was due to forces outside their control, such as a recession, slow recovery, and the September 11 attacks. But many analysts believe that a good portion of the shift from surplus to deficits that occurred under President Bush can be attributed to policy choices such as tax cuts, the wars in Afghanistan and Iraq, and a new prescription drug program for those on Medicare.[16] In addition, the president called for Social Security reform, which also would have budgetary implications if adopted. Through all of this, the administration had favored the maintenance or even an extension of these tax cuts, while the two major presidential candidates in 2008 held different views on the matter: John McCain favored retaining the tax cuts and Barack Obama opposed doing so for those with high incomes. Democrats and fiscal conservatives have been highly vocal in raising their concerns about these economic policies. Was it justifiable to give large benefits to the rich, especially in light of a growing gap between the rich and the poor? How will these decisions affect policymaking in the coming years? These are crucial questions that will continually need to be evaluated.

Responses to the Deficit

As mentioned, one consequence of the Reagan tax cuts was a tremendous growth in the federal budget deficit. While fixing a deficit is theoretically a simple matter—either increase taxes or decrease government spending so that revenues are more in line with expenditures—politically, these two policy choices can be difficult. President Reagan was in office and holding the line against any significant tax increases. Democrats, on the other hand, were unwilling to go along with any additional cuts in the programs they supported. In essence, the political will to decrease the deficit was not there. In an effort to deal with the situation, in 1985 Congress enacted the Balanced Budget and Emergency Deficit Control Act, otherwise known as Gramm-Rudman-Hollings (GRH) for the three senators who cosponsored the legislation.

The idea behind GRH was to require progressive reductions in the deficit over five years to ensure a balanced budget by 1991. Supporters hoped that requiring relatively small reductions in the deficit (about $30 to $40 billion a year) might prove to be politically feasible. The real innovation with the legislation, however, was an enforcement mechanism that cut spending if Congress and the president failed to make reductions through the budget process. This mechanism, referred to as "sequestration," required automatic spending cuts to ensure achievement of the deficit target in any given year split evenly between defense and domestic spending.[17] The General Accounting Office was to implement sequestration, but in *Bowsher v. Synar* (1986) the Supreme Court ruled this part of the legislation unconstitutional. This decision led to the enactment in 1987 of Gramm-Rudman-Hollings II, which gave the sequestration function to the Office of Management and Budget and extended the deficit targets.

The primary goal of GRH and GRH II was to restrain congressional spending and ultimately to achieve a balanced budget. Did it succeed? By almost all accounts, the answer is "no." In reality, the deficit almost doubled by 1992. Many believed that sequestration would enforce discipline in the budget process because members of Congress or the administration would not want to see forced cuts in their programs. But the law provided too many loopholes to avoid sequestration. In addition, many legislators saw that forced percentage cuts in their favorite programs were better than targeted cuts that could be larger (Thurber 1996b).

When it became clear that GRH was not going to provide the deficit reductions required, in 1990 Congress and President George H. W. Bush formulated a new budget plan called the Budget Enforcement Act (BEA). The BEA also attempted to reduce the federal deficit, which was approaching $200 billion by then. Among the law's most important reforms was a "pay-as-you-go" provision that required all tax and spending legislation to be deficit neutral. In other words, if new legislation increased expenditures for a particular program, the new spending had to be offset either by subsequent increases in revenue or decreases in expenditures in another program. The BEA also established spending ceilings for each discretionary spending category (defense, domestic, and international). If spending went higher, the sequestration process would be applied only to the category of the offending area. Sequestration could occur only by changes to legislation, not by changes in economic conditions (Thurber and Durst 1993).[18]

The effectiveness of the BEA in reducing the deficit has been the subject of serious debate. On the one hand, the deficit was reduced during the late 1990s and the Treasury had a surplus. Some credit the BEA and President Clinton's extension of its components through 1998 as the reason for the country's economic turnaround. On the other hand, others argue that credit for the deficit reduction should go to the nation's economic growth during this time. The reality is that a combination of both factors (and others) improved the country's deficit situation for a few years. Politically, many have been able to take credit for the economic prosperity at the turn of the century. Perhaps the only person who directly experienced negative political ramifications as a result of the BEA was the first President Bush, who broke his "read my lips, no new taxes" pledge when he signed the law. One aspect of the BEA that has become more important over time is the definition of what constitutes an exemption under the law. The BEA always provided for exemptions, situations in which a budget ceiling could be exceeded. For most of the 1990s these situations were limited to true natural or economic disasters. Since then, according to a former deputy director of the CBO, "the definition was discarded and any semblance of discipline abandoned."[19] By expanding the definition of what constitutes an emergency, policymakers are able to spend well beyond the limits of the original budget.[20]

ECONOMIC ISSUES AND CHALLENGES

Looking at economic policy is always interesting because of the new or renewed challenges that must be faced from year to year. Market swings occur all the time, and changes in economic growth and inflation can affect the overall economy. In addition, what is termed "consumer confidence" plays a role in the health of the economy because consumer spending accounts for about 70 percent of economic activity in the United States. All of these factors point to the dynamic nature of the economy and economic policy. What might this term hold in regard to economic challenges and issues for the United States? In addition to the changing nature of budgetary politics, where surpluses can become deficits in a matter of months, there are many other issues to consider.

Maintaining Economic Growth

America's years of strong, sustained economic growth produced many positive benefits: tax receipts were up, unemployment was low, the deficit was eliminated, and there were decreases in the national debt. People across the nation saw the benefits of a strong economy as their wages rose and opportunities for personal advancement expanded. It is clear, however, that this kind of sustained growth could not go on forever.

Growth is a cornerstone of not only a strong economy but also a satisfied electorate, which can translate to a stable political system. The economic growth of the 1990s facilitated action

WORKING WITH SOURCES

VIEWS ON ECONOMICS AND BUDGETING

Many of the economic and budget sites available on the Web represent various partisan and ideological perspectives. Some focus on macrobudget issues, such as unemployment and inflation, while others are concerned with the budget's effects on specific programs and policy areas. Explore the sites and try to identify the partisan or ideological orientation of the organization that sponsors each of them. You can usually find this information in the site's "mission" or "about" links. A short comment from the organization's Web site follows below. How evident are the differences in political orientation? What kind of information tells you most reliably what each organization's political leanings are?

www.cbpp.org. Center on Budget and Policy Priorities

"... is one of the nation's premier policy organizations working at the federal and state levels on fiscal policy and public programs that affect low- and moderate-income families and individuals."

www.concordcoalition.org. The Concord Coalition

"... a nationwide, non-partisan, grassroots organization advocating fiscal responsibility."

www.whitehouse.gov/administration/eop/cea/. Council of Economic Advisers

See site.

www.nber.org. National Bureau of Economic Research

"... is a private, nonprofit, nonpartisan research organization dedicated to promoting a greater understanding of how the economy works. The NBER is committed to undertaking and disseminating unbiased economic research among public policymakers, business professionals, and the academic community."

www.taxfoundation.org. The Tax Foundation

"The mission of the Tax Foundation is to educate taxpayers about sound tax policy and the size of the tax burden borne by Americans at all levels of government."

on many of the nation's problems such as the deficit. The strong economy also made possible the action on welfare reform in 1996 and related policies. Many analysts point out that states were able to meet the caseload reduction requirements of the law because of the strong economy and its effect on employment. When jobs are plentiful people can move off the welfare rolls. The strong economy also allowed Congress to spend money on highway construction and maintenance, budget items that had been deferred because of deficits. These expenditures not only help local communities but also allow members of Congress to score political points with their constituents.

The real challenge for the United States and its economy is what to do when economic growth begins to lose momentum or the nation enters a recession. Economic slowdowns over the past eight years—which eventually led to an economic recession—demonstrate that it is not realistic to expect a high level of growth to continue indefinitely. Changing economic conditions should cause policymakers to evaluate priorities and perhaps make changes. But doing so forces them to confront difficult political choices, and not everyone necessarily agrees on the best way to get the economy moving again. What types of expenditures might be directly linked to job

One of the hardest hit segments of the economy in 2008 and 2009 was housing; home values declined substantially, and many homeowners found themselves unable to keep up with mortgage payments and also unable to refinance their home loans to reduce those payments. This was particularly likely in cases in which the value of the mortgage loans exceeded the current value of the homes, or those instances in which individuals lost their jobs or suffered a medical emergency. Foreclosure rates rose sharply across the country, especially in areas like Las Vegas, where home prices had risen substantially over the previous few years. The photo shows a sign outside a foreclosed home in North Las Vegas, Nevada, in February 2009. Home prices in Las Vegas fell by 33 percent compared to the same period the year before. This slide was the second worst of twenty cities tracked by a commonly used housing value index. Policymakers in Washington struggled to figure out what they might be able to do to help the ailing housing sector.

creation and economic development? Is increased spending for higher education an investment in economic development, or is the effect too indirect? How do policymakers balance a perceived need for government intervention with an ever-increasing deficit? How does one cut or eliminate popular programs backed by an alert and powerful constituency? Can and should revenue be raised through tax increases? How much emphasis should be placed on reducing the federal deficit and debt? These are the kinds of questions policymakers ask when budget problems exist. The box "Working with Sources: Views on Economics and Budgeting" provides some additional sources of information from a variety of organizations interested in budget and economic policy.

Growth of Entitlements

Entitlement programs are very pronounced in the United States. An **entitlement program** is one with payment obligations determined by the law that created it, not by the budget associated with that program. Under an entitlement program, any person who meets the eligibility requirements is entitled to receive benefits from the program. The clearest example of an entitlement program is Social Security. When people reach a certain age, they are eligible to receive Social Security payments. A major difference between an entitlement program and other government programs is how it is funded. The usual budget process does not apply; in other words, Social Security administrators do not determine their annual budgets as other agencies do. To change the amount of money spent on an entitlement program, Congress has to amend the authorizing law.

Entitlement programs account for a large portion of the federal budget. Unless policymakers decide to change the substance of the law, much of the federal budget is out of their hands at the start. Moreover, entitlements have grown tremendously. In 1968 entitlements made up approximately 28 percent of the budget, and today they are well over 50 percent of the federal budget. This is a dramatic increase that is expected to grow as the baby boomer generation ages and increases demands on Social Security and Medicare. One of the major concerns about the ever-expanding entitlement programs is that they crowd out other budget expenditures. These other programs must go through the typical budget process and may take the brunt of any cuts because of their more precarious position. So-called discretionary spending, which includes funding for defense, the environment, national parks, and upgrading air traffic control systems, among other programs, has decreased significantly as a percentage of the budget partly because of the growing entitlement expenses. How likely is it that the government can get entitlements under control? Economically, it makes sense to do this because policymakers would probably want more authority over government spending. From an equity perspective, it seems only right that no government expenditures receive special treatment in the budget process. The real issue is political: Why did policymakers decide to make programs such as Social Security and Medicare entitlements in the first place? The answer to this question explains why it is so difficult to make changes now.[21] Figure 7-2 shows where the money in the fiscal 2009 federal budget comes from and where it is spent.

Home Mortgage Crisis

In 2007 it became clear to economists and politicians around the country that there was a growing problem related to home mortgage defaults and to the securities that financial institutions had issued that were based on shaky mortgages. A large number of people had purchased homes through "subprime mortgages" that often come with deceptively low adjustable lending rates (which can rise over time and impose a so-called balloon payment or other penalties) or higher than usual rates that are imposed for poor credit risks. Subprime mortgages are generally provided to individuals who do not qualify for traditional loans because of insufficient income, inability to make a down payment, or poor credit rating; they are therefore riskier. As a result, those with these types of mortgages are more likely to be adversely affected by a downturn in the economy (for example, by losing their jobs or incurring unexpected medical expenses), and therefore default on their loans. As economic problems continued, the United States saw a sharp increase in home foreclosures as a result of such developments. The secondary effect is that this can harm other homeowners, even those not at risk of defaulting on their mortgages, because home prices in an entire neighborhood could fall.[22] Declining home values may prevent homeowners from refinancing or using their homes for equity purposes

FIGURE 7-2

Fiscal 2009 Proposed Federal Budget by Category (in billions of dollars)

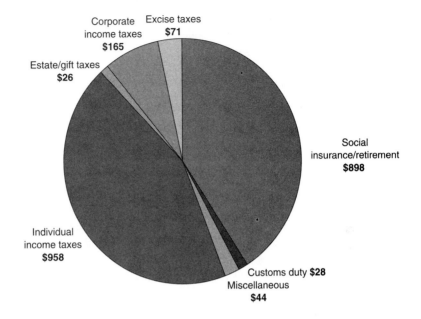

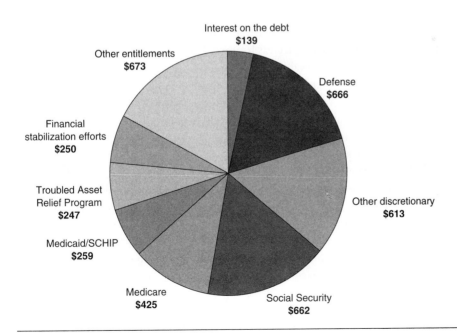

Source: Office of Management and Budget, Budget of the United States Government, Fiscal Year 2010, available online at www.gpoaccess.gov/usbudget/fy10/pdf/fy10-newera.pdf, p. 114. The data represent the estimated fiscal 2009 amounts.

(for example, to borrow money to purchase a car or pay for college tuition) because banks could no longer justify such lending practices in light of the reduced value of the homes. This, in turn, can decrease consumer confidence, further harming the overall economy.

Much of the fallout from the housing debacle can also be traced to what now seems like poor consumer choices when people purchased homes that were more expensive than they could afford only because they were enticed to do so when mortgage rates were low and they believed home values would continue to rise indefinitely. As home values declined, however, many were stuck. They could not make their mortgage payments, refinance, or sell their homes. Some chose to walk away and hand the keys over to the banks, particularly when home values fell to a point where people owed more on their mortgages than the homes were worth in this market, a situation commonly called "being underwater." This meant additional homes would likely be foreclosed and expand the number of homes on the market even more—in addition to ruining the credit rating of those homeowners who found themselves in this unfortunate situation.[23] While it is clear that such issues most directly affect the individual homeowners, especially those who face losing their homes, and the banks and financial institutions holding the mortgages or mortgage-backed securities, there is a very substantial national economic impact as well, as the country—and the world—discovered in 2008.

In both 2008 and 2009, Congress debated various alternatives to this problem. One proposal was the development of a fund that lenders could tap into to help refinance mortgages that were worth more than the home's value. This could allow the lender to offer a lower interest rate so that individuals could stay in their homes. Opponents argue that such a solution would reward lenders that made bad decisions and would be a "bailout" and poor use of taxpayer money. While some who are perhaps unworthy might have benefitted from such a policy, it is equally clear that a large number of people acting in good faith and trying to pursue the "American dream" of owning their own home would benefit as well.

At a minimum, the home mortgage crisis has caused policymakers, once again, to reexamine existing laws and regulations regarding banking and financial services. Some have argued that the deregulatory banking policies of the 1980s and 1990s are partially to blame for the crisis because so many of the newer and exotic financial arrangements widely used on Wall Street and around the world (various forms of mortgage-backed securities) were either not regulated at all or only minimally. Thus it is understandable that many have called for a total revamping of the nation's financial regulatory system, including enhanced authority for the Federal Reserve, the Securities and Exchange Commission, and the Commodity Futures Trading Commission. Many proposals have been made, for example, by President Bush's Treasury secretary, Henry Paulson, and President Obama's Treasury secretary, Timothy Geithner. Those proposals are sure to get careful consideration throughout 2009 and into the future.[24] What does seem clear is that the results of this mortgage crisis as well as its potential policy solutions may be with us for years to come. In addition, the potential economic, political, and ethical implications all need to be considered.

Challenges for State Governments

State governments continue to face challenges, some old and some new. The states have always been obliged to keep their fiscal houses in order, and this task became more problematic during President Reagan's devolution movement, which led to more responsibilities for the states but not necessarily to more funding to carry them out. The 1980s also saw an increase in the number of unfunded mandates imposed on states. As noted in chapter 2, unfunded mandates are federal requirements (often regulatory) placed upon the states without federal funding to pay for them. The result was that many states had to either cut services in other areas or raise their own taxes to ensure compliance. Unfunded mandates were alleviated to some extent with passage of the Unfunded Mandates Reform Act in 1995.

States found relief from their financial woes during the strong economic growth period of the late 1990s, which also helped the federal government deal with its deficit. Many states were running budget surpluses, providing tax relief to their citizens, and expanding services. The passage of welfare reform in 1996 (see chapter 9), while transferring still more responsibilities to the state governments, came with federal money attached. In many states, the strong economy allowed public officials to reduce their welfare caseloads while using only a fraction of their allotted federal dollars. Many states, in fact, began to use the money for experimental programs such as subsidized day care.

Because states typically may not run deficits, the economic bust at the turn of the century was harder on state governments than on the federal government, which can spend money it does not have. The economic slowdown had detrimental impacts on state tax revenues, and deficit projections quickly became the rule for many states. According to the National Association of State Budget Officers, by the end of fiscal year 2008 a number of states were experiencing fiscal difficulties, with projections that forty-five out of fifty were facing shortfalls. Some states had to reduce enacted budgets, a number are assuming negative budget growth for fiscal year 2009, and Medicaid spending is continuing to grow.[25] There are still tremendous spending pressures on the states, such as increases in support for education and entitlement programs, and these pressures often prevent investment in other areas, such as education or infrastructure. These burdens will require state policymakers to use all the fiscal tools at their disposal to ensure budgetary integrity in the years ahead.

FOCUSED DISCUSSION: HOW TO ADDRESS THE BUDGETARY SHORTFALL

For a while it seemed that the numbers would keep getting larger. During 2000 each estimated surplus number stating what the surplus would be for the next ten years was greater than the last. In February the Clinton White House projected $746 billion; then in June the figure rose to $1.87 trillion. By July the nonpartisan CBO projected the highest level yet, with the ten-year surplus estimated to reach $2.2 trillion. A number of conditions backed up these rosy scenarios, including a strong economy, higher tax revenues, and prudent fiscal policies during the 1990s. But, as has been stressed throughout the chapter, the picture can change quickly with regard to surpluses and deficits. In 2005 the nonpartisan CBO was projecting annual deficits until 2015. President Bush stated that he wanted to halve the size of the deficit by 2009. These claims came before the projected $200 billion it may take to rebuild New Orleans following Hurricane Katrina and before the true costs of the new Medicare prescription drug program were revealed. Now, with deficits being projected at over a trillion dollars in 2009 and with deficit spending likely to continue for the next ten years, it is clear that policymakers may need to rethink the deficit issue. Quick fixes are unlikely, and it will take a long-term strategy that may not be seriously considered until the current economic environment improves.

Be that as it may, eventually talk will turn to deficit reduction and the question must be asked: How will this happen? Coming up with solutions to deficits is a common exercise among think tanks. Some have argued that a considerable amount of money would be saved if the government were just more efficient. There have been numerous reports, for example, of the rush to spend money in response to the September 11 attacks and in relief efforts following Hurricanes Katrina and Rita. In trying to respond quickly to these demands, policymakers probably wasted a substantial amount of money. These examples notwithstanding, it is hard to conceive of reducing a trillion-dollar deficit through greater efficiency.

Generally, reducing the deficit requires that the government either bring in more revenue or cut expenditures. As noted earlier, neither of these options is politically popular. This focused discussion explores a few of the general alternatives—each with multiple choices—to reduce our federal deficit. These choices are relatively straightforward and not necessarily mutually exclusive. In fact, one may want to explore all of these options:

- decrease entitlement expenditures;
- decrease discretionary expenditures;
- increase revenue through taxes or other devices.

Decreasing entitlement expenditures is an important option to explore because of the size of the entitlement budget in the United States. As mentioned, over 50 percent of federal expenditures are entitlements, so it is in this category that one may be able to get significant reductions in federal spending. Upon entering office, President Obama stressed the importance of reforming Medicare and Social Security as one step toward long-term economic recovery. Reducing discretionary spending is what generally has been occurring in the United States for the past thirty years as entitlements have grown. Discretionary funds include a wide range of expenditures such as those for the environment, most education, foreign aid, and a range of other programs. Some would even classify military expenditures as discretionary (although it could be its own category), and if so they would represent a significant percentage of the budget. It is important to recognize that much of the 2009 economic stimulus plan would typically be characterized as discretionary expenditures. Critics of government waste and pork-barrel expenditures often look to this category to find cuts. Finally, there is always the option of bringing in more revenue. This may occur painlessly through economic growth, but more than likely it may require an increase of taxes or fees. One may be able to make the argument for increased taxes from the perspective that U.S. citizens are taxed at a far lower level than in other industrialized nations. Critics argue the additional taxes will probably just lead to more spending and slow down economic growth.

All of these choices involve complex economic relationships that need to be better understood in order to comprehend the arguments put forth and the consequences of each choice. We have stated that policy analysts can use a number of different criteria in evaluating policy alternatives including efficiency, effectiveness, and equity. For this case study on how to decrease the deficit we use economic, political, and ethical criteria as we examine the three alternatives.

Economic Issues

The economic issues associated with how to decrease the federal budget deficit may be a bit different from those of the other public policy areas discussed in the following chapters. Here, the discussion does not necessarily attempt to address a problem of a market failure, such as a negative externality, but the budget has obvious economic implications that should be understood when considering the alternatives provided.

As stated earlier, one of the biggest economic arguments for decreasing entitlement spending is the overall size of this part of the budget. Of course, there are many entitlements from which to choose, including such popular programs as Social Security and Medicare, as well as a number of agricultural subsidies. Social Security is the government's largest program, and there are a number of options available to reduce outlays for it. One would be to decrease the cost of living adjustment (COLA) paid to beneficiaries each year. The COLA occurs every year in response to the consumer product index. According to the CBO, reducing this adjustment by a mere 0.3 percentage points would save $26 billion over five years.[26] Another option might be to further increase the retirement age or to reduce benefits. The downside to these options is that such reductions in benefits may have a detrimental effect on the economy because beneficiaries will have less money to spend. For Medicare, some have argued for an increase in the age at which one becomes eligible for the program. Similar changes have occurred in Social Security, which has slowly increased the required age for full benefits from sixty-five to sixty-seven. A similar change in Medicare could substantially reduce the program's outlays. President Obama called for a "fiscal responsibility" summit to discuss Medicare and Social Security in particular.

Of course, reducing any of these entitlement programs may have other kinds of economic impacts beyond reducing the deficit. Those who rely on agricultural subsidies might argue that their crops are not viable without government supports. Raising interest rates on federal student loans may decrease the number of students attending college, which would limit their future earning potential. The real problem with changing any entitlement program is that in order to make these adjustments, legislators have to change the authorizing statute. All of these programs are either very popular or have a well-represented constituency that benefits from the programs, which makes such changes difficult.

Reducing discretionary spending is another option. A large variety of programs are categorized as discretionary, and it would be impossible to discuss every one of them as a proposal for elimination or decrease. Some have argued that too much is spent on military expenditures, which make up a sizable portion of the budget. There have been large increases in discretionary military spending since 2000, some of which supports the war on terrorism. Reduction in military spending is often difficult because of the strong support such spending generates from many in Congress as well as the Department of Defense. In addition, military spending acts as a major economic boost for local communities. A related area is homeland security. It is clear that a large amount of money has been spent since the attacks of September 11, but it is equally clear that problems still exist with security, and more funding may be needed in the years ahead.

One issue regarding other areas of discretionary spending is that during the previous era of large deficits, these programs did not receive major funding increases. Because discretionary spending is just that—discretionary—it was easier for policymakers to ignore the needs of these areas than of the entitlement programs. As such, while some of these programs may have seen some increases in funding, the level of the increase may not have met program needs. A good example may be in the area of education funding. As we will discuss in chapter 10, the federal government has increased its support for primary and secondary education as a result of the No Child Left Behind Act. But, while support has increased, many states argue that the increases do not provide sufficient money to implement the requirements and goals of the act. Some of these discretionary expenditures, such as for education and job training, may represent investments that could improve the nation's economic performance in the future. Others, such as environmental spending, protect important resources and the health of the nation's citizens, which also have economic value even if they are not calculated as part of the budget. In some situations, one could argue that the amount budgeted for an activity is insufficient to alleviate the existing market failure. For example, perhaps the amount budgeted for environmental protection is inadequate to address the negative externalities associated with the production of goods and services. Another example may be that the funds to ensure a capable military are currently insufficient and that it is the government's responsibility to provide this pure public good. All of which is to say that many times these decisions come down to the political priorities of those in office.

Increasing revenue through an increase in taxes or fees also has obvious economic implications. In a deficit situation there is not enough revenue to meet expenditure demands, so one might think the best course of action would be to increase revenues. As discussed earlier in the chapter, a change in fiscal policy that increases taxes takes money out of the pockets of individuals. This could then lead to less spending and potentially a slowing down of the economy. Slower economic growth can then translate to less revenue generated through taxes. This is why many conservatives and antitax groups suggest decreasing taxes in order to increase economic growth and as an alternative way to increase revenue. Naturally, there are definite political implications to the tax question. These will be addressed in the next section.

Political Issues

To say that politics drives most of the debate surrounding the budget deficit alternatives would be a vast understatement. All of the alternatives being discussed have strong advocates and opponents both within government as well as in the interest group community. In addition, while sometimes the deficit itself does not generate much public interest, cutting desired programs or proposals to increase taxes will quickly gain the public's attention.

From a political standpoint, suggesting cuts to existing entitlement programs may be the most volatile option. This is especially true since many of these programs are projected to be underfunded in the future and not able to provide the current level of benefits. The political debate in cutting these programs is certain to be highly contentious, and because cuts in entitlement programs would require changes to the law itself, there is an extra burden placed on Congress for enacting such cuts. It is no secret that any suggestions to reform programs such as Social Security and Medicare are often met with accusations that the supporters of the so-called reforms are trying to harm senior citizens. One only has to look at the Social Security debate in 2005 as an illustration (see chapter 9 for more information). By suggesting cuts in these popular entitlement programs, proponents are opening the door to intense criticism from politically active groups such as AARP. In addition, elected policymakers, because of the political sensitivity, are reluctant to suggest decreases in these programs for fear that they will lose their positions. Balancing the budget on the backs of the elderly is usually not seen as politically acceptable. It is a foregone conclusion that presidential backing is necessary for changes in these types of entitlements, and as mentioned earlier, President Obama appears to want to tackle these issues as part of the larger economic policy concerns.

The same can be said for many other entitlement programs, such as agricultural subsidies. Policymakers do not want to be labeled "anti-farmer," especially in a country that holds the family farmer in such high regard. It tends not to matter that a large proportion of these subsidies go not to the family farmer but to agribusiness. On the other hand, because of the size of these programs, one could gain a lot of benefits with relatively modest changes, which can be appealing. In addition, since many people are not currently eligible for these entitlements, there could be a chance to gain public support for the cuts. Regardless, is it any wonder why policymakers tend to shy away from these kinds of choices?

Political debate about cutting discretionary programs can also be contentious. Generally, though, these debates are more limited because the programs are smaller and, depending on the program, may have less support and even opposition. For example, a proposal to decrease spending in environmental protection programs will generate an uproar, particularly from environmental interest groups, but industry and property rights groups, as well as others who want to see limited government intervention, may applaud such a proposal. Likewise, suggestions to cut funding to advance the use of Amtrak and other high-speed railroad systems will be a concern to a few focused organizations but may be supported by the automobile and airline industries, which are worried about competition. The extent to which any discretionary spending can be labeled as "pork" or "wasteful" tends to maximize the chance of it being slashed. Cuts in military spending or homeland security are politically more difficult. Policymakers do not want to be labeled weak on defense, and as noted earlier, the economic effects of some of this spending can be substantial. In addition, politicians will not likely stop trying to "bring home the bacon." More so than entitlements, discretionary programs are left to the preferences of those who are in power.

Raising taxes is never seen as a savvy political proposal, even if the result ultimately leads to a better economic outcome. Politicians have seen the political benefits of proposing tax cuts and the dire consequences of those, such as former presidential candidate Walter Mondale, who suggest tax increases. As such, this proposal may politically be the most difficult one to enact as a way to decrease the deficit. Such proposals are easy to attack in thirty-second sound bites, especially in an era where it appears that any budgetary problem should be addressed by a tax cut. On the interest group front, a number of organizations such as Americans for Tax Reform and the National Taxpayers Union continuously advocate for smaller government and lower taxes. These groups are also joined by conservative think tanks such as the Cato Institute and the Heritage Foundation. On the other hand, one rarely hears of interest groups that advocate tax increases. The general public seems to share a distaste for tax increases.

The only area related to revenue increases that sometimes generates public support is in the category of user fees and, to a lesser extent, calls for increases in "sin taxes" such as those on cigarettes. People are more willing to support user fee increases because the users are getting a particular service for what they pay for (such as entry and use of a national park) or because others do not perceive that they will ever use the good, so the tax has no effect on them. Similarly, for nonsmokers, a proposal to increase the sales tax on cigarettes has no direct effect on them, so they are more likely to support it. Some user fee increases may make economic sense and garner public support. In areas such as grazing and mining on public lands, it is generally accepted that these are government-subsidized programs; an increase in the fees to use these public lands would generate more revenue and would likely be supported by the general population, if not by the industries getting the subsidies.

Equity and Other Ethical Issues

As is often the case with equity and related ethical issues, people have different ideas of what is fair or moral. For example, is it fair to have the government increase taxes and take more revenue to cover expenditures? Is it moral to retreat from a promise made years ago by cutting entitlements? When the question is what the government should do about the deficit and how to decrease it, equity and ethics can inform the discussion.

Reducing the deficit by cutting entitlement programs may raise the strongest ethical argument, especially as it relates to Social Security and Medicare. Supporters of Social Security, for example, state that the program is a promise the government makes to the American public or a contract it has with workers: if employees contribute during their working lives, the program will pay benefits upon their retirement or disability. If the funds are not available because too many people have become eligible, has the government broken its word? Is its action unfair? On the other hand, some may argue that these programs have outlived their usefulness and the nation needs to turn to other ways of financing them that may better provide the necessary benefits. Why should certain segments in society such as the elderly receive so many government benefits without fully paying for them?

Fairness arguments to decrease discretionary spending come down to whether we should continue to underfund programs that over the past thirty years have already been subject to budget cuts according to proponents. For years these programs have suffered from budget austerity. Proponents argue that now is the time to make up for their financial neglect, not to cut them further. The nation's infrastructure is in serious disrepair; education spending is not keeping pace with inflation; and, some argue, military spending and preparedness have suffered. On the other hand, some of these expenditures may include programs that some would say represent an oversized government or illustrate government intrusion. To the extent that one can show that some of these programs are unnecessary or wasteful, the ethical argument can be very persuasive, especially in times of budget austerity. What about military expenditures? It may be difficult to cut such funding during times of war. Policymakers want to ensure that the military has the necessary resources, especially if their safety is an issue. Reports of understaffed and undersupplied troops in Iraq illustrate this. Once troops are committed, many argue that there is a moral obligation to ensure they have the necessary supplies.

Addressing the deficit by increasing taxes runs into issues of fairness and personal freedom. Typically, those supporting limited government also push for citizens to be taxed at the lowest possible level. It is easy to argue against this choice because it plays on many people's fears of an overzealous government that taxes too much and may intrude excessively into citizens' lives through a variety of public policies. On the other hand, people generally are asking for these programs and there should be an obligation to pay for them. Many of the same people who decry taxes and would rally against a proposed tax increase oppose cuts in programs providing them with benefits. Some, for example, may argue that the government should not be spending money to fund renewable energy research, perhaps arguing that the private sector should finance these efforts. Others, though, would say that the coal and oil energy industries have little incentive to fund such research and it is up to the government to contribute to this effort. If policymakers can increase revenue by decreasing taxes and thus spur economic growth, the equity issues shift to who should receive the tax cuts. While some argue that the rich should receive the greatest tax cuts because they pay the highest taxes, others counter that the poor will benefit most from the cuts. There is some debate as to which of these choices will better promote economic growth.

Clearly, all three of these alternatives for addressing the deficit have merit, and it is difficult to know which is best. From a political standpoint, policymakers have been reluctant to address the deficit at all because of what may befall them if they propose cutting a preferred program or increasing taxes. There is a strong incentive to do nothing and hope that strong economic growth returns and makes the problem disappear. Whether relying on economic growth to solve the deficit problem is realistic is something that will be evident only with the passage of time. If policymakers want to address the deficit using the alternatives suggested above, then ideally combining multiple policy alternatives might be the best choice. Sharing the pain through a wide range of program cuts and tax increases will lessen the overall effect on any one program and perhaps diffuse the political situation somewhat. There is also an intuitive trait of fairness and equity with such a solution. Of course, given the economic conditions in 2009 and proposals to deal with the recession, it would appear as if any discussion regarding decreasing the deficit will need to be placed on the back burner until the economy recovers sufficiently.

It is important to keep in mind that budget estimates for deficits or surpluses are just that—estimates. They are based on economic assumptions that may or may not prove to be reasonable. According to the Congressional Budget Office, if economic growth was 0.1 percentage points a year higher than the rate assumed, the CBO's baseline projection for the deficit would decrease by $58 billion by 2015.[27] In addition, spending decisions change all of the time, as one can see from the increases in spending for homeland security, the wars in Afghanistan and Iraq, and the economic stimulus plans. There are also political pressures to increase popular programs that policymakers may have a hard time ignoring. All of these issues require the public policy student to keep abreast of changes and be willing to continually ask questions and seek justification for program decisions.

CONCLUSIONS

This chapter is the first in the text to consider a substantive public policy issue. Its purpose is to demonstrate the different ways to examine problems, alternatives, and policies related to economic policy and budgeting. In other words, it shows how to apply the tools of policy analysis to real issues and the decisions policymakers reach.

Economic policymaking is a bit different from most of the other substantive areas the next chapters discuss. It is almost always a starting point for other policy areas because money or the lack of it influences what government policymakers do at all levels. The best solutions to deal with issues such as prescription drugs for the elderly, terrorism within U.S. borders, or the disposal of nuclear waste cannot be adopted and implemented without adequate funding. This chapter shows that budget data and projections change frequently and this information affects how policymakers address a particular problem or fail to do so.

Policy analysis can help policymakers make informed decisions about how to use a limited budget with a number of competing goals. It can also help citizens to better understand how and why these decisions are made. Why, for example, did Congress spend billions of dollars on homeland security measures without any semblance of analytical thought? How can local leaders justify to their communities an increase in a sales tax to build a new professional sports stadium? Should the deficit be a concern, and if so, what is the best way to address it? Is it best to stimulate the economy through tax cuts or additional government spending? Policy analysis of economic and budget matters can help people appreciate the difficulties of these kinds of questions and understand the policies proposed to address them. In the chapters that follow, students will find similar arguments about the importance of thinking critically and creatively about possible solutions to challenges in a range of policy areas.

DISCUSSION QUESTIONS

1. The Federal Reserve Board is somewhat independent of political and citizen control in the making of monetary policy. Why do you think the system was set up this way? Is the independence of the Fed a problem or a strength?

2. Examine your state's current budgetary situation. Would you say the state budget picture is healthy? Why or why not? What are the largest budgetary issues affecting your state? How have these issues affected state programs?

3. Economic policy, as shown in this chapter, depends heavily on projections of future developments, for example, of economic growth and tax revenues. What questions would you ask about any such forecast to determine its reliability? Can these forecasts be used for political purposes? How so?

4. Why do you think entitlement programs have grown so large in the United States? Is the growth of such entitlements equitable? Why or why not?

5. The recession of 2008 and 2009 has raised a number of issues regarding the role of the federal government and how best to address the situation. What are the relative merits of either cutting taxes or increasing government spending as a way to stimulate the economy?

SUGGESTED READINGS

Jeffrey H. Birnbaum and Alan S. Murray, *Showdown at Gucci Gulch: Lawmakers, Lobbyists, and the Unlikely Triumph of Tax Reform* (New York: Vintage, 1987). A journalistic account of the politics of tax reform and how interest groups try to get their most important goals enacted.

Scott Bittle and Jean Johnson, *Where Does the Money Go? Your Guided Tour to the Federal Budget Crisis* (New York: HarperCollins, 2008). Written by the editors of Public Agenda Online, this book is a very accessible discussion of the major issues associated with budgetary policy, with an emphasis on the issues brought about by the United States' current entitlement programs.

Jeffrey E. Cohen, *Politics and Economic Policy in the United States,* 2nd ed. (Boston: Houghton Mifflin, 2000). A comprehensive and understandable overview of economic policy, organized around the theme of equity versus efficiency in economic decisions.

Marc Allen Eisner, Jeff Worsham, and Evan J. Ringquist, *Contemporary Regulatory Policy,* 2nd ed. (Boulder, Colo. Lynne Rienner, 2007). One of the few books on regulatory policy, with a focus on the idea of regulatory change and why it occurs. Includes chapters on substantive regulatory policies, such as environmental protection, telecommunication, workplace safety, and consumer product safety.

John M. Rothgeb Jr., *U.S. Trade Policy: Balancing Economic Dreams and Political Realities* (Washington, D.C.: CQ Press, 2001). A concise text covering international trade, the political tensions related to it, and its historical roots.

Aaron Wildavsky and Naomi Caiden, *The New Politics of the Budgetary Process,* 5th ed. (New York: Longman, 2003). A classic in the field of budget politics and development. Promotes incrementalism as a way of government budget development.

SUGGESTED WEB SITES

www.cbo.gov. The Congressional Budget Office provides analysis of economic and budget issues. This site has a variety of data, projections, reports, and analyses on economic issues. This is also the place to get specific budget analysis publications on a range of government issues.

www.cbpp.org. The Center on Budget and Policy Priorities is a policy organization that examines how federal and state fiscal policies affect low- and moderate-income families.

www.epi.org. The Economic Policy Institute is a nonpartisan think tank that examines strategies to promote a fair and prosperous economy. The site contains reports relating to economic and budget issues as well as other substantive policies and how they affect economic issues.

www.federalreserve.gov. The main Web site for the Federal Reserve Board provides a variety of information on monetary policy, how the Fed works, and how it uses its tools to affect the economy.

www.ustreas.gov. The U.S. Department of the Treasury site provides general information on economic issues such as taxes, financial markets, and current events. Access the Public Debt Online link to get information on the public debt, including what the debt is at a specific moment.

MAJOR LEGISLATION

Balanced Budget and Emergency Deficit Control Act of 1985 (Gramm-Rudman-Hollings)   210
Budget Enforcement Act of 1990   210
Congressional Budget and Impoundment Control Act of 1974   206
Economic Recovery Tax Act of 1981   208

KEYWORDS

balance of trade   193
Consumer Price Index (CPI)   193
entitlement program   213
fiscal policy   198

full employment   190
line-item veto   206
monetary policy   199
national debt   196

NOTES

1. For a good and accessible discussion of these issues, see Scott Bittle and Jean Johnson, *Where Does the Money Go?* (New York: HarperCollins, 2008).

2. See U.S. Congressional Budget Office, "The Budget and Economic Outlook: Fiscal Years 2009–2019," 2009, available at www.cbo.gov/doc.cfm?index=9957.

3. David Stout and Edmund L. Andrews, "$1.2 Trillion Deficit Forecast as Obama Weighs Options," *New York Times* online edition, January 7, 2009.

4. Gardiner Harris, "Peanut Product Recall Grows in Salmonella Scare, *New York Times* online edition, January 28, 2009.

5. See U.S. Department of Labor, Bureau of Labor Statistics, "Gross Domestic Product: Percent Change from Preceding Period," 2008, available at www.bea.gov/national/xls/gdpchg.xls.

6. See U.S. Department of Labor, Bureau of Labor Statistics, "Labor Force Statistics from the Current Population Survey," 2008, available at http://data.bls.gov/PDQ/servlet/SurveyOutputServlet?data_tool=latest_numbers&series_id=LNU04000000&years_option=all_years&periods_option=specific_periods&periods=Annual+.

7. Additional information can be found at Louis Uchitelle, "Economist's Survey Supports Theory That Inflation Is Overstated," *New York Times,* February 13, 1997.

8. To get information on the current federal debt and the interest on the public debt, see the following Department of the Treasury Web sites: www.publicdebt.treas.gov/opd/opdpdodt.htm, for information on the public debt; www.publicdebt.treas.gov/opd/opdint.htm, for information on interest on the debt.

9. This is discussed in James L. Rowe Jr., "Holding the Purse Strings: Our Money and Our Economic Lives Depend on the Federal Reserve," *Washington Post National Weekly Edition,* June 28, 1999, 6–9.

10. For additional information see Stephen Slivinski, "The Corporate Welfare State: How the Federal Government Subsidizes U.S. Business," *Cato Institute Policy Analysis* 592, May 14, 2007.

11. Alan K. Ota, "Cost of IRS Overhaul Has Former Backers Wary," *CQ Weekly,* September 2, 2000, 2017–2019; and Joseph J. Schatz, "IRS Set to Lean Harder on Wayward Taxpayers," *CQ Weekly,* April 25, 2005, 1055–1056.

12. To see tax burdens for these and other countries, see Organisation for Economic Co-operation and Development, "OECD Countries' Tax Burden Back Up to 2000 Historic Highs," available at www.oecd.org/document/16/0,3343,en_2649_201185_39495248_1_1_1_1,00.html.

13. There are many resources on the Internet regarding the budget process. If you want more detail, these Web sites provide additional information on the budget process: the U.S. House of Representatives Committee on Rules, "How Congress Works: The Budget Process," available at www.rules.house.gov/budget_pro.htm; and the Center on Budget and Policy Priorities, "Policy Basics: Introduction to the Federal Budget Process," December 17, 2008, available at www.cbpp.org/3-7-03bud.htm.

14. The Supreme Court case was *Clinton v. City of New York.* For a brief discussion of the line-item veto law, see http://rs9.loc.gov/home/line_item_veto.html.

15. For additional information see Jonathan Weisman, "Erosion of Estate Tax Is a Lesson in Politics," *New York Times,* April 13, 2005.

16. See Jonathan Weisman, "The Tax-Cut Pendulum and the Pit," *New York Times,* October 8, 2004.

17. Although the spending cuts were split between defense and domestic spending, a large portion of the budget was considered off-limits in regards to sequestration. This part of the budget included most entitlement programs, such as Social Security, and interest payments on the debt (Thurber 1996b). The result was that sequestration had an even larger effect on those programs that could be sequestered.

18. In other words, if the law was changed to provide for greater benefits for a particular program, it could trigger sequestration. But if the economy soured, increasing unemployment and therefore the number of people eligible to receive benefits, that would not trigger sequestration.

19. See U.S. Congressional Budget Office, "CBO Testimony: Budgetary Discipline," 2002, available at www.house.gov/budget/hearings/anderson02.pdf.

20. For example, in fiscal year 1999 the total emergency appropriation was just over $34 billion—the largest since 1991, the year of Desert Storm. See U.S. Congressional Budget Office, "Emergency Spending Under the Budget Enforcement Act: An Update" (1999), available at www.cbo.gov/showdoc.cfm?index=1327&sequence=0.

21. For a larger and accessible discussion of the issue of entitlements and their effect on the budget, see Scott Bittle and Jean Johnson, *Where Does the Money Go? Your Guided Tour to the Federal Budget Crisis* (New York: HarperCollins, 2008).

22. See Michael R. Crittenden, "Bracing for Default Day," *CQ Weekly* online edition, April 23, 2007, 1168–1177, available at http://library.cqpress.com/cqweekly/weeklyreport110-000002494661.

23. See Adriel Bettelheim and Benton Ives, "The Crisis of Choice." *CQ Weekly* online edition, July 7, 2008, 1834–1840, available at http://library.cqpress.com/cqweekly/weeklyreport110-000002911199.

24. See Richard Rubin and Benton Ives. "Paulson's Overhaul Plan Gets Reserved Praise," *CQ Weekly* online edition, April 7, 2008, 882–883; and Alan S. Blinder, "Six Blunders en Route to a Crisis," *New York Times,* January 25, 2009, Business Section, 8. For an especially thorough review of the U.S. and global financial calamity and its various causes, see Anthony Faiola, Ellen Nakashima, and Jill Drew, "What Went Wrong: Washington Policymakers Disagreed about Intervention in the Markets," *Washington Post National Weekly Edition,* October 20–26, 2008, 6–9.

25. See National Association of State Budget Officers, *The Fiscal Survey of States,* June 2008, available at www.nasbo.org/Publications/PDFs/Fiscal%20Survey%20of%20the%20States%20June%202008.pdf.

26. This and a number of other options are discussed in U.S. Congressional Budget Office, *Budget Options,* 2005, available at www.cbo.gov/showdoc.cfm?index=6075&sequence=0.

27. See U.S. Congressional Budget Office, *The Budget and Economic Outlook: Fiscal Years 2006 to 2015,* 2005, available at www.cbo.gov/showdoc.cfm?index=6060&sequence=0.

CHAPTER 8

HEALTH CARE POLICY

IN A RARE BIT OF GOOD NEWS, THE FEDERAL CENTERS FOR MEDICARE and Medicaid Services reported in early 2009 that national health spending grew in 2007 at the lowest rate in nine years. The reason was that prescription drug cost increases rose at the slowest rate since 1963 as people turned to generic drugs, and drug prices in general increased more modestly than had been the case. Nonetheless, spending on health care rose to a total of $2.2 trillion, or 16.2 percent of the nation's gross domestic product (GDP). That was a record high. The United States spent $7,421 per person for health care in 2007, a rise of 6.1 percent over spending in 2006; a comparable increase was expected for 2008, for which the total is expected to be $2.4 trillion, or 16.6 percent of the GDP. The 2007 figures were released just before President Barack Obama took office after promising sweeping changes in health care policy during the presidential campaign of 2008.[1]

The high cost of health care in the United States is a big part of the challenge facing the new president and Congress, especially at a time of economic retrenchment and rising federal deficits that will constrain enactment of new and expensive programs. But spending more money is not necessarily the best response. The United States already spends twice as much per person on health care as most other industrialized nations, and achieves less for it. As the chief executive of the Mayo Clinic stated: "We're not getting what we pay for. It's just that simple." Another health care expert put it this way: "Our health care system is fraught with waste," with as much as half of the money spent today doing nothing to improve health. If large sums of current spending were shifted to preventive health care and wellness activities, the outcomes could be far better. This is because about 75 percent of health care costs go to treatment

The United States spends twice as much per person on health care than any other developed country and yet on average gets worse results. Thus merely spending additional money on health care is not likely to fully solve the problems of access to medical services or the quality of citizens' health even if we are willing to pay more. However, a large portion of health care spending goes to treatment of preventable illnesses, so among the actions that could make a big difference is putting more money and effort into preventive health care and wellness activities. Doing so could improve people's health and well-being over time and reduce the demand for health care services. These workers are taking a yoga class at a large garment factory in Los Angeles in 2004. The employees of this particular factory work standard forty-hour weeks, are paid more when they are more productive, and have benefits that other similar factories don't offer, including massages, yoga, and soccer teams.

of preventable chronic illnesses, such as diabetes and heart disease.[2] Would you favor such a change in priorities? Are there reasons not to make such a change?

The long-recognized gap between health care spending and results is striking. In a 2008 report, for example, the Commonwealth Fund evaluated the United States on thirty-seven different health care measures and found that it did not measure up very well. The United States placed last among industrialized nations in preventing deaths through the use of timely and effective health care. Among all nations in similar studies, the United States ranked twenty-ninth in infant mortality and forty-ninth in life expectancy. Many other similar comparisons in recent years have come to the same conclusions. One reason for these findings is that some seventy-five million people in the United States either lack health insurance or are underinsured, and therefore have limited access to health care services.[3] Another is that the quality of health care people receive and what they pay for it depends on where they live and personal characteristics such as race, income, and education.[4] What should the nation do to correct such an important inequity? Who should pay for the added cost?

The combination of the high cost of and unequal access to quality health care has become a quiet crisis in public policy. In 2008, the average health insurance premium for a family of four under employer-provided health plans averaged $12,700, with workers contributing about $3,400 of that amount—an increase of 12 percent in one year. The health insurance costs alone exceed the gross earnings for a full-time, minimum-wage worker ($10,712).[5] It is little wonder, then, that reform of health care policy has regularly appeared at the top of issues that voters consider to be important, even if the nation has yet to resolve the problem.

Most people rely on employer-provided health care insurance, for which they pay a portion of the cost, or on government programs to meet essential health care needs. Federal and state health care policies also affect the uninsured and those who pay for their own insurance. Government policies influence not only access to and quality of health services across the country, but also the pace of development and approval of new drugs and medical technologies and the extent of health research that could lead to new life-saving treatments. Whether the concern is periodic medical examinations, screening for major diseases, or coping with life-threatening illnesses, health care policy decisions eventually affect everyone.

This chapter examines some of the problems associated with health care services and the public policies designed to ensure that citizens have access to them, and at a reasonable cost. The two major political parties disagree over the proper degree of government involvement and how much should be left to the private sector—to individuals, physicians, hospitals and clinics, insurance companies, and pharmaceutical houses. In addition, among the major controversies in health care are how best to deal with escalating costs, how to ensure sufficient access to health services, and how to maintain the quality of health care services while containing costs. The chapter begins with background information about the evolution of major public policies, such as Medicare and Medicaid, and then turns to some of the leading policy disputes: the role of managed care, patients' rights, the high cost of prescription drugs, and the potential of preventive health care and other strategies to keep people healthy and save money. In this chapter we give particular attention to the effectiveness of current public policies, and we use the criteria of economic efficiency and equity to examine these disputes and recommendations for improving health care policy.

WORKING WITH SOURCES

HEALTH CARE POLICY INFORMATION

As is the case with other public policy issues, there are hundreds of Web sites providing information on health care policy. The easiest way to learn about what information is available and its reliability is to visit one or more of the leading sites listed below and at the end of the chapter. Select one of the sites and try to find information about a major health care issue such as the ones highlighted below. How easily can you locate the information? Is coverage of the issue adequate or too limited to tell you what you need to know? Is the information provided at the site objective or biased in some way?

www.ahip.org. America's Health Insurance Plans, a leading industry trade association, has broad and excellent coverage of and links to the full range of health care policy issues. Select the link to Issues and Advocacy, then to AHIP Plan to Improve Health Care Quality and Safety, where you can find the industry's position on how to improve patient care, or AHIP Plan to Cover the Uninsured, to deal with access to health care by those without insurance.

www.citizen.org/hrg. Public Citizen's Health Research Group site, with extensive links to policy issues and citizen activism. Select a topic such as food safety, drug safety, or health care delivery.

www.iom.edu. The Institute of Medicine, a component of the National Academies and a major source for reliable health care studies. Includes links to related sites for health care studies and reports. Select Child Health, Women's Health, or Healthcare and Quality, and then a particular topic, such as saving women's lives, the consequences of uninsurance, or health literacy.

www.kaisernetwork.org. One of the premier online resources for coverage of health policy news and debate. Select Issue Spotlight, then Children's Health, Long-Term Care, Medical Malpractice, State Health Policy, or Minority Health and Health Care Disparities, and look for a specific report.

www.nytimes.com/pages/health/index.html. The *New York Times* health news page. Select a specific news report.

www.policyalmanac.org/health/index.shtml. The *Almanac of Policy Issues* health care page, with many useful links to news, organizations, government agencies, health care statistics, and a range of health policy issues. Select a topic listed under the directory, such as abortion, health insurance, HMOs, privacy, or medical professions.

BACKGROUND

Health care policy includes all of the actions that governments take to influence the provision of health care services and the various government activities that affect or attempt to affect public health and well-being. Health care policy can be viewed narrowly to mean the design and implementation of the range of federal and state programs that affect the provision of health care services, such as Medicare and Medicaid. It also can be defined more broadly and more meaningfully by recognizing that government engages in many other activities that influence both public and private health care decision making. For example, the government funds health science research and public health departments and agencies; subsidizes medical education and hospital construction; regulates food, drugs, and medical devices; regulates health-damaging environmental pollution; and allows tax deductions for some health care expenditures (which makes them more affordable). The box "Working with Sources: Health Care Policy Information" lists some useful Web sites to begin a policy investigation.

As a government activity, health care policy is relatively recent, even though governments at every level long ago established public health agencies to counter the threat of infectious diseases and related problems. They also dealt with such seemingly mundane but critical functions as providing safe drinking water supplies, sanitation, and waste removal. Those agencies continue such work today, largely without much public notice. Consider the Food and Drug Administration (FDA), the National Institutes of Health (NIH), and the Centers for Disease Control and Prevention (CDC).

Since 1862, when it employed a single chemist and was housed in the U.S. Department of Agriculture, the Food and Drug Administration has overseen the development of new drugs and medical devices as well as the nation's food supply (other than meat and poultry, which the USDA regulates). The modern FDA dates from 1906, when it was authorized by the Federal Food and Drugs Act and regulatory functions were added to the agency's scientific mission. The agency is now part of the Department of Health and Human Services (HHS). In addition to food and drugs, the agency is responsible for regulating biologics (vaccines and blood products); the labeling and safety of cosmetics once they come to market; medical devices, including contact lenses; and radiation in consumer products such as microwave ovens and cell phones. Later in the chapter we offer a steps-to-analysis exercise on how the FDA regulates the approval of new drugs.

The federal government also has been actively engaged in health science research for years. Generous budgets allowed the government to expand its research into the causes of various diseases and possible treatments. The NIH, the primary vehicle for federal health science research, was founded in 1887 and consists of twenty-seven separate institutes and centers. The NIH is one of eight health agencies of the U.S. Public Health Service, itself a component of HHS. The NIH supports health research across the nation at colleges and universities, medical research centers, and on the NIH main campus in Bethesda, Maryland. The agency took on a national security role following the bioterrorism scares of October 2001.

The federal CDC has been part of the Public Health Service of HHS since 1973. The CDC was established in 1946 as the Communicable Disease Center. It focuses on the development and application of disease prevention and control, environmental health, and health promotion and education. The CDC has long been involved in programs dealing with immunization, the prevention and control of AIDS and other infectious diseases, chronic disease prevention, birth defects and developmental disabilities, occupational safety and health, and the compilation of a treasure trove of national health statistics. After the anthrax scare of 2001, the CDC took on expanded responsibilities for threats of bioterrorism and emergency operations.

As the work of the three agencies shows, the federal government has been involved in public health, if not the actual provision of health care services, for a long time. The same is true of state and local governments. Government involvement in funding or provision of direct health care services, on the other hand, is relatively recent. In many ways, despite expenditures of more than $700 billion a year, it is a limited form of intervention into what is still predominantly a private health care system.

Evolution of Health Care Policy

What we consider the core of health care policy developed in the United States only after the 1930s, with the idea of health insurance. Individuals could take out an insurance policy, much as they did for their lives, houses, or cars, that would defray the cost of health care should an illness develop or an injury occur. Most of those early policies covered only catastrophic losses. Health insurance works much the same way now, though instead of individual policies, most people are insured through their jobs, and the insurance policies cover routine medical services as well as preventive health care. Employer-sponsored health insurance became popular in the 1950s after the Internal Revenue Service ruled that its cost was a tax-deductible business expense. By the early 1960s the push was on for federal health insurance policies, primarily to aid the poor and the elderly, two segments of the population that normally would not benefit from employer-provided health plans. It is clear that equity concerns in access to health care services were important as health care policy developed. Those efforts culminated in the enactment of the federal Medicare and Medicaid programs in 1965 (Marmor 1999).

Even with adoption of these two programs, the U.S. health care system remains distinctive in comparison to other industrialized nations, where **national health insurance,** also known as single-payer (the government) insurance, is the norm. Campaigns to adopt national health insurance in the United States date back to 1948, when the Democratic Party platform endorsed the idea. Members of Congress began to introduce bills to create such a program, but they were unsuccessful, except for the decision in 1965 to establish insurance programs for the poor and the elderly.

One of the more recent efforts to create a national health insurance program occurred in 1993, when President Bill Clinton submitted the National Health Security Act to Congress after extensive analysis by a presidential health care task force headed by his wife, Hillary Rodham Clinton. The plan would have guaranteed health insurance to every American, including the thirty-four million who were uninsured at the time. It proposed doing so through a system of health care alliances that would function much like current managed care organizations. The plan called for individuals to pay about $1,800 a year for coverage, and families about $4,200; both amounts were less than private insurance rates for most of the population. Most employers would have been required to cover their employees under the plan (a so-called employer mandate), with subsidies for small businesses that otherwise could not afford to pay.

Republicans in Congress argued that the Clinton plan was too expensive, bureaucratic, and intrusive. The health insurance industry also criticized it. The insurance companies lobbied intensely against the plan and mounted an expensive television advertising campaign designed to turn the public against it. In the end the Clinton recommendations failed to win congressional approval, as did the many alternatives that members of Congress proposed (Hacker 1997; Rushefsky and Patel 1998). The failure was a classic story of the kind of policy gridlock described in chapter 2. Divided government cannot be blamed for the result because Democrats controlled both the White House and both houses of Congress at the time. However, the president was unable to persuade his party members to support him, even though a number of states (among them Hawaii, Massachusetts, and Minnesota) had set an example by establishing comprehensive health care programs that combined public and private insurance and by developing innovative approaches to controlling health care costs.[6]

With the victory of Barack Obama and gains in Democratic seats in the House and Senate in the 2008 elections, national health care policy reform once again was in the spotlight, although with competing proposals that reflected deep differences between the two parties. During the campaign Obama offered proposals that mandated parents to insure their children; allowed individuals and businesses to purchase health coverage through a new national health insurance exchange program; required most employers to make a "meaningful" contribution for their employees' health insurance or contribute to a public plan; ordered medical providers to compile data on costs, quality, preventable errors, nurse-patient ratios, and hospital-acquired infections; and required the use of disease management programs in federal health care plans, among other ideas. The plan's high costs were to be covered by allowing President George W. Bush's tax breaks to expire for those earning more than $250,000 a year. In comparison, Republicans, including presidential candidate John McCain, emphasized individual choice through tax incentives for purchase of health care insurance (combined with taxation on employer-provided health benefits that have long been tax free) and use of personal health savings accounts. They too favored requiring medical providers to make available more information about costs, outcomes, and quality to help individuals make wiser choices.[7]

A Hybrid System of Public and Private Health Care

Another way to consider the history of health care in the United States and the nation's present health care system is that it continues to rely largely on the private market and individual choice to reach health care goals, as we indicated in the chapter's opening paragraphs. The U.S. government plays a smaller role in health care than the governments of Great Britain or Canada, nations that have national health insurance programs that provide comprehensive health services. Their systems are often criticized for the lack of timeliness and quality of care, however, because the demand for health care can exceed the supply of available services, forcing people to wait for nonemergency health care services or even to forgo them. In contrast to government-run systems, most health care services in the United States are provided by doctors and other medical staff who work in clinics and hospitals that are privately run, even if some are not-for-profit operations. Indeed, the United States has the smallest amount of public insurance or provision of public health services of any developed nation in the world (Patel and Rushefsky 2006). The result is a health care system that is something of a hybrid. It is neither completely private nor fully public. It does, however, reflect the unique political culture of the nation, as first discussed in chapter 1. Americans place great emphasis on individual rights, limited government authority, and a relatively unrestrained market system. Those who favor a larger government role to reduce the current inequities in access to health care services are in effect suggesting that health care should be considered a so-called **merit good** to which people are entitled. In short, they tend to believe that normal market forces should not be the determining factor in the way society allocates such a good.

The majority of U.S. adults (about 158 million people) have employer-sponsored, private health insurance, and others purchase similar insurance through individual policies. But with rising costs, employer coverage is likely to be less widely available in the future. About 63 percent of employers offered health benefits in 2008, down somewhat from 69 percent in 2000; the rate is higher for companies with unionized employees.[8] The annual premium for covered workers in 2008 averaged $4,704 for single coverage and $12,680 for family coverage—an increase of about 5 percent from 2007, with the employee paying 16 to 27 percent of the cost, the higher amount for family coverage.[9] These premiums have been rising substantially for the past several years, leading employers to cut back on some benefits and to shift more of the cost to employees. That trend will likely continue.

Employer and other private health insurance policies generally cover a substantial portion of health care costs, but not all. Some services, such as elective cosmetic surgery, are not covered at all, and partial payment may apply to others. The federal government can specify particular services that must be included in private insurance plans, but there are major gaps in coverage, such as assistance with expensive prescription drugs and provision of long-term care in nursing homes and similar facilities that may follow a disabling injury or illness, or simple aging. People are living longer, and the demand for these services is expected to rise dramatically in the future. Most policies also have a lifetime cap that could be exceeded in the event of serious medical conditions.

The Perils of Being Uninsured

The number of individuals and families without any insurance coverage has risen significantly since 1990. In recent years about forty-seven million individuals, or 17 percent of the population under the age of sixty-five, had no health insurance. The percentage of people without health insurance varies widely from state to state. In some states, more than 25 percent of the population is uninsured (New Mexico and Texas), and in others the rate is 10 percent or less (Hawaii, Massachusetts, Minnesota, and Wisconsin).[10]

As the cost of medical care continues to grow, what happens to the uninsured? The consequences for them can be devastating—a higher lifelong risk of serious medical problems and premature death. A review of the health consequences for uninsured, working-age Americans conducted by the Institute of Medicine in 2002 found that they are more likely than the insured to receive too little medical care, to receive it too late, to be sicker, and to die sooner. Indeed, they are 25 percent more likely to die than those with insurance coverage. That difference translates into about eighteen thousand deaths per year that can be attributed to being uninsured. These estimates may even be too low. An Urban Institute study that sought in early 2008 to update the Institute of Medicine report put the number at twenty-seven thousand preventable deaths in America each year attributable to being uninsured.[11]

The uninsured also are more likely than the insured to receive less adequate care when they are in a hospital, even for acute care, such as injuries from an automobile accident. They are more likely to go without cancer screening tests, such as mammograms, clinical breast exams, Pap tests, and colorectal screenings, and therefore suffer from delayed diagnosis and treatment. That finding helps to explain why uninsured women with breast cancer have a 30–50 percent higher risk of dying than women with private health insurance (Institute of Medicine 2002).

In addition, the uninsured do not receive the care recommended for chronic diseases such as diabetes, HIV infection, end-stage renal (kidney) disease, mental illness, and high blood pressure, and they have worse clinical outcomes than patients with insurance. "The fact is that the quality and length of life are distinctly different for insured and uninsured populations," the report said. It added that if this group obtained coverage, the health and longevity of working-age Americans would improve (Institute of Medicine 2002).

Policymakers are aware of some of these risks and the inequities they present to the U.S. public. As the failure of the Clinton health policy initiative shows, however, reaching agreement on extending insurance coverage to the entire population is not an easy task. What should the government do about the uninsured? Should it consider health care to be a merit good and put it beyond the market? If so, how should the nation pay for extending services to the uninsured? The debate is likely to continue for years, and the rising costs of health care may force reconsideration of current policies that leave so many citizens without health care insurance.

Strengths and Weaknesses of the U.S. Health Care System

No one seriously doubts that the United States has one of the finest health care systems in the world by any of the conventionally used indicators, such as the number of physicians per capita, the number of state-of-the-art hospitals and clinics, or the number of health care specialists and their expertise. The United States also has a large percentage of the world's major pharmaceutical research centers and biotechnology companies, which increases the availability of cutting-edge medical treatments.

Despite these many strengths, patients and physicians alike frequently complain about the U.S. health care system. As noted at the beginning of the chapter, the United States is ranked well below the level of other developed nations despite spending more on health care per person.[12] Such findings reflect the highly unequal access of the population to critical health care services, from prenatal care to preventive screening for chronic illnesses. The poor, the elderly, minorities, and those living in rural areas generally receive less frequent and less adequate medical care than white, middle-class residents of urban and suburban areas. Because of such disparities, among others, the fifty states vary widely in the health of their populations, with Minnesota, New Hampshire, and Vermont at the top in recent rankings, and New Mexico, Mississippi, and Louisiana at the bottom.[13]

As noted earlier, comparisons of U.S. health care costs to those in other nations force the question of what U.S. citizens are getting for their money. Just how effective are current programs, and are health care dollars being well spent? How might the programs be modified to improve their effectiveness and efficiency and to ensure that there is equitable access to health care services? Plenty of controversy surrounds each of these questions, and they remain at the center of policymakers' concerns about the future of the U.S. health care system. The Web sites listed in the box "Working with Sources: Health Care Policy Information" (see page 231) cover health care developments and policies and offer a wealth of information on these issues.

A Pluralistic Health Care System

Before we turn to a description and assessment of specific U.S. health care programs, we start with an overview of the health care system itself. The individual health care programs are complicated enough to confuse even the experts, but they do not represent the totality of government activities that affect the health and welfare of the U.S. public. A broad view of health care policy suggests that many other actions should be included as well. Table 8-1 lists the collection of agencies and policies at the federal, state, and local levels.

Especially noteworthy in the table is the diversity of departments and agencies involved in health-related services. As is often the case with U.S. public policies, authority is diffused rather

TABLE 8-1	Major Government Health-Related Programs

Level of Government	Agency and Function

Federal	Department of Agriculture
	    Food safety inspection (meat and poultry)
	    Food stamp and child nutrition programs
	    Consumer education
	Department of Health and Human Services
	    Food and Drug Administration
	    Agency for Healthcare Research and Quality
	    Centers for Medicare and Medicaid Services
	    Health Resources and Services Administration (health resources for underserved
	        populations)
	    Indian Health Service
	    Substance abuse programs
	    Health education
	    U.S. Public Health Service (including the Surgeon General's office, the National
	        Institutes of Health, and the Centers for Disease Control and Prevention)
	Department of Labor
	Occupational Safety and Health Administration (regulation of workplace safety
	    and health)
	Department of Veterans Affairs
	    Veterans Health Administration (VA hospitals and programs)
	Environmental Protection Agency (regulation of clean air and water, drinking water,
	    pesticides, and toxic chemicals)

State	Medicaid and State Children's Health Insurance Program (SCHIP) State hospitals State mental hospitals Support of state medical schools State departments of health Health education State departments of agriculture and consumer protection State environmental protection programs
Local	City and county hospitals and clinics Public health departments and sanitation Emergency services City and county health and human services programs

than concentrated, and is shared among all levels of government. The programs most frequently in the public eye, such as Medicare and Medicaid, are only part of what governments do to promote the public's health. Many activities, such as those sponsored by state departments of public health and federal medical research, are far less visible to the average citizen. Others, such as environmental protection, are not always considered in terms of their public health orientation, even if they do affect people's health.[14]

It is important to think in these broader terms about government health care activities. Doing so suggests that solutions to U.S. health problems are not to be found solely in expanding and modifying the established Medicare, Medicaid, and Veterans Healthcare System programs. Other actions also are possible, including those that rely on preventive health care. These include personal decisions related to diet and exercise, detection of disease at its earliest stages, health education, medical research, environmental protection, and a host of public and private programs to improve mental and physical health. We will return to a discussion of such preventive health care below.

MAJOR GOVERNMENT HEALTH CARE PROGRAMS

The following sections describe the major federal and state programs that deal directly with health care services. In addition to the programs' goals and provisions, the discussion tries to evaluate them in terms of the major public policy criteria we set out earlier in the text: effectiveness, efficiency, and equity. Public policy students who want a fuller account and assessment of the programs can find additional information at government agency Web sites and others such as those listed at the end of the chapter. Of particular value for the two most prominent federal programs is the site for the Centers for Medicare and Medicaid Services (www.cms.gov).

Medicare

The federal **Medicare** program began in 1965, following authorization by that year's amendments to the Social Security Act of 1935. It was intended to help senior citizens, defined as those age sixty-five and older, to meet basic health care needs. It now includes people under age sixty-five with permanent disabilities and those with diabetes or end-stage renal disease—for example, patients who need dialysis treatment or a kidney transplant. Medicare had nearly forty-five million beneficiaries in 2008, a number certain to rise appreciably over the next two decades as the baby boom generation—those born between 1946 and 1964—begins reaching age sixty-five. In 2008, the three major entitlement programs—Social Security, Medicare, and Medicaid (counting the State Children's Health Insurance Program [SCHIP])—already accounted for over 42 percent of federal expenditures.

Medicare Program Provisions. The Medicare program has two main parts, one standard and the other optional. Medicare Part A is the core plan, which pays partially for hospital charges, with individuals responsible for a deductible and co-payments that can be substantial. The program is paid for by Medicare trust funds, which most employees pay through a payroll deduction, much like the Social Security tax, which employers match. Part A also covers up to one hundred days in a nursing care facility following release from the hospital, but again with co-payments. Part A of Medicare covers people who are eligible for the federal Social Security system or Railroad Retirement benefits.

The optional part of the Medicare program, Part B, is supplemental insurance for coverage of health care expenses other than hospital stays. These include physician charges, diagnostic tests, and hospital outpatient services. The cost of Part B insurance is shared by individuals who choose to enroll in it (they paid $96.40 per month for it in 2009) and by the government, which covers about three-fourths of the cost from general federal revenues. Part B also has both deductibles and co-payments, but it does not cover routine physical examinations by a physician. Even with its limitations, about 95 percent of eligible recipients opt for coverage under Part B of Medicare. Under the Balanced Budget Act of 1997, Congress included additional services for Medicare recipients, particularly preventive diagnostic tests to detect major health problems such as diabetes, breast and colon cancer, and osteoporosis, but payment schedules have been lower than health care providers believe to be essential.

Medicare uses a fee schedule of "reasonable" costs that specifies what physicians, hospitals, nursing homes, and home services should charge for a given procedure, and the government pays 80 percent of that amount. Individuals are responsible for the difference, which can be a significant expense for people living on modest retirement incomes. Physicians are free to charge more than this "reasonable" amount, passing along the higher costs to patients. Some physicians choose not to participate in the Medicare system because they believe the fee schedule is too low and their options for raising patient fees unrealistic.

Equally important is the fact that the regular Medicare program does not cover many other medical expenses, including prescription drugs used outside of the hospital, dental care, and eyeglasses. It also pays for only the first ninety days of a hospital stay and limited nursing home care. Because of these restrictions and the deductibles and co-payment charges, Medicare historically has covered only about two-thirds of the health care costs for the elderly. Individuals must therefore pay for the rest of the costs, or purchase supplementary private insurance policies to cover the gaps in Medicare. Many of the Medigap insurance policies are expensive, and few of them have offered prescription drug coverage. Low-income elderly also may be eligible for state Medicaid programs, which cover some of these costs. Despite the many restrictions, Medicare is a bargain for the elderly, who would have to pay much higher fees for a full private insurance policy—if they are insurable at all, considering the chronic and serious health problems they are likely to face.

As we discussed earlier, the costs of health care in general, including Medicare, continue to rise, and this trend poses major challenges to the solvency of the Medicare trust fund as the population ages and the ranks of Medicare recipients swell. In an effort to reduce health care expenses, since 1985 Medicare has encouraged its participants to join health maintenance organizations (HMOs), preferred provider organizations, and similar managed care plans rather than to rely on the traditional fee-for-service arrangement. In 1997 Congress created Medicare + Choice, Part C of the program, to facilitate this change. It used to be the only Medicare program that offered a prescription drug benefit until the new drug plan discussed below went into effect. The program also exemplified the value of disease prevention, disease management, and "personal nurse" programs that are intended to improve patient compliance with medical advice. According to surveys at the time, those enrolled in it were quite satisfied.

With the enactment of the Medicare prescription drug benefit program in 2003, the Medicare + Choice program was replaced with a Medicare Advantage program, managed care programs run by private health insurance companies, which is called Medicare Part C, and which requires enrollees to have both Medicare Parts A and B coverage; most of these plans also include prescription drug coverage, called Medicare Part D. About one-quarter of those on Medicare have signed up for a Medicare Advantage plan, and about three-quarters have chosen instead to remain with a traditional fee-for-service Medicare plan (Part B). Medicare has paid the private plans about 13 percent more than similar programs in traditional Medicare, and for that reason, among others, Democrats have tended to criticize the Medicare Advantage program as unjustifiable. Congress may cut the subsidy soon.

Medicare Part D took effect on January 1, 2006. Approved by Congress in late 2003 in response to the rapid rise in drug prices, particularly for senior citizens, the Medicare Prescription Drug, Improvement, and Modernization Act of 2003 has several key elements. It is intended to provide discounts for routine prescription drugs and also to protect those who enroll against the extremely high costs that come with a serious illness. Through 2008 it barred the government from negotiating lower prices for drugs going to Medicare recipients, although this provision may change in the future. But the program does subsidize the cost of those drugs.

Prescription drug benefits include a $295 annual deductible and a monthly premium expected to average about $28 in 2009. For 2009, the government covers 75 percent of the drug cost up to $2,700, after which the beneficiary pays the full cost. However, once the beneficiary has paid a total of $4,350 in out-of-pocket expenses, the government will pay for most of the remaining drug costs except for a small co-payment. Health plans must offer the base plan, but they have the freedom to offer other plans that eliminate this coverage gap. All of these dollar amounts are adjusted annually to reflect rising drug costs for Medicare recipients.

Beneficiaries in the new program choose among many different private drug plans that vary by region of the country and that are partially subsidized by HHS to provide an incentive to offer plans in areas that are hard to serve; beneficiaries must stay in a chosen plan for a year. Premiums may also change from year to year. Where no private plan is available, the government would offer one. Low-income beneficiaries who qualify for Medicaid as well as Medicare ("dual eligibles") may be eligible, depending on income level, for a full subsidy of the plan's lowest cost premium and also have no deductibles or gaps in coverage; however, they must pay a small amount for each prescription drug.[15]

Fraud and Abuse under Medicare. Another perennial problem is fraud and abuse committed under Medicare. Less-than-scrupulous health care providers charge the government for services that were not performed or order tests and procedures that may not be necessary but for which the health care provider knows Medicare will pay. The Centers for Medicare and Medicaid Services has estimated that such fraud accounts for more than $100 billion annually. In a telling commentary about a 1998 HHS investigation into abuses by community mental health centers, Donna Shalala, then secretary of the department, noted there was "extensive evidence of providers who are not qualified, patients who are not eligible, and services billed to Medicare that are not appropriate," including services "that weren't covered, weren't provided or weren't needed."[16] Many recent assessments of Medicare spending echo those concerns. The program continues to be deficient in its monitoring and enforcement of quality standards and in its oversight of spending even though it spends over $1 billion annually to combat fraud, waste, and abuse. Researchers at Dartmouth Medical School have estimated that as much as $1 of every $3 in the program is wasted by spending on inappropriate or unnecessary care; others put the figure even higher.[17] Part of the explanation is that the federal government simply does not spend enough to inspect facilities properly and often is unable to correct deficiencies that are found because of complex rules and procedures.[18]

In response, the federal government has begun to devote substantial resources to criminal and civil actions against health care fraud. Health care centers have responded to charges of fraud and abuse by saying the government's billing procedures are so complex that it is difficult to avoid making errors. They also say they worry about the government creating a climate of fear in the health care industry that would be detrimental to patient care.[19] Federal agents who investigate Medicare fraud are not persuaded by such arguments. They charge that health care providers intentionally put services into a higher-paying category, or "up code" their billing, and engage in other illegal practices to increase profits. Ending such abuses will not be easy.[20]

Medicare's Future. Given the projections of an aging population, the cost of the Medicare program represents one of the most important issues in health care policy. Unfortunately, aside from the new prescription drug plan, there has been little agreement on how to modify the program to expand its benefits and to improve its effectiveness. Bipartisan cooperation on health

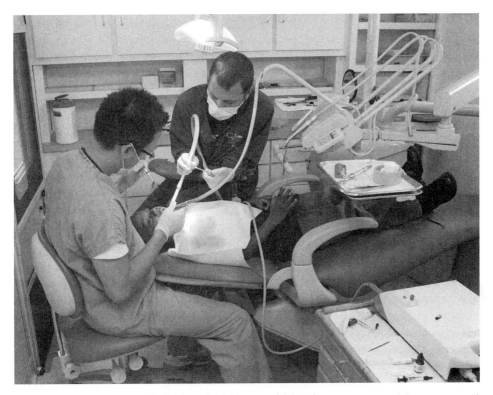

The economic downturn of 2008 and 2009 put additional pressures on state government spending for Medicaid and for the State Children's Health Insurance Program (SCHIP), which helps to ensure that children living in poverty have medical coverage. Many states had reduced their funding of the SCHIP program in recent years, as they struggled with budget constraints and competing priorities. New funds that Congress provided in 2009 when it expanded SCHIP helped to ease these pressures, but the challenge of paying for health care services for those in poverty remains. The photo shows an elementary student receiving treatment in the mobile dental group Help a Child Smile in Conyers, Georgia, in August 2007. The future of the dental group, which primarily serves children on Medicaid, was uncertain after two of the state's three care management organizations for Medicaid dental service announced they were terminating contracts with the group.

care policy is made difficult by intense ideological disagreements over the role of government in health care and the different constituencies to which each of the major parties tries to appeal. The debate is certain to continue. Based on the description of the Medicare program offered here, do you think it provides sufficient coverage to be termed an effective and efficient health insurance program for senior citizens? Is it sufficiently equitable? What else could be done to improve the program's coverage and operation to make it more effective, efficient, and equitable?

Medicaid

Medicaid is the other major program of the U.S. health care policy system. Like Medicare, it was established in 1965, as Title XIX of the Social Security Act. It is designed to assist the poor and disabled through a federal-state program of health insurance. It differs from Medicare in one critical way: Medicare serves all citizens once they reach age sixty-five, regardless of income, and is therefore a form of national health insurance for senior citizens, but Medicaid is a specialized health care program for the poor and disabled.

Medicaid Provisions and Controversies. Under Medicaid the federal government establishes standards for hospital services, outpatient services, physician services, and laboratory testing, and it pays about half of the cost. States pay the remainder and set standards for eligibility and overall benefit levels, which vary significantly from state to state. If a state chooses to have a Medicaid program—and all have since 1982—it must also extend benefits to welfare recipients and to those receiving Supplemental Security Income because of blindness, another disability, or age. Medicaid provided coverage for about fifty-five million people in 2009, a number expected to increase substantially in the years ahead. About half of the Medicaid beneficiaries are children in low-income families. By default, Medicaid has become the major payer for long-term health care provided in nursing homes and similar facilities, and it accounts for about half of the nation's spending for such services. Because of the rising demand and cost for these services, some states are changing their Medicaid programs to reduce use of nursing homes and to encourage health care in the home or community. These and other innovative approaches to help keep costs down will likely become more prevalent in the years ahead.[21]

In some respects, the state Medicaid programs are more generous than Medicare. The federal government requires states to cover hospitalization, nursing home services, physician services, diagnostic and screening tests, and X-rays. States may opt to cover prescription drug and other expenses, for which the cost can be exceedingly high. For example, New York's spending on prescription drugs under its Medicaid program doubled in five years and was nearly $4 billion by 2004; in 2008 the state spent a total of $47 billion on its Medicaid program, more than any other state in the nation.[22] States are also required to cover children under the age of eighteen if the family income falls below the poverty level. States may set limits on the health care services that are provided, and most offer the minimum level stipulated by federal law.

Much like Medicare expenses, Medicaid costs continue to rise at a rapid pace. Expenditures reached $339 billion in 2008, and they are expected to continue rising over the next decade at about 8 percent a year.[23] As might be expected in such a program, the states are constantly at odds with the federal government over the imposition of additional burdens. Medicaid is one of the largest programs in most state budgets. As states and counties spend more on Medicaid, they must cut back on the program's optional services, reduce the rate of reimbursement for physician and other services, and curtail funding elsewhere. Education, welfare, and other programs may suffer as Medicaid costs continue to rise, as they did in the 2008 economic recession.[24] As with Medicare, Medicaid recipients have been encouraged to join HMOs and other managed care organizations as a way to deal with those rising costs. The initiative has been controversial, however, as some policymakers continue to oppose shifting recipients over to the slightly more restrictive managed care alternative. However, the states are allowed to require Medicaid recipients to join managed care organizations to reduce the cost of the program. Well over half of Medicaid recipients have joined managed care groups, though with wide variation in participation rates among the states.

In response to concern over the rising costs of Medicaid, in late 2005 Congress approved broad changes that give states new power to reduce their costs through imposition of premiums and higher co-payments for many of Medicaid's benefits; these include prescription drugs, physician services, and hospital services, such as use of emergency rooms for nonurgent care. Higher costs for beneficiaries are expected to reduce their demand for those services. States also were authorized to cap or eliminate coverage for many services that previous federal law guaranteed within the program. In addition, the new law will make it somewhat more difficult for senior citizens to qualify for Medicaid nursing home care by transferring their assets to their children or other relatives.[25]

As part of the Balanced Budget Act of 1997, a new Title XXI was added to the Social Security Act to create the **State Children's Health Insurance Program** (SCHIP), which helps to ensure that children living in poverty have medical coverage. The federal government provides funds to the states, which the states match. The states are free to set the eligibility levels, which can include families that earn up to three times the poverty level. More than six million children have been covered under SCHIP in recent years, but the states vary widely in their ability to enroll children in the program. As has been the case for Medicaid in general, many states have reduced their funding of SCHIP in recent years, as they have struggled with budget constraints and competing priorities. In 2007 Congress twice passed legislation to extend and expand SCHIP, especially for families that work but remain too poor to pay for health insurance and make too much to enroll in Medicaid; the bills were vetoed by President Bush. In early 2009 Congress was once again working on similar legislation, with the cost to be financed largely by an increase in the federal tobacco tax. By the end of January, both the House and Senate had approved the measure by large margins and with bipartisan support, and President Obama signed it on February 4, 2009.[26]

Issues of Medicaid Fraud and Abuse. The Medicaid program, like Medicare, is vulnerable to fraud and abuse by service providers, such as filing inaccurate claims for reimbursement. Although the money lost to fraud is less than in the Medicare program, the costs are nevertheless substantial. The service providers defend themselves by arguing that they are the victims of an excessively complicated system of eligibility requirements and reimbursement procedures. In chapter 6 we cited the example of the New York State Medicaid program. The state failed to pursue many opportunities to reduce the program's high costs and to monitor its operation carefully. The result has been billions of dollars in fraud and abuse. One former state Medicaid investigator estimated that at least 10 percent of the New York program's dollars were spent on claims that were fraudulent and that another 20 to 30 percent had been wasted in "abuse," or unnecessary, if not criminal, spending. Thus as much as 40 percent of New York's Medicaid claims could be questioned, totaling some $18 billion each year in what may well have been wasteful spending. Following the highly visible criticism of its program, New York State pledged to substantially cut fraud over the next several years, and it seems to be making some progress.[27] It should be said that the states vary widely in how they administer the Medicaid program, and New York's experience does not imply that such waste exists in other states.[28]

What should the government do to reduce the incidence of Medicaid fraud and abuse? Spending more money to investigate suspected fraud and abuse would be a good start. With so many hospitals, clinics, and other health care providers, one of the few ways that states can protect themselves is to hire more auditors. Such efforts can easily pay for themselves, so there is little reason not to do so. Nonetheless, most states have not invested in auditor programs that would help to recover fraudulent payments.[29] What other actions do you think the states should take to reduce fraud and abuse?

In early 2007 veterans hospitals received a great deal of negative publicity when deplorable conditions were found at Washington, D.C.'s Walter Reed Army Medical Center. The problems extended well beyond this facility and in part reflected funding cuts during the Bush administration and the rising number of veterans in need of care as a result of the wars in Iraq and Afghanistan. The photo shows Jeremy Duncan, a wounded army specialist who was assigned a room in Building 18, a facility used by Walter Reed to house wounded soldiers recovering from their injuries. Other rooms in Building 18 were found to be rat- and cockroach-infested, and some had stained carpets, cheap mattresses, and black mold on the walls. A few had no heat or water.

Veterans Health Care

With all the attention paid to Medicare and Medicaid, policymakers and journalists sometimes forget that one of the oldest programs of federal health care service is similar to the national insurance programs that are the rule in Canada and Great Britain, but this one is for veterans only. The **Veterans Healthcare System** is designed to serve the needs of U.S. veterans by providing primary medical care, specialized care, and other medical and social services, such as rehabilitation. The Veterans Health Administration operates veterans' hospitals and clinics across the nation and provides extensive coverage for veterans with service-related disabilities and diseases and more limited coverage for other veterans, particularly those with no private health care insurance. It also engages in diverse medical research. In early 2007 the quality of care at veterans' hospitals received considerable media coverage when substandard conditions and practices were discovered at the Walter Reed Army Medical Center, in Washington, D.C. President Bush promised that improvements would soon follow, but Democrats complained that the problems were not unique to Walter Reed and that poor care for veterans could be traced to funding cuts in the Bush administration and poor planning for the number of injured veterans returning from the wars in Iraq and Afghanistan.[30]

One other consequence of these wars became clear by 2009. There would be a major and costly expansion of service to veterans, many of whom suffered debilitating brain injuries and other serious battle wounds that would take years of treatment and recovery. The projected increase in veterans' health care needs is all the more reason to insure that these health care programs are both effective in meeting veterans' needs and efficient in the use of federal health care dollars.[31]

Congress expanded the existing veterans' health programs by enacting the Veterans Health Care Eligibility Reform Act of 1996. That legislation created a medical benefits package, an enhanced health benefits plan that is available to enrolled veterans. The health care plan emphasizes preventive and primary care, but it also offers a full range of services, including inpatient and outpatient medical, surgical, and mental health services; prescription and over-the-counter drugs and medical and surgical supplies; emergency care; comprehensive rehabilitative services; and even payment of travel expenses associated with care for eligible veterans. The Department of Veterans Affairs (VA) health care benefits extend to preventive care and include periodic physical examinations, health and nutrition education, drug use education and drug monitoring, and mental health and substance abuse preventive services. Medical needs attributable to service-related injuries and disease typically are free of individual deductibles and co-payments. VA uses a priority group structure and a financial means test to set co-payment charges for other veterans (see www.va.gov). Its medical system has undergone a major transformation in recent years and is now widely considered to be a model for a national health care system. This is especially so because of its use of electronic medical records, its strong focus on preventive care measures (for example, for cancer, diabetes, and heart disease), and its high scores on health care quality indicators.[32]

At the request of senior military leaders, in 2000 Congress approved another health care program for career military personnel. It expands the military's health plan, known as **TriCare,** to include retirees with at least twenty years of service once they become eligible for Medicare. TriCare pays for most of the costs for medical treatment that are not covered by Medicare, except for $3,000 per year in out-of-pocket expenses. The plan also includes generous prescription drug coverage. One health care policy analyst, Henry Aaron of the Brookings Institution, summed up what many would conclude about this action: "It's interesting that Congress recognizes that for this one group the Medicare benefit package isn't adequate," he said. "One might well ask that if [Medicare] isn't good enough for men and women who served in the armed forces, why is it good enough for men and women who spent a lifetime paying federal payroll taxes?" [33] The answer would seem to be that Congress thought this initiative was politically attractive in an election year but feared that providing comparable benefits for the entire nation would be extremely costly and far more difficult.

OTHER HEALTH CARE POLICY ISSUES

Several major health care policy issues do not directly involve government insurance programs such as Medicare, Medicaid, and the Veterans Healthcare Services, but instead affect the way private medical insurance operates and the legal rights of policyholders. Two issues merit special attention: the portability of insurance as individuals leave one job for another and the rights of patients to seek legal recourse for decisions made by a managed care or other health organization.

Portability

Given the large number of people whose health care services are provided under employer-sponsored insurance plans, the possible loss of benefits when an employee switches jobs is a persistent concern. One employer's plan might not be the same as another's in cost or quality. People with preexisting medical conditions, such as heart disease, hypertension, or cancer, might find that a new employer's insurance company is unwilling to cover them at all or will charge higher premiums. To address some of these problems, in 1996 Congress approved the Health Insurance Portability and Accountability Act (HIPAA). The law guarantees that employees who change jobs have the right to insurance coverage, even if that coverage comes at a higher cost. That is, they have the right of **portability** for their insurance coverage; they can take guaranteed coverage with them if they change jobs. And they do not have to endure the waiting period that policies often impose to limit coverage of preexisting conditions.

Each state establishes the arrangements for providing these guaranteed-issue individual insurance policies. Typically, an individual must first use all benefits provided under yet another federal policy from the mid-1980s, the Consolidated Omnibus Budget Reconciliation Act (COBRA). This program allows individuals who leave their jobs to remain on the employer's health insurance policy for as long as eighteen months, but the employee is responsible for the premiums. The time period is thirty-six months in the case of spousal rights following divorce or death and twenty-nine months for a disability severe enough to qualify for the Social Security disability program. About forty states have adopted mini-COBRA laws that give employees similar rights. The main problem with the policies purchased under HIPAA or COBRA, even though they are guaranteed, is their cost.

Patients' Rights

One of the most common complaints about managed care health systems, such as HMOs, has been the inappropriate denial of care. More than 150 million Americans rely on HMOs and similar health care plans, which are designed to save money by providing affordable, high-quality health care through a consolidated organization of physicians and other professionals. Critics claim that HMOs are so focused on cost reduction that they deny patients needed medical care. Dissatisfaction with what seemed like the HMOs' callous behavior led to the movement to guarantee **patients' rights.** Patients who are denied the right to see a specialist or to have medical treatment argue that they should be able to inquire into the financial arrangements that may affect referrals to specialists and have a right to sue the health care provider either to gain those services or be compensated for their loss.

The Employee Retirement Income Security Act of 1974 (ERISA) allows individuals to sue health insurance companies for such decisions, but only in federal court. ERISA says that federal regulations supersede state laws that govern employee health plans and that no punitive damages may be sought beyond compensation for actual medical expenses. This provision exempts many health plans from state laws, and millions of patients can sue for damages only in federal court, which is difficult, and not for punitive damages. Advocates of expanding patients' right to sue have argued that the right should be extended to state courts and that individuals should be allowed to sue for punitive damages. Democrats tended to favor expanding patients' rights in this way, and Republicans resisted the efforts. Employers argued that extending the right to sue would greatly increase their costs and force them to cut back on insurance coverage. HMOs also resisted the proposals and lobbied intensely against them for similar reasons. Their arguments have been better received as health care costs have risen sharply.

Nevertheless, everyone agrees that health care plans should be held accountable for decisions that deny patients needed medical care. The disagreement comes over when patients should be allowed to sue and the appropriate damages. Despite the prolonged debate on Capitol Hill, neither political party has shown much willingness to compromise on patients' rights. Ultimately, however, the courts seem to have resolved the conflict. The Supreme Court ruled in two cases in 2004 that patients could sue their health plans over a decision to deny them coverage, but only in federal court, consistent with ERISA. The ruling overturned patients' rights laws in ten states. Given this ruling, further protection of patients' rights will likely require a new act of Congress. However, in recent years HMOs have been less willing to deny patients access to

TABLE 8-2	National Health Expenditures, 1980–2007, in nominal dollars			
Item	1980	1990	2000	2007
Total national health care expenditures (in billions)	$253.40	$714.10	$1,353.20	$2,241.20
Per capita health care expenditures	$1,100	$2,813	$4,789	$7,421
Health care expenditures as percentage of GDP	9.1%	12.3%	13.8%	16.2%

Sources: Drawn from current and historical tables prepared by the Centers for Medicare and Medicaid Services, Office of the Actuary Web site (www.cms.hhs.gov), January 6, 2009. Projections of health expenditures are offered for ten years out from the time of publication, or through 2017 for the most recent year of data (2007). The documents are updated annually.

health care services, making the issue less salient by 2009. The overall cost of health care has received more attention of late than patients' rights.[34]

What is the equitable solution to the patients' rights dispute? Should HMOs and other managed care organizations be able to deny coverage they deem unnecessary? Should patients be allowed to challenge such decisions in court if no other dispute resolution process is provided? What impact do you think the extension of such patients' rights will have on health care costs?

RISING HEALTH CARE COSTS

As this chapter has emphasized, one of the most difficult issues in health care policy disputes is cost. To make matters worse, the cost of providing health care services is rising inexorably. Health care is expensive enough that individuals whose employers do not provide full coverage can easily find themselves unable to pay for private insurance or for all the medical services they need. The result can be financially devastating should a major medical emergency arise from an acute illness or an accident. Indeed, such circumstances often are a major reason for personal bankruptcy filings.[35] Even those with relatively generous health care insurance policies can find themselves facing enormous medical bills because of required deductible expenses and co-payment fees, for example, for prescription drugs.

Table 8-2 shows the trend in health care costs. It lists total U.S. health care expenditures for the years 1980 to 2007, as well as per capita expenditures, indicating that health care costs rose substantially over this period.

As might be expected, soaring costs deeply affect the leading federal health care programs. Medicare expenditures alone totaled $427 billion in 2007, with the overall cost for federal and state spending on Medicare, Medicaid, and SCHIP combined at $770 billion. Among the largest increases has been spending for prescription drugs, which rose from $88.5 billion in 1998 to $231.3 billion by 2007 and is expected to reach $515.7 billion by 2017.[36] So-called **third-party payers**, that is, insurance companies, employers, governments, or other parties that pay for care, are now responsible for a much greater share of drug costs than in 1990. This practice contributes to increasing demand that is expected to rise further as the population ages and as new therapies are introduced.

As many television viewers have noted, pharmaceutical manufacturers have changed their marketing strategies and now advertise directly to consumers, instead of only to health professionals. In sometimes deceptive advertisements, viewers are urged to ask their doctors for the new medications.[37] The practice has been a success for the pharmaceutical companies, as the public demand for expensive new prescription drugs grew, even though many of them are only marginally more effective than cheaper, over-the-counter medications and generic versions of similar drugs. For example, commonly used (and heavily advertised) medications such as Celebrex, Lunesta, Nexium, Plavix, Prevacid, and Zocor can cost nearly $1,000 per year, and it is by no means clear that they are preferable to cheaper products, including over-the-counter medications, or better diet and exercise. As one illustration, Celebrex is a COX-2 inhibitor used for arthritis pain and inflammation. According to its manufacturer, on average some one million prescriptions are filled each month; the daily costs of the medication are about $2.40, or $72 for a month's supply. Yet many people might find equal relief with ordinary aspirin or ibuprofen at one-hundredth of the cost.[38] Of course, the cost of drugs for cancer treatment and other serious illnesses can dwarf even these medications. The drug Avastin, for example, is used for patients with advanced lung, colon, or breast cancer, and its cost can reach $100,000 per year. Cerezyme, a drug used to treat Gaucher Disease, a rare inherited disorder, can cost $500,000 a year.

What is the future of health care costs? The Centers for Medicare and Medicaid Services offer projections for U.S. health care costs ten years out, through 2017, and they show no change in the upward trend. Total health care expenditures are expected to grow at a substantially higher rate than the economy as a whole, rising from an estimated $2.2 trillion in 2007 to $4.3 trillion in 2017, per capita expenditures from $7,421 to $13,103, and expenditures as a percentage of GDP from 16.2 percent to 19.5 percent.[39] The government projects that pressure will increase on both public and private payers to cover accelerating health care costs, and it anticipates additional need to reconsider health care priorities in the years ahead.

State Policy Innovations

The federal government is not the only policy actor trying to contain health care costs; the states also have a role to play, and some states have adopted innovative public policies. For example, as we pointed out in chapter 6, Oregon approved a state health plan that offered Medicaid recipients and others universal access to basic and effective health care. Based on a public-private partnership, the plan included state-run insurance pools, insurance reforms, and a federal waiver allowing for the expansion of Medicaid. The system featured rationing of services based on a ranking of medical procedures that the state and its residents believed to be cost effective. In 2002 Utah also received permission from the federal government to reduce benefits under its Medicaid program and use the savings to bring additional low-income people into the program. Oregon's program has since suffered, as the state's economy deteriorated in the early 2000s and it was forced to cut back on benefits, and by early 2009 state legislators in Utah were under similar pressure to reduce funding for its program, already one of the most generous in the nation.[40]

As an illustration of the capacity of state governments to develop innovative public policies when the federal government often cannot or will not do so, some states have targeted smoking as a preventive health measure, and they have used creative ways to do so. The photo shows an e-card from the Tobacco-Free California Web site. The site also has ads, videos, message boards, and other information about quitting smoking and the harmful effects of tobacco. California has used higher taxes on tobacco to fund various types of advertisements in an effort to discourage teenagers from starting to smoke. They have worked. Smoking in California has dropped substantially since the beginning of the campaign, and teen smoking has been cut greatly as well.

In one effort to keep its Medicaid expenses in check, in 1994 Tennessee began a demonstration program that was to move all of its Medicaid recipients to a managed care program called TennCare. It used the savings to expand the number of people who could be served by the state program. For example, it covered the uninsured and uninsurable in the state who were not eligible for Medicaid, and eventually TennCare covered 23 percent of the state's population, more than any other state in the nation. However, as the program's costs escalated and the state's economy suffered, by 2005 Tennessee was forced to institute major reforms in the program to reduce its spending; critics said the reforms in effect dismantled the program.[41] This is a good example of how a policy decision to improve economic efficiency also helped to improve equity in access to health care services. Unfortunately, the state's budget dictated a dramatic shift in policy, at least for the short term.

Other states, such as California, have long promoted policy innovation. California, for example, developed an aggressive antismoking media campaign and raised tobacco taxes in an effort to get people to stop smoking, a preventive health care action. The goal is to reduce the number of people needing expensive medical services in the future, and thus to improve the economic efficiency of health care programs. By all accounts, the effort has been successful, and the state will likely face a declining rate of lung cancer and other serious illnesses as a result. States have also taken measures to deal with rising rates of obesity, such as limiting access to calorie-laden fast food in public schools.

Some states, as noted early in the chapter, have gone well beyond these limited measures to adopt comprehensive health care plans. Most notably, a landmark plan enacted in Massachusetts in 2006 requires all state residents to purchase health insurance coverage and imposes a financial penalty on those who do not. There is a state subsidy for low-income residents, the poorest of whom are enrolled automatically into the program. The plan also requires employers with eleven or more employees to make a "fair and reasonable" contribution toward their health insurance coverage or to pay a "fair share" contribution annually per employee. Although the plan is potentially costly, supporters point to its coverage of more than 350,000 state residents who previously did not have health insurance. They also highlight the plan's Health Care Quality and Cost Council, which sets goals for improving quality, containing costs, and reducing inequities in health care. Many other states are looking closely at the Massachusetts plan despite what has been a difficult experience in its implementation.[42]

These and many other examples illustrate the pivotal role that the states can play in finding solutions to the emerging health care crisis. Where the federal government is often unable to act because of the constraints on policymaking that we discussed in chapter 2, states have been able to try different approaches and demonstrate their merits. Some states, as noted, are limiting coverage for the Medicaid programs, but others have adopted or are considering bold ventures to expand insurance coverage, rein in costs, and relieve employers of some of the burden they now bear for insuring employees.[43] What should states do to try to improve public health and reduce the long-term costs of health care? Examine one or more of the Web sites listed in the box "Working with Sources: Health Care Policy Information" (see page 231) and at the end of the chapter to see some of the innovative policies states are trying and how well they are working.

Regulation of Prescription Drugs

Given the already high and rapidly rising cost of prescription drugs, another way to control health care costs is to change the way the federal government and drug manufacturers develop and approve new medicines. The current process of drug development is long and expensive, forcing drug manufacturers to charge high prices to cover their cost of research and development. For example, the arthritis drug Embrel, developed by the Immunex Corporation, costs a patient over $10,000 a year. New drugs that stave off AIDS cost even more, as do some cancer therapies, as noted earlier. In defense of their pricing policies, the drug companies note that, for every successful product, dozens of others never make it to market despite millions of dollars in development costs. Moreover, even drugs that are approved have patent protection against generic competition for only about eleven years.

Is there a way to reduce such costs without jeopardizing the public's health? Or is it more important to maintain a rigorous and demanding drug approval process regardless of the time and cost it imposes? Congress addressed the need for such balancing when it passed legislation in 2007 aimed at expanding the FDA's regulatory powers and budget, particularly for its monitoring of prescription drugs and medical devices.[44] Adding to the concerns that prompted the policy change, some news accounts in 2008 questioned the validity of new drug studies, with allegations that pharmaceutical companies often were ghostwriting medical research studies about their own drugs that were later published in medical journals as objective scientific evaluations.[45] The box "Steps to Analysis: Regulation of New Drug Approval" deals with these kinds of issues. It focuses on the difficult trade-offs that the FDA faces in trying to move new drug treatments to market. How carefully should it review the safety and effectiveness of new drugs prior to their approval? Is it better to err on the side of caution or to help ensure that we have early access to new medical treatments?

REGULATION OF NEW DRUG APPROVAL

The Food and Drug Administration (FDA) requires pharmaceutical and biotechnology companies to conduct elaborate, lengthy, and costly testing of new drugs before they can be approved for patient use. The justification for this process is to ensure the safety and effectiveness of new drugs prior to marketing. Drug manufacturers have often complained that the FDA procedures are too demanding and delay the availability of new treatments, prevent some of them from reaching the market at all, and contribute to the high cost of new drug development. They also report that a new drug may take as long as ten to fifteen years to develop, with research and development costs reaching $800 million or more.

In response to some of these concerns, Congress enacted the Prescription Drug User Fee Act in 1992, which imposed tight deadlines for new drug evaluation at the agency, but also required pharmaceutical companies to pay fees that would permit the agency to hire more drug reviewers, thus reducing the time needed to evaluate and approve new drugs. Reviews are now expected to be completed within ten months, half the time that was common before the act. Priority drugs may be reviewed even more quickly. Yet one consequence of the new procedures is that some drugs are approved even where questions remain about their safety, efficacy, or quality.

Has the United States struck an acceptable balance between the need for a speedy approval process and the necessity to ensure drug safety and efficacy? Is the FDA too cautious? Should the FDA use a special, expedited procedure to approve so-called breakthrough drugs that offer great promise for serious illnesses, such as cancer and heart disease? What about drugs that might be used to combat bioterrorism?

To explore these questions, consider two examples of recent FDA and company actions. In 1999 the FDA approved the pain relief drug Vioxx, a non-steroidal anti-inflammatory medication. Vioxx was widely used, even though the majority of those taking it could have chosen instead to use safer, more effective, and cheaper drugs that had long been on the market. Then, in 2004, new information appeared on serious side effects of using the drug; those taking Vioxx for a long time faced a doubled risk of heart attack or stroke. The manufacturer, Merck, withdrew Vioxx from the market and the FDA issued a public health advisory to warn patients to consult with their physicians about use of the drug. Merck faced at least seven thousand lawsuits over the drug, with a potential financial liability of perhaps $50 billion. In 2007 it settled the cases for nearly $5 billion. Was the FDA approval process insufficient in this case? Was its post-approval monitoring of the drug's safety inadequate?[1]

Other drugs present the opposite situation. A drug that may have broad benefits to the population faces a long testing and approval process, thereby denying treatment to those in need of it. Or a drug may be removed from the market because of safety concerns for a segment of the population, leaving others who need the drug with no medication for their disease. One example of the latter is the drug Tysabri, made by Biogen Idec. In late 2004, the company received FDA approval to market Tysabri, one of the few drugs that proved to be effective in treating multiple sclerosis (MS). In February 2005, however, the company voluntarily suspended sales of the drug after concerns arose over extremely rare (but serious) side effects. It then designed new studies to clarify the side effects before seeking FDA approval for more limited use of the drug, which came back on the market in July 2006. In the meantime, Biogen Idec reported that MS patients complained that they could no longer get the drug, or anything else that would help them, and they pleaded with the company to bring the drug back to market as quickly as possible. Should the FDA have demanded such stringent safety testing for the drug even if it meant it would not be available to those in need of it?

1. For a review of similar problems with the FDA approval process, see "Prescription for Trouble," *Consumer Reports,* January 2006, 34–39. For the Vioxx settlement as well as allegations that the drug studies may not be as valid as once thought, see Stephanie Saul, "Merck Wrote Drug Studies for Doctors," *New York Times,* April 16, 2008, C1, 6.

MANAGED CARE ORGANIZATIONS

Managed care, now a fixture of modern health care services and policy, was proposed as one way to contain rising health care costs that had soared under the old system of unrestrained **fee-for-service,** in which the patient or an insurance company pays for the medical service rendered. Over the past several decades, the United States has shifted from fee-for-service to a system dominated by managed care, typically with the costs borne by third-party payers. By most measurements, the transition has been successful, particularly in holding down health care costs and promoting preventive health care.

Managed care organizations provide health care by forming networks of doctors, other health care providers, and hospitals associated with a given plan; monitoring their treatment activities; and limiting access to specialists and costly procedures. The best-known managed care organizations are the **health maintenance organizations** (HMOs). Along with other managed care companies, such as **preferred provider organizations** (PPOs), they promote health services that are the most cost effective, such as ensuring regular physicals and certain medical screening tests, limiting access to costly services and specialists, and negotiating lower fees with health care providers. PPOs differ from HMOs in that enrollees have a financial incentive to use physicians on the preferred list but may opt to see other health professionals at a higher cost. By most accounts, HMOs and PPOs save the nation billions of dollars a year in health care costs, an important achievement. By the late 1990s the number of workers in managed care health plans dwarfed those in traditional fee-for-service plans. The ratio was about six to one, with the fee-for-service plans declining steadily throughout the 1990s and into the 2000s.

Managed care still has its critics, even if by most indications it has been a highly successful design that balances quality health care service with the concern over how to constrain costs. Recent criticism of HMOs has focused on limits placed on patients' stays in hospitals—routinely, only twenty-four hours following childbirth, for example—and denying or limiting coverage for certain procedures. HMOs counter that they are trying to ensure that limited health care dollars are spent efficiently and fairly and that patients be provided with only safe and proven treatments. They fear that expanding patients' rights might lead to the use of unnecessary and possibly dangerous procedures, resulting in higher insurance fees and injuries to patients. They also argue that laws guaranteeing patients the power to select physicians and to sue their health care plans will raise premium costs and leave more people uninsured and vulnerable to health risks.

Following patient complaints and adverse publicity in the 1990s and early 2000s, however, managed care companies changed some of their policies to become more accommodating than in the past. The evidence suggests they are not denying care in many cases, even though the occasional horror story to that effect pops up in a movie or on television. Indeed, some states, including Connecticut, New Jersey, and New York, require managed care plans to report incidents of care denial and how they were resolved. In these states, plan administrators seem to be reluctant to second-guess physicians, but the plans still deny access to physicians outside of their networks and nonessential or experimental treatments. Economists concerned about rising health care costs think that HMOs and other plans need to be much tougher in overseeing physician decisions to minimize the use of needless and risky surgery and unnecessary and expensive diagnostic tests (Bettelheim 1999).

REDUCING HEALTH CARE COSTS: BEYOND HMOS

If managed care has not succeeded in restraining the rise in health care costs, other strategies may emerge to reach that goal. Four of these merit brief mention: (1) passing on additional costs to health care consumers; (2) setting up personal health accounts; (3) managing disease more effectively; and (4) using preventive health care.

Everyone complains about the cost of health care, but the fact is that few people ever see the full price tag because insurance plans take care of most of it.[46] Of course, even simple surgeries can cost thousands of dollars, and many prescription drugs, such as new antibiotics, can run to hundreds of dollars per month. So these relatively low burdens on individuals can escalate quickly if a major health care need arises. But under more normal circumstances, these modest costs borne by individuals suggest that one way to reduce rising demand for health care services and prescription drugs is to pass along more of the cost to them. For example, if employees had to cover more of the costs now paid by their employers' insurance policies, they might have an incentive to reduce their demand for health services that are not essential, such as visiting a hospital emergency room for a nonemergency situation, demanding exotic new drugs when less expensive alternatives exist, or requesting expensive diagnostic tests that a physician believes are unnecessary. Raising the policyholder's share of the cost with higher deductibles and higher levels of co-payments would inject "market discipline" into health care coverage.[47]

A variation on this theme is that individuals who use health services more frequently than average should pay more of the cost, for example, through higher insurance premiums. In other words, the sicker should pay more, just as those with more driving citations or accidents pay higher automobile insurance premiums and those with safe driving records get a break. Is this proposal fair? It might be if the health care consumers brought on their conditions through poor choices over which they had reasonable control. But what about individuals with inherited diseases, or accident victims, or those who simply have the misfortune of suffering from a rare (and expensive) illness? Is it ethical to pass the costs of treatment along to them and their families?

Many employers seeking ways to cope with rising premium costs are setting up personal health accounts for their workers. The employers deposit money into an account that is used to pay for each employee's health expenses that the regular insurance does not cover. The money can be used for prescription drugs, physician visits, dental work, and other health-related bills. Employees make their own decisions about how best to spend the limited funds. Once the money is gone, the employee is responsible for any additional charges that year. These plans may come with a very high deductible, which would make them essentially catastrophic insurance policies; if so, the employee is better off using the plan for a highly unusual major medical need, not routine services. Those who make poor choices, or are unlucky and suffer from a serious injury, or need continuing medical care, may be worse off under such a plan. Is this kind of plan likely to be effective as a compromise to control costs and still cover catastrophic illness or injury?

Disease management programs focus on a few chronic diseases associated with high costs. The programs promise to reduce employers' costs by bringing employee diseases under control more effectively than is likely through conventional medical treatment. Managed care organizations have led the way in developing these kinds of programs. Surveys indicate that a majority of them have implemented programs for managing conditions such as asthma, diabetes, heart disease, end-stage renal disease, cancer, and depression. Their goal is to train patients to take better care of themselves by monitoring their diseases, watching their diets, and seeking appropriate and timely medical care. Some critics are concerned that singling out employees with chronic conditions for the training programs may pose a threat to them. Even some insurance programs believe that disease management of this kind raises difficult ethical issues involving medical privacy and employee-employer relationships. But few question that such programs make many individuals healthier and also reduce health care costs. How would you weigh the ethical issues of disease management?

The compelling logic of preventive care is addressed more fully at the end of the chapter. All agree that if people take good care of themselves throughout their lives, they are likely to be healthier and need less medical care than those who do not. Preventive care health plans usually allow regular physical examinations and diagnostic tests; education and training in diet, exercise, and stress management; and smoking cessation programs. Some employers emphasize preventive care, while others seem to give it little thought, even though the potential to reduce long-term health care costs is substantial. Moreover, most HMO and PPO plans fully cover preventive health care, including educational programs on health and wellness, prenatal care, nutrition, and smoking cessation. Do you think most employees would take advantage of preventive health care if it were offered?

QUALITY OF CARE

The issue of quality in medical care is easy to understand. At a minimum, every patient should expect to receive professional and competent care that is consistent with good medical practice. The physician or other health care professional should be well trained, up-to-date on new research and treatments, and able to spend sufficient time with a patient to properly diagnose and treat medical conditions that arise. These expectations are particularly reasonable in the United States, given the vast amounts of money invested by government, insurance companies, and individuals in one of the best medical care systems in the world.

The evidence suggests, however, that quality care is not as routinely available as many would like to believe. Patients complain about poor-quality care, and even the American Medical Association concedes that errors in diagnosis and treatment occur at a significant rate. In addition, studies indicate that many physicians rely excessively on costly medical technology and drugs, in part to increase revenues for physician offices and hospitals and in part as "defensive medicine," to guard against liability in malpractice claims. Indeed, a 1991 study put the cost of defensive medicine in the United States at $25 billion per year.[48] Another study in 2002 by the Juran Institute, a group representing large employers, found that $390 billion a year was wasted on outmoded and inefficient medical procedures. The authors argued that poor quality in health care at that time cost the average employer some $1,700 to $2,000 for each covered employee each year. More recently, studies by Dartmouth Medical School questioned the effectiveness of aggressive medical care found in some regions of the country. Patients receiving such care were at increased risk of infections and medical errors, and they didn't benefit appreciably compared to those who received less aggressive care.[49]

Part of the general problem of insufficient quality of care is that physicians and state medical associations find it difficult to discipline colleagues who may be guilty of malpractice.

Despite the federal law requiring HMOs and hospitals to report any disciplinary action taken against doctors for incompetence or misconduct, few incidents are reported.[50] California and other states, however, have succeeded in reforming medical liability laws without compromising quality patient care. These reforms suggest what can be done if the public and policymakers take the issue of quality health care seriously. For example, as early as the 1970s California chose to limit noneconomic (pain and suffering) awards to $250,000, an approach that apparently has kept malpractice insurance in the state lower than in many others.

If, as patients in HMOs sometimes complain, doctors spend less time with them and access to specialists is limited, are these problems evidence of lower-quality care? They might be, if physicians and other health care professionals are too busy to properly diagnose and treat their patients. It is true that, to cope with rising patient demand and to compensate for lower rates of reimbursement, medical professionals must see more patients per day than they did in the past. Still, it is difficult to measure the quality of medical care.[51] The issue is not likely to go away because the amount of care and patients' perceptions of its quality are closely tied to the factors that escalate health care costs, such as seeing physicians more frequently, gaining access to specialists, benefiting from new medical technology and treatments, and using the latest prescription drugs.

Medical Errors

One element of the concern about the quality of medical care is more concrete and disturbing—the incidence of medical errors. A widely circulated and influential report released in 1999 by the Institute of Medicine (IOM), which is part of the National Academy of Sciences, estimated that between forty-four thousand and ninety-eight thousand patients die each year as a result of medical errors made in hospitals. The errors include operations on the wrong patient or the wrong side of a patient, incorrect drug prescriptions or administration of the wrong dosages, malfunctioning mechanical equipment, and nursing and other staff errors. The study did *not* include medical errors in other health care settings, such as physician offices, clinics, pharmacies, nursing homes, and urgent care facilities, which presumably would add considerably to the overall numbers. Nor did it include the estimated 1.7 million infections acquired in the nation's hospitals each year, which the CDC claims lead to some ninety-nine thousand deaths. The CDC findings have led many hospitals to adopt new procedures to try to cut infection rates.[52]

To put the IOM study into perspective, using the lower number of forty-four thousand deaths per year would make medical errors in hospitals the eighth leading cause of death in the United States, higher than motor vehicle accidents, breast cancer, or AIDS.[53] Aside from the dire consequences for the patients, including injuries as well as death, medical errors are expensive. The IOM study estimated that they cost the nation $37.6 billion each year, about $17 billion of which is associated with preventable errors. Generally, the preventable medical errors are not attributable simply to individual negligence or misconduct but to the health care delivery system, such as the way patient and drug information is handled.

The IOM called for a new federal law to require hospitals to report all such mistakes that cause serious injury or death to patients, just as they are supposed to report disciplinary actions against doctors. Initially, federal health officials were unwilling to back such a proposal without further study.[54] In 2005, however, Congress approved and President Bush signed legislation that establishes procedures for voluntary and confidential reporting of medical errors to independent organizations that are to submit the information to a national database. After analysis, recommendations for improving patient safety are likely to follow. It is not clear that such a reporting system would reduce the number of errors, but it has the potential to do so. That seems to be the lesson from the twenty-two states that already have laws intended to identify and deal with medical errors.[55] Further evidence of government commitment to deal with the problem came in late 2008, when the federal Medicare program announced that it would no longer pay for medical errors—what it called "reasonably preventable" conditions on a list it made available to hospitals. Four state Medicaid programs, and some of the nation's largest health insurance companies, also announced that they would not pay for what they called "never events," that is, medical errors that should never occur.[56]

Boutique Health Care

Another aspect of health care quality is noteworthy, if only because of its sharp contrast to the situation affecting those without health insurance or those who find the standard services of HMOs wanting. What is known as **boutique health care,** or concierge care, is the upscale and often expensive health care provided to the wealthy. It may include easier access to "concierge" physicians who limit the number of patients they agree to see; luxury suites in hospitals; spa-like stress reduction services; or certain cosmetic surgeries and treatments, such as Botox injections to minimize facial wrinkles. Insurance companies rarely cover such boutique services if they are medically unnecessary or exceed the specified minimal hospital and other charges they would normally pay. However, those who want these services and can afford them do not worry about the expense.[57]

Some providers of boutique health care offer special care to patients willing to pay a retainer of several thousand dollars a year. They promise their patients twenty-four-hour availability seven days a week and no waiting to see a physician. Doctors with boutique practices can increase earnings that have been constrained by government policies and managed care rules and regulations. In addition, some doctors say they are tired of the mandates imposed by managed care, which often dictate that they see more patients per day than they believe is compatible with quality care. They genuinely want to spend more time with patients than otherwise possible.

Boutique health care is a reminder that the nation has long had a multitier health care system in which those with sufficient money can buy almost any health services they desire, from a comprehensive physical exam at the Mayo Clinic to a visit to a plastic surgeon to receive a breast enhancement. People of limited means are forced to settle for basic care or even less than what is minimally necessary. Policy analysts differ in their appraisals of boutique health care. Conservative analysts, such as those at the Cato Institute, have argued that "people should be able to get as much [health care] as they can pay for." In contrast, liberal analysts are just as likely to criticize what they call "wealth-care" services as inequitable and inappropriate.[58] Which argument is more persuasive? The box "Working with Sources: Ethical Issues in Health Care" examines the issue of embryonic stem cell research to illustrate how ethical and scientific concerns are intertwined in health care policy decisions.

ETHICAL ISSUES IN HEALTH CARE

Some of the most contentious issues in health care involve ethical rather than economic issues. One of the prominent debates in recent years has concerned embryonic stem cell research. Advocates of such research point to the potential for discovering possible treatments for life-threatening disease, and polls indicate that more than two-thirds of the American public approve of expanding use of human embryonic stem cells in research. Yet conservative religious groups, among others, are critical of such exploration because some researchers use tissue from aborted fetuses. They successfully lobbied the George W. Bush White House to set stringent limits on the use of stem cells in federally sponsored medical research. The state of California, however, took a strikingly different position, endorsing stem cell research and setting up an elaborate state-funded institute to further it. In March 2009 President Barack Obama revoked Bush's federal limits on funding for stem cell research.

Cases such as stem cell research raise broad questions about decision making in government. How do policymakers decide what to do about such controversial issues? How much weight do they give to science, and how much weight do they give to the views of organized interest groups that are active on the issues?

To determine the roles of science and interest groups' pressure in the case of stem cell research, first examine the arguments presented at two Web sites: www.stemcellresearchnews.com and www.cc.org. The first is a private site that covers scientific research from around the world, and the second represents the conservative Christian Coalition (where you can use the search engine to find statements and news reports on stem cell research). Then turn to the Web sites that report on policymakers with different positions on the issue. The state of California has strongly supported stem cell research. See the program description at the state's Center for Regenerative Medicine: www.cirm.ca.gov. In contrast, the states of Louisiana, Michigan, North Dakota, and South Dakota, among others, have restricted such research. For reports of recent developments in these and other states at a site supportive of such restrictions, go to www.lifenews.com, an independent news agency that is devoted to reporting news that affects the pro-life community. Do you find any differences in references to science or the position of key interest groups? What conclusions can you draw about the relative roles of science and interest groups in decision making for this issue? For a detailed summary of all state policies on stem cell research, see this site on state health facts at the Kaiser Family Foundation: www.statehealth facts.org/comparetable.jsp?ind=111&cat=2.

FOCUSED DISCUSSION: SHOULD THERE BE GREATER EMPHASIS ON PREVENTIVE HEALTH CARE?

Throughout the chapter we have highlighted many of the weaknesses of the U.S. health care system, particularly its high costs and the forecasts for increasing costs as the baby boom generation ages. Much of the debate over health care policy actions, from government programs such as Medicare and Medicaid to employer-provided health insurance plans, focuses on how to pay for expensive health care services. One of the most promising ways to constrain health care costs and also to keep people healthy would be to give greater emphasis to **preventive health care**, or the promotion of health and prevention of disease in individuals. This would include routine screening for serious diseases such as diabetes, heart disease, or high blood pressure; better treatment of chronic illnesses; improved health care education; and more attention to the role of diet, exercise, smoking, and other lifestyle choices that can affect individuals' health. Put otherwise, ill health and premature death are not merely functions of genetics or exposure to disease-causing microbes or environmental pollutants over which individuals have little control. They also reflect choices people make in their daily lives.

For this focused discussion we turn to selected efforts of this kind, particularly those involving smoking and diet. We evaluate them in terms of the criteria we have emphasized in the chapter and throughout the book: effectiveness, economic efficiency, and equity and other ethical issues. That is, we want to see how effective preventive health care measures might be in improving health; what they might save in costs to the nation; and how we can appraise the wisdom of such policy actions in terms of ethical issues, including possible infringement on individuals' right to behave as they choose without government regulations or pressures to change their lifestyles.

Effectiveness

One way to appreciate the importance of preventive health care is to consider the leading causes of death in the United States. As the data in Table 8-3 indicate, heart disease and cancer dominate the list, followed by stroke and chronic respiratory diseases such as emphysema. Among the leading contributing factors in all of these cases are smoking, diet, lack of exercise, stress, and exposure to environmental pollutants. Moreover, even where the causes can be found elsewhere (such as in genetic predisposition to certain diseases), early detection and treatment can both save lives and lower the costs of treatment. For chronic diseases such as diabetes and high blood pressure, regular monitoring of those conditions and use of appropriate medical treatments could improve the quality of patients' lives, reduce premature death rates, and save money, all at the same time.

Take the issue of smoking. It is widely recognized to be the single most preventable cause of premature death in the United States, accounting for more than 438,000 deaths annually, according to the CDC. Secondhand smoke takes an additional health toll, particularly in children. Roughly half of those who smoke die prematurely from cancer, heart disease, emphysema, and other smoking-related diseases.[59] If there is good news related to smoking it can be found in the number of Americans who have quit. An estimated forty-six million people have stopped smoking, while about the same number continue to light up. Of those eighteen years of age or older, smokers account for about 20 percent, the lowest level since the mid-1960s. The U.S. surgeon general's reports indicate that smoking cessation at any age conveys health benefits; for example, quitting at even age sixty-five can reduce the risk of dying from some diseases by as much as 50 percent.[60]

Or consider the role of diet and insufficient exercise to prevent excessive weight gain. The surgeon general has observed that, left unabated, "overweight and obesity may soon cause as much preventable disease and death as cigarette smoking." [61] Recent studies by the CDC indicate that about 34 percent of those age twenty or older, some seventy-two million people, are obese. Another 32 percent of the adult population is overweight, and the number of young

TABLE 8-3	Percentage of U.S. Deaths Attributed to the Ten Leading Causes, 2005		
Rank	Causes of Death	Number of Deaths	Percentage of Total Deaths
	All causes	2,448,017	100.0
1	Heart disease	652,091	26.6
2	Cancer	559,312	22.8
3	Stroke	143,579	5.9
4	Chronic lung disease	130,933	5.3
5	Accidents	117,809	4.8
6	Diabetes	75,119	3.1
7	Alzheimer's Disease	71,599	2.9
8	Influenza and pneumonia	63,001	2.6
9	Kidney disease	43,901	1.8
10	Septicemia (blood poisoning)	34,136	1.4

Source: The data are drawn from Hsiang-Ching Kung, Donna L. Hoyert, Jiaquan Xu, and Sherry L. Murphy, "Deaths: Final Data for 2005," *National Vital Statistics Reports* 56, no. 10 (April 24, 2008). Death rates vary by age, and similar statistics are available for different age groups.

people who are overweight has tripled since 1980. Other trends are on the upswing as well. For example, the number of people categorized as overweight increased by 61 percent from 1991 to 2000 alone, and the percentage categorized as obese increased by 65 percent during the same period. The CDC reports that many children are severely overweight as well, and it has launched a research program to study the causes of a seeming epidemic in weight gain. Rates of childhood obesity leveled off in 2008 after years of sharp increases.[62] The rates of obesity and overweight vary from state to state, with some states such as Colorado having low rates (less than 19 percent) and others such as Mississippi having high rates (32 percent). Being overweight, which for some is beyond their control because of genetic and other factors, increases the risk of many health problems. Among them are hypertension, high cholesterol levels, Type 2 diabetes, coronary heart disease, and stroke. Taken together these are so important that one study released in 2005 projected an eventual decline in U.S. life expectancy because of obesity trends and their associated health problems.[63]

The American diet is a strong contributing factor in obesity for both children and adults, with increasing reliance on prepared foods high in calories, fat, and cholesterol. Some critics single out the $800 billion food industry for much of the blame, saying it undermines good nutrition by strongly promoting sales of unhealthy food (Nestle 2002). Not surprisingly, the food industry rejects the charge, and it has fought hard in Congress and state legislatures to protect itself against any legal liability for the nation's collective weight gain.[64] The industry also has fought recommendations by the World Health Organization, reflecting an international scientific consensus, to limit the intake of fat and sugar. In these instances the industry says the real focus should be on individual responsibility for one's diet rather than on food processors and restaurants.

By most accounts, Americans also fall well short of the recommended levels of physical exercise and fitness, and they drink too much alcohol. Both habits contribute to poor health. About one in ten adults reports consuming alcohol excessively, with higher percentages among younger adults. Despite these habits, life expectancy in the United States reached an all-time high of 78.1 years in 2008—which, however, placed it only forty-ninth among the nations of the world. Life expectancy is slightly higher for women and somewhat lower for men, and there are large and growing disparities between rich and poor citizens, which parallels growth in U.S. income inequality over the past two decades.[65] It is reasonable to assume that average life expectancy would be even higher if people took better care of themselves throughout their lives.

Do the facts presented in this section convince you that preventive health care measures directed at smoking, diet, and exercise could be effective in promoting good health? What particular preventive actions should the federal and state governments, employers, insurance companies, or others consider taking? For example, should states try to do what California has done successfully, directing antismoking education programs at teenagers to prevent them from starting to smoke? Should employers help employees enter smoking cessation programs or weight loss programs, or encourage more exercise and other wellness activities? Should public schools try to limit the availability of high-fat and high-calorie foods available in campus vending machines, as some have tried to do? Should the schools require more physical activity of their students?

Economic Efficiency Issues

Consistent with the information provided in the previous section, many advocates of preventive health care defend such initiatives as providing economic benefits. That is, spending money on preventive health care would pay substantial dividends, both financially and in improved health and well-being. For example, a 2003 article in *Health Affairs* put the cost of obesity at 5.7 percent of health care spending in the United States, and other studies say that treating illness related to obesity costs more than $100 billion per year. In addition, some studies make clear that health care for obese and overweight individuals can cost considerably more (about 37 percent more on average) than for those of normal weight.[66] As one example, diabetes, strongly associated with being overweight, ranks as number one in direct health care costs, consuming about 14 percent of health care spending. Studies like the ones cited here have helped to convince the federal government to spend more on anti-obesity therapies and to increase support for research on obesity.

Experience at the state level tells much the same story. The state of West Virginia, for example, found that the cost of obesity for its state employees more than doubled since 1995; it is now almost one-fifth of the health plan's cost. An even more striking study comes from California. In 2005, a report put the cost of obesity to businesses and the state itself at $22 billion per year in lost productivity, increased medical costs, and higher insurance payments. The report was the first to link such weight problems to increases in employer costs. The study concluded that a 5 percent increase in physical activity could save businesses and the state $6 billion each year; a 10 percent increase could save nearly $13 billion.[67] Numbers like these suggest that both state governments and businesses would be wise to give serious thought to programs that promise to reduce weight gain. Analysts have long made similar arguments about the costs of smoking, which are estimated to result in about $150 billion in health-related economic losses each year.

The economic logic of preventive health care seems plain enough. To the extent that health care costs are rising, does it not make sense to direct a greater portion of health care dollars to disease prevention and to encouraging lifestyle changes? Doing so should save money in the long run. But which of many policy instruments should be emphasized? Should government focus on public education and information provision, such as revising the food pyramid to emphasize healthy eating and weight loss? Or should it try to limit the sale of fast food in schools and impose stricter nutritional standards, for example, in the national school lunch program? Or toughen requirements for physical fitness? What about employers, who provide much of the nation's health insurance and who must deal with rising costs? Many will likely try to do more to keep their employees healthy, if only out of concern for the bottom line. In some cases, employer and government actions raise ethical issues.

Equity and Other Ethical Issues

As suggested in the discussion above, taking action on preventive health care should be evaluated not only on the grounds of effectiveness and efficiency, but also in terms of ethics. One of the concerns is equity, or fair treatment for all groups in the population, and another is whether governments (or employers) are justified in taking actions that may impinge on individual rights.

Consider the case of smoking. Do the statistics presented above make for a strong case for further government intervention to reduce smoking and therefore smoking-related disease? For example, should government further raise the price of cigarettes to discourage their use? Studies show that increasing the price of cigarettes can substantially decrease the number of young people who become smokers, and that restrictions on smoking in workplaces and public places can decrease smoking by young adults (Tauras 2005). But does this mean that it is right for government to restrict smoking, particularly among adults who choose to smoke? Should state and local governments become more aggressive in restricting smoking in public places? Would it be right for employers to refuse to hire employees who smoke, or to fire those who do, based on the impact on their health and the cost to the employer? In all of these illustrations, it is easy to see that smokers might well feel they are being treated unfairly as a group even if they acknowledge the possible health care costs of their habit.

As noted in the discussion of obesity, the food industry has fought what it asserts are frivolous lawsuits by individuals seeking to blame the industry (such as fast food restaurants) for their obesity. It also has sought protection through federal and state legislation, so-called cheeseburger bills, that would bar such lawsuits. But is the food industry's argument that the weight-gain trend is entirely a matter of personal responsibility a defensible position? Is the industry really so blameless? Should it do more to help educate consumers on nutritional issues? For example, should restaurants be required to provide some basic nutritional information on their menus, such as calories in a serving of each food item?

Lifestyle choices and wellness activities also are part of the equity question when it comes to provision of generous prescription drug coverage or other health care insurance benefits. Some would argue that heavily subsidized coverage of drugs and other medical expenses discourages individuals from making sensible lifestyle decisions regarding diet, weight, exercise, and smoking. Individuals may believe that medical science will be able to treat any resulting illness with no cost to them, so they have little incentive to take responsibility for such choices. However, if they were responsible for more of the eventual cost, they might make different choices.[68]

Given the arguments here for effectiveness, efficiency, equity, and other ethical issues, would you favor a major shift on the part of government, employers, and insurance companies toward emphasizing preventive health care? What reasons do you find most persuasive? What reasons might lead you to challenge such a recommendation?

CONCLUSIONS

This chapter traces the evolution of government health care policies and examines the leading programs. It emphasizes issues of cost, access, and quality, and the diverse ways government activities affect the public's health and well-being. The present array of health care programs, from Medicare and Medicaid to innovative state preventive health measures, may seem complex and confusing to many, and it strikes health care professionals the same way. Students of public policy, using the criteria discussed in the text, can evaluate all of these programs against standards of effectiveness in delivering quality health care services, efficiency of present expenditures in terms of the benefits received, and equity in access to and payments for those services. Many analysts, policymakers, health care professionals, and patients alike find strengths and weaknesses in this system in terms of all three criteria. The strengths merit the praise they have received, but the weaknesses need to be addressed as well.

Rising costs alone suggest the imperative of change. As we have shown, the costs threaten to bankrupt the Medicare system as the baby boom generation ages. Employers and individuals face similar hurdles in meeting the anticipated increases in insurance policy premiums and almost certainly higher deductibles and co-payments. Health care policy therefore would profit greatly from critical assessments that point to better ways of providing affordable and high-quality health care to the U.S. public in the future. The questions posed throughout the chapter encourage such assessments, from how best to reform Medicare and Medicaid to the effectiveness of many state efforts to constrain costs to the promotion of health education, wellness training, and other preventive health care measures. Fortunately for the student of public policy, information to help design more appropriate health care policies and institutions is widely available on the Internet through government and independent sites.

DISCUSSION QUESTIONS

1. Consider the data provided in this chapter on the rising cost of health care services. What are the most effective ways to control these costs? Try to think of several alternative ways to do so, and then compare them in terms of the criteria of effectiveness, efficiency, and equity.

2. In light of the chapter's discussion of the consequences of being uninsured, what should governments do to meet the needs of the forty-seven million Americans without health care insurance? Why do you think so?

3. Should employers continue to carry the burden of providing health care benefits to employees, or should the government institute a form of national health insurance instead? What difference might this make for the ability of U.S. companies, such as automobile manufacturers, to compete internationally when most other developed countries provide national health insurance?

4. Do you think it is fair that those who can afford it should be able to arrange for high-end concierge health care when many Americans have minimal or no access at all to health care services?

5. What kinds of public policies might be designed to give individuals more incentives to remain healthy and reduce demand for costly health care services?

SUGGESTED READINGS

Thomas S. Bodenheimer and Kevin Grumbach, *Understanding Health Policy,* 5th ed. (New York: McGraw Hill, 2008). A broad introduction to the field of health care policy.

Jacob S. Hacker, *The Road to Nowhere: The Genesis of President Clinton's Plan for Health Security* (Princeton: Princeton University Press, 1997). A review of the failure of Clinton's national health care plan of 1993.

Theodore R. Marmor, *The Politics of Medicare,* 2nd ed. (Hawthorne, N.Y.: Aldine de Gruyter, 1999). An insightful assessment of Medicare's history and success.

Jack A. Meyer and Elliot K. Wicks, eds., *Covering America: Real Remedies for the Uninsured* (Washington, D.C.: Economic and Social Research Institute, 2001). Includes an array of leading analysts specializing in health care policy. Full text available online at www.esresearch.org/RWJ11PDF/full_document.pdf.

Kant Patel and Mark E. Rushefsky, *Health Care Politics and Policy in America,* 3rd ed. (Armonk, N.Y.: M. E. Sharpe, 2006). A major text in health care policy that covers the full spectrum of issues.

SUGGESTED WEB SITES

www.ahip.org. America's Health Insurance Plans, a leading industry trade association, with excellent coverage of and links to the full range of health care policy issues.

www.citizen.org/hrg. Public Citizen's Health Research Group, with extensive links to policy issues and citizen activism.

www.cms.hhs.gov. Centers for Medicare and Medicaid Services within the Department of Health and Human Services, with extensive links to federal and state health care programs.

www.kaisernetwork.org. One of the best sites for timely, in-depth coverage of health care news and policy debates, with extensive links to policy organizations, research, public opinion, and advocacy.

www.kff.org. Kaiser Family Foundation, respected by both liberals and conservatives for its health care studies and reports. Written for the general public.

www.milbank.org/quarterly/links.html. Links to major health care policy journals.

www.rwjf.org/index.jsp. Robert Wood Johnson Foundation; research and policy analysis on health care issues, with a progressive leaning.

MAJOR LEGISLATION

Balanced Budget Act of 1997   238
Children's Health Insurance Program Reauthorization Act of 2009   243

KEYWORDS

NOTES

1. Robert Pear, "Spending Rise for Health Care and Prescription Drugs Slows," *New York Times,* January 6, 2009, A17. The cost estimates come from the federal Centers for Medicare and Medicaid Services, Office of the Actuary. Many different figures on the nation's health care costs can be found at the centers' Web site: www.cms.hhs.gov. Look for reports under the Research, Statistics, Data & Systems link.

2. Ceci Connolly, " 'We're Not Getting What We Pay For': Experts Say U.S. Health Care Is Inefficient, Wasteful, and Sometimes Dangerous," *Washington Post National Weekly Edition,* December 8–14, 2008, 33.

3. Reed Abelson, "While the U.S. Spends Heavily on Health Care, a Study Faults the Quality," *New York Times,* July 17, 2008, C3; and Connolly, " 'We're Not Getting What We Pay For.' " The Commonwealth Fund study, "Why Not the Best? Results from the National Scorecard on U.S. Health System Performance, 2008," can be found at the group's Web site: www.commonwealthfund.org.

4. Kevin Sack, "Research Finds Wide Disparities in Health Care by Race and Region," *New York Times* online edition, June 5, 2008.

5. The data come from the Web site for the National Coalition on Health Care (www.nchc.org/facts/cost.shtml), which summarizes data from the Henry J. Kaiser Family Foundation employee health benefits survey of 2008.

6. For a description of the much-touted Massachusetts plan, see Marilyn Werber Serafini, "The Mass.-ter Plan," *National Journal,* June 10, 2006, 22–27.

7. Robert Pear, "Daschle Lays Out a Plan to Overhaul Health Care," *New York Times,* January 9, 2009, A18. For a sense of the likely partisan differences that will affect these reform efforts, see Marilyn Werber Serafini and James A. Barnes, "Judging the 2008 Health Plans," *National Journal,* October 27, 2007, 20–37; Serafini, "Divergent Paths," *National Journal,* June 7, 2008, 44–48; and Robert Pear, "Obama's Health Plan, Ambitious in Any Economy, Is Tougher in This One," *New York Times,* March 2, 2009, A14. After initially considering former senator Tom Daschle, Obama named Gov. Kathleen Sebelius of Kansas as head of Health and Human Services, and thus the point person on health care reform. See Kevin Sack, "For Obama Pick, Second Chance for Progress on Health," *New York Times,* March 2, 2009, 1, A14.

8. The data come from the annual Employer Health Benefits survey conducted by the Kaiser Family Foundation, available at its Web site: www.kff.org.

9. Ibid.

10. The numbers come from the Kaiser Family Foundation Web site (statehealthfacts.org) and represent the uninsured from ages zero to sixty-four for the period 2003–2004.

11. Stan Dorn, "Uninsured and Dying Because of It: Updating the Institute of Medicine Analysis on the Impact of Uninsurance on Mortality" (Washington, D.C.: Urban Institute, 2008), available at www.urban.org/UploadedPDF/411588_uninsured_dying.pdf.

12. World Health Organization press release, June 21, 2000. The results are published in "The World Health Report 2000—Health Systems: Improving Performance," available at the WHO Web site: www.who.int/whr.

13. CQ Press news release, March 26, 2008. The rankings are found in *Health Care State Rankings 2008: Health Care Across America* (Washington, D.C.: CQ Press, 2008).

14. For empirical evidence of the connection between environmental policy and improved public health, see Neal D. Woods, David M. Konisky, and Ann O'M. Bowman, "You Get What You Pay For: Environmental Policy and Public Health," *Publius: The Journal of Federalism* 39, no. 1 (2008): 95–116.

15. For a clear discussion of all these provisions, see Mary Agnes Carey, "Provisions of the Medicare Bill," *CQ Weekly,* January 24, 2004, 238–243. It is interesting that Congress chose to devise such a complex drug plan when the federal government already has one that is widely considered a model. This is housed within the veterans' health care program. See Robert Pear and Walt Bogdanich, "Some Successful Models Ignored as Congress Works on Drug Bill," *New York Times,* September 4, 2003, 1, C6.

16. Robert Pear, "Cost of Rampant Mental Health Care Fraud Soars in Medicare," *New York Times,* September 30, 1998, A12.

17. Gilbert M. Gaul, "Medicare's Chronic Condition," *Washington Post National Weekly Edition,* August 1–7, 2005, 6–9.

18. Gilbert M. Gaul, "Which Gets Inspected More Often: Hospital or Taco Truck?" *Washington Post National Weekly Edition,* August 8–14, 2005, 9. Another persistent problem for Medicare is that it often pays excessive prices for medical equipment (such as walkers and oxygen tanks) because of the way Congress has written the fee schedule for durable equipment. See David Leonhardt, "High Costs, Courtesy of Congress," *New York Times,* June 25, 2008, C1, 5.

19. Jennifer Steinhauer, "Chasing Health Care Fraud Quietly Becomes Profitable," *New York Times,* January 23, 2001, A1, A17.

20. See a statement before the House Budget Committee by Timothy B. Hill, chief financial officer at CMS, on "Medicare Health Care Fraud and Abuse Efforts," July 17, 2007, available at www.hhs.gov/asl/testify/2007/07/t20070717b.html. See also Charles Duhigg, "Report Rejects Medicare's Boast of Cutting Fraud," *New York Times,* August 21, 2008, 1, A18.

21. A recent comprehensive review of Medicaid and its perilous future can be found in Rebecca Adams, "Medicaid on the Edge: Balancing Cost and Coverage," *CQ Weekly,* May 22, 2004, 1223–1238.

22. See Michael Luo, "Under New York Medicaid, Drug Costs Run Free," *New York Times,* November 23, 2005, 1, A26.

23. The data come from an October 17, 2008, CMS press release, available at the CMS Web site: www.cms.gov.

24. See, for example, Kevin Sack and Katie Zezima, "Growing Need for Medicaid Strains States," *New York Times,* January 22, 2009, 1, 25.

25. Robert Pear, "Budget Accord Could Mean Payments by Medicaid Recipients," *New York Times,* December 20, 2005, A22.

26. Alex Wayne, "Congress Defies Bush on SCHIP," *CQ Weekly* online edition, October 1, 2007; and Robert Pear, "Health Bill for Children Is Passed by Senate," *New York Times,* January 30, 2009, A18.

27. Clifford J. Levy and Michael Luo, "New York Medicaid Fraud May Reach into Billions," *New York Times,* July 18, 2005, A1, A18–A19.

28. Gaul, "Medicare's Chronic Condition."

29. See, for example, Michael Luo and Clifford J. Levy, "As Medicaid Balloons, Watchdog Force Shrinks," *New York Times,* July 19, 2005, 1, A21.

30. John Holusha, "Congress Hears of Neglect in Veterans' Care," *New York Times* online edition, March 5, 2007.

31. On the projected cost of veterans' health care resulting from the wars, see David Herszenhorn, "Estimates of Iraq War Cost Were Not Close to Ballpark," *New York Times* online edition, March 19, 2008. For a much fuller treatment of the subject, see "VA Health Care: Long-Term Care Strategic Planning and Budgeting Need Improvement" (Washington, D.C.: Government Accountability Office, January 2009).

32. Gilbert M. Gaul, "Back in the Pink: The VA Health Care System Outperforms Medicare and Most Private Plans," *Washington Post National Weekly Edition,* August 29–September 4, 2005, 29.

33. Elizabeth Becker, "Congress Approves Plan to Insure Military Retirees," *New York Times,* October 13, 2000, A16.

34. Kate Schuler, "High Court Rules Against State Efforts to Broaden Patients' Legal Rights," *CQ Weekly,* June 26, 2004, 1558–1559.

35. David U. Himmelstein, Elizabeth Warren, Deborah Thorne, and Steffie Woolhandler, "MarketWatch: Illness and Injury as Contributors to Bankruptcy," *Health Affairs* online edition, February 2, 2005, available at http://content.healthaffairs.org/cgi/content/full/hlthaff.w5.63/DC1.

36. The data come from the Centers for Medicare and Medicaid Services and are reported in their annual report, available at www.cms.hhs.gov/NationalHealthExpendData. The report includes health care expenditure projections through 2017.

37. Robert Pear, "Investigators Find Repeated Deception in Ads for Drugs," *New York Times,* December 4, 2002, A22. The article summarizes findings from a Government Accountability Office report.

38. Robert Pear, "Study Finds Top Drugs for Aged Easily Outpace Inflation," *New York Times,* June 25, 2002, A21. See also Jerry Avorn, *Powerful Medicines: The Benefits, Risks, and Costs of Prescription Drugs* (New York: Knopf, 2004).

39. Extensive data on these trends can be found at the CMS Web site: www.cms.gov.

40. See Carol Anderson, "Squeeze Play," in Outlook: Health Care, a special supplement to *CQ Weekly,* June 2005, 24–26; and Lisa Rosetta, "Medicaid Programs May Be on Chopping Block: Cuts Pondered, Poor Utahns Could Find It Difficult to Qualify for Coverage," *Salt Lake Tribune,* January 12, 2009.

41. The information comes from the TennCare Web site: http://tn.gov/tenncare.

42. The plan and its implementation are described in a May 2008 report by the Kaiser Family Foundation, "Massachusetts Health Care Reform: Two Years Later," available at www.kff.org/uninsured/upload/7777.pdf. See also Kevin Sack, "With Health Care for Nearly All, Massachusetts Now Faces Costs," *New York Times,* March 16, 2009, 1, A13.

43. William C. Symonds, with Howard Gleckman, "The Health-Care Crisis: States Are Rushing In," *Business Week,* November 28, 2005, 49; and Joe Klein, "The Republican Who Thinks Big on Health Care," *Time,* December 12, 2005, 31. The Kaiser Family Foundation keeps track of health care policy innovation in the fifty states. Its Web site would be a good place to see what the states are doing: www.kff.org.

44. Drew Armstrong, "FDA Bill Clears after Intense Negotiations," *CQ Weekly* online edition, September 24, 2007.

45. See Stephanie Saul, "Merck Wrote Drug Studies for Doctors," *New York Times,* April 16, 2008, C1, 6.

46. Steven R. Machlin and Marc W. Zodet, "Family Health Care Expenses, by Size of Family, 2002," Statistical Brief 63, Medical Expenditure Panel Survey, Agency for Healthcare Research and Quality (January 2005).

47. Cited in "The Unraveling of Health Insurance," *Consumer Reports,* July 2002, 48–53. See also Charles Morris, "The Economics of Health Care," *Commonweal* 132, online edition, April 8, 2005, for insightful analysis of the need to find more creative ways to limit overuse and misallocation of health care resources.

48. See Richard E. Anderson, "The High Cost of Defensive Medicine," posted on the Web site of the Health Care Liability Alliance: http://64.177.60.131/html/hcla061498.htm.

49. Milt Freudenheim, "Study Finds Inefficiency in Health Care," *New York Times,* June 11, 2002, C12. The Dartmouth study is reported in "Too Much Treatment? Aggressive Medical Care Can Lead to More Pain, with No Gain," *Consumer Reports,* July 2008, 40–44.

50. Robert Pear, "Inept Physicians Are Rarely Listed as Law Requires," *New York Times,* May 29, 2001, 1, A12.

51. For research on health care quality and discussions of national commitment to quality health care, see the Web site for the Agency for Healthcare Research and Quality: www.ahcpr.gov/qual/measurix.htm.

52. Kevin Sack, "Swabs in Hand, Hospital Cuts Deadly Infections," *New York Times,* July 27, 2007, 1, A16.

53. See Linda T. Kohn, Janet M. Corrigan, and Molla S. Donaldson, eds., *To Err Is Human: Building a Safer Health System* (Washington, D.C.: National Academy Press, Institute of Medicine, 2000). A summary is available online at http://books.nap.edu/books/0309068371/html/index.html. The high numbers of deaths reported in these studies represent an extrapolation from several state-level studies, including analysis of deaths in hospitals in Colorado, New York, and Utah. Some critics charge that the estimates are too high, and others believe they may be too low.

54. Robert Pear, "U.S. Health Officials Reject Plan to Report Medical Mistakes," *New York Times,* January 24, 2000, A14.

55. Marilyn Werber Serafini, "First, Do No Harm," *National Journal,* February 19, 2000, 542–545.

56. Kevin Sack, "Medicare Rules Say, 'Do No Harm,'" *New York Times,* October 1, 2008, 1, A19.

57. See Abigail Zuger, "For a Retainer, Lavish Care by 'Boutique Doctors,'" *New York Times,* October 30, 2005, 1, 21; and Ceci Connolly, "The Best Care Money Can Buy," *Washington Post National Weekly Edition,* June 3–9, 2002, 8.

58. The quotations come from Jim Avila, "Boutique Medical Practices on Rise," reported on the MSNBC Web site, April 3, 2002.

59. The figures come from the CDC, which reports regularly on smoking-related deaths and economic losses, and are available at the CDC Web site: www.cdc.gov/tobacco.

60. These statistics are taken from the surgeon general's extensive report of 2004, and are available at the CDC Web site: www.cdc.gov/tobacco.

61. Quoted in a review of Marion Nestle's *Food Politics: How the Food Industry Influences Nutrition and Health* (Berkeley: University of California Press, 2002), by Ben Geman, *National Journal,* June 22, 2002, 1899.

62. The CDC regularly reports on the prevalence of obesity and overweight among Americans on its Web site: www.cdc.gov. Use the search engine at the page to find information on these conditions. A significant proportion of Americans, about 66 percent, can be classified as obese or overweight. Obesity is defined as having a body mass index (BMI) of 30 or greater, and being overweight is defined as having a BMI of 25 or higher. On the trend in childhood obesity, see Tara Parker-Pope, "Hint of Hope as Obesity Rate among Children Hits Plateau," *New York Times,* May 28, 2008, 1, A18.

63. Charles C. Mann, "Provocative Study Says Obesity May Reduce U.S. Life Expectancy," *Science* 307 (March 18, 2005): 1716–1717. See also Susan Levine and Rob Stein, "Obesity's Toll on a Generation: Experts Predict an Epidemic of Earlier Deaths and Higher Health Costs," *Washington Post National Weekly Edition,* May 26–June 1, 2008, 6–9.

64. Melanie Warner, "The Food Industry Empire Strikes Back," *New York Times,* July 7, 2005, C1, C3.

65. The National Center for Health Statistics in the CDC releases these figures each year. The national rankings come from the CIA, *World Fact Book* (available at www.cia.gov), and the life expectancy differences are reported in Robert Pear, "Gap in Life Expectancy Widens for the Nation," *New York Times* online edition, March 23, 2008.

66. The cost estimates come from the journal *Health Affairs* and are reported on its Web site: www.healthaffairs.org. See also Levine and Stein, "Obesity's Toll on a Generation."

67. David M. Drucker, "A Fat and Lazy State: Obesity Costly for California," *LA Daily News,* April 13, 2005.

68. Morris, "The Economics of Health Care."

9

WELFARE AND SOCIAL SECURITY POLICY

OVER TEN YEARS HAVE PASSED SINCE THE ENACTMENT OF THE PERSONAL Responsibility and Work Opportunity Reconciliation Act of 1996 (PRWORA). Often referred to as "welfare reform," this law was seen as a major shift in the way the United States deals with welfare spending and recipients of these benefits. As we will discuss in more detail later in the chapter, the law provides the states with more responsibility for welfare programs and also institutes a work requirement as a condition for benefits. Perhaps not as explicit, welfare reform was yet another attempt to address issues of poverty in the United States. Following Hurricane Katrina in August 2005, it appeared as if poverty issues would rise on the government's agenda. The pictures out of New Orleans and the surrounding areas were strong evidence that poverty continued to be a major concern for the nation and raised public awareness of the issue. As Jonathan Alter stated at the time in *Newsweek*, "It takes the sight of the United States with a big black eye—visible around the world—to help the rest of us begin to see again. For the moment, at least, Americans are ready to fix their restless gaze on enduring problems of poverty, race, and class that have escaped their attention." [1] But as then-senator Barack Obama, D-Ill., stated in the same article, "I hope we realize that the people of New Orleans weren't just abandoned during the hurricane. . . . They were abandoned long ago."

National poverty has been on the agenda since the mid-1960s, and a variety of programs have addressed the issues related to it. Following Hurricane Katrina, all sorts of aid went to the New Orleans region. Yet the question must be asked, has the nation yet adequately addressed the poverty issue? Former presidential candidate John Edwards answered no and made poverty and income discrepancy between the "haves" and the "have nots" the centerpiece of his unsuccessful campaign, arguing that the nation needed to do much more to help

In addition to the physical effects of 2005's Hurricane Katrina on New Orleans, Louisiana, and other parts of the Gulf Coast, the storm demonstrated the enormous impact that such disasters can have on unusually vulnerable populations, including the poor in neighborhoods such as the Ninth Ward of New Orleans, where many lost their homes and others their lives, and where adverse health and economic effects continue. This teenager sits in front of a demolished section of the B. W. Cooper housing projects in May 2008, in New Orleans. B. W. Cooper and the three other major New Orleans housing projects are being torn down to make way for "mixed-income developments." The demolition has sparked protests and lawsuits as affordable housing stocks have dwindled and homelessness has doubled in the wake of Katrina.

the poor. Candidates Hillary Clinton and Obama also explicitly campaigned on the issue. Since taking control of the House of Representatives in 2006, the Democratic Congress has held several hearings on poverty and related economic issues. While the rhetoric surrounding poverty issues is loud and clear, many are questioning the government's response, and some statistics concerning the poor continue to be disturbing.

According to 2007 U.S. Census data, one in eight Americans (37.3 million) live below the poverty line, and a third of them are children. Those living in "deep" poverty, defined as below one-half the poverty line, number 15 million.[2] When the economy is sputtering, as was the case starting in 2007 and continuing through 2009, and the middle class perceives some danger of becoming one of these statistics, these issues take on even greater importance—particularly from the political perspective. The role of the government in addressing poverty in the United States has always been delicate, as the nation has debated whether the suffering is due primarily to personal decisions or inadequate government policies and economic inequalities.

A number of government policies are geared toward income maintenance and support in the United States. Some of these, such as Temporary Assistance for Needy Families (TANF) or welfare, are need-based programs based on the recipient meeting a certain income test. But Social Security is also considered a program to provide financial stability, and most of these recipients meet their eligibility requirements in other ways. This chapter examines the issue of poverty generally and some of the major programs implemented by the United States to address income issues. As you will see, the general population often perceives these programs quite differently, and as a result the politics surrounding them vary as well.

BACKGROUND

As noted, Social Security is one of a number of federal programs designed to help individuals maintain a minimal level of income after retirement or, if they are unable to continue working, before they reach retirement age. The other major program associated with income maintenance is the welfare system, currently administered under PRWORA and reauthorized in 2006. This law was a major reform of the old Aid to Families with Dependent Children (AFDC), and it provides support to individuals with low incomes. These two programs are the chief components of social welfare in the United States, and they are designed largely to help combat poverty. The programs differ on a number of levels, however, including general public acceptance, sources of financing, and potential challenges they face in the future.

To better understand the social welfare programs, one first needs to know something about poverty in the United States. With the United States' large economic engine, it can be difficult to believe that a substantial number of Americans live in poverty. The fact is that poverty exists and needs to be addressed, and it becomes an even greater concern during times of economic downturns. This chapter begins with some information about poverty in the United States and then discusses Social Security and welfare programs.

Poverty

The United States has always had different viewpoints regarding poverty. The American cultural and social perspective that encourages individualism and promotes equality of

FIGURE 9-1 U.S. Poverty Rates by Age, 1959–2006

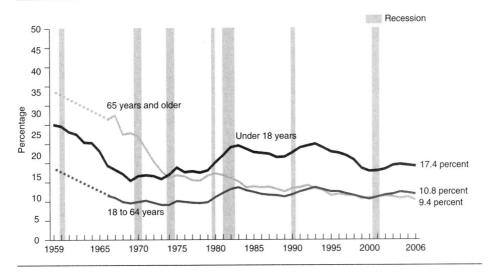

Note: The data points are placed at the midpoints of the respective years. Data for people aged 18 to 64 and 66 and older are not available from 1960 to 1965.
Source: U.S. Census Bureau, Current Population Survey, 1960 to 2007. Annual Social and Economic Supplements.

opportunity leads to a tendency to blame the poor for their own circumstances. On the other hand, some say there is really inequality of opportunity that prevents many from increasing their standard of living. Hurricane Katrina and its aftermath, as well as the economic recession of 2008 and 2009, have focused America's attention on this question once again.

There are a number of different ways to examine **poverty** in the United States, starting with the official definition, as noted in chapter 5. For 2007, the Census Bureau placed a family of four below the poverty line if its annual income was less than $21,200 in the 48 contiguous states. The bureau adjusts this number for factors such as the number of people in a family, the composition of a family, and inflation from year to year. Others look at poverty from an income distribution perspective: the more unequal the distribution of income, the greater the potential poverty problem. Still others examine poverty in terms of demographic characteristics such as race, gender, and age.

As an issue, poverty in the United States came to a head during the mid-1960s when President Lyndon Johnson declared a "war on poverty." The government initiated a number of programs to deal with the problem. Between 1965 and 1973 the poverty rate fell from 17.3 percent to 11.1 percent (Haveman 1999), and it appeared that the nation was winning the war (see Figure 9-1). Unfortunately, the United States has not achieved a poverty rate this low since 1973. The rate has improved significantly in certain demographic categories; for example, the elderly and intact minority families have made definite advances. Single mothers, children, and poorly educated young people, however, still have a hard time rising out of poverty (Haveman 1999).

TABLE 9-1	Income Distribution in the United States, 2007	
Income Quintiles	Percentage of Income	Cumulated Percentage
Lowest	3.4%	3.5%
Second	8.7	12.1
Third	14.8	26.9
Fourth	23.4	50.3
Highest[a]	49.7	100.0

Source: U.S. Census Bureau, Current Population Report, P60-221, *Income, Poverty, and Health Insurance Coverage in the United States: 2007,* available at www.census.gov/prod/2008pubs/p60-235.pdf.

[a]The distribution of income in the United States is even more unequal than the data in the table suggest. If one examines the gain in income over the past thirty years of the top 10 percent of Americans, one discovers that most of the gain went to the top 1 percent of taxpayers, and 60 percent of the gains of the top 1 percent went to the top 0.1 percent. The disparity between the very rich and the average American has been growing significantly in recent years. For a commentary about the erosion of equality in income distribution, see Paul Krugman, "For Richer: How the Permissive Capitalism of the Boom Destroyed American Equality," *New York Times Magazine,* October 20, 2002, 62–67, 76–77, 141–142.

Some statistics concerning children in poverty help to drive this point home. In 2007, 18 percent of all children in the United States were poor. Children make up only 25 percent of the population, but they comprise 35 percent of the nation's poor. Moreover, minority populations in the United States also suffer higher poverty rates than whites,[3] which may indicate something about the weaknesses of government programs to reduce poverty as well as those aimed at improving the status of minorities. Figure 9-1 shows the United States' poverty rate by age over the past fifty years.

Many look at poverty as an income distribution problem. In other words, a large number of people are living on limited resources, while a smaller percentage of people earn a large proportion of the nation's combined income. Economists often use the **Gini coefficient** (see Figure 9-2) as a way of demonstrating a nation's income equality and inequality. Income equality is represented by a forty-five degree line, on which each percentage of the population is making the same percentage of the income. As a curve deviates away from the forty-five degree line, it shows an increase in income inequality. The implicit interpretation of the curve is that if a few people are making a large percentage of the income, more people are put at risk of poverty.

Based on 2007 data from the Census Bureau, the richest 20 percent of the population makes close to 50 percent of all of the income in the United States, and the poorest 20 percent make only 3.5 percent. Another way to state this is that the top quintile is making as much income as the other 80 percent of the population (see Table 9-1).

Some analysts and policymakers have begun to look at the poverty problem in a way that they believe will change the debate on the issue. Although levels of poverty, as defined by the Census Bureau, have decreased, other data sources indicate real challenges for the poor. For example, the U.S. Conference of Mayors reported in 2002 that instances of hunger and homelessness had increased dramatically over the previous year, citing a 23 percent increase in emergency food assistance.[4] While the Census Bureau has considered revising its definition of poverty, no real changes have occurred and it is unclear when or if a new definition will be

FIGURE 9-2 | Gini Coefficient for U.S. Income Distribution, 2007

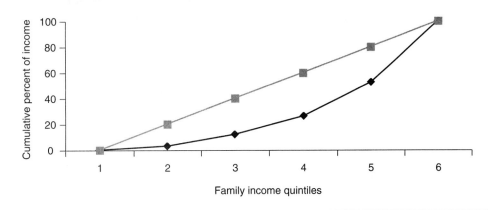

used. Based on analyses using some different definitions of poverty, the income threshold in 2007 would be between $23,465 and $25,849, minimally $2,000 greater than the stated rate. Estimates suggest that using a different definition of poverty could increase the poverty rate by 3 percent.[5] Such changes in the poverty-line calculations may be necessary because the original poverty line is based on a number of assumptions made in the mid-1960s that may no longer be valid. In addition, the poverty level is the same for the lower forty-eight states and does not take into consideration cost-of-living differentials across the country. Discussions continue on this effort, but if poverty is redefined, it would be the first major adjustment, not counting inflation, in how poverty is calculated since creation of the formula.[6] It is probably safe to say that even the proposed increase in the income threshold and the resulting additional assistance may not be sufficient to cover a family's expenses—housing, food, clothing, child and medical care, and everything else.[7]

Another way to examine poverty is from an ideological perspective, or what some might say are the root causes of poverty. Is poverty due to broad economic circumstances or to individual behavior and choices not to work? Liberals and conservatives have different ideas about why poverty exists and consequently make different proposals for addressing the problem. Conservatives see poverty in part as a personal choice; they believe that little poverty exists in the United States that is involuntary. Some may also believe in the **culture of poverty**, meaning that those brought up in poverty learn how to be poor and work the current system to their benefit, and that they choose to remain poor as adults. In addition, conservatives tend to blame government programs for encouraging people to remain poor, in part by not requiring any kind of responsibility in exchange for received benefits. Liberals, on the other hand, see poverty as a problem brought on by economic and social conditions over which individuals have little or no control. Liberals recognize that not everyone has the same opportunity for quality education or job training, and they favor government intervention to help equalize the playing field. They believe as well that the high number of minorities who are poor indicates that discrimination also contributes to poverty.

As discussed in chapter 6, equity is one of the criteria used to analyze problems or policies, but the word can have multiple meanings. In the case of poverty, should the concern be whether the process is fair regarding resource distribution? This view is perhaps more ideologically conservative. Or, from the more liberal perspective, does equity mean moving toward a more equal distribution of resources? By now, the public policy student knows that, depending on how one sees the causes of the problem and defines the evaluating criteria, the various alternatives to address it will seem more or less appealing.

Many of the social programs developed throughout U.S. history have attempted to deal with the poverty issue from different perspectives. Social Security, for example, was developed specifically to address poverty among the elderly. By this measure, the program has been somewhat successful. According to an analysis conducted by the Center on Budget and Policy Priorities using Census data, 38 percent of the elderly population was kept out of poverty specifically because of their Social Security benefits.[8] One of the goals of the food stamp program is at least to address issues of severe hunger that could occur as a result of poverty. The **Earned Income Tax Credit** (EITC) supplements wages of the working poor to lift recipients out of poverty. Programs such as AFDC or the newer TANF have attempted to deal with the poverty of all individuals who happen to fall below a certain income level or who have no income at all.

SOCIAL SECURITY

Social Security is the single largest federal government program today, providing money for retired workers, their beneficiaries, and disabled workers. While almost everyone these days is covered by Social Security, some federal, state, and local government employees and certain agricultural and domestic workers are not. For a majority of beneficiaries, however, Social Security provides more than half of their total income, and it is the largest share of income for the aged (see Figure 9-3). The presidential budget request for Social Security for fiscal year 2009 was $695 billion,[9] which provides some idea of the size and budgetary impact of the program. Social Security was enacted in 1935 during the New Deal period as a way to ensure that certain segments of society were guaranteed an income after their working years. The perception of Social Security both at its birth and today is that it is a social insurance program. Other examples of such programs are unemployment insurance and workers' compensation. With these programs, citizens pay into a fund from which they expect to receive money back when they are eligible. Because of this designation, the public has always looked upon Social Security as more acceptable than other government welfare programs. Social Security is not regarded as a government handout but as money returned based on an individual's contribution or investment. It should be noted, however, that in most cases a Social Security recipient eventually receives more money than he or she contributed as a worker.

Social Security is typically classified as a redistributive policy program. In this case, however, money is being redistributed across generations—that is, from workers to nonworkers or young to old—rather than between economic classes. Many people believe that their personal contributions are going into a benefits account to be paid out upon retirement, but that is a misconception. Social Security is a pay-as-you-go program; someone's current contributions are paying for someone else's current benefits. The program is also considered an entitlement. That is, if a person meets any of the eligibility requirements for Social Security, he or she is entitled to its benefits. The program is typically associated with payments to the elderly, and in fact this is the system's largest outlay, but other people are eligible as well.

| FIGURE 9-3 | Shares of Aggregate Income by Source, 2004 |

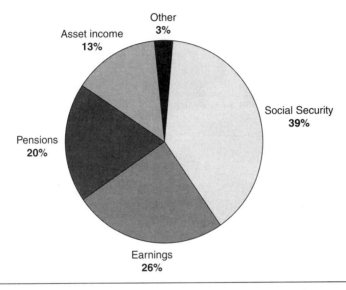

Other
3%

Asset income
13%

Social Security
39%

Pensions
20%

Earnings
26%

Note: Social Security provides the largest share of income for the aged. Aggregate income for the aged population comes largely from four sources. Social Security accounts for 39 percent, earnings for 26 percent, pensions for 20 percent, and asset income for 13 percent. Only 3 percent comes from other sources.
Source: Income of the Aged Chartbook, 2004.

Who is entitled to Social Security? Qualifying for the program is based partially on the number of years one has worked and contributed to the program. As individuals work, they earn "credits" toward Social Security. They can earn a maximum of four credits a year, and most people need forty credits to be eligible for benefits. Benefits fall into five major categories:

- *Retirement:* full benefits currently provided at age sixty-six plus a few months. The minimum age will gradually increase to sixty-seven in future years.
- *Disability:* benefits are provided to people who have enough credits and have a physical or mental condition that prevents them from doing "substantial" work for a year or more.
- *Family:* if an individual is receiving benefits, certain family members such as a spouse or children may also be eligible for benefits.
- *Survivor:* when individuals who have accumulated enough credits die, certain family members—for example, a spouse sixty years or older—may be eligible for benefits.
- *Medicare:* Part A (hospital insurance) is paid through part of the Social Security tax. Typically, if individuals are eligible for Social Security, they also qualify for Medicare.

The Social Security Administration also administers the Supplementary Security Income Benefits program for low-income individuals who are at least sixty-five years old or disabled. The program is not financed through Social Security taxes.

The Social Security program has two major goals, and in some ways these goals conflict with each other. First, the level of benefits individuals receive is related to the amount they put into the system. In other words, the greater their contributions, the higher their benefits. Second, the program was supposed to ensure that lower-income individuals had at least minimal financial protection (Light 1995; Derthick 1979). Both goals are included in the benefits formula, and, although the rich receive higher total benefits, the amounts are not proportionally higher. The poor, on the other hand, get a much greater return on their investment.

Most of Social Security is financed by a specific tax on income. The rate of this tax has remained stable since 1990, with no significant increases since 1985. Currently, the government taxes individuals and employers 7.65 percent of their income. Theoretically, this tax is earmarked, meaning the money collected goes specifically toward the benefits; these taxes also are the only source for these benefits. In reality, the federal government collects more revenue through Social Security taxes than it is currently spending to pay benefits. The government uses the excess dollars for various purposes—most commonly to reduce the size of the federal deficit.

The Social Security tax is capped at an annual income of $106,800 (the 2009 amount, which normally increases each year based on inflation) for a maximum contribution total of $6,621 per year. If an individual's income is greater than $106,800, he or she pays the maximum tax and no more for that year. In other words, a person making $1 million or $10 million pays the same amount of Social Security taxes as a person making $106,800. And everyone is paying the same rate of tax; as discussed in chapter 7, this formula makes the Social Security tax regressive. Is the Social Security tax fair in light of some of the considerations on tax policy introduced in chapter 7? Keep in mind that there are also limits imposed on the amount of money that each person can receive each month from the program.

Social Security is often referred to as the political "third rail" because of the potential danger associated with attempts to reform it, a reference to the subway that receives its power from this rail. Likewise, politicians foolish enough to touch the issue of Social Security reform will likely find themselves voted out of office—in other words, "fired." Whenever policymakers suggest changes, intense debate arises, and the proposals often anger the people who are currently benefiting from the program or expect to in the near future. From a political standpoint, there are two closely related reasons for the controversial nature of any proposal to change the Social Security system. First, the majority of the recipients are senior citizens, who are demographically the people most likely to vote in the United States. Politicians are necessarily wary about crossing such a politically active group. Second, the power of AARP, the major interest group representing the concerns of seniors, is formidable. AARP claims a membership of more than forty million people, and it is one of the most influential interest groups in the nation. It also has a large professional staff involved in lobbying. With these political resources, it should be clear why efforts to make major reforms to Social Security can be challenging. The box "Steps to Analysis: AARP as an Advocacy Group" suggests some ways to become familiar with the group's activities. Nevertheless, almost everyone believes that something must be done to reform Social Security, because it is not sustainable under its current model. As noted in chapter 7, President Obama has indicated a desire to examine Social Security and other entitlements as part of a broader economic plan.

Social Security's Changing Demographics

The Social Security program and the number of people eligible for it have changed dramatically since its inception in 1935. In 1945 the program had fewer than five million beneficiaries, but

STEPS TO ANALYSIS

AARP AS AN ADVOCACY GROUP

AARP, formerly called the American Association of Retired Persons, is an advocacy organization adept at developing and using policy analysis to promote its positions on issues such as Social Security reform and health care for the elderly. Visit AARP's Web site at www.aarp.org and select the Policy and Research page toward the bottom of the page. Here, you will find a number of reports and responses to reports on many issues of interest to older people, including long-term health care, economic security, and prescription drug coverage. In the Social Security Reform section, select the Reform Options for Social Security link. Read this report with the following issues and questions in mind:

- Why is it important to consider reform options for Social Security?

- Which of the options presented in the AARP paper make sense to you? Why? Does AARP do a good job presenting the options in an unbiased way?
- Can you discern what AARP's preferred position is on reform? What is it, and what is the basis of the group's support?

Now turn to the Concord Coalition site at www.concordcoalition.org. Select the Issues and Social Security links. What does this organization say about Social Security and its reform? Do its ideas match those of AARP? Go to the home pages of members of Congress, particularly those for your home state. What do they say on the issue? Given these similarities and differences, how much influence does AARP seem to have on policymaking on this issue?

by 2008 the number had grown to approximately fifty-five million.[10] The reason for this increase is simple: life expectancy is higher today than it was fifty years ago. As more people live beyond the age of sixty-five, larger numbers are entitled to Social Security benefits. What this has meant is that Social Security, as a program, has grown enormously since the New Deal years and, by all estimates, will continue to grow well into the future. Analysts are especially worried about the impending retirement of the baby boom generation. The first wave of Americans born between 1946 and 1964 will start retiring in 2011.

Social Security is obviously larger now in terms of total dollars. But it also makes up a larger percentage of government expenditures; it grew from about 14 percent of the federal budget in 1969 to almost 21 percent in 2008.[11] More problematic for Social Security is that while the number of beneficiaries is growing larger, the number of workers contributing to the program is becoming smaller, leaving fewer workers per beneficiary. In fiscal year 2007 the ratio of workers to retiree was approximately 3.3:1; that is, 3.3 workers were supporting each recipient. Compare this to 1960, when the ratio was 5.1:1, or to 1950, when the ratio was 16.5:1, and the problem becomes apparent. Projected estimates indicate that with no change to Social Security, by 2040 each recipient will be supported by only two workers,[12] when the typical 2009 college graduate will be only in mid-career. The graying of the U.S. population is actually quite staggering when examined over time. Figure 9-4 shows the ratio of workers to Social Security beneficiaries since 1945 and the dramatic decrease in that ratio.

FIGURE 9-4   Fewer Workers per Retiree, 1945–2075

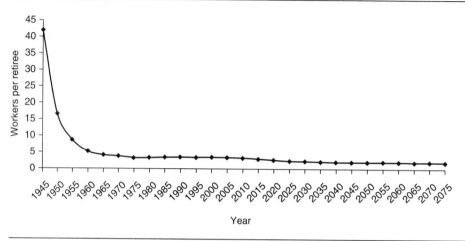

Because of these changing demographics, projections suggest that the amount of revenue coming into the Social Security system will finance only 75 percent of the benefits. For younger workers today to receive full benefits, it might be necessary to increase the withholding tax. This issue will affect people not only in the long term upon their retirement, but also in the short term if Social Security taxes go up. Would these moves be fair and equitable? If not, what are the alternatives to increasing the Social Security tax?

Problems with Social Security

Beneficiaries and policymakers have acknowledged for years that even though the government has addressed some of its problems, Social Security as it currently exists has a number of flaws. In 2000 Congress and the president changed the rule regarding the employment of retired workers and how it affects their Social Security benefits. Under the old rules, beneficiaries who chose to work to supplement their income would lose part of their Social Security benefits if they made more than a certain amount of money during the year. Workers under age sixty-five would lose $1 of benefits for every $2 they earned above $10,048 a year. Workers between the ages of sixty-five and seventy lost $1 of benefits for every $3 earned above $17,000 a year. Currently, everyone sixty-six and over (the full-benefit or normal retirement age for those born between 1943 and 1954) can earn as much as they want without forfeiting part of their Social Security benefits. Naturally, this change in the law benefits only those senior citizens who continue to work.

Another Social Security issue the government addressed is the fixed retirement age. Historically, the official age for collecting Social Security benefits was sixty-five, but changes to the law have gradually raised the age of eligibility to between sixty-six and sixty-seven, depending on the year of birth, in recognition of the population's longer life expectancy and people's tendency to continue to work.[13] Raising the age provides two major benefits for Social Security's solvency. First, if people cannot receive full benefits until sixty-seven, they will not receive as much money over their lifetimes. Second, if they continue to work, they will also continue to contribute to the program.

Increasing the retirement age raises other issues, however, such as equity. Is it fair to the current working generation to demand that they work until age sixty-seven when their parents or grandparents could retire at sixty-five? What about quality of life? If people cannot retire until relatively late in life, they may be less able to enjoy their retirement years because of illness or physical limitations. Some social commentators have already raised concerns about the amount of time people spend working in American society, compared to most European countries. For example, Americans consider forty hours the typical full-time workweek, whereas in many European countries the norm is closer to thirty-five hours. In addition, a policy that encourages later retirement may exacerbate problems affecting family life and employment opportunities for younger people.

A third major problem with Social Security is the potential gender inequity built into the system. When Social Security was enacted few married women worked outside the home, but by the mid-1990s more than 60 percent did, and the number today is higher still.[14] Why is this a concern? Under the current Social Security system, a married woman who does not work receives half of her husband's Social Security benefits (on top of what the husband receives) when she reaches age sixty-five. A working woman will receive her full benefits upon reaching this age, but the nonworking woman (or spouse) will be receiving a significant entitlement without paying anything to the system. Depending on the Social Security contributions of the working person, the nonworking spouse could get a larger payment than a working person. Women in the workforce could conceivably receive less money than a spouse who never worked. The issue has equity implications, because working women may not be receiving a fair return on their investment in Social Security.

For unmarried women, the issue is that women do not earn as much as men. In 2006 women's annual median earnings reached a peak of 81 percent of men's annual earnings.[15] Women, whether married or single, are also more likely to take extended periods away from work because of family obligations. The result is that, in general, women will be contributing less to Social Security and subsequently will receive lower payments than men upon retirement.

Financing Social Security

Obviously, the biggest problem with Social Security and the one that gets the most attention is the financing of the program and the projections showing the system running out of money. The strong economy during the 1990s partially improved the situation of Social Security by increasing its solvency. Recent projections by the Social Security Administration, however, show that by 2017 the benefits that must be paid out will exceed the program's revenue from current workers. By 2041 the trust funds, which are in reality a promise to pay, will be depleted, and the revenue coming into the program will pay only about 75 percent of the benefits that are due to retirees and other recipients.[16] These kinds of numbers spark concern among many younger Americans who say they do not believe that Social Security will be around when they are eligible to collect it after they paid a lifetime of taxes into the system.

Solutions to financing Social Security are particularly problematic from a political perspective. Like any other budget problem, the "simple" solution to deal with the coming deficit in

Social Security would be to increase revenues flowing into the program or to cut expenditures. In the context of Social Security, how might that be done? To bring in more money, policymakers could increase the tax on individuals and employers by raising either the withholding percentage or the maximum income that can be taxed, or both. If, however, the government makes a subsequent change in the benefits to which retirees are entitled, then the additional revenues would be partially offset. As discussed in other chapters, Congress always finds it politically difficult to raise taxes even to protect a popular program such as Social Security.

The other course of action is to reduce expenditures, which can be done in a number of ways. As discussed earlier, the age of eligibility for benefits has already gone up, which postpones the outlay of funds for a number of years. Another idea, which has been used in the past, is to delay the **cost of living adjustment** (COLA). Social Security benefits go up annually, and the amount is linked to changes in inflation, as measured by the Consumer Price Index (CPI). By not implementing the COLA for a period of time, the Social Security Administration could save billions of dollars. Another solution would be to decrease the COLA outright. In other words, it might only be a partial, not a full, inflationary adjustment.

The reasons for exploring the COLA option are worth considering. First, many workers in the United States do not receive inflationary adjustments in their wages. Is it fair that retirees get regular increases in their income while those who are working do not? Second, as discussed in chapter 7, many policy analysts believe the government's current indicators, such as the CPI, overstate inflation. This means that the COLAs are actually higher than the true rate of inflation. For the sake of illustration, if Social Security pays out $400 billion in benefits this year and the inflation rate is determined to be 3 percent, it would mean an automatic increase in benefit payments the following year (disregarding new beneficiaries or deaths) to $412 billion. Delaying the payment of the COLA increase for six months would save $6 billion a year. Adjusting the COLA down by 1 percent would save $4 billion a year. If either of these proposals were adopted for a number of years, significant savings in the program would materialize.

Privatization is another approach to Social Security financing. The idea here is that individuals would be allowed to invest some of their withholding tax in mutual funds of their choosing, or the government might be permitted to invest Social Security funds in the stock market or other private instruments to generate a higher rate of return than is now possible. Currently, the money collected for Social Security is invested in government bonds with a relatively low yield (albeit with little risk). Many people believe that a partially privatized system would increase the return and extend the financial life of the system.

Following the 2004 election, President George W. Bush proposed the idea of personal accounts as a major agenda item. According to the president, these personal accounts would have allowed workers to contribute up to four percentage points of their payroll taxes into a larger range of account options that potentially would have provided them with a greater return upon their retirement. Currently, the money is invested in government Treasury bills that earn only about 2 percent. President Bush's proposal would have partially changed the structure of Social Security from pay-as-you-go to more of a 401K plan; it sets up a private account for each person from which he or she can draw upon retirement. Many analysts and public officials endorsed this proposal. The Social Security Advisory Council (1997)[17] included it as one of its proposals, although not all of the committee members supported it. In addition, the National Commission on Retirement Policy

THE FUTURE HOME of YOUR SOCIAL SECURITY NEST EGG.

One of the Bush administration's proposed reforms that proved to lack public support was the addition of a personal savings account option to the Social Security system. This partial privatization of Social Security was to involve a combination of the traditional government-managed program and personal accounts that individuals could invest in different types of investment funds, including treasury bills, corporate bonds, and stock market funds. Proponents argued that individuals could obtain considerably higher returns on their investments than what could be expected from the conservative Social Security fund. The proposal was much discussed in 2005 and 2006 when the stock market was doing well. Even so, it never gained traction and was never approved by Congress. By late 2008, the plan's critics, and cartoonists, were saying, "I told you so," as the stock market sank and many saw their investments, including their 401(k) or 403(b) personal retirement accounts, plummet by 40 to 50 percent or more.

(1999), which addressed a number of issues on how to fund retirement, also included a plan to allow for private investment of a portion of the withholding tax. Much of the Bush plan was based on the commission's proposal, which would direct approximately one quarter (or two percentage points) of the current 7.65 percent payroll tax into individual savings accounts for which people could make choices about investment strategies for their money.

There are some things to consider with this type of Social Security reform. A system that permits individual retirement accounts and siphons off a portion of the Social Security withholding tax changes the investment picture. These accounts would be specifically earmarked for the individual retiree. In other words, the four percentage points withheld plus interest is dedicated directly to each worker, who will want to get the largest return possible on these investments. Doing so would likely mean investing outside of government securities, particularly in the stock market. Is this a good idea? Related to this, in the absence of other policy changes, and with four percentage points of the withholding tax going into individual accounts, the solvency of the current Social Security funds becomes even more fragile. The funds would be depleted earlier than under current projections. The Center on Budget and Policy Priorities estimated that such a change would deplete the reserves in 2030 rather than 2041.[18] On the positive side, if individuals make good investment choices, they will receive a higher rate of return from Social Security and subsequently a higher standard of living upon retirement. The negative effects are equally obvious, and the most important of these is the impact on financial markets of a prolonged economic downturn. For example, the markets suffered some of the steepest losses in 2008 when the economy soured in the United States and abroad. The losses demonstrated that there are large potential risks associated with these kinds of investments. This situation raises new questions: Will people be able to manage their investments? How many will make poor choices on where to invest their money? Will financial advisers pressure people to make unwise decisions? Under this proposal, the investment part of people's Social Security donations will not be protected, and retirees could receive less money than they would under the current plan. Would society be willing to redirect money into programs to ensure that people can make ends meet? Will action be taken to provide any protection for these self-invested funds? If the answer is "yes" to either of these questions, it may require so much money from the federal budget that the purpose of the legislation is defeated.[19]

The politics of Social Security reform also merits attention. We have already mentioned the sensitive politics associated with Social Security and potential reform efforts. Senior citizens are an attractive target for politicians because, as a group, they turn out to vote in large numbers. Not surprisingly, seniors and the interest groups representing them, such as AARP, have been wary of Social Security reform efforts that may decrease their benefits. AARP raises many of the issues discussed above in regards to privatization. According to AARP, its members should be concerned about privatization reform plans for two reasons: the potential unpredictability of the stock market and fears that such accounts would take money out of the Social Security account and pass the bill along to future generations.[20] It seems clear that any reform option that includes a form of privatization would need to proceed cautiously, assuring the current beneficiaries and people close to retirement that their benefits will continue at the same rate. Privatization programs tend to be more popular with younger voters who have the time to take advantage of these investments, are more likely to invest in the market, and are concerned about the current pay-as-you-go system and its future solvency. But there is one problem with this analysis. While the young should be more supportive of such a plan, they are likely to be the least engaged in the political debate because it is a program where they will not see benefits for decades.[21]

When the nation was experiencing surpluses, some argued that the time and political situation might be right to reform Social Security; the budget surpluses accumulated in the late 1990s provided the necessary financial cushion. Yet even with the planets aligned, the Social Security system resisted reform, and we have now returned to budgetary deficits in the United States. Senior citizens and AARP make a powerful team that supports the present system. The program itself is often held up as a significant achievement in public policy, which adds to the difficulty of making major changes in it. In addition, politicians often use the program as a wedge issue in their campaigns against their opponents, which makes sensible discussions for reform difficult.

Each of the numerous and conflicting perspectives on proposals to privatize Social Security comes with plenty of supporting data and reports, but the debate is not only about personal retirement and investment but also, and perhaps more important, how the program will continue to survive for future generations. Social Security has been, and will continue to be, a highly politicized issue, which makes major reforms exceedingly difficult. Any reform effort, whether it is privatization or less drastic changes such as increasing the withholding tax or changing the benefit structure, also has multiple economic implications for individuals and for the nation as a whole. In addition, the perceived success of the program in providing for the elderly and those who cannot work raises important equity issues. All of these problems will become even more significant both to individuals and to the nation as the baby boom generation nears retirement.

WELFARE

Welfare policies, as most Americans think about them, concern **means-tested programs.** To qualify for a means-tested program, a potential recipient usually must meet an income test—perhaps better described as a lack-of-income test. These programs include food stamps, job training, housing benefits, and direct cash payments to the poor. Means-tested programs differ from social insurance programs such as Social Security: eligibility for these programs is based on need rather than contributions made to the program.

Because of this distinction, welfare programs do not engender the same level of public support as Social Security. Most people do not see welfare as a social insurance program but as a government handout or charity, which has different connotations for many. These programs are also redistributive, but in this case funds are being transferred to the poor from those who are paying taxes.

Food Stamps

One of the largest federal programs for the poor is the **food stamp program** administered by the Department of Agriculture (USDA). The plan provides low-income households with coupons that they can use to purchase food. Eligible recipients are allotted a dollar amount based on the size of their household. In 2008 the food stamp program served approximately twenty-six million people at a cost of about $37 billion. One of the changes made to the welfare program is that food stamp recipients are expected to register for work and take available employment.

The food stamp program has been controversial throughout its history. One concern was fraud such as food stamp counterfeiting and theft. As a result, the system now distributes benefits electronically, rather than using paper coupons. Clients and others have criticized the program for being overly bureaucratic and making potential recipients jump through hoops to receive benefits. For example, applicants must produce eleven pieces of eligibility verification and may have to recertify several times during the year (Koch 2000). These requirements have convinced many potential applicants that the benefits are not worth the effort. Many eligible

Despite the major overhaul of federal welfare policy in 1996, states continue to struggle with how best to assist families in need. These children are part of a demonstration in front of a state building in Oakland, California, in August 2007. Demonstrators were protesting the state budget, which included possible cuts to welfare and other social services. The California budget process in recent years has been exceptionally conflict ridden as the state's economy has suffered. Enormous state budget deficits in 2008 added to the usual difficulty that the state has had in funding welfare and related human services programs.

people, therefore, may forgo benefits they are entitled to receive, and either they do not get adequate nutrition or turn to other sources for help.[22]

The food stamp program is only one of many public programs geared to meet the nutritional requirements of individuals. The USDA also administers the federally assisted national school lunch and school breakfast programs, which provide well-balanced, nutritional meals at either no cost or reduced cost to low-income children. The school lunch program was first aimed at assisting schools to purchase food for nutritious lunches. The passage of the National School Lunch Act in 1946 gave the program a permanent funding basis and stipulated how funds would be apportioned to the states. The purpose of the law was to ensure the "safety and well-being of the nation's children" through a program that encouraged consumption of nutritious commodities and assisted states to provide such food and necessary facilities.[23] The program, as it is currently conceived, started in 1971, when subsidized meals were tied directly to the poverty guidelines. Today, children in a family below 130 percent of the poverty level ($27,560 for a family of four in FY 2008) are eligible for free meals. More than thirty million children benefit from these programs.[24] This program is clearly directed at children living below or near the poverty line, but it is also part of the government's larger effort to provide valuable nutrition education to all Americans, including yet another revamping of the food pyramid in 2005. Providing information and education is one tool policymakers use to address public problems. The federal government has even set up a centralized Web site (www.nutrition.gov) where anyone can access nutrition information.

Aid to Families with Dependent Children

For years, the nation's major means-tested program was Aid to Families with Dependent Children, which was what most people referred to as "welfare." AFDC was intended to provide financial aid to low-income mothers and children. The program benefited about fourteen million people in its last year in existence and cost about $14 billion annually (Peters 2000).

Until the government replaced the AFDC program in 1996, critics had denigrated it for years on numerous grounds. First, AFDC provided funds to individuals but expected little in return. Welfare programs are not popular with voters in the first place, because they believe the recipients are getting something for nothing. Widespread media accounts of people taking advantage of the system in various ways made the public angry. The stories included allegations that some women had additional children as a way of increasing their benefits. Although little systematic evidence existed to prove that these practices were common, the stories persisted and helped lead to the program's elimination. Other critics disapproved of several of the program's practices. In particular, they said AFDC stigmatized the beneficiaries by requiring them to respond to personal questions, home inspections, and other administrative intrusions to qualify for the benefits (Cochran et al. 1999; Peters 2000). Another frequently raised issue was that AFDC seemed to provide a disincentive to work. Under AFDC, beneficiaries could work only so many hours a month. If they earned more than the specified amount, they would lose a part of their benefits. The incentive therefore was to work only up to the point of losing benefits. A related problem was that attempts to move off welfare by taking a job were not necessarily a rational solution for beneficiaries. By the time individuals paid for child care, transportation, and perhaps health care, they often had little money left, especially if they were being paid minimum wage. The smart financial decision, therefore, was to remain in the government welfare program.

Staying on public assistance may have been a rational decision for individuals, but it did not mean that the money provided was adequate. Even those who supported public assistance pointed out that the amount of financial aid was not enough to move people out of poverty. Statistics showed that the purchasing power of AFDC payments and food stamps had declined over time. During the 1980s and 1990s, the gap between the government poverty line and the welfare benefits provided grew wider (Cochran et al. 1999).

Welfare Reform Options

The concerns with AFDC led to calls for reform from many ideological perspectives. Liberals saw the program as inadequate to provide enough benefits to ensure an adequate standard of living and protect the children who were supposed to be the primary beneficiaries. Conservatives, on the other hand, were more interested in correcting the disincentives for adult beneficiaries to work and try to become self-sufficient. R. Kent Weaver (2000, 45) discussed this conflict as the "dual clientele trap" associated with calls for welfare reform:

> Policymakers usually cannot take the politically popular step of helping poor children without the politically unpopular step of helping their custodial parents; they

cannot take the politically popular steps such as increasing penalties for refusal to work or for out-of-wedlock childbearing that may hurt parents without also risking the politically unpopular result that poor children will be made worse off.

Attempts to reform the welfare system in general, and AFDC in particular, occurred numerous times. During the 1990s, however, major forces came together to get welfare reform onto the government agenda, and the result was a new policy. As Randall B. Ripley and Grace A. Franklin (1986) state, in the U.S. system of government, presidential leadership is often needed to propose any major changes to redistributive programs. The election of President Bill Clinton in 1992 and the subsequent Republican victories in the 1994 congressional elections set the stage for change. Clinton had campaigned as a New Democrat, meaning he was more centrist than many of his colleagues. On the issue of public support for the poor, Clinton said he wanted to "end welfare as we know it" (Clinton and Gore 1992). His ideas to require work to receive benefits and "demand responsibility" (p. 164) were in some ways more in line with the Republicans than with traditional Democratic constituencies. The Republicans had made welfare reform a tenet of their Contract with America, a set of proposals that formed the basis of their campaign. Their version of welfare reform emphasized work even more firmly than the Clinton proposals (Weaver 2000). The ideological changes in Congress likely also forced some movement in Clinton's position. The eventual outcome, after much negotiation, political posturing, and strong opposition by many liberal interest groups, was the Personal Responsibility and Work Opportunity Reconciliation Act of 1996 (PRWORA).

Welfare Reform Law

The PRWORA ended the old AFDC program and welfare as most people know it, replacing it with a block grant program, Temporary Assistance for Needy Families (TANF), which provided state governments with additional flexibility to run their welfare programs. The law also imposed work requirements for beneficiaries and put lifetime limits on receiving benefits (Weaver 2000). The law included the following new rules:

- Teenage parents are required to live with their parents or in an adult-supervised setting.
- States are required to ensure people are moving off the welfare rolls and into work. For example, 50 percent of the families were to be working thirty hours a week by 2002. States not meeting the requirements are penalized by reductions in their TANF block grant funds.
- Adult recipients are limited to a total of five years of receiving federal TANF funds, and states can either impose additional limits or use their own money to fund recipients beyond the five-year period.
- The entitlement structure would change from a system in which individuals who meet the eligibility requirements are entitled to AFDC funds to one in which the states receive the entitlement based on a federal block grant formula (Weaver 2000).

As part of the Deficit Reduction Act of 2006, Congress reauthorized TANF and approved changes that made the program stricter, made it more difficult for states to meet the established goals, and took away some state flexibility. These changes included:

WORKING WITH SOURCES

WELFARE CHANGES AND STATE EFFECTS

As noted in the chapter, the Deficit Reduction Act of 2006 made some major changes to PRWORA and TANF. The states will be responsible for implementing many of these changes, and there are numerous resources available for students to understand the effect on the states. Go to the following sites and study the information provided:

Center on Budget and Policy Priorities (www.cbpp.org/pubs/tanf.htm)

National Conference of State Legislatures (www.ncsl.org/statefed/welfare/welfare.htm)

Urban Institute (www.urbaninstitute.org/welfare/index.cfm)

Consider the following questions:

- What are these organizations saying about the effect of the reauthorization on the states?
- How can the states best plan for these changes and meet the goals set forth in the policy?
- What concerns are being raised by either these organizations or the states regarding the reauthorization?
- What is your assessment of the change? Is it an improvement over the original law?

- Work participation rates are based on caseload declines after 2005 rather than 1995. Since significant case reductions occurred particularly in the late 1990s, the result will be that it will be more difficult for states to meet the goals.
- Work participation rates will be based on both TANF and state-funded programs. In the past, state-funded programs did not count toward the work rate.
- Uniform methods for reporting hours, type of work accepted, and other issues are adopted.
- A new penalty of up to 5 percent is established for states that do not implement internal procedures and controls consistent with the secretary of health and human services' regulations.[25]

The box "Working with Sources: Welfare Changes and State Effects" presents opportunities to examine this issue in more depth.

Analysis of the Welfare Reform Law

The welfare reform policy incorporated a number of components of interest to public policy students. In terms of economic efficiency, the Congressional Budget Office estimated that the new law would save $54 billion by fiscal year 2002 (U.S. Congressional Budget Office 1996), with most of the savings coming from reductions in benefits to legal immigrants and other changes to existing programs such as food stamps (Weaver 2000). These savings obviously pleased many in the Washington community, especially conservatives who wanted to cut funding for welfare programs. It is also interesting to note, however, that many of the suggestions for reforming welfare, such as providing job training, child care benefits, or medical care to ensure that adults could work, would actually be more expensive to implement in the short run than the previous AFDC program. Kent Weaver calls this problem the "money trap." Former governor Tommy Thompson of Wisconsin—a state at the forefront of welfare reform—made similar assertions about the changes in his state's welfare programs. According to Thompson, states that are serious about welfare reform needed to spend more money on health care, child care, transportation, and training.[26] The PRWORA, however, did not fully endorse many of the high-cost provisions being pushed by advocates of the work requirement.

Politically, the public supported and continues to agree with the changes to the welfare program. Remember, most of the general public is wary of a program that gives benefits with no strings attached. The public also supported the work requirement that would provide people with the skills they needed to become self-sufficient, not to mention the reduction of the number of out-of-wedlock births that seemed to come as a result (Weaver 2000). On the other side of the fence, many individuals and groups worried about the welfare reforms. Liberal politicians and interest groups, especially child advocacy groups, expressed concerns that the reforms could lead to higher levels of poverty for the affected populations, because of their inability or unwillingness to follow the new requirements such as finding work. The supporters of welfare reform, however, constituted a much larger coalition, which included nearly all Republicans and conservative and moderate Democrats. Moreover, the Clinton administration was feeling pressured to follow through on one of its major policy proposals, especially as the president was running for a second term.

Looking at the law from the point of view of individual freedom, it is clear that in some ways the welfare reforms impinged on a measure of the beneficiaries' freedom. In fact, many parts of the law reflected what has been called "new paternalism," whose adherents had found the permissiveness in the welfare state appalling (Mead 1986). Requiring work to receive benefits not only takes away part of an individual's freedom but also imposes a different set of values—the government's values—over how people should live. On the other hand, taxpayers prefer a program that has clear guidelines and requirements for what it takes to receive benefits. Ethically, the questions that inevitably arise are what happens to children under this program if their parents do not meet their obligations or if they exceed their time limits for receiving benefits. Is the nation willing to cut off benefits to this vulnerable population?

Ultimately, one needs to evaluate the success of welfare reform based on the goals of the program. According to Lawrence Mead, there were three major goals associated with welfare reform based on what the government did: (1) enforce work requirements, (2) reduce dependency, and (3) promote marriage. A fourth goal, to reduce poverty, would follow from the previous conditions (Mead 2007). Goals one and two relate very explicitly to the important question of whether the PRWORA has been effective in moving people off the welfare rolls. The initial numbers showed a dramatic decrease in the welfare caseloads since the enactment of the law in 1996. By the end of 1998, for example, caseloads had decreased by 38 percent, and many states experienced caseload reductions higher than 50 percent (U.S. Department of Health and Human Services 2000). These decreasing trends in the welfare rolls continued into 2004 even with the sluggish economy and increases in unemployment and poverty.[27] The changes to TANF made in 2006 that link program goals and caseload reductions will make it more difficult for states to claim success or perhaps to make some hard decisions regarding how they will meet the new work rules. States could choose to assist fewer poor families in order to meet new requirements.[28]

These positive caseload numbers led many to announce that welfare reform was a major success. The Government Accountability Office, however, cautioned against making such grand assessments at this stage. According to the GAO (1998), the success documented by its studies might be a factor of the positive economic conditions that prevailed during the mid- to late 1990s. In addition, the first beneficiaries who moved from welfare to work were likely to have been the easiest people to place.

Moreover, much "remains unknown about how families fare after leaving welfare with respect to economic stability and child and family well-being" (U.S. Government Accountability Office 1998, 8). For example, according to the health care advocacy group Families USA, "nearly a million low-income parents have lost Medicaid coverage and have probably become uninsured" since the welfare system was overhauled.[29] Another GAO report (1999) found that people were indeed getting jobs after being on the welfare rolls, but the jobs paid so little that the families were still relying on other forms of aid, such as food stamps and the Earned Income Tax Credit, to maintain a semblance of economic stability. One analyst at the Urban Institute described the situation as follows:

> Figuring out whether welfare reform is a success means looking beyond how fam-
> ilies that recently left welfare are faring today. For those families that have left wel-
> fare and joined the workforce, success will depend on whether they move into
> jobs with higher wages and benefits so that they can be not just better off than
> when they were on welfare but move further toward self-sufficiency.[30]

It goes without saying that evaluation of the PRWORA will continue for some time. As is often the case in determining the impact of public policies (Sabatier and Jenkins-Smith 1993), sufficient time must pass before analysts can accurately assess how well the welfare reform act is working. A major test of the law occurred when the country's economic growth slowed. During 2001 and 2002, for example, the unemployment rate inched upward, and advocates for the poor were concerned that this would cause problems with the TANF program and its beneficiaries. According to the Center on Budget and Policy Priorities, for example, by 2002 thirty-three states had already experienced an increase in the number of cash assistance case-loads during that recessionary period.[31] Will the states be able to weather a surge in people needing cash assistance as jobs decrease in an economic slowdown? Many states had used their TANF funds to provide services to people who moved off the welfare rolls into work. These funds supported services such as child care or medical care and have helped former recipients move into jobs. For example, Baltimore transferred $90 million of its federal TANF money to child care and other family support services.[32] If more people need cash assistance because jobs are scarce, will these services be reduced? Another issue that merits serious thought is the time limit imposed on beneficiaries. As the country once again experienced major economic down-turns in 2008 and 2009, it is fair to say that a number of people were negatively affected and had to turn to government support. What kind of impact will the limit have on individuals? What will the public response be to entirely cutting off benefits to children?

More recent studies of welfare reform show a level of success, but also caution about the future. Former welfare recipients are entering the job market in higher numbers and seem financially better off. Much of the reason has to do with the financial support provided by other programs such as food stamps and the Earned Income Tax Credit. Yet, while economi-cally more comfortable than before, many of these people still hover around the poverty line (Rodgers 2005). The poorest households in particular seem not to have benefited from the changes to welfare (Murray and Primus 2005), and the question about what to do with this most difficult category of individuals needs to be addressed. While states have decreased their caseloads, studies from a number of states have found former welfare recipients struggling in low-income jobs or having no jobs at all.[33]

There have been a limited number of evaluations of welfare reform in the last five years, and this has somewhat hindered further discussions about its effectiveness. This question of effectiveness is critical as policymakers decide what may be the next step in addressing poverty and welfare issues. Did welfare reform work? From the federal government's perspective, the stricter requirements were paramount in decreasing the caseloads. But state officials see the greater flexibility provided through block grants as a primary reason for its success. This flex-ibility allowed states to develop their own solutions based on local conditions.[34] How this question is resolved can affect future decisions. Should requirements be even stricter to receive benefits, or should states be provided with additional funding and flexibility? Additional data and analysis are critical to better understand the wide range of issues. The Urban Institute has suggested five major areas for additional research: (1) improving data capacity; (2) understand-ing changes in welfare participation; (3) tracking current and former welfare recipients to identify persistent needs and problems; (4) understanding how specific state initiatives affect the well-being of current and former recipients; and (5) expanding beyond TANF to learn more about how other public programs are serving low-income families.[35]

As one can imagine, the discussions and debate over the law are highly partisan, with each person using a different study to promote his or her perspective. For example, debate in the Senate Finance Committee revealed diverse opinions about the success of welfare reform. Sen. Max Baucus, D-Mont., pointed to a study in his state that found only 10 percent of families leaving the welfare rolls were earning enough to be self-sufficient, whereas Sen. Charles Grassley, R-Iowa, countered that in his state, families leaving welfare had more money and greater self-esteem.[36] Even with these different opinions, many seem to agree that the direc-tion welfare reform took in 1996 was the correct one. Welfare caseloads have gone down sig-nificantly from the early 1990s, and more people are working for their benefits. But are these changes the best way to evaluate success? Remember that the purpose of these programs was to lift people out of poverty. Did that happen? As mentioned earlier, poverty continues to be a problem in the United States, and deep poverty seems to be increasing. There are other prob-lematic signs regarding the state of the poor. Families leaving the TANF rolls more recently seem less likely to find a job, and caseloads for other poverty programs, such as food stamps and Medicaid, are increasing.[37] Growing poverty rates with continued decreases in TANF case-loads seem counterintuitive and may suggest a need for a different standard to measure the success of these programs (Murray and Primus 2005). A large number of people, even those that have found work as a result of welfare reform, still remain impoverished. In addition, what remains unclear is how well the families that left welfare are doing economically.[38]

It is of interest that the original PROWRA had no requirements to track these families, a seri-ous matter from the perspective of policy design and evaluation. Instead, the only available data came from the states, and only from states that chose to present the information. These data may display only snapshots of welfare recipients and their conditions (McQueen 2001). They continue to come in, but if the information is inadequate, how will policymakers know what changes to make in welfare programs? Are former welfare recipients better off or worse off? What has been the effect on family lives? Should work requirements be increased? On the positive side, think tanks and other nonprofit groups are also collecting and analyzing data on these problems.

FOCUSED DISCUSSION: WE'VE REFORMED WELFARE, NOW WHAT? ADDRESSING POVERTY

Throughout the chapter we have discussed a variety of issues surrounding what is often called the "social safety net." How does the nation, whether through government, nonprofits, or other organizations, ensure an acceptable standard of living for its citizens, especially those most at risk, such as children? Poverty remains a reality in the United States, as the dramatic pictures following Hurricane Katrina showed. Trillions of dollars have been spent since the "war on poverty" was initiated more than forty years ago. More recently, the passage of the PRWORA in 1996 instituted major changes to how the government implements its major welfare programs. By some measures, welfare reform was highly successful. TANF caseloads are down, more people are working, and states have increased flexibility. But

U.S. Speaker of the House Nancy Pelosi (left), D-Calif., and Senate Majority Leader Harry Reid, D-Nev., attend a July 2007 rally on Capitol Hill to celebrate the first raise in the federal minimum wage. The new rate instituted that month increased pay from $5.15 per hour to $5.85, then in July 2008 to $6.55 per hour, and, finally, in July 2009 to $7.25 per hour. States are free to set their own minimum wage levels, and many of them have been more generous than has the federal government. Yet as the text notes, such actions remain controversial. Supporters say the minimum wage should be set at a level that provides for a suitable standard of living, or a "living wage." On the other side of the debate, small business owners in particular say that raising the minimum wage may force them to hire fewer workers.

poverty continues to be a major concern; over thirty-seven million people live below the poverty line, and many of them are working adults.

As noted earlier in the chapter, the presidential campaign of 2008, particularly the Democratic primaries, included rhetoric on the state of poverty in the United States. As the economy continued its downward trend in 2008, gas prices fluctuated dramatically, and with the increase in home foreclosures it became clear that the economy would once again be the primary issue in the general election. This harped back to 1992, when the campaign staff of then-candidate Bill Clinton claimed, "It's the economy, stupid," forcing almost every issue to be examined from this context. While these general economic issues are often focused on the middle class, there are obvious implications for the poor as well.

For the sake of this focused discussion, we will assume that those in poverty are willing and able to work in order to get a wage. But we also need to consider that many of those in poverty are working and not getting a sufficient wage to survive. On July 24, 2008, the government increased the **minimum wage** to $6.55 per hour, and in July 2009 it will increase to $7.25 per hour. Assuming a full-time schedule working fifty weeks, the pay in 2008 of someone working at minimum wage would be $13,100 ($14,500 in 2009), nowhere near the poverty line for a family of four. So what might be the solution?

This section will examine a few potential solutions to the scenario above. The solutions include two existing programs within our government's safety net policies: the Earned Income Tax Credit (EITC) and the minimum wage. In both cases, the focused analysis will examine increases to these programs as a way to reduce poverty. The EITC is a refundable federal income tax for low-income working individuals and families. For those who qualify, if the EITC is greater than the amount owed in taxes, the beneficiary receives a tax refund. The government implemented the EITC as a way to encourage people to work by providing additional benefits to do so. In 1938, the government implemented a minimum wage to ensure a certain level of income. It has been increased periodically (though on an irregular basis) since then in recognition of the higher cost of living. There is an ongoing debate regarding the minimum wage; it concerns its effect on business and whether it is an effective way to ensure an adequate wage to employees. Yet a number of policymakers and organizations concerned about poverty advocate for additional increases. Policymakers need to think about a range of options to reduce the incidence of poverty in the United States, keeping in mind that the political environment makes it difficult to suggest even modest reforms, let alone major initiatives. This section analyzes a number of issues concerning these policy proposals and touches on a couple of others using the criteria of economics or efficiency, political feasibility, and ethics and equity.

Economic and Effectiveness Issues

The economic and effectiveness criteria are intricately linked for these antipoverty policies. In many cases, the effectiveness criterion is based on the ability of these policies to improve the economic positions of the beneficiaries. The EITC was implemented over thirty years ago as a way to encourage work and to provide recipients with some tax relief and in some cases even a tax refund. In 2007 the maximum tax credit was $4,716 for a family with two or more qualifying children. For those in deep poverty, the tax credit is probably not significant enough to provide much improvement to living conditions, but it could make a difference for low-wage workers. Minimum wage legislation has been around much longer, but there is some question as to whether it has done much to reduce poverty. In both cases, these are policies to ensure additional income to people who are willing to work. The question that must be asked, though, is whether these two programs as they currently exist do enough to lift people out of poverty.

The Center for American Progress, a liberal think tank, has put forth a series of proposals aimed at cutting poverty in half. Among them are suggestions to expand the EITC and increase the minimum wage. This expansion of the EITC includes proposals to increase it for childless workers, young adults, and families with three or more children. In addition, the center suggests an adjustment for two-parent families so that half of the lower-wage spouse's income is excluded. The argument for this last point is that the current policy dissuades marriage because it could reduce the EITC benefit. On the minimum wage front, the center proposes an increase to half the average hourly wage (in 2009 this was $9.25 an hour).[39]

As noted earlier, the EITC is particularly useful for low- to moderate-income families in that it alleviates a tax burden and in many cases provides a tax refund. An expansion in the program would therefore put additional money in the wallets of these recipients. For example, the current policy makes no distinction between families with two children and families with three or more. Obviously, there is a greater cost associated with raising more children. Therefore, a family's financial benefits associated with this change are clear. Proponents of the EITC also point out that this program may provide families with the ability to "save for a rainy day" and protect them from short-term monetary problems. At the macroeconomic level, more money can lead to additional expenditures or savings, both of which can have a positive effect on the overall economy. In addition, families may be less likely to enter other, more expensive government support programs.

An increase in the minimum wage would also put additional money in the wallets of those working at this wage and would have similar individual and macro-level benefits. While $9.25 an hour would still not provide a minimal standard of living wage for a one-parent family, it would be a significant increase. In addition, for two-parent families in which both parents are working, the annual wage would be nearly $34,000, which is well above the current poverty line. The Center for American Progress, along with others, argues that the minimum wage has not kept up with the cost of living in real dollar terms. As Figure 9-5 shows, the real value of the minimum wage has decreased substantially.

Of course, the EITC is an appropriated item in the budget, and any expansion of the tax credit will have budgetary implications and potentially increase the federal deficit unless it is offset in some way. In examining the Center for American Progress's recommendations, the Urban Institute estimated that its major proposals would cost approximately $90 billion a year—a significant sum but less than 1 percent of the nation's gross national product. The institute also estimated that implementing three of the major proposals would decrease poverty by 26 percent.[40] The question comes down to one of priorities for government spending and whether addressing poverty in this way is one of them.

Increasing the minimum wage has always generated different opinions regarding the economic impacts. A minimum wage is similar to setting a price floor—the minimum price at which a product can sell. In this case, individuals represent a supply of workers, and setting a minimum wage could lead to a situation where the number of workers is greater than the demand for those workers. More simplistically, employers may be less willing to hire workers when wages are higher because of the additional costs. Opponents to minimum wage increases have often raised this issue as a burden, particularly on small businesses, that would have adverse economic consequences. There is research available, however, that suggests otherwise. A number of states have minimum wage policies higher than the federal level, and have seen faster job growth.[41] Not everyone agrees with some of this research,[42] but it does raise the issue of whether the traditional economic arguments

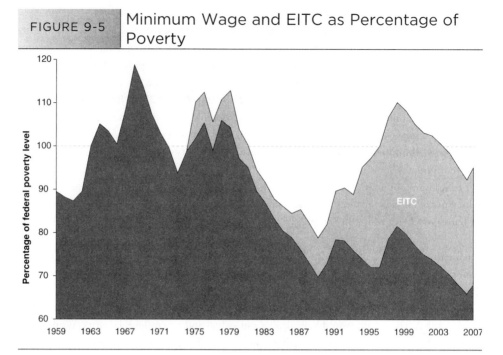

FIGURE 9-5   Minimum Wage and EITC as Percentage of Poverty

Mark Greenberg, Indivar Dutta-Gupta, and Elisa Minoff. This material was published by the Center for American Progress, www.americanprogress.org.

against minimum wage increases represent the entire story. Another common argument for those opposing a minimum wage increase is that it has a limited effect on those in poverty who really need relief. They argue that a low percentage of workers actually earns this wage, and those that do are mainly teenagers working for extra spending money, not to make ends meet. In addition, opponents state that an increase in the wage will lead to employee layoffs, particularly in entry-level positions. Therefore, the policy would actually do more harm to those it is intended to aid because they will not have the skills necessary for higher-wage positions.

The economics of these proposals not only highlight disagreements about their effects—they also show differing political positions. In addition, there are also differing opinions regarding how effective these policies would be in dealing with poverty problems in the United States. Some relate directly to how the problem has been defined for purposes of this focused discussion. As noted throughout the book, politics often enters into problem definition and can affect how one examines potential solutions. We turn now to some of these political issues.

Political Issues

The politics of the proposals introduced above are relatively straightforward. As noted throughout the chapter, means-tested programs are generally less popular with the population than something like Social Security. This is particularly true for programs that appear not to have any requirements associated with the benefits received. Welfare reform in 1996 was mainly predicated on this concern. Both expanding the EITC and increasing the minimum wage have the political advantage of being related to work requirements. Obviously, in order to receive an increased minimum wage, one must be working. And if the minimum wage increases, so too would a person's income. In the case of the EITC, the credit increases as income increases up to a certain amount before the credit decreases. For example, based on the "EITC estimator" provided on the Center on Budget and Policy Priorities' Web site, a single person (with two children) making $5,000 will receive an estimated credit of $2,010, and one making $15,000 will receive a credit of $4,716. So in general there may be greater political support for these programs than there is for traditional welfare programs.

General population support is important because the beneficiaries of these programs often are not adequately represented by interest groups and have a more difficult time getting their voices heard. Political organization can be difficult when those in poverty are worrying about their next meal or whether they may be out on the street. While there are organizations, such as the National Coalition for the Homeless, that represent the poor, mobilizing this population for political purposes can be difficult. These types of policies are generally classified as "redistributive programs," meaning that as one group of people benefits, some other group may lose. In the case of minimum wage, for example, those getting a higher minimum wage are benefiting at the expense of the employer paying the wage. According to Ripley and Franklin (1991), enactment of redistributive policies often requires a strong advocate, such as the president, to take the lead and push it through the legislative process. A president has to sell this type of program to the general population in order for it to succeed.

On the other side of the political equation will likely fall those stressing free-market economies that would set wages based on the supply and demand of the labor market. These groups and individuals would argue that government should not be involved, particularly in minimum wage policies. Organizations such as the National Small Business Association argue that increases in the minimum wage will force small businesses to cut their workforce because of the increased cost of not just minimum wage workers but of all workers.[43] Some organizations and think tanks state that an increase in the minimum wage may actually increase poverty if more people are thrown out of work as a result of such policies.[44]

The EITC raises more general budgetary issues that the government needs to take into consideration, as well as potential concerns by organizations worried about the federal deficit. While the program encourages work and is generally supported, an expansion of it could have budgetary effects, particularly an increase in the federal deficit. As noted above, this will require some important discussions regarding government priorities, including just how much of a role government should play in ensuring that people do not live in poverty. These issues are also obviously tied to the ethical questions associated with poverty, especially regarding equity or equality.

Ethics and Equity Issues

At first glance, one might think the ethical and equity issues associated with programs dealing with poverty would be somewhat simple and agreed to by all. Shouldn't we live in a society where people no longer need to live in poverty? Who could argue against this or, for that matter, the programs that address poverty? Of course, as is true with most public policy questions, especially as they relate to issues of ethics and equity, matters are never quite so simple. The devil is in the details, and your perspective on this issue may depend on how a problem is defined and the types of solutions that are offered.

As noted earlier, questions of equity often examine the difference between equality of opportunity and equality of results; and as we stated, the United States has focused historically more on equality of opportunity. One might argue that training or educational programs provide additional opportunities for people to increase their income status and potentially lead them out of poverty. Are programs such as the EITC and increases in the minimum wage similar? Equity questions often arise regarding the role of government in the free market, and programs that require a specific minimum wage directly insert the government into matters of employer-employee contracts as they relate to a fair wage based on supply and demand. Of course, the other equity issue that should be considered is what effect these policies have on businesses or employees if they find themselves out of a job as a result of a minimum wage requirement. Should government step in if a person is willing to work for less than the minimum wage? Isn't a low wage better than no wage?

These are questions that have been part of our nation's history for a long time. For a number of years, the idea of government imposing itself in any kind of an employer-employee transaction, including a wage requirement, was strenuously opposed. In fact, when President Franklin Roosevelt first tried to do so, the Supreme Court ruled it unconstitutional. While free-market arguments and questions about the appropriate role of government have dissipated to some extent, they have been replaced with the potential economic effects of a minimum wage (positive or negative). In a society that values work, the idea that someone could work a full-time job and not make ends meet is a contradiction. The ethical question comes down to one of fairness. If someone is willing and able to work, and is in fact doing so, shouldn't the wage be sufficient to live? This is the argument made by proponents of increasing the minimum wage, and it resonates with many. In fact, for this very reason some have advocated for a "living wage," an amount that would keep a family of four above the poverty line. While there may be a significant number of minimum wage earners who are not impoverished, they do not change the fact that some heads of households are working at minimum wage.

As one can see, there are a number of interrelated issues surrounding the question of how to address poverty. The programs discussed above—the minimum wage and the EITC—are two that have general support, although their expansion raises other concerns. There are additional proposals—such as subsidizing child care for low-wage workers, promoting marriage, and investing in early childhood education—that have also been raised as potential solutions to poverty.[45] These actions might raise issues similar to those discussed above, and additional ones. It does appear, though, that the issue of poverty is once more on the political agenda, partly because of the struggling economy, and the time is ripe for some new or different kinds of government action.

CONCLUSIONS

This chapter examines the challenge of poverty and some of the major programs designed to address it. These programs aim to ensure an adequate income to make ends meet, and they have enjoyed different levels of support from the general public. Social Security is often heralded as a prime example of successful government intervention to deal with a public problem. While most agree that the nation needs to maintain a guaranteed income for senior citizens based on their previous working lives, they would also agree that the current Social Security program has some deficiencies and faces serious problems. Welfare programs, on the other hand, have not experienced the same level of public support, and this attitude is apparent in the debates over welfare programs and subsequent changes in how they are administered.

Poverty continues to exist in the United States, despite the programs aimed at relieving it and getting people into the workforce. The welfare rolls are smaller, but it remains unclear whether fewer people are living in poverty. With Social Security, the debate continues regarding its financing and how to ensure its solvency in the future. Every student of public policy needs to understand the issues and know how to find and assess the available data to make informed decisions about these programs.

DISCUSSION QUESTIONS

1. President Obama has suggested that the time has come to solve some of the problems associated with entitlement spending. Why do you think it has been so difficult to address these issues? What has changed to perhaps make it more likely that federal policymakers will do so now?

2. What explains the demographic discrepancies in poverty rates across the nation, for example, among racial and ethnic groups? How else might the United States address issues of poverty other than through its means-tested programs?

3. The level of individual income subject to the Social Security tax was capped at about $106,000 in 2009. Should the income level be raised to help address anticipated shortfalls in the Social Security trust fund? Would doing so constitute an unfair taxation on current workers? Would it be more equitable to meet anticipated future demand for Social Security by reducing the level of benefits?

4. One purpose of the welfare reform law was to provide more flexibility to states in administrating their programs. What kinds of policies has your state adopted? What can you say about their effectiveness, political support, or fairness?

SUGGESTED READINGS

Mary H. Cooper, "Social Security Reform," *CQ Researcher*, September 24, 2004. Examines issues of Social Security reform particularly from the perspective of financing. Focuses on the privatization alternative as one way to address this issue.

Sarah Glazer, "Welfare Reform," *CQ Researcher*, August 3, 2001. Examines welfare reform a few years after passage of the welfare reform law, with special attention to issues likely to be faced in the future and the effectiveness of the reform effort.

Paul Light, *Still Artful Work,* 2nd ed. (New York: McGraw-Hill, 1995). Examines the 1983 Social Security reforms to put the system on sounder footing. The book focuses on the politics involved in these policy changes and assesses more recent concerns about financial issues.

National Commission on Retirement Policy, *The 21st Century Retirement Security Plan: Final Report of the National Commission on Retirement Policy* (Washington, D.C.: U.S. Government Printing Office, March 1999). This U.S. government commission report looks at the elements of Social Security and offers some alternatives for addressing the financial issue.

Review of Policy Research 22, no. 3 (May 2005). This entire issue examines welfare reform from a variety of perspectives, including the recent trends, innovations, and research in welfare reform.

R. Kent Weaver, *Ending Welfare as We Know It* (Washington, D.C.: Brookings Institution, 2000). Examines the welfare reform movement and the politics affecting it, including innovations developed and used by state governments.

Alan Weil and Kenneth Finegold, *Welfare Reform: The Next Act* (Washington, D.C.: The Urban Institute, 2002). Examines some of the results of the 1996 Welfare Reform Act in the context of the reauthorization of the law that needs to occur.

SUGGESTED WEB SITES

www.aarp.org. AARP is an advocacy group for senior citizens. The site contains data and research on a variety of issues of concern to this constituency.

www.acf.hhs.gov. HHS site for the Administration for Children and Families, with links, data, and information on welfare issues.

www.concordcoalition.org. The Concord Coalition is a nonpartisan think tank advocating fiscal responsibility for programs such as Social Security and Medicare. The site contains data and analysis concerning Social Security and reform options.

www.financeproject.org/index.cfm?page=24. The Economic Success Clearinghouse (formerly the Welfare Information Network) is a clearinghouse of data and analyses on a wide range of welfare and welfare reform issues.

www.socsec.org. The Social Security Network provides a large number of reports and analyses on Social Security; provides a link to other Web sites with Social Security information.

www.ssa.gov. U.S. Social Security Administration site, with a wide range of information on the Social Security program and its history; also reports and data on projections for the future.

www.urban.org. The Urban Institute is a policy research organization. The site contains analyses of Social Security and welfare issues.

MAJOR LEGISLATION

Aid to Families with Dependent Children (AFDC)   270
Deficit Reduction Act of 2006   286
National School Lunch Act of 1946   284
Personal Responsibility and Work Opportunity Reconciliation Act of 1996 (PRWORA)   269

KEYWORDS

cost of living adjustment (COLA)   280
culture of poverty   273
Earned Income Tax Credit (EITC)   274
food stamp program   283
Gini coefficient   272

means-tested programs   283
minimum wage   292
poverty   271
Social Security   274

NOTES

1. See Jonathan Alter, "The Other America," *Newsweek,* September 19, 2005, 42.
2. For additional information, see T. J. Billitteri, "Domestic Poverty," *CQ Researcher* 17, online edition, September 7, 2007, 721–744.
3. This and additional information regarding poverty statistics can be found at the U.S. Census Web site: www.census.gov/hhes/www/poverty/poverty.
4. For additional information on poverty, other measures related to the poor, and potential problems of the current estimate of poverty, see Deepak Bhargava and Joan Kuriansky, "Drawing the Line on Poverty," *Washington Post National Weekly Edition,* September 23–29, 2002, 23.
5. See the U.S. Census Bureau Web site: www.census.gov/hhes/www/povmeas/tables.html.
6. Louis Uchitelle, "Economist's Survey Supports Theory That Inflation Is Overstated," *New York Times,* February 13, 1997.
7. There has been a tremendous amount of research and work done on the issue of how best to calculate poverty. For more information, see the Welfare Reform Academy site, particularly the Income and Poverty link: www.welfareacademy.org/pubs/poverty.
8. See Arloc Sherman and Isaac Shapiro, "Social Security Lifts 13 Million Seniors above the Poverty Line: A State-by-State Analysis" (Washington, D.C.: Center on Budget and Policy Priorities, 2005), available at www.cbpp.org/2-24-05socsec.htm.
9. U.S. Social Security Administration, "President's Budget Press Statement," February 8, 2008, available at www.ssa.gov/budget.
10. See U.S. Social Security Administration: www.ssa.gov/policy/docs/quickfacts/stat_snapshot.
11. See Center on Budget and Policy Priorities, 2008, available at www.cbpp.org/4-14-08tax.htm.
12. Estimates according to the annual report issued by the OASDI Trustees. See U.S. Social Security Administration, "The 2008 OASDI Trustees Report," available at www.socialsecurity.gov/OACT/TR/TR08.
13. The full-benefit or normal retirement age for those born between 1955 and 1960 increases slowly from sixty-six to sixty-seven. For those born in 1960 or later, the full-benefit or normal retirement age is sixty-seven.
14. See U.S. Government Accountability Office, *Social Security: Issues Involving Benefit Equity for Working Women* (Washington, D.C.: U.S. Government Printing Office, 1996).
15. See U.S. Department of Labor, "Highlights of Women's Earnings in 2006," available at www.bls.gov/cps/cpswom2006.pdf.
16. See U.S. Social Security Administration, "The 2008 OASDI Trustees Report," available at www.ssa.gov/OACT/TR/TR08/index.html.
17. For further information on this report, see www.ssa.gov/history/reports/adcouncil/index.html.
18. You can review the CBPP report in Jason Furman, "The Impact of the President's Proposal on Social Security Solvency and the Budget," Center on Budget and Policy Priorities, available at www.cbpp.org/5-10-05socsec.htm#fig.
19. Several reports go into further detail on the potential economic impacts of the private investment plan. For details see Henry Aaron, Alan Blinder, Alicia Munnell, and Peter Orszag, *Governor Bush's Individual Account*

Proposal: Implications for Retirement Benefits, 2000, available at www.socsec.org/facts/Issue_Briefs/ PDF_versions/11issbrf.pdf; Barry Bosworth and Gary Burtless. 2000. "The Effects of Social Security Reform on Saving, Investment, and the Level and Distribution of Worker Well-Being" (Boston: Center for Retirement Research at Boston College, 2000), available at http://crr.bc.edu/images/stories/Working_Papers/wp_2002-02.pdf?phpMyAdmin=43ac483c4de9t51d9eb41 and Concord Coalition, "Issue Brief: Social Security Reform," available at www.concordcoalition.org/socialsecurity/ 000628issuebriefsocsecrefgorebush.pdf.

20. You can find a variety of research reports on this issue prepared by AARP at www.aarp.org/research/social security/reform.

21. *CQ Weekly* covered this political issue regarding Social Security. For more information, see Adriel Bettelheim, "No Market for Next New Deal," *CQ Weekly,* April 4, 2005, 828.

22. For more information on hunger and the food stamp program, see Kathy Koch, "Hunger in America," *CQ Researcher,* December 22, 2000.

23. This information comes from the U.S. Department of Agriculture's National School Lunch Program Web site: www.fns.usda.gov/cnd/Lunch/AboutLunch/ProgramHistory.htm.

24. See U.S. Department of Agriculture, "National School Lunch Program," available at www.fns. usda.gov/cnd/Lunch/AboutLunch/NSLPFactSheet.pdf.

25. See Center on Budget and Policy Priorities, "Implementing the TANF Changes in the Deficit Reduction Act: 'Win-Win' Solutions for Families and States," 2nd ed., available at www.cbpp.org/2-9-07tanf.htm. This site also provides more details on the changes to welfare as a result of the Deficit Reduction Act of 2006.

26. See E. J. Dionne, "Welfare Reform: The Clues Are in Wisconsin," *Washington Post,* September 23, 1997.

27. See Robert Pear, "Despite Sluggish Economy, Welfare Rolls Actually Shrank," *New York Times,* March 22, 2004.

28. See Sharon Parrott and Arloc Sherman, "TANF's Results Are More Mixed Than Is Often Understood," *Journal of Policy Analysis and Management* 26, no. 2 (2007): 374–381.

29. See Robert Pear, "A Million Parents Lost Medicaid, Study Says," *New York Times,* June 20, 2000.

30. See Pamela Loprest, "Long Ride from Welfare to Work," *Washington Post,* August 30, 1999.

31. This information comes from a report by Zöe Neuberger, Sharon Parrott, and Wendell Primus, "Funding Issues in TANF Reauthorization," Center on Budget and Policy Priorities, February 5, 2002, available at www.centeronbudget.org/1-22-02tanf5.htm.

32. For a full discussion of the potential of a recession's impact on the nation's programs designed to help the poor, see Mark Murray, Marilyn Werber Serafini, and Megan Twohey, "Untested Safety Net," *National Journal,* March 10, 2001.

33. According to a *Washington Post* article, studies show problems with those former recipients that might be considered the poorest of the poor. See Evelyn Nieves, "The Limits of Welfare Reform," *Washington Post Weekly Edition,* August 1–7, 2005, 29.

34. For additional information see Corine Hegland, "What Works for Welfare?" *National Journal,* January 10, 2004, 106.

35. This study also provides a comprehensive summary of a number of welfare reform studies and also conducts its own analysis of some welfare issues. See Urban Institute, "TANF Caseload Composition and Leavers Synthesis Report," March 28, 2007, available at www.urban.org/UploadedPDF/411553_tanf_caseload.pdf.

36. See Anjetta McQueen, "Welfare Law's Big Question: Has Success Been Real?" *CQ Weekly,* March 30, 2001, 869–870.

37. See Shawn Fremstad, "Recent Welfare Reform Research Findings," Center on Budget and Policy Priorities, January 30, 2004, available at www.cbpp.org/1-30-04wel.pdf.

38. For further studies on the evaluation of PRWORA, see the May *Review of Policy Research* (May 2005), which examines a number of areas relating to welfare reform.

39. For additional information on these proposals and others, see Mark Greenberg, Indivar Dutta-Gupta, and Elisa Minoff, "From Poverty to Prosperity: A National Strategy to Cut Poverty in Half" (Washington, D.C.: Center for American Progress, April 2007), available at www.americanprogress.org/issues/2007/04/poverty_report.html.

40. The costs associated with this proposal include more than just an expansion of the EITC and the minimum wage and includes other recommendations made by the Center for American Progress. See "From Poverty to Prosperity: A National Strategy to Cut Poverty in Half," Center for American Progress,

41. See David Card and Alan Krueger, *Myth and Measurement: The New Economics of the Minimum Wage* (Princeton: Princeton University Press, 1995), 1-4; and Fiscal Policy Institute, *States with Minimum Wages above the Federal Level Have Had Faster Small Business and Retail Job Growth* (Washington, D.C.: Fiscal Policy Institute, March 30, 2006).

42. For example, see Donald Deere, Kevin M. Murphy, and Finis Welch, "Sense and Nonsense on the Minimum Wage," *Regulation* 18, no. 1 (1995).

43. See National Small Business Association, "Minimum Wage," available at www.nsba.biz/docs/minimum_wage.pdf.

44. See James Sherk, "Raising the Minimum Wage Will Not Reduce Poverty" (Washington, D.C.: The Heritage Foundation, 2007), available at www.heritage.org/Research/Labor/bg1994.cfm.

45. See Isabel Sawhill and Ron Haskins, "Attacking Poverty and Inequality: Reinvigorate the Fight for Greater Opportunity" (Washington, D.C.: Brookings Institution, February 28, 2007), available at www.brookings .edu/papers/ 2007/0228poverty_haskins_Opp08.aspx.

IN EARLY 2002, PRESIDENT GEORGE W. BUSH SIGNED THE NO CHILD LEFT Behind Act (NCLB) with great fanfare and strong bipartisan support from Congress. In fact, one of the key players in the U.S. Senate was Massachusetts's liberal senator Edward Kennedy. It was clear at the time that support for this law, a reauthorization of the Elementary and Secondary Education Act (ESEA), was strong, and many believed in the goals of the legislation to improve the nation's education system. These goals were to be achieved through the following demands, all placed upon the states by the federal government: establishment of state standards and increase in testing requirements for students in all grades between three and eight (once in high school, requirements for public reporting of the test results were broken down into various subgroups, such as economically disadvantaged students); state accountability requiring proficiency in math and reading and closing achievement gaps between different groups of students; "highly qualified" teachers in the classroom; and financial sanctions (loss of federal funds) placed upon the states if "adequate yearly progress" was not being met by schools.

A few years later, though, the across-the-board support for this new policy had lessened significantly, with Senator Kennedy leading the opposition. He stated that the federal government in general, and the Bush administration in particular, had not kept its promise to provide appropriate funding for the policy's implementation (Mantel 2005). Opposition and concern also had arisen in many of the states. NCLB represented a major shift in the role that the federal government plays in K–12 education. Historically the purview of state and local governments, NCLB involved the federal government in the management of local schools and tested states' rights issues. Perhaps the larger problem from many states' perspectives concerned the perceived inadequacy of the funds provided to fully implement the federal

Four third graders listen as their teacher explains a reading lesson at Eagle Elementary School in West Bloomfield Township, Michigan, in March 2006. Under the federal No Child Left Behind Act, all students are to achieve proficiency in reading and math by 2014. Public schools must periodically test students in reading and math and report their overall measure of success. The law says that no student's scores can be excluded from the overall measure. As the text makes clear, controversy continues over this federal education law and the requirements for testing that it imposed on the nation's schools. Sharp divisions within Congress have kept policymakers from renewing and revising the law to respond to the critics. The Obama administration has pledged to reform the law and substantially increase funding for it.

mandate. A number of states introduced, and in some cases passed, bills challenging the legality of certain aspects of NCLB. Utah, where Republicans are in firm control of the legislature and governorship, passed legislation that allows schools to ignore NCLB in the event that it conflicts with state education laws or if it requires the state to use its resources to implement it (Mantel 2005). Connecticut actually sued the federal government and accused the Bush administration of being "rigid, arbitrary and capricious" in its enforcement of the law.[1]

In a report on NCLB the National Conference of State Legislatures raised a number of the state governments' concerns associated with this law. These range from funding levels and the federal government's role as noted just above to the stringency of standards and the lack of flexibility states have in meeting these standards.[2] Other criticisms of the law include concern over the requirement for what some see as overtesting, "teaching to the test," and disregarding other subject areas, to name but a few.

On the other hand, supporters of the law claim that it is leading to education improvements through better accountability of the school systems. How can we know how well the education system is working without such measures? In addition, they argue, federal funding for public education has increased 30 percent since NCLB was enacted. Many supporters of the law would argue that still more needs to be done. President Bush in 2004 proposed that testing should be expanded to include all high school years, intensifying much of the debate surrounding NCLB. There have also been calls for more accountability in the area of higher education as well, with some suggesting additional testing mechanisms for those attending college. On the other hand, there have been instances where the Department of Education has recognized some of the reporting concerns associated with NCLB and has provided more leeway to states and schools than what was considered during the initial years of the program. In addition, President Barack Obama has stated that he wants to "fix the broken promises of No Child Left Behind." Suffice it to say that there continues to be much discussion and debate about education, how to improve its quality, and how best to proceed. Time will tell how an Obama administration may try to address these issues.

Education is one of the public services that people take for granted. For some students, it provides the knowledge and skills that enable them to continue their studies in college. For many others, however, receiving a quality education is a difficult, if not impossible, task. Since the release of the federal report "A Nation at Risk" in 1983, concern has been growing about the quality of education in the United States. Although most people living in the United States are products of a public education system that has been in existence for almost as long as the nation itself, critics claim that the system is broken and that students are suffering from its inadequacies. Indeed, statistics suggest that U.S. students are not performing at the same levels as their counterparts in other countries. This chapter explores a number of different issues associated with education in the United States, but it returns to the primary issue: the quality of education and what policies, such as testing requirements imposed by NCLB, can be adopted to improve it for all students.

BACKGROUND

Education, especially public education, fulfills many of the nation's basic goals and has done so since the country's founding. First, according to the beliefs of Thomas Jefferson, it provides an avenue to ensure the continuation of U.S. democracy (Mayo 1942). How can people be active, engaged participants in democratic processes if they lack the ability to read and understand the issues? Second, education helps to assimilate large numbers of immigrants. Finally, it is the primary mechanism for social mobility in the United States, as the educated are better able to secure jobs that raise their economic and social status. This goal fits nicely with the American ideal of upward mobility and rewarding those who work hard. An educated population has a better chance of being productive and taking care of itself. Such people are less likely to need government assistance.

If one asks why government took it upon itself to provide education, it becomes apparent that the reasons were both moral and political. Morally, education was seen as a way to help individuals and groups in the population to understand the nation's ideals and to give them a chance to better themselves. Politically, education not only informed people about the U.S. system of government but also imparted the nation's political culture. In addition, it served the needs of certain political parties and helped those running for office to get elected. As we pointed out in chapter 1, public education also has been a response to market failure in that it is an example of a positive externality. Society benefits from a well-educated population, which justifies the government's involvement and support. The reasons for providing public education that existed years ago are still relevant as government policymakers deal with education policy today.

Traditionally, public education has been in the hands of state and local government. Policymakers at these levels have guarded this responsibility throughout the years and raised concerns whenever the federal government has attempted to interfere in education policy, especially in primary and secondary schools. State governments have the major responsibilities in education policy with respect to curriculum, teacher training and certification, and—to a greater degree than before—funding public schools. And a great deal of education policy remains under local control. Schoolteachers employed by local government comprise the largest category of public workers. There are close to fifteen thousand local school boards across the United States, all shaping education policy to some degree within their districts.[3]

This is not to say that the federal government has been completely absent from public education, but its involvement is relatively recent, and growing. Congress had passed ESEA, its first major education legislation, in 1965. The law raised the amount of federal funding for primary and secondary education (Thomas 1975). In 2005, for example, ESEA provided $25 billion in public school funding.[4] With federal funding came a variety of contentious issues, including whether the federal government would dictate what was taught and whether parochial schools should receive funding. ESEA also signaled the beginning of increased federal interest in public education. In fact, many elected officials and candidates for office from both political parties regard education as a high-priority issue and want to enact programs designed to improve it.

Historically, however, the federal government has demonstrated a greater interest in higher education than in primary or secondary education. Because education is associated with positive externalities, policymakers want to encourage individuals to attend college and to help defray the cost of doing so; in the end, the better-educated population stimulates economic growth. The national government also provides billions of dollars in research grants to universities every year that cover nearly all disciplines. These grants support basic research in the biomedical and other sciences through the National Institutes of Health (NIH) and the National Science Foundation (NSF). Grants from the NSF and other agencies fund applied research in support of space exploration, national defense, and environmental protection goals.

Among the early programs in support of higher education was the Morrill Act, approved in 1862. It helped to develop the nation's land-grant college system, which in turn contributed significantly to economic development during the nineteenth and twentieth centuries. Land-grant colleges focused initially on practical fields such as agriculture and engineering, but they eventually broadened their scope to include the full range of arts and sciences. Institutions such as Cornell University, Rutgers University, the University of Kentucky, and the University of Wisconsin were first established to foster research, development, and training to improve the practice and productivity of agriculture. These schools, and many others with similar backgrounds, have since blossomed into major centers of higher education. In addition, the federal government fully funds the service academies, such as the U.S. Military Academy at West Point, New York, and the U.S. Naval Academy at Annapolis, Maryland. It costs the government close to $60,000 per year for each student attending the naval academy.[5]

The federal government also assists the general student population and specific categories of individuals by making money available through direct payments and subsidized loans. Programs such as the GI Bill and the Pell Grant provide money directly to eligible students to make attending college more affordable. The GI Bill, originally the Servicemen's Readjustment Act of 1944, was instrumental in the decision of tens of thousands of veterans to attend college after World War II. Congress continues to update the law to help fund higher education programs for eligible veterans. The Pell Grant program offers awards—not loans—of as much as $4,731 (the 2008–2009 amount) to eligible undergraduates, depending on financial need and costs of attending college. Many other students benefit from guaranteed student loan programs. With federal guarantees for the loans, private financial institutions agree to lend money to students at a reduced interest rate, making college more accessible.

As even this brief introduction indicates, the federal government typically pays more attention to higher education than to elementary and secondary education, which state and local governments traditionally control. In recent years, however, the federal government has begun to respond to the problems in public education at all levels. For example, student performance statistics show wide variation in the quality of education from state to state, and the government has attempted to impose higher standards where needed. The federal government's participation has raised not only suspicion on the part of policymakers who oppose it but also questions about equity and freedom. Does increased federal involvement represent a genuine concern about the quality of education for all students? Or is it an unwarranted intrusion by federal policymakers into an area of public policy where state and local government officials are better able to determine public needs?

The federal government's role in primary and secondary education brings up many issues relating to the goals of education policy and the government's obligations in ensuring an educated public. In today's world, what are, or should be, the goals and objectives of education policy regardless of the level of government with primary responsibility? It would be easy to say that the goals of education policy are to provide a high-quality education to all students,

EDUCATIONAL GOALS:
DEFINITION AND EVALUATION

Goals are often difficult to define and evaluate. An abbreviated list of the goals associated with the Educate America Act appears below. In addition, you can find the detailed goals for the legislation at the Department of Education site: www.ed.gov/legislation/GOALS2000/TheAct/sec 102.html.

Goal 1: School Readiness
Goal 2: School Completion
Goal 3: Student Achievement and Citizenship
Goal 4: Teacher Education and Professional Development
Goal 5: Mathematics and Science
Goal 6: Adult Literacy and Lifelong Learning
Goal 7: Safe, Disciplined, and Alcohol- and Drug-Free Schools
Goal 8: Parental Participation

As you examine the details of the goals, you also can get a better sense of the type of measures being used to help evaluate whether or not success has been achieved. These goals were set with a deadline of 2000. How is the United States doing? Examine a couple of the goals below. For example, Goal 2: School Completion states:

(A) By the year 2000, the high school graduation rate will increase to at least 90 percent.
(B) The objectives for this goal are that—
   (i) the Nation must dramatically reduce its school dropout rate, and 75 percent of the students who do drop out will successfully complete a high school degree or its equivalent; and

(ii) the gap in high school graduation rates between American students from minority backgrounds and their nonminority counterparts will be eliminated.

Or Goal 5: Mathematics and Science states:

(A) By the year 2000, United States students will be first in the world in mathematics and science achievement.
(B) The objectives for this goal are that—
   (i) mathematics and science education, including the metric system of measurement, will be strengthened throughout the system, especially in the early grades;
   (ii) the number of teachers with a substantive background in mathematics and science, including the metric system of measurement, will increase by 50 percent; and
   (iii) the number of United States undergraduate and graduate students, especially women and minorities, who complete degrees in mathematics, science, and engineering will increase significantly.

How is the United States performing on these goals? Information for some of these goals can be accessed at the Department of Education's site on research and statistics at www.ed.gov/rschstat/landing.jhtml?src=rt. You may also want to visit sites for the National Center for Education Statistics and the National Assessment of Educational Progress. As you read these goals, also consider whether there may be other ways to measure success.

but that statement raises many additional questions, the most basic of which is, what constitutes "high quality"? The Department of Education, based on the Goals 2000: Educate America Act of 1994, established a list of national educational goals that can be found in the box "Steps to Analysis: Educational Goals: Definition, and Evaluation."

While the goals provided in this report provide some relatively specific ideas about the preferred direction for education, they tend to deal with a broad range of educational issues, including teacher training, not an overriding "theme" of the purpose of education in the United States.

PROBLEMS FACING EDUCATION

To provide the means for elementary and secondary schools to do the best they can for each student, policy analysts and policymakers need to address a number of problems and issues. Among them are funding for public schools, the separation of church and state, the quality of education, school vouchers, and the merit of a host of proposals—such as teacher standards and testing requirements—for improving the performance of public schools.

Funding

Traditionally, a significant portion of funding for public schools in the United States comes from local property taxes. In fact, it is this characteristic of education policy that has ensured that state and local governments maintain a large measure of control over school curriculums in their jurisdictions. This form of financing, however, has run into problems. First, in general, the property tax does not keep pace with the inflationary costs of providing an education; or, to use a tax policy term discussed in chapter 7, it is not *buoyant*. So while teacher salaries, textbooks, school supplies, and other costs continue to increase, the amount of money provided through property taxes remains unchanged. In essence, schools find themselves having to provide more services with fewer resources. This can be particularly problematic with increasing costs and an unwillingness of local or state government to increase revenue by raising property or state taxes.[6]

The second problem is equity. Property tax revenue directed to public schools varies considerably among the fifty states and within states. For example, in 2005–2006 New York spent $14,884 per student on public education, while Utah spent only about $5,437.[7] The result is that students from poor areas may be receiving a lower-quality education. Many believe that financing education with local property taxes is inequitable and should be replaced with a system of state or federal funding to ensure greater equality. Education funding is a topic ripe for policy analysis. The box "Steps to Analysis: State Education Funding" provides some guidance for engaging in this topic.

In response to political and legal pressures, some states have begun to change the way they finance their public schools. Michigan, for example, adopted a statewide sales tax that is to be distributed to the state's school districts according to need. Other states continue to use the property tax to fund schools, but have worked out a system of redistributing a portion of the revenue to poorer districts within the state. This egalitarian approach puts some politicians on the defensive. They have to explain why their constituents' property taxes are being used to

STATE EDUCATION FUNDING

The discussion of how states fund their public education systems suggests the importance of the different evaluative criteria discussed throughout the book. Questions of equity, political feasibility, economics, and effectiveness are particularly pertinent to this discussion. Which criteria do you think are the most important in examining education funding? Is one typically the "driving force" in making decisions regarding funding sources? States use a variety of ways to finance public education. Policy analysis can help you learn about these systems and what issues may be most important for specific states. Using the criteria discussed throughout the text, examine how two states fund their educational systems (elementary and secondary) and what criteria seem to be driving these decisions.

Search a particular state with the words *school funding* to get a listing of sites that address this issue. For each state you select, respond to the following questions:

- How does the state finance its public education system? What types of taxes or funding mechanisms are used?
- What criteria do you believe were the most important in making these funding decisions for the state?
- What challenges does the state now face regarding funding? What about future challenges?
- How has the state balanced issues of effectiveness, equity, and politics in making these decisions?

finance another child's education elsewhere in the state. When this issue arose in Vermont, its state supreme court ruled that an equal educational opportunity is a right that must be guaranteed by the state. Following the ruling, the state legislature passed Act 60, which uses a portion of the tax money from richer communities to help fund the schools in poorer districts. Some of the "gold towns" objected, and for a while they refused to provide their designated amounts to the state.[8] The squabble over tax money in Vermont is just one symptom of a more serious nationwide concern, which is the wide discrepancies between districts and the many school districts that are not adequately funded. State courts have decided that these differences are illegal and have sought solutions. Some have even suggested that state governments take on a greater role in the funding of public education to ensure greater equity.[9]

School funding has a direct bearing on the quality of education. School districts have to deal with growing costs and flat budget resources; some have to face the low end of unequal funding. Without adequate resources, schools cannot hire well-qualified teachers and other staff, provide the needed books and supplies, make use of computers and other technological resources, or even give students a clean and safe building in which to learn.

Separation of Church and State

The First Amendment to the U.S. Constitution provides, among other strictures, "Congress shall make no law respecting an establishment of religion, or prohibiting the free exercise thereof." These two clauses dealing with freedom of religion, the **Establishment Clause** and the **Free Exercise Clause,** established the concept that church and state are separate in the United States. Certain policies have come into conflict with these First Amendment clauses, and the conflicts continue to this day. Prayer in public schools and government funding of religious institutions of learning are the two leading areas of education policy that have caused disagreements and have led to Supreme Court cases.

The issue of prayer in public schools relates to both religion clauses. Opponents to school prayer argue that it represents an establishment of religion by government. If a public school or an official of the school, such as a teacher or principal, requires prayer in the classroom, then, according to judicial interpretations, the practice is state sponsorship of religion and a violation of the Establishment Clause. Even though a majority of the public supports some form of prayer in the schools, since the Supreme Court case *Engel v. Vitale* (1962), the courts have consistently ruled against any kind of school-sponsored prayer. The prohibition extends to student-led prayer in an officially sanctioned event such as a football game, as the Court ruled in *Santa Fe Independent School District v. Doe* (2000). The courts also have dealt with the so-called moment of silence or moment of reflection, and whether this practice also violates the Constitution's Establishment Clause. Politically, the moment of silence may be more acceptable because it involves no established prayer that could violate an individual's religious freedoms. It should also protect an individual's rights for the same reasons. Is there any reason to be opposed to school use of a moment of silence? Are the issues similar to school require-ment of a prayer?

But what about school prayer and the Free Exercise Clause, which states that the gov-ernment cannot prohibit the practice of religion? In theory, students who choose to pray on their own should have that right; that is, the school cannot prohibit students from engag-ing in prayer. In the *Santa Fe* case, the school district argued that preventing students from expressing their views amounted to an unconstitutional censorship of their speech. The Court did not agree with the argument, saying that the practice not only constituted an endorsement of religion but also was coercive in that it forced students who wished to attend school-sponsored activities, such as football games, to conform to a state-sponsored religious activity.

Public funding of religious schools is the other major issue related to the separation of church and state in education, and here the courts have been more lenient than on school prayer, despite some contradictory rulings. In general, if public money is being used for a secular purpose and the money is being provided to students rather than to the religious insti-tutions that run the schools, the courts have ruled public funding allowable. This issue took on added importance because of the growing popularity of school vouchers. The voucher pro-gram provides parents with public funds in the form of vouchers that they can use to send their children to private schools. Proponents of the voucher movement see it as a way to intro-duce competition into education and improve the quality of education across the board (Chubb and Moe 1990). The constitutional question is whether parents can use these pub-licly funded vouchers to send their children to parochial schools. The Supreme Court said yes, they could, when in *Zelman v. Simmons-Harris* (2002) it upheld the Cleveland voucher sys-tem, which the justices said did not violate the First Amendment. Even with the Supreme Court's ruling, though, this issue continues to be raised at the state level, where voucher opponents have brought suit in states such as Florida, stating that these programs violate state constitutional protections.

It should be clear that even a constitutional issue, such as the separation of church and state, relates to concerns about educational quality, especially public funding for parochial schools. Parents who believe their children are trapped in a poor public school have a strong incentive to look for alternative ways to improve their education and opportunities for the future.

Quality

Statistics support the concern about the quality of education in the United States. According to the Trends in International Mathematics and Science Study, conducted in 2007, U.S. eighth grade students scored above the international average in math and science but significantly below such countries as Chinese Taipei (Taiwan), Japan, and Korea in math. U.S. students trailed these countries, England, and the Russian Federation in science scores but outperformed thirty-seven other countries. Unfortunately, other studies suggest that U.S. students fall behind as they move into high school. The Program for International Student Assessment, conducted in 2003, shows that fifteen-year-old U.S. students had fallen below the Organisation for Economic Co-operation and Development's average in mathematics scores.[10] In addition, SAT scores, often used as a measure of college preparedness, went down for a number of years during the 1980s. Scores rebounded slightly during the 1990s and continued into the new century, but more recent years (2006 and 2007) have seen decreases in performance. Although these statistics may be questioned in terms of the validity of the measurements used, they do correspond with qualitative accounts of public education's failings in the United States. Does the information in the box "Steps to Analysis: Don't Know Much about History" prove that the lack of competence extends to social studies?

One problem is that defining what a quality education means is not so easy, but as public policy students have learned, it is necessary. The way a public problem is defined affects the appraisal of it, the alternatives that are considered, and the policies that might be adopted to deal with it. In that regard, education is no different from any other policy area. Education traditionalists suggest that quality is decreasing because schools are not emphasizing the basics such as math, English, reading, writing, and science in their teaching. By offering flexibility and electives, especially for secondary school students, the traditionalists say that the education system has moved away from its responsibilities of teaching the fundamental skills and subject matter and allowed quality to slip. Others argue that students need to be encouraged to learn and provided with opportunities to pursue their interests. The abilities to access, understand, and judge information and to work with others are more important than simply memorizing geometric theorems, chemical formulas, and the steps for how a bill becomes a law. These kinds of skills, proponents argue, create lifelong learners and will ultimately be of greater value to society. Unfortunately, such goals are much more difficult to measure and typically are not "tested" through the traditional quality measures.

So is the quality of education in the United States better or worse than in the past? This question may get a different answer, depending on what the respondent believes are the ultimate goals of the education system. But if one assumes that education quality *is* a problem

STEPS TO ANALYSIS

DON'T KNOW MUCH ABOUT HISTORY

The standards movement may be a direct result of national surveys of academic material that educators (and others) believe everyone in the population should know. In 2000 the American Council of Trustees and Alumni conducted a U.S. history poll of college seniors at what *U.S. News and World Report* names as the fifty-five top institutions. The results were not very promising. Eighty-one percent of the seniors received a D or an F. They could not identify Valley Forge and the principles of the Constitution. A more recent study by the nonprofit Intercollegiate Studies Institute found a similar lack of knowledge from college seniors. Here are several specific results from the two studies:

- Less than a quarter could identify James Madison as the father of the Constitution.
- Only 22 percent were able to identify the line "Government of the people, for the people and by the people" as part of the Gettysburg Address.

- More than a third did not know that the Constitution provides for a division of power in the United States.
- While more prestigious universities performed better, the highest school average was only a D+.

Why might college seniors not have a thorough knowledge of history? Is there another level of education that stresses history more than college? How important is this kind of knowledge? Do the results suggest that college seniors are not prepared to exercise their roles as citizens? As a policymaker, how could you respond to such a report? What initiatives are currently in place to address history education, and what could be done to strengthen them?

If you are interested in the Intercollegiate Studies Institute study, you can take the full quiz at www.americancivicliteracy. org/resources/quiz .aspx.

Sources: American Council of Trustees and Alumni, "Losing America's Memory: Historical Illiteracy in the 21st Century," 2000, available at www.goacta.org/publications/downloads/LosingAmerica'sMemory.pdf; and Tracey Wong Briggs, "College Students Struggle on History Test," *USA Today,* September 19, 2007, available at www.usatoday.com/ news/education/ 2007-09-17-history-test_N.htm.

compared to the past, why is this so? What variables might be explored to improve the education system? What can be changed to help students learn more effectively?

One area of exploration is **teacher quality.** Some analysts assert that current teachers have less skill and knowledge than teachers did in the past. A study conducted by the American Council on Education, for example, found that more than half of the students in grades seven through twelve have unqualified teachers for the physical sciences. Another study by the Education Trust found that a quarter of all high school classes are taught by out-of-field instructors—teachers who did not major or minor in the subject area—and the rate increases dramatically for schools in poorer areas. In fact, the study also found that no progress had been made on this score since the 1993–1994 academic year and that the problem is worse in middle schools than in high schools, with 44 percent of the classes taught by out-of-field instructors. A more recent report continues to show a concern with out-of-field teachers, particularly in high minority–high poverty schools. The problem remains more pervasive in middle school.[11]

If the quality of teachers is lower today, what are the reasons? Another study provided a different perspective. It showed that one in five teachers leaves the profession after only three years, and those who do so are more likely to have been in the top of their education classes when they graduated.[12] A common explanation is that teachers are paid far less than those in other professions with comparable educational requirements. From an economic standpoint, why should good students become teachers and earn a starting salary in the high twenties when they can choose another field and make substantially more money? Another reason may be the level of respect for the teaching profession. The old adage "Those who can, do; those who can't, teach" suggests that people become teachers by default because they cannot succeed in other professions. Outsiders may see teaching as an easy job because teachers get the summers off. What they do not see is that teachers are on nine-month contracts and get paid accordingly. Moreover, teachers may become discouraged about their jobs. The classroom atmosphere is different from the way it was thirty or forty years ago. School violence, crowded classrooms, and pupils' unstable family situations have made it more difficult for students to learn, and fewer of them are inspired to become teachers than in the past.

Another explanation for the disappointing quality of education centers on the students themselves. Teachers who have been in the field for some time often compare the present situation to how things "used to be." Students today spend more time watching television, working, texting, going online and "Facebooking" with friends, or playing video games and less time reading and focusing on schoolwork.[13] In addition, the increase in families headed by one parent or in which both parents work, along with other changes in home life, have likely hindered the ability of students to learn.

As mentioned at the beginning of the chapter, one response to poor-quality education has been moving toward increased testing requirements for students. In order for students to move on to the next grade or perhaps to graduate, they must meet the appropriate standards. President Bush's signing of NCLB in 2002 ushered in this movement at the federal level and involved the federal government more directly in educating the nation's children than in the past. NCLB requires student testing as one mechanism to try to close the education gap. The law requires states and school districts to be accountable for student performance. Under its provisions, all states will administer a single test, the **National Assessment of Educational Progress,** to determine if the schools are meeting the appropriate standards. Schools that fail to improve for two years in a row could receive more federal funds, but if improvement still does not occur, the money could be used to provide tutoring or to move students to different schools. One goal of the standards movement is to prevent "social promotions." According to the testing proponents, the requirements ensure that students are promoted based on their understanding of the material.

Many other issues affect the quality of education. Inadequate facilities, increases in student violence, and high student-faculty ratios are just a few of the many variables frequently associated with school quality. All are fruitful areas for investigation and public policy analysis.

HIGHER EDUCATION ISSUES

Unlike primary and secondary education, attending college is not a requirement; rather, it is a student's personal choice. But it is becoming increasingly clear that a higher education may be necessary for a wider range of careers and jobs than before. Perhaps this is one reason why governments get involved by encouraging students in many ways to continue their education. President Obama has also made higher education a policy priority. In his first speech to Congress as president, he stated his goal of having the highest proportion of college graduates in the world by 2020. The achievement of that goal is directly affected by the one of the issues discussed below—the cost of going to college. The other issue concerns doing a better job in making higher education a goal for a wider diversity of people in the United States.

Affirmative Action

For years, many colleges and universities, in the name of promoting diversity in their student bodies, have given admissions preferences to certain demographic groups such as African Americans or Hispanic Americans. Many administrators and faculty members argued that a more diverse student body adds value to the education of all the students at a college or university. For that reason, they believed it was justifiable, indeed essential, to admit some students whose academic work or test scores may not have been at the same level as others but whose other qualities enriched the campus community.

A number of states have moved to eliminate these kinds of preference programs from their state institutions. Many college administrators at other institutions, such as former University of Michigan president Lee Bollinger, believe that racial diversity is critical to the goals of education (Jost 2001). At most schools, the effect of eliminating these programs is likely to be minor. It is at the more selective institutions—the elite schools—where they currently have the greatest effect. Do declines in minority admissions, especially at elite schools, pose a significant problem? Some worry about fostering even greater inequalities between elite and nonelite universities than have existed for some time. Those who favor the abolition of affirmative action programs, however, see nonaffirmative action admissions practice as more equitable to all the applicants. The students who score lower on SATs and other admission criteria are not being denied a higher education, but they may have to choose a less competitive institution.

From a policy analysis perspective, how might one examine the issue of affirmative action programs in higher education? There are obvious ethical and fairness issues associated with affirmative action, but naturally, proponents and opponents of affirmative action programs both defend their positions in terms of equity. Proponents of affirmative action might point out that in the past minorities were excluded from many institutions of higher learning. In addition, many minorities have faced discrimination and inadequate preparation to attend elite schools, and affirmative action programs help to level the playing field. Opponents argue that it is unfair to give preferences just because of racial characteristics. They strongly defend the position that admission to college should be based on individual abilities rather than demographic characteristics. Any other method, they say, is unfair.

Have affirmative action programs been effective? That depends on one's definition of the problem. More minorities are attending college than ever before, and these increases are across the board in terms of the quality of the institution. A study by William G. Bowen and Derek C. Bok (1998) found that affirmative action programs in highly selective institutions have been successful in educating and promoting the students who benefited from the admissions policy. This particular study, however, is somewhat limited because it concentrates on selective institutions rather than a broader range of schools. Many institutions assert that affirmative action programs are effective because they reach the goal of diversified student bodies. But are the programs effective if they also deny admission to qualified students?[14]

College admissions are partially a zero-sum game. In any given year or program, each university has only so many openings, and competition can be fierce for the highly selective schools. One person's admission results in another's denial. In June 2003, the Supreme Court ruled on two University of Michigan cases dealing with affirmative action admission procedures. The ruling was somewhat complex: it stated that minorities could be given an edge for admissions but limited the extent that race could play as a factor in selecting students. Subsequent years have found that schools such as the University of Michigan and Ohio State University saw only slight decreases in the number of minority students accepted, but that they spent considerably more time on the applicant evaluation process.[15]

Costs of Higher Education

Most readers of this text need no reminder that the costs of college education are substantial and continue to rise. For much of the past several decades, they have been rising faster than the rate of inflation. In 2007, for example, public higher education costs rose 4.2 percent, which was about twice the rate of inflation.[16] Because a college education is regarded as essential for a competitive and productive workforce and for maintaining economic growth, the ever-higher price tag for a college degree is alarming. The cost of attending a private college or university can be prohibitive. For example, at Harvard University the 2008–2009 comprehensive fee (tuition and room and board) was over $47,000—although, as with other private institutions, scholarships often lower the cost. Many students who might have considered private institutions have turned instead to public colleges and universities, which almost always cost less. Attending the University of Wisconsin in 2008–2009, for example, cost a little more than $19,000 for tuition and room and board for in-state residents and more than $33,000 for out-of-state residents.

Given the costs, one of the most important issues in higher education is the level of state support provided to students, especially those attending state institutions. Students may consider such support to be unexceptional, much as they expect the public to pay for the cost of elementary and secondary education, but public support for higher education raises important questions of equity. Should state governments be providing such subsidies for individuals to attend college? Or should individuals be responsible for paying their own college costs on the grounds that they are getting the benefits, such as enhanced social and economic status, that a college education usually provides? If some amount of subsidy is warranted, how much is justifiable? Equity questions like these arise because public subsidies for higher education involve a transfer of income from those who do not attend college to those who do; that is, state residents pay the taxes that support higher education, but not all the residents or members of their families attend college. To be sure, everyone

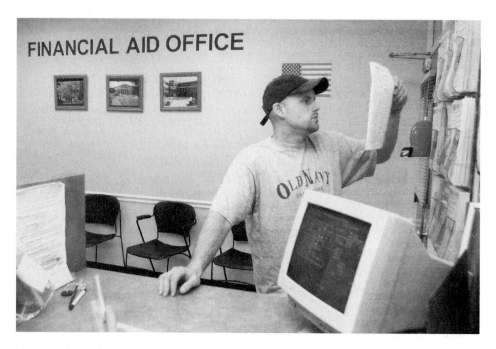

Like countless other students nationwide, this undergraduate at Middle Tennessee University knows well that the costs of higher education—from tuition to books, housing, and special fees—keep rising. This puts more students in need of more scholarships and loans to cover the bills. The situation is not likely to get better anytime soon as most states face looming deficits and are unlikely to increase their budgets for higher education. State support for higher education has declined appreciably over the past several decades in the face of competing demands, including rising state Medicaid and incarceration costs.

benefits from having a well-educated population, but even taking that point into account, inequities exist.

Even though the subsidies continue, in almost every state they cover a smaller percentage of college and university operating budgets than they did in the past. State support for higher education has gone down over the past twenty years as competition for funding has increased, particularly from the prison systems and state support for Medicaid and other social service programs. Colleges and universities therefore raise tuition to make up for the shortfall. According to the Postsecondary Education Opportunity, between fiscal years 1976 and 2005, every state had cut its appropriations to higher education from a low of 3.4 percent to as much as 69.6 percent. The average cut across all states was 34.7 percent.[17] A more recent study by the State Higher Education Executive Officers reported similar results comparing state support in 2007 to that of 2002. On average, states decreased their support per full-time equivalent by 7.7 percent, and only fifteen states increased their support, although states did better in 2007.[18] Finally, a 2008 study by the National Center for Public Policy and Higher Education gave every state but California a failing grade when it came to the criteria of affordability.[19] For public institutions to continue to operate at the same level as in previous years, one must expect future increases in tuition. According to the authors of the study, if this trend continues, state funding for higher education will reach zero by the year 2036, a frightening possibility.

As many colleges and universities have attempted to compete for students, there has also been a tendency to provide more scholarship money based on merit than on need. While it is difficult to argue against merit-based scholarships, it is also clear that a larger proportion of these dollars is likely to go to middle- to upper-income families, thus providing less financial help for low-income students. Is the decrease of government funding, coupled with the increase in merit-based financial aid, pricing some students out of going to college? Are we in danger of a college education being a good only the elite can afford?

Some state and federal programs have helped to ameliorate the impact of these rising costs. Georgia, for example, offers Hope Scholarships to seniors graduating with better than a B grade-point average. President Bill Clinton signed into law a similar policy that provides a tax credit for part of the costs of the first two years of attending college. Other federal financial programs have also been put into place to help alleviate the costs of higher education. These kinds of programs raise the same equity concerns as the state-supported plans because such policies involve a redistribution of income. In addition, which students are more likely to achieve a B average or higher and thus qualify for the HOPE Scholarship program? Students from a middle or upper-middle-class background or from a working-class or blue-collar background? Students from cash-strapped inner-city schools or from well-supported suburban high schools? Can such programs be justified on the basis of equity or fairness?

Although higher education costs provoke considerable debate, the value of a college education cannot be overestimated. On average, students with a bachelor's degree or higher earn substantially more than those who only complete high school. Based on 2007 data, both men and women over the age of twenty-five with a bachelor's or higher degree earn on average over 50 percent more than those without a college degree.[20] Although it seems apparent that a college education is highly valued, the box "Steps to Analysis: Where Are the Guys?" points out that one group of potential students is becoming smaller.

It is also evident that many students place a high value on attending some of the most prestigious colleges and universities despite what other people believe are exorbitant costs. Clearly, they think their investment in such a college degree will prove to be worth it over time. Much the same is true of students who pay high tuition costs to attend professional graduate programs in law, medicine, or business administration. They expect to recoup their investment many times over once they graduate and begin work.

As mentioned, education is also a positive externality in that society benefits from a more educated population. Individuals typically will make more money with a college degree, but what about the return on a state's investment through tuition subsidization? A number of studies have examined the economic impact of higher education spending, and they suggest that such spending is a good investment for the state. For example, it is estimated that the state of Texas receives a $5.50 return for every dollar spent on higher education. Another study of the University of Wisconsin system found a number of positive economic benefits as a result of state support. These included a $9.5 billion economic contribution, direct and indirect job creation, and a positive state tax revenue generation. This economic benefit of over $9 billion compares to an approximate $1 billion state expenditure provided to the University of

WHERE ARE THE GUYS?

The Mortenson Research Seminar has observed a disturbing trend in higher education today, other than increasing costs. The Mortenson seminar documents the decreasing percentage of men going to college and receiving degrees. In 1950 more than 76 percent of the bachelor's degrees were awarded to men. In 1996 this percentage fell to just under 45 percent, and it is projected to continue to shrink.

The good news is that women are taking advantage of opportunities for higher education, but one must wonder why the rate for men is falling. The trends for college attendance are evident across a variety of demographic characteristics and academic disciplines. Although the traditionally male-dominated academic fields, such as engineering and business, continue to have a higher percentage of men, the gender gap is disappearing. For example, in 1970 men received more than 91 percent of the business degrees, but in 1996 nearly equal numbers of men and women received business degrees.

If these statistics have not alarmed you, try this one: if the current trend continues (which is highly unlikely), all of the graduates in 2068 will be women. The trend also raises important social and family issues. If all women college graduates choose to marry after college, 66 percent of them will not marry a male college graduate. Christina

Hoff Sommers of the American Enterprise Institute asks, "What does it mean in the long run that we have females who are significantly more literate, significantly more educated than their male counterparts? It is likely to create a lot of social problems" (Fletcher 2002).

Think about the following issues regarding this information. You can find additional information at www.ecs.org/html/offsite.asp?document=http%3A%2F%2Fwww%2Ences%2Eed%2Egov%2Fpubs2005%2F2005169%2Epdf.

- Why is using forecasting or trend analysis problematic in evaluating the number of males attending college?
- What might be some of the reasons why there have been decreases in the percentage of male participants in college and increases in female participation? How can the public policy student find out what is causing the shift in male and female college attendance?
- What types of "social problems" might Sommers be referring to in her comments above?
- Does the situation constitute a problem that merits government concern, or is this an issue in which government should not intervene? Why or why not?

Source: Mortenson Research Seminar on Public Policy Analysis of Opportunity for Postsecondary Education, "Where Are the Guys?" *Postsecondary Education Opportunity* 76 (October 1998).

Wisconsin system, which would suggest that state support for the university is a good economic investment.[21] These represent tangible returns to a state economy and may justify political movements to try to stop the downward trend of state support for higher education. This belief is likely shared by other nations of the world that provide free or greatly reduced tuition to their students and in some cases a monthly stipend to continue their education. In some cases, these nations, such as those in the European Union, may even pay for the education for students not from their own country.

EDUCATION POLICY REFORMS

It is not surprising that many of the education reforms that policymakers and others have proposed, debated, and implemented originated as a response to their concern over the quality of education. This section assesses some of these ideas for reform and their potential impact.

Merit Pay

One of the most divisive issues concerning education and quality is the system most public schools use to pay their teachers. In general, teachers get raises based on their years of service. Although there may be good reasons to provide raises based on longevity, critics say that teachers have little incentive to change their methods to improve their teaching. Many workers in the United States get raises based on performance, but teachers, regardless of the quality of their work, generally are not held to such a standard. To correct what they see as a flaw in the system, some reformers have promoted the idea of tying teacher salary increases to merit. **Merit pay,** according to supporters of this plan, should lead to better education as teachers improve themselves to be eligible for greater raises or promotions. Some states have implemented merit pay systems in their school districts with varying success. Districts in Denver and Douglas County, Colorado, have claimed success in implementing such systems with the help and support of the teachers.[22] As a presidential candidate, Senator Obama proposed that some form of merit pay should be implemented to help improve the education system, and it will be interesting to watch during his administration if this support will continue. The current chancellor of the Washington, D.C., public school district, Michelle Rhee, has promoted such a system, as well as a potential elimination of the tenure process. Due to the physical location, President Obama's support for this initiative may be necessary for such reforms in the nation's capital's school district.

Opponents raise several issues about linking pay increases to performance. First, no objective or agreed-upon measurement has yet been formulated for what constitutes an effective or quality teacher. Using student performance as an indicator of quality disregards other factors that may affect how students perform in the classroom. In addition, tying merit pay to student performance may produce some possibly undesirable incentives in the education system as the pressure mounts on schools to ensure high scores or for teachers to receive bonuses. A *Newsweek* article spotlighted a number of situations in which teachers cheated by providing answers to students during standardized tests or by teaching to the exam. According to a related *Newsweek* article, students reported that a principal told them, "You might want to look at this one again," held up a map, and pointed to the country about which the students were being questioned.[23] Without some agreement as to what makes a quality teacher, bias and inequity could taint the assessments. Second, many argue that until teacher salaries are competitive with those of other occupations, merit pay will not succeed in attracting and retaining highly qualified people. Third, opponents point out that merit pay does not achieve the stated goal. A report from the California State University Institute for Education Reform found that merit pay systems reward a small percentage of the teachers as individuals (in contrast to recognizing the value of team-based activities) without addressing the overall problems of education quality. In addition, the study reported that funding for such programs is not maintained, resulting in "pervasive cynicism among teachers about new pay schemes."[24]

The American Federation of Teachers has promoted a related proposal that would provide significant salary increases to those who become board certified by the National Board for Professional Teaching Standards. This nonprofit organization has set standards for teacher excellence and is analogous to boards that certify doctors.[25] By having specific standards that teachers must meet and demonstrate, this process is not only objective but also offers a monetary incentive for teachers to pursue excellence in the classroom. In addition, it brings an element of professional status that sometimes is lacking in the education field. For more information regarding the standards, access the organization's Web site at www.nbpts.org.

Teacher Standards

Related to merit pay are proposals for teachers to meet certain standards to become and remain certified in the profession. Requiring a uniform level of competency for teaching should ensure a better quality education for the students. For example, the standards would end the practice of assigning teachers to courses in fields that are not among their specialties.

Requiring a **competency test** for teachers is not without its problems. The validity of any kind of standardized test, for example, can be questioned. One can also ask which kind of expertise is more important, knowledge of the content (substance) or ability to transmit that knowledge (pedagogy)? The quick answer is that they are equally important. But the reality is that the nation already suffers from a teacher shortage in some subject and geographical areas, and imposing additional requirements may intensify the problem. Rather than using a test to certify teaching competence, states such as Indiana and Connecticut have focused on programs that help current teachers improve their skills. The development of more stringent standards can be part of this process. Indiana, for example, adopted a rigorous set of standards developed by the National Board for Professional Teaching Standards as part of its licensing system. Connecticut adopted similar standards that teachers must meet within three years, and the state can dismiss them if they fail (Billitteri 1997). School districts need to maintain a balance because if the standards become too onerous, the schools may not have enough qualified teachers, at least in the short term. A teacher shortage is not all bad news, however. Over time it would likely cause teacher salaries to rise, which in turn might make the profession more attractive to those who would not otherwise consider it.

Teacher Salaries

Few would dispute the importance of ensuring that the nation's children receive a quality education and develop a capacity to participate actively in the economy and government, and few doubt that the majority of U.S. residents strongly support a better education system. Even so, teacher salaries continue to seriously lag behind what other professions earn. Table 10-1 shows starting salaries for selected occupations in 2006. Proponents of higher teacher salaries argue that if teachers are professionals, their school districts must pay them as such.

The pay scale has likely contributed to a mismatch between the great demand for teachers, especially in urban school districts, and the supply of individuals willing to accept such

TABLE 10-1	Median Salaries of Selected Occupations, 2006	
Occupation		**Median Salary**
Computer scientist		$93,950
Electrical engineer		75,930
Chemical engineer		78,860
Accountant		54,630
Mathematician		86,930
Teacher		46,135

Source: U.S. Bureau of Labor Statistics, *Occupational Outlook Handbook,* 2008-2009, available at www.bls.gov/OCO.

positions. According to the report *The Urban Teacher Challenge,* most of the major-city school districts reported teacher shortages in special education, math, and science. The study also estimated that approximately seven hundred thousand new teachers would be needed in major urban school districts in the coming decade. Similar concerns are also present in rural districts and in certain fields such as science and math.[26] Without pay raises, the teacher shortage problem will likely continue. The right salaries, however, can turn the situation around quickly. In 2002 New York City nearly eliminated its teacher shortage by offering attractive financial incentives to recruit new teachers despite the difficult working conditions in many parts of the city. By offering higher salaries, New York City could draw qualified people from other teaching jobs and in other professions who were willing to change careers.[27]

School Vouchers, School Choice, and Charter Schools

Local school boards have traditionally drawn district lines that determine which school each student attends. Unless parents decide to send their children to a private school, students go to the school generally closest to where they live in the district. One way to look at the students in a particular school district is as a captive market whose single provider (a monopoly) supplies their public school education. Americans traditionally mistrust business monopolies, believing that they can increase prices indiscriminately or offer lower-quality goods and services, but consumers have little or no choice. Monopolies are seen as inefficient in a market system, and such companies have no incentive to improve on quality if consumers have nowhere else to turn. Some analysts see the same lack of competition in education (Chubb and Moe 1990). Schools do not need to improve their product because they have a guaranteed market. In essence, public schools are a government-sponsored monopoly.

Many have argued that in order to break up the public school monopoly, society needs to reform the system in a way that gives parents options about where to send their children to school. Among the suggested reforms are school choice, school vouchers, and charter schools. Supporters argue that when parents can exercise choice, the schools will compete for students by providing higher-quality education, and the competition will raise the level of quality for everyone. The No Child Left Behind Act brought school choice to the forefront by giving parents the ability to switch schools if their original school does not meet the appropriate standards. The offending schools must take on the financial burden of transporting these students to new schools.

School choice programs allow parents to send their children to any public school in a particular area. The competition is among public schools only, not between public and private schools, but these programs do foster competition. With school choice programs, school selection is no longer based on school districts but where the child might get the kind of education desired. If the chosen school also receives government funding associated with the child, then this arrangement should spur competition. The various schools might try to improve the education they offer to maintain or even increase the size of their student body. It should be noted that many education reformers use the term *school choice* to encompass all reform efforts that provide parents with options about where to send their children, including charter schools and voucher programs.

School vouchers, theoretically, are also intended to improve education by promoting competition among schools. The major difference is that with school vouchers, the government provides a certain dollar amount that parents can then apply to private or parochial school tuition or as part of the full cost of a public school education. The government voucher normally is not enough to cover the full cost of tuition, but it allows parents the choice of sending a child to a private school by relieving the family of part of the financial burden. In this way, the government encourages competition by bringing private schools into the education market. In addition, proponents argue that the voucher system will improve the quality of all schools; to entice students to enroll, administrators will do everything they can to improve their schools and compete in this open market.

Most school voucher systems currently in place in the United States, including the best-known plans in Cleveland and Milwaukee, are limited in that they are aimed at assisting low-income students. For example, to be eligible for a voucher in the Milwaukee program, a family of four must have an income no higher than about $37,400 a year. School voucher purists would support a universal voucher system in which every family would receive a designated amount of money for their children's education.

The school voucher programs became politicized when opponents, who see them as unconstitutional, took the school boards to court asserting that the school voucher programs could violate an individual's religious freedom and the principle of separation of church and state. They argued that giving public money to parents to send their children to parochial schools is a clear violation of the First Amendment because, no matter what the religious denomination, the funds are being used to promote religion. *Zelman v. Simmons-Harris,* the Supreme Court's 2002 decision regarding Cleveland's voucher system, perhaps has clarified the legal environment surrounding school voucher programs. The decision affected the voucher debate, but it remains unclear exactly what the full effects will be. Voucher opponents had hoped that the constitutional issues would be resolved in their favor. With that option gone, the debate moved into other policy-making arenas, such as state courts, state legislatures, and referendums.[28] A number of questions remain regarding school vouchers: Are resources being transferred from the public to the private schools, and is this equitable? Who should be eligible for vouchers? Should it be based on need?

Of course, a primary issue must be whether voucher programs have been successful. Often, the different sides of the voucher debate use the same researchers or studies to

President Barack Obama and First Lady Michelle Obama read aloud to second graders during a visit to Washington, D.C.'s Capital City Public Charter School in February 2009. Charter schools, independent schools authorized to provide educational services with limited control by a school board, have become increasingly popular in many cities as parents have found the public schools falling short of their expectations. Yet questions remain about whether charter schools are more effective than public schools, and the evidence to date is mixed.

prove their point. Opponents cite a number of studies suggesting that voucher programs have minimal effects at best in improving education programs.[29] Studies by John F. Witte et al. (1995, 1997, 2000), Cecilia E. Rouse (1997), and Kim Metcalf et al. (1998) all find that voucher programs are not as effective as proponents claim and that other, more accessible programs can provide better results. Witte's study of the Milwaukee voucher program found that, in relation to student outcomes, "There is no consistent and reliable evidence that the students differed in achievement from randomly selected Milwaukee Public School students" (Witte 2000, 143). According to this collection of studies, therefore, the current school voucher programs have had somewhat limited results. Naturally, supporters of school voucher programs point to their own set of studies, or even parts of the same studies, that contradict the arguments of their opponents. The Heritage Foundation, for example, cites studies by Kim Metcalf (1999) and Paul E. Peterson, William G. Howell, and Jay P. Green (1999) that found positive effects associated with voucher programs. According to Heritage, the Metcalf study found that "Cleveland scholarship students show a small but statistically significant improvement in achievement scores in language and science," and Peterson et al. claim that parents are more satisfied with many aspects of the school they chose (Shokrail Rees 2000). A study by Cecilia E. Rouse (1998), using data from the Milwaukee school choice program

similar to that used by Witte, found a positive effect on math scores for students participating in the choice program. Finally, a major study conducted by William G. Howell
and Paul E. Peterson (2002) found that the use of vouchers had a significant impact on
the success of African American students. Using this measure of effectiveness, that is,
whether the program improves educational success for a particular demographic group,
is another way researchers can present their results and voucher proponents can claim
success. When making policy, one must be careful with the results of such studies.
Researchers later found the study by Peterson et al., for example, to be inconclusive in
terms of improving scores.[30] Unfortunately, organizations with a particular bias will take
advantage of some of these nuances when making their claims in support of or in opposition to the voucher programs.[31]

The **charter school** is another way of introducing choice into education. Charter schools
are unique in that they are government supported but independent. A state board of education gives an independent entity the responsibility of establishing a school and delivering
education services with limited control by the school board. The state funds these schools,
but the regulations that typically govern public schools are significantly reduced to allow the
schools to have a particular focus. Some examples of charter schools in Illinois illustrate their
variety. The Academy of Communications and Technology seeks to prepare students for
careers in communications and computer technology. The Young Women's Leadership
Charter School follows the small schools' model and focuses on academic achievement. It
offers a rigorous career and college preparatory curriculum that emphasizes math, science,
and technology; leadership; and personal and social development. Charter schools may
choose to pursue certain educational needs or strategies to improve student performance, and
they are responsible for meeting the standards they develop. The number of charter schools
is growing, with more than 4,300 operating in 2008.[32] Some see charter schools as just
another form of voucher system because the state is paying for them while perhaps reducing
the funding for traditional public schools. The question of whether charter schools are a
more effective way to educate students is still open to debate. The evidence to date is mixed
regarding whether students in charter schools perform significantly better. This is a difficult
question to research because of the different types of state laws and schools that are in existence. This is also the case for voucher schools. The other question relates to whether the existence of these schools may be improving educational effectiveness for the public schools; the
evidence here is also mixed.[33]

FOCUSED DISCUSSION: SCHOOL TESTING AND EDUCATIONAL QUALITY

This chapter opened with a discussion of the No Child Left Behind Act (NCLB). It
specifically addressed the issue of standardized testing as a potential way to improve failing schools and prevent inadequate quality in the U.S. public education system. When
enacted in 2002, NCLB represented a dramatic shift in the role of the federal government in public education. The testing requirement was one of the largest changes to
education policy and, in some ways, probably the most controversial. This controversy
increased in subsequent years as states complained about inadequate federal funding and

One of the more pressing issues in education policy today concerns the relationship between testing and educational quality. As the No Child Left Behind Act is further evaluated and Congress takes on the task of reforming the law, the value of testing and how it should be imposed on the nation's schools is sure to be among the major questions addressed. Here, tenth grade students take a chemistry test at Springfield High School in Springfield, Illinois. A 2007 Associated Press analysis of state data found a 28 percent gap on average between the percentage of elementary pupils meeting or exceeding standards on tests and high school students doing the same. Nationwide, schools have struggled to raise achievement levels and test scores in anticipation that the federal law could impose penalties on underachieving schools in the near future.

many educators questioned the relevance of standardized testing in improving education quality.

The Bush administration has come to an end and the Obama administration is in its early stages, but debate concerning whether the school testing requirements imposed by NCLB improve education continues. President Bush defended the testing requirement up to his final days in the White House and even warned incoming president Obama against any major changes to the law. President Bush argued that without tests, or some other form of measurement, how can one be sure that students are getting the appropriate education? Shouldn't parents be made aware if their children's schools are not adequate? Not everyone agrees, however, that testing—or perhaps the term is *overtesting*—is the right policy choice. Will the increase in testing lead to less classroom instruction? Will teachers "teach to the test" to be sure the children will pass? Another concern causing discord is the threat of losing federal aid. Should the government stop funding schools that do not improve? What additional problems could arise as a result of cutting aid to schools to ensure compliance with the standards?

Standardized testing creates its own problems. First, the way the exams are written and graded may introduce racial or cultural bias. Second, is the imposition of such standards an infringement on state and local education? Third, the testing is expensive. Could the resources be put to better use in the classroom? A related issue is the amount of classroom time devoted to testing, which can then not be used for content instruction. The federal requirements also have encouraged states to reassess their existing standards or issue new ones that students must meet in specific subject areas. Given that these state standards may differ considerably from one another, is it wise to allow such variation, given that people frequently move to pursue employment opportunities or for other reasons?[34] Anna Quindlen argued in a *Newsweek* column that "constant testing will no more address the problems of our education system than constantly putting an overweight person on the scale will cure obesity."[35] Her point was that testing is occurring for the sake of testing and not to make curricular changes that may improve learning. But what if the results of these tests are being used to improve the curriculum?

The policy analysis framework used throughout the book can be used to explore the major questions in this ongoing debate. In this case, some of the major analytic criteria used to study this issue include economic costs or efficiency, politics and political feasibility, effectiveness, and equity. What are the economic impacts of these testing programs on state governments? Are they adequately funded, or is this an unfunded mandate? What are the political issues surrounding the testing debate? Perhaps most important, are such testing programs effective in improving education?

Economic Issues

In terms of school testing, the economic issues that need to be considered are the cost of this expanded testing and who is responsible for bearing it. It is clear that the federal government is providing more resources as a result of NCLB, but federal funding of education is still a minor proportion (about 8–9 percent) of all K–12 funding. In addition, the increase in federal funding, as a result of NCLB, represents only a 2 percent increase in aggregate K–12 revenue.[36] The concern raised by many states and interest groups is the adequacy of this funding. Even legislators who originally supported NCLB are now opposing the law, mainly because of the funding issue. The issue comes down to determining the true costs of implementing the law compared to the amount of funding being provided.

Determining the cost of a program often involves questions of measurement. As we have discussed in previous chapters, appropriate measurement is extremely important in policy analysis and policymaking in order to fully understand the nature of a problem. Several studies have examined funding levels, and in every case their cost estimates differ. This is often due to different interpretations of what to include as costs. Estimates have ranged from surpluses to major shortfalls in funding (Mantel 2005). As mentioned earlier, the National Conference of State Legislatures claimed that funding was a concern in the implementation of the law. While the increase in federal dollars may "marginally" cover the administrative or compliance costs of the law, not enough funding is provided for states to offer appropriate programs to raise the proficiency of their students. Compliance costs include administering tests, data analysis and reporting, and getting teachers to meet the "highly qualified" standards. Proficiency costs are associated with activities the schools implement to increase student achievement; they can include a wide range of programs. What are the legitimate costs that states should expect the federal government to fund as a result of NCLB?

Advocates of NCLB question the claims that states are not adequately funded. They believe the argument regarding the proficiency costs is irrelevant because schools can reallocate existing funding if necessary to implement new programs. In addition, meeting the 100 percent proficiency is not a requirement of the law, so including costs to get to this level is inaccurate and not justified. A number of studies have shown NCLB funding to be adequate to meet current goals of the program.[37]

The other component related to costs and economic efficiency concerns the administration of the program by various state education departments. In many cases, these bureaucracies have not implemented testing to the degree required by NCLB. It is possible that many of these agencies need more staff to deal with the additional workload as well as to acquire the appropriate expertise to run the programs. It is unlikely that the additional federal funding will provide the resources for these administrative needs.

Political Issues

The political issues surrounding NCLB and particularly student testing have been at the forefront of the discussion. Education quality is something that almost everyone can agree needs to be improved, but many disagree on how to measure quality or what mechanisms to use to try to improve it. When President Bush was governor of Texas, he implemented a statewide testing requirement that some data suggested led to the "Texas miracle." According to then Governor Bush, testing and similar accountability measures were the primary reason for an improvement in the public schools in Texas. And if it can work in Texas there is no reason to believe that it would not work for all of the United States. Education quality generally has been on the agenda, and a number of policymakers from both parties were looking for some major changes that would improve quality. Hence, during the development of NCLB there was strong bipartisan support that facilitated its passage in Congress and ultimately its approval by President Bush. However, political support has since weakened.

Within the interest group community, some conservative organizations and think tanks support standards and testing requirements, perhaps out of loyalty to the former president. On the other hand, libertarian think tanks such as the Cato Institute are not strong supporters of these federal standards and testing requirements and have even called for not reauthorizing the law.[38] In Cato's view, this is an area of policy best left to the states, one in which the federal government has no place.

Organizations representing teachers, such as the National Education Association (NEA) and the American Federation of Teachers (AFT), have not been strong supporters of the testing requirements. While supporting the goals of raising student achievement and performance gaps, the NEA questions whether the current approach of testing and punishment is the right way to achieve the desired outcomes. The NEA raises concerns regarding standardized tests being the only means of determining student learning. These tests can provide important information that may be used to help instruction, it claims, but they should not be used as the only accountability measure.[39] This has been an issue in some states that have required students to pass tests in order to graduate from high school. In a number of cases, good students have been denied their high school diploma because of their performance on one exam and in other cases on material they may not even have covered in class. As an example, in 2003 Nevada had 12 percent of its senior class denied their diplomas because they failed the math portion of the Nevada high school graduation test.[40] While state graduation tests are not part of the original NCLB law, they reflect the law's emphasis on measures to determine proficiency.

Another issue raised by critics of the testing requirement regards the pedagogy in the classroom that such standards may create. They raise concerns about teachers "teaching to the test" and eliminating the creativity that can occur in the classroom. In addition, and related to the state–local control issues, educators raise concerns about curriculum control. Finally, some have expressed reservations about impacts on the "richness" of the curriculum. Are schools shifting their focus to math and reading, where most of the testing occurs, at the cost of other subjects such as social studies or art (Mantel 2005)?[41]

The political fallout associated with NCLB was met with some concessions by the Bush administration as it entered its second term. Secretary of Education Margaret Spellings, who served from 2005 to 2009, showed more willingness to work with state education departments to help them meet the intention of NCLB. She was less willing, however, to allow states to be waived from the testing requirements for third through eighth grade students—what she called the "law's central provision." [42] Another development has been the Education Department's willingness to accept "growth models" for determining whether a state is making adequate yearly progress. These growth models provide credit to schools that show academic improvement in individuals even if their test scores are below state standards.[43] It would appear that the administration responded to some of the political pressure raised by critics of the legislation.

It remains to be seen how some of these political issues may affect education policy in the future. President Bush suggested that testing be extended into high schools, but with a new administration and a Democratic Congress that has been less supportive of the NCLB's testing requirements, it is unclear what the future may hold. In addition, states and many federal policymakers continue to express concern regarding the adequacy of funding, and it is clear that budgetary shortfalls can spark political controversy, especially in times when many states are facing severe budget constraints. Finally, evaluation of the law—has it been effective in improving education?—may affect the ongoing political debate. It is this effectiveness issue to which we now turn.

Effectiveness

According to supporters, the purpose of testing requirements is to ensure that student education is improving toward proficiency, or to put it another way, to ensure that students are learning the appropriate material before being passed along to the next grade. These tests ensure a form of accountability of the education system by having a systematic measure of student performance—albeit a measure that is subject to controversy, as mentioned above. Accountability of the nation's schools also may include a number of issues. Among these are overall student performance and closing achievement gaps among different groups of students (for example, urban, suburban, white, and minority). While states had to meet "adequate yearly progress" in improving achievement since 1994, NCLB set a deliberate timetable during which to meet such progress.

Something to keep in mind as one looks at the effectiveness of testing is that states are responsible for determining their own standards, the tests used, and what it means to be proficient (Mantel 2005). This makes comparisons across states a difficult, if not meaningless, task. Evaluation, therefore, may need to center on what is occurring within particular states. Debate around the success of NCLB and its testing requirements continues. But as the program continues, more studies question whether NCLB is meeting its identified goals. As noted throughout the text, though, advocates and opponents are quick to point to the evidence that best bolsters their positions.

The Center on Education Policy (CEP) bills itself as a nonpartisan organization concerned about public education and more effective public schools. The organization has completed a number of studies regarding the effectiveness of NCLB to help meet the goals of improving public education. Its June 2008 study reported on student achievement trends from 2006–2007. Among a variety of indicators, it specifically looked at two major factors: Did math and reading scores increase since 2002, and has there been a decrease in the achievement gap between subgroups of students? CEP found that since 2002, math and reading achievement test scores have gone up in most states. In other words, more states have a higher percentage of students scoring at the proficiency level. The center also found that achievement gaps had narrowed in more states than where they had widened. It is important to note the language in the report, because it did not claim that these gaps have narrowed in every state. The final main conclusion of the report, and the one likely to spark the most debate, was that it is impossible to determine whether or not these improvements are a direct result of NCLB. This is because during this time there have been a number of efforts at the state and local levels to improve education as well, and it would be difficult to separate the effects of these reform efforts from those associated with NCLB.

The Education Trust, another nonprofit organization, found that while progress is being made at the elementary school level, the results are not as promising at the middle and high school levels. This is particularly true in terms of closing gaps of achievement. Another study conducted by the Northwest Evaluation Association also found mixed results a few years after the passage of NCLB. While test scores are up as each class does better than the one before, it appears that less progress is being made during the school year than before NCLB. A more recent report also raised the issue of states defining the term *proficiency* differently. If this is the case, then it becomes difficult to ascertain how effective NCLB is nationwide. Another result in this same report indicated that tests in eighth grade are significantly more difficult for students to pass compared to elementary school tests. Another concern raised by reports of this organization suggested that the achievement gap between white and nonwhite students could soon widen.[44]

These studies are examining the effectiveness of NCLB and testing at the student level. Of course, another way to measure effectiveness could be by looking at the school or district-level data. Schools must make adequate yearly progress according to the law. If they fail to do so after two years, they must provide transportation for students wanting to transfer to other schools. According to the Center on Education Policy, 25 percent of the districts receiving Title I funding in the United States had at least one school that did make adequate yearly progress. A larger proportion of these schools are in urban school districts. If these percentages continue, school districts will need to spend a substantial amount of money either in transporting students to other, higher-testing schools or in providing programs such as tutoring in efforts to improve. An issue related to transferring students concerns the capacity of the schools that may need to accept these students. Since the law was only passed in 2002, it is a bit too early to determine whether this is, or will be, significant.[45]

Finally, the issue of federalism and states' rights is affecting the determination of effectiveness of NCLB and education proficiency. While states are required to administer the federal National Assessment of Education Progress exam, states determine their goals toward meeting proficiency based on their own state-administered exams. Thus students within a state may be rated differently with two separate exams. Such was the case in Tennessee, where 87 percent of the eighth grade students performed at or above proficiency on the state-based test but only 21 percent were considered proficient in math on the federal test. In addition, some states have set the bar relatively low regarding the stringency of their test in order to show improvement over time. While states may show progress by having scores increase over time, if they started at a very low level the scores may be meaningless.[46]

As one can see, the issue of effectiveness of school testing is complex. While initial data and studies seem to show gains in student scores overall, the evidence is mixed when it comes to closing achievement gaps. In addition, researchers warn of the preliminary nature of these reports. It is not unusual to see changes in performance at the initial stages of a new program. While supporters of testing and the law may trumpet these initial gains, policy analysts will want to see the results sustained over a longer period of time before being willing to accept them as a byproduct of NCLB.

Equity and Ethical Issues

Proponents of testing and NCLB often raise the issue of equity when discussing the importance of these policy changes. Their argument is that the achievement gap that has occurred in the nation's schools for a number of years is not right. By focusing attention on this gap, schools will see the data and respond. Shining the light on this problem, along with NCLB requirements to reduce the gap, will lead to a more equitable education system. Urban schools, which tend to be more diverse and contain more subgroups, have a more difficult time meeting the adequate yearly progress requirements. But as a member of the Education

Trust has asked, "Is it fair to expect less of schools that are educating diverse student bodies? Is it fair to those students?" (Mantel 2005).

On the other hand, we have noted throughout the book that equity is sometimes seen as freedom from government intervention. For NCLB, these are requirements that are being imposed by the federal government in a policy area that traditionally has been the purview of state and local governments. States that have made strides in improving their education systems prior to enactment of NCLB have found themselves labeled as "failing" because they are missing one federal standard. This is what happened in Virginia, where the Tuckahoe Middle School was identified as failing because only 94 percent of its students took the test; NCLB requires 95 percent. Yet 99 percent of the students were proficient in math and 95 percent in English.[47] It is this type of inflexibility and what some would call federal government "nit-picking" that concerns many state lawmakers and others responsible for implementing the law.

No one can argue that education should be somewhat equal in quality regardless of race, locality, or some other variable. Education is often looked upon as the great equalizer, and to the extent that testing requirements and accountability will improve equity, these are noble goals. What many states wonder, though, is whether the federal government should take such a primary role in ensuring that this is taking place. In other words, might the states do it better?

CONCLUSIONS

This chapter examines education policy and a number of associated issues. The heart of the debate is this question: What is the best way to improve the quality of education in the nation's schools? Whether it is raising standards for students and/or teachers, increasing teachers' pay, or providing additional choices for parents, all of the alternatives address what is perceived to be a problem of less-than-adequate quality.

Traditionally, education issues are the responsibility of state and local governments, but with the passage of NCLB federal policymakers are much more involved in education issues and taking a greater interest in this policy area. Their rhetoric on the subject reflects differing partisan and ideological views, and the conflicts over education policy show little sign of dissipating. Given the high level of public concern over education, this response by federal officials is not surprising, but state and local government officials continue to be guarded about the federal role in education policy. They welcome any increase in federal dollars flowing their way, but they remain wary of national programs and the possible threat they pose to their long-standing control over education policy. They would much prefer federal funds that they can use at their own discretion. We also cannot ignore the effect an economy in recession can have on issues of education. A large percentage of state budgets goes toward education—and as much as politicians want to protect this policy area, sometimes there is little choice but to cut spending in this area.

Given the partisan and ideological differences over education policy goals and growing federal involvement, policy change will depend on which party controls the White House and Congress. The bipartisan effort that led to the new federal law on education standards is no longer apparent but could rise again in the future. No Child Left Behind represents a major departure in education policy, particularly in federal-state relations. But partisan differences remain, and it will be interesting to watch how a new Obama administration along with a Democratic Congress may make adjustments to NCLB. Interest groups, particularly ones such as the National Education Association, will also contribute to this debate. If the conflicts make the future of education policy somewhat unpredictable, it is nevertheless certain that policymakers and the public will continue to seek more effective ways to reach education goals, and very likely with an eye toward efficient use of scarce resources and the promotion of equity in education programs.

DISCUSSION QUESTIONS

1. Should education policy remain primarily a state and local government concern, or should the federal government be involved? What are the arguments for the federal government to be more involved in education policy? What advantages do states have in maintaining their responsibility in this policy area?

2. Should government continue to support higher education and students who attend college? What factors should be considered when making such a policy decision? What are the arguments for and against such government support?

3. Should school districts change the usual expectations for teacher training to recruit a sufficient number of applicants? What might be done beyond increasing pay to ensure high-quality applicants?

4. What are the major advantages and disadvantages of adopting a school voucher program? How would you design such a program so that it can address most of the criticisms? Is this an issue of improving education quality, or is it related more to moral questions in our education system? Discuss.

5. Should school testing be expanded into all the high school years? What are the implications of increasing such testing requirements? What about standardized testing for college students? Are students overtested, and do the results matter in terms of curriculum?

SUGGESTED READINGS

William G. Bowen and Derek C. Bok, *The Shape of the River: Long-Term Consequences of Considering Race in College and University Admissions* (Princeton: Princeton University Press, 1998). Explores affirmative action policies in some of the nation's selective institutions; states that the policies had a positive effect on the lives of the benefited students.

John E. Chubb and Terry M. Moe, *Politics, Markets, and America's Schools* (Washington, D.C.: Brookings Institution, 1990). One of the first scholarly books to discuss the issues of the nation's public school systems and how these monopolies could be improved by the introduction of school choice and voucher programs.

R. Kenneth Godwin and Frank R. Kemerer, *School Choice Tradeoffs: Liberty, Equity, and Diversity* (Austin: University of Texas Press, 2002). An overview and appraisal of school choice; examines a number of issues related to this education policy alternative and the trade-offs associated with it, such as equality of opportunity and religious freedoms.

William G. Howell and Paul Peterson, with Patrick J. Wolf and David E. Campbell, *The Education Gap: Vouchers and Urban Schools* (Washington, D.C.: Brookings Institution, 2002). A comprehensive analysis of different school voucher programs around the country. The study finds, among other things, that voucher programs have a consistent positive benefit on African American students who participate in such programs.

Barbara Mantel, "No Child Left Behind," *CQ Researcher,* May 27, 2005, 469–492. This article explores the major issues of No Child Left Behind, focusing on effectiveness of the law and adequacy of its funding. In addition, it provides the history that led to its passage in 2002.

National Conference of State Legislatures, "Task Force on No Child Left Behind Final Report," (February 2005). This report from the NCSL discusses a number of issues regarding No Child Left Behind and also suggests improvements for Congress to consider.

John F. Witte, *The Market Approach to Education* (Princeton: Princeton University Press, 2000). Examines the school voucher issue—primarily within the Milwaukee system—and begins the process of evaluating the success or failure of the program.

SUGGESTED WEB SITES

www.acenet.edu. The site for the American Council of Education, which is the coordinating organization for higher education. It also conducts research on issues of higher education and provides a clearinghouse for news related to higher education.

www.aft.org. Site of the American Federation of Teachers, an advocacy group that conducts research and publishes studies on a range of education issues.

www.cep-dc.org. Site of the Center for Education Policy, a national, independent advocate for public education and for more effective public schools. The center conducts a range of research on the issue of public education, which can be accessed at this site.

www.ed.gov. U.S. federal government site for the Department of Education, with links to resources, news, policies, and statistics. Users can also access information about No Child Left Behind.

http://edreform.com. Nonprofit organization founded to support teachers, parents, and communities trying to bring reform to the public schools. Information available on education issues, reports, current news and updates, and links to other organizations.

www2.edtrust.org/edtrust. Nonprofit organization that focuses on schools in low-income areas and schools with high numbers of minority students. Reports, data, and news on these issues are provided on this site.

www.heritage.org/Research/Education/index.cfm. Heritage Foundation's portal to its reports and information regarding its ideas on education policy.

www.nbpts.org. National Board for Professional Teaching Standards site. Provides information regarding professional standards for the teaching profession.

http://nces.ed.gov. The National Center for Education Statistics is part of the U.S. Department of Education. A wide range of information is available at this site.

www.nea.org. Major organization representing teachers and supporting public education. Reports and information available on a number of education issues.

www.pta.org. National organization for the Parent-Teacher Association, a child advocacy group that promotes engagement in the school system as a way to help children. Resources, news, and links to other organizations available.

www.publicagenda.org/citizen/issueguides/education. General public policy site that provides resources, options, data, and links regarding issues of education.

MAJOR LEGISLATION

Elementary and Secondary Education Act of 1965 (ESEA)   303
GI Bill (Servicemen's Readjustment Act of 1944)   306
Goals 2000: Educate America Act of 1994   308
Morrill Act of 1862   306
No Child Left Behind Act of 2001   321
Pell Grant   306

KEYWORDS

charter school   324
competency test   320
Establishment Clause   310
Free Exercise Clause   310
merit pay   319

National Assessment of Educational
   Progress   313
school choice   322
school vouchers   322
teacher quality   312

NOTES

1. See Sam Dillon, "Connecticut Sues the U.S. Over School Testing," *New York Times,* August 23, 2005.
2. For access to this report, see National Conference of State Legislatures, *Task Force on No Child Left Behind Final Report,* February 2005.
3. This information is found at the National School Board Association, "About NSBA," 2005, available at www.nsba.org/site/page.asp?TRACKID=&CID=625&DID=9192.
4. Further information regarding school funding can be found at U.S. Department of Education, "10 Facts About K–12 Education Funding," 2005, available at www.ed.gov/about/overview/fed/10facts/index.html.
5. This figure is provided by U.S. Department of Education's Executive Peer Tool and can be accessed at http://nces.ed.gov/ipedspas/ExPT/index.asp?w=1. The Naval Academy subsidy is actually relatively low compared to the other military academies. The subsidy for a West Point student, for example, is over $200,000.
6. For additional information on school financing in different states, see "Rankings and Estimates: Rankings of States 2004 and Estimates of School Statistics 2005," available at the National Education Association site: www.nea.org/edstats/images/07rankings.pdf.
7. Information about state school funding can be found at U.S. Census Bureau, "Federal, State, and Local Governments: Public Elementary-Secondary Education Finance Data," available at the bureau's Web site: www.census.gov/govs/www/school.html.

8. See "Vermont Town May Blink in Dispute with State," *Boston Globe,* December 20, 1998. Additional information on Act 60 can be found at the state of Vermont's Department of Education site at http://education. vermont.gov/new/html/laws/act60_fact_sheet.html.

9. An increase in state support would require a dramatic shift in how many states currently fund their public education systems and likely cause states to raise taxes. For more information, see William C. Symonds, "Closing the School Gap," *Business Week,* October 14, 2002, 124.

10. For those interested in these reports and who want to explore further, see Patrick Gonzales, Trevor Williams, Leslie Jocelyn, Stephen Roey, David Kastberg, Summer Brenwald, and Westat, *Highlights from the Trends in International Mathematics and Science Study (TIMSS) 2007* (Washington, D.C.: U.S. Department of Education, National Center for Education Statistics, 2009), available at http://nces.ed.gov/pubs 2009/2009001.pdf; and M. Lemke, A. Sen, E. Pahlke, L. Partelow, D. Miller, T. Williams, D. Kastberg, and L. Jocelyn, *International Outcomes of Learning in Mathematics Literacy and Problem Solving: PISA 2003 Results from the U.S. Perspective* (Washington, D.C.: U.S. Department of Education, National Center for Educational Statistics, 2004).

11. Additional information can be found at American Council of Education, "To Touch the Future: Transforming the Way Teachers Are Taught," 1999, available at www.acenet.edu/bookstore/pdf/teacher-ed-rpt.pdf; and Craig D. Jerald, "No Action: Putting an End to Out-of-Field Teaching," *The Education Trust,* August 2002, available at www.edtrust.org/main/documents/AllTalk.pdf; Richard M. Ingersoll, "Core Problems: Out-of-Field Teaching Persists in Key Academic Courses and High-Poverty Schools," *The Education Trust,* November 2008, available at www2.edtrust.org/NR/rdonlyres/0D6EB5F1-2A49-4A4D-A01B-881CD2134357/0/SASSreport CoreProblems.pdf.

12. See Kenneth J. Cooper, "'Best and Brightest' Leave Teaching Early, Study Says," *Washington Post,* January 13, 2000.

13. According to a 2005 report by TV-Turnoff Network, an anti-TV advocacy group, the average American spends nearly four hours per day watching television. Children between the ages of two and seventeen spend about twenty hours a week watching television.

14. For additional information, see Peter Katel, "Affirmative Action," *CQ Researcher 18, online edition, October 17, 2008,* 841–864, available at http://library.cqpress.com/cqresearcher/cqresrre2008101711.

15. See Greg Winter, "After Ruling, Three Universities Maintain Diversity in Admissions," *New York Times,* April 13, 2004.

16. More detailed information on college pricing can be found at College Board, *Trends in College Pricing,* 2007. Retrieved November 28, 2008, from www.collegeboard.com/prod_downloads/about/news_info/trends/ trends_pricing_07.pdf.

17. These percentages are based on the amount of state tax funds for operating expenses of higher education per $1,000 of personal income. This information comes from Thomas G. Mortenson, "State Tax Fund Appropriations for Higher Education FY1961–FY2005," *Postsecondary Education Opportunity,* January 2005, 151.

18. See State Higher Education Executive Officers, *State Higher Education Finance FY 2007.* Retrieved November 28, 2008, from www.sheeo.org/finance/shef_fy07.pdf.

19. See the National Center for Public Policy and Higher Education, *Measuring Up 2008: The National Report Card on Higher Education,* 2008, retrieved December 3, 2008, from http://measuringup2008.highereducation. org/print/NCPPHEMUNationalRpt.pdf.

20. This information is based on U.S. Census Bureau data from its historical data tables. Men over the age of twenty-five with a high school diploma make on average $44,016 compared to $89,900 for those with a bachelor's degree or higher. For women, a high school diploma average is $31,548 and with a bachelor's or higher it is $59,015. To access this information, go to www.census.gov/hhes/www/income/histinc/p26.html.

21. See Texas Comptroller of Public Accounts, "The Impact of the State Higher Education System on the Texas Economy," February 2005, available at www.window.state.tx.us/specialrpt/highered05/; and Dennis K. Winters and William A. Strang, *The University of Wisconsin System's Economic Contribution to Wisconsin,* September 2002, available at www.northstareconomics.com/UWSsum.pdf.

22. For information on how merit pay has worked in parts of Colorado, see Ellen R. Delisio, "Pay for Performance: It Can Work—Here's How," *Education World,* 2003, available at www.educationworld.com/a_issues/ issues374c.shtml.

23. For additional information, see Barbara Kantrowitz and Daniel McGinn, "When Teachers Are Cheaters," *Newsweek,* June 19, 2000; and Evan Thomas and Pat Wingert, "Bitter Lessons," *Newsweek,* June 19, 2000.

24. See California State University Institute for Education Reform, *Paying for What You Need: Knowledge- and Skill-Based Approaches to Teacher Compensation,* September 1997, 9.

25. The AFT's perspective on merit pay can be found at American Federation of Teachers, "Pay for Performance," retrieved on December 3, 2008, from www.aft.org/topics/teacher-quality/compensation/performance-pay.htm.

26. Information on urban-area teaching can be found at Elizabeth F. Fideler, Elizabeth D. Foster, and Shirley Schwartz, *The Urban Teacher Challenge,* Urban Teacher Collaborative, January 2000, available at www.cgcs.org/pdfs/utc.pdf. In addition, this more recent article discusses continuing concerns for certain districts and fields of study. For additional information, see Jonathan Watts Hull, "Filling in the Gaps," *Threshold* (spring 2004).

27. See Richard Rothstein, "Teacher Shortages Vanish When the Price Is Right," *New York Times,* September 25, 2002, A16.

28. For additional information regarding the role of state constitutions, their legal environments, and the effect on school vouchers, see R. Kenneth Godwin and Frank R. Kemerer, *School Choice Tradeoffs: Liberty, Equity, and Diversity* (Austin: University of Texas Press, 2002).

29. The NEA provides a list of studies suggesting either zero or minimum positive effects of voucher programs (see www.nea.org/issues/vouchers/index.html).

30. There was quite a bit of controversy surrounding the results by Peterson et al. and their interpretation. For additional information see Michael Winerip, "What a Voucher Study Truly Showed, and Why," *New York Times,* May 7, 2003.

31. For additional information on this, students should see Brian Gill, P. Mike Timpane, Karen E. Ross, Dominic J. Brewer, and Kevin Booker, *Rhetoric versus Reality: What We Know and What We Need to Know about Vouchers and Charter Schools* (Santa Monica, Calif.: Rand Corporation, 2007), available at www.rand.org/pubs/monograph_ reports/2007/RAND_MR1118-1.updatedfindings.pdf.

32. Additional information on charter schools can be found at the National Alliance for Public Charter Schools, available at www.publiccharters.org.

33. See Gill, et al., 2007.

34. Kenneth Jost discusses many of the issues regarding standardized testing in "Testing in Schools," *CQ Researcher,* April 20, 2001.

35. See Anna Quindlen, "Testing: One, Two, Three," *Newsweek,* June 13, 2005, 88.

36. This is according to the National Conference of State Legislatures. See National Conference of State Legislatures, *Task Force on No Child Left Behind Final Report,* February 2005.

37. See James Peyser and Robert Castrell, "Exploring the Costs of Accountability," Education Next (spring 2004); and Accountability Works, "NCLB Under a Microscope," January 2004.

38. See Neil McClusky and Andrew J. Coulson, "End It, Don't Mend It: What to Do with No Child Left Behind," *Policy Analysis,* Cato Institute, September 5, 2007, available at www.cato.org/pub_display. php?pub_id=8680.

39. The National Education Association and the American Federation of Teachers have a number of resources on the issue of federal standards and education testing. For additional information, see National Education Association, "No Child Left Behind ACT (NCLB)/ESEA," available at www.nea.org/home/NoChild LeftBehindAct.html; and the American Federation of Teachers, "The AFT on NCLB," available at www.aft.org/topics/nclb/index.htm.

40. Similar issues occurred in other states in the nation that required graduation exams. For more information, see Michael A. Fletcher, "When Good Students Can't Graduate," *Washington Post National Weekly Edition,* June 9–15, 2003, 29.

41. See also Sam Dillon, "Schools Cut Back Subjects to Push Reading and Math," *New York Times,* March 26, 2006; and Alex Tehrani, "How to Fix No Child Left Behind," *Time,* March 24, 2007.

42. See Sam Dillon, "New U.S. Secretary Showing Flexibility on 'No Child' Act," *New York Times,* February 14, 2005.

43. For additional information, see Nick Anderson, "Bush Administration Grants Leeway on 'No Child' Rules," *Washington Post,* November 22, 2005, A1.

44. There are a variety of reports associated with the evaluation of NCLB. The ones mentioned here can be found at Center on Education Policy, "Has Student Achievement Increased Since 2002?" (June 2008), available at www.cep-dc.org/document/docWindow.cfm?fuseaction=document.viewDocument&documentid=241& documentFormatId=3881; and Education Trust, "Stalled in Secondary: A Look at Student Achievement since the No Child Left Behind Act" (January 2005). The Northwest Evaluation Association studies cited are: "Achievement Gaps: An Examination of Differences in Student Achievement and Growth" (November 2006), available at www.nwea.org/assets/research/national/achgap_11.11.061.pdf; and "The Proficiency Illusion" (October 2007), available at www.edexcellence.net/doc/ The_Proficiency_Illusion.pdf.

45. The Department of Education provides additional information regarding the assessment of state progress for NCLB at www.ed.gov/admins/lead/account/cornerstones/index.html.

46. See Sam Dillon, "Students Ace State Tests, But Earn D's from U.S.," *New York Times,* November 26, 2005. The article also claims that, according to research by the Northwest Evaluation Association, states that set proficiency standards prior to NCLB's passage tended to set them high, and that since then states have set lower standards.

47. See Michael Winerip, "Superior School Fails a Crucial Federal Test," *New York Times,* November 19, 2003.

In late May 2008, the George W. Bush administration released a new report on global climate change. This one was different from many others that the administration had produced. In contrast to the usual skepticism the president and his advisers had expressed over the reality of climate change and the urgency of addressing it, the 2008 report pointed to the substantial and harmful impacts that could be expected as a result of human activities that are slowly warming the planet and threatening both the environment and public health. Most of the findings were well known to scientists and had been thoroughly documented over the years, especially by the UN-sponsored **Intergovernmental Panel on Climate Change** (IPCC), most recently in its fourth assessment report issued in 2007 (DiMento and Doughman 2007; IPCC 2007).[1] The administration did not choose to release the climate report; rather, it was forced to do so by a federal court after it was sued by environmentalists for not issuing periodic climate change assessments required by law. The Bush White House had argued that it already had met its legal obligations by publishing many other scientific studies of climate change. A federal judge disagreed, saying those reports fell short of requirements set out in a 1990 law. As a result, the judge ordered that a comprehensive report on the effects of climate change in the United States be published by the end of May, and the administration complied with the order.

Environmentalists and their political allies were cheered by the court's decision, and they used the opportunity to criticize the Bush administration for not taking climate change seriously enough. Sen. John Kerry, D-Mass., the lead author of the Global Change Research Act of 1990 that required such reports, and the Democratic nominee for president in 2004, was particularly blunt in his assessment: "The three-year delay of this report is sadly fitting for an administration that has wasted several years denying the real threat of global climate change," he said.[2]

U.S. president Barack Obama and Vice President Joe Biden join Namasté Solar CEO Blake Jones on a tour of the solar array at the Denver Museum of Nature and Science in February 2009. Climate change and energy use were discussed often during the 2008 presidential election campaign, and during his inaugural address, President Obama pledged to "harness the sun and the winds and the soil to fuel our cars and run our factories." As one sign of that commitment, the president allocated a large share of the February 2009 economic stimulus package to development of renewable energy sources, and he said he would seek congressional approval of a climate change policy that would gradually move the nation away from reliance on carbon-based fuels.

For its part, the Bush administration had long maintained that scientific evidence on the causes and consequences of climate change was too uncertain to warrant policy action beyond voluntary measures by industry and funding of additional research, which it supported. It also argued that dealing with climate change would be prohibitively expensive for the United States. This was especially so, it said, under the stipulations of the Kyoto Protocol, an international agreement on climate change that exempted developing nations, such as China and India, from a requirement imposed on industrialized nations to reduce greenhouse gas emissions. This unequal treatment of developed and developing nations was the basis for the administration's rejection of the protocol in early 2001 as "fatally flawed" and particularly harmful to the economic interests of the United States.[3]

The administration's stance on climate also was reflected indirectly in its energy policy proposals, which emphasized the need to *increase* the use of fossil fuels to meet the nation's growing energy demands; the burning of fossil fuels such as oil, coal, and natural gas releases large quantities of carbon dioxide, the chief greenhouse gas. Environmentalists and most Democrats had argued that the United States instead should concentrate on improving energy efficiency and encouraging conservation and use of renewable energy sources such as wind, solar power, and biofuels. After four years of bitter partisan debate, with rising public frustration over high gasoline prices and with new concerns about the national security and economic implications of relying heavily on imported oil to meet national needs, in 2005 Congress approved most of President Bush's energy policy proposals. Was the Bush administration right about the perils of acting on climate change in light of inequitable requirements and high economic costs? Was it correct to emphasize an expansion of fossil fuels over energy efficiency, conservation, and use of renewable energy sources? Or were the administration's critics on more solid ground in these debates?

In some respects, the American public reached its own conclusions in the 2008 presidential election. Climate change and energy use were far more visible during the campaign than in previous years, as gasoline prices soared to over $4.00 a gallon, and both Republican candidate John McCain and Democratic nominee Barack Obama pledged to change public policies on climate change and energy.[4] During his inaugural address, President Obama stated that he would "restore science to its rightful place" (a clear reference to criticism that the Bush administration had not listened to scientists sufficiently on climate change and other environmental issues) and work to "harness the sun and the winds and the soil to fuel our cars and run our factories." Within days of taking office, Obama sought to overturn the Bush administration's stance on climate change by urging the U.S. Environmental Protection Agency (EPA) to reconsider the administration's denial of California's request for a federal waiver that would allow it—and many other states—for the first time to limit greenhouse gas emissions from automobiles, essentially raising fuel economy standards; the Bush White House had blocked the EPA from issuing such a waiver.[5]

As we discuss later in the chapter, Obama's shift from Bush policies was even sharper in an economic stimulus package approved by Congress in February 2009; it included tens of billions of dollars for energy efficiency, research and development of renewable energy sources, modernization of the nation's electricity grid, and support for mass transit, among other actions. In addition, Obama pledged in a message to Congress later that month that he would seek approval for a national climate change policy that included a mandatory cap-and-trade program to reduce greenhouse gas emissions. He indicated as well that the United States would play a strong leadership role in forging a new international agreement on climate change to replace the dated Kyoto Protocol.[6]

These reports and policy decisions in 2008 and 2009 underscore the strong relationship between energy and environmental policy; that is, the amount of energy Americans use and its sources—especially fossil fuels and nuclear energy—can have profound environmental impacts, including climate change, increased urban air pollution, production of toxic chemicals and hazardous wastes, and damage to ecosystems. Some reports in late 2005 even linked the devastation wrought by Hurricane Katrina to climate change: warmer water in the Gulf of Mexico can intensify the severity of tropical storms.[7] By the same token, environmental policy, such as air and water regulations, can influence the production and use of energy by setting high standards that can affect which sources of energy may be used and what they will cost. During the 2008 campaign, Republicans, for example, strongly favored increased drilling for oil in off-shore public lands, captured in the memorable chant during the party's nominating convention: "Drill, baby, drill." Such drilling had been long prohibited out of concern for the possible environmental impacts, but Congress ended the restriction in 2008.

This chapter describes and evaluates U.S. environmental and energy policies. It discusses their evolution in some detail because this history, especially since the 1970s, is necessary to understand the conflicts and struggles to rebuild and redirect environmental policy for the twenty-first century. These conflicts center on the impacts of regulatory policies adopted largely during the 1970s and 1980s, the cost of those policies, the burdens they impose on industry, the promise of alternative policies, and the potential for integrating economic and environmental goals through sustainable development in the United States and around the world. In keeping with our emphasis throughout the text on several core criteria for judging policy alternatives, the chapter gives special consideration to the effectiveness of current policies and to economic, political, and equity issues in evaluating policy ideas and proposals.

BACKGROUND

Environmental policy is not easy to define. As is the case with health care policy, its scope is much broader than one might see at first glance. Many people believe the environment, and therefore environmental policy, refers only to humans' relationship to nature—which they see as wilderness and wildlife, parks, open space, recreation, and natural resources such as forests. Or perhaps they understand that much environmental policy deals with human health concerns; the Clean Air Act, for example, could be described as a public health law.

Environmental scientists, however, argue that a more useful way to understand the environment is to see it as a set of natural systems that interact in complex ways to supply humans and other species with the necessities of life, such as breathable air, clean water, food, fiber, energy, and the recycling of waste. To put it another way, humans are intimately dependent on environmental systems to meet their essential needs. People cannot survive without these systems but often fail to recognize their functions or to place a reasonable value on the natural services that everyone takes for granted (Daily 1997). In a striking example of how important it is to recognize these natural services and their value, New York City avoided construction of a $6 billion water filtration plant in the 1990s by deciding to invest $1 billion over ten years in better land management practices around an upstate watershed that supplies 90 percent of the city's water.[8]

Numerous scientific reports in recent years also tell us that human beings are now so numerous and use nature to such an extent to meet their needs that they threaten to disrupt these natural systems and lose the services on which life depends. In the late 1990s, Jane Lubchenco, President Obama's selection to head the National Oceanic and Atmospheric Administration and a former president of the American Association for the Advancement of Science, observed that "humans have emerged as a new force of nature." She argued that people are "modifying physical, chemical, and biological systems in new ways, at faster rates, and over larger spatial scales than ever recorded on Earth." The result of these modifications is that humans have "unwittingly embarked upon a grand experiment with our planet" with "profound implications for all of life on Earth" (Lubchenco 1998, 492).

At the 1992 United Nations Conference on Environment and Development (the Earth Summit), delegates from 179 nations pledged support for an elaborate plan of action for the twenty-first century called Agenda 21 (United Nations 1993). It addresses environmental concerns by emphasizing **sustainable development,** or economic growth that is compatible with natural environmental systems and social goals. The objective of sustainable development is "meeting the needs of the present without compromising the ability of future generations to meet their own needs" (World Commission on Environment and Development 1987, 43). Given the continued growth of the human population and the economic expansion that must occur to provide for the roughly 9.4 billion people who are expected to inhabit the planet by 2050, that will be no easy task. In September 2002, the tenth anniversary of the Earth Summit, a new World Summit on Sustainable Development was held in Johannesburg, South Africa, and continued to define that challenge in light of persistent worldwide poverty. The box "Steps to Analysis: The UN Division for Sustainable Development" suggests some ways to study and evaluate issues raised at the 1992 Earth Summit, the 2002 World Summit, and other meetings on global environmental and development issues. As we discussed earlier in the book, communities across the United States and hundreds of colleges and universities have adopted similar sustainability initiatives, with special emphasis on those that promote energy conservation and efficiency, use of renewable energy resources, recycling, water conservation, improved growth management, use of mass transit, and similar actions (Mazmanian and Kraft 2009).[9]

Put in this broader context, environmental policy can be defined as all government actions that affect or attempt to affect environmental quality and the use of natural resources. The policy actions may take place at the local, state, regional, national, or international level. Traditionally, environmental policy was considered to involve the conservation or protection of natural resources such as public lands and waters, wilderness, and wildlife. Since the late 1960s, however, the term has also been used to refer to governments' environmental protection efforts that are motivated by public health concerns, such as controlling air and water pollution and limiting exposure to toxic chemicals. In the future, environmental policy is likely to be tightly integrated with the comprehensive agenda of sustainable development at all levels of government. Environmental policy will extend to government actions affecting human health and safety, energy use, transportation and urban design, agriculture and food production, population growth, and the protection of vital global ecological, chemical, and geophysical systems

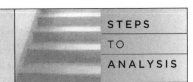

THE UN DIVISION FOR SUSTAINABLE DEVELOPMENT

STEPS TO ANALYSIS

Visit the Web page for the UN Division for Sustainable Development (DSD), which promotes sustainable development as the secretariat to the UN Commission on Sustainable Development (CSD). The CSD was established after the 1992 Earth Summit to track national and international action to promote global sustainable development—economic growth that is compatible with natural environmental systems as well as social goals. The DSD keeps track of implementation of the summit's Agenda 21, the Rio Declaration on Environment and Development, and the Johannesburg Plan of Implementation from the 2002 World Summit held in that city. Starting at the home page (www.un.org/esa/dsd/index.shtml), see the section on DSD in Focus and click on one of the issues, such as climate change, energy, or water. Alternatively, see a longer list under the tab for Comprehensive List of Sustainable Development Projects, which includes health, poverty, sustainable tourism, and demographics (population), among many other topics.

What are the major issues that are identified, and how do they relate to the long-term goal of sustainable development?

What positions did the world's nations endorse at the 1992 or 2002 summits, and how do they compare to those advocated by environmental groups? By conservative or probusiness organizations? For an example of an environmental group's perspective on international issues of this kind, see the Natural Resources Defense Council Web page: www.nrdc.org/international/default.asp. For a conservative and probusiness group's perspective, see the Competitive Enterprise Institute's statement on sustainable development at http://cei.org/gencon/025,01439.cfm.

What justifications are offered for these positions, and how persuasive do you find them?

(Brown 2008; Chasek, Downie, and Brown 2006; Starke 2008; Vig and Kraft 2010). Almost certainly, environmental policy is going to have a pervasive and growing impact on human affairs in the twenty-first century.

To address these challenges effectively, however, policy analysts, policymakers, and the public need to think in fresh ways about environmental and energy policies and redesign them where needed. Many existing policies were developed three to four decades ago, and criticism of their effectiveness, efficiency, and equity abound. Not surprisingly, some complaints come from the business community, which has long argued that stringent laws dealing with clean air, clean water, toxic chemicals, and hazardous wastes can have an adverse impact on business operations and constrain their ability to compete internationally (Kraft and Kamieniecki 2007). Others, however, are just as likely to find fault, including state and local governments that must handle much of the routine implementation of federal laws and pay a sizable part of the costs. Critical assessments come as well from independent policy analysts who see a mismatch between what the policies are intended to accomplish and the strategies and tools on which they rely (Davies and Mazurek 1998; Durant, Fiorino, and O'Leary 2004; Eisner 2007).[10] In addition, groups concerned about environmental justice both within the United States and internationally have objected to the inequitable burden placed on poor and minority communities here as well as impoverished people in developing nations. They argue that these populations often bear a greater public health risk from pollution and are likely to suffer more from climate change and other global environmental threats; hence they believe future environmental policy must address such inequities more effectively than is now the case (Axelrod, Downie, and Vig 2005; Ringquist 2006).

For more than three decades, environmental policy has been bitterly contested, with no clear resolution on most of the major policies; energy policy has been similarly disputed, although congressional action in 2005 and again in 2009 indicated more consensus on policy goals and means even if the two major parties continued to see matters differently. Piecemeal and incremental policy changes have improved some existing environmental programs, such as regulating pesticide and providing safe drinking water, but what remains is a fragmented, costly, often inefficient, and somewhat ineffective set of environmental and energy policies. During the 1990s President Bill Clinton's EPA tried to "reinvent" environmental regulation to make it more efficient and more acceptable to the business community. For example, it experimented with streamlined rulemaking and more **collaborative decision making,** in which industry and other stakeholders worked cooperatively with government officials. The experiments were only moderately successful. Clinton's successor, George W. Bush, likewise proposed a "new era" of more flexible and efficient regulation and a greater role for the states, but few experts thought Bush's efforts were more effective than Clinton's. Clinton and Bush preferred different kinds of reforms of the major environmental laws to make them more appropriate for the twenty-first century, but political constraints prevented both of them from realizing their goals (Fiorino 2006; Vig and Kraft 2010).

As this brief review suggests, environmental policy has reached an important crossroads, as have energy policies, particularly as they relate to the use of fossil fuels and climate change. More than ever before, policymakers and analysts need to figure out what works and what does not and to remake environmental policy for the emerging era of sustainable development both within the United States and internationally. How Congress, the states, and local governments will change environmental and energy policies in the years ahead remains unclear. Much depends on the way leading policy actors define the issues and how the media cover them, the state of the economy, the relative influence of opposing interest groups, and whether political leadership can help to forge a national consensus. Until policy breakthroughs occur, however, today's environmental and energy policies are likely to continue in much their present form. Yet some of the most innovative and promising policy actions, rooted in the kind of comprehensive and coordinated thinking associated with sustainability, are taking place at the regional, state, and local levels, and they provide a glimpse of what might eventually be endorsed at higher levels of government (Klyza and Sousa 2008; Mazmanian and Kraft 2009; Rabe 2010).

THE EVOLUTION OF ENVIRONMENTAL AND ENERGY POLICY

Modern environmental policy was developed during the 1960s and shortly thereafter became firmly established on the political agenda in the United States and other developed nations. During the so-called environmental decade of the 1970s, Congress enacted most of the major environmental statutes in effect today. Actions in states and localities paralleled these

Environmental protection policies developed during the 1970s focused on industrial sources of air and water pollution, such as this coal-fired power plant in Shippingport, Pennsylvania. The photo shows a resident examining the damage resulting from acid rain at a playground as coal smoke and steam vapor pour out of the Bruce Mansfield Power Plant in September 2008. The park is rarely used because of the pollution from two nearby plants. The plant shown here is one of the top twelve emitters of carbon dioxide in the United States, and according to a local investigation, since 1998 it has consistently violated one of its air pollution permits related to the release of health-damaging fine particulates. The U.S. Environmental Protection Agency considered the plant to be a "high-priority" violator, and the plant has subsequently paid nearly $1 million in fines.

developments, as did policy evolution at the international level (Axelrod, Downie, and Vig 2005; Chasek, Downie, and Brown 2006; Kraft 2007; McCormick 1989). Energy policy experienced a somewhat different history, but here too it has been considered in a comprehensive manner only since the 1970s.

Early Environmental and Energy Policies

Although formal environmental policy in the United States is a relatively recent development, concern about the environment and the value of natural resources can be traced back to the early seventeenth century, when New England colonists first adopted local ordinances to protect forest land (Andrews 2006a). In the late nineteenth and early twentieth centuries, conservation policies advanced to deal with the excesses of economic development in the West, and new federal and state agencies emerged to assume responsibility for their implementation, including the U.S. Forest Service in 1905 and the National Park Service in 1916. In 1892 Congress set aside two million acres in Idaho, Montana, and Wyoming to create Yellowstone National Park, the first of a series of national parks. Many of the prominent conservation organizations also formed during this period. Naturalist John Muir founded the Sierra Club in 1892 as the first broad-based environmental organization, and others followed in the ensuing decades.

In contrast to some of the criticism directed at modern environmental policy, none of these early actions challenged prevailing U.S. values relating to the sanctity of private property, individual rights, a limited role for government, and the primacy of economic growth—all of which impose important cultural constraints on environmental policy. They did, however, signal the emergence of new social forces that eventually collided with these long-standing values and by the early twenty-first century led to the government's strong role in environmental protection and resource management. The first policy actions in the nation's youth and the creation of new bureaucracies did, however, establish the important principle that resources in the public domain, such as the national forests, should be used for the benefit of all citizens. In urban areas, by the late nineteenth century, cities began to recognize the importance of establishing services such as providing clean water, managing waste, and treating wastewater. Consistent with these activities to promote urban public health, the first air pollution statutes, dating from the 1880s, were adopted to control smoke and soot from furnaces and locomotives.

Following a number of natural disasters, most memorably the Dust Bowl of the 1930s, President Franklin Roosevelt expanded conservation policies to deal with flood control and soil conservation as part of his New Deal. Congress created the Tennessee Valley Authority (TVA) in 1933 to stimulate economic growth by providing electric power development in that region. The TVA demonstrated a critical policy belief: that government land-use planning could further the public interest. Other measures followed, including the Taylor Grazing Act of 1934, intended to end the overgrazing of valuable rangelands and watersheds in the West, and the Bureau of Land Management in 1946, created to manage vast public lands in the West.

Prior to the 1970s, energy policy was not a major or sustained concern of government. For the most part it consisted of federal and state regulation of coal, natural gas, and oil, particularly of the prices charged and competition in the private sector. The goal was to stabilize markets and ensure both profits and continuing energy supplies. The most notable exception was substantial federal support for the commercialization of nuclear power. Beginning in the late 1940s, Congress shielded the nascent industry from public scrutiny, spent lavishly on research and development, and promoted the rapid advancement of civilian nuclear power plants through the Atomic Energy Commission and its successor agencies, the Nuclear Regulatory Commission and the Department of Energy (DOE). The Price-Anderson Act of 1957 greatly restricted the industry's liability and allowed it to flourish (Duffy 1997).

The Modern Environmental Movement and Policy Developments

By the 1960s the modern environmental movement was taking shape in response to changing social values. The major stimulus was the huge spurt in economic development that followed World War II (1941–1945). During the 1950s and 1960s the nation benefited further from the rise in consumerism. An affluent, comfortable, and well-educated public began to place a greater emphasis on the quality of life, and environmental quality was a part of it. Social scientists characterize this period as a shift from an industrial to a postindustrial society. In this context, it is easy to understand a new level of public concern for natural resources and environmental protection. Scientific discoveries also helped. New studies, often well publicized in the popular press, alerted people to the effects of pesticides and other synthetic chemicals. Rachel Carson's influential book *Silent Spring,* which documented the devastating effects that such chemicals had on songbird populations, was published in 1962, and for many it was an eye opener.

The initial public policy response to these new values and concerns focused on natural resources. Congress approved the Wilderness Act of 1964 to preserve some national forest lands in their natural condition. The Land and Water Conservation Fund Act, also adopted in 1964, facilitated local, state, and federal acquisition and development of land for parks and open spaces.[11] In 1968 Congress created the National Wild and Scenic Rivers System to preserve certain rivers with "outstandingly remarkable" scenic, recreational, ecological, historical, and cultural values.

Action by the federal government on pollution control issues lagged in comparison to resource conservation, largely because Congress deferred to state and local governments on these matters. Congress approved the first modest federal water and air pollution statutes in 1948 and 1955, respectively. However, only in the late 1960s and 1970s did it expand and strengthen them significantly. International environmental issues also began to attract attention in the 1960s. In his 1965 State of the Union message, for example, President Lyndon Johnson called for federal programs to deal with "the explosion in world population and the growing scarcity in world resources." The following year Congress authorized the first funds to support family planning programs in other nations (Kraft 1994).

These early policy developments were a prelude to a wholesale shift in the political mood of the nation that led to the present array of environmental protection, natural resource, and energy policies. Public opinion was the driving force in most of this policy advancement. Membership in environmental organizations such as the Sierra Club and the Audubon Society surged during the 1960s, reflecting a growing public concern about these issues. By the early 1970s newer groups, such as the Natural Resources Defense Council (NRDC), were established, and almost all of them saw their budgets, staffs, and political influence soar. As a result, policymakers became aware of a concerned public that demanded action, and they were eager to respond and take political credit (Bosso 2005; Dunlap 1995).

Congress approved most of the major federal environmental laws now in effect between 1969 and 1976 in a stunning outpouring of legislation not repeated since then. Policymakers were convinced that the public favored new federal regulatory measures that would be strong enough to force offending industries to clean up. In many respects, this development illustrates the kind of market failure discussed in chapter 1. The public and policymakers demanded that the federal government intervene to stop rampant pollution by industry that constituted a market externality. Most of the states also were constrained from taking action. As we noted in chapter 2, the states either lacked the necessary policy capacity at that time, or they chose not to act because of pressure from local industry. Eventually, Congress decided that only national policy action would suffice (Davies and Davies 1975). The development of environmental and resource policies during the 1960s and 1970s, therefore, grew out of the same factors that led to other public policies: market failures (economic reasons), a belief that government action was the right thing to do (ethical reasons), and the eagerness of elected

| TABLE 11-1 | Major U.S. Environmental Laws, 1964–2009 |

Year Enacted	Legislation
1964	Wilderness Act, PL 88-577
1968	Wild and Scenic Rivers Act, PL 90-542
1969	National Environmental Policy Act (NEPA), PL 91-190
1970	Clean Air Act Extension, PL 91-604
1972	Federal Water Pollution Control Act Amendments (Clean Water Act), PL 92-500
	Federal Environmental Pesticides Control Act of 1972 (amended the Federal Insecticide, Fungicide, and Rodenticide Act [FIFRA] of 1947), PL 92-516
	Marine Protection, Research, and Sanctuaries Act of 1972, PL 92-532
	Marine Mammal Protection Act, PL 92-522
	Coastal Zone Management Act, PL 92-583
	Noise Control Act, PL 92-574
1973	Endangered Species Act, PL 93-205
1974	Safe Drinking Water Act, PL 93-523
1976	Resource Conservation and Recovery Act (RCRA), PL 94-580
	Toxic Substances Control Act, PL 94-469
	Federal Land Policy and Management Act, PL 94-579
	National Forest Management Act, PL 94-588
1977	Clean Air Act Amendments, PL 95-95
	Clean Water Act (CWA), PL 95-217
	Surface Mining Control and Reclamation Act, PL 95-87
1980	Comprehensive Environmental Response, Compensation, and Liability Act (Superfund), PL 96-510
1982	Nuclear Waste Policy Act, PL 97-425 (amended in 1987 by the Nuclear Waste Policy Amendments Act, PL 100-203)
1984	Hazardous and Solid Waste Amendments (RCRA amendments), PL 98-616
1986	Safe Drinking Water Act Amendments, PL 99-339
	Superfund Amendments and Reauthorization Act (SARA), PL 99-499
1987	Water Quality Act (CWA amendments), PL 100-4
1988	Ocean Dumping Act, PL 100-688
1990	Clean Air Act Amendments, PL 101-549
	Oil Pollution Act, PL 101-380
	Pollution Prevention Act, PL 101-508
1992	Energy Policy Act, PL 102-486
	The Omnibus Water Act, PL 102-575
1996	Food Quality Protection Act (amended FIFRA), PL 104-120
	Safe Drinking Water Act Amendments, PL 104-182
2002	Small Business Liability Relief and Brownfields Revitalization Act, PL 107-118
2003	The Healthy Forests Restoration Act of 2003, PL 108-148
2005	Energy Policy Act of 2005, PL 109-58
2007	Energy Independence and Security Act of 2007, PL 110-140
2009	The American Recovery and Reinvestment Act of 2009 (for its funding of energy policy), PL 111-5
	The Omnibus Public Lands Management Act of 2009, PL 111-11

Note: For a more complete list, with a summary description of major features of each act, see Norman J. Vig and Michael E. Kraft, eds., *Environmental Policy,* 7th ed. (Washington, D.C.: CQ Press, 2010), Appendix 1. We list two acts from early 2009 because of their importance, but otherwise the table is intended to report on major actions only through 2008. Other actions may follow later in 2009.

officials to respond to strong public demand (political reasons). Table 11-1 lists the most important of the federal environmental laws enacted between 1964 and 2008. Comparable policy developments took place at the state level and abroad (Axelrod, Downie, and Vig 2005; Rabe 2010; Vig and Faure 2004).

Policymakers also appeared to believe at the time that pollution problems and their remedies were fairly simple. Few would make such assumptions today, because they understand the
complexity of environmental problems and the difficulty of solving them. But in the 1960s
and 1970s policymakers and the public had more confidence that the chosen solutions would
work. They thought that application of technological or engineering know-how would do the
trick and that little or no change would be required in human behavior, for example, in using
personal automobiles in urban areas or in creating far-flung suburbs (Paehlke 2010). These
policy beliefs dominated legislative debates, although it was evident to some even then that
the necessary technical knowledge did not always exist and that government agencies sometimes lacked the necessary resources and skills to take on the many new responsibilities mandated by these laws (Jones 1975; Mazmanian and Sabatier 1983).

On the one hand, these policy actions are a remarkable testimony to the capacity of government institutions to move quickly to approve major legislation when public and partisan
consensus demands a policy such as pollution control. On the other hand, this history of policy development suggests why so many of these environmental laws later came under forceful
criticism from business groups and conservatives, and why economists worried about the cost
they imposed on society, not to mention their limited success in reaching the ambitious policy goals they embodied (Higgs and Close 2005; Portney and Stavins 2000).

Some thoughtful environmental philosophers offer a different perspective, which is more
closely attuned to current concepts of sustainable development. They argue that environmental policies can never succeed as long as human population growth and material consumption
continue and society's institutions remain unchallenged. Mere reformist policies of pollution
control and ecological management, they say, are doomed to failure because they do little to
alter human attitudes and behavior or to confront the economic and political systems that
contribute to environmental degradation in the first place (Ophuls and Boyan 1992). In chapter 4 we referred to one of the dilemmas facing policy analysts—whether to deal with fundamental or root causes of public problems or to focus on the more manageable proximate
causes. Environmental policies to date have dealt primarily with the latter.

FROM CONSENSUS TO CONFLICT IN ENVIRONMENTAL POLICY

If consensus on environmental policy was the norm during the 1970s, by the 1980s political
conflict became the new standard in policymaking. The shift in perspective had many causes,
but chief among them were the conservatives' growing concern about the strong role of government and its implications for the private sector, increasing doubts among policy analysts
about the effectiveness and efficiency of the dominant command-and-control regulation, and
the business community's resentment over the burdens and costs of the new policies. Industry
representatives frequently argued that the costs could not be justified by what they saw as the
limited benefits produced in improved public health or environmental quality.

Reagan and Bush Administration Policies

These new ideas about environmental policy rose to prominence during Ronald Reagan's presidency (1981–1989), when environmental agencies suffered deep budget cuts, lost experienced

professional staff members, and saw their program activities slow down. Reagan's agenda was largely one of providing temporary relief to the business community and to western resource development interests such as mining, logging, and ranching. His administration demonstrated little persistent interest in genuine reforms of environmental programs to make them more effective and efficient (Vig and Kraft 1984). That goal would have been much tougher. To work toward it would have meant rewriting the basic environmental laws, and that in turn would have required broad agreement among the major policy actors, which did not exist.

Ultimately, the Reagan administration was ineffective in rolling back environmental policy, primarily because the U.S. public continued to favor strong environmental protection, and Congress in response blocked many of the president's efforts (Dunlap 1995). The result, perversely, was a *strengthening* of the major environmental laws and adherence to the same command-and-control policy strategy that policy analysts and other critics were questioning. That reaction was particularly evident in the 1984 amendments to the Resource Conservation and Recovery Act, which established demanding standards and detailed requirements for the handling of hazardous wastes.

This pattern of policy enhancement continued through 1990, as George H. W. Bush, who served as Reagan's vice president for eight years, worked closely with Congress to enact the Clean Air Act Amendments of 1990. That law was a major expansion of the original 1970 act, and it is discussed below. Environmentalists cheered their success in keeping the policies and programs of the 1970s intact and in some instances expanding them. But policy analysts continued to argue that additional reform of those policies was essential to make them more effective and to control their substantial and rising costs (Durant, Fiorino, and O'Leary 2004; Portney and Stavins 2000).

Partisan Conflict over Environmental Policy

Partisan conflict had much to do with the inability to focus seriously on the real reform agenda and to chart new environmental policy directions for the future. The two major political parties grew further apart over environmental policy, even though they had worked together in the 1970s to advance environmental protection. President Richard Nixon, for example, created the Environmental Protection Agency at the end of 1970 through an executive order that consolidated government agencies and expanded their role. He also cooperated with a Democratic Congress in enacting the Clean Air Act Extension of 1970, although the lawmakers had to pass the 1972 Clean Water Act over his veto. By the 1990s a widening gulf divided the parties on fundamental issues such as the legitimacy of government regulation to protect the public's welfare, the sanctity of private property rights, and even whether environmental problems posed a real and substantial risk to the public's health and well-being.[12]

These differences were evident in congressional voting on all major environmental protection and natural resource issues. A comprehensive analysis of voting records in Congress shows that the gap between the parties grew from the early 1970s through the late 1990s. On average the parties have differed by nearly 25 points on a 100-point scale, and the differences increased during the 1980s and 1990s (Shipan and Lowry 2001). Scores compiled by the League of Conservation Voters (LCV) in more recent years show the same pattern, with Senate

	STEPS
VOTING RECORDS ON THE ENVIRONMENT	TO
	ANALYSIS

The League of Conservation Voters (LCV) is a leading environmental organization. For nearly four decades it has kept tabs on how members of Congress vote on the environment. Each year the group compiles the National Environmental Scorecard, which records members' choices on ten to fourteen key votes. Go to the league's Web site (www.lcv.org) to see a recent scorecard. You can view the full report as a pdf file or see the scores of individual members or state delegations as html files. Look up the voting records for one or more members in the House of Representatives and Senate from your state or a state you find interesting. If using the full report, you can see how these votes compare to the average for the member's state, the scores of the chair and ranking minority member on each of the leading environmental policy committees of the House and Senate, or each party's House or Senate leaders. The report also indicates which issues and particular votes were used to compile these scores. Why do you think the member you selected has the score he or she does? Does it reflect the nature of the constituency, the locally active environmental or business groups, or the member's own political philosophy or ideology?

The LCV scores reported on the site represent how often a member of Congress voted in accordance with the position taken by the league and the coalition of environmental group leaders on which it relies to select an annual list of important environmental votes. Look at the votes the LCV selected in a particular year and the way it compiles the environmental voting score. These are described at the beginning of the full report.

Do you think the score fairly represents the voting record of members of Congress on environmental and energy issues? Compare the voting records of Democrats and Republicans, either nationwide or within your own state. Why do you think Republicans consistently have much lower LCV scores than Democrats? Do you think there is a bias in the way votes are selected and the scores calculated? Do the differences in scores reflect the nature of the constituencies within each of the major parties? Their political philosophies? Something else?

Democrats averaging about 85 percent support for the positions the LCV and the environmental community favored, and Senate Republicans around 8 percent. In the House, Democrats averaged about 86 percent, and Republicans 10 percent.[13] Clearly, the parties no longer saw eye to eye on environmental issues. The box "Steps to Analysis: Voting Records on the Environment" explains how these scores are compiled and points to the Web site where students can find the environmental voting record of any member of Congress.

The differences between the two parties on environmental votes were especially sharp in the latter half of the 1990s, as the Republicans gained control of both houses of Congress and aggressively sought to curtail environmental policy actions, much as the Reagan administration had done. Once again, Congress cut agency budgets and tried to rein in what it described as regulatory bureaucracies run amok. The EPA was a prime target. As was the case during the 1980s under Reagan, however, the anti-environmental agenda won too few converts to succeed. The U.S. public continued to demonstrate strong support for environmental protection, the Clinton White House fought hard to defend existing programs, and lobbying by environmental groups such as the Sierra Club and NRDC prevented enactment of the most severe measures considered by Congress. The most common result during the 1990s was policy gridlock, as the opponents of environmental policy could not muster the votes to repeal or significantly change the established policies and programs. But this outcome also meant that Congress could not enact the much-needed reforms of the Clean Air Act, the Clean Water Act, and the Endangered Species Act, among others (Kraft 2010).

Environmental Policy under George W. Bush

Heated battles over the direction of environmental policy continued after the 2000 election of George W. Bush. This time, however, the efforts to weaken environmental policy came at least as much from the White House as from congressional conservatives. Democrats in Congress strongly opposed the president's initiatives, including substantial budget cuts for environmental programs. They successfully blocked many of them, often in alliance with moderate Republicans.

Like his father, who had served as president a decade earlier, Bush acknowledged popular support for environmental protection and resource conservation, but as a conservative Republican he could not ignore his party's ideological and financial base in the business community, particularly industrial corporations and timber, mining, agriculture, and oil interests. In fact, Bush drew heavily from those constituencies, as well as from conservative ideological groups, to staff the EPA and the Interior, Agriculture, and Energy departments. In addition, he sought to deregulate environmental protection through what he called a new era of voluntary, flexible, and cooperative programs and to transfer more responsibility for enforcement of federal laws to the states. Environmentalists criticized the president's approach as unlikely to be effective and far too generous to the business community.

As noted earlier in the chapter, the election of Obama brought a strikingly different perspective and set of priorities to the White House, suggesting that environmental policy might be quite different in the next several years. His appointees to key positions in the Departments of Energy and Interior, at the EPA, and within the White House itself all suggested much stronger support for environmental policy than had been the case under Bush (Vig and Kraft 2010).[14]

MAJOR FEDERAL ENVIRONMENTAL POLICIES

Environmental policy consists of the many different statutes enacted during the 1960s and 1970s and their later amendments, but there is no single consolidated policy on the environment that describes the nation's goals and the strategies needed to reach them. Nor is environmental policy concentrated in one executive department or agency; rather, at the national level, responsibility for the environment is divided among twelve cabinet departments and the EPA, the Nuclear Regulatory Commission, and other agencies. The EPA has the lion's share of responsibility, but it must work with other departments and agencies, especially the Departments of Agriculture, Energy, and the Interior, to carry out its mission.

Because so many agencies contribute to U.S. environmental policy, the best way to survey the subject is to highlight the major elements within each of three areas: environmental protection policy or pollution control, natural resource policy, and energy policy. Only one

EXECUTIVE AGENCIES WITH ENVIRONMENTAL RESPONSIBILITIES

Visit one or more of the Web pages of the leading federal environmental and natural resource departments and agencies to learn more about their missions, the laws they administer, the agencies and programs under their jurisdiction, and their programs' achievements or shortcomings. The Department of the Interior, for example, includes the U.S. Geological Survey, Fish and Wildlife Service, National Park Service, and Bureau of Land Management. The U.S. Forest Service and the Natural Resources Conservation Service are parts of the Department of Agriculture. The Department of Energy (DOE) sponsors a large number of energy research and development programs and has broad responsibilities for cleaning up former defense installations, including heavily contaminated nuclear weapons production facilities. The DOE is also in charge of studying the site at Yucca Mountain, Nevada, for the anticipated federal nuclear waste repository.

All of the agency Web sites have links to current programs and issues, studies and reports, internal organization issues, related programs at other departments and agencies, or White House positions on the issues. In interpreting information provided by these sites regarding program accomplishments, you should bear in mind that government agencies—federal or state and local—almost always offer a positive assessment of their activities and say little about their weaknesses or failures.

To find environmental and natural resource agencies at the state level, visit the Web site for the Council of State Governments (www.csg.org) and look for the link to State Pages, where all fifty state governments are listed. Once on the state government home page, look for agencies dealing with the environment, natural resources, or energy.

As you examine these pages, consider what might be the telltale signs that the agency is providing only one side of an issue or putting a positive spin on the agency's achievements or current actions. For example, the DOE site describes in very positive terms President Obama's initiatives that were part of the economic stimulus package of early 2009. Click on the tab for Environment, and then Climate Change. How does the DOE describe the Obama administration's approach to climate change policy? What does the agency have to say about the potential contribution of nuclear power? Can you tell from these descriptions how effective the action taken has been and whether it promises to be a major component of a U.S. policy on climate change?

www.doi.gov (U.S. Department of the Interior)
www.energy.gov (U.S. Department of Energy)
www.epa.gov (U.S. Environmental Protection Agency)
www.nrc.gov (U.S. Nuclear Regulatory Commission)
www.usda.gov (U.S. Department of Agriculture)

major statute, the National Environmental Policy Act, cuts across these categories. For each of the three categories, this chapter emphasizes the broad goals that policymakers have adopted and the policy strategies or means they use to achieve them. It also evaluates selected policy achievements and considers policy options for the future. Students who want a more complete description of the major environmental or energy policies should consult the suggested readings listed at the end of the chapter or visit the Web sites of the implementing agencies, where summary descriptions as well as the full statutes are usually available. The box "Working with Sources: Executive Agencies with Environmental Responsibilities" lists the Web sites for the leading executive agencies with environmental responsibilities and suggests how public policy students might evaluate the information they find at those sites.

The chapter focuses on national environmental and resource policies, even though, as noted earlier, some states, such as California, Minnesota, New Jersey, Oregon, Vermont, and Wisconsin, often are at the forefront of policy innovation. One of the best ways to compare state environmental policies is to visit the Web site for the Council of State Governments (www.csg.org) for links to all the state home pages. Those pages in turn describe environmental policy within the state. Another source for state environmental policy is the Web site for the Environmental Council of the States (www.ecos.org), a national nonpartisan association of state environmental commissioners that reports on a range of issues concerning state environmental policy activities and federal-state relations.

The National Environmental Policy Act

One law that might appear to constitute a coherent national policy on environmental issues is the National Environmental Policy Act of 1969 (NEPA). The enactment of this six-page statute signified the beginning of the modern era in environmental policy. NEPA acknowledged the "profound impact of man's activities on the interrelations of all components of the natural environment" and the "critical importance of restoring and maintaining environmental quality" for human welfare. The instrument for achieving these goals, however, is procedural rather than substantive: the preparation of an **environmental impact statement** (EIS), which is then used in government agency planning and decision making. Such statements are required for major federal actions "significantly affecting the quality of the human environment." They are intended to offer a detailed and systematic assessment of the environmental effects of a proposed action, such as building a highway, and alternatives to the action that might be considered. In effect, NEPA mandates that agencies engage in policy analysis before they make decisions. Its real effect, however, comes less from the preparation of these impact statements than from a requirement that they be made public. Doing so means that agencies have to give serious consideration to the consequences of their decisions and anticipate how critics of those decisions might respond.

NEPA requires only that such EISs be prepared and be subject to public review; it does not prevent an agency from making an environmentally harmful decision. Nevertheless, most evaluations of the policy find that it has had a substantial effect on decision making by government agencies such as the U.S. Forest Service, the Federal Highway Administration, and the Army Corps of Engineers (Bartlett 1989; Caldwell 1998). In a way, NEPA symbolized environmental policy action during the late 1960s and 1970s by establishing new decision-making procedures that opened the policy process to public scrutiny and assured widespread consultation with affected parties, including environmental groups and local governments. The old subgovernments, long dominant in many areas of natural resource management such as logging, mining, and ranching, were forever changed as a result of these procedural requirements.

NEPA also created a presidential advisory body for environmental issues called the Council on Environmental Quality (CEQ). The CEQ is charged with supervising the EIS process, and it works with executive agencies to define their responsibilities under the act; in recent years, however, the CEQ has had a relatively low profile among executive agencies. As might be expected, not all agencies adapted quickly to the new requirements for impact statements and public review, but over time most have significantly altered their decision making. Still, about one hundred court challenges to agency decisions under NEPA are filed every year. The most common complaints are that no EIS was prepared when one should have been or that the EIS was inadequate. For more information on how NEPA works, visit the CEQ Web site (www.whitehouse.gov/administration/eop/ceq). Many states have adopted "little NEPAs," or NEPA-like statutes, with much the same purpose—to assess the likely environmental impacts of development projects such as highways. This is yet another reminder that states have considerable independent authority to act on environmental protection challenges, and many have gone well beyond what the federal government has done (Rabe 2010).

Environmental Protection Statutes and the EPA

Congress has enacted and, over time, strengthened with amendments seven major environmental protection, or pollution control, statutes: the Clean Air Act; Clean Water Act; Federal Insecticide, Fungicide, and Rodenticide Act; Safe Drinking Water Act; Resource Conservation and Recovery Act; Toxic Substances Control Act; and Comprehensive Environmental Response, Compensation, and Liability Act. This is a diverse set of public policies, but they have much in common: the EPA develops regulations that affect the current and future use and release of chemicals and pollutants that pose a significant risk to public health or the environment.[15]

The Clean Air Act Amendments of 1970 (CAA) required for the first time the development of national ambient air quality standards that were to be uniform across the country, with enforcement shared by the federal and state governments. These standards were to "provide an adequate margin of safety" to protect human health, and cost was not to be a consideration. The CAA also set emissions standards for cars, trucks, and buses—the mobile sources of pollution—and it regulated fuels and toxic and hazardous air pollutants. In addition, it set emissions limits on stationary sources of pollution such as power plants, oil refineries, chemical companies, and other industrial facilities. The extensive 1990 amendments added acid rain controls and set new deadlines for improving urban air quality and controlling toxic air pollutants.

The Clean Water Act of 1972 (CWA) is the major federal program regulating surface water quality. Like the Clean Air Act, the CWA established a national policy for water pollution control. It set 1985 as the deadline for stopping the discharge of pollutants into navigable waters (a stipulation that allows federal jurisdiction) and sought to make all surface water "fishable and swimmable" by 1983. The act encouraged technological innovation and comprehensive regional planning for attaining water quality. And like the Clean Air Act, the CWA gave the states primary responsibility for implementation as long as they followed federal standards and guidelines. Essentially, these involve water quality standards and effluent limits set by a permit system that specifies how much each facility is allowed to discharge and the control technologies it will use. For years the CWA also provided substantial subsidies and loans to the states to help construct new wastewater treatment plants.

The Federal Insecticide, Fungicide, and Rodenticide Act of 1972 (FIFRA) was similarly ambitious and limited. It required the EPA to register the pesticides used commercially in the United States. The pesticides had to not pose "any unreasonable risk to man or the environment," but the law allowed consideration of the economic and social costs and benefits of pesticide use. The EPA had to balance the benefits of using pesticides against their impact on public health, and the government had the burden of proof to show harm if it attempted to ban an existing pesticide. FIFRA was modified significantly by the Food Quality Protection Act of 1996, which required the EPA to apply a new, uniform "reasonable risk" approach to regulating pesticides used on food, fiber, and other crops. The new standard is more stringent than the old one. In addition, the agency is required to give special consideration to the impact of pesticide residues on children and to set higher standards for these residues. The law gives the EPA greater authority to suspend a pesticide believed to pose a public health hazard, and the agency must review all pesticide registrations at least once every fifteen years.

The Safe Drinking Water Act of 1974 was designed to ensure the quality and safety of drinking water by specifying minimum health standards for public water supplies. The EPA sets the standards for chemical and microbiological contaminants for tap water. The act required regular monitoring of water supplies to ensure that pollutants stay below safe levels, and it regulated state programs for protecting groundwater supplies that many areas use for drinking water. To assist states and localities in meeting these goals, the act provided loans and grants to defray the costs. A 1996 amendment established a more flexible approach to regulating water contaminants based on their risk to public health and allowed consideration of the costs and benefits of proposed regulations. It also added a "right-to-know" provision that requires water systems to provide customers once a year with a report of any contaminants in the local water supply.

The Resource Conservation and Recovery Act of 1976 (RCRA) is the nation's main hazardous waste control policy. The law was intended to regulate existing hazardous waste disposal practices and promote the conservation and recovery of resources through comprehensive management of solid waste. It required the EPA to develop criteria "necessary to protect human health and the environment" for the safe disposal of solid waste and to set standards for the treatment, storage, and disposal of hazardous wastes. The 1984 amendments to RCRA made the act even more demanding and set tight new deadlines, largely because the EPA had made insufficient progress toward the goals that Congress initially set.

The Toxic Substances Control Act, also approved in 1976, gave the EPA comprehensive authority to identify, evaluate, and regulate risks associated with commercial chemicals. The idea was to help develop a national database of chemicals posing an "unreasonable risk of injury to health or the environment," but without unduly burdening industry or impeding technological innovation. Policymakers combined these two competing goals and saddled the EPA with a difficult and time-consuming set of procedural requirements that greatly limited the act's effectiveness.

The last of the seven statutes, the Comprehensive Environmental Response, Compensation, and Liability Act of 1980, also known as Superfund, is perhaps the most criticized of the lot. It was enacted after the public became alarmed about toxic waste dumps, such as the one at Love Canal in New York that was highlighted at the beginning of chapter 2. Superfund is directed at the thousands of abandoned or uncontrolled hazardous waste sites in the nation. Congress gave the EPA responsibility to respond to the problem by identifying, assessing, and cleaning up these sites. If necessary, the EPA can draw from a special fund for that purpose, which is how the program got its nickname. The fund originally was financed through a tax on the petrochemical industry and other chemical manufacturers. One of the central principles of Superfund is that polluters should pay the costs of cleanup, and the act's financial liability provisions have caused controversy for years.[16] In 1986 Congress strengthened the act, put more money into the fund, and added an entirely new provision on the public's right to know about toxic chemicals made by, stored within, or released through local businesses. The Toxics Release Inventory, or TRI, is published each year and can be accessed on the EPA's Web site and elsewhere. The TRI describes toxic chemicals that industrial facilities release to the air, water, and land in communities across the country, and the information can be displayed on a local map that shows the location of each facility (Hamilton 2005). After 1995, however, Congress declined to renew the taxes on chemical and oil companies that support the Superfund trust fund, resulting in a slowdown of action on site cleanups and a shifting of the financial burden to the public through general tax revenue.

Common Themes in Environmental Protection Policy. Separately and collectively, these seven policies created diverse regulatory actions that touch virtually every industrial and commercial enterprise in the nation. They also affect ordinary citizens by regulating air, food, and water quality, and the cars and other consumer products everyone buys. In other words, almost every aspect of daily life is affected by the way these statutes were written and how the EPA and the states implement them. It should not be surprising, therefore, that routine implementation of the policies and their periodic renewal in Congress usually spark contentious debates. People argue over the extent of the risks that citizens face, the appropriate standards for protecting public health and the environment, the mechanisms used to achieve these standards, and how the benefits of these policies should be weighed against the costs of compliance and other social and economic values. The box "Working with Sources: Environmental Policy Advocacy" lists some of the environmental and industry groups that have been active in these policy debates. Their Web sites are included as well.

These disagreements put the EPA, whether fairly or not, at the center of fractious political fights. The agency is a frequent target of criticism by members of Congress, the business community, and environmental groups, all of whom often fault its scientific research and regulatory decision making (Rosenbaum 2010). The **Environmental Protection Agency** is an independent executive agency, but its administrator reports directly to the president, and its decision making tends to reflect White House priorities. The agency is the largest of the federal regulatory agencies, with a staff of nearly eighteen thousand and a total budget in 2008 of about $7.4 billion. However, in his first budget outline of February 2009, President Obama proposed a 34 percent increase in EPA's funding, to raise it to $10.5 billion, with most of the additional funds going to support clean water initiatives and a new Great Lakes Initiative. By most accounts, the EPA handles its job fairly well and is among the most professional of the federal environmental agencies. Policy analysts have long observed, however, that the EPA's resources are insufficient to handle its vast responsibilities. They have also concluded that to succeed at its demanding tasks, the agency must adopt new policy approaches and work with Congress to ensure that it has the authority and tools it needs (Durant, Fiorino, and O'Leary 2004; Fiorino 2006; National Academy of Public Administration 1995, 2000; Rosenbaum 2010).

WORKING WITH **SOURCES**

ENVIRONMENTAL POLICY ADVOCACY

Many organizations play an active role in shaping environmental policy in Congress, federal executive agencies, federal courts, and state and local governments. To learn more about what positions they take and what they do, visit some of the following Web sites. We list environmental groups first and then several groups that normally oppose the environmentalist position. Comparable groups are involved at state, local, and regional levels, and you might try the same exercise in these locales for advocacy organizations.

ENVIRONMENTAL GROUPS
www.edf.org/home.cfm (Environmental Defense Fund)

www.greenpeace.org/usa (Greenpeace)
www.nrdc.org (Natural Resources Defense Council)
www.nwf.org (National Wildlife Federation)
www.sierraclub.org (Sierra Club)

INDUSTRY GROUPS
www.nam.org (National Association of Manufacturers)
www.nfib.com (National Federation of Independent Business)
www.uschamber.com (U.S. Chamber of Commerce)

The core environmental protection policies have over time produced substantial and well-documented environmental and health benefits, which are especially evident in dramatically improved urban air quality and control of point sources of water pollution. Not every policy has been equally effective, however, and those dealing with control of toxic chemicals and hazardous wastes have been the least successful. Moreover, existing policies barely touch some substantial environmental risks, such as indoor air pollution, even though the cost of these policies has been relatively high. In 1992 the U.S. Government Accountability Office estimated that between 1972 and 1992 the cumulative expenditures for pollution control exceeded $1 trillion. By the late 1990s, the EPA put the continuing cost to both government and the private sector at more than $170 billion per year, and by most estimates more than half of that cost is paid by the private sector, which no doubt passes it along to consumers as higher product prices. Is the cost too high? Are the benefits worth it? Might the costs be reduced through adopting different policies?

The seven major environmental protection statutes share a common approach to problem solving. All rely on a regulatory policy strategy, or what critics call **command and control;** economists would call it a system of **direct regulation.** What this means is that environmental quality standards are set and enforced according to the language of each statute, and each specifies how the agency is to make its decisions. Generally, Congress gives the EPA discretion to set standards that are consistent with the law, and the EPA is expected to base its decisions on the best available science. Invariably, however, setting environmental quality standards involves an uncertain mix of science and policy judgment about how much risk is acceptable to society (Andrews 2006a; Rosenbaum 2010). The cost of implementing the standard is also usually considered. These kinds of judgments are necessary whether the issue is the amount of pesticide residues allowed on food, the level of lead or arsenic in drinking water, or how much ground-level ozone in the air is acceptable. That is, the laws do not aim for the elimination of risks to public health or the environment; instead, they seek to reduce the level of risk to a point that is reasonable in light of the costs.

Because the science is almost never complete or definitive, agency officials must make policy or political judgments about how stringent a standard ought to be. These kinds of decisions are never easy, and they invariably cause disagreements. Business groups criticize the standards for being too stringent, and environmental and health groups say they are too weak. One side or the other in a dispute, and sometimes both, may decide to challenge the standard in court. As might be expected, EPA decision making operates under somewhat different expectations in Democratic and Republican administrations. For example, Clinton's EPA was more likely than Bush's EPA to adopt tough environmental standards. As stated earlier, Obama's administration is likely to have priorities that are much closer to Clinton's than to Bush's; certainly, Obama's early actions suggest as much (Vig and Kraft 2010). Once a standard is set, the EPA and the states take various actions, through issuing rules and regulations, to ensure that it is met.

The elaborate laws and regulations for environmental protection actions might lead one to believe that the government is protecting the public against the most significant risks. Unfortunately, that is not always the case. Several comparative environmental risk studies, which weigh the risks to the public against EPA program priorities, have shown that the agency tends to focus on highly visible risks about which the public is concerned, rather than on those most dangerous to the public's health. For example, people worry about hazardous wastes and abandoned waste sites, and Congress has told the EPA to deal with these problems. According to the professionals' rankings of environmental risks, however, hazardous wastes are not as dangerous as the public believes, while other risks that the public barely recognizes are near the top of the list. These problems include indoor air pollution from radon and secondhand (passive) smoke, as well as ecological concerns such as climate change, stratospheric ozone depletion, habitat alteration, and species extinction and loss of biological diversity (U.S. EPA 1990).[17]

To put the matter in slightly different terms, the way people perceive environmental risks is often at odds with how professionals see them (Slovic 1987). Public perceptions tend to drive the policy-making process, which sometimes results in distorted priorities that do not adequately protect the public's health. The solution to this dilemma may lie in educating the public better on environmental and health risks and involving the public in environmental decision making at all levels of government. Many analysts also argue that Congress needs to rewrite environmental laws to give the EPA more discretion to act on the most important risks to public and environmental health (Davies 1996; Durant, Fiorino, and O'Leary 2004; National Academy of Public Administration 2000).

How Well Do Environmental Protection Programs Work? With all the criticism that has been directed at environmental protection policy and command-and-control regulation, one would think the programs have been dismal failures. But the evidence suggests that they have been quite successful on the whole. Granted, environmental policies are difficult to evaluate, in part because they entail long-term commitments to broad social values and goals that are not

WORKING WITH SOURCES

EVALUATING ENVIRONMENTAL POLICY

As stated throughout the text, it is important to evaluate how well policies have worked and what they have achieved. The organizations and Web sites listed here offer such information from many different perspectives. Government Web sites usually have official reports and databases, such as the annual EPA report on air pollution. The Government Accountability Office conducts independent evaluations of executive agencies and programs for Congress. Many other groups evaluate environmental and resource programs in terms of economic costs, efficiency, and effectiveness (Resources for the Future); the role of government and regulatory burdens (Cato Institute, Competitive Enterprise Institute, and the Heritage Foundation); and environmental science and advocacy (Environmental Defense Fund, Natural Resources Defense Council, and the Union of Concerned Scientists); or some combination of these criteria.

www.cato.org (Cato Institute)
www.cei.org (Competitive Enterprise Institute)
www.doi.gov (Department of the Interior)
www.edf.org (Environmental Defense Fund)
www.epa.gov (Environmental Protection Agency)
www.gao.gov (Government Accountability Office)
www.heritage.org (Heritage Foundation)
www.nrdc.org (Natural Resources Defense Council)
www.rff.org (Resources for the Future)
www.sierraclub.org (Sierra Club)

www.ucsusa.org (Union of Concerned Scientists)

Go to the EPA Web site and to the Office of Air and Radiation's annual air trends report (www.epa.gov/air/airtrends/index.html), and click on Reports and Data. You will see a list of the annual air quality trends reports. Examine some of the data on air trends for the major or criteria air pollutants such as ozone, sulfur dioxide, and fine particulates. Considering the trends over time and the EPA's own assessment of this information, would you conclude that the Clean Air Act has been effective? What other information would you need to determine the effectiveness of the act?

Now visit one or more of the other sites to see how environmental organizations and industry view the Clean Air Act and its achievements. For example, visit the National Resources Defense Council (NRDC) site and click on Air or Air Pollution. What is its position on the effectiveness of the act, or on industry influence on the act's implementation in recent years? Now compare the NRDC evaluation of the act to that of a conservative think tank such as the Competitive Enterprise Institute (CEI). Click on Issues, then Environmental Policy, and finally on Air Quality. How would you compare the CEI's view of the act's success with that of NRDC, especially its view of the costs and efficiency of the current national policies on air pollution? Why do you think each of these groups selects the information and the focus that it offers at its Web site?

easily quantified. Short-term and highly visible costs tend to attract more attention than long-term gains in public and environmental health—another source of debate over the value of environmental programs.

Some environmental conditions, such as air and water quality, are regularly monitored, but it is still difficult to assess how well present programs are achieving other objectives. For many critical natural resource concerns, such as protection of biological diversity, accurate measures are still being developed and national inventories are not yet available. The uncertainties over environmental trends mean that scientists and policy advocates frequently debate whether the environment is deteriorating or improving. Many state-of-the-environment reports addressing such conditions and trends can be found on Web sites for government agencies and environmental research institutes. The box "Working with Sources: Evaluating Environmental Policy" lists some of the most useful sources of such data and analysis of what the information means.

Fairly good information is available for air and water quality even if disagreement exists over which measures to use. For air quality, the EPA estimates that, between 1970 and 2004, aggregate emissions of the six principal, or criteria, air pollutants decreased by 54 percent even while the nation's population grew by 40 percent, the gross domestic product (GDP) rose by 187 percent, vehicle-miles traveled increased by 171 percent, and energy consumption grew by 47 percent.[18] Progress generally continues. Between 1990 and 2007, for example, monitored levels of the six criteria pollutants (that is, ambient air concentrations) showed improvement, with most declining during this period. Yet despite these impressive gains in air quality, as of 2007 some 158 million people (more than half of the U.S. population) lived in counties with pollution levels above the standards set for at least one of these criteria pollutants, typically for ozone and fine particulates. Do such figures tell you that the Clean Air Act is working well? Should the nation have done even better after forty years since its enactment?

The nation's water quality also has improved since passage of the Clean Water Act of 1972, although more slowly and more unevenly than has air quality. Monitoring data are less adequate for water quality than for air quality, with the states collectively assessing, for example, only 23 percent of the nation's rivers and streams. Based on these limited studies, water quality clearly falls short of the goals of federal clean water acts. For example, only 52 percent of the rivers and streams were considered to be of good quality and 47 percent were impaired.[19] Prevention of further degradation of water quality in the face of a growing population and strong economic growth could be considered an important achievement. Would you draw a different conclusion?

Policy Options for the Future. What kinds of policy alternatives should be considered for the future to replace or, more likely, to supplement environmental regulation? Critics of regulation frequently mention the greater use of market incentives or market-based approaches, more reliance on public information disclosure, more flexible and cooperative approaches to regulation, and further decentralization of power to the states (Dietz and Stern 2003; Durant, Fiorino, and O'Leary 2004; National Academy of Public Administration 2000). Such alternatives may be especially appropriate where conventional regulation works poorly. Two examples are reducing indoor air pollution and cleaning up nonpoint water pollution, which cannot be traced to a single source. Either there are too many sources to regulate or regulation simply is impractical; for example, no government can regulate indoor air quality in every U.S. dwelling. What might work instead are subsidies, public education campaigns, and tax credits, which are a form of market incentive. The federal government and the states have experimented with such policy options. As one illustration, Wisconsin has used a combination of educational outreach programs directed at changing farming practices, providing technical assistance, and partially subsidizing the cost of new nonpoint source controls to improve surface water quality.

The 1990 Clean Air Act revision incorporated market incentives by allowing marketable permits for emissions of sulfur dioxide. The idea behind the permits is that some companies will find it cheaper than others to make needed changes to reduce emissions, and they can then sell the "extra" permits to other companies. The program operates in two ways: the market incentives improve economic efficiency by reducing the overall cost of environmental improvement, and the government reduces the number of permits over time to ensure that the goal of lower emissions is reached. Although the federal program is thought to have worked well, a similar effort in the Los Angeles metropolitan area through a regional air quality management system has not entirely lived up to expectations (Mazmanian and Kraft 2009). Nevertheless, environmental economists have high hopes for these efforts because they provide important economic incentives for industry to work toward environmental goals, even to go "beyond compliance" to make greater improvements than the law requires (Portney and Stavins 2000). Is their assessment persuasive?

As a policy strategy, information disclosure is another useful supplement to regulation. The nation uses this strategy by compiling the Toxics Release Inventory; by publishing automobile fuel efficiency standards, which are also attached to the windows of new cars; by promoting appliance efficiency standards developed as part of the federal ENERGY STAR program; and in other ways.[20] The hope here is that individuals and organizations will use the information to press industry and government to move more aggressively on environmental and energy improvements than they might otherwise be inclined to do. Or, acting proactively to avoid embarrassment, those same parties might undertake initiatives to head off criticism, such as reducing pollution or improving fuel efficiency.

The use of flexible regulatory approaches and collaborative regulatory approaches was a hallmark of the Clinton administration's EPA, and the Bush administration also favored these techniques (Vig and Kraft 2010). The general idea is to reduce conflict between regulators and those being regulated and to work cooperatively to develop appropriate environmental standards, regulations, and action programs. The intention is to move from the contentious, legalistic system of regulation to one in which the various stakeholders work together to seek solutions. Environmentalists are sometimes skeptical of these arrangements, fearful that they will endanger what has been achieved in environmental quality, but business interests, state and local governments, and many policy analysts think highly of the promise of flexible regulations and collaborative decision making. What is the case for relying on such collaborative approaches rather than always using regulation to achieve environmental quality goals? Would you favor doing so?

Further decentralization of environmental responsibilities to the states is also controversial. Over the past two decades, a major transfer of environmental authority from the federal government to the states has taken place. How much more is desirable and what the likely effects will be are questions yet to be answered. Policymakers in both parties favor increased decentralization, but many analysts are skeptical about whether giving additional powers to the states will improve policy effectiveness. They also raise questions of equity. Many states have a greater capacity for environmental policy than they did four decades ago, but the performance from state to state is uneven. As noted, California, Minnesota, New Jersey, Oregon, and Wisconsin have been leaders in environmental policy innovation and enforcement, but other states lag behind and may be subjecting their citizens to preventable health risks. The tendency of states to compete with one another economically could constrain enforcement of environmental laws. In addition, many environmental problems—including acid rain, toxic air pollutants, and water pollution—cross state lines, suggesting that a national or regional approach might be both more effective and more equitable than leaving the solution to the states. Ultimately, what is needed is a sorting out of which environmental functions are best suited for state and local governments and which require national, or even international, management (Rabe 2010).[21]

Natural Resource Policies

Many of the concerns that arise in pollution control also pertain to natural resource policies that govern the management of public lands, forests, and parks, and the efforts to protect species and biological diversity. Public policies for the management of natural resources developed in response to concerns over their abuse. After more than a century of policies that encouraged exploitation of resources in the vast federal lands of the West, the twentieth century brought a new ethic of **environmental stewardship,** the protection of resources for the future. That change has taken effect only slowly, however, and the resource development interests, such as timber, ranching, agriculture, mining, and oil and gas drilling businesses, often disagree with conservation organizations over what policies best promote the public's welfare. Indeed, some of the strongest opposition to environmentalists over the past several decades has come from development interests and their supporters in the so-called wise use, county supremacy, and property rights movements (Brick and Cawley 1996; Cawley 1993; Switzer 1997).

Most of the current federal natural resource policies are grounded in the principle of **multiple use,** which Congress intended to use to help balance competing national objectives of economic development and environmental preservation. Should old growth forests in the Northwest be cut for timber or preserved as wildlife habitat? To what extent should mining for gold, silver, and other minerals, which can cause extensive environmental damage, be permitted on public lands—and how much should developers pay the Treasury for the right to do it? Should the government protect the Arctic National Wildlife Refuge (ANWR), and other similar lands, from oil and gas development, or is expansion of energy sources a more important priority? Using the guidance found in the various natural resource laws, the officials in federal resource agencies, mostly in the Interior and Agriculture departments, are charged with answering these questions.

One of the major federal policies that governs these kinds of debates is the National Environmental Policy Act, discussed earlier. Through the environmental impact statement process this legislation mandates, agencies are forced to consider a broader set of issues and to open decision making to a wider group of stakeholders than before. As noted earlier, NEPA helped to break up some of the subgovernments and diminish the influence that, for example, the mining industry had long exercised in federal decisions on mineral leasing and the timber industry in decisions on federal forest management.

Two other major statutes, the Federal Land Policy and Management Act of 1976 (FLPMA) and the National Forest Management Act of 1976 (NFMA), had comparable effects in changing the way the government makes natural resource decisions. These acts set out new procedures for government planning and management of resources, including extensive public participation, and they established a mission for long-term stewardship of public resources. In effect, these policies required government officials to consider diverse values in managing resources, not just the highest dollar return (Clarke and McCool 1996; Davis 2001). For example, the NFMA helped to shift the U.S. Forest Service away from an emphasis on timber production. The law requires the Forest Service to prepare long-term, comprehensive plans for the national forests and to involve the public in its decision making through meetings and hearings. The FLPMA gives the Bureau of Land Management greater authority to administer federal land under a broad, multiple-use mandate that leans toward environmental values and away from its previous practice of favoring grazing as the dominant use.

These two policies did not end the disputes over public lands and forests, however. Environmentalists continue to battle with timber, ranching, mining, and oil and gas interests, and the winners often depend on which party is in the White House. Republican administrations tend to side more often with the forces of development, and Democratic administrations with those of land preservation. For example, President Clinton used his executive authority under the Antiquities Act of 1906 to establish nineteen new national monuments and enlarge three others. In all, he protected more than six million acres of public land this way. In addition, just before he left office, Clinton issued an executive order protecting nearly sixty million acres of roadless areas in the national forests from future development. President Bush challenged Clinton's policies, reversed many of his initiatives, and was far more receptive to development interests than to conservation (Lowry 2006; Lubell and Segee 2010; Vig 2010). Indeed, a comprehensive examination of his natural resource policies after his first year in office found that Bush was "aggressively encouraging more drilling, mining, and logging on much of the seven hundred million acres controlled by the Interior Department and the Forest Service." [22]

One of the most controversial of the natural resource policies is also one of the toughest. The Endangered Species Act of 1973 (ESA) in many ways symbolizes the nation's commitment to resource conservation goals, and perhaps for that reason it has become a lightning rod for anti-environmentalists. The ESA broadened federal authority to protect threatened and endangered species and established procedures to ensure the recovery of all species threatened with extinction. It prohibited the "taking" of such species by fishing, hunting, or habitat alteration or destruction whether the species inhabited state, federal, or private land. The U.S. Fish and Wildlife Service (FWS) administers the ESA for land-based species, and the agency has struggled to achieve its goals amidst frequent congressional criticism and perennially inadequate budgets. Despite condemnation from conservatives who see the ESA as a threat to property rights, most decisions under the act have been made without much controversy, and the act has prevented few development projects from going forward. More recently, the FWS has made good use of collaborative decision making in developing habitat conservation plans to avoid such confrontations.

Evaluating Success. As is the case with pollution control policies, evaluating the success of natural resource policies is not easy. The kinds of measurements available, such as the number of acres of protected lands set aside in national monuments and parks, are not good indicators of what really matters. Still, these laws have brought about considerable achievements. For example, the national park system grew from about 26 million acres in 1960 to over 84 million acres by 2008. Since adoption of the 1964 Wilderness Act, Congress has set aside 108 million

One of the most recognized of the natural resource policies is the federal Endangered Species Act (ESA), enacted in 1973. It was designed to identify and help to protect those species that might be lost, most often from human activities that adversely affect their habitat. In May 2008, the Bush administration listed the polar bear as a threatened species under the ESA because of a decrease in sea ice coverage. Polar bears depend on sea ice to hunt for their favorite food, seals. Changes in the abundance and distribution of sea ice threaten the bears' existence and eventually will put them at risk of becoming endangered. The decrease in sea ice is attributed to climate change brought about by human activities that release greenhouse gases. The Bush administration, however, was reluctant to admit this connection, which would have opened the door to a challenge that the bears' habitat can be protected only by reducing greenhouse gas emissions from the use of fossil fuels.

acres of wilderness through the national wilderness preservation system. Since 1968 it has designated over 165 wild and scenic rivers with more than 11,000 protected miles. The FWS manages more than 93 million acres in about 540 units of the national wildlife refuge system—triple the land area managed in 1970. State and local governments have also set aside large amounts of open space for parks and recreational purposes, some of them funded through the federal Land and Water Conservation Fund Act of 1964 (Fairfax et al. 2005; Press, 2002). By late 2008, thirty-five years after passage of the Endangered Species Act, more than 1,300 U.S. plant and animal species had been listed as either endangered or threatened, over 520 critical habitats had been designated, nearly 950 habitat conservation plans had been approved, and more than 1,100 recovery plans had been put into effect. Despite all of that activity, however, only a few endangered species have recovered fully, and recent studies indicate that as many as 80 percent of species on the list are conservation reliant; that is, they will need to remain on the list indefinitely.[23]

Still, the true measurement of success or failure is whether an ecosystem is healthy or sustainable, but even ecologists cannot agree on what that means or the indicators to use.

Ecologists are attempting to develop such standards so that communities across the nation can determine whether, or to what extent, a lake, river, bay, or land area should be preserved or restored to a healthy condition. Many communities are already trying to make those kinds of decisions. Massive federal and state efforts to restore damaged ecosystems such as the Great Lakes, the Florida Everglades, and the Chesapeake Bay testify to the need for accurate ecological indicators.[24]

Policy Options for the Future. Even without the most accurate indicators to judge the success of natural resource policies, suggestions abound for reforming the policies to make them more effective, efficient, and fair. Among the most frequently proposed are reduction or elimination of subsidies for resource development or exploitation; the imposition of **user fees,** which is a form of market incentive; devolution of resource decisions to the state, county, or local level; the use of ecosystem management; and greater reliance on collaborative decision making and collaborative planning.

Natural resource policies have long incorporated generous **resource subsidies** to users—such as ranchers, mining and timber companies, and oil and gas exploration companies. Often, the user pays the government less in fees than the cost to taxpayers of providing services to these businesses. For example, for years the Forest Service realized less money from timber sales than it cost the agency to build and maintain access roads for loggers. Because of the General Mining Law of 1872 (little has changed since its adoption), the mining industry has paid only nominal sums for the right to mine public lands and has paid no royalty on the minerals extracted from them; moreover, it has caused extensive environmental damage. Critics argue that the government should reduce or end resource subsidies. These subsidies are hard to defend on equity or efficiency grounds, and often they contribute to environmental degradation.[25] Environmentalists say that development interests should pay the full cost of access to public resources through higher user fees. Although the argument seems reasonable, the developers stoutly defend their long-standing subsidies, arguing that changing the rules at this time would be unfair to them and the industries they represent and would harm the economy in many rural areas of the West.

The idea of imposing user fees extends to charges for entering national parks and other federal lands. Historically, visitors paid a small fee that was well below what they would pay for comparable recreation on private land and hardly sufficient to cover the costs of park maintenance. Fees have gone up, but is this fair? Some argue that people already pay for the national parks with their federal taxes. Should they have to pay again when they enter a park? From the perspective of equity, the answer might be yes, those who use public services should pay a premium for them. Otherwise, taxpayers who do not use the parks are subsidizing those who do. What is fair in this case?

Devolution proposals, as noted in regard to pollution control policies, call for decentralization of resource decision making to state and local governments. The assumption is that these governments are more alert to the needs of their populations and more capable of taking appropriate action. Critics charge that state and local governments are likely to favor development interests within the state and would not necessarily represent those of the nation. How the states would use their additional power will no doubt vary. Some may be inclined to support development interests more than the federal government does at present. A good example is drilling for oil in ANWR. Alaska strongly favors doing so, but support is not nearly as strong within other states and in Congress. Given the level of public concern over the environment, it is also likely that conflict over natural resources will continue (Lowry 2006; Lubell and Segee 2010).

As a policy, **ecosystem management** means a shift in emphasis toward principles of protecting habitat and maintaining biological diversity. Among its supporters are natural scientists, particularly biologists and ecologists concerned about the loss of biological diversity and the fragmentation of ecosystems that do not coincide with the boundaries of national parks and wilderness areas. Essentially, ecosystem management is a long-term, comprehensive approach to natural resource management, with a priority on ecosystem functioning rather than human use (Cortner and Moote 1999). Protection of old growth forests in the Pacific Northwest is one example. Critics of ecosystem management include economic development interests that predict less access to natural resources and conservatives who question the wisdom of increasing government agencies' authority over public and private lands. Some policy analysts also question just how effective ecosystem management has been, reminding us that even good ideas do not always translate into effective policy. Much depends on how programs are designed and implemented (Layzer 2008).

Collaborative decision making and planning aspires to resolve conflicts over local and regional natural resource issues. It brings the various stakeholders together in an ad hoc and voluntary process characterized by cooperation and consensus building. Policymakers have used it to develop successful habitat conservation plans, protect and restore damaged ecosystems, and plan for the future of river basins, among many other activities (Sabatier et al. 2005; Weber 2003; Wondolleck and Yaffee 2000). The parties have an incentive to cooperate because collaboration may speed up the decision-making process and allow them to avoid costly litigation. Although the principle is generally applauded, critics of collaboration argue that not all interests are necessarily represented and that the most powerful interests may dominate the process. Nevertheless, such collaboration holds considerable promise for the future, and its use is likely to continue (Lubell and Segee 2010).[26]

ENERGY POLICY

Energy policy is part environmental protection and part natural resource policy, but most analysts would probably agree that the United States has no real energy policy. Instead, individual and corporate decisions in the marketplace largely determine energy use, with each sector of energy influenced to some extent by a variety of government subsidies and regulations. For example, since the 1940s nuclear power has benefited substantially from government subsidies; indeed, the financial aid made its commercial development possible. Other subsidies have promoted coal, natural gas, and oil, often in ways that those outside the industries barely recognize.[27] As discussed below, even more recent energy policies enacted by Congress in 1992 and 2005 continued this pattern.

Energy policy is something of an anomaly compared to the collection of broadly supported environmental policies listed in Table 11-1. For energy, the prevailing pattern was policy gridlock from the 1970s through the early 2000s. Presidents Richard Nixon, Gerald Ford, and Jimmy Carter all attempted to formulate national energy policies to promote energy independence by increasing domestic supplies, primarily fossil fuels. Following the oil embargo imposed by the **Organization of Petroleum Exporting Countries** (OPEC) in 1973 and the subsequent sharp increases in the cost of oil, Carter, who was elected in 1976, undertook the most sustained and comprehensive of these presidential policy efforts, but for the most part they failed. The reasons were Carter's inability to overcome public disinterest in energy issues, the combined force of organized group opposition to policy action, and his poor relations with Congress on energy and other issues (Kraft 1981). Congress did create the Department of Energy in 1977 to consolidate previously independent energy agencies, but the DOE's chief mission was national defense (nuclear weapons development), not energy.

The other major outcomes from the energy policy debates of the 1970s were enhanced federal research support for energy conservation and efficiency and automobile fuel efficiency requirements. The **corporate average fuel economy (CAFE) standards** had long required passenger cars to average 27.5 miles per gallon, but those in the light truck category, which includes vans and sport utility vehicles (SUVs), needed to average only 20.7 miles per gallon. Efforts by environmental and other groups to raise the CAFE standards generally were not effective, although a slight rise in requirements for light trucks was approved in 2003 (22.2 miles per gallon for the 2007 model year). After an initial improvement in fuel economy, the average mileage rating for all vehicles sold in the United States declined during the 1990s, as buyers came to favor vans and SUVs, which at one point accounted for more than 50 percent of passenger vehicles sales. Rising gasoline prices in 2008 appeared to close that trend as buyers sought more fuel-efficient vehicles and abandoned trucks and SUVs, a change that dramatically hurt U.S. automobile companies that had come to depend on those vehicles for healthy profits. Would the government be more effective in reducing gasoline consumption (and oil imports) if it raised gasoline taxes instead of relying on the CAFE standards? This decision represents a classic choice between two of the most common policy options: regulation and the use of market incentives.

The result of the efforts made during the 1970s was that the United States adopted no national energy policy worthy of the name. Nor did the Reagan administration pursue such a policy during the 1980s, because President Reagan and his advisers preferred to defer to the free market rather than use government authority to chart a particular energy path. Moreover, as long as energy prices were low, there was little public interest or policymaker support for acting on energy issues. The George H. W. Bush administration adopted a modest measure, the Energy Policy Act of 1992, that created new energy conservation programs aimed chiefly at electric appliances, lighting, plumbing, and heating and cooling systems, as well as efficiency programs for alternative-fuel fleet vehicles. It did nothing, however, to curtail U.S. reliance either on imported oil or on fossil fuels in general (Kraft 2007).

About ten years later, the George W. Bush White House began a major energy policy initiative. In early 2001, following a short-term energy crisis in California and rising gasoline prices, the White House sent a national energy policy proposal to Congress. As discussed earlier, the president's plan called for an increase in the production and use of fossil fuels. It also favored a greater reliance on nuclear energy, gave modest attention to the role of energy conservation, and sparked intense debate on Capitol Hill with its emphasis on oil and gas drilling in ANWR. Four years of partisan conflict in Congress followed, with agreement seemingly out of reach. Democrats, opposed to drilling in ANWR, pressed for increases in automobile fuel efficiency standards and greater attention to conservation and efficiency.

Republicans were just as insistent on keeping the drilling provisions and the emphasis on increasing energy supplies.

Finally, in July 2005 Congress approved much of the president's proposal, other than oil and gas drilling in ANWR, and at twice the cost of the president's initial recommendation. Consistent with White House preferences, the Energy Policy Act of 2005, the first major overhaul of national energy policy since 1992, emphasized greater production and use of oil, natural gas, and coal, and strongly boosted federal support for nuclear power. It also streamlined—some would say weakened—environmental requirements as they affect energy production. In addition, it required utilities to modernize the nation's electricity grid to ensure reliable delivery of electric energy. Even the president conceded that the complex law, running to over 1,700 pages, would do little to lower gasoline or other energy costs, or U.S. dependency on imported oil, in the short term. But he was nonetheless optimistic about the act's potential: "This bill is not going to solve our energy challenges overnight," he said. "It's going to take years of focused effort to alleviate those problems."[28]

By February 2006, the president declared in his State of the Union message that the nation was "addicted to oil, which is often imported from unstable parts of the world." Yet Bush remained opposed to an increase in the federal gasoline tax or to higher fuel efficiency standards; Congress adopted the higher CAFE standards anyway in December 2007 in the Energy Independence and Security Act of 2007, and they may well go higher in the future as the nation responds to the risks of climate change. The California waiver initiative noted in the chapter's introduction, if successful, would impose what amounts to a standard of about forty-two miles per gallon by 2020.

Action on climate change implies movement away from the practices and policies discussed here and toward eventual reliance on renewable energy sources, but it will take time for such a shift to occur. Debate continues both on the goals themselves (what targets to set for energy use and what mix of energy sources to use) and on the means to reach them. As noted early in the chapter, Republicans have favored an emphasis on increasing supplies of energy, primarily fossil fuels and nuclear power. Democrats have argued somewhat more for decreasing demand for energy with measures on energy conservation and efficiency as well as supporting the development of renewable energy sources. Yet it is fair to say that neither party wants to move quickly to end reliance on fossil fuels or believes such an action is feasible in the short term, even though former vice president Al Gore and others have argued that such change is urgent. In July 2008, for example, Gore called for a crash program equivalent to the *Apollo* moon project to end U.S. dependence on fossil fuels for the generation of electricity.[29] President Obama did not go that far, but soon after taking office he did initiate substantial changes in U.S. energy policy as part of his massive $787 billion economic stimulus package that Congress approved in February 2009. The bill included some $80 billion in energy and climate change–related initiatives: spending, tax incentives, and loan guarantees for energy efficiency programs, renewable energy sources, mass transit, and technologies for capture and storage of greenhouse gases produced by coal-fired power plants, among others. The *New York Times* observed that had the energy components been a stand-alone measure, they would have amounted to "the biggest energy bill in history" and one decidedly different from energy policies under the Bush administration.[30] We address one element of this ongoing dialogue on energy policy in the focused discussion.

FOCUSED DISCUSSION: CLIMATE CHANGE AND ENERGY POLICY ALTERNATIVES

Climate change is probably the most important environmental challenge of the twenty-first century, and policymakers are only just beginning to deal with it seriously. As we indicated in the chapter's opening paragraphs, each new study or report illustrates continuing controversy over the extent of the problem and its possible solutions. Many scientists and environmentalists are convinced that enough is already known about the risks of climate change to justify taking strong measures now to reduce future harm to people and the environment. Skeptics have argued that climate science is inadequate to forecast such risks with much precision. They support more research on the subject and voluntary efforts by industry, but they oppose most other policy actions as premature and excessively costly. They also argue that the United States can adapt to climate change once it occurs and need not be overly concerned about preventing it.

Although commentators and public officials do not always make the link clear, climate change policy is closely tied to energy policy. Acting on climate change means reducing the world's emissions of greenhouse gases, with attention focused on carbon dioxide. Most experts, including those who work under the auspices of the Intergovernmental Panel on Climate Change, argue that one of the surest ways to slow the rate of climate change and reduce its harmful effects is to cut back on the use of fossil fuels, which produce large amounts of carbon dioxide when burned.[31] If coal, oil, and natural gas remain the dominant energy sources, carbon dioxide emissions will continue. Because about 85 percent of the energy used in the United States comes from fossil fuels, many policymakers are reluctant to endorse a reduction in fossil fuel use for fear that it will significantly harm the economy. They also argue that the nation at this time has no other major fuel sources to substitute for fossil fuels other than nuclear power, which generally has faced strong public opposition. Concern also continues over the unresolved issue of how to dispose of the spent fuel rods (nuclear waste) that result from the operation of nuclear power plants. Congress approved use of the proposed Yucca Mountain, Nevada, nuclear waste repository, and President Bush supported it as well. However, President Obama has opposed it, and it is not yet clear whether the Nuclear Regulatory Commission will approve the opening of the site. Any expansion of nuclear power in the United States will be constrained if the facility is not available for waste disposal, although temporary storage is an option as well.

Has science supplied enough information about climate change and its effects on public health and the environment for policymakers to take action? What kinds of public policies should be considered, and which of them is likely to be the most effective? Which is likely to be least costly? How can the benefits of taking action be balanced against the costs? What about ethical issues? Is it fair for people today to continue their dependence on fossil fuels and to pass along the risks of climate change to future generations? The discussion below addresses some of the economic issues, questions of political feasibility, and equity and other ethical issues. We focus on these three criteria because they are at the heart of most debates today. However, it is equally important to ask how climate change actions stand up to other criteria, such as probable effectiveness and environmental impacts.

Economic Issues

If policymakers focused solely on reducing the use of fossil fuels to cut carbon dioxide emissions, what actions might they suggest? Among the most common policy recommendations are to increase taxes on fossil fuels to reduce their use (a market incentive approach) and to raise energy efficiency standards that apply to motor vehicles (a regulatory approach). Other proposals would probably include government support for alternative energy sources, research and development funds, tax credits for buying energy efficient appliances and cars, and the like. Bills introduced in Congress also have emphasized the use of a market-based, cap-and-trade program that would resemble the one noted above for sulfur dioxide under the 1990 Clean Air Act. Such a program might give away and/or sell through auctions various credits for the right to release greenhouse gases, which could be bought and sold by coal-fired power plants, refineries, and manufacturers. Money generated by the government's sale of such credits could be distributed to industries, states, and consumers to encourage use of renewable energy, conservation, and energy efficiency. But to keep things simple, let us consider the first two approaches.

As a result of public concern over higher fuel costs and the consequences of using fossil fuels to power vehicles, automobile manufacturers are looking to a new generation of cars that might appeal to potential buyers. One promising technology is the plug-in hybrid, which combines the high fuel economy of hybrid (gasoline and electric) vehicles with the convenience of plugging the car into an electrical outlet for recharging the battery. This Chevy Volt is on display at the 2008 New York International Auto Show. General Motors plans to begin selling the Volt late in 2010. It is designed to travel about forty miles using only electric power, but the battery can be recharged by the Volt's gasoline engine for longer trips. This means the car will use no gasoline for most daily trips and will emit no pollutants.

Should the federal government, for example, raise gasoline taxes by a substantial amount, perhaps 50 cents to $1.00 per gallon, or more? Gasoline in the United States would still be far cheaper than it is in most other industrialized nations, where it is usually two to three times higher because of government taxes. Raising gasoline taxes has several benefits, including providing additional revenues for government support of other environmental and energy programs. More important is the impact on consumer behavior. A large increase in the cost of gasoline should be a strong incentive for consumers to change their conduct. As noted earlier, a spike in gasoline prices in 2008 appeared to have more of an effect of this kind than did earlier price rises. With higher gasoline prices, consumers might look for fuel-efficient vehicles, or perhaps use mass transit or find other ways to use their cars less often. According to recent studies, traffic congestion already costs the nation more than $78 billion a year in wasted fuel and extra travel time, a figure that is expected to soar over the next twenty years as the U.S. population grows and the number of vehicles keeps pace.[32] Reducing the use of motor vehicles could bring many economic benefits, as well as improve air quality in urban areas.

What about raising automobile fuel efficiency standards once again? Studies by the National Academy of Sciences conclude that the technology has long existed to raise fuel efficiency substantially without sacrificing vehicle performance or safety, for example, by using variable valve timing, variable transmissions, tires with low rolling resistance, and unibody construction to reduce vehicle weight. These results were feasible, the academy said, if automakers had the ten to fifteen years necessary to further develop and refine the technologies. Most automakers, however, have strongly opposed higher government efficiency standards, and they successfully lobbied Congress to block them through 2007, when they lost that battle.[33] Many economic analyses reach similarly skeptical conclusions about the benefits of higher fuel economy standards in comparison with their costs to the economy, but their authors also acknowledge that great uncertainty surrounds such calculations (Parry 2005).

Even without new standards, consumers can choose higher efficiency vehicles. New gas-electric hybrid vehicles such as a Honda Civic model and the Toyota Prius (and many others that will arrive over the next several years) get substantially higher mileage than conventional cars, but at a premium in purchase price. Even hybrid SUVs that have now reached the market do better than their nonhybrid siblings, and within a decade or so we may see fuel-cell-powered vehicles; prototype models were being tested as early as 2005. Plug-in hybrids, which can be charged in the garage overnight, offer a suitable compromise between all-electric vehicles (with no emissions) and conventional hybrids that can still be driven for extended distances when needed. But because most vehicles sold over the next twenty years or so will run on gasoline engines, higher efficiency standards could make a big difference in greenhouse gas emissions. Should the government adopt tougher fuel efficiency standards that go beyond those set in 2007 to force automakers to build vehicles that use less gasoline? Would you be willing to pay more for a car that got better mileage but otherwise had the same performance and safety features as present cars?

Political Feasibility

During debates in recent Congresses on President Bush's national energy policy, proposals to raise automobile fuel efficiency standards did not fare well through 2007. Until Congress acted at that time, CAFE standards had not changed since 1990 except for the minor increase in the light truck requirements noted earlier, and the average gas mileage of vehicles sold in the United States continued to drop. Policymakers also have shown no enthusiasm for raising gasoline taxes by any substantial amount. Indeed, during the 2008 presidential nominating campaign, candidates John McCain and Hillary Clinton argued strongly for a summer federal gasoline tax "holiday" to ease the burden created by high gasoline prices at the time; nearly all economists opposed such a move, as did candidate Barack Obama, who described such proposals as merely pandering to the public. As noted, automobile manufacturers, with the exception of Honda, generally have adamantly opposed higher fuel economy standards as an unwarranted intrusion into the marketplace.[34] Their multimillion-dollar lobbying and advertising campaigns, in association with autoworkers' unions, emphasized the importance of individual choice and implied that, if such standards were adopted, people would be forced to drive small cars. Sen. Trent Lott, R-Miss., was the Senate minority leader when he criticized Democratic proposals for higher efficiency standards as examples of "nanny government" that would deprive him of the SUV he used to drive his three grandchildren. Some of Lott's colleagues said that higher efficiency standards would drastically reduce vehicle size and weight and increase traffic fatalities.[35] Automakers worried that higher economy standards would reduce the sales of large SUVs, a major industry moneymaker. They were right to worry. When gasoline prices rose sharply in mid-2008, mostly due to rising global demand and short supplies, the public deserted those SUVs in droves. Gas prices plummeted in late 2008 as a result of declining global demand in the midst of a worldwide recession. But few anticipated they would stay at those levels once economic growth began to resume.

As for gasoline taxes, policymakers fear the voters' wrath over any tax increase, especially one that will annoy them every time they fill their gas tanks. When gas prices rose sharply in the fall of 2005, many policymakers once again reacted with horror at the possible political implications, and they promised to take any number of actions to ensure that prices dropped. However, as was the case a year earlier when prices rose, there was little they could do in the short term.[36] Some states suspended or lowered the state gasoline tax, which varies substantially from state to state. President Bush even opened the nation's Strategic Petroleum Reserves to bring more oil to the market and push prices down, and he urged Americans to conserve gasoline by driving less.[37] Previous legislative debates indicate that a large gasoline tax increase is not politically feasible at this time, but would it be more acceptable if it were clearly linked with a decrease in other taxes—a move known as "tax shifting"? In other words, if the gas tax had a neutral impact on overall taxation rates, would the public accept it? What about if the tax increase were linked in the public's mind with action on energy policy or climate change? Would that make a difference, and would policymakers be more likely to favor some kind of gas tax hike under these circumstances? A 2006 *New York Times/CBS News* poll addressed such questions. If asked directly whether they favored an increase in the federal tax on gasoline, only 12 percent of the public did. But if told the increased tax would "reduce the United States' dependence on foreign oil," 55 percent were in favor. And if told the increased tax would "cut down on energy consumption and reduce global warming," 59 percent were in favor. What is the message here? On this and many other issues, we should be careful not to dismiss policy alternatives that we think would not attract public or political support. Circumstances can change quickly, and policymakers may find the public more amenable to some ideas than they imagined would be the case. Much depends on the context and how policymakers explain a proposal to the public.[38]

Democrats have supported raising fuel efficiency standards more than Republicans typically have, but neither party has favored higher gasoline taxes. With intense partisan disagreement over some aspects of national energy policy, particularly opening ANWR and coastal areas to oil and gas drilling, and with no consensus so far on how to reduce the use of fossil fuels and greenhouse gas emissions, state legislators have taken on energy issues themselves, and with some success. For example, in 2002 California approved legislation that for the first time would compel automakers to limit emissions of carbon dioxide by building more fuel-efficient vehicles. In 2005 the California Air Resources Board developed regulations to implement the policy, which call for the "maximum feasible reduction" in emissions of greenhouse gases.[39]

In addition to California's unique approach, many other states (and cities) have adopted or are considering policies to reduce greenhouse gas emissions, including offering subsidies for the purchase of alternative-fuel vehicles such as natural gas cars, gasoline and electric hybrids like the Prius and Civic, and fuel-cell cars. Indeed, several recent analyses conclude that the states were taking the lead on climate change policies by offering more innovative and far-reaching policies than the federal government (Rabe 2004 and 2010; Rabe and Mundo 2007). By 2008 the states had enacted dozens of laws that established specific strategies, from electricity generation to transportation, forestry, and agriculture, to reduce greenhouse gases. Oregon, for example, established a tough standard for carbon dioxide releases from new electric power plants. Massachusetts also set limits on carbon dioxide emissions for many of the state's power plants.

Aside from action at the state level, there is evidence that the political feasibility of acting on climate change may be shifting. As noted, both candidates in the 2008 presidential election favored new policy commitments. In June 2008, major climate change proposals were debated on the floor of the Senate, and legislation will be seriously considered in both the House and Senate in 2009.[40] Rising support can also be seen in the business community, which had long opposed action. One journalist who has followed these developments summed up the trends this way: "On Capitol Hill, in corporate America, and in cities and state capitols across the country, a growing chorus of leaders is calling for aggressive action to limit U.S. emissions of carbon dioxide and other 'greenhouse gases' which are blamed for global warming."[41] Since that summary account in 2005, the science of climate change has improved, and support has grown to the extent that many commentators today claim that a political "tipping point" has been reached, with strong prospects for imminent action, even though the issue continues to be of low priority to most of the public (Guber and Bosso 2010).[42]

In recognition of the obstacles that remain to forging political consensus on climate change and energy policies, President Obama named former EPA administrator Carol Browner to a new position in the White House as coordinator of energy and climate policy, informally called the "climate czar."[43] Moreover, as a reminder of how domestic and international policies are intertwined on the issue, thus complicating the political negotiations, early in the Obama presidency the Brookings Institution and the Pew Center on Global Climate Change issued reports calling for a new partnership between the United States and China (the world's two largest emitters of greenhouse gases) and a presidential summit to produce a broad plan to reduce emissions and concrete steps toward that end. One of the Brookings authors captured the timing of the reports' release and the expectations many held for the new administration: "New leadership and new technologies are creating unprecedented opportunities for action."[44] Within a few weeks, Secretary of State Hillary Clinton made her first trip abroad, and it included a stop in China to begin discussing such possibilities.[45]

Ethical Issues

The ethical issues of climate change and energy policy concern how the various policy proposals affect different groups of citizens now and in the future. For example, many point out that the gasoline tax is regressive, that it has an adverse effect on the poor. Will raising this tax make driving to work prohibitively expensive? What about people who live in sparsely populated rural areas and need to drive farther to work and for other necessities, or who need to use heavy-duty pickup trucks and vans that get lower mileage? Will adding new technologies to make cars more fuel efficient push the price of already expensive vehicles beyond the reach of many people?

Some of the most intriguing ethical issues relate to the U.S. role in climate change. The United States, which comprises less than 5 percent of the world's population, uses almost 25 percent of its commercial energy and produces more than 20 percent of global greenhouse gas emissions. Was its refusal to sign the **Kyoto Protocol** and decision to defer action on climate change under the Bush administration justifiable on equity grounds? Environmentalists argue that it is not right for U.S. citizens to use so much energy and contribute so much to global climate change while doing so little about it. Do you agree?

Also to be considered is **intergenerational equity,** or what is fair to future generations. Climate change forecasts suggest that the adverse impacts will be felt most by people fifty to one hundred years or more in the future. Taking action on climate change, however, would impose economic burdens on those living now. Is it more equitable to defer action on climate change to improve economic well-being today or to take action now to protect future generations from an unreasonable risk of climate change and its effects? What obligations does the present generation have to the future in this regard? A related issue concerns the role of the United States as an international leader. As the wealthiest and most powerful nation in the world, does the United States have an obligation to take a leadership role on climate change and promote sustainable development? What impact does the U.S. role have on the likelihood that other nations will commit themselves to plans to reduce greenhouse gas emissions?

Those opposed to a strong climate change policy for the United States raise a different kind of equity concern. Why should the United States lead in these efforts when so little is required (for example, under the Kyoto Protocol) of rapidly developing nations such as China and India? It is true that the United States and other developed nations have been the main generators of greenhouse gases and thus could fairly be said to be obliged to play a greater role in reducing emissions now. Yet in the future China, India, and other developing nations may well exceed the U.S. level of emissions. So does equity call for those nations to take substantial action today rather than to place most of the burden on the United States and other rich nations?

CONCLUSIONS

This chapter traces the evolution of environmental and natural resource policies to explain how current policies came to be adopted. It surveys the broad range of policies now in force and their strengths and limitations. It highlights an important shift from political consensus during the 1970s to a greater degree of conflict in the 1980s and 1990s. Disagreement about environmental and resource policies continues in the twenty-first century, as shown by congressional challenges to the Bush administration's policy actions and Republican opposition to measures advocated by President Obama in early 2009. Nevertheless, it is clear that the U.S.

public is concerned about environmental and health risks and continues to support strong public policies. When the Gallup Poll in 2000 asked people to name what they thought would be the most important problem facing the United States twenty-five years in the future, more people named the environment than any other issue. Still, polls in early 2009 found that the environment and climate change were not very salient to most people in light of the severe economic crisis that held their attention at the time.[46]

The chapter also emphasizes the need to modernize environmental, resource, and energy policies for the twenty-first century. From many perspectives, including that of policy analysis, the policies are neither as effective nor as economically efficient as they could be. Policymakers need to evaluate them and consider alternative approaches that hold more promise for better performance in the future. Among the changes the U.S. environmental policy system needs is a set of priorities that is more in tune with the reality of risk to public and environmental health, including policies to deal with climate change and the protection of biological diversity. Ultimately, these and other policy changes must also be consistent with the widely recognized, long-term goal of sustainable development.

DISCUSSION QUESTIONS

1. What are the strengths and weaknesses of U.S. environmental policies? What policy elements do you think are most in need of change? For example, should the nation rely more on the use of market incentives rather than regulation? Should more responsibility for environmental policy be devolved to the states?

2. Consider a specific environmental protection policy, such as the Clean Air Act or Clean Water Act. What kind of information would allow you to determine how successful the policy has been?

3. Consider a specific natural resource policy, such as the Endangered Species Act or the National Environmental Policy Act. Answer the same question posed above. What kind of information would you need to have to determine how effective the policy has been?

4. What approach should be at the heart of a U.S. national energy policy? Increasing energy supplies? Decreasing demand? Shifting emphasis to renewable energy resources such as wind and solar? Whichever goal you consider to be most important, which policy alternatives are most promising? For example, should policy be based on provision of market incentives (such as higher gasoline taxes) or regulation (such as CAFE standards)?

5. What should the United States do about climate change? Should it adopt strong policies to reduce the use of fossil fuels and thus to limit the emissions of greenhouse gases? Or should it encourage more research for now, and hold off on adopting strict requirements until the scientific evidence about climate change and its effects is more certain? Other than requirements or incentives for reducing fossil fuel use, what kinds of policies should the federal or state governments consider?

SUGGESTED READINGS

Lester R. Brown, *Plan B 3.0: Mobilizing to Save Civilization* (New York: W. W. Norton, 2008). A comprehensive survey of global environmental challenges accompanied by a range of far-reaching yet practical solutions.

Joseph F. C. DiMento and Pamela Doughman, *Climate Change: What It Means for Us, Our Children, and Our Grandchildren* (Cambridge: MIT Press, 2007). A short and highly readable collection that clearly explains climate change and societal responses to it.

Michael E. Kraft, *Environmental Policy and Politics,* 4th ed. (New York: Pearson-Longman, 2007). A short text that focuses on the major environmental problems and their consequences for society, the policy-making process, the evolution of U.S. policies, and current issues and controversies.

Judith A. Layzer, *The Environmental Case: Translating Values into Policy,* 2nd ed. (Washington, D.C.: CQ Press, 2006). A collection of intriguing case studies in environmental politics and policy that emphasizes conflicts in values and how they are resolved in pollution control and natural resource management.

Paul R. Portney and Robert N. Stavins, eds., *Public Policies for Environmental Protection,* 2nd ed. (Washington, D.C.: Resources for the Future, 2000). An excellent collection of studies of air and water pollution control, hazardous wastes and toxic chemicals, climate change, and solid waste policies by leading experts in the field, with an emphasis on economic issues.

Norman J. Vig and Michael E. Kraft, eds., *Environmental Policy: New Directions for the Twenty-first Century,* 7th ed. (Washington, D.C.: CQ Press, 2010). A collection of original studies covering U.S. political institutions and policymaking, the role of the states and local communities, natural resource policies, climate change, global population growth and economic development, Chinese environmental policy, and environmental security.

SUGGESTED WEB SITES

www.api.org. Web site of the American Petroleum Institute, a trade association representing the oil and natural gas industry, with much information on U.S. energy issues. Includes valuable links to energy statistics, industry statistics, and policy issues.

www.energy.gov. Department of Energy portal, with news links and access to DOE studies and reports on energy and the environment, and debates over national energy policy.

www.epa.gov. Home page for the U.S. Environmental Protection Agency. Contains the full text of the agency's major laws and their associated rules and regulations. Includes useful links to all major environmental problems and current government activity on them.

www.interior.gov. Department of the Interior portal, with news links and access to the department's agencies such as the National Park Service, U.S. Geological Survey, Fish and Wildlife Service, and Bureau of Land Management.

www.nam.org. National Association of Manufacturers site; includes a page on resources and environmental issues that provides business commentary on a range of current policy disputes.

www.nrdc.org. Natural Resources Defense Council site, with an extensive set of links to environmental issues, recent events, news releases, and reports.

www.ucsusa.org. Union of Concerned Scientists portal, with extensive reports and analyses related to the use of scientific information in environmental and energy policy.

MAJOR LEGISLATION

KEYWORDS

NOTES

1. For a broad review of climate change and policy action on it, see Henrik Selin and Stacy D. VanDeveer, "Global Climate Change: Kyoto and Beyond." In Norman J. Vig and Michael E. Kraft, eds., *Environmental Policy*, 7th ed. (Washington, D.C.: CQ Press, 2010). The Bush administration report is "U.S. Climate Change Science

Program Revised Research Plan: An Update to the 2003 Strategic Plan," May 29, 2008, available at www.climatescience.gov.

2. The story of the climate change report is recounted in Andrew C. Revkin, "Under Pressure, White House Issues Climate Change Report," *New York Times*, May 30, 2008, A16. See also Revkin, "U.S. Report Foresees Effects of Climate Shift," *New York Times,* May 28, 2008, A14, which describes a different report, also released in May 2008: "The Effects of Climate Change on Agriculture, Land Resources, Water Resources, and Biodiversity," available at www.climatescience.gov.

3. Katharine Q. Seelye, "President Distances Himself from Global Warming Report," *New York Times,* June 5, 2002, A19. The Kyoto Protocol was set to expire in 2012, and by 2009 negotiations were well underway for its replacement, providing the United States with new opportunities to revise the treaty. See Joseph E. Aldy and Robert Stavins, "Climate Policy Architectures for the Post-Kyoto World," *Environment* 50, no. 3 (May/June 2008): 7–17.

4. Andrew C. Revkin, "McCain and Obama Agree on Real Need to Address Issue of Global Warming," *New York Times,* October 19, 2008, 20.

5. John M. Broder and Peter Baker, "Obama's Order Is Likely to Tighten Auto Standards," *New York Times* online edition, January 25, 2009. By mid-February, the EPA indicated that it might as well initiate regulation of carbon dioxide using its authority under the Clean Air Act. But the agency much prefers that Congress adopt a separate climate change policy to deal with the issue. See John M. Broder, "E.P.A. Expected to Regulate Carbon Dioxide and Other Heat-Trapping Gases," *New York Times,* February 19, 2009, A13.

6. John M. Broder, "Obama's Greenhouse Gas Gamble," *New York Times,* February 28, 2009, A13; and Elizabeth Rosenthal, "Obama's Backing Increases Hopes for Climate Pact," *New York Times,* March 1, 2009, 1, 10.

7. See Juliet Eilperin, "Katrina May Be Just the Beginning," *Washington Post National Weekly Edition,* September 26–October 2, 2005, 35.

8. See Kirk Johnson, "City's Water-Quality Plan Working So Far, U.S. Finds," *New York Times,* June 1, 2002, A14.

9. See also Ann Rappaport, "Campus Greening," *Environment* 50, no. 1 (January/February 2008): 7–16.

10. Although somewhat outside the mainstream, conservative positions on environmental policy can be found in Huber (1999) and Higgs and Close (2005). The latter is a collection of conservative commentary on a range of environmental and natural resource issues, published by the Independent Institute, a conservative think tank in California.

11. For a fascinating history of land acquisition, see Fairfax et al. (2005). The authors critically assess the potential and limitations of both public and private land acquisition strategies.

12. For a good introduction to conservative views of environmental issues, see Peter Huber, *Hard Green: Saving the Environment from Environmentalists, a Conservative Manifesto* (New York: Basic Books, 1999).

13. "National Environmental Scorecard" (Washington, D.C.: League of Conservation Voters, November 2004, and later years). The scorecards are available at the LCV Web site (www.lcv.org). The LCV used to report party averages in its annual scorecard, but it has stopped doing so. The sharp difference between the parties remains evident, however, within most state delegations, between the two parties' leadership on the key environmental committees, and between the House and Senate leaders of each party. The group's report on the 110th Congress, second session (2008), showed the same party divisions that have existed for years.

14. See, for example, John M. Broder, "Obama Team Set on Environment," *New York Times,* December 11, 2008, 1, A22; and David A. Fahrenthold, "Ready for Challenges: Obama's Environment Team: No Radicals," *Washington Post National Weekly Edition,* December 22, 2008–January 2, 2009, 34–35. For a retrospective look at the Bush administration's environmental policy legacy, see John M. Broder, "Environmental Views, Past and Present," *New York Times,* February 7, 2009, A12. The one Obama nomination that was not well received by environmentalists was Harvard law professor Cass Sunstein, who is to head the Office of Information and Regulatory Affairs. Sunstein is a strong proponent of using cost-benefit analysis in evaluating proposed government regulations, which in previous administrations often meant opposition to new environmental rules.

15. For a fuller description of each of these statutes and recent changes either proposed or approved, see Kraft (2007). These and other environmental protection statutes, and the regulations used to implement them, are also available in full at the EPA Web site: www.epa.gov/epahome/laws.htm.

16. In 2002 the Bush administration announced it would not seek reauthorization of the Superfund tax. It would sharply curtail the number of Superfund sites to be cleaned up and cover the costs through general Treasury funds. In an op-ed article, former Clinton EPA administrator Carol Browner called the Bush action "an enormous windfall for the oil and chemical companies." See "Polluters Should Have to Pay," *New York Times,* March 1, 2002, A23.

17. For a direct comparison of the EPA risk ranking to public concerns drawn from poll data, see Leslie Roberts, "Counting on Science at EPA," *Science* 249 (August 1990): 616.

18. U.S. Environmental Protection Agency, "Air Emissions Trends—Continued Progress through 2003," January 2005, available at www.epa.gov/airtrends/econ-emissions.html.

19. U.S. Environmental Protection Agency, "Watershed Assessment, Tracking, and Environmental Reports: National Summary of State Information," available at http://iaspub.epa.gov/waters10/attains_nation_cy.control# total_assessed_waters.

20. See Mary Graham and Catherine Miller, "Disclosure of Toxic Releases in the United States," *Environment* 43 (October 2001): 8–20; and Mary Graham, "Regulation by Shaming," *Atlantic Monthly,* April 2000, available online at www.theatlantic.com.

21. See also Denise Scheberle, "Devolution," in Durant, Fiorino, and O'Leary (2004).

22. See Margaret Kriz, "Working the Land: Bush Aggressively Opens Doors to New Mining, Drilling, and Logging on Federal Lands, as Green Activists Despair of Even Keeping Track," *National Journal,* February 23, 2002, 532–539.

23. Erik Stokstad, "Will Many Endangered Species Recover?" *Science* 323 (February 20, 2009): 998–999.

24. For one effort to produce a comprehensive survey of the health of U.S. ecosystems, see *The State of the Nation's Ecosystems, 2008,* released by the Heinz Center and available at www.heinzctr.org.

25. A case in point is the gold mining industry in Nevada, which has consumed huge quantities of precious groundwater and left behind massive amounts of toxic mercury in mining wastes. See Kirk Johnson, "A Drier and Tainted Nevada May Be Legacy of a Gold Rush," *New York Times,* December 30, 2005, 1, A20.

26. See the chapters by James Meadowcroft and DeWitt John in Durant, Fiorino, and O'Leary (2004). For a review of Bush administration actions touting "cooperative conservation" and environmentalist concern, see Paul Singer, "Beyond a Catchy Slogan," *National Journal,* December 10, 2005.

27. *National Energy Policy: Inventory of Major Federal Programs and Status of Policy Recommendations,* GAO-05-379 (Washington, D.C.: U.S. Government Accountability Office, 2005).

28. See Rebecca Adams, "Hard-Fought Energy Bill Clears," *CQ Weekly,* August 1, 2005, 2108–2110; Michael Grunwald and Juliet Eilperin, "A Smorgasbord with Mostly Pork," *Washington Post National Weekly Edition,* August 8–14, 2005, 18–19; and Ben Evans with Joseph J. Schatz, "Details of Energy Policy Law," *CQ Weekly,* September 5, 2005, 2337–2345. The president's remarks on signing the bill can be found in Richard W. Stevenson, "Bush Signs an Energy Bill That Had Been a Longtime Priority," *New York Times,* August 9, 2005, A12.

29. David Stout, "Gore Calls for Carbon-Free Electric Power," *New York Times* online edition, July 18, 2008.

30. "An $80 Billion Start," *New York Times,* February 18, 2009, A22.

31. The IPCC reports can be found at www.ipcc.ch. The IPCC issues a new report every five years, with separate studies on the scientific aspects of climate change, the impacts that such change could have, and policy actions that could mitigate those impacts.

32. See Mark Murray, "Road Test," *National Journal,* May 25, 2002, 1548–1553.

33. John Lancaster, "Debate on Fuel Economy Turns Emotional," *Washington Post,* March 10, 2002, A12. The National Academy of Sciences report is *Effectiveness and Impact of Corporate Average Fuel Economy (CAFE) Standards* (Washington, D.C.: National Academy Press, 2002). See also Winston Harrington and Virginia McConnell, "A Lighter Tread? Policy and Technology Options for Motor Vehicles," *Environment* 45, no. 9 (November 2003): 22–39; and Steven Ashley, "On the Road to Fuel-Cell Cars," *Scientific American* (March 2005): 62–69.

34. Honda's unique role in supporting higher fuel economy standards, even for SUVs, is detailed by Danny Hakim in "Honda Takes Up Case in U.S. for Green Energy," *New York Times,* June 12, 2002, C1, C4.

35. Lancaster, "Debate on Fuel Economy Turns Emotional," and David Rosenbaum, "Senate Deletes Higher Mileage Standard in Energy Bill," *New York Times,* March 14, 2002, A26.

36. Martin Kady II, with Isaiah J. Poole, "Record Gas Prices Immune to Any Legislative Magic," *CQ Weekly,* June 12, 2004, 1388–1396.

37. David Leonhardt, Jad Mouawad, and David E. Sanger, "To Conserve Gas, President Calls for Less Driving," *New York Times,* September 27, 2005, 1, A20.

38. The poll was published in the *New York Times* on February 28, 2006, and it was conducted in February of that year.

39. Danny Hakim, "Battle Lines Set as New York Acts to Cut Emissions," *New York Times,* November 26, 2005, 1, A14.

40. Margaret Kriz, "Changed Climate," *National Journal,* February 7, 2009, 40–43.

41. Margaret Kriz, "Heating Up," *National Journal,* August 6, 2005, 2504–2508.

42. See also an editorial by former vice president Al Gore on this point, "The Climate for Change," *New York Times,* November 9, 2008, Week in Review Section, 10.

43. For example, see John M. Broder and Andrew C. Revkin, "Hard Task for New Team on Energy and Climate," *New York Times,* December 16, 2008, A22. See also a profile on Browner by Margaret Kriz, "Power Player," *National Journal,* January 31, 2009, 16–23.

44. Andrew C. Revkin, "First Trip for Clinton Aims at China, Climate," *New York Times*, February 4, 2008 (Dot Earth blog).

45. Edward Wong and Andrew C. Revkin, "Experts in U.S. and China See a Chance for Cooperation against Climate Change," *New York Times,* February 5, 2009, A13. See also Rosenthal, "Obama's Backing Increases Hopes for Climate Pact."

46. Andrew C. Revkin, "Environment Issues Slide in Poll of Public Concerns," *New York Times*, January 23, A13.

CHAPTER 12

FOREIGN POLICY AND HOMELAND SECURITY

ONE OF THE MOST DISTINCTIVE FEATURES OF THE WAR IN IRAQ WAS THE George W. Bush administration's unprecedented reliance on private contractors. From the U.S. invasion of Iraq in 2003 through the end of 2008, the United States spent over $100 billion on contractors for the military and other government agencies, or more than one in every five dollars devoted directly to the war effort. This was a far larger role for contractors than in any previous military conflict; if anything, these estimates by the Congressional Budget Office may well be too low. One analyst put it this way: "I don't think there have been any credible cost numbers for the Iraq war. There was so much money spent at the beginning of the war, and nobody knows where it went." Another expert, Peter Singer, a foreign policy analyst at the Brookings Institution and author of *Corporate Warriors: The Rise of the Privatized Military Industry,* said the administration contracted out so much work that little thought had been given to an overall strategy to determine precisely which jobs should be handled by the U.S. government itself and which could be given to private contractors without compromising the military effort.[1] Whatever the precise budgetary numbers or explanations for this experiment in privatization, there is little question that after 2003, the United States entered a risky new era in the use of private contractors in a war zone, with important consequences for military personnel, the conduct of the war, and U.S. foreign policy.

How many contractors did the United States employ in Iraq? By one count, the number totaled over 180,000 people, or more than the U.S. military force in that nation, with most of their activities largely shielded from public view. Who were these contractors? Some estimates said about 50,000 of them were "private security" operatives, that is, mercenary fighters working for companies such as Blackwater USA, DynCorp, and hundreds of more obscure companies from around the world.[2] However, most of the contractors were not security personnel; rather, they filled jobs essential to the conduct of any war and to the economic rebuilding

In this photo from February 2005, members of the U.S.-based private security firm Blackwater Worldwide take in an aerial view of Baghdad. Blackwater employees were involved in a shoot-out in Baghdad in September 2007 that resulted in the deaths of seventeen Iraqi civilians; the Iraqi government subsequently canceled the firm's license to operate in that country. In late 2008 Iraq also decided to end legal immunity from Iraqi law for such private contractors. As the text notes, the war in Iraq has relied heavily on the use of private contractors, including tens of thousands of security personnel such as those employed by Blackwater.

efforts that were part of U.S. policy in Iraq. These included preparing and serving meals, transporting supplies, cleaning buildings, driving vehicles, and serving as translators and bodyguards. Many others were hired to help rebuild schools, hospitals, pipelines, roads, bridges, and other infrastructure in Iraq. Only about 17 percent of the workers were Americans; about half were Iraqis and the rest came from other nations. However, the percentage of Americans was expected to drop sharply after the Iraqi government chose in late 2008 to end the contractors' legal immunity from Iraqi law. That decision could be traced to a widely publicized incident in September 2007, where security guards working for Blackwater Worldwide were involved in a shooting in downtown Baghdad that led to the deaths of at least seventeen Iraqi civilians. Blackwater held a contract to protect U.S. diplomats in Baghdad.[3]

Aside from violent incidents of this kind, contractors were blamed for other misdeeds, most notably poor construction work that took a toll on U.S. military personnel in addition to wasting billions of dollars. One report concluded that shoddy electrical work by private contractors operating on U.S. bases in Iraq was both widespread and dangerous. In one six-month period from 2006 through early 2007, some 283 electrical fires damaged or destroyed military facilities. Two soldiers died in one electrical fire, and at least thirteen Americans were electrocuted in Iraq and many more injured by electrical shocks.

As it turns out, these problems were only the tip of the iceberg. An official history of Iraq rebuilding efforts circulated in late 2008 pointed to numerous failures, which it attributed to bureaucratic turf wars, poor planning and management, growing violence in Iraq, and a fundamental lack of understanding of both Iraqi society and infrastructure needs.[4] A parallel study by the RAND Corporation on the effort to rebuild Iraq was submitted to the army in 2005, and it reached similar conclusions. The army never acted on the study, saying that it adopted too broad a perspective to be useful in setting army policies, programs, or priorities.[5] In a similar development, the Defense Department's inspector general found that the number of Pentagon auditors who were charged with overseeing military contracts simply did not keep up with the increased level of defense spending during the Bush administration. Insufficient auditing would seem to invite waste, fraud, and abuse.[6]

A lot of questions about employment of contractors in Iraq come to mind. In retrospect, was such a substantial use of private contractors in the Iraq war a smart policy choice? Could it be justified as an efficiency move—a way to save money? That is one of the most common arguments in favor of privatization of government functions. Was it more effective in reaching policy goals in comparison to the alternative of using government personnel? How much accountability is possible when the key personnel are private contractors rather than government employees? And if the government does not properly supervise or oversee the work of contractors, does it in effect invite poor-quality work, overbilling, and other kinds of fraud and waste? If so, is there a way for the military to prevent such abuses in the future, for example, through better use of competitive bidding and more careful management or oversight of contractors?

As should be evident at this point in the text, these are the kinds of questions that students of public policy ought to ask about the use of private contractors in the Iraq war. Important changes have occurred in foreign and defense policy in recent years, and in homeland security as well. The 9/11 terrorist attacks meant that, as many have said, "the world has changed." The goals of U.S. foreign policy, national defense, and homeland security need fresh and critical examination. Policy tools that were widely used in the past, from diplomacy and international

STEPS TO ANALYSIS

THE USE OF PRIVATE CONTRACTORS IN THE IRAQ WAR

To learn more about the use of private contractors in the Iraq war, examine an August 2008 report by the Congressional Budget Office (CBO) on the subject (www.cbo.gov/ftpdocs/96xx/doc9688/08-12-IraqContractors.pdf), which is a good example of the kinds of reports issued by the CBO. Alternatively, go to the CBO Web site (www.cbo.gov), search for "private contractors in Iraq war," and locate the August 2008 report. Reports are listed in chronological order. The report is about thirty-six pages long, but look for information of particular interest to you, such as the amount of money spent on contractors; the particular activities that consumed the most money; the government agencies (Defense, State, or AID) that employ the most contractors; where the contractors come from (United States, Iraq, or other nations); contractor use in Iraq compared to other U.S. military operations going back to the Revolutionary War; the legal issues related to contractor use in a war; or restrictions on the arming of contractors. What conclusions can you draw about the use of contractors in Iraq? How distinctive is their use in this war? For future military engagements, what kinds of restrictions would you place on the use of contractors or how they are monitored and managed?

economic assistance to military intervention abroad, need to be rethought as well to ensure that they are as effective as they can be. At the same time, use of new policy tools, including reliance on private contractors in Iraq, clearly calls for careful assessment and re-evaluation when the results are less than satisfactory. The box "Steps to Analysis: The Use of Private Contractors in the Iraq War" suggests some ways to gather information and reach your own conclusions on these questions.

Similarly, government agencies and offices responsible for foreign and defense policy, such as the Departments of State and Defense, the Central Intelligence Agency, and the new **Department of Homeland Security** (DHS), need to be thoroughly examined to make sure they are as capable as they can be of carrying out U.S. policy and protecting the nation from security threats. Based on recent assessments, the DHS has a long way to go in that regard. As we noted in chapter 2, it is an exceptionally large and unwieldy department (with about a $50 billion budget and over two hundred thousand employees) that was assembled in 2002 from twenty-two different federal agencies, many of which had never worked together.[7] One 2008 assessment of the DHS concluded that it continued to be hindered by a "crisis-of-the-moment environment," which led it to rush to meet each new threat or mandate without sufficient attention to strategic planning and effective management.[8] Surveys of federal employees that seek to measure the best place to work in the federal government have placed the DHS near the bottom of the list: twenty-ninth among the thirty large agencies studied for 2007.[9] Aside from capacity to do their jobs and satisfy employees, it is imperative that these agencies be able to weigh and balance their missions against long-standing concern for the rights of citizens. As we will see, critics have questioned the trade-offs between security and liberty in debates over the USA PATRIOT Act, both at the time of its adoption in 2001, just a few weeks after the terrorist attacks, and its renewal in 2006.

Because of the scope of the topic, this chapter is organized differently from those that precede it. Instead of the major policies and programs, we emphasize vital issues in foreign policy and homeland security and address questions about the effectiveness of new policies adopted in the years following the terrorist attacks of 2001. We also place those policies within the larger context of new and complex global challenges that confront the United States in the twenty-first century, including national security threats posed by the growth of international **terrorism,** often defined as the unconventional use of violence for political gain. In addition, we provide a brief historical overview of U.S. foreign and defense policy since the end of World War II in 1945 that helps to explain the changing policy agenda in recent years, particularly following the collapse of the Soviet Union in 1991 and the end of the cold war that dominated U.S. thinking about foreign policy for decades.

We emphasize as well that policy analysis can help in understanding contemporary challenges in foreign policy and homeland security, much as it can in domestic policy areas such as education and health care. Analysts and policymakers need to be alert to the available policy tools and think about which are most likely to be effective, which are justifiable in terms of economic costs and efficiency, and which are likely to be fair or acceptable on ethical grounds. There is an obvious need to think clearly and imaginatively about such questions, yet much of the current political debate over foreign policy and homeland security continues to be grounded in simplistic assessments of the situation faced. If this pattern continues it will serve the nation poorly in the years ahead.

BACKGROUND AND POLICY EVOLUTION

We start with some basic definitions. **Foreign policy** refers to the collection of government actions that affect or attempt to affect U.S. national security as well as the economic and political goals associated with it. Foreign policy can deal with matters as diverse as international trade, economic assistance to poor nations, immigration to the United States, building of political alliances with other nations, action on human rights abuses around the world, global environmental and energy issues such as climate change, and strategic military actions abroad. As the list of topics suggests, foreign policy involves a great diversity of policy actors, among the most important of which are the president, the secretary of state, the president's national security adviser, the National Security Council (see below), and key congressional committees. Among the most commonly used policy tools are diplomacy (high-level communication among policymakers), economic relations (such as imposing trade restraints or providing economic assistance), and threats of military intervention. Foreign policymaking also has some distinctive qualities, among them a greater need than in other policy areas for secrecy or a lack of transparency, more of a reliance on policy professionals (for example, in the State Department and in intelligence and defense agencies), considerably less opportunity for public input, greater involvement by foreign policy actors, and dominance by the president over Congress.

Defense policy, considered part of foreign policy, refers to the goals set (usually by civilian policymakers in the White House and Congress) and the actions taken by government officials directed at the conduct of military affairs. Here too the issues are diverse, ranging from decisions to build and deploy a variety of strategic weapons systems such as nuclear missiles and manned bombers to the maintenance of suitable military force levels, domestically and abroad, and the planning and conduct of military operations such as the wars in Iraq and Afghanistan. Among the major policy actors in defense decisions are the secretary of defense, other members of the National Security Council, and the Joint Chiefs of Staff (representing the military services). The **National Security Council** (NSC) is chaired by the president. Attendees usually include the vice president, the secretary of state, the secretary of the Treasury, the secretary of defense, and the assistant to the president for national security affairs (also called the president's national security adviser). The chair of the joint chiefs by statute is the military adviser to the council and the director of national intelligence is the intelligence adviser. The Barack Obama administration is planning to alter the NSC substantially by extending its scope beyond traditional foreign policy issues (for example, to climate change and energy concerns) and including other agencies in its work. Members of Congress who serve on defense-related committees also are influential policy players.[10]

Although it is something of a simplification, the chief purpose of U.S. foreign policy since the end of World War II can be described as the promotion of national security through a diversified economic, political, and military strategy. The United States emerged from the war in 1945 as one of the world's leading military and economic powers, and it sought to ensure that the security it won at such a high price in World War II would not be lost. For most of the postwar era, that goal was associated with five essential activities: (1) the rebuilding of a war-devastated Europe through the Marshall Plan and the formation of the North Atlantic Treaty Organization (NATO); (2) the formation of and support for the United Nations; (3) a military buildup to ensure adequate capacity to deal with security threats; (4) the development and growth of the nation's intelligence agencies to provide reliable knowledge about potential enemies; and (5) the initiation of economic and military assistance to other nations for humanitarian and strategic purposes. We briefly review each of these in turn.

The Marshall Plan, NATO, and the Cold War

The **Marshall Plan,** named after Secretary of State George Marshall, was authorized by the Economic Cooperation Act of 1948 to help rebuild Europe after the defeat of Nazi Germany by the allied forces, which included the United States and the Soviet Union. Europe continued to suffer greatly from the effects of the prolonged war, which had caused unprecedented loss of life and destruction across the continent. The plan was to offer humanitarian aid to assist in Europe's recovery and to encourage nations in Europe to work together to improve economically. This was an early form of economic cooperation that led decades later to the European Union. The United States offered up to $20 billion in aid, and by 1953 it had spent some $13 billion, enough to put Europe back on its feet.[11] The United States also was aware that a stronger Europe could help to block the expansion of communism from the East as well as stimulate the U.S. economy, because so much of what European nations bought was made in the United States. The plan was one of the first clear demonstrations after the war that foreign policy could reflect idealistic goals but also be grounded in *realpolitik,* a hardheaded or practical appraisal of national interests that emphasizes competition among nation states.

By 1949, in response to the threat of aggression by the Soviet Union, the United States and Western European nations created a formal alliance to pursue their security interests cooperatively: the **North Atlantic Treaty Organization** (NATO), also called the North Atlantic Alliance or the

Western Alliance, which was signed in Washington, D.C., in April. By 1955, NATO welcomed West Germany to the pact, but East Germany remained under the domination of the Soviet Union. The divided Germany would come to symbolize the deep ideological and political differences between NATO nations and the Soviet Union and its satellite states, the communist nations of Central and Eastern Europe. In response to West Germany's entry into NATO, and with Soviet concern about a "remilitarized" West Germany, in 1955 these nations formally established their counterpart, called the Warsaw Pact. The two collections of nations, West and East, were on opposing sides during the rest of the cold war. The Warsaw Pact itself was formally dissolved in 1991 with the end of the Soviet Union (the Union of Soviet Socialist Republics, or USSR).

The **cold war** was so named because the conflicts between the United States and the Soviet Union never emerged into direct military confrontation between the two, or a "hot" war. Rather, the conflicts that were fought were between surrogate nations, such as North and South Korea in the early 1950s and North and South Vietnam in the 1960s and early 1970s. This is not to say there was an absence of real war-like activities. In place of military engagement between the two superpowers, the cold war relied on a variety of other policy tools. These included diplomatic actions, communication strategies (propaganda), economic and military aid to nations to secure their support, and covert intelligence and military operations in advance of each nation's interests. The cold war lasted from 1947 until the collapse of the Soviet Union in 1991 (Gaddis 2006).

The United Nations and Globalization

At the end of World War II, the United States and its European allies concluded that future conflicts might be resolved without war through the establishment of an international organization. In 1945 the United States and fifty other nations formed the **United Nations** (UN), headquartered in New York City and governed under the United Nations Charter, its constitution. Today, the UN describes itself as a "global association of governments facilitating cooperation in international law, international security, economic development, and social equity." In 2009, the UN consisted of 192 member states, and it had a vast array of agencies and programs to further its purposes, such as the World Health Organization, the United Nations Children's Fund (UNICEF), and the UN Development Programme. In addition to these agencies, the UN sponsors periodic international conferences on issues of special importance such as the World Summit on Sustainable Development discussed in chapter 11 and the Fourth World Conference on Women, held in Beijing, China, in 1995.

Several affiliated organizations work toward goals similar to those of the UN, especially economic development of poor nations. Most prominent among them are the World Bank and the International Monetary Fund, which are controlled by leading developed nations, such as the United States. The World Bank was created at about the same time as the UN, in 1945, and loans money to developing nations for certain kinds of development projects. As is the case with the UN itself, these organizations are criticized for a variety of reasons. Some argue that they impose Western political and economic values on developing nations, such as a demand for democratic institutions and free-market economic systems that do not necessarily benefit the people of those nations. Others complain that they have worsened environmental conditions by fostering wasteful and damaging projects, such as the construction of large hydroelectric dams. There is no question, however, that the World Bank remains a highly regarded financial institution with an enormous impact on world economic development strategies. The same could be said of its related financial institutions.

As we discussed in chapter 7, one of the most important economic aspects of foreign policy, though not restricted to work through the United Nations, is an attempt to manage the effects of **globalization,** defined here as the growing interrelationship of all nations through global trade and other kinds of interaction and communication. Increasingly, national barriers to trade, such as tariffs (customs duties or taxes imposed on imports), have been lowered, facilitating the development of an international marketplace in what one journalist has called an increasingly "flat" or connected world (Friedman 2006 and 2008). Yet the nations that compete in this marketplace do so with greatly varied economic circumstances, particularly their cost of labor and reliance on different national health, safety, and environmental regulations. These variations can lead to conflicts over what is considered to be fair trade. Today such conflicts often are presented to the **World Trade Organization** (WTO). The WTO was established in 1995 and administers trade agreements among about 150 nations to settle conflicts over trade disputes, such as imposing unreasonable restrictions on other nations' trade with the United States. Its very existence testifies to the global marketplace of the twenty-first century, the effects of which sometimes become topics of intense debate. One example is the United States' increasing reliance on importation of Chinese-made goods, which are ubiquitous in discount department stores across the nation such as Wal-Mart and Target. Concerns have been raised about issues as disparate as China's record on human rights abuses; its lax environmental, health, and safety protection; and the economic impact on the United States when importation of goods greatly exceeds purchase of U.S.-made products in China and other nations (thus contributing to the United States' trade deficit).

The membership of the UN Security Council—the most important of the UN policy-making bodies—reflects the history of the UN's formation. The council has a rotating membership of ten nations selected from the UN General Assembly (which consists of all member states) in addition to five permanent members: France, the People's Republic of China, Russia (replacing the former Soviet Union), the United Kingdom, and the United States; each of the five has veto power over the council's actions.

Military Buildup and Nuclear Weapons

Following the end of World War II, at $5 trillion (in 2008 dollars) the most expensive war in U.S. history, military spending declined somewhat but remained high for decades.[12] Measured as a percentage of the federal budget, spending rose in the early 1950s during the Korean War (1950–1953) and stayed at high levels during the 1950s and 1960s. It then declined steadily after the formal end of the Vietnam War in 1975. In 1960, defense spending was over 52 percent of the federal budget, and it remained at over 40 percent by 1965. By 2009, however, the Department of Defense budget stood at 17 percent of federal spending, a shift explained in part by the end of the Soviet Union and the cold war and in part by the soaring costs of federal entitlement programs such as Social Security, Medicare, and Medicaid (these programs comprise about 41 percent of the total budget). Adding expenses for the global war on terrorism would raise the total to about 25 percent of the entire federal budget and over 50 percent of discretionary spending (that is, spending other than what is mandated by entitlement programs). Federal defense spending in

Retired Air Force general Thomas McInerney is shown here arriving at the FOX News Channel event in January 2009 in Washington, D.C. In recent years, McInerney and other retired officials have gone to work for consulting companies and defense contractors and have spoken out on defense spending and related military issues. The media usually describe the officials as independent military analysts whose opinions should be given consideration in light of their experience and expertise, even though they now may have a conflict of interest. Their involvement has raised questions about the influence of a so-called military-industrial-media complex on public policy. For example, the Bush administration provided special briefings and information to these officials in the hope that their media appearances would benefit the administration's policies and programs.

President Barack Obama's 2010 budget request was about $664 billion (counting the cost of the wars in Iraq and Afghanistan), making it one of the most costly programs in the budget. The Bush administration had put much of the cost of the wars "off budget" by funding them through supplemental or emergency appropriations rather than the usual budgetary process. Obama promised instead to deliver "honest" budgets that accurately reported defense spending.

In 2008, that budget supported some 1.4 million active duty personnel and over 850,000 in the National Guard or other military reserves. Military service is voluntary or professional, but at times in U.S. history the nation has used conscription or "the draft" to fill service needs. This was the case during the Vietnam War (1964–1975). The United States has had no draft since the 1970s, yet male U.S. citizens ages eighteen through twenty-five, and many male resident aliens, are still required to register with the Selective Service System. The purpose is to have information about potential military personnel in the event of a crisis. Congress has shown no interest in recent years in reinstituting the draft.

Those with a serious interest in defense programs and spending levels might peruse the federal budget documents for the Department of Defense and related programs in the Departments of State, Energy, and Homeland Security, all available at the Web site for the

Office of Management and Budget (www.omb.gov). The annual budget documents provide elaborate descriptions of defense programs and priorities. These also include an accounting of homeland security funding by each department and agency.[13]

The high cost of defense and the increasing reliance on technologically advanced weapons systems as well as the corporations that manufacture them became a prominent issue as early as the 1950s and 1960s. In his farewell address to the nation in January 1961, President Dwight Eisenhower, who had served as commanding general of U.S. forces in Europe in World War II, famously complained about the nation's "military-industrial complex," a form of iron triangle discussed in chapter 2. It was, he said, a "permanent armaments industry of vast proportions," and with great political influence. Even if no dominance by military or industrial elites is suspected, cumulative military spending during this period was without precedent. Today, defense contractors work closely with members of Congress and the Pentagon and continue to press for their costly weapons systems, even when the Pentagon seeks to shift spending to newer and more appropriate technologies. For example, believing it no longer suitable for modern conflicts, senior military officials want to end production of the F-22 Raptor fighter jet that was first conceived during the cold war. Yet members of Congress who represent the states and districts where the fighters are built have insisted on funding it; tens of thousands of jobs in some forty-four states are linked to the F-22. There are many examples of these kinds of spending earmarks in defense appropriations bills that defy economic and military logic but are driven by political needs in Congress.[14]

In an unusual update of the Eisenhower criticism, in 2008 some journalists began referring to a "military-industrial-media complex," to describe the efforts of retired military officials to use the nation's communications media to further the interests of the military and of defense contractors with whom many now worked. These individuals, such as Barry R. McCaffrey, a retired four-star army general, appeared on news shows as independent "military analysts" to offer their assessments in a bid to affect public opinion. Their efforts received considerable support from the military establishment during the Bush administration, including access to special briefings, tours of military installations, and being provided with talking points about important issues. The positive media coverage they received proved to be highly beneficial to the administration's policies and programs.[15]

Issues related to the use of nuclear weapons no longer get the attention they once did, yet they remain among the most important in foreign and defense policy. The potential of nuclear weapons was vividly demonstrated by their use in Japan at the end of World War II, and the United States and the Soviet Union began a decades-long effort to achieve superiority in the number and destructive potential of nuclear weapons. This part of the arms race between the two nations was intended to serve one major purpose: to deter an attack by one against the other by creating fear of a counterattack. The key idea is that of mutually assured destruction, and it is based on an application of the rational choice theory that we discussed in chapter 3. In such strategic and foreign policy decisions, policymakers need to understand the interests, perceptions, and motivations of nation states and other international actors, whether they are terrorists or multinational corporations. In the case of nuclear weapons, the assumption is that a strike by one nation would likely be followed by an equal strike by the other, so that both nations are assured of destruction. If the nations are rational actors, neither should be motivated to engage in a first strike. Hence, having sufficient weapons would promote

deterrence, and there would be no nuclear war.[16] The United States relied on the policy of deterrence to prevent the outbreak of such a war.

The number, increasing power, and location of these weapons on land and on or under the sea were some of the most closely protected military secrets during the cold war and a vital component of defense strategy. Each side was attentive to the possibility that the other might acquire more or better weapons or place them in areas where they could not easily be destroyed in a nuclear strike, such as within reinforced missile silos, on manned bombers, or in nuclear-powered submarines that could remain hidden for long periods of time under the sea. Thus, pressure on both nations led to an enormous investment in the building of nuclear stockpiles and the vehicles that would deliver them. The United States also placed nuclear weapons in strategic locations throughout Europe in the 1950s and 1960s, with over seven thousand nuclear warheads at the peak in 1971. By most accounts, today there are fewer than five hundred U.S. weapons remaining in Europe.[17]

Beyond the stockpiled weapons in internationally recognized "nuclear weapons states" (China, France, Russia, the United Kingdom, and the United States), there is continuing concern over nuclear proliferation; this is the spread of nuclear weapons knowledge and technology to new nations such as India and Pakistan. The interest is particularly great over those nations that are politically unstable or that for other reasons may pose a threat to regional or world peace. The U.S. government is alert to the possibility that "rogue" nations, such as Iran and North Korea, might eventually be able to threaten others with nuclear weapons. The U.S. decision to deploy a still-developing missile defense system was based in part on concern over the possibility of such an attack.[18]

The enormous buildup of nuclear stockpiles led over time to a number of talks and treaties to try to reduce their numbers; the manufacture and maintenance of those weapons were costly and inefficient uses of defense funds, and their numbers posed a continuing security risk. Both the United States and the Soviet Union had a reason to favor arms limitations, but they also distrusted each other, so the various arms talks went slowly and yielded mixed results. Eventually, both the United States and the Russian government agreed to limit their nuclear weapons arsenals to 1,700 to 2,200 warheads each. Critics have complained, however, that such agreements are only loosely enforced, with no provisions for verification. Thus despite considerable progress in reducing the number of nuclear weapons, concern persists over the risk posed by the existence of so many old weapons and the security of the stockpiles, especially in nations of the former Soviet Union. During his campaign in 2007, President Obama proposed setting a goal of eliminating all nuclear weapons in the world, in part to lower the risk of terrorism. In doing so, the president added his support to a bipartisan effort to rethink the nation's reliance on nuclear weapons that has become "increasingly hazardous and decreasingly effective." In April 2009, shortly after a North Korean missile test, the president called for reducing the role of nuclear weapons in U.S. national security policy and urged other nations to do the same. He also began negotiations with Russia to decrease the number of warheads and stockpiles of nuclear weapons in both nations.[19]

The Intelligence Agencies and the War in Iraq

In addition to the formation of NATO and the United Nations, and the buildup of military forces, the post–World War II era also saw a transition from temporary intelligence services during the war to the organizations that operate today. The National Security Act of 1947 created the **Central Intelligence Agency** (CIA) to replace the Office of Strategic Services that had performed more limited operations during World War II. The act also established the National Security Council (NSC) to advise the president on security issues. Under the act the CIA was charged with coordinating the nation's intelligence activities and "correlating, evaluating and disseminating intelligence which affects national security."[20] Other intelligence agencies were created as well, many operating in relative secrecy for much of their existence. For example, according to its Web site, the **National Security Agency** (NSA) "coordinates, directs, and performs highly specialized activities to protect U.S. government information systems and produce foreign signals intelligence information."[21] Created by President Harry Truman to unify the nation's codemakers and codebreakers, the agency began operating in 1952, during the Korean War. It is widely viewed as one of the most secretive of the intelligence agencies, working on the cutting edge of intelligence data analysis.

For years the intelligence agencies were considered to be highly professional and effective in their work. Yet the terrorist attacks of 2001 cast them in a completely different light. Several major assessments of their organization and decision making were launched, including one by a joint congressional panel representing the House and Senate intelligence committees. It reported in July 2003 with a scathing critique of the Federal Bureau of Investigation (FBI) and the CIA, saying they had failed to pay attention to repeated warnings that the terrorist organization al Qaeda was planning to attack the United States. It said the attacks might have been prevented if the agencies had done their jobs better.[22] A second nineteen-month investigation was undertaken by a bipartisan commission chaired by former New Jersey Republican governor Thomas H. Kean, called the 9/11 Commission; it issued its final report on July 23, 2004. It too focused on the many failures of the FBI, the CIA, the Pentagon, the NSC, and almost every other agency charged with defending the nation. The commission called for a major overhaul of the intelligence agencies, and it argued that without such a restructuring the United States would be vulnerable to an even more damaging attack in the future.[23]

In response to the 9/11 Commission report, Congress enacted a sweeping overhaul of the agencies called the Intelligence Reform and Terrorism Prevention Act of 2004. It was the most extensive reorganization of the intelligence community since World War II. The law focused on establishing a new management structure to coordinate and oversee the disparate agencies. The director of national intelligence is to develop the budgets of the nation's sixteen military and civilian intelligence agencies (said to employ about one hundred thousand people and to have a budget of more than $40 billion a year, although the budgets have long been secret), advise the president on intelligence matters, coordinate intelligence activities worldwide, and set an overall strategic direction for the U.S. intelligence system.[24] The agencies themselves are to improve their analysis of intelligence data and develop mechanisms for coordinating activities and sharing their information with one another. The law also calls for a variety of new efforts to improve transportation and border security and better protect the nation against terrorism.[25]

Time will tell if the new institutional arrangement will succeed in improving what was widely thought to be unacceptably weak performance and lack of coordination by the CIA, FBI, and other agencies in anticipating the 2001 attacks and communicating critical information to policymakers. Dennis Blair, a retired admiral and President Obama's choice as director of national intelligence, called for a number of changes in intelligence operations and counterterrorism efforts, including making the agencies operate "in a manner consistent with our nation's values, consistent with our Constitution, and consistent with the rule of law." He also indicated that he would seek an "extremely important balance" for the various agencies and would use so-called soft power (diplomacy and economic development assistance) as well as the "hard power" of tough counterterrorism efforts associated with the Bush administration. One reason for the mix of policy tools is a growing recognition that global instability and terrorism can be linked to economic and social unrest in developing nations as well as to the independent actions of terrorist organizations.[26]

Where does the nation now stand in relation to future terrorist attacks? In 2005, the 9/11 Commission issued a "report card" that faulted the federal government on its efforts to protect the nation from another terrorist attack. The report criticized both Congress and executive agencies for not taking further action, such as ending pork-barrel spending in federal antiterrorism grants and resolving persistent communications problems that afflict police and firefighters during disasters. The 2005 report said the nation's political leadership had been "distracted" and that the country remained vulnerable to attack. Former panel chair Kean concluded that it was "scandalous" that so little had been done since 2001. Even members of congressional homeland security committees seemed to agree that the issues faded in importance the further the nation moved from 9/11.[27] A similar assessment was released in March 2005 by a nine-member commission appointed by President Bush to investigate the intelligence agencies. Chaired by Judge Laurence Silberman and former senator Charles Robb, it concluded that major flaws remained in the U.S. intelligence agencies, which it said were deeply affected by chronic dysfunction. It recommended further radical reorganization of the agencies, with a special focus on how their legendary turf battles, which had divided them and weakened their capabilities, could be overcome.[28] To the extent that these criticisms are equally justifiable today, and there is no reason to believe they are not, the Obama administration will have its hands full addressing the problems.

By some accounts, these serious weaknesses in the intelligence agencies also played a large role in U.S. decisions about how to mount the global war on terrorism. Flawed intelligence as well as misuse of intelligence data led to the Bush administration's assertion that Iraq was linked directly to al Qaeda and that it possessed weapons of mass destruction (nuclear, chemical, or biological) that could be used to attack the United States. A five-year inquiry by a U.S. Senate committee drew essentially these conclusions in 2008.[29] At about the same time, however, on the fifth anniversary of the war, President Bush acknowledged that its costs in lives and money were higher and that it lasted longer than he had anticipated, but he nonetheless remained convinced that the 2003 invasion was justifiable and had made the world and the United States safer: "The answers are clear to me. Removing Saddam Hussein from power was the right decision, and this is a fight that America can and must win."[30] The case against Afghanistan was far stronger than the one the president made against Iraq. It clearly did harbor and support those responsible for the attacks. In October 2001 the United States sent troops to Afghanistan in what the U.S. military called Operation Enduring Freedom. It was the beginning of the U.S. war on terrorism. U.S. forces sought to remove the Taliban organization from power and to track down and capture the leaders of al Qaeda responsible for the 9/11 attacks, especially Osama bin Laden. U.S. forces worked intensely with the Afghan Northern Alliance and with a number of Western allies. As of early 2009, there were thirty-eight thousand U.S. troops in

A U.S. soldier from the 2nd Battalion/87th Infantry searches male Afghans as Afghan women sit off to the side at a checkpoint near Ghazni, Afghanistan, in April 2004. The city has a population of about 300,000 people and was a former stronghold of the Taliban regime. U.S. military personnel have tried to foster good relations with local populations in cities and villages as part of the reconstruction of Afghanistan. Afghans ask for help with various issues, and in return they provide intelligence that may be useful for the military campaign. President Obama favors an increase in troop strength in Afghanistan even as U.S. forces in Iraq are reduced in anticipation of a withdrawal of all combat forces from that country by August 2010.

Afghanistan, which President Obama wanted to increase by an additional seventeen thousand to continue the fight against Taliban forces in that nation.

The Iraq war itself has been more controversial. On March 20, 2003, after Iraqi president Saddam Hussein refused to agree to U.S. terms (particularly to surrender suspected weapons of mass destruction) or to adhere to a United Nations demand for disarmament, the United States invaded Iraq. It was supported by a number of coalition allies, chief among them the United Kingdom, in what the United States called Operation Iraqi Freedom. Hussein's elite Republican Guard troops were quickly defeated, and the Iraqi capital, Baghdad, fell on April 9. On May 1, 2003, President Bush declared the end of major combat operations in Iraq, a statement that would later prove to be wildly optimistic. The coalition forces eventually captured Saddam Hussein in December 2003, and he was brought to trial in late 2005 and later executed.

For the United States, Hussein's capture was a milestone in the war, particularly in light of the earlier Persian Gulf War in 1991. At that time U.S. forces, leading a United Nations coalition, intervened to thwart an Iraqi invasion of neighboring oil-rich Kuwait, but the United States did not attempt to invade Iraq and remove Hussein from power. President George H. W. Bush argued that to do so would go beyond the stated mission of the war, violate international law, and impose "incalculable human and political costs" on the United

States. So the United States limited its role to removing Iraqi troops from Kuwait. After the war, Hussein brutally repressed Iraqi factions that opposed his rule, including Kurds in the North and Shiites in the South.

Following the military success of the first few weeks of the war in 2003, the situation quickly deteriorated. Iraq came to be plagued by continuing violence, much of it launched by the Sunni Muslim insurgency and its supporters, including al Qaeda. If al Qaeda was not active in Iraq prior to the war, there was little question that the war itself, and hatred for the United States in many Muslim nations, made it easier for the terrorist group to recruit volunteers in that nation and in neighboring states. As many analysts have argued, one of the greatest weaknesses of the U.S. war on terrorism in Iraq and elsewhere has been a failure to truly understand the adversaries that the United States faces, and thus to determine what would be most effective in countering the threats they pose.[31] The box "Working with Sources: Has the Iraq War Been Successful?" reviews different arguments about the success of the Iraq war and points to several Web pages where you can judge how successful the war has been.

Over time, public support for the war withered, and President Obama pledged to withdraw all U.S. combat forces by August of 2010, somewhat later than he had promised during the presidential election campaign of 2008 but still a significant departure from policies of the Bush administration. Obama planned to leave about 35,000 to 50,000 support troops in Iraq for another year. As of May 2009, 4,300 Americans had lost their lives in Iraq and over 30,000 had been wounded. Beyond the obvious human toll, there have been varying estimates of the costs of the Iraq war, some as high as $4 trillion when both short-term and long-term costs (such as medical care and disability payments for veterans and interest on the national debt) are included.[32] But even if only direct and short-term costs are counted, by 2008 the war was costing $10 to $12 billion per month, and it remained unclear how much of that expense would be saved with the drawdown of U.S. troops in 2009 and 2010.[33] Most of these cost estimates do not attempt to put a value on the number of Americans and other coalition forces killed or wounded, or the very large number of Iraqi civilians who died as a result of the war.

The box "Steps to Analysis: What Is the Cost of the War on Terrorism?" raises questions about how best to measure the costs of the Iraq war. In light of the objectives of the war, the successes and failures, and the overall costs, would you say the war was worth fighting or not? Can the methods of cost-benefit analysis be applied to questions like this, or are such methods not really suitable for determining whether a war is justifiable or not? By 2008, both policy analysts and elected officials began asking questions like this, in effect asking what else the country might have done with the money being spent on the Iraq war. On the campaign trail in West Virginia in March 2008, for example, Obama made that argument: "Just think about what battles we could be fighting instead of this misguided war." On the opposite side of support for the war, Sen. John McCain, R-Ariz., at that time the likely Republican nominee, stated repeatedly that success in Iraq justified any cost and that pressures on the federal budget should be relieved by cutting wasteful domestic programs, not spending for the war. For their part, journalists and policy analysts began counting what the $12 billion per month would buy in other federal programs, such as health care reform, relief for homeowners unable to pay their mortgages, development of renewable energy sources, or fixing the Social Security system. The congressional Joint Economic Committee examined the same kinds of questions in 2008, concluding in one example that the money spent on the war in one day would be enough to enroll

WORKING WITH SOURCES

HAS THE IRAQ WAR BEEN SUCCESSFUL?

As the discussion in the text indicates, people use different ways to judge the success of any policy or program, including those involving foreign affairs and defense. What is the best way to determine whether the military campaign in Iraq, the economic reconstruction of Iraq, or the effort to initiate democratic practices in the nation have been successful?

Defenders of U.S. action in Iraq would surely point to one of the key successes: Saddam Hussein and his authoritarian regime were removed from power and he was brought to justice in an Iraqi courtroom. They would also highlight investment by the United States and its allies of billions of dollars in Iraqi economic reconstruction (highways, schools, water and sewer lines, and the like), with much of the work taking place under extremely adverse conditions. Finally, they would likely cite the fact that in 2005 Iraq went through what President Bush called a political transformation without precedent. It adopted a constitution, held national elections, and began a credible effort to build an Iraqi security force that will permit U.S. and other troops to withdraw from the nation in 2010. The Bush administration developed several key indicators to measure progress in the Iraq war, which were reviewed in a Government Accountability Office report in 2008.[1]

Critics of the war would point to its many failures. As noted, they have questioned the president's initial arguments for the conflict as well as the administration's continuing justifications for it. They have faulted the planning for the war and what many consider to be its poor management that has put U.S. troops in harm's way (for example, from insufficiently armored vehicles). They

also identify moral and ethical concerns, especially involving the treatment of prisoners of war and the soaring costs of the conflict. And they worry that with its "go it alone" posture, the United States has sacrificed its reputation and lost the good will around the world that it will need in years ahead to face other foreign policy and security challenges.

You can compare arguments for and against the Iraq war at many Web sites. We suggest that for the former you visit the George W. Bush Presidential Library site (www.georgewbushlibrary.gov/whitehouse) and search for presidential statements on the war. You can also see continually updated reports by the Department of Defense (www.defenselink.mil) and the Department of State (www.state.gov). Other possibilities include the House and Senate committees with foreign and defense policy jurisdiction, where you will find arguments on both sides: Senate Armed Services Committee (http://armed-services.senate.gov), Senate Foreign Relations Committee (http://foreign.senate.gov), House Armed Services Committee (http://armed services.house.gov), and House Committee on Foreign Affairs (http://foreignaffairs.house.gov). For arguments critical of some parts of the war and Iraqi reconstruction, in addition to the House and Senate committees, see the Institute for Policy Studies Web page (www.ips-dc.org), where you can search for its reports and commentary on the Iraq war, and the Web sites for the following senators, all Iraq war opponents: John Kerry (http://kerry.senate.gov), Edward Kennedy (http://kennedy.senate.gov), or Russell Feingold (http://feingold.senate.gov). At all the sites you can easily search for statements and actions on the Iraq war.

Note:

1. The Government Accountability Office's June 2008 study, "Securing, Stabilizing, and Rebuilding Iraq: Progress Report," is available at the GAO Web page (www.gao.gov/new.items/d08837.pdf). See also James Glanz, "Government Study Criticizes Bush Administration's Measures of Progress in Iraq," *New York Times*, June 24, 2008, A6.

an additional 58,000 children in the Head Start program, make a year of college affordable for 160,000 low-income students through Pell Grants, or pay for 14,000 more police officers.[34] Do you think these are fair comparisons to make in trying to decide to continue a war?

The United States also mounted a parallel campaign to rebuild Iraq economically and politically, with emphasis, as noted earlier in the chapter, on the Iraqi infrastructure and oil production facilities, and with initial steps toward building democratic institutions. At least some of the vast rebuilding effort was to be subsidized by Iraqi oil revenues, but as of 2008 relatively little Iraqi money was being spent in that way.[35] Even here the challenge was formidable in light of the insurgency and ethnic and religious strife within the nation. Many insurgent attacks targeted vital oil pipelines and other key facilities, and sought to block U.S. success in rebuilding the nation. Similarly, U.S. efforts to train Iraqis for law enforcement and military service often were thwarted by the insurgents, who tried to discourage any cooperation by Iraqis with the U.S. government. The insurgent forces sought to hinder the political development process as well by discouraging Iraqi citizens from participating in the budding democratic experiment of constitution building and holding of elections. Regardless of how these conflicts play out in the short term, the United States will have a long-term interest in the nation and in the region. Iraq is of great strategic importance and has the second-largest proven oil reserves in the world after Saudi Arabia. Hence it is certain to remain of keen interest to U.S. policymakers for years to come.

Economic and Military Assistance: Foreign Aid

One of the most recognizable aspects of U.S. foreign policy today is economic and military assistance to other nations, or foreign aid. The United States has long helped other countries in need, and for many reasons. The one that is easiest to understand is humanitarian assistance, for example, following a natural disaster such as the tsunami that struck South Asia in late 2004. But U.S. assistance more often than not has also served the nation's strategic interests. That is, aid often is given to nations where it can help to support U.S. foreign policy goals. For many years, a large percentage of foreign aid went to the Middle East, especially to Egypt and Israel, and a similar pattern continues today, with Afghanistan, Iraq, Jordan, and Pakistan now receiving much larger shares of the pie (see Figure 12-1). According to figures compiled by the Congressional Research Service for 2008, in recent years about 18 percent of foreign aid money has gone for military purposes (for example, to acquire U.S. military equipment and training); about 36 percent for development purposes (such as health, family planning, environmental protection, and economic reform); about 14 percent for humanitarian ends (such as assistance for refugees and for food); about 6 percent for multilateral aid through international organizations; and most of the remainder (about 27 percent) for other political, economic, or security purposes (for example, to advance U.S. strategic goals in the Middle East). These allocations reflect presidential and congressional policy priorities, which can shift from year to year.[36]

The Clinton administration, for example, gave special emphasis to the promotion of sustainable development as a new strategy in the post–cold war period, with attention to achievement of broad-based economic growth, stabilization of the world population, protection of human health, sustainable management of natural resources, and building of human capacity through education and training. The Bush administration modified these goals to focus on

WHAT IS THE COST OF THE WAR ON TERRORISM?

STEPS
TO
ANALYSIS

Although decisions to go to war rarely are based on economics alone, the costs of war are hardly insignificant. Here we look at several different estimates for the Iraq war. Before the war's launch in 2003, the Bush administration offered a worst-case estimate of $200 billion, and in September 2005 the Government Accountability Office (GAO) reported that the Pentagon's estimate for what had been spent by that date on the global war on terrorism (most of which was for the Iraq war) was $191 billion. This estimate did not include the cost of rebuilding war-torn Iraq and many other indirect costs of the war; the GAO also expressed concern that the Pentagon's cost estimates were of "questionable reliability."[1] By December 2005, military outlays alone totaled over $250 billion, a number that rose considerably over the next several years.

In late 2005, two independent economic analyses of the cost of the war in Iraq were completed. They reached different conclusions, both offering much higher estimates of the war's costs. This is chiefly because they included not only direct expenditures such as payments for military hardware and supplies and support for the troops, but some indirect and long-term costs as well. These included lifelong disability and health care payments to injured soldiers, the effects of the war on the price of oil, and interest payments on the national debt (money borrowed to pay for the war). Both studies acknowledged the difficulty of making such calculations with all of the intangible factors involved, such as loss of life and the value of a stable and democratic Iraq. They also stated that many assumptions have to be made in the conduct of such analysis, as we discussed in chapter 6. Still, the

conclusions were remarkable. One of the studies, noted in the text, put the cost at $3–4 trillion by 2008, much higher than the initial 2005 estimate.[2]

Which of these different ways of measuring the costs of the war makes the most sense? Is it fair to consider indirect and long-term costs when trying to estimate what a nation pays for a war, or should only direct costs be counted? Why do you think so?

Aside from such professional economic analysis, there are many organizations offering estimates for costs of the war. All have significant limitations in light of the controversial subject matter and the role that partisan views may play. To compare different estimates of the war's costs, visit several of the Web pages devoted to the topic. One is sponsored by the liberal National Priorities Project and includes a running tally of the costs as well as a comparison of what the money invested in the war could pay for if spent on alternative policy areas. Go to http://national priorities.org and click on the link to Cost of the War in Iraq. For a similarly critical approach to the mounting costs of the Iraq war, visit the Web site for the Institute for Policy Studies at www.ips-dc.org, and search for studies on the cost of the Iraq war.

For a contrary and far more positive assessment of the war and its costs, visit the Defense Department Web page, www.defenselink.mil, and search for recent fact sheets on the war and assessments of the global war on terrorism. You might also look at the CIA Web site for similar information: www.cia.gov. Finally, you could look for the most recent cost estimates by the authoritative GAO. Go to its Web page at www.gao.gov and search for Iraq war costs or estimates for the war on terrorism.

Notes:

1. U.S. Government Accountability Office, "Global War on Terrorism: DOD Needs to Improve the Reliability of Cost Data and Provide Additional Guidance to Control Costs" (Washington, D.C.: GAO, GAO-05-882, September 2005).

2. Linda Bilmes and Joseph E. Stiglitz, "The Economic Costs of the Iraq War: An Appraisal Three Years after the Beginning of the Conflict" (New York: Columbia University, 2005). The study was updated in 2008 and reported in an editorial by the authors and a book: Linda J. Bilmes and Joseph E. Stiglitz, "Day of Reckoning," *Washington Post National Weekly Edition*, March 17–23, 2008, 27; and *The Three Trillion Dollar War: The True Cost of the Iraq Conflict* (New York: W. W. Norton, 2008). Excerpts from these studies can be found on Professor Stiglitz's Web page: www2.gsb.columbia.edu/faculty/jstiglitz.

FIGURE 12-1 | Top Foreign Aid Recipients, 1998 and 2008

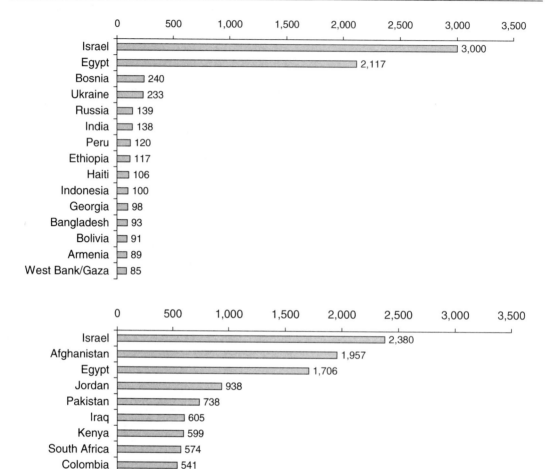

Source: Taken from Curt Tarnoff and Marian L. Lawson, "Foreign Aid: An Introduction to U.S. Programs and Policy" (Washington, D.C.: Congressional Research Service, February 10, 2009), 14. The original sources of the data are USAID and the Department of State.

three "strategic pillars": (1) economic growth, agriculture, and trade; (2) global health; and (3) democracy, conflict prevention, and humanitarian assistance. Later, the administration identified five "core" elements of U.S. foreign assistance:

- promoting transformational development, especially in the areas of governance, institutional capacity, and economic restructuring;

- strengthening fragile states;
- providing humanitarian assistance;
- supporting U.S. geostrategic interests, particularly in countries such as Afghanistan, Egypt, Iraq, Israel, Jordan, and Pakistan; and
- mitigating global and international ills, including HIV/AIDS.[37]

Early in his administration, President Obama signaled his intention to change U.S. foreign policy and foreign aid significantly, and a new set of goals and priorities is emerging.

The **U.S. Agency for International Development** (USAID) is the principal vehicle for the distribution and management of what is called bilateral economic aid, that is, where the United States sends money directly to other nations. Most multilateral (or multination) aid is handled by the U.S. Treasury Department, and the U.S. Departments of State and Defense separately administer military and other security-related aid programs. Some of the multilateral aid goes to the United Nations or to other international organizations, which in turn distribute it through their own programs. The history of foreign aid dates back to the Marshall Plan and the reconstruction of Europe after World War II, and the agency took its current name in 1961 when President John F. Kennedy signed the Foreign Assistance Act and created the USAID by executive order. The USAID is an independent federal agency but works closely with the Department of State.

There is widespread misunderstanding over the level of foreign aid today, which also explains why the program is so broadly criticized as being excessive. Polls taken over the past decade have shown that most people think the amount the nation spends on foreign aid is too much; however, they have also believed that the nation devotes far more than it does to such programs. When told the United States spent about 1 percent of the federal budget on foreign aid, a large majority said that was about the right amount if not too little; few thought it was too much. By 2008, however, the United States was spending only about one half of 1 percent of the federal budget on foreign aid, although the Congressional Research Service says this amount is about 2.4 percent of federal discretionary spending and 0.19 percent of the national gross domestic product (GDP).[38] One poll taken in 2005, like others in previous years, found that a strong majority of Americans favored spending 0.7 percent of the nation's GDP—the UN target level—on foreign aid, or about four times the present level. Of course, public support is likely to be much weaker during times of economic hardship and uncertainty.[39]

Such findings are important for several reasons. It is clear that foreign aid is not popular, even if there is much misunderstanding about it. People tend to argue that unmet needs at home (for health care, education, job training, improving the nation's highways, and much more) require that the money be spent here rather than abroad. There is also a widely shared belief that foreign aid does not reach those in need abroad but goes instead to corrupt officials or is simply wasted on inefficient and ineffective projects. It has been extremely difficult, therefore, to build public support for ambitious new goals to end world destitution, such as those adopted at the 2002 World Summit on Sustainable Development, set out in the UN Millennium Development Goals to end world poverty and hunger and described in recent books on the subject (Sachs 2005).

U.S. spending on foreign aid is substantially lower today than it has been historically, particularly when viewed as a percentage of the nation's GDP, and yet the nation is still among the leading contributors to developing countries. According to the Organisation for Economic Co-operation and Development, in 2007 the United States gave 0.16 percent of its gross national product to developing nations, far below the UN target level of 0.7 percent. This put the United States below nearly every other developed nation in the world, down sharply from the level of 0.54 percent it donated in 1960 and the 1 to 2 percent it gave during the Marshall Plan era.[40] However, the actual dollar amount of U.S. aid was easily the highest in the world at about $22 billion a year.[41] How would you interpret these data? Should the United States be applauded for providing more money in aid than any other developed nation, or should we focus on the amount of aid given as a percentage of a country's overall economy, which suggests that the United States is not as generous as many other countries?

SELECTED ISSUES IN HOMELAND SECURITY

Homeland security as a focus of public policy did not begin with the terrorist attacks of September 2001. It has always been an important component of foreign and defense policy and of law enforcement activity at all levels of government. However, the level of government activity in homeland security and the kinds of efforts made were completely transformed after the 2001 attacks. In this section we review the major activities and programs not already touched on earlier and examine several of the most prominent issues that have arisen in the past few years. Among these are the diverse responsibilities of the Department of Homeland Security (DHS), the varied homeland security threats that the nation faces, the special case of transportation security, and the conflict between pursuit of security goals and protection of citizens' civil liberties.

Most people probably associate the term *homeland security* with antiterrorist actions of the nation's intelligence agencies, military, and law enforcement bodies. Yet even the DHS defines its job in broader terms. It is responsible for dealing with natural disasters, protecting the nation's borders, handling immigration services, managing transportation security at airports, directing the movement of international trade across U.S borders in ports and waterways, and supporting scientific and technological research that could improve the nation's capacity for security protection. Even the Secret Service is now part of the massive new department.

This form of organization and the preoccupation with international and domestic terrorism is problematic. The department is an awkward conglomeration of offices and programs, and many of its component agencies appear to have lost the professional capabilities they once had. One consequence can be seen in the ineffective response of the Federal Emergency Management Agency (FEMA), made part of the DHS at its creation, to Hurricane Katrina in September 2005. With its massive toll in lives lost and economic damage, Katrina was a sign to many not only that FEMA was ill prepared to deal with natural disasters but that the DHS itself was organizationally dysfunctional and unable to handle similar threats to the nation's citizens.

For example, a preliminary report by the Government Accountability Office (GAO) in February 2006 concluded that no one from the federal government was firmly in charge of the response to Katrina. The GAO criticized the homeland security secretary, then Michael Chertoff, for waiting until the day after the storm hit New Orleans to call Katrina an "incident of national significance." Such a designation would more clearly have made the DHS responsible for the government's action. The GAO study found that government agencies "did not act decisively or quickly enough to determine the catastrophic nature of the incident" and to make appropriate decisions to deal with it.[42] The problems associated with FEMA that Katrina brought to light so vividly have led some members of Congress to call for its abolishment and replacing it with a new emergency management agency.

Clearly many hope fervently that the department gains greater administrative capabilities over time, learns better how to communicate with the American public, and figures out how to set meaningful priorities in homeland security. In its early efforts to signal concern about possible security threats, the department became something of a national laughingstock for its ineffective use of color-coded security announcements that most people could never figure out. By July 2005 the DHS had set out a six-point agenda that was designed to reverse its fortunes and to ensure some degree of coherence in its diverse activities. Its new agenda included: (1) an increase in overall preparedness, especially for catastrophic events; (2) the creation of better transportation security systems; (3) the strengthening of border security and reform of immigration processes; (4) enhancement of information sharing with other government agencies; (5) improvement in departmental management; and (6) realignment of the DHS organization to "maximize mission performance." Critics of the department would doubtless say that such tasks are admirable but also difficult to attain. In October 2006, President Bush signed into law the Post-Katrina Emergency Management Reform Act, which established some new leadership positions within the DHS, brought some additional duties to FEMA, and modified other responsibilities of the department. The law also amended the Homeland Security Act in other ways that affect the department's organization and functions. Time will tell if the DHS succeeds in meeting both its own and Congress's expectations.

Comparing Homeland Security Threats: How Vulnerable Are We?

As the DHS itself openly acknowledges, the nation must learn how to identify and measure the various security risks it faces and also find a way to set priorities among them. No agency or government can possibly protect the United States fully against all threats to its security. So which ones are most important? For which might government action realistically prove to be effective? Which can be addressed at moderate cost? To its credit, the DHS is beginning to grapple seriously with such questions.

Consider the following list, which is derived from one account in 2005 of "troubling vulnerabilities that have yet to be seriously addressed" by the nation despite the great attention to security issues and the large investment of public funds:

- Large chemical plants that could endanger one million or more individuals in a worst-case attack. The Environmental Protection Agency has identified 123 such plants, but little has been done to protect them. The chemical industry has resisted the imposition of stronger safety measures.
- Use of a so-called dirty bomb, a compact nuclear device, in a major urban center. The concern here is the international capacity to identify and secure nuclear materials, especially in nations of the former Soviet Union.
- Nuclear power plants that could become the focus of an attack from the air or ground. Current security measures may prove ineffective.

- Insufficient security at the nation's ports. The question is whether sufficient security exists to prevent a weapon of mass destruction from being brought into the country through one of the millions of shipping containers that arrive every year, mostly without inspection (discussed below).
- Hazardous waste transport, in trucks and on rails, much of it through populated urban areas. How adequate are the regulatory measures for the movement of such material?
- Bioterrorism, especially release of a deadly toxin in an urban area. The concern here is the adequacy of security at laboratories that house such materials.[43]

Is one of the risks of greater importance than the others? How would you go about determining that? Recall the discussion in chapter 6 on risk assessment as you consider these issues.

The DHS itself has lent support to such expressions of concern, and it is beginning to try to address the issues. In March 2005, one of its internal studies that the department did not intend for public release was inadvertently posted on a state government Web site and picked up by the press. The National Planning Scenarios identified fifteen possible threats to the nation, some by terrorists, some by natural disasters, and some by disease outbreaks. It then estimated the likely economic and human costs of each. At the upper end of the scenarios was a biological disease outbreak not related to terrorism, a flu pandemic that could kill eighty-seven thousand people, hospitalize three hundred thousand, and cost the nation $70 to $160 billion in economic impacts. Several natural hazards could be equally devastating, such as a 7.2 magnitude or higher earthquake in a large city. Yet various forms of terrorism could exact a very high toll as well, particularly actions directed at chemical storage tanks near urban areas or detonation of a small nuclear device.[44]

One thing that such a comparison of risks and costs tells us is that despite the many actions taken since 9/11, the nation remains vulnerable to a variety of harmful events, many of which have not been directly addressed with current federal priorities. One account in 2004, for example, described the United States as "woefully unprepared to protect the public against terrorists wielding biological agents despite dramatic increases in biodefense spending in the Bush administration and considerable progress on many fronts."[45] Could the same statement be made in 2009? Probably, even though the DHS and other agencies have learned much since then about how to prevent such attacks or how to respond to them should they occur. The DHS has indicated, however, that local and state governments around the nation would soon be required to plan for such possibilities, and to work collaboratively to deal with them. The department also has been trying to implement a new risk-based strategy to help ensure that money and effort are directed at the greatest risks.[46]

The Case of Transportation Security

One way to assess the effectiveness to date of antiterrorism efforts is to examine transportation security, which has been a high priority following the hijacking of the airliners used in the 9/11 attacks. Since that time, airport security has undergone a dramatic transformation, as anyone who has traveled by air in recent years is well aware. Airport security was federalized and the number of airport security agents increased substantially. There is now elaborate, costly, and time-consuming screening of baggage and passengers. Other airport personnel have undergone special training, airliners have been retrofitted to reduce the risk of hijacking, and armed federal agents now travel on selected flights. The task is massive. The Transportation Security Administration (TSA) at the Department of Homeland Security reports that it screened more than seven hundred million people traveling on commercial aircraft during 2006 and more than five hundred million checked pieces of luggage. These are impressive numbers, but do they tell us how effective the TSA has been in reducing security risks? Is it even possible to know that?

By one important measure, the TSA has been remarkably effective. As of early 2009, there have been no further hijackings of aircraft and no further terrorist incidents at airports. But the added security for aviation comes at a substantial price and does not necessarily protect the United States adequately.

First, because of the rush to secure the nation's airports, a great deal of money was wasted. Numerous reports indicate that the TSA in effect "lost control of the spending" in an effort to meet a congressional deadline for added safety. High costs also have been linked to reliance on private contractors and a lack of sufficient management of them, much as we saw for the Iraq war effort.[47]

Second, the TSA itself reports that in recent years it has spent far more on airport security than for any other form of transportation. For example, in 2005 it spent $4.6 billion on aviation security but only $115 million on passenger rail service, buses, and other modes of surface transportation; that is about 98 percent for aviation. Is such an imbalance in security spending warranted? Would the nation be better served by spending a greater share of the funds on other forms of transportation that might also become terrorist targets? The box "Steps to Analysis: Should Passenger Aircraft Be Equipped with Antimissile Defense Systems?" explores a terrorist risk that most people probably have not thought much about: possible attacks on passenger aircraft in the United States.

The DHS also has reported that there are about eleven million trucks and two million rail cars that cross into the nation each year and also 7,500 foreign flagships that make over fifty thousand calls in U.S. ports annually. Some of those ships carry shipping containers, a common way to move goods around the world today. More than six million cargo containers enter the United States annually at seaports around the nation, reflecting the fact that about 90 percent of global trade is shipped via such containers. Until recently, relatively few of them were inspected—and for good reason. U.S. Customs and Border Protection said that inspecting the average twenty-to-forty-foot container would take four customs inspectors four hours. With sixteen thousand containers entering the country *every day,* routine manual screening is not feasible. By 2009, more attention was being given to the ports and how best to deal with shipping containers by means of a container security initiative as well as to consideration of a number of new detection technologies.[48]

Some of the same criticisms and concerns have been directed at agencies charged with protecting U.S. borders, which is one reason why immigration has become such a hot topic in the last few years. U.S. Customs and Border Protection says it is intent on "keeping terrorists and terrorist weapons from entering the United States," and that as the nation's unified border agency, it is "strategically positioned at and between our ports of entry to prevent further terrorist attacks on our nation." According to the agency, it is adopting a number of new initiatives to live up to those expectations. Yet, according to independent accounts, costly programs

STEPS TO ANALYSIS

SHOULD PASSENGER AIRCRAFT BE EQUIPPED WITH ANTIMISSILE DEFENSE SYSTEMS?

There is rising concern about the spread of shoulder-fired missiles around the world (also called man-portable air defense systems, or MANPADS). More than seven hundred thousand such missiles have been manufactured worldwide, and many thousands are unaccounted for, including some that the United States sent to Afghanistan during that nation's fight against the Soviet Union in the 1980s. An attack using any of these missiles could kill several hundred passengers on an airliner and also create an enormous economic impact on the nation, because airline travel would likely be severely restricted following such an attack.

Given these possible consequences, some have argued that the nation should seriously consider equipping passenger aircraft with defensive systems to guard against such missiles. The concern increased after September 11, 2001, for obvious reasons. There are several ways to thwart an attack through use of lasers to jam a missile's guidance system and other technology, and some are currently used for military aircraft. But none of these antimissile systems would be cheap. There are also many technical issues that would have to be resolved to make such systems workable for commercial airliners.

Would it be a good idea to better protect passengers on commercial aircraft by making such antimissile systems available or even mandating that airlines use them? The RAND Corporation, a policy analysis institute widely respected for its work on defense and foreign policy concerns, studied the proposal during 2004. It concluded that such systems are both too expensive and too unreliable to justify such action. Its calculations are interesting. RAND researchers found that installing such systems on the entire fleet of commercial airlines (about 6,800 planes) would require up to $11 billion, with operating costs running an additional $2.1 billion per year. Over twenty years, it said, the cost could be as high as $40 billion. To put that amount into perspective, the federal government has been spending about $4.4 billion annually on all of its transportation security programs.

These numbers force the question of whether it would make sense to spend such large amounts of money on an unproven technology when spending funds in other ways could do much more to safeguard the nation. The director of RAND's homeland security program emphasized the need to consider such efficiency criteria: "Resources available for homeland security are limited, so we must strive to get the most benefit from our investment," he noted. "There may well be other strategy alternatives that could prove to be less expensive and considerably more effective." One alternative to the airliner-equipped antimissile defense system is to install systems at the nation's major airports. Shoulder-fired missiles are only effective during an airliner's takeoff or landing (where they are close enough to strike the plane), so a land-based system might work as well.

By 2008, the Department of Homeland Security (DHS) had funded the first-ever tests of shoulder-fired missile defense systems for commercial aircraft carrying passengers. The DHS signed a $29 million contract for the laser systems, which were being installed on selected American Airlines aircraft flying between New York and California.

Sources: Drawn from a news release from the RAND Corporation, January 25, 2005, "RAND Study Says Airliner Anti-Missile Systems Too Expensive and Unreliable," and other news accounts.

involving the use of new technology have not proven to be very effective to date. Indeed, critics have complained that the use of new and untested (and expensive) technology as well as continued reliance on computer systems that are out of date and ineffective have created an "illusion of security" and that more needs to be done. Members of Congress also have called for strengthening of border defenses, even if money for transportation security has to be decreased to provide for it. In one such initiative, the DHS is completing construction of a nearly seven-hundred-mile fence along the U.S.-Mexican border, an effort that has attracted plenty of critics who doubt its effectiveness.[49]

FOCUSED DISCUSSION: CIVIL LIBERTIES IN AN AGE OF TERRORISM

As discussed earlier in the chapter, a perennial issue for any national security action beyond its actual success in protecting the nation's security and whether the money is spent efficiently is the degree to which it may infringe on the civil liberties of citizens. Several recent policy developments have illustrated the potential conflict and how policymakers appraise sometimes necessary trade-offs between security and liberty. These concern the use of surveillance technology as authorized by the USA PATRIOT Act and other legislation where the chief purpose is to detect possible terrorist activity. We examine arguments related to the likely effectiveness of such surveillance as well as legal and ethical concerns.

Effectiveness and Efficiency

There are few direct measures of effectiveness in the nation's war on terrorism, including policy actions to improve homeland security through the use of surveillance technology. That is, government agencies such as the FBI, CIA, and NSA make thousands of decisions and accumulate untold quantities of data on possible terrorists and their activities. But it would be exceptionally difficult to determine just how effective these efforts have been or whether the investments of agency budgets and staff time are worth the results achieved. Consider this possibility. The vast majority of actions taken by the NSA and FBI are not very effective, but a few of them are vitally important in identifying and apprehending suspected terrorists. Would you say that the overall effort is effective, or at least defensible? What about the efficiency of having government agents spending so much time on actions that prove to be fruitless? Is this of concern? The difficulty of evaluating the effectiveness or efficiency of many antiterrorist policy efforts has significant implications. It means that policy proposals and defense or criticism of existing policies, such as the PATRIOT Act, often are framed in terms of support for the intelligence or law enforcement agencies, a determination to stop terrorism at any cost, or an equal determination to defend the civil rights of citizens under any circumstances that may exist.

Rep. James Sensenbrenner Jr., R-Wis., has been one of the most fervent supporters in Congress of the PATRIOT Act, and as a high-ranking member of the House Judiciary Committee, held an influential policy-making position. "It is not by luck that the United States has not been attacked since September 11, 2001," he said in July 2005, following terrorist bombings in London. "It is through increased cooperation and information sharing among law enforcement and intelligence agencies as well as the enhanced domestic security and investigative tools contained in legislation such as the PATRIOT Act." [50]

Like Sensenbrenner, the Bush administration was convinced that the act was working, and in 2005 it sought congressional approval to make all of its provisions permanent, without any major changes. Indeed, it asked for additional legal authority to track terrorists. Former attorney general Alberto Gonzales put the case this way in his testimony before the Senate Judiciary Committee in April 2005: "The tools contained in the USA PATRIOT Act have proven to be essential weapons in our arsenal to combat the terrorists, and now is not the time for us to be engaging in unilateral disarmament [by not renewing the act's provision]." At least some members of Congress were not persuaded, in part because the administration was reluctant to share information with Congress about just how it had used the act and what effects its provisions had. Said long-time critic of the act, Sen. Russell D. Feingold, D-Wis.: "I do think the administration, by its lack of candor and its unwillingness to provide basic information, has caused the movement across the country against the PATRIOT Act to grow." [51] Based on these kinds of statements, how effective do you think the PATRIOT Act has been? What kind of information would you need to determine that with some confidence?

In late 2005, as Congress was deeply immersed in debates over renewal of the act, President Bush made a startling announcement. He acknowledged that he had ordered the NSA to conduct electronic eavesdropping on individuals *without* first requesting a warrant from judges who serve on the special Foreign Intelligence Surveillance Court as the law seems to require. He claimed the action was essential in the war on terrorism and that his authority for such orders came from his role as commander in chief: "I think most Americans understand the need to find out what the enemy's thinking," the president said. [52] His actions meant that the NSA could intercept international communications of those with known links to al Qaeda and other terrorist organizations, which Bush defended as a "vital tool in our war against the terrorists." That is, the president strongly believed that such surveillance was not only effective in reaching its goals but also critical to the nation's security. Is the argument convincing?

Concerns about the efficiency of such surveillance also were voiced, particularly by the FBI, which had the task of dealing with massive amounts of information sent to it by the NSA. According to news accounts, in the months after the September 11 attacks, FBI officials "repeatedly complained to the spy agency that the unfiltered information was swamping investigators." The agency reported that virtually all of the thousands of tips it received each month led to "dead ends or innocent Americans," and thus diverted agents from counterterrorism work that they considered to be more important. The NSA itself, however, continued to view the surveillance program as a valuable source of information that was not available anywhere else. [53]

Legal and Ethical Concerns

In addition to judgments about the effectiveness or efficiency of government efforts in the war on terrorism, policy debates turn on questions of legality with respect to several elements of current law and the Constitution. Closely aligned with these questions are concerns over one of the ethical aspects of policy that we have discussed throughout the text. This relates to individual rights, or liberty in the face of government actions to pursue policy goals.

The USA PATRIOT Act is the short name (and acronym) for the Uniting and Strengthening America by Providing Appropriate Tools Required to Intercept and Obstruct Terrorism Act of 2001. This law, rushed through Congress forty-five days after the 2001 terrorist attacks, has sweeping implications for both national security and civil liberties, as the statements above suggest. There was limited debate over its provisions at that time, but a belief among policymakers that something extraordinary was needed to protect the nation after the shocking experience of 9/11. In particular, President Bush argued that the administration needed additional tools to combat terrorism, including expansion of federal investigating authority. Congress approved the act after extended and difficult negotiations both within Congress and between Congress and the administration. There was, however, a great deal of concern expressed within Congress over how the act would be implemented and how it would affect both presidential power and individual rights (Wolfensberger 2005).

The PATRIOT Act emphasized empowering the government to monitor communications, detect signs of terrorist activities, and take action against suspected terrorists. Clearly there was a belief in Congress and in the White House that such surveillance would help in the difficult task of identifying suspicious individuals, gaining critical information about them and their activities, and preventing possible terrorist attacks. A minority of members expressed concern about the implications for civil liberties and the necessity to place limits on the exercise of executive authority.

Well before the news of late 2005 regarding presidential approval of NSA surveillance practices, many critics of the PATRIOT Act had voiced these concerns about civil liberties. For example, the American Civil Liberties Union (ACLU) pointed to a "lack of due process and accountability [that] violates the rights extended to all persons, citizens and non-citizens, by the Bill of Rights." Among other complaints, it said the PATRIOT Act threatened a return to illegal actions by the FBI in the 1950s, 1960s, and 1970s, where it "sought to disrupt and discredit thousands of individuals and groups engaged in legitimate political activity."[54] Some four hundred resolutions expressing some kind of opposition to parts of the act were approved by state and local governments around the nation, from both political parties and all points on the ideological spectrum. Although they had varying reasons for their opposition, opponents included civil libertarians, gun rights advocates, the American Conservative Union, librarians, doctors, and business organizations. As the press reports put it, the biggest complaint about the act was that it would not sufficiently protect civil liberties.[55]

When the controversies of late 2005 hit the newspapers, many members of Congress raised other legal and political issues. For one thing, some charged that the president's actions were illegal under current law, the Foreign Intelligence Surveillance Act of 1978 (FISA), unless first authorized by the Foreign Intelligence Surveillance Court. In early 2006, after several members of Congress asked it to weigh in on that particular dispute, the nonpartisan Congressional Research Service concluded that Congress did not appear to have given the president the legal authority to order such surveillance without a court-issued warrant.[56] The president's defense of his actions did little to convince his opponents in Congress, and the year ended with only a temporary extension of the act. The debate continued in 2006 and is ongoing today, though it is much less visible. In March 2006 Congress voted overwhelmingly to renew the PATRIOT Act, giving the Bush administration most of what it had sought. However, critics in Congress also promised an investigation into the president's use of domestic surveillance without court approval.

In 2007 and 2008, Congress considered several key amendments to FISA to bring it up to date by explicitly covering Internet communication, which was not addressed in the original 1978 legislation. That action raised anew the many conflicts between the Bush administration and Congress over the president's assertion that he had the legal authority to intercept any telephone calls or e-mail communications from citizens without first obtaining a warrant. The revised law also protected telecommunications companies that cooperated with the Bush administration's warrantless wiretapping program by granting immunity from lawsuits. Ultimately, Congress acquiesced to most of the president's demands, making it easier for the government to wiretap U.S. phone and computer lines in its search for possible terrorists. This was the most significant revision of the law in a generation; yet, as a political compromise, it skirted some of the most controversial elements, and even people familiar with the issues reported that they found the new policy hard to understand. The law is up for revision in 2012, when it is likely to divide policymakers again.[57]

The debate over precisely what legal rights exist in such circumstances is not new. A balance of sorts had been reached in earlier years to govern such actions by the NSA. After the end of the Vietnam War, where government surveillance of opponents of the war was a common practice, a new policy was set. Government spying on citizens would be prohibited unless very special circumstances required it. Those circumstances were to be examined, and the process regulated and supervised, by the courts to ensure that there was no abuse of power on the part of the executive branch. By one tally in 2004, the Foreign Intelligence Surveillance Court had issued more than 1,700 warrants since the September 11 attacks and had turned down only a handful of government requests for wiretaps. Moreover, under the 1978 law that created the court, the administration could initiate emergency wiretaps and then seek approval retroactively from the court. The White House argued, however, that in practice this process was too cumbersome to permit quick response to terrorist threats.[58] Would you be inclined to give the president the benefit of the doubt in this dispute, or to question the need to act without a court warrant?

In a parallel development that did not attract quite as much attention in the nation's press, much concern was expressed in 2005 about the FBI's increasing use of so-called national security letters (NSLs) to gather data on U.S. citizens. Recently, the FBI has issued about thirty thousand NSLs each year—one hundred times the historical rate—in what one assessment called "a growing practice of domestic surveillance under the USA PATRIOT Act."[59] A single such letter, for example to a librarian, can be used to mine or acquire data on many people at once, including the books they borrow from libraries and the Web sites they browse. Recipients of NSLs are permanently barred from disclosing their content, making it difficult to determine whether they are being used responsibly.[60]

The point of such data mining is to look for evidence of terrorist activities. However, the FBI needs no approval by a prosecutor, grand jury, or judge to issue such letters, nor is there any review of their use after the fact by the Department of Justice or Congress. Moreover, the data gathered in such broad searches are deposited into government databases, which are widely shared within the federal government and beyond it with state, local, and tribal governments, and even with private sector entities. The data gathered on innocent citizens and companies are not destroyed, but are kept in this system.

Is the FBI justified in using such NSLs in the search for terrorist activities? What potential is there for abuse of the information by the FBI or other agencies and organizations that have access to it? Are such broad sweeps of data collection a threat to the nation's civil liberties? It is no surprise that groups such as the ACLU have denounced the practice as potentially having "a profound chilling effect" on people's behavior. But does the war on terrorism require such unusual methods?

Even though they draw the line differently, both liberals and conservatives agree that it is imperative that the nation improve its gathering of information related to possible terrorism, including domestic intelligence. The essential question they must address is how best to balance competing needs of security and civil liberties. As the nation's intelligence agencies chart a new path under the reorganization plans discussed earlier, both the agencies and their overseers in Congress and the White House will be struggling to figure out how to combat the threat of terrorism without weakening the nation's historic commitment to citizens' rights.

There was little doubt that President Obama would change many of the Bush administration's policy choices on these issues, as he signaled on his first day in office by ordering the closure of the Guantánamo Bay detention facility in Cuba. The facility had long been a source of criticism for its treatment and prosecution of prisoners in the war on terrorism.[61] It is not fully evident how Obama might change domestic surveillance operations, but here too he has indicated his administration will draw the line much closer to civil liberties than did President Bush. For example, in his first few months in office, his attorney general, Eric Holder, indicated that he would critically review the practice of warrantless surveillance and run the Justice Department with "transparency and openness." He also stated that he saw no reason why the war on terrorism could not be pursued without sacrificing American freedoms. Consistent with these beliefs and goals, in April 2009 Holder authorized the release of secret Justice Department documents that were used during the Bush administration to guide the CIA's interrogation of terrorism suspects (including the use of torture), an era that President Obama referred to as a "dark and painful chapter in our history."[62]

CONCLUSIONS

This chapter surveys the evolution of U.S. foreign policy and some of the key institutions involved in its formation and implementation and examines selected issues in homeland security. It emphasizes questions of policy effectiveness, the efficiency with which government funds are invested in a diversity of competing programs, and ethical and political concerns that invariably arise as nations try to balance foreign and national security policy needs against the rights of citizens, as evident in debates over renewal of the USA PATRIOT Act. The number of departments and agencies involved in foreign and national security policy, particularly when homeland security is added to the mix, also suggests the imperative of developing more effective organizational arrangements, with improved communication and decision making. The September 11 attacks on the United States, attributable in part to such institutional failures, speak powerfully to those needs.

Beyond the threat of terrorist attacks and military involvement abroad, the next several decades are likely to present the United States with formidable challenges for which it is not as well prepared as it could be. Although they appraise the risks differently and call for varied forms of action, analysts of all stripes point to a similar set of international problems with which the nation must come to terms. These include economic globalization and its consequences for the United States; worldwide threats of diseases that spread more easily today than in earlier years; rising global use of energy, particularly fossil fuels that contribute to climate change; persistent poverty in developing nations; increasing demands on the world's natural resources to meet rising human needs; cultural and religious conflicts that threaten regional and world peace; and escalating international terrorism. The severe worldwide recession of 2008 and 2009 served as a brutal reminder of the economic relationships that now bind the United States to other nations, and it signaled the clear need for international cooperation in addressing problems. All of these current and future challenges call for creative thinking, better analysis, and stronger leadership to discover viable solutions and to build public and political support for a new generation of public policy actions.

DISCUSSION QUESTIONS

1. Consider the use of private contractors in the Iraq War as discussed in the chapter opening. Why do you think the United States decided to rely so heavily on such contractors? Is it a good idea to use contractors as private security forces? What about for rebuilding the Iraqi infrastructure, such as roads, pipelines, and schools? For supporting troops by preparing and serving meals, cleaning buildings, driving vehicles, and transporting supplies?

2. Consider the USA PATRIOT Act, enacted just after the terrorist attacks of 2001 to give the government greater authority to investigate possible terrorist activities. How should government and its citizens resolve the conflict between providing sufficient security to the nation and protecting civil liberties? What information would you need to have to know how to answer that question?

3. Based on the changes made in airport security since 9/11, do the more elaborate security systems appear to be working well? On the whole, do the new procedures seem to be justifiable? Does the emphasis on airport security appear to be excessive in light of other threats to transportation security, as discussed in the chapter?

4. Has the war in Iraq been a success? How would you determine that? What standards would you use, and what kinds of information do you think you need to make that judgment?

5. Review the data on foreign economic and military assistance provided in the chapter. Is the United States providing sufficient foreign assistance to developing nations? Should the nation do more? What do you think is the best way to determine an appropriate level of foreign aid?

SUGGESTED READINGS

Daniel Benjamin and Steven Simon, *The Next Attack: The Failure of the War on Terror and a Strategy for Getting It Right* (New York: Times Books/Henry Holt, 2005). A critical assessment of the Bush administration's war on terrorism and the war in Iraq by two experts on terrorism who were members of the Clinton administration's National Security Council.

William O. Chittick, *American Foreign Policy: A Framework for Analysis* (Washington, D.C.: CQ Press, 2006). Text that explores the history of U.S. foreign policy and the policy-making process in terms of three interrelated motivations: security, economic, and political concerns.

Commission on the Intelligence Capabilities of the United States Regarding Weapons of Mass Destruction, *Report to the President of the United States* (Washington, D.C.: Government Printing Office March 31, 2005). A scathing indictment of dysfunction in the intelligence agencies and extensive recommendations for reform. The commission was cochaired by Lawrence H. Silberman and former senator Charles S. Robb, and the full report is available at a federal government archive site: http://govinfo.library.unt.edu/wmd/pr.html.

Samuel P. Huntington, *The Clash of Civilizations and the Remaking of World Order* (New York: Simon and Schuster, 1997). A modern classic, assessing the clash of world cultures as a major theme of the post–cold war era, where ideology matters less than conflict among different cultures.

Mark M. Lowenthal, *Intelligence: From Secrets to Policy,* 4th ed. (Washington, D.C.: CQ Press, 2009). An intelligence veteran writes about the sources and uses of intelligence in government policymaking.

National Commission on Terrorist Attacks upon the United States, *The 9/11 Commission Report: Final Report of the National Commission on Terrorist Attacks upon the United States.* An independent and bipartisan analysis ordered by Congress in the aftermath of the September 2001 attacks, released in July 2004, that called for a sweeping overhaul of intelligence agencies. The full text of the report is available at the commission's Web site: www.9-11commission.gov.

Jeffery D. Sachs, *The End of Poverty: Economic Possibilities for Our Time* (New York: Penguin Press, 2005). A leading development economist calls for a strong commitment to ending world poverty. Many articles related to the book are available via the author's Web site for the book at Columbia University: www.earth.columbia.edu/pages/endofpoverty/reading.

SUGGESTED WEB SITES

www.brookings.edu. Brookings Institution. Select "research topics," and follow the link to "defense" for studies on defense strategy, homeland security, military organization and management, and military technology issues.

www.cia.gov. The Central Intelligence Agency home page, with information about the agency, its history, its organization, its activities, and a variety of agency publications.

www.csis.org. Center for Strategic and International Studies, a major independent research organization that studies defense and security policy, international affairs, and world trends.

www.defenselink.mil. U.S. Department of Defense home page, with links to the war on terrorism, military news, U.S. military forces and capabilities, a variety of fact sheets on the military and the Pentagon, and links to each of the military services and other defense-related agencies.

www.dhs.gov/index.shtm. U.S. Department of Homeland Security portal, with links to major issues such as immigration and borders, emergencies and disasters, security threats and protection, and travel and transportation.

www.fbi.gov. Federal Bureau of Investigation. Select the link to "counterterrorism" for detailed information about FBI programs and activities related to homeland security.

www.rand.org. The RAND Corporation, an independent policy analysis organization that has long studied military and national security threats. Does extensive and high-quality work on terrorism, international affairs, defense, and science and technology issues.

www.state.gov. U.S. Department of State home page, with links to a variety of international issues, the department's bureaus and offices, press and public affairs, travel and living abroad, countries and regions, and more.

www.un.org/english. United Nations portal, with exhaustive links to UN programs and activities, from the establishment of Millennium Development Goals to end world poverty to actions of the World Health Organization in combating disease and promoting public health in developing nations.

http://worldpublicopinion.org. A Web site sponsored by the Program on International Policy Attitudes, located at the University of Maryland, that provides information and analysis of public opinion on international issues.

MAJOR LEGISLATION

Economic Cooperation Act of 1948 (the Marshall Plan)   387
Foreign Intelligence Surveillance Act of 1978 (FISA)   409
Intelligence Reform and Terrorism Prevention Act of 2004   393
National Security Act of 1947   393
Uniting and Strengthening America by Providing Appropriate Tools Required to Intercept and
   Obstruct Terrorism Act of 2001 (USA PATRIOT Act)   409

KEYWORDS

Central Intelligence Agency (CIA)   393
cold war   388
defense policy   386
Department of Homeland Security
   (DHS)   385
deterrence   392
foreign policy   386
globalization   389
Marshall Plan   387

National Security Agency (NSA)   393
National Security Council (NSC)   387
North Atlantic Treaty Organization
   (NATO)   387
terrorism   386
United Nations (UN)   388
U.S. Agency for International Development
   (USAID)   401
World Trade Organization (WTO)   389

NOTES

1. The Congressional Budget Office cost estimates are described in James Risen, "Use of Contractors in Iraq Costs Billions, Report Says," *New York Times,* August 12, 2008, A13. The CBO report found that the government awarded about $85 billion in contracts between 2003 and 2007 and was awarding around $15 to $20 billion each year since then. Singer's book was published in 2003 by Cornell University Press.

2. That estimate was reported by the *New York Times* in an editorial on October 1, 2007, "Subcontracting the War." See also James Glanz, "Report on Iraq Security Lists 310 Contractors, from U.S. to Uganda," *New York Times,* October 29, 2008, A5. The Public Broadcasting System's *Frontline* program aired a film on this subject in 2005 called "Private Warriors," available online at www.pbs.org/wgbh/pages/frontline/shows/warriors.

3. James Risen, "End of Immunity Worries U.S. Contractors in Iraq," *New York Times,* December 1, 2008, A14. On the rising use of private security forces in war, see Rafael Enrique Valero, "Hired Guns," *National Journal,* January 5, 2008, 22–28.

4. James Glanz and T. Christian Miller, "Official History Spotlights Iraq Rebuilding Blunders," *New York Times,* December 14, 2008, 1, 16. The report, entitled "Hard Lessons: The Iraq Reconstruction Experience," was prepared by the Office of the Special Inspector General for Iraq Reconstruction, which Congress created in 2004 to oversee the use and potential misuse of the Iraq Relief and Reconstruction Fund. The report was presented at a February 2009 hearing of the Commission on Wartime Contracting. A summary of the report and testimony is available at www.wartimecontracting.gov. The commission is to report its findings to Congress.

5. Michael R. Gordon, "Army Buried Study Faulting Iraq Planning," *New York Times,* February 11, 2008, 1, A8.

6. Jon Ward, "Pentagon Spending Growth Outpaces Auditors: Report: Lack of Oversight Opens Door to Fraud, Abuse," *Washington Times* online edition, October 20, 2008. Other reports suggested that the State Department's inspector general's office may have blocked investigations of suspected fraud and abuse on the part of contractors in Iraq and Afghanistan. See Peter H. Stone, "Inspecting the Inspector," *National Journal,* October 20, 2007, 47–48. In one particularly outrageous case, a small, Miami-based defense contractor named AEY, Inc. received contracts worth some $300 million under a program intended for small, disadvantaged businesses (essentially those run by disadvantaged racial minorities), even though the company did not qualify as such a business. No one in the government bothered to check on its status, and the company was awarded a Defense Department contract to supply ammunition to Afghanistan's army and police forces. Much of what they supplied was obsolete and defective ammunition manufactured in China in 1966. See Elizabeth Newell and Robert Brodsky, "The Advantage of Disadvantage," *National Journal,* May 3, 2008, 45–46.

7. For an overview of the challenges that the DHS faces, see Jeff Stein, "The Nation's First-Responder," *CQ Weekly,* June 20, 2005, 1634–1641. A survey of federal employee satisfaction with agency or departmental operations put the DHS dead last. See David E. Rosenbaum, "The Mood at Homeland Security? Bleak, a Study Says," *New York Times,* October 16, 2005, 17.

8. Spencer S. Hsu, "Department of Crisis Management," *Washington Post National Weekly Edition,* March 10–16, 2008, 10.

9. The study methods and the ranking can be found at www.bestplacestowork.org/BPTW/rankings.

10. See the NSC Web site for a description of its work, membership, and history: www.whitehouse.gov/administration/eop/nsc.

11. The numbers come from the U.S. State Department's history of the Marshall Plan, available at http://usinfo.state.gov/usa/infousa/facts/democrac/57.htm.

12. In comparison, the Korean War cost $408 billion, the Vietnam War cost $584 billion, and the Persian Gulf War in 1991 cost $82 billion (with allies covering most of the cost). The varying estimates of the Iraq war costs are discussed in the chapter. The source is the Congressional Research Service, as reported in *CQ Weekly,* May 8, 2004.

13. The budget documents can be found at www.whitehouse.gov/omb. Click on the latest fiscal year budget. Budget documents include "historical tables" that can provide a good idea of how spending has changed over time.

14. R. Jeffrey Smith and Ellen Nakashima, "Pentagon's Unwanted Projects in Earmarks," *Washington Post,* March 8, 2009, A1.

15. David Barstow, "One Man's Military-Industrial-Media Complex," *New York Times,* November 30, 2008, 1, 26–27.

16. Of course, part of the concern in strategic analysis is that not all nations are rational in this way. One might think it can win with a first strike despite the likelihood of severe retaliation. Similarly, some nations may be so motivated by ideology or other political and cultural beliefs that they are prepared to launch such an attack despite the consequences.

17. Robert S. Norris and Hans M. Kristensen, "U.S. Nuclear Weapons in Europe, 1954–2004," *Bulletin of the Atomic Scientists* 60 (November/December 2004): 76–77.

18. John M. Donnelly, "Debate Yields to Deployment as Missile Defense Takes Off," *CQ Weekly,* September 11, 2004, 2090–2096.

19. Jeff Zeleny, "Obama to Urge Elimination of World's Nuclear Weapons," *New York Times,* October 2, 2007; and Helene Cooper and David E. Sanger, "Obama Seizes on Missile Launch in Seeking Nuclear Cuts, *New York Times,* April 5, 2009.

20. The Central Intelligence Agency, "History," available at www.fas.org/irp/cia/ciahist.htm.

21. Taken from the NSA Web page: www.nsa.gov/home_html.cfm.

22. David Johnson, "Report of 9/11 Panel Cites Lapses by C.I.A. and F.B.I," *New York Times,* July 25, 2003, 1, A12–13.

23. See also Philip Shenon, "9/11 Report Calls for a Sweeping Overhaul of Intelligence," *New York Times,* July 23, 2004, 1, A13. The full report of the 9/11 Commission is cited in the recommended readings at the end of the chapter. It is available at www.9-11commission.gov.

24. One estimate in late 2008 put the annual budget for intelligence operations at $47.5 billion, and this did not include use of satellites that fall under the Pentagon's budget. See Joby Warrick, "A New Wave of Threats," *Washington Post National Weekly Edition,* November 24–30, 2008, 6. Some critics also charge that a sizeable portion of this intelligence budget is outsourced, going to private-sector contractors and consultants such as Booz Allen and S.A.I.C.—many of whom are exempt from public oversight. See Harry Hurt III, "The Business of Intelligence Gathering," *New York Times,* June 15, 2008, Business Section, 5.

25. See Philip Shenon, "Next Round Is Set in Push Toward Intelligence Reform," *New York Times,* December 20, 2004, A19. A summary of the law can be found in Martin Kady II, "Details of the Intelligence Overhaul Law," *CQ Weekly,* February 21, 2005, 464–468.

26. Scott Shane, "Blair Pledges New Approach to Counterterrorism," *New York Times* online edition, January 23, 2009; and Warrick, "A New Wave of Threats."

27. Tim Starks, "Sept. 11 Panel Says Country Still at Risk," *CQ Weekly,* December 12, 2005, 3330–3331.

28. The report is included in the recommended readings at the end of the chapter. See also Scott Shane and David E. Sanger, "Bush Panel Finds Big Flaws Remain in U.S. Spy Efforts," *New York Times,* April 1, 2005, 1, A10.

29. See Mark Mazzetti and Scott Shane, "Bush Overstated Evidence on Iraq, Senators Report," *New York Times,* June 6, 2008, 1, A11.

30. Steven Lee Myers, "Marking 5 Years, Bush Insists U.S. Must Win in Iraq," *New York Times,* March 20, 2008, 1, A11.

31. See, for example, Bruce Hoffman's *Inside Terrorism* (New York: Columbia University Press, 1999), and work by the RAND Corporation's Center for Terrorism Risk Management Policy. Hoffman directs RAND's Washington, D.C., office.

32. David M. Herszenhorn, "Estimates of Iraq War Cost Were Not Close to Ballpark," *New York Times,* March 19, 2008, A9. The $4 trillion estimate comes from Nobel Prize–winning economist Joseph E. Stiglitz. The Congressional Budget Office and some others put the total at $1 to $2 trillion, depending on the length of U.S. involvement in Iraq. As noted in the text, the high estimates include long-term health care and disability costs for veterans; the impact of the rising national debt attributable to the war; and wider economic effects, such as part of the cost of rising oil prices. See also Linda J. Bilmes and Joseph E. Stiglitz, "Day of Reckoning," *Washington Post National Weekly Edition,* March 17–23, 2008, 27. Bilmes and Stiglitz are the authors of *The Three Trillion Dollar War: The True Cost of the Iraq Conflict* (New York: W. W. Norton, 2008).

33. For one cost estimate as of March 2009, see James Glanz, "The Economic Cost of War," *New York Times,* March 1, 2009, Week in Review Section, 1, 4.

34. John M. Broder, "Views on Money for Iraq War, and What Else Could Be Done with It," *New York Times,* April 14, 2008, A21; and Bob Herbert, "The $2 Trillion Nightmare," *New York Times,* March 4, 2008, A25.

35. James Glanz and Campbell Robertson, "As Iraq Surplus Rises, Little Goes into Rebuilding," *New York Times,* August 6, 2008, 1, A13.

36. See Curt Tarnoff and Larry Nowels, "Foreign Aid: An Introductory Overview of U.S. Programs and Policy" (Washington, D.C.: Congressional Research Service, April 15, 2004).

37. Ibid.

38. Curt Tarnoff and Marian L. Lawson, "Foreign Aid: An Introduction to U.S. Programs and Policy" (Washington, D.C.: Congressional Research Service, February 10, 2009), available at www.fas.org/sgp/crs/row/index.html.

39. Program on International Policy Attitudes (PIPA), "Americans Support U.S. and G8 Countries Committing to Spend 0.7% GDP on World Poverty," June 30, 2005. The poll data are archived at www.worldpublicopinion.org.

40. Celia W. Dugger, "Discerning a New Course for World's Donor Nations," *New York Times,* April 18, 2005, A10.

41. The rankings of nations on development assistance can be seen in annual data from the Organisation for Economic Co-operation and Development, which are displayed on the Web page of the nonprofit organization RESULTS, at www.results.org/website/article.asp?id=3558.

42. Susan B. Glasser and Michael Grunwald, "Prelude to Disaster: The Department of Homeland Security Had a Weak Mission from the Start," *Washington Post National Weekly Edition,* January 9–15, 2006, 6–8. The GAO report is described in Eric Lipton, "Investigators Criticize Response to Hurricane," *New York Times,* February 2, 2006.

43. The list comes from the *New York Times,* February 20, 2005, but similar lists have been compiled by other sources.

44. See Eric Lipton, "U.S. Lists Possible Terror Attacks and Likely Toll," *New York Times,* March 16, 2005, 1, A14. See also Benjamin and Simon (2005) on the failure of the war on terrorism and a review of continuing terrorist threats.

45. John Mintz and Joby Warrick, "Are Our Biodefenses Up?" *Washington Post National Weekly Edition,* November 15–21, 2004, 6–7.

46. For example, see Eric Lipton, "New Rules Set for Giving Out Antiterror Aid," *New York Times,* January 3, 2006, 1, A12; and a DHS fact sheet released on December 18, 2008, where the department lists its achievements for the year, available at www.dhs.gov/xnews/releases/pr_1229609413187.shtm.

47. Scott Higham and Robert O'Harrow Jr., "Securing the Homeland: The Government's Rush to Private Contracting Led to Abuse and Fraud," *Washington Post National Weekly Edition,* May 3–June 5, 2005, 6–7.

48. Ibid. See also the U.S. Customs and Border Protection Web page for a description of the container initiative: www.cbp.gov/xp/cgov/trade/cargo_security/csi.

49. Robert O'Harrow Jr. and Scott Higham, " 'An Illusion of Security': Technology Problems Limit the Effectiveness of a Costly Program to Screen Visitors," *Washington Post National Weekly Edition,* June 6–12, 2005, 9–11; and Tim Starks, "Committee Realigns Homeland Priorities," *CQ Weekly,* June 20, 2005, 1652. On the fence project, see Randal C. Archibold and Julia Preston, "Homeland Security Stands by Its Fence," *New York Times* online edition, May 21, 2008; and John Pomfret, "Two Sides to the Border Fence," *Washington Post National Weekly Edition,* October 23–29, 2006, 30.

50. Quoted in Keith Perine, "Attacks Loom over Anti-Terrorism Law," *CQ Weekly,* July 8, 2005, 1902.

51. Both quotes are taken from Perine, "Attacks Loom."

52. David E. Sanger, "In Speech, Bush Says He Ordered Domestic Spying," *New York Times,* December 18, 2005, 1, 30; and Eric Lichtblau, "Bush Defends Spy Program and Denies Misleading Public," *New York Times,* January 2, 2006, A11.

53. Lowell Bergman, Eric Lichtblau, Scott Shane, and Don Van Natta Jr., "Spy Agency Data After Sept. 11 Led F.B.I. to Dead Ends," *New York Times,* January 17, 2006, 1, A12.

54. The language comes from a flyer on the ACLU Web page: "The USA PATRIOT Act and Government Actions That Threaten Our Civil Liberties," available at www.aclu.org/FilesPDFs/patriot%20act%20flyer.pdf.

55. Perine, "Attack Looms," and Michael Sandler, "Another Setback for Anti-Terrorism Law," *CQ Weekly,* December 9, 2005, 3325.

56. Eric Lichtblau and Scott Shane, "Basis for Spying in U.S. Is Doubted," *New York Times,* January 7, 2006, 1, A28.

57. For a description of the new surveillance law, see Shane Harris, "Explaining FISA," *National Journal,* July 19, 2008, 66–70. For a history of a two-decades-long battle over domestic surveillance or wiretapping and limits placed on government's authority, see Shane Harris, "Surveillance Standoff," *National Journal,* April 5, 2008, 21–27.

58. See Eric Lichtblau, "Judges and Justice Dept. Meet Over Eavesdropping Program," *New York Times,* January 10, 2006.

59. Barton Gellman, "The FBI Is Watching," *Washington Post National Weekly Edition,* November 14–20, 2005, 7–10.

60. Barton Gellman, "FBI Mines Records of Ordinary Americans," *Washington Post,* November 6, 2005, A1.

61. Mark Mazzetti and William Glaberson, "Obama Issues Directive to Shut Down Guantánamo," *New York Times* online edition, January 21, 2009.

62. Greg Miller and John Meyer, "Memos Reveal Harsh CIA Interrogation Methods," *New York Times,* April 17, 2009.

IN MAY 2002 VOTERS IN PORTLAND, OREGON, WERE PRESENTED WITH A ballot initiative that would have overturned a three-decades-old regional growth policy that was widely recognized as a national model for controlling urban sprawl. The developers who placed the initiative on the ballot were frustrated with the strict local rules that limited housing developments in the area around the city. State law in Oregon required larger cities and towns to create an urban growth boundary for the purpose of maintaining free-of-development farmland and forests outside the city. Consistent with these goals, a regional government body called Metro regulates land use and transportation within the Portland metropolitan area. On three previous occasions, voters in Portland turned down efforts to weaken or eliminate their local growth plan.

This time, however, builders, property rights advocates, and even some environmentalists complained that Portland's stringent regulation of new housing construction was leading to lofty home prices and high population density. They wanted to change the plan to allow new development outside the city in the greenbelt. Supporters of the existing land-use plan defended it as essential for allowing Portland to accommodate new housing while protecting the rural character and open spaces at the edge of the city. As a result of the long-standing plan, Portland resembles many European cities, with an efficient and popular mass transit system, compact urban residential neighborhoods, and abundant forests and farms just outside the urban boundary. In part because of these qualities, Portland regularly appears near the top of rankings of the most livable cities in the United States.

In the end, 57 percent of voters in the Portland metropolitan area opposed the ballot initiative, and 43 percent voted in favor.[1] Just a little over two years later, however, in November 2004, voters once again had the opportunity to express their views, this time on a statewide land-use ballot measure. Confirming that voters in Portland are not necessarily representative of the entire state of Oregon, the pro-development initiative was approved by 61 percent to 39 percent. Ballot Measure 37 was backed by a conservative property rights group called Oregonians in Action, and it called for compensation by local governments to property owners who could prove that zoning

Residents of Portland, Oregon, have long defended their strict urban land-use policies in the face of criticism about their impact on property values and the constraints they place on regional growth. Because of the statewide ballot initiative approved by voters in November 2004, however, the city will face new challenges in managing its growth. The photo, taken in 2002, shows newly constructed homes on what were once forestlands west of Portland. Rural property owners, timber companies, and builders argue that land-use plans in the Portland area have been too restrictive and result in congestion, crowded schools, and inflated housing prices.

ordinances or environmental laws harmed their investment in the land. Property rights groups across the nation cheered their victory, and defenders of strict zoning laws and smart growth policies expressed deep concern about the consequences of the vote; this was particularly so because the measure allowed for retroactive claims for compensation, a rarity in these kinds of laws.[2]

But the story does not end there. In October 2005, the Marion County Circuit Court (in Salem, the state capital) overturned Measure 37 on the grounds that it violated both the Oregon and U.S. Constitutions. The state of Oregon announced that it would appeal the decision to the state supreme court, but this was doubtless a reluctant move on its part; state law requires that the state's attorneys defend voter-approved initiatives. Oregonians in Action also entered the fray to defend the initiative it drafted and supported.[3] In February 2006 the Oregon Supreme Court reversed the county circuit court and upheld Measure 37, which took effect the following month.

As of March 2007, over 7,500 Measure 37 requests for payments or land-use waivers had been filed under the new law, which together covered about 751,000 acres in Oregon. These included shopping malls to be built in what was farmland and gravel pit mines located in residential neighborhoods. One Hood River County fruit farmer filed a Measure 37 claim demanding payment of $57 million for his land or approval of his request to build 800 houses on his 210-acre property. Because local governments cannot afford to compensate land owners, the laws that would otherwise restrict such developments have to be waived. Not unexpectedly, in the Portland area, many of the requests were filed by major land developers. In yet another turn of events, in a special election in November 2007, Oregon voters approved Measure 49, which modified some aspects of the earlier ballot measure by restricting the circumstances under which property owners must be compensated for a change in land-use regulations. This time it was placed on the ballot by action of the state legislature, and it was strongly opposed by Oregonians in Action. Nonetheless, it received overwhelming approval by the electorate—62 percent of voters. It seems that the citizens of Oregon changed their minds to some extent after seeing the consequences of their earlier vote for Measure 37.[4]

The Portland growth management initiative and the subsequent statewide ballot measures illustrate a number of points that we address in this concluding chapter. The first concerns the substance of policy choices and the critical nature of policy design. As we have shown throughout the text, the way policymakers design public policies can make them more or less effective, efficient, and fair. There is no guarantee that policies will work or have the impact for which policymakers and the public hope. But careful thought and design of public policies, whether they address welfare reform, health care, education, or foreign policy, make a big difference. The second point concerns the impact that policies have on society, that is, on children receiving benefits under the State Children's Health Insurance Program, patients accepting health care services under Medicaid or Medicare, students relying on federal grants and loans, homeowners struggling to pay their mortgages, and veterans depending on the federal government for disability services and other health care. How these policies affect people's lives depends on the choices made about policy goals and the means used to achieve them. What goals make the most sense and reflect a justifiable role for government? What is the best way to achieve those goals through public policy? In the example above, the Oregon state law and the Portland land-use plan made a real and important difference in the quality of life for the city's residents. So too did the many other federal, state, and local policies we have discussed in the text, even if they are often unrecognized and unappreciated.

The growth management initiative and the later statewide ballot initiatives also illustrate the potential for policy analysis to clarify the problems that citizens face and to help people find and assess possible solutions to them. Whether applied to contemporary challenges such as how best to promote the nation's economic recovery, how to ensure that the nation's food supply is safe, or how to combat global terrorism, or to problems that will arise in the future, analysis can help to define the issues more sharply, focus public debate, and help the public and policymakers find the best solutions.

Finally, the Portland and statewide ballot measures provide a clear demonstration of the dynamics of the policy-making process as well as the opportunities that it affords to citizens. As we have stated often throughout the text, policymaking never really ends. It is an ongoing process of defining problems, developing solutions to them, selecting what we prefer to do, putting those solutions into effect, and then considering whether to continue or modify those policies depending on how well they are working and whether we find the results acceptable. Precisely because policy decisions can have important and often critical effects on people's lives, those who feel aggrieved by a decision are moved to take action to amend it or overturn it. Individuals and organized groups on either side of a given dispute will make the best case they can and use whatever arguments and data—and political tactics—they believe will strengthen their position.[5] The political parties and elected officials are, of course, deeply involved in this process of policymaking, and ultimately politics in this sense strongly affects what kinds of public policies we have. Policies advocated by the Barack Obama administration, for example, are very different from those favored by the George W. Bush administration.

All this is mostly good news for citizens. It means that at all levels of government they can choose to play an active role in decision making, sometimes by the simple act of voting on a ballot initiative and sometimes through deeper involvement in the political process, in government decision making, and in civic or community affairs in general. Initiatives, such as Ballot Measure 37 in Oregon, are unusual in that they offer citizens the chance to vote directly on public policy measures; but even if they are less directly involved in other kinds of policymaking, individuals can choose to participate in countless ways, particularly at state and local levels, where opportunities often are abundant. As the presidential election of 2008 clearly showed, however, modern Internet technologies facilitate a much greater level of involvement even in national elections and governing. Voter turnout in 2008 was the highest in decades, especially among Democratic voters excited by their candidate, Barack Obama. Interest in the election, participation in the campaign, and voting in 2008 were particularly strong among younger voters, indicating an emerging potential for political activism among this segment of the electorate.[6]

In this chapter we revisit the core arguments of the book and extend them to several contemporary challenges, especially as they relate to government's capacity to act on public problems, and what might be done to improve that capacity as well as to build a vital democratic process for the future. The questions are exceptionally important today. The last few months of the Bush administration in 2008 and the first few months of the Obama administration in 2009 made crystal clear that government is not always prepared to deal with the problems it faces, whether they concern the Iraq and Afghanistan wars or the U.S. and global financial collapse. Policymakers do not always fully understand the causes of the problems, as was evident in the initial financial rescue plans directed at Wall Street banks, and they may be incapable of designing a coherent and comprehensive approach that stands much chance of working—simply because of the enormity and complexity of the economic system today. Even the economic experts are unsure of what to do.

At the same time, at least some analysts and policymakers viewed the dire conditions of early 2009 as offering a unique opportunity to institute major policy changes and to do so quickly. For example, the economic recovery plan that Congress approved in February 2009—the American Recovery and Reinvestment Act—and the budget message that Obama delivered to Congress shortly thereafter offered an ambitious policy agenda to "build a new foundation for lasting prosperity." It included sweeping changes in the nation's use of energy resources; a long-delayed plan to address climate change; a proposed overhaul of the nation's health care system; and plans to sharply increase spending on childhood education and college loan programs, to "ensure that every child has access to a complete and competitive education, from the day they are born to the day they begin a career." [7]

PUBLIC POLICIES AND THEIR IMPACTS

Chapter 1 defined public policy as what governments and citizens choose to do or not to do about public problems. Such choices are made at every level of government through the kinds of policy-making processes outlined in chapter 3 and elsewhere in the book. General descriptions of policymaking are somewhat abstract, however, and do not convey how important those choices can be, especially the great impact they can have on people's lives. The examples are myriad. Social Security policy has enormous consequences for the ability of senior citizens to live in dignity and meet their most essential needs during what is often a financially difficult period in life. So too do health care policies such as Medicare and Medicaid, which provide insurance coverage when health care is urgently needed, expensive, and often beyond the means of many individuals. Education policies can affect every public school in the country, what children learn, and how well prepared they are for college or employment. Economic and environmental policies that shape human well-being in the short term can also have serious long-term effects, as the discussion of climate change in chapter 11 indicated. In short, even though many people may not be aware of it, government and public policy matter.

Because policymaking involves a specification of policy goals as well as the means used to achieve them, a natural part of it is disagreement in every policy area. Should the Endangered Species Act continue to require stringent measures to protect threatened species and biological diversity, and if so, should Congress add provisions to protect the rights of property owners? The federal Medicare program now includes prescription drug benefits, but how generous should those benefits be? What regulations might the government adopt to control the rising cost of drugs? As these and countless other examples illustrate, policy design can make a big difference in how much policies cost and how well they work to meet people's needs. Particular statutory or regulatory provisions can have significant effects on the way policies are implemented, how individuals and institutions comply with the law, and the impacts those laws have on society.

Policy Conflicts and Incremental Decision Making

Conflict arises when policy actors have differing views about the substance of public policies or whether government intervention is justifiable at all. Conflicts over the role of government and public policy underscore the inherently political nature of policymaking. Inevitably, policymaking involves choices about social values as well as calculations about policy design. In the heat of public debate, the differences are not always clear, even to those most directly involved. Policymakers and interest groups may disagree intensely about whether government intervention is warranted and about broad policy goals such as homeland security or equality in the workplace. Forging consensus is more difficult on fundamental goals and values than it is on the specific policy tools that might be used, such as provision of market incentives, regulation, privatization, or government management. The history of policy gridlock in areas as diverse as energy policy and health care reflects the inability of policymakers to resolve some of these deep conflicts, particularly when organized groups on each side subject the policymakers to intense lobbying.

Because political conflict is endemic to policymaking, almost all policies represent a compromise on the goals being sought as well as the policy tools proposed to achieve them. Compromise means that the policies are likely to be only partially effective and that the debate over further changes will continue. Thus elected officials enact policies to remove agricultural subsidies, only to put them back again a few years later when farmers complain that the free market that policymakers anticipated is not working well. Congress approved the Clean Air Act Amendments in 1970 but debated two decades later whether to add acid rain controls to the act's provisions and how to improve its dismal achievements in curbing toxic air pollutants. The nation seems to alternate between periods when policymakers impose tough requirements on food safety and the marketing of drugs, for example, and when there is no effective regulation. When weak policies result in public exposure to unreasonable risks of contaminated food, as happened with some peanut products in 2008, the pendulum swings the other way as public outrage convinces policymakers to take action. This is true of financial regulation as well. Lax oversight of Wall Street banks and their reliance on exotic financial instruments was a major cause of the economic collapse in 2008, and the eagerness of mortgage loan officials across the country to offer risky or abusive home loans free from state or federal regulation was a key factor in the fall of the housing market. Now we are likely to see a period of strong government regulation of financial institutions and also of health, safety, and environmental practices.[8] Such examples tell us that policymaking is never complete but an ongoing process, in which new problems emerge, old ones are seen in a different light, and arguments are advanced once again about how best to further the public interest (Anderson 2006; Kingdon 1995). These and other characteristics of U.S. politics almost always mean that public policies change in small steps over time.

Incremental policymaking of this kind can be a sensible way to act on public problems. It can provide short-term political stability by minimizing conflict over social values and policy goals. It can forge compromises that help diverse policy actors gain something that they want while delivering needed services to the public. It subjects policy proposals to careful evaluation of their likely effectiveness, costs, and impacts, thus reducing the risk of serious mistakes. It can help to build political legitimacy and confidence in the policy-making processes. Finally, it can encourage policy experimentation and learning, the kind of trial-and-error decision making that allows policymakers, especially at the state level, to try new approaches to see how they work before committing to a particular course of action (Lindblom and Woodhouse 1993). Programs that are successful or broadly supported, such as Head Start, can be expanded over time, and those that fall short can be curtailed or modified in other ways.

Policy Strategies with No Crystal Ball

Incremental policymaking, the dominant style in the U.S. political system, is suitable for many public problems and circumstances, but it also has its limitations. Some critics suggest that it may be least appropriate when governments face new problems for which they are ill prepared and where considerable uncertainty exists over the risks, the costs of trying to reduce them, and the likely effectiveness of policy measures (Ophuls and Boyan 1992). Others may be tempted to say that this is precisely when incremental policy change makes more sense than a radical departure from the status quo.

Global climate change offers a context in which to consider the relative advantages of incrementalism and radical change. Climate science is still developing, and forecasts of future climate scenarios are necessarily somewhat uncertain. But opting for minimal policy responses while awaiting more definitive scientific evidence on the seriousness of the problem may be catastrophic to societies around the world. Adopting radical changes that could be quite costly, however, poses a different kind of risk to society, that of spending money that could be better used for other purposes (DiMento and Doughman 2007; Selin and VanDeveer 2010). What should governments do in these circumstances?

Luckily, a middle course is available. Many recent proposals in a range of policy areas have emphasized the value of policy flexibility and adaptive management, meaning that policymakers can continue to evaluate the situation while taking incremental policy steps. For climate change, this type of policymaking might mean a real effort to promote energy efficiency and conservation, which are relatively cheap to achieve and for which technologies already exist. Or it might mean funding a research program to develop alternatives to fossil fuels, as President Obama favored in 2009 as part of his economic stimulus measure and initial budget proposals. Whatever policies are adopted could have enough built-in flexibility to allow program changes as new knowledge develops. Administrators might be given the discretion to alter course when conditions justify doing so. Policymakers can always revisit the policy when they have enough evidence to warrant a change in direction.

At the same time, some analysts cite the **precautionary principle** as a guideline. This principle was developed as a way of dealing with uncertain future risks. It encourages a prudent or conservative response to potentially serious threats, with a bias in favor of protecting human health and the environment rather than advancing proposals for new technologies or economic development activities (Raffensperger and Tickner 1999). It also reflects a belief that ethical standards may be able to inform policy debates that otherwise might center on economic issues.

Another way of thinking about responses to an uncertain future is evident in the example of Portland's land-use plan discussed earlier. Because their policy decisions have long-term effects, city and state governments need methods for making reasonable predictions about the future. They can turn to forecasting methods to determine what the city and state might look like in twenty or fifty years if present trends continue. They can also work with citizens to define what they prefer to see in the future. Once a preferred vision or ideal for the city or state is identified, officials can develop plans and policies to help realize it. Chapters 5 and 6 discussed a similar trend in many localities to shape their futures around the idea of sustainable development or how best to enhance the quality of life for citizens on an enduring basis. The movement toward sustainable communities is a striking testimony to the belief that citizens can affect their futures through cooperation and local action that includes adopting policies that attempt to integrate economic development, environmental protection, and social well-being. Hundreds of communities across the country have tried to chart their futures in this way, and scholars have begun to assess their success and the conditions that foster it (Mazmanian and Kraft 2009; Portney 2003; Paehlke 2010).[9]

In this vein, one of the most frequently observed limits of decision making is that it tends to focus on events or developments that are closest to people in time and space. Commentators often fault policymakers for having a short-term time horizon, by which they mean that elected officials tend to think about impacts only through the next election. This is a common explanation offered for why the president and Congress have been unable to reform entitlement programs such as Social Security and Medicare. The dire effects of the present policies will be felt in the future, but any attempt to revise the policies invites short-term political controversy. Still, this kind of bias, even if exaggerated, exists throughout society. Corporations, for example, focus heavily on short-term profits shown in quarterly and annual financial reports. As a result, they may lose sight of long-term goals, which are not highly valued in the marketplace. The financial meltdown of 2008 and 2009 clearly showed major banks and other financial institutions taking on enormous risks for short-term gains, a gamble that turned extremely negative for them, but only after they profited handsomely from those very calculations.

As understandable as such a fixation on the short term is, public policy of necessity must look ahead. It must also adopt a broader perspective that includes people and institutions located at some distance, geographically and culturally, from policymakers and citizens. As the nation has learned since 9/11, fighting global terrorism means more than guarding domestic airports or taking military action against specific targets in other countries. It involves trying to understand and respond to cultural and economic forces around the world that breed resentment toward the United States and sympathy and support for terrorists.

The September 2002 World Summit on Sustainable Development, mentioned at the beginning of chapter 11, is a good example of forward-looking and wide-ranging policymaking. The world's population is expected to climb to over nine billion by 2050, and the Census Bureau projects a U.S. population of about 439 million by then. To provide for all these people, nations will have to foster more economic development to meet the demands for energy, food, water, clothing, housing, transportation, jobs, and other essentials. To be sustainable, economic development around the globe would have to be designed to avoid the severe environmental and social strains that would likely come with reliance on conventional growth. The World Summit was arranged to try to identify and build support for this new kind of economic development.

As these examples illustrate, public policy aims at a moving target. Public problems change over time, in part because economic, cultural, social, and political conditions are dynamic. New values and perspectives arise, for example, about welfare and work or the right to health insurance, and policy processes shift accordingly. In the mid-1990s, many Republicans in Congress wanted to abolish the Department of Education, which was created during the Jimmy Carter administration in part as a way of showing support for teachers, a major Democratic constituency. Yet many of these same Republicans took the lead in supporting additional federal power for education with the passage of the No Child Left Behind Act of 2001, which required national testing of students. What changed? The American public said it was tired of failing public schools, and Republicans, interested in broadening their party's base, were now prepared to back a stronger federal role in education.

Policies also change in response to the development of new technologies, which in turn stimulate new public demands for government intervention. For example, cities and states try to regulate the use of cell phones by drivers, protect individual privacy rights on the Internet, subsidize stem cell research, advance passenger rail service, or provide high-speed highway lanes for those willing to pay for them.[10] The federal government is forced to define its position on human cloning and use of embryonic stem cells as medical science advances and new technologies raise ethical concerns.

Because the targets of public policy are always shifting, analysts, policymakers, and citizens need to be alert to changing situations and consider new policy ideas. As the substantive policy chapters showed, too often old policies continue long after they are outdated. If the nation truly values effective and efficient public policies, it must be open to evaluating those policies and changing them as needed. The same argument applies to addressing new concerns about the equity of public policies, whether the concern is over environmental justice for poor communities or equal access to opportunities in education.

POLICY ANALYSIS AND POLICY CHOICES

Making public policies more effective, efficient, and equitable raises once again the subject of policy analysis and its role in policymaking. As we discussed in chapters 4 through 6, policy analysis can bring greater clarity to public problems and their solutions than might otherwise be the case. Analysts acknowledge the political character of the policy-making process, but they also believe that objective knowledge can reveal the nature of problems and their causes and help guide the search for public policies that promise a measure of success. If nothing else, policy analysis can clarify the issues and sharpen political debates. The potential for using policy analysis in state and local problem solving may be even greater than at the national level because state and local governments often lack the same level of expertise seen in the federal government.

Oregon's land-use case indicates that potential. In deciding whether to continue or alter the thirty-year-old growth management policy, voters benefited from reliable knowledge of what the policy had achieved to date and a fair assessment of how changing the policy would affect the quality of life in the metropolitan area. For example, how would additional residential development outside of the city affect highway travel, congestion, and air pollution? Would businesses migrate from the central city to suburban shopping malls, as they have done in most other urban areas around the country? Given the vote on the state's land-use policy initiative in 2004, how might development in the greenbelt around the city affect recreational opportunities? How likely are farmers to sell their land to developers to meet the growing demand for housing? In this case and many others like it, local officials and the citizens who voted on either of the ballot initiatives could have benefited from unbiased information that addressed such questions.

Evaluating Public Policy

Among other evaluative criteria, this book has placed special emphasis on three: effectiveness, efficiency, and equity. Effectiveness, or how well a policy works or might work, is always difficult to address, but it is obviously an important consideration at a time when many critics doubt the capacity of government to solve any problem. At the earliest stages of the policy process, when policy alternatives are proposed, effectiveness is necessarily based on various assumptions and projections of the future that may or may not come to pass.

At periodic stages of the policy process, effectiveness is the criterion analysts use to determine how well a policy has lived up to expectations. Did it succeed in producing the desired results? Even after a reasonable period of time, it is not easy to identify and measure a policy's impacts and compare them to the initial policy goals. Policymakers and independent analysts in and out of government conduct such evaluation studies, which have great value, despite their limitations. Whether use of school vouchers or the operation of charter schools are effective in improving educational outcomes, for example, depends on what one measures. Should analysts consider parental support, improvement by participating students, or progress of all students? The difficulty in measuring success means that students of public policy need to think critically about such studies and their findings.

Efficiency is probably the criterion most likely to receive attention in contemporary policymaking as policy alternatives and existing programs are assessed. The reasons are clear. Government budgets are almost always under tight constraints, and it is a rare politician or taxpayer who favors tax increases, so policymakers want to ensure a good return on the money spent. This has long been true, but with rising federal deficits and a doubling of the national debt during the 2000s, the constraints on spending today are far greater than they have been. Policymakers almost certainly will want to know how much proposed programs cost and where the money will come from to pay for them. They will demand some kind of comparison of the costs with the benefits of government action. They may even compare different programs according to which are most efficient in producing good results for the same dollar amount invested. Policy analysis can contribute to answering those questions. While this is all well and good, public policy students already know that measuring and comparing costs and benefits are rarely simple; not all can be identified and measured, and it is difficult to compare them over time. Policymakers and the public need to exercise care in the way they use such studies and pay attention to their assumptions and methods so that they understand the studies' limitations.

Equity issues are addressed less frequently than effectiveness and efficiency, but they are no less important in public policy. As we have seen, equity can be defined in several different ways, and therefore it may include concerns that range from protecting individual freedom to regulating how policy costs and benefits are distributed among groups in a population, such as the urban and rural residents or rich and poor taxpayers. The issue of individual (or corporate) freedom arises frequently when a new program is proposed or an old one expanded. For example, federal health care policies offer benefits to Medicare and Medicaid recipients, but they impose constraints on health insurance companies and health professionals. Federal and state environmental regulations can help to protect the public's health, but at some cost to the rights of corporations to make decisions about the technologies they use and the kinds of products they make. Policy analysis can facilitate policy choices by clarifying these kinds of trade-offs. Analysis can be similarly useful in describing the way many programs, such as Social Security, welfare, and education, either redistribute wealth in society or try to promote equity in some other ways.

This November 4, 2008, photo shows young supporters of Democratic presidential candidate Barack Obama early on election day in New York. Some commentators described the day as a defining moment for the generation of youth, as voter turnout for the election was particularly high among younger voters. The 2008 election relied heavily on modern Internet technologies for fundraising and mobilizing supporters. Obama's campaign was especially adept at using the technologies to communicate frequently with supporters to maintain their enthusiasm for the candidate and his message of change.

Improving Policy Capacity

Policy analysis also can help improve the performance of government and its responsiveness to citizen concerns. Now might be as good a time as any to consider how to improve the **policy capacity** of government. Public trust and confidence in government institutions fell almost steadily from the 1960s to the late 1990s, with a small upward trend only in the fall of 2001, following the terrorist attacks on the United States and the U.S. response to them (Mackenzie and Labiner 2002). After the financial crisis of 2008 and 2009, and growing public frustration over government's seeming ineptitude in figuring out what to do and which industries and companies deserved a federal bailout, it would be remarkable if trust and confidence in government returned to its former levels any time soon. Yet on the campaign trail in 2008, then-candidate Barack Obama pledged to "make government cool again." In support of such a goal, some policymakers and citizen activists are supporting a new civilian service academy, analogous to the Peace Corps but devoted to training a new generation of public servants. The United States Public Service Academy would offer a free four-year college education if individuals who attend are prepared to commit to five years of government service. In early 2009, the idea was attracting support, and legislation is pending in Congress to create such a program.[11]

Despite the many criticisms of government performance, the evidence on how well government programs have done is clearly mixed. Some programs have indeed fallen short of expectations, but others, as we have shown in previous chapters, have produced significant benefits to the public, from public education and environmental protection to health care services delivered through Medicare and Medicaid. A 2007 article in the *National Journal* on ten notable successes in public policy put it this way: "Not every problem is intractable. Progress *is* possible."[12] In a similar vein, in 2000 the Brookings Institution released a study of government's greatest achievements of the past half-century. Among the most notable were rebuilding Europe after World War II; expanding the right to vote; promoting equal access to public accommodations, such as hotels and restaurants; reducing disease; ensuring safe food and drinking water; increasing older Americans' access to health care; enhancing workplace safety; increasing access to higher education; and reducing hunger and improving nutrition. The study's point was simple: it is easy to ignore some of the most important public policy actions because they are not very visible as they become routine parts of American life; yet examining such a list confirms the important role that government and public policy can play in improving everyday life.[13]

Still, there is little doubt from public commentary and political rhetoric that many people believe to the contrary that government is not working well (Bok 2001). In response to this skeptical public mood, policymakers at all levels of government have struggled with how to improve public policies and programs and better meet citizens' needs. Various efforts to "reinvent" government and to improve its efficiency were tried during the 1990s, and they continue today. As indicated earlier, President Obama began his administration determined not only to operate with openness and transparency, but to ensure that all programs would be as effective and efficient as possible. Over time, this will require more than a determined White House. It will mean developing a broader policy capacity to define and respond effectively to public problems, both present and future, and ensuring that government agencies, from the military to Social Security, are as well managed as they can be.

How can policy analysis contribute to improving the policy capacity of government? One way is through the analysis of proposed institutional reforms, such as changes in the electoral process, campaign finance, term limits for legislators, and opportunities for citizens to participate in decision making. This is a task at which political scientists excel (Levi et al. 2008). Yet too often their analyses fail to reach the public or even policymakers, who then must act without benefit of what the analysis has uncovered. The box "Steps to Analysis: Money in Politics" illustrates these needs.

Other chapters have suggested that policy capacity can also be improved through better evaluation of the agencies charged with implementing policies and programs. Thanks to the Government Performance and Results Act of 1993, the federal government is likely to conduct more evaluations of this kind than in the past, though probably of varying quality (Radin 2006). For many reasons, think tanks and other independent bodies carrying out external evaluations may be better able to identify institutional strengths and weaknesses and to suggest meaningful paths to reform. For example, chapter 11 noted that a series of studies by the National Academy of Public Administration (1995, 2000) identified many elements of the U.S. environmental protection system that could be changed to improve the effectiveness and efficiency of the Environmental Protection Agency (EPA) and other agencies. Studies by

MONEY IN POLITICS

No other aspect of politics may be as well documented as the role of money. The Center for Responsive Politics allows you as a citizen to examine the data to see how money is donated and spent to influence the policy-making process. The center's Web site, www.opensecrets.org, lists the amounts of money donated to campaigns, dollars spent on lobbying activity, and soft money contributions. This kind of information can give voters a great deal of insight into the politics of policymaking. The center believes that turning the "sunshine" on these activities will get policymakers thinking about how they go about making decisions and just who is supplying not only the money but also the information they use to make them.

The Web site also provides research and reports on political issues, and you can make your own assessments of the information. For example, during the 2008 election year cycle, the oil and gas industry contributed over $10 million to candidates through their political action committees (PACs). Counting all forms of campaign contribution, the industry gave more than $34 million to candidates and parties at a time when energy issues such as off-shore drilling were prominent in the campaigns. Much was at stake in the election outcomes, and the industry was fully aware of that.

Go to www.opensecrets.org and click on Influence and Lobbying, and then on Industries. Select Oil and Gas. Examine the data presented in the table and figures. How do PAC donations compare to individual donations? Which political party received the majority of money from this industry in 2008, and how does that compare to previous years? You will see the results presented both in the total amount of dollars donated and as a percent for each major party. On the top bar, click on Recipients to see who received the most money from this industry. You can examine the presidential contest as well as donations to members of Congress. Compare the donations to Barack Obama and John McCain. Now look at the contributions to all members of Congress. Who are the leading recipients? Do you see any pattern here? Now go to the Background link and read what this industry thinks about money and policymaking regarding this area of public policy. Do you agree or disagree with what it has to say?

Go back to the main page of the site and click on Politicians and Elections. Then select the tab for Congress. You can examine any of those members in leadership positions whose names and photos are on the main page. Or you can find your member of Congress, or the candidate who challenged that member, by using the box on the right and entering part of the member's or candidate's name. How much did he or she spend on the last election campaign, and where did the money come from? Click on the member's name to see the leading contributors to the campaign. What conclusions would you draw? How do you think the sources of election funding might affect decisions on public policy issues before Congress?

Resources for the Future have reached similar conclusions (Davies and Mazurek 1998). Chapter 12 highlighted a number of studies by the Government Accountability Office and the Congressional Budget Office on the use of contractors in the Iraq war and spending on foreign aid.

Sometimes evaluations of government institutions and processes come from citizen groups such as Public Citizen and Common Cause, which favor reforming laws on campaign finance and lobbying. Policy entrepreneurs such as Ralph Nader and John Gardner, longtime representatives of those two groups, helped to get these issues on the political agenda, attract media coverage of reform proposals, and pressure Congress to act. The organizations scored a major victory with the enactment of the Bipartisan Campaign Finance Reform Act of 2002, which imposed new restrictions on contributions of funds to political parties and campaigns.

One of the central tasks in improving policy capacity in government is in the hands of the people. If citizens lack interest in public affairs and fail to educate themselves on the issues, government is likely to continue to respond to organized groups and special interests. What citizens see as faulty performance in government sometimes reflects the influence of organized groups that work to ensure that policies affecting them are *not* effective or that they inflict minimum constraints on their activities. A well-known example from the late 1990s was the influence of corporations in weakening government oversight of their financial operations. The weaker financial regulations provided the opportunities for corporate abuses at companies such as Enron and WorldCom that shocked and disgusted the public in 2002. The best way to counter such self-serving actions by special interests is for citizens to get involved. There is no question that the public and Congress will now demand much greater transparency and accountability on the part of financial institutions. In fact, we are likely headed to an era of bigger government and more regulation, as noted earlier, which the public seems to favor. Every well-publicized story about failed food-safety regulation, weak financial oversight, or national security risks stimulates a new round of public demands to deal with the situation.

CITIZEN PARTICIPATION IN DECISION MAKING

The final perspective this chapter emphasizes is the politics of policymaking, that is, how policy choices are made. The decision-making process affects what kinds of decisions are made and, ultimately, what impacts they have on society. The policy outcomes reflect who participates in the process, who does not, and the different resources that each policy actor brings to the decision-making arena. In a democracy, one would expect public policies to be consistent with public preferences and to meet the needs of citizens. As noted, however, policymakers are often more responsive to organized interests—the agriculture industry, the mining industry, the oil industry, health insurance companies, or the music recording industry—than they are to the general public. The discussion of subgovernments, elites, and the role of interest groups in chapters 2 and 3 highlighted these patterns.

Citizen Capacity and Policy Engagement

How might that situation be changed? One way is to strengthen **citizen capacity** to participate in policy-making processes. The level of public participation in policy processes, whether voting in elections or taking active roles in civic affairs, has declined over the past several decades (Putnam 2000; Skocpol 2003; Skocpol and Fiorina 1999). Of all the age groups, the youngest—including college students—generally has had the lowest level of interest in politics and policymaking and active participation in these processes. However, as stated earlier, there are some contrary indicators of citizen interest in public affairs, especially in their local communities. The movement toward sustainable communities often involves extensive citizen involvement in local decision making, and it captures recent interest in redesigning communities in terms of mass transit, energy efficiency, use of open space, and rehabilitation of older buildings and neighborhoods. There also are encouraging signs from surveys by the Pew Partnership for Civic Change, demonstrating that Americans have a "profound sense of connectivity to their communities and neighbors" and are willing to work with others to solve problems.[14] Additional evidence comes from the 2008 election campaigns, where candidates proved they could spark intense interest and participation by younger voters.[15]

There is no shortage of analyses about why the American public has been so disengaged from politics and civic affairs for so long. At least part of the explanation lies in the disconnect between the policy process and people's daily lives. That is, most citizens either do not see how government affects their lives, or they do not believe they can do much to change it. As we have argued, public policies unquestionably have a great impact on people's lives. The question is whether people see these impacts, and also whether they really believe their opinions and actions can make a difference. Looking at the election results in November 2008, many commentators anticipated a rebirth of citizen enthusiasm about government and politics. Its arrival may have been tempered to some extent by the economic downturn, and time will tell if we are in the early stages of a new era of active citizenship.

In addition to making the connection between policy choices and individual lives clearer, improving the public's access to government information might encourage more people to participate. Consider the activities of the public interest group Environmental Working Group (EWG), which in 2002 became heavily involved in congressional debates over agricultural subsidies. Frustrated by the lack of public attention to what it believed were inequitable payments to wealthy farmers, the group secured access to the raw data for the government's farm subsidy payments and placed the information on its Web site (www.ewg.org). Members of Congress frequently cited the data and the EWG Web site when considering the bill, probably because they had heard from their constituents on the subject. Particularly important was the revelation that hundreds of farmers and absentee landlords were receiving millions of dollars in subsidies.[16] It is noteworthy that by early 2009 President Obama made a point of urging Congress to end such subsidies.

Later in the year, as Congress began debating whether to approve construction of the Yucca Mountain nuclear waste repository, the same group put information about possible nuclear waste shipment routes on its site. It included an interactive map that allowed citizens to determine how close the shipments would come to their communities. The site also provided data on the amount of nuclear waste in each state, the likely number of shipments of waste by truck and rail through the state, the number of people who lived within one mile of a transportation route, and similar information. Once again, the Web site attracted a great deal of media coverage, along with plenty of criticism. Critics said the information was misleading because the government has yet to approve any transportation routes for the nuclear waste shipments and that the maps therefore were speculative. Whether one thinks that the group's efforts were praiseworthy or not, its strategy suggests the potential political power of Web-based citizen education and lobbying. The box "Steps to Analysis: Using Web Sites to Influence Public Opinion and Policy Debate" illustrates yet another group effort to shape public opinion and policy debate.

USING WEB SITES TO INFLUENCE PUBLIC OPINION AND POLICY DEBATE

Back in 2002, the groups Public Citizen and Government Accountability Project analyzed testing records from the U.S. Department of Agriculture (USDA) for Salmonella bacteria found at ground-beef processing plants. They acquired the data with a Freedom of Information Act request. The groups' 2002 report cited many plants that failed the tests, some repeatedly, because of lax USDA enforcement. They placed the list of failing plants on the Public Citizen Web site to highlight what they considered to be a serious threat to public health.

In 2008, another public health scare received enormous media attention. This again involved Salmonella bacteria, but this time the concern was tainted peanut butter at a plant in Georgia whose ingredients wound up in thousands of food products across the country. Eventually, the Food and Drug Administration (FDA) recall of those products became the largest in U.S. history. The FDA set up a special Web page on the recalls (www.fda.gov/oc/opacom/hottopics/Salmonellat yph.html) as a way to provide important information for the public.[1] Visit the site and scan the list of recalled products. How understandable are the FDA's product lists? Review the other topics on this page, including the "resources for consumers." Or, should the FDA discontinue the special peanut butter site, see its Spotlight Archive page for this and previous food product recalls (www.fda.gov/oc/opacom/hottopics). What conclusions can you draw from the information

provided here? Do you believe the FDA did a good job on the peanut butter recall action or on previous product recalls or comparable agency action? Should the FDA have done even more in this case? Should it have more carefully inspected the peanut plant in Georgia to prevent the spread of contaminated peanut products in the first place? Why do you think it did not? Why do think the state of Georgia was not more vigilant or more thorough in inspecting the plant? What about the state of Texas? A peanut processing plant in that state run by the same company, the Peanut Corporation of America, operated for years without any inspection or state license from government health officials.

According to the U.S. Centers for Disease Control and Prevention, improperly handled ground beef and other foods contaminated with pathogens such as Salmonella, Listeria, and E. coli bacteria are implicated in 14 million illnesses, 60,000 hospitalizations, and about 1,500 deaths in the United States every year. Illness and death are particularly high among newborn infants, the elderly, and those with weakened immune systems. The information is on the CDC Web site (www.cdc.gov/ncidod/eid/vol5no5/mead.htm# Figure%201). The CDC also reports, as noted in chapter 6, that all food-related illnesses account for perhaps 5,000 deaths each year. In light of these numbers, why do you think the United States has not done more to reduce the risks of food-borne illness and death?

[1]For an overview of the contaminated peanut story and related problems with food safety inspections, see Michael Moss and Andrew Martin, "Food Safety Problems Slip Past Private Inspectors," *New York Times* online edition, March 5, 2009.

New Forms of Citizen Participation

Public participation in the policy process can go well beyond voting, writing letters or e-mail messages to policymakers, and discussing policy issues. Historically, only a small percentage of the public is even this active. But the percentage could rise as technology makes public involvement easier and as policymakers become more interested in raising public participation in government.

As discussed in many previous chapters, some government agencies already make a concerted effort to promote the use of their Web sites, to offer information and public services through "e-government," and to invite the public to engage in the issues (West 2005). For example, in 2001 the EPA completed an online national dialogue on how to improve public involvement in the agency's decision making.[17] For years the Internal Revenue Service has accepted electronic submission of tax returns, and in 2003 it began a new program called Electronic Account Resolution that allows tax professionals to resolve many kinds of disputes online in minutes. The opportunities to become involved in policymaking are even greater at the state and local levels. In addition to inviting people to public meetings and hearings and asking the public to submit comments on proposed government actions, policymakers also ask citizens to serve on advisory panels and assist them in making often difficult choices.

In the world of campaign and advocacy politics, the 2004 and 2008 elections demonstrated the enormous potential for candidate fund-raising and citizen mobilization through Internet technology. The use of specialized networks and blog sites has greatly expanded, and the potential for citizen involvement in politics and public policy continues to grow. With nearly universal access to the Internet and increasing use of high-speed and wireless connections, citizens should find it even easier to become active in public affairs (Anderson and Cornfield 2002; Kamarck and Nye 2002; Macedo 2005; Tolbert and McNeal 2003).[18]

Of course, there is also a downside to these developments. Citizens face a veritable flood of political and public policy commentary, much of which is biased and partisan, and sometimes blatantly manipulative and misleading.[19] The same could be said for many Internet news sites that bear little relationship to real journalism. The trend is made worse as Americans' interest in news from all sources has declined steadily in recent years.[20] Without an ability to compare information from different sources, and evaluate it objectively, citizens have little protection against the onslaught.

One of the forms of citizen involvement that is most vulnerable to these kinds of risks is voting on ballot propositions, much like the ones in Oregon discussed at the beginning of the chapter. Consider this example that gained national media attention. In 2008 voters in California approved Proposition 8, a ballot measure that revised the state constitution to restrict the definition of marriage to a union between a man and a woman. The vote was 52 to 48 percent in favor, and its approval reversed a decision by the state's supreme court earlier that year permitting marriage by same-sex couples; the court had ruled that banning such marriages was discriminatory under the state's constitution. In early 2009, that same court heard legal challenges to Proposition 8 that sought to declare it invalid.[21] The two sides in the state ballot campaign had spent about $40 million each, making it the costliest state ballot measure ever and, except for the presidential election, the highest-funded election campaign in 2008.

In addition to spending a lot of money, opponents of the measure made use of a new technology that made available on the Internet information on Proposition 8 donations that the state collects and makes public under its campaign finance disclosure laws. Visitors could see donors' names and approximate locations, and as one journalist put it, "That is often enough information for interested parties to find the rest—like an e-mail or home address." Because of public access to the information, donors to groups that supported Proposition 8 said they had been harassed—sometimes with death threats—by some of those who opposed it.[22] Is the use of such information, collected through public disclosure laws that are designed to increase the transparency of the political process, reasonable? Does use of it in this way threaten to undermine democratic values that campaign finance and other similar laws are intended to enhance, as some critics have said? That is, might the practice of making the information public in a very visible way discourage citizens from getting involved by contributing money? Or is it an acceptable way to alert citizens to the identity of those individuals and businesses that stand on one side or the other of a public dispute and contribute money, knowing that such contributions become public information?

As we noted in chapter 4, even public policy think tanks are not immune to some of these trends; some are drawn more than ever into hotly contested partisan and ideological battles (Rich 2004). Thus, as we have argued throughout the book, students of public policy need to develop a strong capacity to think critically about news and policy commentary and train themselves to determine which Web sites and other sources offer the best in public policy information and analysis. Despite the difficulties, there are reasons to be optimistic about the potential of the Internet and citizen access to information about government and public policy.

Policy analysts have long recognized different social goals furthered by public involvement in policymaking and the criteria by which participation can be evaluated. Thomas Beierle and Jerry Cayford (2002) identify five goals: (1) incorporating public values into decisions (a fundamental expectation in a democracy); (2) improving the substantive quality of those decisions (for example, by suggesting alternatives and finding errors of inappropriate assumptions underlying policy proposals); (3) resolving conflict among the various competing interests (by emphasizing collaborative rather than adversarial decision making); (4) building trust in institutions and processes (thereby improving their ability to solve public problems); and (5) educating and informing the public (raising public understanding of the issues and building a shared perspective on possible solutions). The last of these goals can be thought of as enhancing public capacity for participation in policy processes, an example of what Anne L. Schneider and Helen Ingram (1997) refer to as the capacity-building tools that governments possess.

Government agencies and public officials are often unclear about what they expect public participation to accomplish, and citizens might be puzzled as well. Some agencies feign interest in public involvement to appear to be doing the "right thing" and to comply with legal mandates. But they greatly limit the degree to which citizens can affect decision making. They may do so because they do not trust citizens' capacity to understand issues and participate with a sufficient degree of competence (Yang 2005). Responding to that common practice, some analysts have suggested that there are four quite different models of citizen involvement, with increasing degrees of public influence on decision making. The first is the commentary model, in which agencies and proponents dominate; second, the social learning model, in which citizens learn about policy proposals and provide advice on them; third, the joint planning model, in which citizens engage in a dialogue with policymakers and planners and work collaboratively with them; and fourth, the consent and consensus model, in which citizens share authority with government and work together to solve problems.[23] This last model resembles what some scholars call **deliberative democracy,** where citizens are expected to play an intensive role in discussions with each other and with policymakers as part of the process of justifying or legitimizing policy action (Gutmann and Thompson 2004). Which model makes the most sense? Are citizens well enough informed on the issues to share authority with government officials? If not, how might their knowledge be increased enough to permit such a sharing of authority?

CONCLUSIONS

Throughout this book, we have emphasized an integrated approach to the study of public policy rather than focusing on policy history and program details. Although this kind of information is clearly important, policy and program particulars change quickly, and the knowledge learned may be of limited use over time. In the long run, the perspectives and approaches of policy analysis are more helpful in understanding how the nation's policies evolved into their present state and considering what alternatives might work better. The book stresses how to think about policy issues, where to find pertinent information, and how to interpret it. It also underscores the need to develop a robust capacity for critical and creative thinking about public problems and their solutions.

This last chapter revisits some of these points in the context of the policy challenges governments face as they try to make difficult decisions about the future. It focuses on the way policy decisions can affect people's lives, how policy analysis can clarify public problems and possible solutions, and the role of citizens in the policy-making process. Despite a prevailing sense of cynicism toward government and politics, we believe that we live in a time of exceptional opportunity for citizens to get involved in public affairs. New technologies, particularly those based in the Internet, greatly facilitate access to a vast range of policy information. Governments at all levels are welcoming citizen involvement, giving new vitality to the promise of American democracy. We urge you to take advantage of these opportunities and play an active role in designing and choosing public policies for the future.

DISCUSSION QUESTIONS

1. Consider the case presented at the beginning of the chapter on land-use decisions in Portland and the state of Oregon. Is the provision for statewide ballot initiatives such as Ballot Measure 37 a good idea? That is, should citizens be allowed to vote directly on such legislation, or should state governments rely instead on their elected legislators to make such policy choices? What do you see as the major advantages or disadvantages of such state initiatives?

2. Why do you think most citizens do not take more interest in politics and public policy? What might increase their level of interest and participation? What would motivate you to become more active?

3. How much potential do you see in Internet-based political mobilization of citizens, either during election campaigns or for specific advocacy campaigns between elections? What particular kinds of actions are most likely to be successful in reaching voters, especially younger ones? Based on the examples and discussion offered in this chapter, what concerns, if any, do you have?

4. Consider this chapter's discussion of California's Proposition 8 banning same-sex marriage in the state. Should such questions be placed on the ballot for citizens to vote on directly, or should they be decided instead by state legislators? If they are placed on the ballot, is it fair to make public information about individual and business donations to each side of the campaign? Should the state try to restrict the way in which such campaign donation information is made available, or should it leave matters as they now stand—including presenting the data online so that donors to each side can be easily identified?

SUGGESTED READINGS

Derek Bok, *The Trouble with Government* (Cambridge: Harvard University Press, 2001). A perceptive assessment of government and civic shortcomings, with thoughtful recommendations for greater citizen participation in public affairs.

Russell J. Dalton, *The Good Citizen: How a Younger Generation Is Reshaping American Politics,* rev. ed. (Washington, D.C.: CQ Press, 2009). Charts how young Americans are creating new norms of citizenship and engagement, including evidence from the 2008 presidential election.

Stephen E. Frantzich, *Citizen Democracy: Political Activists in a Cynical Age,* 3rd ed. (Boulder: Rowman and Littlefield, 2008). Addresses the myriad ways in which citizens can participate in the political process despite today's prevailing cynicism about government and politics.

Michael J. Kryzanek, *Angry, Bored, Confused: A Citizen Handbook of American Politics* (Boulder: Westview, 1999). A short, refreshing introduction to U.S. government and politics that adopts the perspective of an anxious consumer who seeks to understand and improve government, politics, and public policy.

Paul Loeb, *Soul of the Citizen: Living with Conviction in a Cynical Time* (New York: St. Martin's Press, 1999). Describes how ordinary citizens can make their voices heard and take action in a time of widespread cynicism and despair.

Stephen Macedo et al., *Democracy at Risk: How Political Choices Undermine Citizen Participation, and What We Can Do About It* (Washington, D.C.: Brookings Institution Press, 2005). A short but significant set of commentaries that both analyze the challenges to contemporary U.S. democracy and propose reforms that can revitalize the practice of politics.

Robert D. Putnam, *Bowling Alone: The Collapse and Revival of American Community* (New York: Simon and Schuster, 2000). A best-selling, data-filled treatment of civic disengagement in the United States, the reasons for it, and possible solutions.

SUGGESTED WEB SITES

www.apsanet.org/content_4899.cfm. American Political Science Association's Civic Education Network, with links to civic and political education organizations, centers and institutes, teaching and research resources, and service learning programs.

www.citizen.org. Public Citizen home page, with many links to policy issues and activism.

www.excelgov.org. Council for Excellence in Government, a nonprofit organization working to improve government at all levels and to encourage greater citizen involvement. Has links to other resources and sites, including the Center for Democracy and Citizenship.

www.ipi.org. Institute for Policy Innovation, a research organization that believes in individual liberty and limited government; does research and papers on policy options.

www.usa.gov/index.shtml. FirstGov's citizen portal, with links to public action and e-government services.

KEYWORDS

citizen capacity   431

deliberative democracy   435

policy capacity   428

precautionary principle   424

public participation   433

NOTES

1. Timothy Egan, "Portland Voters Endorse Curbs on City Growth," *New York Times,* May 23, 2002, A25.
2. Felicity Barringer, "Rule Change in Oregon May Alter the Landscape," *New York Times,* November 26, 2004, 1, A26. Other states allow for compensation to be paid to property owners, including Florida, Louisiana, Mississippi, and Texas. But in all cases they set a threshold for making such a claim (such as 25 percent loss of value), and the state is liable only for losses affected by newly approved land-use rules. For other commentary on how the new Oregon law might affect local efforts to control sprawl, see Blaine Harden, "Neighbor vs. Neighbor," *Washington Post National Weekly Edition,* March 7–13, 2005, 30.
3. The key aspects of the ongoing saga of Measure 37 can be read at the Web page for the state's Department of Land Conservation and Development: www.oregon.gov/LCD/MEASURE49/misc_m37_information.shtml#.
4. For those interested, the effects of Measure 37 and the vote on Measure 49 are nicely recounted in a study by the American Land Institute in Portland, "The 'Yes' Vote on Measure 49: Protecting the Geese That Lay the Golden Eggs," July 10, 2008, available at the Oregon State University library: http://ir.library.oregonstate.edu/dspace/handle/1957/9132.
5. As is perhaps evident in this review of the Oregon ballot measure, direct citizen participation of this kind is often fraught with risk. Both sides in such disputes may be tempted to distort the facts, a good deal of money can be spent in ways that can easily mislead voters, and the outcome does not always represent what citizens or the state legislature might choose to do with greater deliberation. The risks of direct policymaking by citizens have not gone unnoticed by scholars. See, for example, Richard J. Ellis, *Democratic Delusions: The Initiative Process in America* (Lawrence: University Press of Kansas, 2002).
6. Scott Helman, "For Democrats, a New Electorate," *Boston Globe* online edition, January 30, 2008.
7. The complex economic recovery measures can be followed on a new government Web site devoted to this effort as part of the Obama administration's pledge to make the actions open to the public, collaborative, and participatory: www.recovery.gov. The text of the Obama speech to Congress is available on the White House Web site: www.whitehouse.gov.
8. See Jackie Calmes, "Both Sides of the Aisle Say More Regulation, and Not Just of Banks, *New York Times,* October 14, 2008, A15.
9. In *Taking Sustainable Cities Seriously: Economic Development, the Environment, and Quality of Life in American Cities* (Cambridge: MIT Press, 2003), Kent E. Portney examined major cities that have "started to take the idea of sustainability seriously as a matter of public policy." These included Austin, Boston, Boulder, Portland, San Francisco, Santa Monica, Seattle, Tucson, and others. Beyond his own analysis, Portney suggests the value of more systematic appraisal that can reveal why cities undertake such efforts and the factors that make some of them more successful than others.

10. For an account of the use of such highway lanes in the metropolitan Washington, D.C., area, see Steven Ginsberg, "A Future Free from Gridlock, for a Price," *Washington Post,* December 12, 2005, A1. For an assessment of California's Proposition 71, a ballot measure that resulted in the state investing heavily in stem cell research, see Connie Bruck, "Hollywood Science," *The New Yorker,* October 18, 2004, 62–80.

11. Jason DeParle, "A Plan to Lift the Lowly Bureaucrat to a Status of Cherished Public Servant," *New York Times,* January 7, 2009.

12. See "10 Successes, 10 Challenges," *National Journal,* January 20, 2007, 18–40. Among the successes were support for higher education, clean air and clean water, the food stamp program, and action against AIDS.

13. The Brookings study, "Government's Greatest Achievements of the Past Half Century," by Paul C. Light, is available at the Brookings Web site: www.brookings.edu/papers/2000/11governance_light.aspx.

14. The Pew study, "Ready, Willing and Able: Citizens Working for Change," is available at www.pew-partnership.org. The site includes similar studies and recommendations for civic engagement.

15. Melissa Dahl, "Youth Vote May Have Been Key in Obama's Win," November 5, 2008, available at the MSNBC Web site: www.msnbc.msn.com/id/27525497.

16. Elizabeth Becker, "Accord Reached on a Bill Raising Farm Subsidies," *New York Times,* April 27, 2002, 1, A11.

17. The EPA dialogue can be found at www.network-democracy.org/epa-pip/welcome.shtml.

18. One of the most active liberal groups that has exploited the potential of the Internet for citizen mobilization is MoveOn.org (www.moveon.org). For an early assessment of its success and the actions of similar groups, see Carl M. Cannon, "Flexing Internet Muscles," *National Journal,* October 9, 2004, 3047–3050.

19. For an argument that the Republican Party has been especially guilty of such manipulation of the American public, see Jacob S. Hacker and Paul Pierson, *Off Center: The Republican Revolution and the Erosion of American Democracy* (New Haven: Yale University Press, 2005). Republicans would counter that liberals and Democrats also manipulate language and political symbols that can mislead the public on policy issues in much the same way.

20. See Frank Ahrens, "Hard News to Digest," *Washington Post National Weekly Edition,* February 28–March 6, 2005, 19–20.

21. Maura Dolan, "California Supreme Court Looks Unlikely to Kill Proposition 8," *Los Angeles Times* online edition, March 6, 2009.

22. See Brad Stone, "Disclosure, Magnified on the Web," *New York Times,* February 8, 2009, Business Section, 3.

23. See Hardy Stevenson Associates, "How to Conduct National Level Consultations," *Social and Environmental Assessment Bulletin* (spring 2002).

REFERENCES

Aaron, Henry, Alan Blinder, Alicia Munnell, and Peter Orszag. 2000. *Governor Bush's Individual Account Proposal: Implications for Retirement Benefits.* Available at www.socsec.org/ facts/Issue_Briefs/PDF_versions/11issbrf.pdf.

AARP. 2004. *Social Security: Where We Stand: An Open Letter to AARP Members.* Available at www.aarp.org/bulletin/socialsec/ss_where_we_stand.html.

Accountability Works. January 2004. "NCLB under a Microscope."

Adams, Rebecca. 2002. "Politics Stokes Energy Debate." *CQ Weekly,* January 12, 109.

Advisory Council on Social Security. 1997. *Report of the 1994–1996 Advisory Council on Social Security, Vol. 1: Findings and Recommendations.* Washington, D.C. Available at www.ssa.gov/history/reports/adcouncil/report/toc.htm.

Alexander, Lamar. 1992. "Merit Pay Programs Would Improve Teacher Performance." In *Education in America: Opposing Viewpoints.* Edited by Charles P. Cozic. San Diego: Greenhaven Press.

American Council of Education. 1999. "To Touch the Future: Transforming the Way Teachers Are Taught. Available at www.acenet.edu/resources/presnet/report.cfm.

American Federation of Teachers. March 2000. "Where We Stand: True Merit Pay." Available at www.aft.org/stand/previous/2000/0300.html.

Ammons, David N. 2009. *Tools for Decision Making: A Practical Guide for Local Government.* 2nd ed. Washington, D.C.: CQ Press.

Amy, Douglas J. 1984. "Why Policy Analysis and Ethics Are Incompatible." *Journal of Policy Analysis and Management* 3: 573–591.

Anderson, Charles W. 1979. "The Place of Principles in Policy Analysis." *American Political Science Review* 73: 711–723.

Anderson, David M., and Michael Cornfield, eds. 2002. *The Civic Web: Online Politics and Democratic Values.* Lanham, Md.: Rowman and Littlefield.

Anderson, James E. 2006. *Public Policymaking.* 6th ed. Boston: Houghton Mifflin.

Andrews, Richard N. L. 2006a. *Managing the Environment, Managing Ourselves: A History of American Environmental Policy.* 2nd ed. New Haven: Yale University Press.

———. 2006b. "Risk-Based Decision Making: Policy, Science, and Politics." In *Environmental Policy.* 6th ed. Edited by Norman J. Vig and Michael E. Kraft. Washington, D.C.: CQ Press.

Asher, Herbert. 2007. *Polling and the Public: What Every Citizen Should Know.* 7th ed. Washington, D.C.: CQ Press.

Associated Press. December 1998. "Vermont Town May Blink in Dispute with State." *Boston Globe.*

Axelrod, Regina S., David Leonard Downie, and Norman J. Vig, eds. 2005. *The Global Environment: Institutions, Law, and Policy.* 2nd ed. Washington, D.C.: CQ Press.

Bardach, Eugene. 2009. *A Practical Guide for Policy Analysis: The Eightfold Path to More Effective Problem Solving.* 3rd ed. Washington, D.C.: CQ Press.

Bartlett, Robert, ed. 1989. *Policy through Impact Assessment: Institutionalized Analysis as a Policy Strategy.* New York: Greenwood Press.

Baumgartner, Frank R., and Bryan D. Jones. 1993. *Agendas and Instability in American Politics.* Chicago: University of Chicago Press.

Baumgartner, Frank R., and Beth L. Leech. 1998. *Basic Interests: The Importance of Groups in Politics and Political Science.* Princeton: Princeton University Press.

Behn, Robert D., and James W. Vaupel. 1982. *Quick Analysis for Busy Decision Makers.* New York: Basic Books.

Beierle, Thomas C., and Jerry Cayford. 2002. *Democracy in Practice: Public Participation in Environmental Decisions.* Washington, D.C.: Resources for the Future.

Berman, Evan. 2007. *Essential Statistics for Public Managers and Policy Analysts.* 2nd ed. Washington, D.C.: CQ Press.

Berry, Jeffrey M. 1997. *The Interest Group Society.* 3rd ed. New York: Longman.

———. 1999. *The New Liberalism: The Rising Power of Citizen Groups.* Washington, D.C.: Brookings Institution.

Berry, Jeffrey M., Kent E. Portney, and Ken Thomson. 1993. *The Rebirth of Urban Democracy.* Washington, D.C.: Brookings Institution.

Bettelheim, Adriel. May 1999. "Managing Managed Care." *CQ Outlook,* 8–28.

Billitteri, Thomas J. 1997. "Teacher Education." In *Issues for Debate in American Public Policy.* Edited by Sandra L. Stencel. Washington, D.C.: CQ Press.

Birkland, Thomas A. 1997. *After Disaster: Agenda Setting, Public Policy, and Focusing Events.* Washington, D.C.: Georgetown University Press.

Bittle, Scott, and Jean Johnson. 2008. *Where Does the Money Go?* New York: HarperCollins.

Bok, Derek. 2001. *The Trouble with Government.* Cambridge: Harvard University Press.

Bond, Jon R., and Richard Fleisher, eds. 2000. *Polarized Politics: Congress and the President in a Partisan Era.* Washington, D.C.: CQ Press.

Borins, Sandford. 1998. *Innovating with Integrity: How Local Heroes Are Transforming American Government.* Washington, D.C.: Georgetown University Press.

Bosso, Christopher J. 2005. *Environment Inc.: From Grassroots to Beltway.* Lawrence: University Press of Kansas.

Bosworth, Barry, and Gary Burtless. 2000. "The Effects of Social Security Reform on Saving, Investment, and the Level and Distribution of Worker Well-Being." Center for Retirement Research at Boston College. Available at http://crr.bc.edu/images/stories/Working_Papers/wp_2000-02.pdf?phpMyAdmin=43ac483c4de9t51d9eb41.

Bowen, William G., and Derek C. Bok. 1998. *The Shape of the River: Long-Term Consequences of Considering Race in College and University Admissions.* Princeton: Princeton University Press.

Bowman, Ann O'M., and Richard C. Kearney. 2005. *State and Local Government.* 6th ed. Boston: Houghton Mifflin.

Bowman, James S., and Frederick A. Elliston, eds. 1988. *Ethics, Government, and Public Policy.* Westport, Conn.: Greenwood Press.

Bowman, Karlyn. April 1999. "Social Security: A Report on Current Polls." American Enterprise Institute for Public Policy Research.

Brennan, Timothy J. November 2001. *The California Electricity Experience, 2000–2001: Education or Diversion?* Washington, D.C.: Resources for the Future.

Brick, Philip D., and R. McGreggor Cawley, eds. 1996. *A Wolf in the Garden: The Land Rights Movement and the New Environmental Debate.* Lanham, Md.: Rowman and Littlefield.

Brown, Lester R. 2008. *Plan B 3.0: Mobilizing to Save Civilization.* New York: W. W. Norton.

Caldwell, Lynton Keith. 1998. *The National Environmental Policy Act: An Agenda for the Future.* Bloomington: Indiana University Press.

California State University Institute for Education Reform. September 1997. *Paying for What You Need: Knowledge- and Skill-Based Approaches to Teacher Compensation.*

Card, David, and Alan Krueger. 1995. *Myth and Measurement: The New Economics of the Minimum Wage.* Princeton: Princeton University Press.

Cato Institute. 2005. "Education and Child Policy." Available at www.cato.org/research/education/testing.html.

Cawley, R. McGreggor. 1993. *Federal Land, Western Anger: The Sagebrush Rebellion and Environmental Politics.* Lawrence: University Press of Kansas.

Center for Education Policy. March 2005. "From the Capital to the Classroom: Year 3 of the No Child Left Behind Act." Available at www.ctredpol.org/pubs/nclby3/press/cep-nclby3_21Mar2005.pdf.

Center for Education Reform. 2005. Available at www.edreform.com/index.cfm?fuseAction=stateStats&pSectionID=15&cSectionID=44.

Century Foundation. 2005. "Social Security Reform: Revised 2005 Edition." Available at www.tcf.org/Publications/RetirementSecurity/SocialSecurityBasicsRev2005.pdf.

Chasek, Pamela. S., David L. Downie, and Janet Welsh Brown, eds. 2006. *Global Environmental Politics.* 4th ed. Boulder: Westview Press.

Chubb, John E., and Terry M. Moe. 1990. *Politics, Markets, and America's Schools.* Washington, D.C.: Brookings Institution.

Chubb, John E., and Paul E. Peterson, eds. 1989. *Can the Government Govern?* Washington, D.C.: Brookings Institution.

Cigler, Allan J., and Burdett A. Loomis, eds. 2007. *Interest Group Politics.* 7th ed. Washington, D.C.: CQ Press.

Clarke, Jeanne Nienaber, and Daniel McCool. 1996. *Staking Out the Terrain: Power and Performance among Natural Resource Agencies.* 2nd ed. Albany: State University of New York Press.

Clinton, Bill, and Al Gore. 1992. *Putting People First.* New York: Times Books.

Cobb, Clifford, Ted Halstad, and Jonathan Rowe. October 1995. "If the GDP Is Up, Why Is America Down?" *Atlantic Monthly,* 59–78.

Cobb, Roger W., and Charles D. Elder. 1983. *Participation in American Politics: The Dynamics of Agenda-Building.* 2nd ed. Baltimore: Johns Hopkins University Press.

Cochran, Clark E., Lawrence C. Mayer, T. R. Carr, and N. Joseph Cayer. 1999. *American Public Policy: An Introduction.* 6th ed. New York: Worth.

Concord Coalition. "Issue Brief: Social Security Reform." Available at http://old.concordcoalition.org/issues/socsec/old-doc000628issuebriefsocsecrefgorebush.pdf.

Congressional Quarterly. November 1999. "ESEA Title I Reauthorization." *CQ Weekly.*

Connolly, William. E., ed. 1969. *The Bias of Pluralism.* New York: Atherton.

Cooper, Kenneth J. January 2000. " 'Best and Brightest' Leave Teaching Early, Study Says." *Washington Post.*

Cortner, Hanna J., and Margaret A. Moote. 1999. *The Politics of Ecosystem Management.* Washington, D.C.: Island Press.

Cronin, Thomas E. 1989. *Direct Democracy: The Politics of Initiative, Referendum, and Recall.* Cambridge: Harvard University Press.

Dahl, Robert A. 1966. *Who Governs? Democracy and Power in an American City.* New Haven: Yale University Press.

Daily, Gretchen, ed. 1997. *Nature's Services: Societal Dependence on Natural Ecosystems.* Washington, D.C.: Island Press.

Dalton, Russell J. 2004. *Democratic Challenges, Democratic Choices: The Erosion of Public Support in Advanced Industrial Democracies.* New York: Oxford University Press.

———. 2009. *The Good Citizen: How a Younger Generation Is Reshaping American Politics.* Rev. ed. Washington, D.C.: CQ Press.

Davidson, Roger H., Walter J. Oleszek, and Frances E. Lee. 2009. *Congress and Its Members.* 12th ed. Washington, D.C.: CQ Press.

Davies, J. Clarence, ed. 1996. *Comparing Environmental Risks: Tools for Setting Government Priorities.* Washington, D.C.: Resources for the Future.

Davies, J. Clarence, III, and Barbara S. Davies. 1975. *The Politics of Pollution.* 2nd ed. Indianapolis: Bobbs-Merrill.

Davies, J. Clarence, and Jan Mazurek. 1998. *Pollution Control in the United States: Evaluating the System.* Washington, D.C.: Resources for the Future.

Davis, Charles, ed. 2001. *Western Public Lands and Environmental Politics.* 2nd ed. Boulder: Westview Press.

deLeon, Peter. 1997. *Democracy and the Policy Sciences.* Albany: State University of New York Press.

Delisio, Ellen R. 2003. "Pay for Performance: It Can Work—Here's How." *Education World.* Available at www.educationworld.com/a_issues/issues374c.shtml.

Derthick, Martha. 1979. *Policymaking for Social Security.* Washington, D.C.: Brookings Institution.

———. 2005. *Up in Smoke: From Legislation to Litigation in Tobacco Politics.* 2nd ed. Washington, D.C.: CQ Press.

Dietz, Thomas, and Paul C. Stern, eds. 2003. *New Tools for Environmental Protection: Education, Information, and Voluntary Measures.* Washington, D.C.: National Academy Press.

DiMento, Joseph F. C., and Pamela Doughman, eds. 2007. *Climate Change: What It Means for Us, Our Children, and Our Grandchildren.* Cambridge: MIT Press.

Dionne, E. J. September 1997. "Welfare Reform: The Clues Are in Wisconsin." *Washington Post.*

———. winter 2000. "Why Americans Hate Politics." *Brookings Review* 18, no. 1.

Dodd, Lawrence C., and Bruce I. Oppenheimer, eds. 2009. *Congress Reconsidered.* 9th ed. Washington, D.C.: CQ Press.

Donahue, John D. 1997. *Disunited States.* New York: Basic Books.

Duffy, Robert J. 1997. *Nuclear Politics in America: A History and Theory of Government Regulation.* Lawrence: University Press of Kansas.

Dunlap, Riley E. 1995. "Public Opinion and Environmental Policy." In *Environmental Politics and Policy.* Edited by James P. Lester. Durham: Duke University Press.

Dunlap, Riley E., Michael E. Kraft, and Eugene A. Rosa, eds. 1993. *Public Reactions to Nuclear Waste: Citizens' Views of Repository Siting.* Durham: Duke University Press.

Dunn, William J. 2004. *Public Policy Analysis: An Introduction.* 3rd ed. Englewood Cliffs, N.J.: Prentice Hall.

Durant, Robert, Daniel Fiorino, and Rosemary O'Leary, eds. 2004. *Environmental Governance Reconsidered: Challenges, Choices, and Opportunities.* Cambridge: MIT Press.

Dye, Thomas R. 2001. *Top Down Policymaking.* New York: Chatham House.

Dye, Thomas R., and L. Harmon Zeigler. 2003. *The Irony of Democracy.* 12th ed. Monterey, Calif.: Brooks/Cole.

Easton, David. 1965. *A Systems Analysis of Political Life.* New York: Wiley.

Eberstadt, Nicholas. 1995. *The Tyranny of Numbers: Mismeasurement and Misrule.* Washington, D.C.: AEI Press.

Edelman, Murray. 1964. *The Symbolic Uses of Politics.* Urbana: University of Illinois Press.

Education Trust. January 2005. "Stalled in Secondary: A Look at Student Achievement since the No Child Left Behind Act."

Ehrlich, Paul R. 1968. *The Population Bomb.* New York: Ballantine.

Eisner, Marc Allen. 2007. *Governing the Environment: The Transformation of Environmental Regulation.* Boulder: Lynne Rienner.

Eisner, Marc Allen, Jeff Worsham, and Evan J. Ringquist. 2007. *Contemporary Regulatory Policy,* 2nd ed. Boulder: Lynne Rienner.

Elazar, Daniel J. 1984. *American Federalism: A View from the States.* 3rd ed. New York: Harper and Row.

Ellis, Richard J. 2002. *Democratic Delusions: The Initiative Process in America.* Lawrence: University Press of Kansas.

Eulau, Heinz, and Kenneth Prewitt. 1973. *Labyrinths of Democracy.* Indianapolis: Bobbs-Merrill.

Fairfax, Sally K., Lauren Gwin, Mary Ann King, Leigh Raymond, and Laura A. Watt. 2005. *Buying Nature: The Limits of Land Acquisition as a Conservation Strategy, 1780–2004.* Cambridge: MIT Press.

Fideler, Elizabeth F., Elizabeth D. Foster, and Shirley Schwartz. January 2000. *The Urban Teacher Challenge.* Urban Teacher Collaborative. Available at www.cgcs.org/pdfs/utc.pdf.

Figlio, David N. 1995. "The Effect of Drinking Age Laws and Alcohol-Related Crashes: Time Series Evidence from Wisconsin." *Journal of Policy Analysis and Management* 14: 555–566.

Fiorino, Daniel J. 2006. *The New Environmental Regulation*. Cambridge: MIT Press.

Fischer, Frank. 1995. *Evaluating Public Policy*. Chicago: Nelson-Hall Publishers.

Fletcher, Michael A. July 2002. "A Cap and Gown Gender Gap." *Washington Post National Weekly Edition*, 30.

Freeman, A. Myrick, III. 2000. "Economics, Incentives, and Environmental Regulation." In *Environmental Policy*. 4th ed. Edited by Norman J. Vig and Michael E. Kraft. Washington, D.C.: CQ Press.

———. 2006. "Economics, Incentives, and Environmental Policy." In *Environmental Policy*. 6th ed. Edited by Norman J. Vig and Michael F. Kraft. Washington: D.C.: CQ Press.

Freeman, J. Leiper. 1965. *The Political Process: Executive Bureau–Legislative Committee Relations*. Rev. ed. New York: Random House.

Fremstad, Shawn. January 2004. "Recent Welfare Reform Research Findings." Center on Budget and Policy Priorities. Available at www.cbpp.org/1-30-04wel.pdf.

Friedman, Thomas. 2006. *The World Is Flat: A Brief History of the Twenty-First Century*. New York: Farrar, Straus and Giroux.

———. 2008. *Hot, Flat, and Crowded: Why We Need a Green Revolution and How It Can Renew America*. New York: Farrar, Straus and Giroux.

Fritschler, A. Lee, with James M. Hoefler. 1995. *Smoking and Politics: Policy Making and the Federal Bureaucracy*. 5th ed. Englewood Cliffs. N.J.: Prentice Hall.

Furman, Jason. 2005. "The Impact of the President's Proposal on Social Security Solvency and the Budget." Center for Budget and Policy Priorities. Available at www.cbpp.org/5-10-05socsec.htm#fig.

Gaddis, John Lewis. 2006. *The Cold War: A New History*. New York: Penguin.

Geiger, Keith. 1992. "Merit Pay Programs Do Not Improve Teacher Performance." In *Education in America: Opposing Viewpoints*. Edited by Charles P. Cozic. San Diego: Greenhaven Press.

Georgia Student Finance Commission. 2005. "Georgia's HOPE Scholarship and Grant Program." Available at www.gsfc.org/hope.

Gerth, Jeff, and Sheryl Gay Stolberg. October 2000. "Drug Industry Nurses Ties to Wide Range of Groups." *New York Times*, 1, A23.

Gill, Brian, P. Mike Timpane, Karen E. Ross, Dominic J. Brewer, and Kevin Booker. 2007. *Rhetoric versus Reality: What We Know and What We Need to Know about Vouchers and Charter Schools*. Available at www.rand.org/pubs/monograph_reports/2007/RAND_MR1118-1.updatedfindings.pdf.

Gilmore, John B. 1995. *Strategic Disagreement: Stalemate in American Politics*. Pittsburgh: University of Pittsburgh Press.

Goggin, Malcolm L., Ann O'M. Bowman, James P. Lester, and Laurence J. O'Toole Jr. 1990. *Implementation Theory and Practice: Toward a Third Generation*. Glenview, Ill.: Scott Foresman/Little, Brown.

Goldenberg, Jacob, David Mazursky, and Sorin Solomon. September 1999. "Creative Sparks." *Science*, 1495–1496.

Gonzales, Patrick, Juan Carlos Guzman, Lisette Partelow, Erin Pahlke, Leslie Jocelyn, David Kastberg, and Trevor Williams. 2004. *Highlights from the Trends in International Mathematics and Science Study (TIMSS) 2003* (NCES 2005-005), U.S. Department of Education, National Center for Educational Statistics. Washington, D.C.: U.S. Government Printing Office.

Gormley, William T., Jr. March 1987. "Institutional Policy Analysis: A Critical Review." *Journal of Policy Analysis and Management* 6: 153–169.

Graham, Mary. 2002. *Democracy by Disclosure: The Rise of Technopopulism*. Washington, D.C.: Brookings Institution.

Graham, Mary, and Catherine Miller. October 2001. "Disclosure of Toxic Releases in the United States." *Environment* 43: 6–20.

Grant, Darren, and Stephen M. Rutner. 2004. "The Effect of Bicycle Helmet Legislation on Bicycling Fatalities." *Journal of Policy Analysis and Management* 23, no. 3: 595–612.

Green, Donald P., and Ian Shapiro. 1994. *Pathologies of Rational Choice Theory: A Critique of Applications in Political Science*. New Haven: Yale University Press.

Greene, Jay, Paul Peterson, Jiangtao Du. 1996. *The Effectiveness of School Choice in Milwaukee: A Secondary Analysis of Data from the Program's Evaluation*. Cambridge: Harvard University Press.

Greenhouse, Linda. June 2002. "Supreme Court Upholds Voucher System That Pays Religious Schools' Tuition." *New York Times*, A1.

Guber, Deborah Lynn, and Christopher Bosso. 2010. "Past the Tipping Point? Public Discourse and the Role of the Environmental Movement in a Post-Bush Era." In *Environmental Policy*. 7th ed. Edited by Norman J. Vig and Michael E. Kraft. Washington, D.C.: CQ Press.

Gutmann, Amy, and Dennis Thompson. 2004. *Why Deliberative Democracy?* Princeton: Princeton University Press.

Hacker, Jacob S. 1997. *The Road to Nowhere: The Genesis of President Clinton's Plan for Health Security*. Princeton: Princeton University Press.

Hadden, Susan G. 1989. *A Citizen's Right to Know: Risk Communication and Public Policy*. Boulder: Westview Press.

Hamilton, James T. 2005. *Regulation through Revelation: The Origin, Politics, and Impacts of the Toxics Release Inventory Program*. New York: Cambridge University Press.

Harris, Richard A., and Stanley M. Milkis. 1996. *The Politics of Regulatory Change: A Tale of Two Agencies.* 2nd ed. New York: Oxford University Press.

Haveman, Robert. fall 1999. "The Poverty Problem after a Forty-Year War: Reflections and a Look to the Future." *The La Follette Policy Report* 10, no. 2.

Heclo, Hugh. 1978. "Issue Networks and the Executive Establishment." In *The New American Political System.* Edited by Anthony King. Washington, D.C.: American Enterprise Institute.

Hedge, David M. 1998. *Governance and the Changing American States.* Boulder: Westview Press.

Hibbing, John R., and Christopher W. Larimer. 2005. "What the American Public Wants Congress to Be." In *Congress Reconsidered.* Edited by Lawrence C. Dodd and Bruce I. Oppenheimer. Washington, D.C.: CQ Press.

Hibbing, John R., and Elizabeth Theiss-Morse. 1995. *Congress as Public Enemy: Public Attitudes toward American Political Institutions.* New York: Cambridge University Press.

———. 2002. *Stealth Democracy: Americans' Beliefs about How Government Should Work.* New York: Cambridge University Press.

Higgs, Robert, and Carl P. Close, eds. 2005. *Re-Thinking Green: Alternatives to Environmental Bureaucracy.* Oakland, Calif.: The Independent Institute.

Hill, Stuart. 1992. *Democratic Values and Technological Choices.* Stanford: Stanford University Press.

Hird, John A. 2005. *Power, Knowledge, and Politics: Policy Analysis in the States.* Washington, D.C.: Georgetown University Press.

Hogwood, Brian W., and Lewis A. Gunn. 1984. *Policy Analysis for the Real World.* Oxford, U.K.: Oxford University Press.

Howell, William G., and Paul E. Peterson. 2002. *The Education Gap: Vouchers and Urban Schools.* Washington, D.C.: Brookings Institution.

Huber, Peter. 1999. *Hard Green: Saving the Environment from the Environmentalists (A Conservative Manifesto).* New York: Basic Books.

Illinois State Board of Education. 2001. "Where Are the Illinois Charter Schools?" Available at www.isbe.state.il.us/charter/charterschoolsinbrief.htm.

Ingram, Helen, and Steven Rathgeb Smith, eds. 1993. *Public Policy for Democracy.* Washington, D.C.: Brookings Institution.

Institute of Medicine. 2002. *Care without Coverage: Too Little, Too Late.* Washington, D.C.: National Academy Press.

Intergovernmental Panel on Climate Change (IPCC). 2007. *Synthesis Report.* Geneva, Switzerland: IPCC. Available at www.ipcc.ch.

Jehl, Douglas. May 2002. "Atlanta's Growing Thirst Creates Water War." *New York Times,* 1, A9.

Jenkins-Smith, Hank C. 1990. *Democratic Politics and Policy Analysis.* Pacific Grove, Calif.: Brooks/Cole.

Jerald, Craig D. August 2002. "All Talk, No Action: Putting an End to Out-of-Field Teaching." The Education Trust. Available at www2.edtrust.org/NR/rdonlyres/8DE64524-592E-4C83-A13A-6B1DF1CF8D3E/0/AllTalk.pdf.

Jones, Charles O. 1975. *Clean Air: The Policies and Politics of Pollution Control.* Pittsburgh: University of Pittsburgh Press.

———. 1984. *An Introduction to the Study of Public Policy.* 3rd ed. Monterey, Calif.: Brooks/Cole.

———. 1999. *Separate but Equal Branches: Congress and the Presidency.* 2nd ed. New York: Chatham House.

Jost, Kenneth. September 2001. "Affirmative Action." *CQ Researcher,* 737–760.

Kamarck, Elaine Ciulla, and Joseph S. Nye Jr., eds. 2002. *Governance.Com: Democracy in the Information Age.* Washington, D.C.: Brookings Institution.

Kelman, Steven. 1980. "Occupational Safety and Health Administration." In *The Politics of Regulation.* Edited by James Q. Wilson. New York: Basic Books.

Kerwin, Cornelius M. 1999. *Rulemaking: How Government Agencies Write Law and Make Policy.* 2nd ed. Washington, D.C.: CQ Press.

Kessler, Glenn. July 2000. "Analysis: Real Surplus May Be in Promises." *Washington Post.*

Kingdon, John W. 1995. *Agendas, Alternatives, and Public Policies.* 2nd ed. New York: HarperCollins College.

Klyza, Christopher McGrory, and David Sousa. 2008. *American Environmental Policy, 1990–2006: Beyond Gridlock.* Cambridge: MIT Press.

Koch, Kathy. April 1999. "School Vouchers." *CQ Researcher,* 281–304.

———. December 2000. "Hunger in America," *CQ Researcher,* 1033–1056.

Kraft, Michael E. 1981. "Congress and National Energy Policy: Assessing the Policy Process." In *Environment, Energy, Public Policy: Toward a Rational Future.* Edited by Regina S. Axelrod. Lexington, Mass.: Lexington Books.

———. 1992. "Technology, Analysis, and Policy Leadership: Congress and Radioactive Waste." In *Science, Technology, and Politics.* Edited by Gary C. Bryner. Boulder: Westview Press.

———. 1994. "Population Policy." In *Encyclopedia of Policy Studies.* 2nd ed. Edited by Stuart S. Nagel. New York: Marcel Dekker.

———. 2000. "Policy Design and the Acceptability of Environmental Risks: Nuclear Waste Disposal in Canada and the United States." *Policy Studies Journal* 28, no. 1: 206–218.

———. 2006. "Environmental Policy in Congress." *In Environmental Policy.* 6th ed. Edited by Norman J. Vig and Michael E. Kraft. Washington, D.C.: CQ Press.

———. 2007. *Environmental Policy and Politics.* 4th ed. New York: Pearson-Longman.

———. 2010. "Environmental Policy in Congress." *In Environmental Policy.* 7th ed. Edited by Norman J. Vig and Michael E. Kraft. Washington, D.C.: CQ Press.

Kraft, Michael E., and Sheldon Kamieniecki, eds. 2007. *Business and Environmental Policy: Corporate Interests in the American Political System.* Cambridge: MIT Press.

Kriz, Margaret. December 2001. "Hot Rod Targets." *National Journal,* 3838–3840.

Lasswell, Harold D. 1958. *Politics: Who Gets What, When, How.* New York: Meridian Books. Originally published in 1936 by McGraw-Hill.

Layzer, Judith A. 2008. *Natural Experiments: Ecosystem-Based Management and the Environment.* Cambridge: MIT Press.

Lemke, Mariann, et al. 2004. *International Outcomes of Learning in Mathematics Literacy and Problem Solving: PISA 2003 Results from the U.S. Perspective.* Washington, D.C.: U.S. Department of Education, National Center for Education Statistics.

Levi, Margaret, James Johnson, Jack Knight, and Susan Stokes, eds. 2008. *Designing Democratic Government: Making Institutions Work.* New York: Russell Sage Foundation.

Levine, Bertram J. 2009. *The Art of Lobbying: Building Trust and Selling Policy.* Washington, D.C.: CQ Press.

Lewin, Tamar. October 2000. "Now a Majority: Families with Two Parents Who Work." *New York Times,* A14.

Lieske, Joel. 1993. "Regional Subcultures of the United States." *Journal of Politics* 55, no. 4: 888–913.

Light, Paul. 1995. *Still Artful Work.* 2nd ed. New York: McGraw-Hill.

Lindblom, Charles E. 1972. "Integration of Economics and the Other Social Sciences through Policy Analysis." In *Integration of the Social Sciences through Policy Analysis.* Edited by James C. Charlesworth. Philadelphia: American Academy of Political and Social Science.

Lindblom, Charles E., and David K. Cohen. 1979. *Usable Knowledge: Social Science and Social Problem Solving.* New Haven: Yale University Press.

Lindblom, Charles E., and Edward J. Woodhouse. 1993. *The Policy-Making Process.* 3rd ed. Upper Saddle River, N.J.: Prentice Hall.

Loprest, Pamela. August 1999. "Long Ride from Welfare to Work." *Washington Post.*

Lowi, Theodore J. July 1964. "American Business, Public Policy, Case Studies, and Political Theory." *World Politics* 16: 667–715.

———. 1979. *The End of Liberalism.* 2nd ed. New York: W. W. Norton.

Lowrance, William W. 1976. *Of Acceptable Risk: Science and the Determination of Safety.* Los Altos, Calif.: William Kaufmann.

Lowry, William R. 2006. "A Return to Traditional Priorities in Natural Resource Policies." In *Environmental Policy.* 6th ed. Edited by Norman J. Vig and Michael E. Kraft. Washington, D.C.: CQ Press.

Lubchenco, Jane. January 1998. "Entering the Century of the Environment: A New Social Contract for Science." *Science,* 491–497.

Lubell, Mark, and Brian Segee. 2010. "Conflict and Cooperation in Natural Resource Management." In *Environmental Policy.* 7th ed. Edited by Norman J. Vig and Michael E. Kraft. Washington, D.C.: CQ Press.

Macedo, Stephen, ed. 2005. *Democracy at Risk: How Political Choices Undermine Citizen Participation, and What We Can Do About It.* Washington, D.C.: Brookings Institution.

Mackenzie, G. Calvin, and Judith M. Labiner. 2002. "Opportunity Lost: The Rise and Fall of Trust and Confidence in Government after September 11." Washington, D.C.: Brookings Institution, Center for Public Service. Available at www.brook.edu.

MacRae, Duncan, Jr., and Dale Whittington. 1997. *Expert Advice for Policy Choice: Analysis and Discourse.* Washington, D.C.: Georgetown University Press.

MacRae, Duncan, Jr., and James A. Wilde. 1979. *Policy Analysis for Public Decisions.* North Scituate, Mass.: Duxbury.

Mantel, Barbara. May 2005. "No Child Left Behind." *CQ Researcher,* 471–491.

Manza, Jeff, Fay Lomax Cook, and Benjamin I. Page, eds. 2002. *Navigating Public Opinion: Polls, Policy, and the Future of American Democracy.* New York: Oxford University Press.

Marmor, Theodore R. 1999. *The Politics of Medicare.* 2nd ed. Hawthorne, N.Y.: Aldine de Gruyter.

Martinez, Gebe. April 2002a. "Playing the Blame Game on Farm-Friendly Politics." *CQ Weekly,* 1008–1014.

———. May 2002b. "Free-Spending Farm Bill a Triumph of Politics." *CQ Weekly,* 1147–1149.

Mayhew, David R. 1974. *Congress: The Electoral Connection.* New Haven: Yale University Press.

———. 1991. *Divided We Govern: Party Control, Lawmaking, and Investigations 1946–1990.* New Haven: Yale University Press.

Mayo, Bernard, ed. 1942. *Jefferson Himself: The Personal Narrative of a Many-Sided American.* Charlottesville: University Press of Virginia.

Mazmanian, Daniel A., and Michael E. Kraft, eds. 2009. *Toward Sustainable Communities: Transition and Transformations in Environmental Policy.* 2nd ed. Cambridge: MIT Press.

Mazmanian, Daniel A., and Paul A. Sabatier. 1983. *Implementation and Public Policy.* Glenview, Ill: Scott Foresman.

McConnell, Grant. 1966. *Private Power and American Democracy.* New York: Random House.

McCool, Daniel C. summer 1990. "Subgovernments as Determinants of Political Viability." *Political Science Quarterly* 105: 269–293.

———. ed. 1995. *Public Policy Theories, Models, and Concepts: An Anthology.* Englewood Cliffs, N.J.: Prentice Hall.

McCormick, John. 1989. *Reclaiming Paradise: The Global Environmental Movement.* Bloomington: Indiana University Press.

McQueen, Anjetta. March 2001. "Welfare Law's Big Question: Has Success Been Real?" *CQ Weekly,* 869–870.

Mead, Lawrence M. 1986. *Beyond Entitlement: The Social Obligations of Citizenship.* New York: Free Press.

———. 2007. "Why Welfare Reform Succeeded." *The Journal of Policy Analysis and Management* 26, no. 2: 370–374.

Meier, Kenneth J. 1993. *Politics and the Bureaucracy: Policymaking in the Fourth Branch of Government.* Pacific Grove, Calif.: Brooks/Cole.

Melville, Keith. 1996. *The National Piggybank: Does Our Retirement System Need Fixing?* National Issues Forums Institute. Dubuque, Iowa: Kendall/Hunt.

Metcalf, Kim K. September 1999. "Evaluation of the Cleveland Scholarship Program, 1996–1999." Bloomington: Indiana University, Indiana Center for Evaluation.

Metcalf, Kim, et al. 1998. *A Comparative Evaluation of the Cleveland Scholarship and Tutoring Program and Evaluation of the Cleveland Scholarship Program, Second Year Report, 1997–98.* Bloomington: Indiana University, Indiana Center for Evaluation.

Mezey, Michael L. 1989. *Congress, the President, and Public Policy.* Boulder: Westview Press.

Millikan, Max F. 1959. "Inquiry and Policy: The Relation of Knowledge to Action." In *The Human Meaning of the Social Sciences.* Edited by Daniel Lerner. New York: Meridian Books.

Miringoff, Marc, and Marque-Luisa Miringoff. 1999. *The Social Health of the Nation: How America Is Really Doing.* New York: Oxford University Press.

Mitchell, Alison. May 2002. "Law's Sponsors Fault Draft of Campaign Finance Rules." *New York Times,* A16.

Mortenson, Thomas G. January 2005. "State Tax Fund Appropriations for Higher Education FY1961–FY2005." *Postsecondary Education Opportunity:* 151.

Murray, Kasia O'Neill, and Wendell E. Primus. 2005. "Recent Data Trends Show Welfare Reform to Be a Mixed Success: Significant Policy Changes Should Accompany Reauthorization." *Review of Policy Research* 22: 301–324.

Murray, Mark. May 2002. "Road Test." *National Journal,* 1548–1553.

Nather, David, with Anjetta McQueen. December 2001. "Social Security Overhaul Panel's Report Lands with a Thud." *CQ Weekly,* 2982–2983.

National Academy of Public Administration. 1995. *Setting Priorities, Getting Results: A New Direction for the Environmental Protection Agency.* Washington, D.C.: National Academy of Public Administration.

———. 2000. *Environment.gov: Transforming Environmental Protection for the 21st Century.* Washington, D.C.: National Academy of Public Administration.

National Commission on Retirement Policy. March 1999. *The 21st Century Retirement Security Plan: Final Report of the National Commission on Retirement Policy.* Washington, D.C.: Center for Strategic and International Studies, CSIS Press.

National Conference of State Legislatures. February 2005. *Task Force on No Child Left Behind Final Report.*

National Education Association. 2002. "Vouchers." Available at www.nea.org/issues/vouchers/index.html.

———. 2004. "Rankings and Estimates: A Report of School Statistics." Available at www.nea.org/edstats/images/04rankings-update.pdf.

National School Boards Association. 2005. "About NSBA." Available at www.nsba.org/FunctionNav/AboutNSBA/aspx.

Nestle, Marion. 2002. *Food Politics: How the Food Industry Influences Nutrition and Health.* Berkeley: University of California Press.

Nozick, Robert. 1974. *Anarchy, State, and Utopia.* New York: Basic Books.

Nye, Joseph S., Philip D. Zelikow, and David C. King, eds. 1997. *Why People Don't Trust Government.* Cambridge: Harvard University Press.

O'Connor, Karen, and Larry J. Sabato. 2006. *American Government: Continuity and Change.* Boston: Allyn and Bacon.

Office of Personnel Management. 2004. *Federal Civilian Workforce Statistics: The Fact Book, 2004 Edition.* Available at www.opm.gov/feddata/factbook/2004/factbook.pdf.

O'Leary, Rosemary. 2010. "Environmental Policy in the Courts." In *Environmental Policy.* 7th ed. Edited by Norman J. Vig and Michael E. Kraft. Washington, D.C.: CQ Press.

Olson, Mancur. 1971. *The Logic of Collective Action.* Cambridge: Harvard University Press.

Ophuls, William, and A. Stephen Boyan Jr. 1992. *Ecology and the Politics of Scarcity Revisited: The Unraveling of the American Dream.* New York: W. H. Freeman.

Orszag, Peter. May 2000. "Impact of 2 Percent Accounts on Social Security Solvency." Center on Budget and Policy Priorities.

Ostrom, Elinor. March 1998. "A Behavioral Approach to the Rational Choice Theory of Collective Action." *American Political Science Review* 92, no. 1: 1–22.

———. 2007. "Institutional Rational Choice: An Assessment of the Institutional Analysis and Development Framework." In *Theories of the Policy Process*. 2nd ed. Edited by Paul A. Sabatier. Boulder: Westview Press.

Paehlke, Robert. 2010. "Sustainable Development and Urban Life in America." In *Environmental Policy*. 7th ed. Edited by Norman J. Vig and Michael E. Kraft. Washington, D.C.: CQ Press.

Page, Benjamin I. 1992. *The Rational Public: Fifty Years of Trends in Americans' Policy Preferences*. Chicago: University of Chicago Press.

Parry, Ian W. H. summer 2002. "Is Gasoline Undertaxed in the United States?" *Resources* 148: 28–33.

———. November 2005. "Should Fuel Economy Standards Be Raised?" *Resources* 159: 15–19.

Patashnik, Eric M. 2008. *Reforms at Risk: What Happens After Major Policy Changes Are Enacted*. Princeton, N.J.: Princeton University Press.

Patel, Kant, and Mark E. Rushefsky. 2006. *Health Care Politics and Policy in America*. 3rd ed. Armonk, N.Y.: M. E. Sharpe.

Patton, Carl V., and David S. Sawicki. 1993. *Basic Methods of Policy Analysis and Planning*. 2nd ed. Englewood Cliffs, N.J.: Prentice Hall.

Pear, Robert. June 2000. "A Million Parents Lost Medicaid, Study Says." *New York Times*.

———. March 2004. "Despite Sluggish Economy, Welfare Rolls Actually Fell." *New York Times*.

Perl, Peter. January 2000. "Packaged Poison: Why Did Regulators Act So Slowly in a Deadly Case of Food Contamination?" *Washington Post National Weekly Edition*, 6–10.

Perrow, Charles. 2007. *The Next Catastrophe: Reducing Our Vulnerabilities to Natural, Industrial, and Terrorist Disasters*. Princeton/Princeton University Press.

Peters, B. Guy. 2000. *American Public Policy: Promise and Performance*. 5th ed. New York: Chatham House.

Peterson, Paul E., William G. Howell, and Jay P. Green. June 1999. "An Evaluation of the Cleveland Voucher Program after Two Years." Cambridge: Harvard University, Program on Education Policy and Governance.

Peterson, Paul E., and Mark Rom. 1988. "Lower Taxes, More Spending, and Budget Deficits." In *The Reagan Legacy: Promise and Performance*. Edited by Charles O. Jones. Chatham, N.J.: Chatham House.

Peyser, James, and Robert Castrell. spring 2004. "Exploring the Costs of Accountability." *Education Next*.

Pianin, Eric. April 2002. "A Yucca Nuclear Showdown." *Washington Post National Weekly Edition*, 30–31.

Pianin, Eric, and John M. Berry. February 1999. "Taking the High Ground." *Washington Post National Weekly Edition*.

Polsby, Nelson W. 1980. *Community Power and Political Theory*. 2nd ed. New Haven: Yale University Press.

Portney, Kent E. 2003. *Taking Sustainable Cities Seriously: Economic Development, the Environment, and Quality of Life in American Cities*. Cambridge: MIT Press.

Portney, Paul R., and Robert N. Stavins, eds. 2000. *Public Policies for Environmental Protection*. Washington, D.C.: Resources for the Future.

Presidential/Congressional Commission on Risk Assessment and Risk Management. 1997. *Risk Assessment and Risk Management in Regulatory Decision-Making, Vol. 2: Final Report*. Washington, D.C.: Presidential/Congressional Commission on Risk Assessment and Risk Management. Available at www.riskworld.com.

President's Council on Sustainable Development. 1996. *Sustainable America: A New Consensus for Prosperity, Opportunity, and a Health Environment*. Washington, D.C.: Government Printing Office.

Press, Daniel. 2002. *Saving Open Space: The Politics of Local Preservation in California*. Berkeley: University of California Press.

Pressman, Jeffrey L., and Aaron Wildavsky. 1979. *Implementation*. Berkeley: University of California Press.

Proctor, Bernadette, and Joseph Dalaker. 2003. U.S. Census Bureau, Current Population Reports, Series P60–222, *Poverty in the United States: 2002*. Washington, D.C.: U.S. Government Printing Office.

Public Agenda Online. 2002. Education Fact Files. Available at www.publicagenda.org/issues/factfiles. cfm?issue_type=education.

———. 2005. "Fewer Workers per Beneficiary." Available at www.publicagenda.org/issues/factfiles_ detail.cfm?issue_type=ss&list=6.

Purdum, Todd S. June 2000. "Booming Economy Helping California Improve Its Schools." *New York Times*.

Putnam, Robert D. December 1995. "Tuning In, Tuning Out: The Strange Disappearance of Social Capital in America." *PS: Political Science and Politics* 28: 664–683.

———. 2000. *Bowling Alone: The Collapse and Revival of American Community*. New York: Simon and Schuster.

Quindlen, Anna. June 2005. "Testing: One, Two, Three." *Newsweek*, 88.

Rabe, Barry G. 2004. *Statehouse and Greenhouse: The Emerging Politics of American Climate Change Policy*. Washington, D.C.: Brookings Institution.

———. 2010. "Racing to the Top, the Bottom, or the Middle of the Pack? The Evolving State Government Role in Environmental Protection." In *Environmental Policy*. 7th ed. Edited by Norman J. Vig and Michael E. Kraft. Washington, D.C.: CQ Press.

Rabe, Barry G., and Philip A. Mundo. 2007. "Business Influence in State-Level Environmental Policy." In *Business and Environmental Policy.* Edited by Michael E. Kraft and Sheldon Kamieniecki. Cambridge: MIT Press.

Radin, Beryl A. 2006. *Challenging the Performance Movement: Accountability, Complexity, and Democratic Values.* Washington, D.C.: Georgetown University Press.

Raffensperger, Carolyn, and Joel Tickner. 1999. *Protecting Public Health and the Environment: Implementing the Precautionary Principle.* Washington, D.C.: Island Press.

Rawls, John. 1971. *A Theory of Justice.* Cambridge: Harvard University Press.

Rein, Martin. 1976. *Social Science and Public Policy.* New York: Penguin Books.

Ricci, David M. 1993. *The Transformation of American Politics: The New Washington and the Rise of Think Tanks.* New Haven: Yale University Press.

Rich, Andrew. 2004. *Think Tanks, Public Policy, and the Politics of Expertise.* New York: Cambridge University Press.

Ringquist, Evan J. 1993. *Environmental Protection at the State Level: Politics and Progress in Controlling Pollution.* Armonk, N.Y.: M. E. Sharpe.

———. 2006. "Environmental Justice: Normative Concerns, Empirical Evidence, and Governmental Action." In *Environmental Policy.* 6th ed. Edited by Norman J. Vig and Michael E. Kraft. Washington, D.C.: CQ Press.

Ripley, Randall B., and Grace A. Franklin. 1986. *Policy Implementation and Bureaucracy.* 2nd ed. Chicago: Dorsey Press.

———. 1991. *Congress, the Bureaucracy, and Public Policy.* 5th ed. Pacific Grove, Calif.: Brooks/Cole.

Rochefort, David A., and Roger W. Cobb, eds. 1994. *The Politics of Problem Definition: Shaping the Policy Agenda.* Lawrence: University Press of Kansas.

Rodgers, Harrell. 2005. "Evaluating the Devolution Revolution." *Review of Policy Research* 22: 275–299.

Rosenbaum, Walter A. 2010. "Science, Politics, and Policy at the EPA." In *Environmental Policy.* 7th ed. Edited by Norman J. Vig and Michael E. Kraft. Washington, D.C.: CQ Press.

Rossi, Peter H., Howard E. Freeman, and Mark W. Lipsey. 2004. *Evaluation: A Systematic Approach.* 7th ed. Thousand Oaks, Calif.: Sage Publications.

Rouse, Cecilia E. 1997. *Private School Vouchers and Student Achievement: An Evaluation of the Milwaukee Parental Choice Program.* Princeton: Princeton University Press.

———. May 1998. "Private School Vouchers and Student Achievement: An Evaluation of the Milwaukee Parental Choice Program." *Quarterly Journal of Economics* 113: 553–602.

Rushefsky, Mark E. 2002. *Public Policy in the United States.* 3rd ed. Armonk, N.Y.: M. E. Sharpe.

Rushefsky, Mark E., and Kant Patel. 1998. *Politics, Power, and Policy Making: The Case of Health Care Reform in the 1990s.* Armonk, N.Y.: M. E. Sharpe.

Russell, Milton. 1993. "NAPAP: A Lesson in Science, Policy." *Forum for Applied Research and Public Policy* 8: 55–60.

Sabatier, Paul A., ed. 2007. *Theories of the Policy Process.* 2nd ed. Boulder: Westview Press.

Sabatier, Paul A., et al., eds. 2005. *Swimming Upstream: Collaborative Approaches to Watershed Management.* Cambridge: MIT Press.

Sabatier, Paul A., and Hank C. Jenkins-Smith, eds. 1993. *Policy Change and Learning: An Advocacy Coalition Approach.* Boulder: Westview Press.

Sachs, Jeffrey D. 2005. *The End of Poverty: Economic Possibilities for Our Time.* New York: Penguin.

Sanger, David E. May 2002. "Bush Was Warned Bin Laden Wanted to Hijack Planes." *New York Times.*

Savas, E. S. 2000. *Privatization and Public-Private Partnerships.* New York: Chatham House.

Schattschneider, E. E. 1960. *The Semisovereign People: A Realist's View of Democracy in America.* New York: Holt, Rinehart, and Winston Press.

Scheberle, Denise. 2004. *Federalism and Environmental Policy: Trust and the Politics of Implementation.* 2nd ed. Washington, D.C.: Georgetown University Press.

Schneider, Anne L., and Helen Ingram. 1997. *Policy Design for Democracy.* Lawrence: University Press of Kansas.

Selin, Henrik, and Stacy D. VanDeveer. 2010. "Global Climate Change: Kyoto and Beyond." In *Environmental Policy.* 7th ed. Edited by Norman J. Vig and Michael E. Kraft. Washington, D.C.: CQ Press.

Sexton, Ken, et al., eds. 1999. *Better Environmental Decisions: Strategies for Governments, Businesses, and Communities.* Washington, D.C.: Island Press.

Shepsle, Kenneth A., and Mark S. Bonchek. 1997. *Analyzing Politics: Rationality, Behavior, and Institutions.* New York: W. W. Norton.

Shipan, Charles R., and William R. Lowry. June 2001. "Environmental Policy and Party Divergence in Congress." *Political Research Quarterly* 54: 245–263.

Shokraii Rees, Nina. March 2000. "School Choice 2000: Annual Report." *The Heritage Foundation Backgrounder,* 1354. Available at www.heritage.org/Research/Education/loader.cfm?url=/commonspot/security/getfile.cfm&PageID=10973.

Shrader-Frechette, K. S. 1993. *Burying Uncertainty: Risk and the Case against Geological Disposal of Nuclear Waste.* Berkeley: University of California Press.

Sinclair, Barbara. 2008. *Unorthodox Lawmaking: New Legislative Processes in the U.S. Congress.* 3rd ed. Washington, D.C.: CQ Press.

Skocpol, Theda. 1995. *Social Policy in the United States: Future Possibilities in Historical Perspective.* Princeton: Princeton University Press.

———. 2003. *Diminished Democracy: From Membership to Management in American Civic Life.* Norman: University of Oklahoma Press.

Skocpol, Theda, and Morris P. Fiorina, eds. 1999. *Civic Engagement in American Democracy.* Washington, D.C.: Brookings Institution.

Skrzycki, Cindy. 2003. *The Regulators: Anonymous Power Brokers in American Politics.* Lanham, Md.: Rowman and Littlefield.

Slovic, Paul. 1987. "Perception of Risk." *Science,* 236: 280–285.

Speth, James Gustave. 2004. *Red Sky at Morning: America and the Crisis of the Global Environment.* New Haven: Yale University Press.

Spinner, Jackie. May 2002. "Don't Mess with Accountants." *Washington Post National Weekly Edition,* 20.

Starke, Linda. 2008. *State of the World 2008: Innovations for a Sustainable Economy.* New York: W. W. Norton.

Starling, Grover. 1988. *Strategies for Policy Making.* Chicago: Dorsey Press.

———. July 2001. "Social Security's Fate Hinges on Investing Plan, Panel Says." *New York Times,* A14.

Stone, Deborah. 2002. *Policy Paradox: The Art of Political Decision Making.* New York: W. W. Norton.

Sundquist, James L. 1986. *Constitutional Reform and Effective Government.* Washington, D.C.: Brookings Institution.

Switzer, Jacqueline Vaughn. 1997. *Green Backlash: The History and Politics of Environmental Opposition in the U.S.* Boulder: Lynne Rienner.

Tanner, Michael. May 2000. "Saving Social Security Is Not Enough." Washington, D.C.: The Cato Institute Project on Social Security Privatization.

Tauras, John A. 2005. "Can Public Policy Deter Smoking Escalation among Young Adults?" *Journal of Policy Analysis and Management* 24, no. 4: 771–784.

Teske, Paul. 2004. *Regulation in the States.* Washington, D.C.: Brookings Institution.

Texas Comptroller of Public Accounts. February 2005. "The Impact of the State Higher Education System on the Texas Economy." Available at www.window.state.tx.us/specialrpt/highered05.

Thomas, Norman C. 1975. *Educational Policy in National Politics.* New York: David McKay.

Thurber, James A. 1991. *Divided Democracy: Cooperation and Conflict between the President and Congress.* Washington, D.C.: CQ Press.

———. ed. 1996a. *Rivals for Power: Presidential-Congressional Relations.* Washington, D.C.: CQ Press.

———. 1996b. "Congressional-Presidential Battles to Balance the Budget." In *Rivals for Power: Presidential-Congressional Relations.* Edited by James A. Thurber. Washington, D.C.: CQ Press.

Thurber, James A., and Samantha L. Durst. 1993. "The 1990 Budget Enforcement Act: The Decline of Congressional Accountability." In *Congress Reconsidered.* 5th ed. Edited by Lawrence C. Dodd and Bruce I. Oppenheimer. Washington, D.C.: CQ Press.

Tolbert, Caroline J., and Ramona S. McNeal. June 2003. "Unraveling the Effects of the Internet on Political Participation?" *Political Research Quarterly* 56, no. 2: 175–185.

Toner, Robin. June 2002. "Why the Elderly Wait . . . and Wait." *New York Times,* 1, 14.

Tong, Rosemarie. 1986. *Ethics in Policy Analysis.* Englewood Cliffs, N.J.: Prentice Hall.

Toor, Will, and Spenser W. Havlick. 2004. *Transportation and Sustainable Campus Communities: Issues, Examples, Solutions.* Washington, D.C.: Island Press.

Tyson, Laura D'Andrea. July 2001. "Bush's Tax Cut: Nickels and Dimes for the Working Poor." *Business Week.* Available at www.businessweek.com.

United Nations. 1993. *Agenda 21: The United Nations Programme of Action from Rio.* New York: United Nations.

U.S. Congressional Budget Office. 1996. *Federal Budget Implications of H.R. 3734, The Personal Responsibility and Work Opportunity Reconciliation Act of 1996* (August 9).

U.S. Department of Agriculture. 2005. "National School Lunch Program." Available at www.fns.usda.gov/cnd/Lunch/AboutLunch/NSLPFactSheet.pdf.

U.S. Department of Education. 1995. *Education Programs that Work: National Goals for Education.* Available at www.ed.gov/pubs/EPTW/eptwgoal.html.

———. 1999. "Annual Earnings of Young Adults, by Educational Attainment." Washington, D.C.: Department of Education, National Center for Education Statistics. Available at www.nces.ed.gov/pubs99/1999009.pdf.

———. 2001. "Digest of Education Statistics, 2001." Washington, D.C. Available at http://nces.ed.gov/pubs2002/digest2001/tables/dt168.asp.

———. 2002. "The Condition of Education." Washington, D.C. Available at http://nces.ed.gov/pubsearch/pubsinfo.asp?pubid=2002025.

————. 2005. "10 Facts About K–12 Education Funding." Washington, D.C. Available at www.ed.gov/about/overview/fed/10facts/index.html.

U.S. Department of Health and Human Services. August 2000. "Annual Report to Congress." Washington, D.C.: Administration for Children and Families. Available at www.acf.dhhs.gov/programs/opre/annual3.pdf.

U.S. Department of Labor, Bureau of Labor Statistics. May 2000. "Occupational Employment Statistics 1998." *National Employment and Wage Data from the Occupational Employment Statistics.* Available at http://stats.bls.gov/news.release/ocwage.t01.htm.

————. September 2004. "Highlights of Women's Earnings in 2003." Available at www.bls.gov/cps/cpswom2003.pdf.

U.S. Environmental Protection Agency. 1990. *Reducing Risk: Setting Priorities and Strategies for Environmental Protection.* Washington, D.C.: EPA, Science Advisory Board.

U.S. Government Accountability Office (formerly the General Accounting Office). 1992. *Environmental Protection Issues, Transition Series.* Washington, D.C.: U.S. Government Printing Office.

————. April 1996. *Social Security: Issues Involving Benefit Equity for Working Women.* Washington, D.C.: U.S. Government Printing Office.

————. 1997. *Social Security Reform: Implications for Women's Retirement Income.* Washington, D.C.: U.S. Government Printing Office (December).

————. 1998. *Welfare Reform: States Are Restructuring Programs to Reduce Welfare Dependence.* Washington, D.C.: U.S. Government Printing Office (June 17).

————. 1999. *Welfare Reform: Information on Former Recipients' Status.* Washington, D.C.: U.S. Government Printing Office (April 28).

————. 2004. *Informing Our Nation: Improving How to Understand and Assess the U.S.A.'s Position and Progress.* Washington, D.C.: U.S. Government Printing Office (November 10).

U.S. Social Security Administration. 2002. "Facts and Figures about Social Security." Available at www.ssa.gov/statistics/fast_facts/2002/index.html#toc.

————. 2005a, "The President's Budget for FY 2006." Available at www.ssa.gov/budget/2006bud.html.

————. 2005b. "The 2005 OASDI Trustees Report." Available at www.ssa.gov/OACT/TR/TR05/index.html.

————. 2006, "Income of the Aged Chartbook 2004" (September).

Van Natta, Don, Jr., and Neela Banerjee. March 2002. "Review Shows Energy Industry's Recommendations to Bush Ended Up Being National Policy." *New York Times,* A16.

Van Natta, Don, Jr., and David Johnston. June 2002. "Wary of Risk, Slow to Adapt, F.B.I. Stumbles in Terror War." *New York Times,* 24–25.

Vig, Norman J. 2003. "Presidential Leadership and the Environment." In *Environmental Policy.* 6th ed. Edited by Norman J. Vig and Michael E. Kraft. Washington, D.C.: CQ Press.

Vig, Norman J., and Michael Faure, eds. 2004. *Green Giants? Environmental Policies of the United States and the European Union.* Cambridge: MIT Press.

Vig, Norman J., and Michael E. Kraft, eds. 1984. *Environmental Policy in the 1980s: Reagan's New Agenda.* Washington, D.C.: CQ Press.

————. 2010. *Environmental Policy: New Directions for the Twenty-first Century.* 7th ed. Washington, D.C.: CQ Press.

Wald, Matthew L. February 2002. "Bury the Nation's Nuclear Waste in Nevada, Bush Says." *New York Times.*

Walker, Jack L. 1977. "Setting the Agenda in the U.S. Senate: A Theory of Problem Selection." *British Journal of Political Science* 7: 423–445.

Weaver, R. Kent. 2000. *Ending Welfare as We Know It.* Washington, D.C.: Brookings Institution.

Weber, Edward P. 2003. *Bringing Society Back In: Grassroots Ecosystem Management, Accountability, and Sustainable Communities.* Cambridge: MIT Press.

Weimer, David L., and Aidan R. Vining. 2005. *Policy Analysis: Concepts and Practice.* 4th ed. Upper Saddle River, N.J.: Prentice Hall.

Weiss, Carol H. 1978. "Improving the Linkage between Social Research and Public Policy." In *Knowledge and Policy: The Uncertain Connection.* Edited by Laurence E. Lynn Jr. Washington, D.C.: National Academy of Sciences.

————. ed. 1992. *Organizations for Policy Analysis: Helping Government Think.* Newbury Park, Calif.: Sage Publications.

Weiss, Edith Brown. 1990. "In Fairness to Future Generations." *Environment* 32, no. 3: 7–11, 30–31.

West, Darrell M. 2005. *Digital Government: Technology and Public Sector Performance.* Princeton: Princeton University Press.

Whiteman, David. 1995. *Communication in Congress: Members, Staff, and the Search for Information.* Lawrence: University Press of Kansas.

Wildavsky, Aaron, 1979. *Speaking Truth to Power: The Art and Craft of Policy Analysis.* Boston: Little, Brown.

————. 1988. *Searching for Safety.* New Brunswick, N.J.: Transaction Books.

Williams, Dennis K., and William A. Strang. September 2002. *The University of Wisconsin System's Economic Contribution to Wisconsin.*

Williams, Juan. 1987. *Eyes on the Prize: America's Civil Rights Years 1954–1965.* New York: Penguin Books.

Wilson, Edward O. 1998. *Consilience: The Unity of Knowledge.* New York: Knopf.

Wilson, James Q. 1977. *Thinking about Crime.* New York: Vintage Books.

———. ed. 1980. *The Politics of Regulation.* New York: Basic Books.

Winerip, Michael. November 2003. "Superior School Fails a Crucial Federal Test." *New York Times.*

Winter, Greg. April 2005. "Study Finds Shortcoming in New Law on Education." *New York Times.*

Witte, John F. 1997. *Achievement Effects of the Milwaukee Voucher Program.* University of Wisconsin–Madison.

———. 2000. *The Market Approach to Education.* Princeton: Princeton University Press.

Witte, John, et al. 1995. *Fifth Year Report: Milwaukee Parental Choice Program.* University of Wisconsin–Madison.

Wolfensberger, Donald R. 2005. "Congress and Policymaking in an Age of Terrorism." *Congress Reconsidered.* 8th ed. Edited by Lawrence C. Dodd and Bruce I. Oppenheimer. Washington, D.C.: CQ Press.

Wolpe, Bruce E., and Bertram J. Levine. 1996. *Lobbying Congress: How the System Works.* Washington, D.C.: CQ Press.

Wondolleck, Julia M., and Steven L. Yaffee. 2000. *Making Collaboration Work: Lessons from Innovation in Natural Resource Management.* Washington, D.C.: Island Press.

World Commission on Environment and Development. 1987. *Our Common Future.* New York: Oxford University Press.

Yang, Kaifeng. May 2005. "Public Administrators' Trust in Citizens: A Missing Link in Citizen Involvement Efforts." *Public Administration Review* 65, no. 3: 273–285.

GLOSSARY

advocacy coalition framework Policy-making theory developed by Paul Sabatier and Hank Jenkins-Smith that focuses on the "interactions of competing advocacy coalitions," particularly within a policy subsystem, such as agriculture, telecommunications, or environmental protection. Each coalition consists of policy actors from different public and private institutions and different levels of government that share a particular set of beliefs about the policies that government should promote.

agenda setting Step in the policy process whereby policy actors attempt to get an issue seriously considered for public action.

assessing alternatives Determining the merit of possible policy choices, often through use of policy analysis.

balance of trade An economic goal related to the role of the United States in an international economy; examines the value of a nation's exports compared to its imports.

bicameral Term used to describe a two-house congress. In the United States this consists of the House of Representatives and the Senate.

block grants Transfers of federal dollars to the states, where the states have substantial discretion in how to spend the money to meet the needs of their citizens.

boutique health care Upscale and often expensive health care options provided to those who can afford them.

brainstorming Used to foster creativity in consideration of policy alternatives. In a small group setting, individuals are encouraged to think of possible solutions without imposing constraints on the discussion or criticizing ideas as they are offered.

cabinet-level departments Offices within the executive branch, such as the Department of the Treasury, that implement policy in specialized areas.

categorical grants Transfers of federal dollars to the states where the funding must be used for specific purposes.

causes Refers to the factors that are thought to bring about a given situation or problem. Used in problem analysis to identify how a problem came to exist and why it continues.

Central Intelligence Agency (CIA) The federal agency established in 1947 to collect, evaluate, and distribute information and analysis related to national security, and to coordinate the nation's intelligence activities.

charter school A school reform idea in which a school is government-supported but independent. A state board of education gives an independent entity the responsibility for establishing a school and delivering education services with limited control by the school board.

circuit court of appeals At the federal level, one of thirteen courts responsible for hearing appeals from the federal district courts; circuit courts only have appellate jurisdiction.

citizen capacity The ability of citizens to participate in policy-making processes; that is, their level of interest and knowledge, and their ability to understand issues and play an active role.

cold war The period of persistent hostility, but not overt "hot" war, between the former Soviet Union and the United States that lasted from 1945 until the Soviet Union's collapse in 1991.

collaborative decision making An approach to environmental or resource decision making in which industry and other stakeholders work cooperatively with government officials. Thought to be more effective and less conflict ridden than more conventional regulation.

collective good The general good of all people in a community, state, or nation. Also refers to goods, such as national defense, that could in principle be private but instead are provided by government because private markets cannot do so. Also called a public good.

command and control The traditional approach to environmental regulation (also called direct regulation) in which government sets and enforces standards for air, water quality, and other resources.

common pool resources Resources that are shared by a society and available to all to consume, such as oceans, lakes, rivers, and public lands. Also represents a type of market failure in which a good is defined by its ability not to be jointly consumed and for which exclusion is not feasible.

competency test An exam used to determine teachers' pedagogical skills or knowledge base.

competitive regulation Regulatory policies that are mostly associated with the regulation of specific industries and their practices.

Consumer Price Index An economic statistic used to measure the inflation rate. The index is calculated by examining percent price changes for a typical market basket of goods.

contingent valuation methods The use of surveys to determine the economic value that people place on certain goods or services for which there is no market value. Used in cost-benefit analysis to consider intangible costs or benefits, such as a safe community or clean water.

cooperative federalism Theory that states that the national government is more involved in different policies through collaboration between the national and state governments.

corporate average fuel economy (CAFE) standards Federal program that mandates achievement of an average level of fuel efficiency for a given automaker's line of vehicles. That is, it sets minimum fuel economy standards, but only for the average of all vehicles produced.

cost-benefit analysis A form of policy analysis in which the costs and benefits of proposed policy actions are considered carefully. Often, although not always, the major costs and benefits are measured quantitatively by their value in dollars.

cost-effectiveness analysis A comparison of the relative value of policy alternatives in terms of a given benefit that is delivered; a method for comparing policy alternatives when a dollar value cannot easily be placed on the benefits of action, such as the value of lives that are saved by requiring safer automobiles.

cost of living adjustment (COLA) Programs with COLAs have benefits tied to the inflation rate so that benefits increase as inflation increases.

creative thinking Refers to a way of analyzing public problems and their solutions that goes beyond conventional ideas. Important for imagining and proposing unusual solutions.

culture of poverty A term used by some to describe how those living in poverty learn to work the welfare system to their benefit and pass this information on to their children, who remain poor.

decentralization The transfer of policy authority from the federal government to the states.

defense policy A major component of foreign policy that encompasses the conduct of military affairs, such as choice of weapons systems and deployment of troops. Intended to achieve policy goals set by civilian policymakers in the White House and Congress.

deliberative democracy The idea that citizens should play an intensive role in discussions with each other and with policymakers as part of the process of justifying or legitimizing policy action. Raises questions of citizen capacity as well as opportunities for public involvement.

democratic political processes Creation of opportunities for citizen involvement in decision making and ensuring public review of policy ideas.

Department of Homeland Security (DHS) The federal executive department created in 2002 and charged with diverse responsibilities related to protection of the nation from security threats.

deterrence A policy strategy used most often in national defense in which the object is to deter or prevent a potential enemy from taking actions harmful to the nation. The strategy of nuclear deterrence, for example, was based on the assumption that no nation would engage in a preemptive, or first-strike, war because the likely retaliation would be too massive to accept.

direct regulation Also called command and control, or simply regulation. Government regulates or controls environmental, health, and safety performance of industry or other facilities through the setting and enforcement of standards and sometimes through requirements for certain technologies to be used.

discount rate A calculation made in conducting cost-benefit analysis that takes into account the changing value of a dollar over time. Future costs and benefits are "discounted" to present value by using estimated inflation rates.

distributive policies Individual programs or grants that a government provides without regard to limited resources or zero sum situations (in which one group's gain is another's loss).

dual federalism Theory that states that the functions or responsibilities of each level of government are distinct; little integration of the two levels of government exists.

Earned Income Tax Credit (EITC) A tax credit for people who work but have low wages; it reduces the amount of taxes they owe or provides a tax refund.

ecosystem management A comprehensive approach to natural resource management that emphasizes the integrated treatment of entire ecosystems and their functions. Contrasted with efforts to deal with a specific species or body of land or water.

effectiveness   Analytical criterion that refers to whether a current policy or program or one that is being considered is likely to work—or the likelihood that the policy's goals will be achieved.

efficiency   Analytical criterion that refers to what a policy or policy proposal costs in relation to its expected benefits to society; or a desire to realize the greatest possible benefit out of the dollars that the government spends.

elite theory   Policy-making theory that emphasizes how the values and preferences of governing elites, which differ from those of the public at large, affect public policy development.

entitlement program   A program in which payment obligations are determined by the law that created it, not by the budget associated with that program. Under entitlement programs, any person who meets the eligibility requirements is entitled to receive benefits from the program.

environmental impact statement (EIS)   A form of impact assessment in which government agencies must provide details on the environmental consequences of major actions, such as highway construction, and make them public prior to a final decision on the project.

Environmental Protection Agency (EPA)   An independent federal regulatory agency charged with enforcement of most environmental protection (such as pollution control) laws.

environmental stewardship   A philosophy of governance based on the belief that the natural environment should be protected for future generations—that is, that the government is the steward of such protection.

equity   An analytical criterion that refers to the consideration of what constitutes a fair or equitable policy choice; how a program's costs and benefits are distributed among citizens; or a way to think about who is allowed to participate in policy-making processes.

Establishment Clause   Part of the First Amendment of the Constitution that states that Congress cannot establish a state religion.

ethical analysis   Policy analysis that is based on ethical principles or norms, such as personal freedom or equality. It can supplement analysis based largely on economic, political, or administrative concerns.

Executive Office of the President (EOP)   A "mini bureaucracy" that consists of the White House offices and agencies, such as the Office of Management and Budget, that assist the president in the development and implementation of public policy and provide the president and the president's staff with vital information and policy ideas in their respective areas.

federal district courts   The federal (national) courts primarily responsible for conducting trials—in the original jurisdiction—for national laws.

fee-for-service   The traditional way to pay for medical services, whereby the patient or health insurer pays for the services rendered with no restraint on overall costs. Managed care programs are offered as an alternative.

filibuster   Senatorial procedure whereby a single senator or group of senators can talk for an extended period of time in hope of delaying, modifying, or defeating a proposal.

fiscal policy   Term that describes the taxing and spending tools at the government's disposal to influence the economy.

food stamp program   Plan administered by the Department of Agriculture that provides low-income households with coupons that they can use to purchase food.

foreign policy   The collection of government actions that affect U.S. national security and the economic and political goals associated with it. Encompasses issues as diverse as international trade, economic assistance to poor nations, immigration to the United States, and action on human rights abuses around the world.

Free Exercise Clause   Part of the First Amendment of the Constitution that states that Congress cannot prevent the exercise or belief of a particular religion.

full employment   A goal of economic policy generally defined as the lowest level of unemployment that can be sustained in light of the structure of the overall economy. Also described as the condition in which everyone who wishes to work at the prevailing wage rates can find a job.

Gini coefficient   A graphical way to demonstrate a nation's income equality/inequality by charting the percentage of income made by quintiles of families.

globalization   The growing interrelationship of all nations through global trade. Facilitates the development of an international marketplace in an increasingly connected world.

group theory   Policy-making theory that sees public policy as the product of a continuous struggle among organized interest groups; tends to believe that power in the U.S. political system is widely shared among interest groups, each of which seeks access to the policy-making process.

health maintenance organization (HMO)   A form of managed care in which an individual chooses or is assigned to a health care provider network that contracts with physicians to deliver health care services. HMOs promote cost-effective health care by negotiating lower fees with health care providers, limiting access to expensive services, and often emphasizing preventative health care.

ideal situation   A reference used in policy analysis whereby a highly preferable or ideal goal or solution to a problem might be set.

impact assessment   A form of policy analysis that examines the likely effects or impacts of proposed or adopted policies. These may be environmental, social, economic, or other significant impacts.

implementation analysis   A form of policy analysis that examines the process and effects of implementing public policy. Can be used to anticipate likely implementation problems prior to adoption or to document actual problems after a policy has been put into effect.

incremental decision making   A way of making decisions that emphasizes consideration of a limited number of policy alternatives and their effects.

incremental policymaking   Policy changes that occur in small steps; adjustments are made at the margins of existing policies through minor amendments or the gradual extension of a program's mandate or the groups it serves.

independent executive agency   An executive branch organization, such as the Environmental Protection Agency, that differs from cabinet-level departments chiefly because it is responsible for a more focused policy area.

independent regulatory commission (IRC)   Another type of executive agency whose commissioners are appointed by the president and confirmed by the Senate for fixed and staggered terms; most IRCs are responsible for the economic regulation of certain industries.

information failure   A type of market failure that occurs when willing buyers and sellers do not possess all of the information needed to enter into a transaction or exchange.

institutional or government agenda   Issues to which policymakers give active and serious consideration.

institutional theory   Policy-making theory that emphasizes the formal and legal aspects of government structures. Institutional models look at the way governments are arranged, their legal powers, and their rules for decision making.

intergenerational equity   An ethical principle that emphasizes fairness or equity among generations. Important for environmental policies that have substantial effects far into the future, such as actions on climate change.

Intergovernmental Panel on Climate Change   The United Nations' scientific body charged with periodic assessment of global climate change and its effects. Its reports are widely considered to reflect scientific consensus on the subject.

issue networks   Term coined by political scientist Hugh Heclo to describe informal arrangements or relationships among policy actors in the making of public policy.

Kyoto Protocol   The major international treaty that commits signatory nations to reducing their greenhouse gas emissions by a specified amount as a way to reduce the risk of global climate change or global warming.

line-item veto   A budgeting tool that allows chief executives to delete specific items from an appropriations bill without rejecting the whole bill.

literature review   A review or assessment of available analyses or writings about a given subject. This can be a way to discover what has been written on a subject and what policy approaches have been tried in various settings.

lobbying   Activities through which interest groups attempt to persuade policymakers to agree with their points of view or support policy proposals they favor, oppose those the group does not, or keep certain issues or policy alternatives off the legislative agenda.

logic of collective action   An interest group theory that suggests that a single individual would be irrational to join an interest group when almost no personal gain would follow.

managed care   Refers to a variety of efforts to organize and manage health care services, for example, through health maintenance organizations. Designed as one way to contain rising health care costs that had soared under the old, unrestrained "fee for service" system.

market failure   Term used when the private market is not efficient; some argue that such a failure provides a justification for government intervention.

Marshall Plan   The plan adopted in 1947 for the economic rebuilding of Europe after the end of World War II. Named for Secretary of State George Marshall.

means-tested programs   Social programs in which recipients must meet an income test in order to qualify for benefits.

Medicaid   A federal state health insurance program that assists the poor and disabled. The federal government sets standards for services and pays about half the cost. States pay the rest, and set standards for eligibility and overall benefit levels.

Medicare   A national health insurance program for senior citizens. Covers basic medical care for those age sixty-five and older, and others with permanent disabilities, diabetes, or end-stage renal disease.

merit good   Refers to a good or service to which people are entitled as a right. Some argue that health care should be considered a merit good and as such be provided by either employers or government regardless of ability to pay.

merit pay   The idea that teacher pay increases be based on performance in the classroom; this is sometimes linked to how students perform on standardized exams.

minimum wage   The lowest wage, typically by the hour, that employers may legally pay to employees or workers; the states may set a level for this wage that is higher than the federal minimum.

monetary policy   Tool used by the Federal Reserve Board to influence economic policy goals; it attempts to control economic fluctuations (through tools such as changes to the reserve requirement) by controlling the amount of money in circulation, also referred to as the money supply.

multiple use   The principle that any natural resource, such as public forestland, can be used simultaneously for multiple purposes or uses, for example, timber harvesting and recreation. A long-standing element of federal land and forest policies.

National Assessment of Educational Progress   The test that is required by the No Child Left Behind Act to determine whether schools are meeting appropriate standards.

national debt   The accumulation of all of the deficits the nation has run historically.

national health insurance   A common health care policy in industrialized nations in which the national government provides health insurance to all citizens. Also called a single-payer system.

National Security Agency (NSA)   A secretive intelligence agency created in 1952 to coordinate, direct, and perform activities to protect U.S. government information systems as well as assess a diversity of foreign communications related to national security.

National Security Council (NSC)   A White House advisory body that focuses on issues of national security. Chaired by the president, it includes the vice president, the secretary of state, the secretary of the Treasury, the secretary of defense, and the assistant to the president for national security affairs (also called the president's national security adviser).

negative externality   A type of market failure that occurs when two parties interact in a market and a third party is harmed as a result, and does not get compensated.

no-action analysis   A policy alternative that considers the advantages or disadvantages of taking no new action, and thus keeping a current policy in place. Maintains the status quo.

North Atlantic Treaty Organization (NATO)   A treaty signed in Washington, D.C., in 1949 by the United States and Western European nations to build a formal alliance to pursue their security interests. During the cold war NATO stood in opposition to actions by the Warsaw Pact, representing the communist nations of Central and Eastern Europe.

operational measures   Refers to a specific way to define and measure a policy problem, such as a rate of poverty or unemployment. Often useful when quantitative measures of problems are needed.

opportunity costs   Common in economic analysis; one considers the value of opportunities that are foregone when time or resources are spent on a given activity. It is what people might have done with the same time or resources if they had had the choice.

Organization of Petroleum Exporting Countries (OPEC)   An association of oil-producing and exporting nations that was established to help fuse their mutual interests, particularly the price of oil on the world market and the stability of oil production and consumption.

patients' rights   A privilege of patients to see medical specialists or have a specific medical treatment, or to sue their health care provider in order to gain those services or be compensated for their loss. This became a legal issue when a 1974 federal law (ERISA) allowed such suits in federal court only.

policy capacity   The ability of government to identify and evaluate public problems, and to develop suitable policies to deal with them.

policy change   The modification of policy goals and/or the means used to achieve them.

policy cycle   Term sometimes used to describe the policy process to indicate that the steps of the process can be continuous and cyclical.

policy design   A form of policy analysis that occurs during policy formulation, where an analyst considers how the various components of a proposed policy fit together and how they are likely to work to solve a problem. Involves consideration of what actions government will take and how they will affect "target populations," or the people most affected by the policy.

policy evaluation or program evaluation   Step in the policy process that assesses whether policies and programs are working well.

policy formulation   Step in the policy process that results in the development of proposed courses of action to help resolve a public problem.

policy gridlock   When political decision makers are unable or unwilling to compromise in a way that permits public policy action.

policy implementation   The actual development of a program's details to ensure that policy goals and objectives will be attained; it is during this part of the policy process when one sees actual government intervention and real consequences for society.

policy instrument   The tool, such as regulation or education, that government uses to intervene in a given problem or issue.

policy legitimation   Step in the policy process that gives legal force to decisions or authorizes or justifies policy action.

policy outcomes   The effects that policy outputs, such as the passing of a law, have on society.

policy outputs   The formal actions that governments take to pursue their goals.

political culture   Widely held values, beliefs, and attitudes, such as trust and confidence in government and the political process.

political feasibility   A calculation of the likely acceptability to policymakers of proposed policy ideas or alternatives. Refers to whether elected officials are likely to support the idea. This is assumed to reflect a broader social acceptability of the same ideas or alternatives.

political systems theory   A policy-making theory that stresses the way the political system responds to demands that arise from its environment, such as public opinion and interest group pressures. Systems theory emphasizes the larger social, economic, and cultural context in which political decisions and policy choices are made.

politics   The exercise of power in society or in specific decisions over public policy; used to refer to the processes through which public policies are formulated and adopted, especially the role played by elected officials, organized interest groups, and political parties. Politics can also be thought of as how conflicts in society are expressed and resolved in favor of one set of interests or social values over another.

portability   A right guaranteed by a 1996 federal law in which employees can take their guaranteed insurance coverage with them (that is, the insurance is portable) if they change jobs.

positive externality   A type of market failure that occurs the same way as a negative externality, but the third party gains something from the two-party interaction and does not have to pay for it.

poverty   The Census Bureau defines poverty as falling below a specified level of annual income that is adjusted each year to reflect the rising cost of living.

precautionary principle   A belief that government should take prudent or precautionary action against problems that pose a serious risk of harm even when scientists and policymakers do not fully understand all the causes or implications.

precedent   The legal doctrine in which judges rely on prior court decisions in the making of current decisions.

preferred provider organization (PPO)   An alternative to an HMO, in which enrollees have a financial incentive to use physicians on an approved list but may opt to see other health professionals (preferred providers) at a higher cost.

preventative health care   The promotion of health and prevention of disease in individuals through such actions as routine screening for serious diseases; better treatment of chronic illnesses; improved health care education; and more attention to the role of diet, exercise, smoking, and other lifestyle choices.

problem   Refers to the existence of an unsatisfactory set of conditions for which relief is sought, either through private means or from the government. Commonly used in discussion of societal issues that call for a governmental response in the form of public policy.

problem analysis   A series of methods that can be used to analyze the causes of public problems, where they exist, what effects they have, and what might be done about them.

problem definition   The step in the policy process whereby a particular issue is defined or explained in a particular way that people can understand. Problems can be defined in a number of ways.

progressive tax   A tax that is based on the philosophy that higher earners should pay higher taxes both in terms of actual dollars and as a percentage of income.

protective or social regulation   Regulatory policies that protect the general public from activities that occur in the private sector.

proximate causes   Those causes of public policy problems that are most direct or immediate, and sometimes easier to handle. Often contrasted with underlying, or root, causes of problems.

public opinion   What the public thinks about a particular issue or set of issues at any point in time.

public or collective good   *See* collective good.

public participation   The involvement of the public in political or governmental processes. It can refer to voting, writing letters or e-mail messages to policymakers, talking with others about policy issues, or assuming a direct role in governmental decisions.

public policy   What public officials within government, and by extension the citizens they represent, choose to do or not do about public problems. This can include passing laws or approving regulations, spending money, or providing tax breaks, among other things.

pure public goods   A type of market failure in which a good, such as police protection, is defined by its ability to be jointly consumed and for which exclusion is not feasible.

rational choice theory   Policy-making theory that draws heavily from economics; assumes that in making decisions, individuals are rational actors who seek to attain their preferences or further their self-interests. The goal is to deduce or predict how individuals will behave under a variety of conditions.

rational-comprehensive approach   A way of making decisions that considers all significant policy alternatives and all of their major consequences. Often contrasted with incremental decision making, which is thought to be more realistic and practical.

rational decision making   An approach to decision making that attempts to follow a series of logical or rational steps: defining a problem, identifying goals and objectives to be sought, evaluating alternative solutions, and recommending one that best achieves the goals and objectives.

redistributive policies   Policies that provide benefits to one category of individuals at the expense of another; often reflect ideological or class conflict.

regressive tax   A tax that, when applied, taxes all individuals at the same rate regardless of their income or socioeconomic standing.

regulatory policy   Government restriction of individual choice to keep conduct from transcending acceptable bounds. Often used in health, safety, and environmental policies.

resource subsidies   Government policies that provide financial incentives (subsidies) to develop and use specific resources, such as land, water, minerals, and forests. Traditionally a major component of federal natural resource policies.

risk assessment   A calculation or estimate of the risks to society posed by a given situation, such as terrorism or natural hazards—for example, hurricanes. A specialized and technical form of policy analysis that can identify risks and estimate their severity.

risk evaluation   Use of various methods to determine the level of risk that is acceptable to the public and policymakers. For example, to what extent should the nation protect its citizens against the risk of air pollution or unsafe food or water? Risk evaluation addresses the question of how safe is safe enough.

risk management   Describes public policies that are adopted to manage or control various risks. For example, antiterrorist policies are designed to lower the risk that terrorism presents for public safety, and pollution-control policies aim to reduce risk to public health posed by various chemicals.

root causes   The basic or fundamental causes of public problems, sometimes referred to as underlying causes. Often contrasted with proximate causes.

school choice   The term used to describe any school reform effort that provides parents with options regarding where to send their children, including charter schools and voucher programs. Sometimes the term is used more specifically to describe programs in which parents can send children to public schools in a particular area.

school vouchers   School reform idea in which the government provides individuals with a certain amount of money that can be applied to a student's education; often associated with a way to provide people with a private school option they may not have been able to afford in the past.

sensitivity analysis A way to adjust policy analysis by making it sensitive or responsive to changes in any one variable so that the consequences can be better understood under varying assumptions. For example, forecasting can be made sensitive to different assumptions about economic growth or inflation.

Social Security Government entitlement program that provides money for retired workers and their beneficiaries and disabled workers.

State Children's Health Insurance Program (SCHIP) A program that helps to ensure that children living in poverty have medical coverage. The federal government provides the states with funds, which the states match. States are free to set eligibility levels.

subgovernments Term used to describe how policymaking occurs in less formal settings or venues and involves policy actors within particular issue areas, such as national defense.

supply and demand perspectives Two views on how to think about public problems. One focuses on the quantity of the good or service that is, or can be made, available (supply) and the other on its use by the public (demand)—which might increase or decrease. For example, energy policy could try to increase the supply or decrease the demand through conservation.

supply-side economics An economic theory that states that the government can increase economic growth by cutting taxes, especially for the richest individuals.

sustainable development Economic growth that is compatible with environmental systems and social goals.

systemic agenda Issues the public is aware of and may be discussing.

tax expenditure A tax subsidy, such as an investment credit or deduction, that is designed to favor a particular industry, activity, or set of persons. Called an expenditure because such a subsidy reduces government revenue and thus is like spending money. Also sometimes called corporate welfare.

teacher quality An issue in education policy that concerns a teacher's ability in the classroom.

terrorism Usually defined as the unconventional or unlawful use or threat of violence to achieve political or social ends. Terrorism encompasses the strategies and tactics of diverse groups around the world.

third-party payers In health care policy, refers to insurance companies, employers, governments, or other parties that pay for most health care expenses.

toll goods A type of market failure whereby a good is defined by its ability to be jointly consumed, and exclusion is feasible. An example is cable television services.

TriCare A health insurance program offered by the U.S. Department of Defense. Includes substantial benefits for retirees with at least twenty years of military service when they become eligible for Medicare.

unfunded mandates Federal requirements placed upon the state governments without sufficient funds for implementation.

United Nations (UN) Established in 1945 by the United States and fifty other nations as a global association of governments to facilitate cooperation in international law, security, economic development, and social equity. Headquartered in New York City.

U.S. Agency for International Development (USAID) The principal office charged with the distribution and management of U.S. economic aid, or foreign aid. USAID is an independent federal agency that works closely with the Department of State.

user fees Specific fees or charges that the user of a natural resource pays. Could be fees for entering a national park, harvesting timber from public lands, or mining minerals on public lands.

Veterans Healthcare System A medical system designed to serve the needs of American veterans by providing primary medical care, specialized care, and other medical and social services, such as rehabilitation.

veto A presidential power to reject a bill approved by Congress; Congress may override the president's veto with a two-thirds vote in both houses.

World Trade Organization (WTO) The WTO was established in 1995 and administers trade agreements among about 150 nations to settle conflicts over trade disputes. Its existence reflects the global marketplace of the twenty-first century.

INDEX

Note: Pages numbers with italicized *f* or *t* indicate figures and tables respectively.